American Minds

American Minds

A HISTORY OF IDEAS

by STOW PERSONS

University of Iowa

ROBERT E. KRIEGER PUBLISHING COMPANY
HUNTINGTON, NEW YORK
1975

Persons, Stow, 1913–
  American minds.

  Reprint of the ed. published by Holt, Rinehart and
Winston, New York.
  Bibliography: p.
  1. Philosophy, American. I. Title.
[B851.P4 1974]   191   74-12326
ISBN 0-88275-203-0

ORIGINAL EDITION 1958
REVISED EDITION 1975

PRINTED AND PUBLISHED BY
ROBERT E. KRIEGER PUBLISHING COMPANY
645 NEW YORK AVENUE
HUNTINGTON, NEW YORK 11743

PRINTED IN THE UNITED STATES OF AMERICA

For D. R. P.

Acknowledgments

A BOOK OF THIS KIND necessarily rests in part on the specialized researches of many scholars. The author acknowledges his obligations to the following: Karl Anderson, Earl Beard, John Berryman, Daniel Boorstin, Edwin G. Boring, Malcolm Cowley, Th. Dobzhansky, Joseph Dorfman, John R. Everett, Ralph H. Gabriel, John Garraty, Harold Lunger, Thomas G. Manning, Perry Miller, Herbert Morais, H. Richard Niebuhr, David Noble, C. P. Oberndorf, John L. Peters, Arnold Rogow, E. N. Saveth, A. M. Schlesinger, Sr., Herbert Schneider, Charlotte Silverman, and George Gaylord Simpson.

The source quotations in Chapter 8, illustrative of the idea of progress, have been taken from Arthur Ekirch's *The Idea of Progress in America, 1815–1860* (New York: Columbia University Press, 1944), with the kind permission of the author.

The writing was facilitated by a Research Professorship appointment at the State University of Iowa in 1956. To Dean Walter F. Loehwing of the Graduate School the author is particularly obligated for kindly encouragement and material assistance.

Professor Oscar Handlin has read much of the manuscript and has saved the author from several errors of fact and interpretation.

Preface

THIS BOOK IS DESIGNED to provide an introduction to the history of American thought. It does not attempt to be encyclopedic in its coverage of the subject; many familiar names of men and books are absent. Its purpose is to describe the principal focal concentrations of ideas, or "minds," that have determined the profile of American intellectual life during its historical development. There have been five of these "social minds," and the five parts of the book describe them as they appeared in chronological succession.

A social mind is the cluster of ideas and attitudes that gives to a society whatever uniqueness or individuality it may have as an epoch in the history of thought. It binds together in an intellectual community those who share its beliefs. This book is concerned principally with the intellectual functions of the social mind. By furnishing a generation of thinkers with a common set of assumptions, the social mind facilitates their task. They can take the assumptions for granted and go about their work with the assurance of mutual understanding and sympathy.

The object of the book is to indicate the leading characteristics of each successive social mind and to illustrate them with discussion of representative thinkers and movements. The method might be described as cross sectional rather than chronological or systematic. No effort is made to explore the formation or dissolution of these systems of ideas or to trace the transitions between them. In the case of the colonial religious mind, the discussion is concentrated on the ideas of the first generation of Puritan settlers who brought with them a fully rounded body of thought. For approximately a century thereafter, the Puritan mind passed through a process of ossification and disintegration, the chronicling of which has no place in the plan of this book. In more recent times, the increasing acceleration in the

vii

tempo of thought has been such that no long gaps separate the successive social minds.

In America, the rapid growth of a population recruited from a hundred sources, and the dispersal of these peoples across the heart of a continent made it extremely difficult to achieve anything like the measure of cultural identity that Europeans had long taken for granted among themselves. In these circumstances, the formation of a social mind was attended by peculiar difficulties; and in the want of one, Americans at many times and places have been forced to remain intellectually mute. The American experience provides strong evidence to support the assertion that the life of the intellect is firmly rooted in community, and that the formation of communities here has been a difficult and precarious achievement.

S. P.

Iowa City, Iowa
January 2, 1958

In the present revised edition discussion of several additional topics has been introduced and the original text emended.

S. P.

February 11, 1975

PART I

The Colonial Religious Mind: 1620-1660

CHAPTER 1

||||||||||||||||||||||||||||||||||||||||||||||||||||||||||||||||||||||||||||

Puritanism

T HE HISTORY OF AMERICAN THOUGHT begins with Puritanism not
simply because the Puritans were the first Americans to have
a coherent system of ideas, but primarily because of the lasting impress of Puritanism on the American mind. The longest continuous
tradition in American intellectual history was that of Puritan-
Congregational theology, stretching for three hundred years from
the arrival of John Cotton in 1633 to the death of George A.
Gordon in 1929. The very survival of the tradition for such a length
of time in a rapidly growing country depended upon its capacity
for modification in successive generations. Each of the thinkers
whose names embellished the tradition—Samual Willard, Jonathan
Edwards, Charles Chauncy, Timothy Dwight, William Ellery Channing, Lyman Beecher, Horace Bushnell, and Newman Smythe, to
mention but a few—occupied a distinctive position of his own. The
direction of change was clearly indicated and consistently held
throughout. It was dictated by the growing strength and prestige
of humanitarian and humanistic values. In the end, although each
thinker firmly believed that his work represented a necessary
restatement of the truth, the cumulative effect was such that
John Cotton would scarcely have recognized George Gordon as a
Christian.

4 / THE COLONIAL RELIGIOUS MIND

Firm institutional support was essential to the continuity of intellectual activity. American Puritanism in the days of its vigor was a communal religion, based upon an autonomous congregation which was in turn the core of an agricultural or commercial community. With a few exceptions in the nineteenth century, when theological seminaries could support academic theologians, the theological leaders of Puritan-Congregationalism were all parish preachers, ministering regularly to the needs of their parishioners, and in intimate contact with their daily activities. Schools and colleges assured the literate congregations and the educated recruits for the ministry, who, prior to the rise of the seminaries, received their professional training by apprenticeship to established clergymen. The flood of printed sermons, tracts, public discourses, and bulky theological tomes together with the rapid proliferation of religious periodicals in the nineteenth century all bear eloquent testimony to the central importance of the printing press as a necessary adjunct to the spoken word. The unquenchable thirst to appear in print paved the way for the Puritan to move over into more secular forms of literary activity.

The English Background

A party of reformers called Puritans arose within the Church of England in the late sixteenth and early seventeenth centuries. It was composed of clergymen and laymen dissatisfied with the partial reforms of Henry VIII and Elizabeth I. The Puritans' object was to restore the primitive purity and simplicity of the early Christian church by ridding the Church of England of its remaining popish ceremonies and compromising morality. They were ardent in their religious piety and uncompromising in their insistence upon a rigorous morality and a life of strenuous Christian endeavor.

The central belief of the Puritans was the conviction that sinners were saved by the grace of God and not through any merit or effort of their own. This theological conviction was the means by which the Puritan expressed his profound sense of the sovereignty, omnipotence, and majesty of God. The belief was not unique to Puritanism but formed one of the major strands of the Christian faith since Apostolic times. The historic function of Puritanism was to reduce this conviction to dogma and to attempt to erect a society upon it.

The doctrine of salvation by God's grace rather than by man's own efforts did not result in a passive acceptance of fate at the hands of an inscrutable deity. The prime purpose of the doctrine was to remind men that they owed their salvation—if they achieved it—to God's infinite mercy and not to their own virtue or effort. In practice, Puritan preachers tended to emphasize the assurance that, if man vigorously sought the grace of God, he would not fail to receive it. His success in this quest was measured in terms of the effect of the search upon his life and conduct. Man could never expect to achieve spiritual or moral perfection, but he could and must wage an unending war upon sin. Intention and inclination, more than overt acts, were the best tests of his spiritual condition. The manner of life resulting from commitment to these doctrines was one of intense activism. Puritan preachers referred to the course of human life with the metaphors of warfare and of pilgrimage, and the release of psychological energy at the height of the movement was one of its most striking features.

Puritanism was not, however, merely a religion of morality and conviction. The conversion that justified the sinner and made the sanctified life of the believer possible was a genuine experience, an event, of which the regenerate Puritan was extremely conscious. It was this experience of conversion to which he testified as the sign of God's mercy to him. Conversion was the turning point of his life, the event that distinguished saints from sinners. The sharpness of these categories in the Puritan mind could not have been so vividly established but for the character of conversion as a concrete experience. As a thoroughgoing supernaturalist, the Puritan might have described the conversion experience as an introduction to a higher form of reality distinct from the external physical reality apprehended by the senses and organized by the rational faculties. Of these two realms, the spiritual, which was the habitat of the redeemed soul, was infinitely the more important.

The earlier English Puritans generally favored a presbyterian form of church organization. The clergy were chosen by the lay church members rather than by bishops; and the lay members participated in church government. Authority for these practices, as for all Puritan doctrines and practices, was believed to be found in a sound interpretation of the Bible. While they disagreed with the Anglicans over church government, however, the Puritans were as firm churchmen as their opponents. They believed in an established church as a divinely ordained institution from which no deviations should be tolerated. The church should be closely associated with the state, but independent of it, and clergymen should possess wide powers to instruct laymen and counsel civil magistrates.

With the passage of time, English Puritans began to disagree about the proper forms of worship and the organization of the true church. While all assumed that Holy Scripture, properly interpreted, contained authoritative standards in matters of doctrine and church polity, the meaning of Scripture was not always clear. A wide variety of opinions began to appear. These differences were accentuated by Queen Elizabeth's policy of neither attempting to stamp out the Puritans nor permitting them to apply their ideas. The result was protracted discussion of theological and ecclesiastical questions that served to bring differences of opinion to the surface.

By the time of the Puritan migrations to New England, between 1628 and 1640, the Presbyterians found themselves on the right wing of a movement divided into many factions. According to their views on church organization and church-state relationships, the Presbyterians on the right might be termed "churchmen." They believed in a state church, established by law and organized on presbyterian principles, from which no deviations were permitted. At the other extreme were groups of separatists: Brownists, Barrowists, Baptists, Millenarians, Seekers, Ranters, Diggers, and, later, Quakers. Each of these sects believed that religious life and religious organization were private matters, and that the state had no right to interfere with the affairs of voluntary religious associations. Between the churchmen and the sectarians were large numbers of Independents or Congregationalists who shared certain features of the groups on either side. Like the Presbyterians, they were churchmen who would maintain the existing parish churches as the official and sole religious organizations of the land, although they would transform them into autonomous bodies free from all episcopalian control. Unlike the Presbyterians, they made a significant concession to the sectarians by proposing to restrict the privileges of church membership to regenerate Christians, as determined by rigorously applied qualifying criteria. Since the Puritan migration to New England came largely from this group, these distinctions acquired great practical importance in the development of an autonomous Puritan society. Puritanism in the New World long retained its peculiar blend of churchly and sectarian elements. (The Plymouth Pilgrims, for example, were sectarians of Brownist persuasion. But their numbers and influence were insignificant in comparison with the Congregationalist Puritans.)

In part, Puritanism was a reflection of the popular unrest caused by the deep social and economic changes that England was undergoing in the sixteenth and seventeenth centuries. It cannot be traced to a single social class. While the bulk of Puritan migrants to America were urban craftsmen and yeoman farmers, the economic changes were producing a new merchant class to which Puritanism also made strong appeal. The dynamic piety and individualistic morality of the movement were well suited to reinforce the psychology of capitalism. The real leaders of Puritanism, however, were drawn from the ranks of the Anglican clergy, a highly privileged class during the sixteenth and seventeenth centuries. Finally, many wealthy landowners and members of the gentry supported the cause, subsidizing the Puritan colleges, protecting outspoken clergymen from Anglican discipline, and furnishing financial support for the migration to New England. Not until well into the seventeenth century did small numbers of social radicals appear on the fringes of the movement, and these were vigorously repudiated by the vast majority of Puritans.

Early Puritanism had no specifically political objectives and displayed little interest in political thought or problems. Concern with ecclesiastical polity, however, did have important political implications. As churchmen, Puritans were unable to separate questions of church organization from the problems of government. The Church of England had been separated from Roman Catholicism in circumstances that left it substantially subordinate to the state. It was controlled by the government, even though it was powerfully represented by the bishops in the House of Lords. Puritanism contended for a larger measure of autonomy for the church. Where Anglican theory had presupposed a single society—political in one of its aspects, religious in another; Puritan theory presupposed two societies —one political, the other religious—though composed of the same people. These societies were independent and coequal; each was official, and neither need tolerate opposition. Puritans at first did not question the validity of the monarchy, but they did expect the monarch to support and enforce religious truth as they understood it.

The subsequent history of Puritanism indicated that the theory of "separate but equal" societies was inherently unstable and unworkable. This was one of the great lessons of American colonial history so far as Puritanism was concerned. The defect of the theory as demonstrated by Puritan experience in New England was the failure to provide adequate means whereby either church or state could effectively guarantee the integrity of the other. It separated church and state much more completely than the Puritans had intended. In theory, two powerful bonds were expected to hold church and state together. One was the influence of the clergy, which was primarily moral and spiritual and only indirectly coercive. All occupations or "callings" were presumed to be sanctified, and on this assumption no activity was outside the legitimate scope of clerical supervision. Although he was acknowledged to be ineligible for political office, the clergyman was expected to be the close and constant adviser of the civil magistrate in all affairs of state. The second bond uniting church and state was the office of the civil ruler. As a sanctified function, the magistracy was expected not only to make and execute good laws but also, as a public example, to display an obedience to God's law comparable to that which it required of the citizen to civil law. The magistrate was to have no determining authority in matters of religious doctrine and ceremony, which were the proper province of the clergy, but he was expected to use civil power if necessary to "keep order" in the church and to preserve the integrity of its doctrines and practices. New England Puritan settlements demonstrated the inadequacy of these theories in practice.

Puritan Piety

The term *piety* refers to the central element in all religion. It might be defined as the worshipful attitude or as the sense of man's dependence on God. It springs from the conviction that the whole of creation and human existence have meaning only with reference to God's purpose; and it refers to those occasions when man's attention is focused upon his relations with God.

According to the Christian interpretation of the drama of life, God created man in His own image, perfect, and admitted him to the intimacy of direct association with, and a full knowledge of, His will. Adam's disobedience resulted in his banishment with his descendants from God's presence into the outer darkness of the mundane world. All Adam's descendants inherited his sinful nature and were, by definition, born sinners. But God in His infinite mercy was not content to leave matters in this sorry state, and He sent His son Jesus Christ to redeem those who would repent and submit themselves to His will. The function of the Christian church was to inform men of their situation and to lead them to Christ, whose sacrifice on the Cross had earned for them vicariously a forgiveness of sins. Those who were saved through Christ would enjoy eternal bliss in heaven; the others would suffer eternal torment in hell.

The piety of the Reformation yielded a special Protestant version of this drama, which came from a deepened sense of the absoluteness of God, with emphasis upon His sovereignty, and from a corresponding conviction of the sinfulness of man. The effort to express these convictions crystallized in the classic dogma of Reformation Protestantism: the doctrine of salvation by the grace of God rather than by the works of man. The more sublime the sense of God's majesty, and the more profound the sense of man's own sinfulness, the more remarkable was the grace of God in Christ whereby men's sins were forgiven and God's love and mercy assured. Certainly nothing man himself was capable of doing could earn such a reward. It was a free gift.

For the Puritan, as for all Christians, salvation was the experience to be sought above all others. From his point of view, it was the climax of the Christian drama of life. Although his attention was focused upon it more than upon any other aspect of human experience, salvation always remained in part an inscrutable mystery. The Puritan could say only that some were saved by God's mercy, through no merit of their own, while the others, perhaps the vast majority of mankind, were damned for their sins. *Regeneration* was the term used to refer to the great event of salvation. Enormous labor was expended by Puritan theologians and teachers in instructing their followers in an understanding of the phases of this process. Briefly, it consisted, first, of the forgiveness of sins, the sinner's justification. Secondly and simultaneously, the justified believer was called to a life of dedicated Christian endeavor, his vocation. Puritans acknowledged both spiritual and worldly vocations or "callings," namely, the obligation of the believer both to worship God and to devote himself wholeheartedly to his daily occupation as a practical means of glorifying God. As a result of these two phases of the process, the believer was said to be "sanctified." By virtue of his justification in the sight of God, a sanctity attached to him and to all his works. Although regeneration was a subjective process, in the long run it became at least partially social and public in the sanctity displayed in the individual's life. From the human point of view, sanctification was proof of regeneration. Sanctification meant "saintliness" of conduct and character. When the Puritans spoke of themselves as "saints," they referred to the sanctity of the regenerate Christian.

Without the divine gift of grace, regeneration was beyond man's capacity. The natural or unregenerate man did indeed have a conscience. Man was not a mere animal; he was susceptible to the pangs of remorse at wrongdoing; and he was capable of making considerable refinement in the theory of virtue as was apparent in the writings of the moralists of classical antiquity. The best men were always aware of the struggle between the conscience and the will. But all this fell far short of the intensity with which the regenerate Christian was aware of the conflict within himself between divine and evil impulses. Nor did the natural man know the sense of strength and exaltation that fortified the believer with a growing assurance that he was truly the unworthy beneficiary of God's mercy.

The weight of evidence from the accumulated testimony of countless numbers of devout saints indicated that, usually if not invariably, regeneration took the form of a concrete and ascertainable experience which the recipient could describe. The early Puritan practice of requiring convincing public testimony of the experience of regeneration as a condition of church membership naturally resulted in somewhat stereotyped but generally acknowledged criteria for testing the validity of these experiences. It was not unusual for regenerating grace to register its impact through the physical senses, to be felt by the justified person. He would see a light, hear a voice, or feel the rush of wind. Occasionally, the violence of these sensations would be sufficient to prostrate him. Admittedly, however, these were subjective experiences not to be relied upon completely. After all, a hopefully aspiring Christian might deceive himself; or Satan might simulate the work of the Holy Spirit. An objective test must be employed to supplement the internal experience, namely, the test of external conduct. Without the capacity to persevere in Christian endeavor, the hope of salvation might well prove to be empty. Here the judgment of the community was brought to bear upon what might otherwise have remained a subjective and personal event. But the social dimension of religious experience was not allowed to displace the central Puritan emphasis upon regeneration as the spiritual rehabilitation of the individual soul. Mere moral conduct in itself was no complete proof of regeneration; it was merely confirming, although necessary, evidence.

The limitations of mere moral conduct as evidence of the condition of regeneration were underlined in the theory of imperfect regeneration. The Puritans affirmed the common Calvinistic dogma that true justification necessarily lasts; when God justifies an individual it is for all eternity. But in this world, the justified man was not at once made perfect, either morally or spiritually. He remained the heir to all his previous weaknesses and temptations, liable to occasional lapses into sin. He could feel within himself, however, a new strength of resistance to sin, which was perhaps for him the best proof of his justification. Thus, although the soul was saved, sin still adhered to the flesh, and few men were able to rid themselves entirely of it in this life.

John Cotton, teacher of the Boston congregation and one of the most prominent of the first-generation Puritans, put the theory of imperfect regeneration forcefully in his *Way of Life* (1641), one of the best general statements of Puritan doctrine. The condition of the newly regenerate person was compared to that of a newborn babe, weak and imperfect, defenseless and full of anguish, and threatened with a sense of imminence of death. "So there is no Christian soul that receives a spirit of Grace, but finds itself compassed about with enemies, the flesh lusting against the spirit, so as there is a great strife in him. Gal. 5.17. Faith strives against doubting, his heart being changed; his heat and zeal against coldness; humility and meekness against pride and wrath; and thus he strives earnestly for the preservation of his life." The gift of grace thus sensitized the soul to an awareness of issues it had not previously taken very seriously. It launched the individual upon a course of persistent spiritual and moral cultivation. Although justification necessarily entailed sanctification, it did not bring immediate moral or spiritual perfection. Rather, the assurance of salvation transferred the perennial struggle to a higher and more refined plane.

Although regeneration was formally regarded as a free gift that man could do nothing to earn or merit, Puritan preachers were constantly exhorting their flocks to seek this gift, with the confident assurance that if they sought it earnestly enough it would not be denied them. Cotton asserted categorically that God would not deny the Holy Ghost to those who beseeched it. If God made a man aware of his sinfulness and of the need for grace, it was "very hopeful" that He would also give the spirit of grace. Thus it was the capacity to ask that was crucial. If God did not intend to save a man, presumably that individual would not find himself induced to seek salvation. In practice, a prime function of the clergy was to train and inculcate in men the state of mind in which they would feel the compulsion and ability to seek grace. Such training consisted chiefly in the regular hearing of the Word preached and in the practice of virtuous living.

Because only a few could be expected to find the path that led to life eternal, the Puritan leaders were determined to do everything in their power to see that all men had an opportunity to find it. Hence the compulsions upon the unregenerate to attend services, to support the clergy, and to submit to the rule of righteousness. Those who failed in spite of these inducements had no one to blame but themselves.

The religious experience as the Puritans understood it had a two-fold character. In one respect, it involved a psychological reorientation of personality. This was a subjective phenomenon, closely related to the sensory "experience" that the justified believer underwent. The reorientation enabled the individual to "get out of himself." The balance of self was shifted from the ego to God in Christ. The regenerate Puritan discovered that when he took up Christ's cross he himself was taken up by Christ. Preachers probed this perennial miracle both in human terms of personal experience and through the formal categories of psychological theory. In a second respect, the religious experience was a moral commitment. The regenerate Christian was pledged to the observance of the moral law. Although Puritan doctrine held that the moral commitment was not an official condition of the covenant, merely a suitable consequence of it, the moral engagement was in fact just as fundamental as the psychological reorientation. As long as the Puritan movement retained most of its original vitality, it looked upon the religious experience shorn of its moral dimension as a monstrous abortion. So strong was this impulse that, with the passage of time, the increasing moralism of Puritanism offered a convenient means of measuring its decay.

The fusion of esthetic and moral impulses pointed toward a central accomplishment of Puritanism, namely, its reconciliation of fate and freedom. Its exalted concept of deity compelled it to acknowledge God's foreordination, His encompassment of all things. But, at the same time, it held tenaciously to the conviction that human life has value only as man has moral freedom to choose between good and evil and therefore is responsible for his acts. This reconciliation was accomplished in part by the character of the official psychological analysis of regeneration (of which something will be said later) and in part by the theory of the covenant.

Covenant Theory

The vast majority of New England Puritans belonged to the group distinguished ecclesiastically by their Congregationalist polity and theologically by their federalism or covenant doctrines. The founders of the tradition were the English Puritans William Ames, William Perkins, and John Preston. Their chief American disciples who wrote treatises on covenant theory were Peter Bulkeley of Concord, Massachusetts (*The Gospel-Covenant*, 2d ed., 1651), and John Cotton (*The Covenant of Grace*, 1655).

A religion that placed as strong an emphasis as Puritanism did upon the sovereignty of God was necessarily obliged to reconcile this emphasis with the regularities of daily life. How was one to square the conception of an arbitrary deity with the reasonably uniform patterns of experience? Why did the almighty God permit men to go about their daily rounds almost as though He did not exist? The doctrine of the covenant, in effect, furnished answers to these questions. The covenant was a compact or contract between God and man. For the Puritan, it supplied the key to the understanding of human history; it opened the secret of revelation. The covenant also performed the practical function of restricting God's attributes with respect to man by binding God to the terms of a contractual agreement. Covenant theory thus permitted the Puritan to compromise theological issues just as his Congregationalism permitted him to compromise ecclesiastical issues.

God had originally made a covenant with Adam, according to the terms of which Adam was to obey the moral law; in return, he should enjoy eternal life. The covenant had specified obedience in conduct, good deeds; hence its designation as the covenant of works. It was by breaking this covenant that Adam had merited his damnation. The substance of the covenant was later contained in the commandments that God delivered to Moses on Mount Sinai. Because of the duties that it prescribed, the covenant of works was sometimes referred to by Puritans as the "law."

Since the fall of Adam, sinful man had been utterly unable to fulfill the conditions of the covenant of works. God in His infinite mercy had consequently entered into a second covenant with Abraham. The stipulation of this covenant was not good works but merely faith in Christ, who would take upon Himself the suffering merited by men for their sins. Thus relieved of their sins, men would be justified and accounted worthy of the free gift of redemption. This was the covenant of grace. It was offered to Abraham in behalf of all his spiritual descendants; as Cotton explained, the covenant pertained not alone to the Jews but to "all the Israel of God." To reap the blessings of this covenant, man need only have faith in Christ. A covenant was, of course, an agreement into which both parties entered freely and as equals. The puritans stressed this aspect of the covenant of grace. It enabled the theologians to depict regeneration as flowing from the free acceptance by man of God's offer of salvation in return for the expression of faith in Christ. The voluntary element was stressed. Grace operated upon the faculties, especially the reason and the will, in such a way that from man's perspective the process seemed to be an offer to which he could give free assent. The contractual relationship of the covenant therefore had the effect of softening the determinism of Calvinistic predestination.

Once within the covenant, the regenerate Christian found that he was still subject to the old covenant of works. This was not a condition of the covenant of grace but simply a rule of conduct, in order that the redeemed soul might continue to grow in sanctity. Although no man since Adam's time had been able fully to satisfy the covenant of works, God continued to hold it up as the rule of conduct. Furthermore, the "law" served an important subsidiary function as a means of conversion, since it was by measuring his conduct against the mandates of the moral law that man gained some sense of the enormity of his sins. So he would turn to Christ, seize the offer of the covenant, and obey the law as best he could in return for justifying grace. In this manner regenerate individuals could ordinarily be identified by their sanctified lives. It was appropriate, therefore, to restrict church membership to them.

In John Cotton's version of covenant theory, the covenant was depicted less as a contract than as a free gift, without any conditions or considerations attached. God did not even require that Abraham's descendants give themselves up to Him. The apparent requirement that men should seek Him was always subsumed under the all-embracing promise that He would be their God. In other words, He was always present to give them the strength and will to satisfy this requirement.

Concerning the relationship between faith and works, Cotton taught that God justified an individual only when He had previously prepared that person by inculcating in him a sense of revulsion from his own sins. The theologian explained that it was "the usual manner of God to give a Covenant of Grace by leading men first into a Covenant of Works." Although the former covenant had technically superseded the latter as the condition of salvation, as a practical matter the believer always felt bound to observe the moral law. If he did lapse momentarily, he would be filled with remorse.

Cotton's insistence upon the practical blending of faith and works reflected his sober second thoughts following the Antinomian controversy of 1636–37 within his own congregation, from which he had emerged with somewhat tarnished reputation (see pp. 46–47). The Antinomians had stridently affirmed that faith in Christ was all sufficient, and that to attempt to display one's gracious condition in a sanctified life was a presumptuous affront to the perfections of the deity. In taking this position they claimed to be merely repeating the instructions of their revered teacher, Mr. Cotton. Although they had clearly distorted Cotton's position, in repudiating his zealous followers the teacher went a considerable distance towards subordinating grace to works. He pointed out that there was a meekness and submissiveness to be observed in a man under the covenant of grace that was consistent with the character of grace as a free gift, whereas a hypocrite living under the covenant of works (such as an Anglican Arminian) would be proud and liable to lapse permanently into sin. The choice of these crucial qualities of meekness and pride throws a strong light on the authoritarian expectations of the Puritan leaders. In any event, a man who was to be justified would first pass under a covenant of works, and, admittedly, it would be very difficult to distinguish such a person from one truly regenerate. In the long run, however, perseverance in sanctity would furnish sufficient public evidence of any man's spiritual condition. Subjectively, the believer's assurance of his own regeneracy was absolutely essential. Cotton insisted that no man was saved without arriving eventually at such an assurance.

Scholars have frequently dwelt upon the individualistic implications of Puritan doctrine. Man was conceived to stand alone before his Maker. The relationship was defined by the terms of the covenant of grace, and it was ultimately the concern of each individual. Some men were to be saved and some were not. No priesthood or authoritarian church held the keys to the Kingdom; the function of the clergy was purely advisory. These features of Puritan doctrine no doubt fostered an individualistic temper that, in the long run, had a decisive influence upon American Protestantism.

But the central emphasis of early Puritan treatises was not upon these individualistic aspects but upon the corporate element. This was especially true of the chief American book on the covenant theory, that of Peter Bulkeley of Concord. As Bulkeley described the covenant of grace, God had offered it not simply to individual men but to a whole people, the spiritual descendants of Abraham. It was extremely important that God's covenant people should be united in a social community. The early American Puritans were incapable of conceiving of a purely individualistic relationship of man to God. This was perhaps the most important practical difference between the Puritans and contemporary sectarians. The miserable condition of the Jews in modern times, according to Bulkeley, stemmed primarily from the fact that they had no national state of their own, due, of course, to their rejection of Christ. Without a complete community, religion could not fully develop in the social dimension.

It was the corporate assumption of their covenant theory that sustained the Puritans in their categorical assertion that the children of regenerate Christians were born within the covenant. The rite of infant baptism, whereby children of believers were baptized in infancy, was called a "seal" or pledge of participation in the covenant. It was assumed that when these baptized infants became adults they would experience regeneration as a matter of course. Increase Mather in 1680 went so far as to say that infant baptism signified regeneration; that some infants were already regenerate. For all infants, however, it was an engagement for future repentance. In defense of the doctrine and practice Mather explained that, if infant baptism were denied, then in order to save the souls of those dying in infancy it would be necessary to embrace the Pelagian heresy and maintain that infants come into the world free of sin. But Mather's arguments reflected the defensive posture of Puritan apologists on this matter in the latter part of the seventeenth century. So long as the corporate bond among believers remained strong, no theological defense of what would otherwise have seemed a paradoxical doctrine was necessary.

In a characteristic attempt to compromise the stern demands of dogma with recalcitrant experience, John Cotton taught that the children of the elect were born under the "outward dispensation" of the covenant of grace, which justified their baptism. Those not actually to be included among the elect would, of course, live by a covenant of works rather than by a covenant of grace. But so would the elect themselves prior to the moment of their effectual calling. The practical significance of this outward dispensation was apparent enough. It served to bind the community through successive generations to a unity of purpose and outlook, regardless of the spiritual distinction between the elect and the unregenerate, which it tended to minimize. It disciplined the community through subjection to the moral law. And it provided the necessary preparation for the conversion of successive generations. Efforts of this kind to reconcile the divergent demands of piety and morality, of subjective experience and social control, afforded the best clues to the essentially moderate spirit of federal Puritanism.

A compromise was perhaps inevitable as a consequence of the Puritan attempt to reconcile two distinct demands of the human psyche: the esthetic and the moral. The first called for a religion of feeling as the immediate response of the personality to the awesome mysteries of experience. The covenant of grace, however inadequate in its bare dogmatic statement, was the theological formulation designed to meet this need. The second requirement was religion as a way of life, as conduct or duty. This was the meaning of the covenant of works. Although grace was held to have superseded works, Puritanism in practice attempted to blend the two together and to assign to each its proper place.

The Puritan conception of piety was a relatively sophisticated theory that did no violence to the facts of life as the faithful were taught to apprehend them. But it was a theory that had to be constantly explained and elaborated by the preachers. It could hold its own against heretical deviations and simplifications of doctrine only as long as its official monopoly was protected by the state. The delicate balance between grace and works proved increasingly difficult to maintain as the drift towards more humanistic and humanitarian attitudes set in. But as long as the piety survived in any form it provided a psychological stimulus of far-reaching effect.

It also shaped a characteristically optimistic outlook on life. The Puritan found life good because God so willed, in spite of its moments of darkness and anguish. He had been taught to believe that all things were comprehended within the purview of God's providence, and that each event, no matter how trivial, displayed His secret will. The course of history was leading inevitably to the final denoucement when evil would be destroyed and the righteous would reign forever. In such a cosmic optimism there was no place for a tragic sense of life.

It may seem paradoxical that a religion teaching total depravity and predestination, which should have resulted in passivity or pessimistic resignation, produced instead a militant activism. Puritanism proved to be well suited to pioneer conditions. Like the Marxist of later times, who blended a sense of historical inevitability with a firm determination to shape the course of events towards their predestined fulfillment, the Puritan conceived of himself as an active participant in the cosmic drama God had foreordained. New England was the "city on a hill" destined to serve as a beacon light for mankind in the latter days, requiring of him a more rigorous and exacting standard of conduct.

Closely related to the paradox of predestination and activism was the problem of conduct. The strong emphasis upon the inherent evils of the flesh, or original sin, did not lead, as one might expect, to ascetic renunciation of the world, as in monasticism. Instead, it resulted in what has been called "worldly asceticism," the conviction that the pleasures and gratifications of the world should be moderately indulged precisely because the measured satisfaction of human needs was necessary to their disciplined regulation. Denial of the gratification of such needs would result merely in selfish craving. Therefore, the criterion by which an act was to be judged was found not in the act itself but in its relation to the great end of life, namely, the glorification of God. Such glorification could receive its most complete expression in a fully rounded life in which all the human faculties and powers received adequate expression. The classical tradition of the liberal arts that was central to the Puritan theory of formal education provided cultivated standards for the measurement of such a career.

Finally, the experience of regeneration as defined and inculcated by Puritan preachers proved to contain so intense an emotional stimulus that it was necessary to be in constant readiness to apply restraints upon those who might be tempted to yield to emotional excesses or doctrinal absurdities. This was one of the most disturbing aspects of the antinomian crisis of 1637. But the effective imposition of such restraints implied the possession of extensive powers by the clergy—or at least the necessary moral and social influence to move the civil officials as the situation might require. In Mrs. Anne Hutchinson's day the clergy exercised such influence. After the middle of the seventeenth century, however, it was no longer possible to use civil means to check heretical deviations, and the disintegration of the doctrinal unity of the Puritan community proceeded apace.

Piety and Intellect

The Puritans were devoted to education. In the midst of the herculean labors of building homes and establishing means of livelihood on the edge of the wilderness, the settlers still found time and wherewithal to organize elementary and grammar schools and to maintain the liberal arts college at Cambridge, Massachusetts. Their zeal for formal learning long survived the disintegration of the original Puritan synthesis. With each successive wave of religious revivalism during more than two hundred years, the descendants of Puritans found spontaneous expression for their renewed piety in the founding of educational institutions, which remained as monuments to the faith that had been carried across successive frontiers. At the same time, men and women of Puritan extraction held a dominant position in the learned professions during the eighteenth and nineteenth centuries.

Religious piety in its more fervent forms has often been indifferent, even hostile, to the life of the intellect. Puritan doctrine, however, was more than a mere rationalization of a form of religious piety. It was an elaborate intellectual system in which there was presumably a place for every aspect of experience. Its conception of the nature of the physical universe was not inhospitable to the prevailing scientific ideas of the age, although Puritans never doubted that all things were governed by the laws of God's providence. A belief in the creation as described in Genesis was blended with a natural philosophy or science derived from medieval Scholasticism and, ultimately, from Aristotle.

The world was conceived to be ordered in a vast coherent hierarchy or chain of being, beginning with the base material stuff of matter and ascending through the realms of plant and animal life to man, and above him to the angels and finally to God Himself. Each part was consistent with the others, their relationships being arranged according to the laws of God's general providence. Man's social, moral, and intellectual life had its place in this great system, and was just as susceptible to scientific investigation as were the facts of nature, since it responded to the same providential oversight.

The Puritans were convinced that as one studied the external world of nature one would find everywhere the evidences of divine plan or design. In this respect, God revealed Himself in nature, and man might apprehend the revelation by means of his intelligence. This was not, of course, a complete revelation of divine purpose. The knowledge of God to be discovered in nature was not sufficient to assure salvation. But it might be a supplemental aid by no means to be slighted. The phrases "light of reason" or "light of nature" frequently recurred in Puritan writings. Sometimes they referred to ideas acquired by observation or induction; sometimes they designated the glimmerings of knowledge of God that man, in spite of his fallen nature, had been able to acquire through the use of reason. The English Puritan John Preston argued that just as the nicely meshing wheels of a watch bore witness to the skill of the watchmaker, so the adaptations to be observed on every hand in nature testified to the cunning contrivances of the Creator. Reason, in short, supplemented revelation and in no way contradicted it.

It would not do, however, to allow the uniformities of nature to bulk too large in the consciousness. God's design might be seen in the general laws or uniformities of nature, but His hand was equally present in each unique event or act. Although many of these events might seem in themselves trivial or meaningless, the Puritan was assured that God had His purpose in every act. Untoward events were to be regarded as special providences, reminding the believer to take stock of his shortcomings and correct his deficiencies. Hence the Puritan penchant for moralizing over trivial occasions. Unlike the modern mentality, which makes allowance for what it calls "chance" as it faces the unknown, the Puritan mind used every occasion to remind itself of God's inscrutability and man's accountability. These special providences were unlike miracles in that God chose to work with natural means. The miraculous setting aside of the natural order of things was believed not to have been employed by God since the days of the Apostles. These doctrines of general design and special providences fixed an acceptable though subordinate place for science in the Puritan system. During the latter part of the seventeenth century, however, as a result of the concurrent decay of vital piety and deterioration in the quality of

Puritan leadership, an increasing emphasis was placed on the role of special providences that, to the modern mind, seems almost pathological.

In his apprehension of God's law in nature, man might be confident that he was not suffering from delusion because he had been endowed by God with a mind capable of conceiving, at least roughly, the true character of external reality. The importance attached in Puritan theory to the role of the critical or reasoning faculty in the religious life had a direct bearing upon the concern with formal learning. Before his fall, Adam had among other blessings enjoyed perfect rationality. The fall not only jeopardized his soul and those of all his descendants, but also deranged their mental faculties, so that in some sense the sinner could be said to be insane. This was a psychological definition of sin quite consistent with the divine attribute of perfect rationality.

In his fallen sinful state man still retained, however, some shreds of his original rationality. He was still possessed of mental abilities that in many instances were capable of considerable refinement. He still possessed a natural conscience that permitted at least rudimentary distinctions between good and evil. In the authors of classical antiquity, whose works formed the staple of collegiate education, there were examples of the best that was to be expected of the unregenerate mentality. With respect to man's spiritual destiny, the function of formal education was to strengthen the natural mental powers. This was especially appropriate because in intellectual terms regeneration consisted of an enlightening of the mind. In this as in other senses regeneration was imperfect; it launched the justified person upon a perpetual course of self-cultivation. With his idealistic philosophical presuppositions, the Puritan recognized no essential incompatibility between natural and spiritual knowledge. The latter was simply beyond the range of the former.

The intellectual challenge confronting the aspiring Puritan convert was not unlike the moral and spiritual challenge. He knew it to be his duty of improve himself in all these respects. With the intellectual faculties he found knowledge of God in nature and in history. He knew that the goal of regeneration was a gift that could never be achieved through mere knowledge. But, at least, whatever achievements could be acquired in this way were aids to assist him along the path on which he trusted that a merciful God would vouchsafe to meet him with saving grace. Natural knowledge in itself could never persuade the will to believe in God. And yet the grace that did incline the will was presumed to operate only through knowledge and in the form of knowledge.

In psychological terms, the receipt of grace usually registered itself through a sense impression. The convert would testify to having seen a light, heard a sound, or felt a presence. These experiences frequently occurred during the hearing of a sermon or while witnessing the administration of the sacraments, both of which were forms of instruction addressed to the mind. For these reasons, Thomas Hooker felt justified in insisting that it was by means of the instructional functions of the ministry that God had chosen to prepare the hearts of sinners to receive saving grace. The effects of regeneration could properly be described as educational. Grace was like logic in that it enabled one to see the truth. It was then possible to understand the great doctrines of the faith with a force and clarity that the unregenerate intellect could never have grasped.

According to Puritan psychological theory, the mind was composed of several faculties. Among them were the physical senses, the common sense, imagination, memory, reason, will (located in the heart), and the passions (located in the viscera). Any mental process involved a kind of chain reaction through these faculties. Each must perform its function properly or the end product would be distorted. In psychological terms, original sin had effected a congenital derangement of the mental faculties, infecting especially the imagination, the passions, and the will. One psychological effect of regeneration was to curb the imagination and to discipline the mind, permitting a closer conformity between the true character of external objects and the mental images produced by them. Another effect was to subdue the unruly passions to the discipline of Christain perseverance. And perhaps most important, regeneration humbled the will, overthrowing its egoistic sovereignty over the other faculties, while at the same time it restored the reason to the supremacy originally intended by the Creator. Thus, while from the theological point of view regeneration represented the forgiveness of sin, psychologically it consisted of a strengthening of the mental, and especially the rational, powers.

These aspects of the Puritan theory of regeneration were not in themselves sufficient to account for the Puritan concern for education. The tradition of Renaissance humanism was firmly fixed in the English universities from which virtually all the original Puritan leaders had graduated, and it was only to be expected that they should undertake to perpetuate that tradition as a matter of course.

Their lay followers were likewise accustomed to the urbane and learned ministrations of men thoroughly trained in the liberal arts and were prepared to make the necessary sacrifices to keep that tradition alive in the New World. Nevertheless, the specific terms in which the Puritans conceived of the phenomenon of regeneration, both in its processes and results, underline the intimate association between piety and learning in Puritan thought. Natural knowledge and the knowledge of holy things were indissolubly linked together. Man could not expect to gain any very deep sense of the one without a firm grounding in the other. The emphasis upon learning furnished one of the most convincing indications of the essentially moderate and practical spirit of early American Puritanism, distinguishing it sharply from the more zealous and single-minded sectarians with their contempt for mere knowledge as a diversion from strictly spiritual objects. The Puritan schools and colleges remained as worthy monuments to the determination of their founders to fuse piety and intellect. They might appropriately have adopted as a motto Solomon's proverb: "the fear of the Lord is the beginning of wisdom."

CHAPTER 2

The Holy Commonwealth

T HE PURITAN MIGRATION to the New World between 1630 and 1660 was the first of a series of religious hegiras that left a distinctive mark on American history. Each sought a wilderness asylum where the faithful might found a holy commonwealth dedicated to the prepetuation of the truth. The migrants brought with them, in the dogmas of the federal Puritan theology, a fully developed system of beliefs by which they proposed to live. To question the validity or the sufficiency of these beliefs was a heresy worthy of summary discipline. It was not to be expected, therefore, that change or modification of doctrine would shortly spring from the transplanting of the faith. Separated by the broad ocean from the rich diversity and ferment of contemporary English religious life, the New England Puritans were free to lay the firm foundations of what later came to be known appropriately as "the standing order." Their object was to preserve the truth, not to experiment with novelties. Within a few years English colleagues were to deplore what, from their vantage point, seemed to be the reactionary attitudes of their American brethren.

But if in matters of religious dogma the purpose of the American Puritans was to perpetuate the truth as they had received it, in social affairs they were unencumbered by commitment to tradition and could follow the bent of their genius. The practical problems of community-building confronted them with issues they had never been called upon to face in England. The very fact that they were unprepared for these eventualities meant that they were free to venture upon unexplored paths where their creative talents had free rein. In this respect, they acquitted themselves well. It would be difficult to overestimate the fruitfulness of the institutional precedents that they established. The institutions of family, church, schools, and state, and the relationships among them, that the Puritans bequeathed to their descendants were a vital part in the development of American society.

The Church Covenant

New England Puritan society was composed of a group of communities each organized around a religious congregation. The peculiar ecclesiastical system was sometimes referred to as "the New England way." This was the set of principles and practices known as Congregationalism. William Ames had been the chief architect of Congregationalism, and the commitment of Congregational principles had fixed the position of his followers as moderates or centrists among the various Protestant parties of England in the years before the Puritan migration. Certain features of original Congregationalism were churchly in character, others were sectarian—a fact that enabled Congregationalists to assume the role of mediators while at the same time subjecting them to opposing pressures from either side.

Congregational theory provided for a church covenant or compact among a group of regenerate Christians who thus formed themselves into a permanent congregation for purposes of worship. The congregation was conceived to be an entirely autonomous body, uncontrolled by bishop, presbytery, or ministerial association. Its members were empowered to elect their ministers and to admit and expel members on due cause. To be admitted to membership, a candidate originally was required to testify convincingly in open meeting concerning his experience of regeneration. The church covenant was founded upon the covenant of grace in the sense that the regenerate person naturally wished to discharge the social obligations of a sanctified life as implied in that covenant. By entering into an agreement with his likeminded fellows, he was thus able to add a social dimension to what would otherwise have remained a purely individualistic experience.

In England, where the nationally established church under the Episcopalian hierarchy professed to hold the entire community within its relatively tolerant embrace, the Congregational theory and pretensions were radical and potentially revolutionary. Although the Congregationalists insisted that they were loyal churchmen and that their congregations were the true Church of England, from the Episcopalian viewpoint this was a miserable deception. In making so clear a distinction between elect and unregenerate, and especially in restricting all ecclesiastical privileges and powers to the elect, the Congregationalists were, in Anglican eyes, indistinguishable from sectarians. John Cotton was less than entirely convincing when he attempted to clarify this relationship by pointing out that the Congregationalists merely separated themselves from the sinners, whereas the sectarians separated from the churches. The practical difference between Anglican and Congregationalist resided in the Anglican conviction that a state church could maintain its exclusive monopoly only if it were reasonably tolerant of the frailties of human nature, and, by refusing to make too sharp a distinction between elect and unregenerate, frankly derived at least part of its power from the toleration of individual shortcomings. The Puritans of course despised such compromise.

But in New England, where they assumed the position and responsibilities that went with legal establishment, the Congregationalists quickly found themselves in the role played by the Episcopalians in England. They were confronted by challenges of a truly sectarian nature and were obliged to realign their forces in order to do battle on the opposite front. This was the chief historical significance of the religious rebellions headed by Anne Hutchinson and Roger Williams. The result of these sectarian attacks was to force significant modifications in Congregationalist theory and practice, especially in the area of church-state relationships. The authoritative discussions of Congregationalist polity, Thomas Hooker's *Survey of the Summe of Church Discipline* and John Cotton's *Way of the Congregational Churches Cleared*, both published in 1648 after their authors had had time to assimilate the meaning of the battles of the previous decade, reflected the tightening of centralized controls over the local congregations that was the practical outcome of the sectarian challenge. Pressure from the sectarians forced the

Congregationalists to adopt practices similar to those they had earlier condemned in the English Episcopalians.

One of the most important of these modifications concerned the qualifications for church membership. An insistence upon a clearcut ecclesiastical and social distinction between the elect and the unregenerate was a chief characteristic of sectarianism. Originally, the Congregationalists had shared this sectarian attitude and had had no doubt of the practical possibility and desirability of separating the saints from the sinners by means of convincing spiritual and moral criteria. This had been one of the principal reasons for the Puritan attack upon the Episcopalians. But now, the sectarians of New England insisted that regeneracy be defined exclusively in spiritual terms, and that the elect themselves possessed exclusive and infallible intuitive knowledge as to who was saved. They accused the Congregationalists of admitting to church membership persons who were merely moral; and, on occasion, they went so far as to accuse orthodox Puritan clergymen of being unregenerate. It was, of course, impossible for the Congregationalist system to operate upon any such elusive and subjective criterion as this without inviting chaos. Congregationalist spokesmen were compelled, therefore, to redefine the qualifications for church membership so as more strongly to emphasize practical moral criteria.

The new definition rested upon an emphatic distinction between visible and invisible saints. The former consisted of all those who professed to be regenerate Christians and who lived lives of exemplary sanctity. It was acknowledged, or rather insisted upon, that a few of these visible saints would prove to be false Christians and perhaps lapse into lives of profligacy. Invisible saints, on the other hand, were the true Christians whose glory was secure but whose character was apparent only to the eye of God. While the two categories overlapped in large measure, there remained an appreciable distinction between them. In response to the sectarian challenge, the Congregationalists of New England held that, in view of man's inability to identify invisible Christians, there was no choice but to build the churches upon the visible saints. In Hooker's words, "visible Saints are the only true and meet matter, whereof a visible church should be gathered." Furthermore, in view of the great difficulty of discerning the spiritual condition of others, charity was always to be exercised. Even a slight measure of grace in an individual entitled him to the benefit of the doubt. Hooker went so far as to say that there were many who never knew the time or manner of their conversion yet expressed the power of grace in their lives and might properly be received into church fellowship. Church order, then, would never be more than a rough approximation of true spiritual order, and men were to make these discriminations with charity and humility.

A congregation once gathered by such prudential considerations was not to be the strictly autonomous and self-governing body that a bald statement of the congregational theory suggested. Powerful internal checks upon the potential democracy of the congregation were at hand, to be emphasized by ecclesiastical statesmen. Hooker provided a detailed description of the powers and responsibilities of church officers. He stressed the fact that their duties were assigned by Christ, as indicated in Scripture, and were not delegated to the officers by the people themselves. It was apparent that the analogy elsewhere drawn between civil and ecclesiastical corporations broke down. The church members might elect their own officers, but the powers and functions of office were ordained of God.

In terms of the quest for congregational discipline, perhaps the most significant passage in Hooker's book was that in which he prescribed the duties of church officers, and especially those of the "Ruling Elder." It was the function of this official to "advise" the congregation in all matters ecclesiastical, to mediate disputes, to screen and approve applicants for church membership prior to action by the members, and to take the initiative in excommunications. The office of ruling elder was clearly designed to be occupied by the most substantial and influential layman in the congregation; and in his respectful deference to the "Preaching and Teaching Elders" he could be expected to set the example of appropriate deferment to clerical authority.

Wherever a congregation was able to afford the luxury, it should maintain two clerical elders, pastor and teacher. The pastor's function, according to Hooker, was "to work upon the will and the affections, and by savoury, powerfull, and affectionate application of the truth delivered, to chafe it into the heart, . . . to speak a good word for Christ, . . . and to let in the terror of the Lord upon the conscience, that the careless and rebellious sinner may come to a parley of peace, and be content to take up the profession of the truth." The teacher's office was to prepare the minds of the congregation with proper instruction in order that they might be ready to entertain the truth as preached. The teacher was also to rule upon any doctrinal controversy that might arise within the congregation. Both clerical officers were qualified to administer the sacraments and to preach the covenant of grace.

In matters of censure of excommunication, the procedure prescribed by Hooker was for the elders as a group to weigh the charges and determine the appropriate course of action before presenting the matter to the congregation. The latter was "bound" to accept the recommendation, unless the elders could be convinced of error. The authority and influence of the clergy in the early days of settlement were if anything strengthened by the generally accepted convention that they were ineligible to hold civil office. In Hooker's opinion, the disqualification was "not because these things are contrary" but simply because clerical duties absorbed all of a man's time.

Hooker's theory of Congregationalism was faintly reminiscent of the contemporary Hobbesean version of the social compact. The saints might voluntarily consent to form a congregation, but once a pastor had been chosen they were obliged to submit to him so long as he observed Christ's rule for the office. The power of clerical office was a unified power and, in its sphere, superior to the divided power of the people. Hooker described the duly constituted and functioning congregation in terms that, in the following century, were to become known as the theory of mixed government. "The Government of the Church, in regard of the body of the people is Democraticall; in regard of the Elders Aristocraticall; in regard of Christ, truly Monarchicall. And its such a compound of all these three, as that a parallel example to the like perfection, is not to be found on earth."

Although the Congregationalists repudiated the presbyterian system of hierarchical organization, they did endorse the formation of regional synods or consociations of congregations. These bodies might properly counsel or admonish their members as circumstances required. They could, if necessary, withdraw the right hand of fellowship from an obstinately uncooperative congregation. But in the face of a truly determined challenge to orthodoxy, the synod could hardly be expected to exert unaided the pressure necessary to assure conformity. This must be the responsibility of the civil power.

The sectarian challenge of the 1630's pushed the Congregational Puritans into a more explicit elaboration of church-state relationships than they had had occasion to develop previously. It was asserted, in the light of the troubles with Anne Hutchinson and

Roger Williams, that a prime function of the state was to support the established church and to guarantee its orthodoxy. The civil magistrate, in Hooker's phrase, was the "nursing father" of the church. It was his duty to nourish and preserve it from contamination. He should require all to attend religious services, and he could, if necessary, compel the officers of a congregation to perform their proper tasks. And yet he was not to usurp the functions of Christ as sole ruler of the church. In practical terms, this meant a close if informal understanding and working alliance between civil and religious officers. In the event of a challenge to orthodoxy, the elders should define the proper steps to be taken, and the civil officials should proceed to take them. Theoretically, the two powers were coequal, each exercising a check upon the other. But should the alliance break down, the magistrate might conceivably oppress the church, and in that case Hooker did not hesitate to concede, so strong was his sense of the need for uniformity, that the congregation must suffer it meekly. Congregational independence, said Hooker, meant that each congregation rightly constituted was competent to exercise all the ordinances of Christ; nothing more.

The spirit of religious toleration that spread rapidly in England during the 1640's posed difficult problems for the New England Puritans because of their ambiguous position. The close alliance of church and state was designed to implement a uniformity of faith and practice that was presumed to be the most effective means of perpetuating the true religion. Opposition to toleration was justified in terms of the underlying conviction that the New England Puritans were possessed of the full truth. Thus it was that Nathaniel Ward, author of *The Simple Cobbler of Aggawam in America* (1647), could say that "to authorize an untruth, by a Toleration of State, is to build a Sconce against the walls of Heaven, to batter God out of his Chaire." Anyone who deviated from the established dogmas or practices must necessarily be an atheist, a heretic, or a hypocrite. To tolerate such persons was to sully the purity of the faith and produce a "meagre and motley" religion. It was further assumed that civil order was impossible without religious uniformity. Religious toleration, said the Simple Cobbler, would inevitably entail a similar latitude in moral principles and conduct, "or else the Fiddle will be out of tune, and some of the strings cracke." That this assumption was untrue was one of the major discoveries of American experience—but more than a century was to pass before New Englanders would care to admit it.

Although the Congregationalists were firm in their opposition to those who, like Roger Williams, carried toleration to its logical fulfillment in complete religious liberty, they presented a different face to the radical sectarians, such as Antinomians and Baptists, who accused them of unwarrantable laxity in admitting to church membership (and hence to political privileges) persons whose spiritual condition was, by any rigorous standard, of doubtful quality. Puritan spokesmen responded with their distinction between visible and invisible saints. John Cotton interpreted the parable of the wheat and the tares in such a way as to justify the toleration of doubtful Christians, on the assurance that the hypocrites would be destroyed at the Judgment Day. Meanwhile, the sectarian criticism of spiritual laxity was branded as the irresponsible chatter of men who had never been called upon to exercise the responsibilities of power. Captain Edward Johnson summed up a generation of experience in the Holy Commonwealth when he advised his fellow Puritans to avoid censorious criticism of the spiritual shortcomings of their neighbors; to be patient with those who had difficulty in assenting to every minute article of faith; but, at the same time, to be persistent in cultivating sound doctrine. The Simple Cobbler put it more succinctly when he observed that "Experience will teach Churches and Christians, that it is farre better to live in a State united, though a little Corrupt, than in a State, whereof some Part is incorrupt, and all the rest divided."

The idea of congregationalism was one of the major contributions of Protestantism to modern social theory and practice. The Puritans believed it to have been authorized by Scripture and to have been the polity of the primitive Christians of the first century. In retrospect, however, we can detect more contemporaneous forces that must have strengthened the pertinence of the idea in the seventeenth century. The intense piety generated by the Reformation sought to express itself in a spiritually perfect church order, in a community of the saints uncontaminated by the claims of more sluggish brethren. Restriction of membership privileges to the elect served this purpose. At the same time, newer political and economic forces were reflected in the individualistic strain in congregationalism, for the Puritans stressed the fact that, ultimately, the congregation was a voluntary association. Another source of the congregational idea of which the Puritans were fully conscious was revealed in the analogy of the corporation, in both its economic and administrative aspects. Thomas Hooker spoke of the congregation as a spiritual and ecclesiastical corporation, with the implied analogy between the charter of incorporation and the church covenant.

The theory and practice of congregationalism played an important practical role in the settlement of New England. The religious congregation formed the hard core of the closely knit little communities that remained the distinctive feature of the life of that region for more than two centuries. So long as the religious impulse remained strong among New Englanders, the autonomous congregation proved itself remarkably adaptable to pioneer conditions. The Puritan Congregationalists shared the institution with more radical Protestant sects, which were less concerned than the Puritans came to be over its potentially divisive implications. In any event, sectarians joined with the Puritans to domesticate congregationalism in the New World and to make it the most characteristic form of religious institutional life in America. Churches of episcopalian and presbyterian forms of polity were gradually forced to make appreciable concessions in practice, if not in form, to the spirit of congregational independence. By the end of the nineteenth century, Roman Catholicism alone of the great American religious bodies had been able to withstand the congregational influence.

Another significant potentiality of seventeenth-century congregationalism as a form of church polity was emphasized by its Anglican and Presbyterian critics. They warned that congregationalism would lead eventually to democracy. The Congregationalists, of course, strenuously denied this smear. They insisted that the elect by definition were agreed as to the necessity of submitting themselves to the leadership of the clergy and the civil magistrates; the unregenerate would be forced to submit. Both in theory and in congregational practice, the Puritans recognized two classes in society: the regenerate and the unregenerate. And as long as the religious impulse lasted, this distinction remained far more vivid to them than differences of economic or social status, although they frequently exhibited a tendency to identify prosperity with sanctity. Samuel Stone, Hooker's colleague at Hartford, Connecticut, summarized the congregationalist attitude when he remarked that the church covenant provided for "a speaking *aristocracy* in the face of a silent *democracy*."

The Social Covenant

The theory of the church covenant had been worked out in England, where Puritans had had little opportunity to put it into practice. Its functions were limited to spiritual and ecclesiastical matters. Although the English Puritans had had little occasion to think about the problems of social and political theory implicit in their Congregationalism, circumstances compelled them to take up these questions when, between 1630 and 1640, some ten thousand of them left for New England. No better proof of their primary loyalty to religious convictions is to be found than in the pragmatic expediency with which the American Puritans confronted and solved their political problems.

England had little thought of a colonial empire in 1630. She had had no experience in colonial administration and had no governmental agencies for the management of colonies. But she did have a vigorous merchant marine engaged in overseas trade. During the previous century, British merchants had been developing a form of organization that gradually evolved into the joint-stock company. These corporations were trading with continental Europe, the Baltic states, and the Levant. In 1607, the Virginia Company of London established its plantation at Jamestown; and in 1620, the separatists known as the Pilgrims migrated under corporate auspices from their temporary refuge in Holland to the New World, although their prime purpose was to preserve their identity as a religious group. Against this background, in 1629 a group of wealthy Puritans obtained a charter of incorporation for the Massachusetts Bay Company, with the deliberate intention of using the Company as a vehicle for settlement. The Puritan migration was thus technically a corporate venture.

A corporation, then as later, was owned by stockholders who met annually in what was called the "Great and General Court" to elect a governor (president) and a board of assistants (directors). The institutional significance of the corporation appeared more clearly in Massachusetts than in Virginia. In the latter, the company was operated by English merchants who merely established a plantation in Virginia in expectation of developing a profitable extractive enterprise. In Massachusetts, the company itself was the agency of migration. A sizable proportion of the freemen (stockholders) came to New England, bringing the company charter with them. The result was a corporation established on American soil, free of effective external control and functioning as a virtually sovereign political entity. The governor of the company was mysteriously transformed into the governor of a political jurisdiction. The assistants functioned as a governor's council. The "Great and General Court" became a colonial legislature. And the freemen of the company became citizens with suffrage privileges. By the middle of the century, when Edward Johnson wrote his history of the founding, the transformation of corporation into commonwealth was complete. Johnson regarded the charter as a purely political instrument, conferring upon the Massachusetts authorities the full range of sovereign governmental powers, including the war-making power. He said nothing of allegiance to the British government.

Virginia and Massachusetts were decisive in shaping the development of other English colonies. The basic structure of American political institutions was derived chiefly from the corporation and not from British parliamentary tradition. It is hard to imagine any other system as flexible and adaptable to the exigencies of frontier existence.

To the Puritan, it appeared as if the good society was a successful corporation in which he fully participated. The nature of this participation involved him in a great contradiction. It was by convincing the members of the congregation of the validity of his regenerating experience that the hopeful convert obtained membership. This was the individualistic aspect of Puritan ecclesiastical theory. Man stood alone before his Maker and could merely testify to the transaction between them. From his pastor he could expect advice and encouragement but no official aid. But at the same time, it was taught that the covenant of grace, according to whose terms salvation was possible, had been made by God with a whole people, the spiritual descendants of Abraham. These were not, of course, Abraham's blood descendants, the Jews who were now suffering the consequences of their repudiation of Christ. Abraham's spiritual descendants were all those redeemed by God's grace. Nevertheless, there was a strong presumption that spiritual descent and blood descent ought to coincide. In practical terms, therefore, the Puritans admitted to full church membership only mature individuals who had experienced conversion, but at the same time they baptized the newborn children of church members on the assumption that these infants were virtually, if not actually, within the convenant. But what if, upon reaching adulthood, many of these baptized persons were unable to testify to the experience of regeneration? In the course of time this contradiction was to become the source of great trouble. The Puritans, like the Jews, thought of themselves as a chosen people. Although only a minority of them in America claimed to be regenerate Christians, they believed intensely that the whole community ought to be saved. Powerful sanctions were employed to compel the sinners to come in. Only so long as these sanctions remained relatively efficacious did the contradiction in the Puritan theory of the community remain concealed.

The adaptation of the corporate machinery to the government of a holy commonwealth was not without symbolic significance. Puritan devotion to the spiritual life was never intended to preclude a hardheaded approach to worldly affairs. In practical terms, the transformation was assisted by an extension of the theory of church covenant to the social and political realms, in order to rationalize what was happening, and to adapt religious purposes to economic instrumentalities.

A basic postulate of the emerging body of Puritan political thought was the assumption that government was necessary because of original sin. No government had been required in the Garden of Eden, nor was any presumably necessary in Heaven. Thus the first function of government was to restrain selfish and sinful men. Government's more positive duty was to advance God's kingdom by effectuating the moral order in the community. This objective was, of course, integrally related to the more strictly spiritual purposes of the church. To this end, the state might properly initiate as well as regulate conduct. Laissez-faire individualism as such was not glorified, but in practice, individual initiative and corporate or group activities were indiscriminately encouraged.

Because the most important distinction that could be made between men concerned their spiritual condition, government was to rest upon this distinction. The Holy Commonwealth was to be a dictatorship of the regenerate. The unconverted should enjoy no political privileges, although no other civil or social disabilities were to be placed upon them as a class. Whenever the policy of the state had been determined, either by statute or by magisterial interpretation of the Word of God as found in Scripture, no deviations were to be permitted. Certainly there was to be no toleration of religious differences. The discussion of controversial questions might properly be suppressed if discussion were deemed by the authorities to be contrary to the public interest. The Puritans had no conception of civil liberties as such. The liberty to sin was precisely what they hoped to persuade men to renounce.

The supremacy of the law of God was doubtless the fundamental Puritan political assumption. All social and political institutions and practices were measured in terms of their effectiveness in promoting the realization of that law on earth. The dominant influence in the Puritan state rested with the clergy as the chief custodians and interpreters of divine law. Holy Scripture was the principal but not the only source of knowledge of that law. Scripture was silent on many subjects, and here the law was to be found in nature or in human reason. But whatever the source of the law, all men, whether màgistrates or citizens, were acknowledged to be subject to it. The idea that there was a fundamental law in the universe, a law above the edicts of rulers, to be found either in revelation, or in reason, or in nature, was destined to play a long and significant role in American thinking.

The theory of social covenant did not prescribe any specific form of governmental organization. The Bible revealed several forms that appeared to be equally suited to divine purposes. The English Puritans had lived under a monarchy; their American brethren readily adapted themselves to the institutions of the corporation.

Beneath the contingencies of formal organization, however, was the insistence that political society was based on a social covenant which incorporated the church covenant. This social covenant enabled the community of the faithful to act in a political capacity, just as the church covenant constituted them a congregation for purposes of worship. Thus the church congregation was made the core of the local community socially as well as religiously. In a sense, the function of the community was to support the congregation. Nonchurch members were expected to attend the services and to pay taxes for the support of the clergy, although before 1664 they possessed no vote, either religious or political. For many practical purposes, the congregation and the local political community were fused together. The term *parish* had both religious and civil connotations. The congregation met in the meetinghouse, where town meetings were also held. Since the freemen were both the church members and the voters, it was not always easy to distinguish between these respective functions, nor would it have seemed important to do so.

Discussions of the social covenant in Puritan writings revealed two aspects of the compact theory, which we may separate for purposes of analysis although such a Puritan as Governor John Winthrop would have regarded the distinction as superfluous if not pernicious. The first aspect of the social-covenant relationship was that of consent. Men freely entered into covenant with one another to form a political society. As John Cotton expressed it: "It is evident by the light of nature, that all Civil Relations are founded in Covenant." Cotton appealed to reason—the light of nature—to justify the covenant as the foundation of civil society. By merely substituting the synonym *compact* for *covenant*, his phrases would have been perfectly suited to the pens of John Locke or of Thomas Jefferson. Just as Puritan theology taught that man was free to seek the gift of grace, so also Puritan political theory based the social covenant on the free consent of the contracting parties. According to Winthrop, "no common weale can be founded but by free consent to," "The foundation of the people's power is their liberty." It was this aspect of covenant theory as consent that was exemplified in the contractual agreement of the freemen in forming the Massachusetts Bay Company.

Winthrop's reference to popular liberty did not mean that he was advocating democracy in the modern sense. In the early seventeenth century, the term *people* clearly did not mean what it came to signify politically by the middle of the twentieth century, namely, all adults. As Winthrop used the word it was clearly intended to designate those other than the magistrates who participated actively in political society—the freemen, who were but a small proportion of the population. We know specifically what Winthrop meant by the term *liberty* because he had occasion to make some famous remarks on the subject. He distinguished two kinds of liberty: natural and civil or federal liberty. Natural liberty he defined as the kind of liberty that men share with animals: freedom of physical movement. In social terms, natural liberty was the freedom to abandon one's fellows and flee in solitude to the wilderness; in moral terms, it was the freedom to sin. Civil or federal liberty Winthrop defined as the sense of the term in which the regenerate Christian freely and gladly submitted himself to the will of God as represented in the clergyman and the magistrate. Only in the latter sense was Winthrop prepared to dedicate government to the defense of popular liberties. The fact that it was necessary to make these distinctions suggests, however, that already the first and more naturalistic meaning of the word *liberty* was beginning to assert its appeal. By Jefferson's time, it had completely displaced Winthrop's federal liberty as the commonly understood meaning.

Nevertheless, in the aspect of covenant theory as consent the voluntary element was always stressed. Although the regenerate alone were included in the covenant, the others had only their own sinful stubbornness to blame for their exclusion. If they would assiduously cultivate the means of grace, the merciful God would doubtless come to their rescue, and they would then be eligible for covenant privileges. The Puritans recognized only one specific for individual and social salvation, that is, regenerating grace; but they acknowledged their obligation so far as it lay within their power to make the remedy palatable by being readily available.

The second major aspect of covenant theory emphasized the mutual obligations that it involved. In this light, the covenant had been entered into not by the people themselves as equals, as in eighteenth-century compact theory, but between the ruler on the one hand and the people on the other. The obligations of the social covenant were also rooted in the covenant of grace. Peter Bulkeley found the authority of the magistrate to be derived from the will of God.

Where the Lord sets himselfe over a people, he frames them into a willing and voluntary subjection unto him, that they desire nothing more than to be under his government. . . . When the Lord is in covenant with a people, they follow him nor forcedly, but as farre as they are sanctified by grace, they submit willingly to his regiment.

The political application of this spiritual obligation was made by John Cotton. "Look what a king requires of his people, or the People of a King, the very same doth God require of his people, and the People of God, . . . that is, a Governor, a Provider for, and a protector of his people. . . . And the people undertake to be obedient to his laws, to whatever he declares to be the counsell of his will." The obligations of the covenant freely accepted thus exemplified Winthrop's doctrine of federal liberty. Entry into such a covenent admittedly involved the renunciation of the natural liberty to assert one's selfish will against the considered judgment of the magistrates. They, in turn, were obliged to rule in accordance with the will of God. In practice, this meant a close working alliance with the clergy and sufficient support among the freemen so that all three groups might present a virtually solid front to the unregenerates. The latter were not expected to be entirely happy with these arrangements and so were to be kindly but firmly held in check.

When both aspects of social covenant theory are kept in mind, it is apparent that, although government was presumed to be constituted voluntarily by the people, its agencies and powers were established by God; the offices were sanctified; and the magistrates were obliged to enforce the law of God however determined, which was assumed to be the wish of the freemen as well. These two aspects of social-covenant theory—the voluntary compact on the one hand, and the submission to the will of God in the magistrate on the other—indicate the way in which the Puritans proposed to reconcile liberty and authority. Every society must make this reconciliation in one way or another. The form that it takes, wherever expressed in words, is one of those ultimate fictions that reveal as well as anything can the spirit and temper of the age. The disintegration of Puritan society in the late seventeenth and early eighteenth centuries paralleled closely the disappearance of the obligatory aspects of covenant theory. All that was left by 1750 was the theory of a society of naturally free men who compacted among themselves to provide government.

The Puritan Ethic

Puritan individualism had a primary religious source. Man stood alone before his Maker. His salvation or damnàtion was a matter between himself and God, without priestly intermediary. It was the duty of every man to seek salvation even though few would find it. This universal obligation meant that, in practical if not in theological terms, man's relationship to God was primarily a moral relationship; grace was a free gift that man in no way merited. In the sight of God, man was a sinner. This was the moral base from which all men started, and no man ever transcended its dimensions. The moral emphasis in Puritanism always remained very strong, so that long after Puritanism as a system of thought was dead people still recognized the type of temperament called the "Puritan conscience." The bonds of obligation were always tight, placing the emphasis upon duties, effort, and self-inspection with a view to improvement.

The intimate bond between piety and morality was cemented in other ways. The Puritan conception of the purpose of life determined its definition of virtue. Unregeneracy in its most hopeless form was frequently displayed in an attitude of complacence and security that preachers struggled to undermine. Once awakened to a sense of his peril, man's aim was to seek salvation, which, according to the doctrine of imperfect regeneration, was a lifelong process. Grace was bestowed in an instant, but it was demonstrated in a subsequent life of virtue. For most men, this would be a practical life lived in the work-a-day world, not in monastic retirement. Eventually, the believer arrived at a comforting sense of assurance as to his spiritual condition, but he never recaptured that security of indifference he had formerly known. He would always be driven by a sense of the insufficiency of his works to show forth his praise of God's glory. The Puritan, in short, had a dynamic sense of life as a moral process originating in sin and proceeding to ultimate hope of salvation through practical Christian endeavor. His morality was inevitably of an activist variety.

The specific content of the Puritan morality, the virtues that reflected the conception of life as a dynamic process, were the creative, disciplinary, self-regarding virtues, such as industriousness, frugality, sobriety, honesty, temperance, moderation, and simplicity. These virtues formed a conspicuously different pattern from that of the virtues generally acknowledged to be the highest Christian virtues, namely, love, self-sacrifice, and humility. In its specific selection of values, the Puritan ethic seemed to partake more of the spirit of the Old Testament than of the New. God's justice was emphasized more than His love. As God's chosen people, the Puritans thought of their mission as one to be accomplished through disciplined and energetic activity.

In view of the obvious pertinence of the Puritan virtues to the moral and psychological characteristics of economic individualism, it was inevitable that eventually students should note the relationship and explore its historical meaning. Max Weber, the modern German sociologist, was the first to expound the thesis that, because of its practical tendency to equate worldly success with regeneration, Calvinism stimulated the growth of capitalism by breaking down the medieval regulations and restraints upon economic activity. The American historian Samuel Eliot Morison, however, vigorously denied the validity of Weber's argument, at least so far as it pertained to the Puritans of the New World. He contended that the Puritans were thoroughly medieval in their economic thinking and policies. Wherever it was possible to do so, the early Puritan churches unhesitatingly regulated business affairs in the interests of religion. Morison cited the occasion in 1639 when Robert Keayne, perhaps the richest merchant in Massachusetts, was fined and up-braided by the General Court for profiteering, although no law against it existed on the statute book. The principles that should govern business practices as laid down by Governor Winthrop were equally alien to the spirit of capitalistic individualism. A commodity has a just price, Winthrop declared, to be computed partly in terms of the current market price and partly in terms of the "true value" of the commodity as determined by the cost of material and the processing, plus a legitimate profit. The merchant's losses on one transaction should not be transferred to other transactions, nor should buyer and seller bargain over the price. These principles and practices reveal a firm intention to subordinate commerce to piety.

It is equally apparent that, both in fact and in purpose, the conception of the good society was distinctly different from that envisaged by the laissez-faire individualist of the nineteenth century. Class distinctions were clearly drawn by the Puritan settlers. They did not reproduce the total class structure of contemporary England, but they did recreate a segment of it, roughly the middle and bottom layers, those classes at and below the rank enjoyed by the leading Congregational Puritans of England. These distinctions were recognized in law and custom and acknowledged in titles of address and in sumptuary legislation. Public economic regulations were employed without hesitation where they preserved these distinctions. Wages were upon occasion fixed by law when they threatened to rise above the level suitable to the status of the laboring class. Prices were also regulated at times, and monopolies were granted either as a stimulus to production or simply as normal perquisites of privileged status. An effort was also made to perpetuate the guild system, although this proved abortive. These practices clearly revealed a society whose conscious thought and aims were precapitalistic.

Nevertheless, the moral virtues described above, the content of the Puritan ethic, were precisely those calculated to stimulate a driving spirit of capitalistic enterprise. The inherited concepts of the Puritans, the subordination of society to the will of God, and the maintenance of class distinctions must inevitably come into conflict with a dynamic economic individualism born of the Puritan ethic and nourished by the abundant resources of the New World. In different ways both Weber and Morison were right. But the

Puritan ethic survived long after the disintegration of Puritan society.

The ethic of individual responsibility was perhaps the major legacy of Puritanism to American civilization. It provided the psychological attitudes, the personal discipline, and the rationale out of which sprang a host of merchants, speculators, and industrialists who never dreamed of the antecedents of their outlook. But John Cotton had written: "There is another combination of virtues strangely mixed in every living holy Christian, And that is, Dilligence in worldly business, and yet deadness to the world; such a mystery as none can read but they that know it. For a man to [take] all opportunities to be doing something, early and late, and loseth no opportunity, go any way and bestire himselfe for profit, this will he do most dilligently in his calling. And yet be a man dead-hearted to the world." This Christian admonition to pursue worldly success while at the same time foreswearing the pleasures and indulgences that success makes possible was precisely the teaching calculated to develop a thriving business civilization in an environment richly endowed to reward the self-disciplined individual who turned to its vigorous exploitation.

More than two and a half centuries passed before the character of business enterprise changed to the degree that for many individuals the Puritan ethic no longer seemed relevant to the facts of economic life. The dawning realization of the discrepancy, at the end of the nineteenth century, with the consequent disintegration of practical values that followed, was one of the chief causes of the moral and intellectual confusion of the twentieth century.

CHAPTER 3

||||||||||||||||||||||||||||||||||||||||||||||||||||||||||||||||||||||||||

Sectarianism

T HE COLONIAL RELIGIOUS MIND expressed itself in two major forms: churchly and sectarian. Puritanism best represented the churchly type, while various offshoots from Puritanism, such as Antinomianism and Quakerism, were aspects of sectarianism. These were the poles about which the ideas of the age crystallized. Neither the churchly nor the sectarian form of the colonial religious mind was native to America, but in the isolation of the wilderness each quickly developed the social and religious implications inherent in its own inner logic. At the same time, the mutual hostility born of radically different religious insights and social purposes became more acute.

The Puritan society of early New England was built around the church. The whole culture was organized and regulated in terms of the values professed by the church. Politics, law, economic behavior—all were expected to display the official religious principles. In practice, however, many compromises were made. The religious elite tended to be the social elite, thanks in part to the peculiar quality of the virtues incorporated in the Puritan ethic. This happy coincidence was of immeasurable assistance to the minority of saints in maintaining control over the unregenerate many. But the intimate involvement of religion in the social affairs of the Puritan settlements resulted inevitably in a coarsening of the spiritual quality of Puritan teaching.

The reaction to the churchly compromises that Puritan Congregationalism was forced to make in order to maintain its governing control over a thriving commercial community appeared in a series of sectarian rebellions. The sectarians proposed to maintain a higher standard of spirituality and morality by refusing to assume responsibility for the sinful surroundings of their fellowship. By washing their hands of the world, they assumed that they would not be contaminated by it. Three of these sectarian challenges to Puritan society were those of the Antinomians, of Roger Williams, and of the Quakers.

The Antinomians

During the first wave of Puritan migration to Massachusetts in 1634, there arrived in Boston one William Hutchinson and his wife Anne, devoted followers of John Cotton. Having been a well-to-do landowner in England, Hutchinson assumed a prominent position in Boston. Mistress Anne was an unusually gifted woman and was, in addition, a midwife, an eminently useful person in a society that regarded the attendance of physicians at childbirth as indecent.

Shortly after her arrival, Anne Hutchinson began the practice of delivering an informal midweek commentary on the previous Sunday's sermons, with considerable success. In itself, this would not have aroused opposition in a society in which religion was all-absorbing. It was reported, however, that Mistress Hutchinson was broaching dangerous theological heresies and questioning the spirituality of the clergy. A party of followers quickly formed about her, which came to include perhaps a majority of the Boston congregation, and the ensuing struggle had political as well as religious aspects. Sir Harry Vane, known to be sympathetic to the Hutchinson or Antinomian party, as it later came to be called, was elected governor of Massachusetts in 1636, unseating the perennial incumbent John Winthrop. On the ecclesiastical front, the Antinomians were unsuccessful in their attempts to replace John Wilson, pastor of the Boston congregation and the chief object of their hostility, with Mrs. Hutchinson's brother-in-law, John Wheelwright. The tide turned in the following year, when the outlying towns were galvanized in support of the orthodox party. Vane was defeated for re-election and Winthrop returned to office. Mrs. Hutchinson and Wheelright were promptly tried for sedition and heresy, convicted, and banished from the colony.

Anne Hutchinson has sometimes been glorified as a defender of freedom of speech against the tyranny of the theocrats. But this interpretation is not accurate when the issues are seen as the participants understood them. The Antinomians accused the ruling clergy and magistrates of being deficient in grace; the latter countered with the charge that the Antinomians were guilty of the heretical teaching that a sanctified life was no evidence of a regenerate condition. The importance of these accusations in the context of Puritan society made the issues serious.

Mrs. Hutchinson was a Christian mystic for whom the experience of direct communion with God was intensely vivid and satisfying. She rejected the prevailing Puritan doctrine of imperfect regeneration, whereby the gift of grace was to be demonstrated indirectly through a life of sanctification. That man's conduct could testify to his redeemed condition seemed to her to imply carnal pride and self-satisfaction. It minimized the necessity of complete dependence upon God. Thus she exposed one of the great churchly compromises of Puritanism, namely, its overt identification of regeneration with the practice of the virtues of the Puritan ethic. The Antinomians insisted that the experience of communion with God was complete and perfect in itself and in no way to be cheapened by identification with sanctification or good works. The orthodox Puritans, they insisted, were presumptuous in attempting to demonstrate God's grace in human conduct. Would it not be more appropriate to allow the gracious gift of an almighty God to sanctify conduct? In other words, the Antinomians broached the dangerous question: How can the regenerate person do wrong? This was one of the most radical forms of Christian perfectionism, and it filled sober Puritans with horror. Finally, Anne Hutchinson believed in direct inspiration, contrary to the usual Puritan teaching that no revelations had been made since the age of the Apostles.

To the leaders of the orthodox party in Massachusetts, these doctrines pointed directly toward social and moral anarchy. If regeneration were to justify the conduct of the regenerate person, chaos would reign. In certain instances, licentiousness and promiscuity were believed to have resulted from the espousal of this pernicious doctrine, although no such charges were leveled at the Hutchinson party. Antinomian perfectionists sometimes maintained that the Mosaic law was meant for Adam's sinful descendants, but that those saved by Christ under the covenant of grace were specifically exempted from the dictates of the law. (Hence the name *Antinomian*, meaning literally *against the law*.) The orthodox Puritans with their code of disciplined self-restraint were appalled by the implications of this perfectionism.

The ambiguous position of the teacher of the Boston congregation with respect to the opinions of his zealous parishioner served to underscore the delicate shades of dogma through which orthodoxy blended into heresy. Throughout her struggle with the authorities, Mistress Hutchinson remained an ardent admirer of John Cotton, stoutly maintaining that she had done no more than reaffirm his teachings. This put the clergyman in an extremely embarrassing position, and he was at great pains then and later to dissociate himself from the taint of heretical views. The synod of the clergy that investigated the Antinomians quizzed Cotton thoroughly to discover whether he was in any degree responsible. Confronted by members of his own congregation, he professed surprise to hear erroneous dogmas attributed to him which he insisted he had never taught. Whatever the likelihood that his parishioners had misunderstood him, it was certainly unusual for the teacher to be as ignorant of current theological opinions in his own congregation as he claimed. Cotton was probably more sympathetic to the Antinomian position than were many of his colleagues. He had been expounding a doctrine of adoption according to which the effect of the spirit of Grace was to render the believer "gracious as [the Lord Jesus] is gracious, holy, wise, and patient as he is, every way like the Father, only reserving to God those excellencies which our natures are not capable of." Thus encouraged, zealous souls might well have been tempted to indulge an extravagant hope for perfection.

Cotton's embarrassment could hardly have been mitigated by the inherent difficulty of maintaining the delicate balance of doctrines that lay at the heart of the Puritan compromise. Surely it was unrealistic to expect every layman (and laywoman) to appreciate all the conflicting claims of piety, morality, and social order that the Puritan system was designed to mediate. Nothing but a statesmanlike sense of the needs of community could furnish a sufficiently firm bond to hold these elements together. Severed from each other, these doctrines pointed in various directions. In Anne Hutchinson's hands, the mystical perfectionism that was inherent in the Puritan theory of regeneration was liberated from the qualifications that disciplined and socialized it, resulting in an ecstatic emotionalism that the clergy feared the more because its effects were so well understood. It was the theological fate of Puritanism in America to be sundered into its various dogmas, each of which was to make its way in isolation through the diverse channels that came to compose the stream of American religious life.

Whatever the implications of Antinomian doctrines, Anne Hutchinson struck directly at the ruling oligarchy of Massachusetts by undermining the spiritual authority of the clergy. She accused all but two of them, Cotton and Wheelwright, of being unregenerate, and she did it with such vigor that John Wilson was constrained to report that "she threw dung in the ministers' faces." Such an attack subverted spiritual authority, for all the clergy must be presumed to be regenerate. The threat of anarchy lurked also in the Antinomian belief in a special organ of perception possessed only by the elect. When Anne Hutchinson declared all but two of the clergy to be unregenerate, how did she know this when by her own definition external conduct was in itself no evidence of regeneration? She replied that the elect possess a faculty that permits them infallibly to recognize the spiritual condition of others. "Christ's sheep know His voice." In actual practice, however, the distinguishing mark of the regenerate person was conduct of a special sort, namely, fervor in devotional exercises and a capacity to arouse the kind of emotionalism that later came to characterize evangelical revivalism. But whatever the theory or practice, the orthodox party regarded all this as sheer obscurantism.

Although they were relatively skilled in theological disputation, the Antinomians held learning in contempt. By concentrating with intense passion upon the all-sufficiency of regenerating grace as the sum and essence of religion, they isolated religious truth from the intellectual heritage. Religion became an entirely personal, subjective experience. Learning made men proud and thus obstructed the free entry of God's grace into the soul. This raised the perennial question whether religion was to be a part of daily life, influencing conduct and social affairs; or whether it was to be a purely private matter between the soul and God, merely an inner illumination to be sought for its own sake. Perhaps there has always been an incipient conflict between piety and intellect. But in the little fringe of settlements clinging precariously to the edge of the wilderness, the outcome of this particular conflict was of peculiar importance for American intellectual history. The year 1636 marked both the Antinomian controversy and the founding of Harvard College. Had the Antinomians carried the day, the federal Congregationalists might not have succeeded in their stubborn determination to maintain the continuity of formal academic learning, and the subsequent cultural history of New England might have followed a far different course.

The Antinomians also caused a major crisis in the Congregational ecclesiastical system. When Mistress Hutchinson succeeded in capturing a majority of the members of the Boston congregation for her views, she uncovered the fundamental defect in the Puritan institutional structure. How was the official principle of congregational independence to be reconciled with the assumption of uniformity of doctrine enforced if necessary by the civil magistrate? The Holy Commonwealth could not possibly survive if the largest congregation was allowed to develop radical heresies unopposed. There could be no question but that the religio-political hierarchy must impose uniformity of doctrine upon the recalcitrant congregation if it could muster the power. Consequently, as soon as the orthodox party gained control of the General Court, the Antinomian leaders were promptly tried for sedition and breach of the peace and banished from the Commonwealth.

The episode underscored the fact that congregationalism was one of the original Puritan concessions to the sectarian spirit. The radical sectarians of that age were invariably congregationalist in ecclesiastical polity. In the face of the Antinomian challenge, the orthodox party did not hesitate to override the independence of the Boston congregation in order to maintain uniformity of doctrine among the churches of the colony. This was the first of several steps whereby New England Congregationalism repudiated its original sectarian elements and thus preserved its religious monopoly. In the long run, however, the congregational principle not only survived this setback but, in the end, outlived Puritanism itself, giving its name to the modern denomination that claims lineal descent from federal Puritanism but retains little else of the spirit or doctrine than the principle and practice of congregational independence.

Driven out of Massachusetts, the Antinomians went to nearby Rhode Island in Narragansett Bay, where they established their own community in 1638. The early history of their settlement revealed a social theory and practice that by Puritan standards was reactionary. The exiles organized themselves as a "Body Politick" and drew up a covenant according to the federal practice in which they had been nurtured. Nineteen individuals signed the covenant. Each contracting party agreed to submit himself to the Lord Jesus Christ and His laws as found in Scripture. The chief officer of the community bore the title of judge. The dispensation of justice in Biblical fashion by this officer illustrated the prevailing conception of politics as living according to the law of God. At the same time, however, the sectarian emphasis upon individual inspiration was reflected in the provision that laws should be enacted by the whole body politic.

Modern students have sometimes professed to find the roots of American democracy in such radical sectarians as the Antinomians, Roger Williams, or the Quakers. While it was true that these rebels resisted the totalitarian discipline of the Puritans, the social institutions with which they replaced it were not necessarily congenial to the democratic temperament; this was not their objective. Freed from the Puritan system, the Antinomians were unprepared to draw up or execute a positive and coherent social philosophy. Because of their sectarian repudiation of the sinful world, they had not equipped themselves with the theoretical system by which men rationalize and explain their social institutions. They had to improvise. Because they were religious zealots, their improvisation revealed a quality of Biblical literalism that had little to do with the rise of secular democracy.

Roger Williams

An intense and uncompromising desire for religious purity was the chief characteristic of the radical Protestant sectarians. Like the Puritans, they made a basic distinction between the elect and the unregenerate, but in order to preserve the purity of the regenerate they disavowed all religious responsibility for the unregenerate. Sectarians knew that the world was the domain of the devil and would remain so until the second coming of Christ. They attempted to redeem sinners by such methods as missionary activity, which would not contaminate the elect, but they were determined not to assume a religious responsibility for the governance of the world. That would only corrupt their religious life.

The sectarian attitude toward worldly responsibility resulted naturally in an insistence upon the separation of church and state. Degrees of withdrawal or separation from the world varied with the brand of separatism, but in all cases the separatist animus was a religious one. Nineteenth- and twentieth-century Americans frequently misunderstood Roger Williams and the separatists by approaching them from a secular point of view. These later students approved of separatism because it divorced the state from religious control. They further tended to assume that the separatists must have had some secular social loyalties like their own. But this would have been irrelevant to the seventeenth-century separatists. To satisfy their thirst for the utmost measure of religious purity, they were prepared to abandon the state and society to the devil. No wonder they paid little attention to social or political philosophy.

It was inevitable that men should inquire what would happen when the sectarian separatist abandoned the state to its own devices. Contemporary Puritans prophesied doom; later, certain twentieth-century historians believed they could detect the seeds of democracy. All, however, would have agreed on the facts: in Europe radical sectarians were usually driven underground, there to form little cells where persecution deepened the chasm between them and the world; in America persecution drove the sectarians into the wilderness where they were on their own. The consequences of the different circumstances were important. In the woods there was no sinful society for the sectarian to disavow. His very coming created a society. What would be its principles? How would he interpret the society growing up around him? To gain an appreciation of the place of Williams in American thought, the student must seek the answer to these questions of perennial significance by inquiring first into the topics that Williams himself deemed important in order to extend the implications of the discussion to matters he did not take up in any detail.

A Congregational Puritan, Williams arrived in Boston in 1631 bearing the reputation of one of the coming young men. But he promptly revealed something of his irregularity by refusing the post of teacher to the Boston congregation on the ground that that body had not sufficiently declared its separation from official Anglicanism. In theological doctrine he seemed to be sound, but on the ecclesiastical side characteristic sectarian scruples quickly appeared. His refined sense of religious values was such that he realized that they could not be upheld if propagated by the police powers of the civil magistrate. Therefore he declared that the state should not undertake to punish such purely religious offenses as idolatry, blasphemy, heresy, or sabbath-breaking. No attempt should be made to maintain religious conformity by law; nor should civil penalties be imposed on sinful persons. The entire religious realm should be removed from the sphere of competence of the state.

In view of these developing scruples, Williams went to separatist Plymouth where he found a more congenial atmosphere. There was no clerical post for him in Plymouth, however, and in 1633 he went to the church in Salem, where he quickly made his views felt. He now challenged the presumed right of the king of England as a Christian monarch to grant the lands of infidel Indians without their consent. Since the landholdings of the settlers rested on the validity of such a grant to the Massachusetts Bay Company, it was not surprising that Williams's views were unpopular, particularly with the more extensive landholders. It was becoming increasingly apparent that this intense and outspoken man was repudiating the emerging New England Puritan social theory of a spiritual-social hierarchy in which the elect governed the unregenerate, Christianizing them so far as possible but in any event ruling them with a firm hand. From Williams's point of view, this was to assume that one could have heaven and prosperity too; it was to attempt to usher in the Kingdom by force. For such cheap compromises he had only disdain. After almost five years of intermittent controversy with the Puritan leaders, Williams was banished in 1635 from the jurisdiction of the Bay colony—"enlarged," as John Cotton preferred to have it. Leaving his family temporarily at Salem, he fled to the head of Narragansett Bay and there established his own settlement, Providence Plantation, on land purchased from the Indians.

Supporting himself in part by trading with the natives, Williams became a sympathetic student of their customs and language. His *A Key into the Language of America*, published in London in 1643, was a pioneer Indian language dictionary in English, and for many years he was the principal intermediary between Indians and white men in New England. Williams journeyed to London in 1643 to secure from Parliament the remarkable charter for Rhode Island that united the little settlements about Narragansett Bay under a colonial government with autonomous powers. He returned again to the homeland in 1651 in order to save the charter in the face of bitter internal dissensions in Rhode Island, the early years of that colony being perhaps the stormiest in all British colonial experience in North America. He served briefly as president of Rhode Island from 1654 to 1657. The last notable episode of his career was a debate in 1672 with Quakers, significant in that it revealed the abiding Puritanism of his theological views. He died in 1683 at the probable age of eighty. During each of his two visits to England he published three books, the most famous being the two defenses of liberty of conscience directed specifically at works of John Cotton: *The Bloudy Tenent of Persecution for Cause of Conscience* (1644), and *The Bloody Tenent Yet More Bloody* (1652). Much of the following discussion is drawn from these books.

With the passage of the years, Williams's religious convictions became increasingly subjective and tenuous on the social and ecclesiastical side. He became a Baptist in 1639, a sectarian deviation to which not a few thoughtful Puritans were prone. But within a few months he abandoned the Baptist belief that a true congregation consisted exclusively of regenerate Christians to whom the rite of baptism was restricted. He then took what was known as the "Seeker" position, namely, that no true church existed because no earthly institution could become the repository of authoritative religious truth. Cotton spoke of Williams contemptuously as "a haberdasher of small questions." The venom was doubtless due in part to the effectiveness of the criticism of Congregational theory that Williams was able to develop from the peculiar vantage point of Seekerism. His criticism aimed chiefly at the inconsistent position at which the Puritans of the Bay Colony proposed to stop in their reform of church practices.

Williams was a Biblical literalist who interpreted the Scriptures in terms of the ancient theory of typology. In orthodox federal Puritan teaching, the doctrine of the covenants united the whole of Scripture, both Old and New Testaments, into a single and coherent revelation of God's will for man. Williams's typological interpretation was heretical in that it made a radical distinction between Old and New Testaments. Williams used the Old Testament ("the law") for allegorical illustrations of principles found in the New Testament ("the gospel"). Old Testament types corresponded to New Testament antitypes. Thus, while Puritan conformists felt free to appeal to the authoritarianism of the ancient Hebraic tradition, Williams set that tradition aside in favor of the radically different spirit of the teachings of Jesus Christ as he understood them. In emphasizing this distinction between the law and the gospel, Williams inaugurated what was to become an important and distinctive strain in American Protestantism. In nineteenth-century perfectionism it was to flower in the conviction that the Gospel promised spiritual and even moral liberation from the restraints of the Mosaic law.

Williams also acknowledged a permissible distinction between personal piety and sound doctrine that more orthodox Puritans were extremely reluctant to admit. He held that a man might be possessed of personal godliness and yet hold views on such important matters as faith, justification, or repentance that were generally regarded as erroneous. Such dissociation of piety from dogma was of great importance. It reflected the typical Seeker uncertainty as to the full measure of truth. It also reflected Williams's personal sense—most unusual for that age—of the relativity of mere doctrines and his extraordinarily deep personal piety. Federal Puritans could not admit the dissociation of piety from dogma without relinquishing an essential prop to the system of enforced conformity.

The Scriptural distinction between law and gospel corresponded to Williams's practical distinction between the world and the church. For his ecclesiastical and social thinking, the latter distinction was of fundamental importance. He drew a sharp typological contrast between Israel on the one hand—the literal offspring or seed of Abraham, a social group bound by ties of blood, propinquity, and tradition—and the modern church on the other hand—composed of true believers, the spiritual seed of Christ, who were to be found anywhere and everywhere. It was the initial absence of any obvious organic or social bonds among spiritual Christians that lay at the heart of Williams's ecclesiastical uncertainty. Drawing upon the analogy of Eden, he spoke of the church or community of the faithful as a garden. Beyond its bounds lay the wilderness of the sinful world from which the garden was preserved by a wall of separation. Should the wall be breached, weeds from the wilderness would invade the garden and choke off its flowers. Thus Williams contended against the Massachusetts practice of compelling the unregenerate to submit to the tutelage of the elect. In his opinion, the elect would be contaminated by the contact.

As in many forms of sectarianism, an eschatological emphasis was strong in Williams's thinking. He eagerly awaited the second coming of Christ. The meaning of experience was to be understood in terms of the full cycle of history from the creation and fall to the Second Coming and day of judgment. Men need not despair to know less than the full truth because Christ would come again soon, and then they would know all. These were the latter days when events would be judged in terms of the prophesied slaughter of the faithful and destruction of Antichrist that were to precede the Second Coming. Williams proposed to emulate the Bereans of

Scripture, who maintained rigorous standards of purity and awaited expectantly the completion of revelation shortly to be consummated. Preoccupied with his millennialist expectations, Williams displayed a casualness, almost indifference, to problems with which more mundane persons concerned themselves. This helps to explain the meagerness of his discussion of social affairs.

In contrast to his millennialism, Williams revealed a strikingly modern feeling for the character of Jesus Christ and the significance of His teaching. The development of his Christology was facilitated by the typological contrast between law and gospel. Christ in many aspects represented the antithesis of the Old Testament emphasis on precept and authority. Christ taught a purely spiritual religion. Williams, of course, did not have the nineteenth-century sense of historical development in his interpretation of Scripture, although in this respect his sense of the significance of Jesus was not unlike that which later historians made familiar. For him, the spirit of Christ was that of love, pity, suffering, and sympathy for the downtrodden. It had little in common with the legalistic transaction by which Christ purchased man's redemption as depicted in the covenant theology. The compulsions of Puritan authoritarianism were contrasted by Williams with the teaching of Him who said: "I came not to destroy men's lives, but to save them." Venerating Christ as the Prince of Peace, the man of sorrows, Williams could not but declare persecution for conscientious belief to be contrary to Christ's spirit.

Finally, certain paradoxes formed an unresolved residue in Williams's Seekerism. Why was it, he asked, that God left men to work out their own salvation in fear and trembling when He could, if He wished, perfect them instantaneously? Why did experience invariably prove that joy, victory, and prosperity were injurious to true piety, while pain, persecution, and poverty were favorable to it? These paradoxes remained as perpetual reminders of the inscrutability of divine purpose. They set Williams apart from all those contemporaries who were so certain of the truth they espoused that they were determined to compel all to acknowledge it. The recollection of these paradoxes assisted Williams in achieving a degree of detachment that enabled him to see the futility of strife among so many contending religious parties, each professing to have the full truth.

The critique of Puritan society that Williams developed from his Seeker point of view was especially effective in exposing the inconsistencies resulting from the Puritan attempt to compromise between church and sect. The effort of the Congregationalists to reconcile their English sectarian origins with their churchly pretensions in the New World resulted in what Williams shrewdly characterized as an attempt "to walke betwixt Christ and Antichrist." These inconsistencies were both ecclesiastical and political.

On the ecclesiastical side, the Puritans were attempting to compromise between separatism and legally established uniformity of worship. They were separatists so far as they restricted church membership and communion to the elect. But at the same time, they were compelling strict observance of the ordinances by all others in the community. This blurred what was to Williams the fundamental distinction between the church and the world and resulted in "confused mixtures of the unclean and clean."

Worse than this, their compromise with churchly uniformity encouraged Puritans to indulge in miserable double talk about liberty of conscience. The Protestant world had by the 1630's so far committed itself to the principle of liberty of conscience in religious matters that New England Puritans were obliged for reasons of public relations to profess allegiance to it in principle even though they might violate it in practice. In fact, they devised an ingenious but not very deceptive evasion. Whenever an individual within their jurisdiction broached a heresy, his error was pointed out to him by clerical authority. If he persisted, he would be further instructed in the truth, solemnly and at length. It was hoped that the logic and reasonableness of officially established truth would be made so crystal clear that, if the obstinate offender still persisted in error, he was violating his own conscience and thus denying liberty of conscience to follow the truth. He might then properly be punished for sinning against his own conscience.

Williams had only to point to the vast welter of contending religious parties in the English-speaking world, each convinced that it had the truth, to show the absurdity of the idea that divine truth was so clear that any instructed conscience would see it in all its details. The only logical and appropriate institutional embodiment of the principle of liberty of conscience was a purely voluntary religious system.

Politically, the revolution inherent in Protestantism expressed itself everywhere in the doctrine of popular sovereignty. The Puritans conceded the civil power to rest upon the will of the people, although in practice they were far from ready to accept the full consequences of the proposition. The political inconsistency that concerned Williams resulted from the use of the civil power to assure religious conformity. According to the doctrine of popular sovereignty, the power of the Puritan magistrate to preserve the church from error came from the people. But, said Williams, so far as the natural man was corrupt and sinful the power of the magistrate must be the power of Satan. The protection of the church could not safely be entrusted to such a power. The Puritans of Massachusetts Bay were, in effect, acknowledging the pertinence of the criticism by restricting political privileges to the elect. But then, as Williams pointed out, the magistrate was merely the church acting in a civil capacity.

The consequence of these ecclesiastical and political inconsistencies, according to Williams, was a coarsening and cheapening of the whole fabric of Puritan piety. The forcible attempt to discipline and indoctrinate the unregenerate involved compromises with sin that inevitably contaminated the elect. At the same time, the coercion of dissenters was a denial of what Williams felt to be the very essence of the Christ spirit. The hatred that the spokesmen for the Massachusetts oligarchy bore their Rhode Island neighbor was sufficient testimony to their sensitivity to his criticism.

Williams's separatism may be more clearly understood by considering what he conceived to be the contemporary situation in Christendom. In his literary controversy with John Cotton, Williams explained that the context of his discussion was not the division of mankind between Christian and pagan, between believer and infidel, but the situation in the Western world wherein large numbers of nominal Christians hated the holiness of the spirit—"the blasphemy of this is so wonderful and dreadful." Consciousness of this unique state of affairs was never absent from Williams's speculations as he deliberated the principles of true church order. He concluded that Christianity had suffered immense harm from the rule of the Christian emperors following Constantine. Their influence had resulted in a wilderness of so-called "Christian" nations. The distinction between the church and the world had become lost. Pure Christian virtue had become adulterated, while the attempt to make everyone Christian by coercion had resulted merely in strife and hypocrisy. The flowers in Christ's garden could flourish only so long as they were kept clear of the noxious weeds from the wilderness.

As a Seeker, Williams never arrived at a personally satisfactory theory or practice of church organization. Since the day that Christ had returned to Heaven without having left precise instructions on this matter, no one could say with authority what were the elements of true church order. Certainly the Massachusetts authorities were in no position to say whether a specific congregation deviated from sound practice. But Williams did at least insist upon the fundamental importance of preserving the distinction between the elect and the unregenerate; for the elect, because they were liable to contamination by contact with sinners; for the unregenerate, because if permitted freely to join the elect in worship they were liable to be eased somewhat of the burden of their sins, to the jeopardy of their immortal souls.

Experience and reflection also suggested to Williams certain other likely features of sound church order. He believed that the Lord generally chose the poor rather than the high and mighty. It was rare indeed to find a king, a governor, or a magistrate who bore even a faint resemblance to the King of Kings! Those churches and individuals most like Jesus were content with poverty and a humble status; they renounced false worship and worldly conversation; they practiced simplicity of worship; and they bore meekly the cross of Christ. Such churches were purely private corporations, conducting their affairs without outside interference. Their pastors received no stipends, whether from tithes or voluntary contributions. The economic nexus was palpably a false one: "no longer penny, no longer paternoster." Although willing to maintain universities as schools of humane learning, Williams, in true sectarian style, would not entrust them with the training of the clergy or with the granting of "degrees" in divinity.

Williams's concept of the church thus rested on his sense of the polar opposition between the rigorous demands of Christian purity and the abiding iniquity of the sinful world. The contrast between heaven and hell was not too great to serve as a comparison for the difference between the church and the world. In practice, in the absence of a convincing Scriptural directive as to church order, Williams resorted to private worship in the family. There was Scriptural warrant for this practice. And furthermore, with few Christians and little agreement among them to be found in the literal and spiritual wilderness of Rhode Island, there was practical justification as well.

Few men who have been forced to deal with public affairs as Williams was, have been more completely preoccupied than he with other-worldly considerations. This is the stubborn fact that confronts those students who profess to find in Williams the seeds of a democratic political philosophy. It is a fact that forces us to interpret his occasional remarks on political affairs in the light of the religious interests that so largely occupied his attention.

In later times, when it became the fashion to extol Williams for his principles of liberty of conscience and the separation of church and state, his fame was celebrated by liberals who would break the remaining shackles of official religious power over the state. But it was precisely the opposite situation that had concerned Williams. It was the release of religion from the incubus of state control for which he contended. The state was the instrument of natural men. It was the wilderness, evil, the domain of the devil. It tended, therefore, in the nature of things to be corrupt. It was the corruption of the church by the world that stood out in Williams's mind as the great fact of modern history. Convinced that God rarely showered his grace upon magistrates, this religious zealot did not concern himself willingly with public affairs. It was his tragedy that a sense of obligation to his neighbors forced him to do so.

One of the fundamental assumptions of the democratic ideology as it developed in the nineteenth century was the conviction that a political order based on universal and equal political privilege is an ethical good. Williams, of course, never discussed this proposition, but in the light of the whole body of his thought it is evident that he would have rejected it as irrelevant if not false. To him, politics was the realm not of value but of expediency. He declared that the civil state, a mere combination of men, should concern itself only with civil affairs. Where it attempted to maintain a religious establishment, chaos and insecurity resulted: witness England under the successive rule of Henry VIII, Edward VI, Mary, and Elizabeth I. Even the sinful world was not without the purview of God's providence, however, for Williams declared that "civil government is an ordinance of God to conserve the civil peace of people so far as concerns their bodies and goods." Under this ordinance, the people were declared to be "the original of all free power and government." In this general sense that political power derives from the body politic, Williams voiced the modern notion of popular sovereignty. The Puritans were in entire agreement with it—as were most moderate as well as radical Protestants of that time. They were united against the reactionary alternative of autocratic authoritarianism.

In the debate between Williams and Cotton, the Puritan spokesman was arguing for a limited toleration of religious differences by established ecclesiastical authority, while Williams stood for full religious liberty and the complete separation of church and state. At one point in the discussion Williams took Cotton on his own terms, observing that a "state policy" which permitted religious freedom in order to avoid civil strife was fully compatible with the teachings of Christ, "the greatest of politicians." The terms *policy* and *politician* had in Puritan circles at that time an invidiously Machiavellian connotation. Williams was suggesting, in other words, that even in the political underworld policies of expediency could be turned to good account, namely, the preservation of civil peace; nor was Christ Himself averse to realizing its practical benefits. Nevertheless, all this suggested an attitude toward the political realm as a lower order of affairs that was far removed from the secular democratic ideology of a later age.

So far as Williams had a political theory, it rested on the idea of the social compact. Unlike the Puritans, he did not define the qualifications for active political participation in religious terms, at least ostensibly. But in the first compact drawn up at Providence in 1636—and at so early a date the founder must have had an influential hand in framing it—active participation was restricted to the heads of families, with bachelors specifically disfranchised. In frontier communities, then as later, the number of bachelors was disproportionately high, and this curious discrimination gave great trouble from the beginning. Perhaps it was another expression of Williams's regard for the head of the family as a religious officer, as reflected in his own resort to family worship. Whatever the explanation, the founder later claimed that he had always advocated "liberty and equality, both in land and government." In general, there is nothing in the long record of his selfless service to his community with which to dispute that claim.

Williams was probably the first American to use the familiar metaphor of the ship of state. In 1655, in the face of threatened Indian depredations, the Baptists of Providence refused to perform militia service on the ground of religious scruple. They claimed that conscience forbade it, an appeal to which Williams might be supposed to be peculiarly sensitive. But they received no aid from that quarter, Williams replying that all the liberty of conscience for which he had ever contended was freedom from religious coercion. Religious freedom to him was the freedom of Turks, Christians, or

Jews on shipboard to attend or absent themselves from the ship's services or to hold their own services. The ship's master was acknowledged to have full authority over all matters pertaining to the ship and its navigation. He might judge and punish seamen who resisted orders or passengers who refused to pay their fares, to follow orders in an emergency, or to aid in the ship's defense. In such circumstances no claim to equality in Christ could exempt them. In brief, religious scruple was no excuse from the obligations of military service. Here Williams fell short of the practice in modern democratic states. Nor does the arbitrary and extensive power enjoyed by a ship's captain strike the modern democrat as a particularly apt symbol for the constitutionally limited state. There were, however, peculiar features of the sea law of the seventeenth century. At the beginning of a voyage it was customary for the crew and passengers to enter into a contractual agreement assenting to the purposes of the voyage and to the jurisdiction of the master. This practice was one of the precedents from which the eighteenth-century idea of constitutional restraint derived its authority, and common knowledge of it might have served to enhance the pertinence of Williams's metaphor.

The assertion that a community based on compact among its members could remain stable and united in civic affairs even though divided into many religious groups was Williams's great contribution to American political theory. It cannot be said, however, that the early history of Rhode Island afforded immediately any very convincing demonstration of the principle in practice. The affairs of that colony long remained in a chaotic state. Liberty and equality in land and government may have been Williams's ideal, but the actual scramble for the pre-emption of land was perhaps more unbridled there than anywhere else. Rhode Island provided instead the first illustration in New England of a trend in early American history: where religion was eliminated as a controlling force in political theory and practice, property reared its ugly head, to remain for about a century and a half the prime prerequisite for participation in political life. As early as 1658 Rhode Island formally restricted its suffrage to property holders.

There is no evidence that Williams was inclined to associate political privilege with economic affluence. On the contrary, all his sympathies lay with the poor, both in land and in spirit. He espoused the principle of equality because in the local circumstances it meant substantial poverty, the principle thus facilitating one of those worldly expediencies that no prudent Christian should ignore. At the same time, however, Williams continued to adhere to the theory that only heads of families should have political privileges. This principle, of course, put him outside the main line of American political development.

The Quakers

The contrast between Puritans and Quakers as expressive of the church-sect dichotomy is particularly instructive because it contained the beginnings of a dynamic social trend that was to characterize American civilization for at least two centuries. In the most primitive sense, it was a contrast between the community and the individual—the community representing those qualities of responsibility, subordination, cooperation, and leadership typical of the Puritan spirit; the individual standing for the self-sufficing independence of classical Quakerism. In the seventeenth century, these divergent tendencies of the religious mind were far from being equipoised. From their first appearance in America, in the middle of the century, the Quakers took the initiative, and they held it consistently until the individual had triumphed over the community and until the name *Puritan* had come to have little more than historical significance.

The seventeenth-century Puritans hated and feared the Quakers. They regarded Quaker religious doctrines as erroneous and socially destructive, for reasons already apparent in their relations with other sectarians. They made every effort to keep Quakers out of the Puritan settlements, and in robust Reformation style punished Quaker missionaries for persistent infiltration. The purely defensive attitude of the Puritans was reflected in the fact that they made no attempt to propagandize among the Quakers. It was the Quakers who seized and held the initiative. Quaker missionaries regularly circulated among the Puritan settlements and were moderately successful to the extent of establishing small but permanent communities of Friends in the Puritan colonies. Puritan teachings, on the other hand, appeared to have no appeal for the Quakers, who seemed impervious to them. As a sectarian offshoot from Puritanism, the Quaker movement had passed through and beyond the Puritan position. But in the very horror with which he recoiled from Quaker antinomianism the Puritan acknowledged his peculiar vulnerability to that insidious heresy. In the late seventeenth-century context, Puritan doctrine seemed to be an unstable compound prone to break up into the simple if improbable elements of sectarian affirmation. This was the fate of American Puritanism during two centuries, for after the Quakers had inaugurated the process of disintegration Baptists, New Lights, and Unitarians appeared successively to continue the work. Thus it was that the Puritans, though far more numerous, wealthy, and powerful than their seventeenth-century adversaries, were left in a purely defensive position. It is in similar ideological circumstances that clues to the source and direction of historical change are often found.

As it worked itself out during the seventeenth century, the Protestant Reformation in England produced a wide variety of religious groups with differing doctrines and social theories. One of the later of the sects was the Society of Friends, commonly known as Quakers, founded by George Fox in 1647. Fox himself had been raised a Presbyterian Puritan, and his followers were recruited largely from those inclined to be dissatisfied with the Puritan compromises. Quaker missionaries first appeared in America in 1656, the vanguard of an intensive and systematic movement that had touched all the English colonies by 1660. By the time of the American Revolution, these efforts had resulted in a distribution of Friends throughout Anglo-America more uniform than that of any other religious group. By that time too, they had dominated the colonial governments of Pennsylvania and Rhode Island. They were numerous enough to have had great influence in New Jersey and the Carolinas. And they existed in appreciable numbers in Maine, New Hampshire, Massachusetts, New York, Maryland, and Virginia. In the history of these regions, the perceptible if intangible influences of the Quaker spirit were apparent.

The Quakers participated fully in the Puritan social ethic. This was perhaps the chief explanation of their rapid accumulation of wealth, with all that this entailed for the modification of their social attitudes. But it is more important to note that the Quakers were the chief source of what later came to be known in popular parlance as the "Puritan morality," or the puritanical attitude toward conduct. The early Quakers were far more rigorous than were the Puritans in enforcing upon themselves simplicity of dress and of speech and the banning of sports, cards, dice, plays, dancing, intemperate drinking, the reading of fiction, instrumental music, and even whistling. The Great Law of Pennsylvania (1682) explicitly prohibited profanity, drunkenness, and gaming. It is one of the ironies of history that the nineteenth-century romantics and their disciples should have succeeded in fixing in popular usage the contemptuous epithet *Puritan* upon a rigorousness of personal asceticism that to the true Puritan mind was but one consequence of sectarian fanaticism.

In his religious affirmations the Quaker, being, like the Puritan, a seventeenth-century Protestant, inevitably started with the experience of regeneration. But he was impatient with the carefully drawn distinctions with which the Puritan theologians defined and, to his mind, diluted this exalted experience. For him it was enough to assert that spiritual regeneration occurred through the agency of the Inner Light, the Seed, which was God's presence in the soul of the believer. The Quaker was a mystic, whose religion consisted in cultivating this experience of direct contact with the divine spirit within. Yet his mysticism was inveterately practical in the sense that the mystical experience was cultivated not simply for its own sake but also, and characteristically, for the light that he believed it shed on his everyday problems. The early Quakers were humble men who had, strictly speaking, no theology. The one Quaker who wrote in the formal theological fashion of the time, the Englishman Robert Barclay, was an ex-Puritan apparently unable to recover from the habit of theologizing. There was a sense in which the movement was an anti-intellectual rebellion of common men against the pretensions of learned theological zealots to mold society according to their sophisticated views. But as soon as this judgment is expressed it must be linked with the acknowledgment of the remarkably positive and pure social and moral convictions that stamped the Quaker movement and that it bequeathed to American society.

Perhaps the most radical feature of early Quaker teaching was its perfectionism. While he was in full agreement with the Puritan that man in the unregenerate state is spiritually, mentally, and morally depraved, the Quaker nevertheless believed that, if man would but subject himself without reserve to the prompting of the light within, he would be perfectly regenerated. Many of the earliest Quakers thought to testify to their faith in God's infinite grace and power by insisting that such perfection in the fullest sense was the instantaneous result of the gift of grace. Anne Hutchinson and her Antinomain followers had been perfectionists in this sense. Several of them later became Quakers.

With the passage of the years, however, and with the accompanying increase in numbers and wealth, the Quakers became more conservative, and the doctrine of instantaneously perfecting grace was modified in the direction of a gradual process of growth. By continuous and assiduous cultivation, the Seed within would flourish and progressively purge the soul and body of sin. This was the view of the great eighteenth-century Quaker John Woolman. Quakers had no use for the sophisticated Calvinistic doctrine of perseverance. Because they thought of the religious experience in emotional and ethical terms, they assumed that it was always possible for the believer to backslide into sin, at least until the perfecting process was complete.

The Quaker was also a universalist who believed that the Inner Light at least flickered in the souls of all men. God in His infinite love for man had made it possible for all to be saved. Any savage or heathen who heeded the light within would be saved, even though he had never heard of Christ's sacrifice. This was the Quaker reply to the logical Christian assertion that heathens ignorant of the saving grace of God in Christ must necessarily if unfortunately be damned. It was perhaps the earliest appearance in America of a kind of cosmopolitanism, characteristic alike of rationalists and romantics, which would come to look with increasing embarrassment upon the provinciality of exclusive claims of historic spiritual insight. Quaker universalism underscored a conception of deity that was quite distinct from that of the Puritan; whereas the latter emphasized God's omnipotence and justice, the Quaker stressed His mercy and love.

The final distinguishing feature of Quaker religious thought was its voluntarism. The Puritan testified in part to his sense of the omnipotence and justice of God by emphasizing the insignificance and impotence of man. Contrariwise, the Quaker glorified his Maker's love and mercy by insisting that Christ's sacrifice was made for all men and that ultimate responsibility for salvation or damnation rested with each individual. Children were not born with the taint of Adam's sin; they sinned by their own first responsible acts. Such voluntarism made religion primarily a moral matter, and the religious "experience" itself became a clue to righteous conduct.

The social consequences of Quaker doctrines provide an apt illustration of the influence exercised by ideas over conduct and institutional behavior. The peculiar features of Quaker sectarianism are among the more important contributions of the seventeenth century to the formation of a distinctive American culture. Quakers

accepted the Puritan theory of congregational independence in ecclesiastical organization and in practice developed it to its logical
extreme. This involved not only the complete autonomy of each
congregation (or meeting, as they preferred to call it) but also by
implication the rigid separation of church and state. The meeting
was a purely voluntary association composed exclusively of believers. Because the prompting of the Inner Light took precedence
over the Scriptures, no formal clergy with authoritative powers to
interpret the Word of God was necessary. In organization and spirit,
the Quaker meeting was entirely democratic. None but the convinced believers need attend; and each member would be scrupu-
lously consulted on common affairs.

The importance of Quaker sectarianism for American institutional
development lay in the social implications of Quaker church organization. The private meeting of believers pointed toward a society
composed of voluntary, autonomous, unrelated organizations, such
as corporations, schools, clubs, labor unions, and religious bodies,
none claiming any authority or jurisdiction over the others. As
a religious man, the Quaker felt a supreme concern for the welfare
of his meeting; as a citizen, he might or might not take any interest
in the political affairs of his province. In short, Quaker sectarianism
presupposed a pluralistic, tolerant, flexible form of society precisely
the opposite of the seventeenth-century Puritan theocracy or the
twentieth-century totalitarian state. The Quaker cared supremely
for the spiritual welfare of his meeting, but he was willing to entrust its fate to an encompassing social milieu that might well prove
hostile to his interests, and in fact frequently did so. The first two
generations of Friends were confident in their expectation of converting mankind to Quakerism. They were among the first Protestant groups to enter systematically into missionary activity.
Restrained by his own principles from the use of such official agencies as the state, the sectarian normally turned to individual and
informal proselytizing as a means of propagating the truth. The
perseverance of Quaker missionaries in hostile territory was the
cause of their persecution. To keep them out of Massachusetts,
the Puritan authorities imposed punishments of progressive severity,
culminating in execution, in order to discourage habitual offenders
from returning.

While these indirect social implications of Quaker sectarianism
for subsequent American society seem fairly obvious, the direct
political contribution of the movement to late seventeenth-century

governmental practices is more difficult to assess. Quaker historians have sometimes claimed with pardonable enthusiasm that the Quakers were the first to introduce universal manhood suffrage in America, pointing to William Penn's constitution of 1682 for his proprietorship of Pennsylvania. But although in practice sectarianism appropriately oriented itself in this direction, evidence of a positive Quaker democratic political theory is difficult to find. Instead there are indications of typical sectarian improvisation and of an indifference to political matters that easily lent itself to passive acquiescence in corruption. Penn himself, as the preamble of his constitution showed, was not yet prepared to rely upon a secular political theory; and the advice that he gave to his heirs who were to succeed him as hereditary proprietors reminds us of a Victorian father warning his son of the perils of sex: "Meddle not with government; never speak of it, let others say or do as they please. . . . I have said little to you about distributing justice, or being just in power or government, for I should desire you should never be concerned therein."

In the light of this advice it is no wonder that the Penns became the most hated proprietors in America. At the same time, Penn's words suggest the ease with which the sectarian could refuse responsibility for the conduct of those aspects of society he might choose to ignore. There is, of course, a sense in which American democracy has thrived upon such indifference, but this should not obscure the recognition of the necessity for implicit agreement upon certain positive if minimal affirmations before any political system can function in practice. Although Quaker sectarianism in its most characteristic features was calculated to stimulate the drift toward an individualistic and democratic society, the early Quakers were not yet able to produce a positive theory for such a society.

Other social consequences of Quaker doctrine help to fill out the picture of the radically new society that was to emerge in the eighteenth century and to which the Quaker movement made significant contributions. The first of these was an individualism far more uncompromising than that implied in Puritanism. The Inner Light in the souls of all men, the source of direct inspiration, was the religious basis of the great Quaker affirmation of the dignity and worth of the individual.

Equalitarianism was another consequence of Quaker practice. Within the religious meeting complete equality prevailed. Action upon religious matters was taken only after reaching unanimous agreement. Women were accorded complete equality with men. Such equalitarianism was symbolized by the custom of refusing to remove the hat and the use of the familiar *thee* and *thou* as terms of address.

Finally, the early Quakers were distinguished for their practical humanitarianism. Their scrupulous dealings with the Indians are well known, and their pioneer opposition to Negro slavery is even more worthy of respect. It was not an easy position for the Quakers of Rhode Island to take, since many of them had become slave owners. As early as 1657, certain Friends began to question the compatibility of slavery with the spirit of Christianity and to inaugurate an agitation that spread throughout the movement. Because of the principle of unanimity, it was impossible for a simple majority in Rhode Island to abolish the practice by resolution. But discussion of the issue never ceased until more than a century later, when, by 1773, the last holdouts were convinced and the practice of slaveholding was abandoned. Such a combination of perseverance and self-restraint may well stand as an object lesson to impatient political majorities everywhere.

Witchcraft

Modern historians have generally agreed that the witchcraft episode of 1692 in Salem Village was a pitiful delusion born of ignorance and superstition that should have been confined to simpleminded people. The educated leaders of the community should have known better. From this point of view the greatest tragedy lay in the fact that the clergy in particular did not intervene to prevent the mania from getting out of hand. Increase Mather and his son Cotton Mather, the most influential Puritan clergymen of the day, have been singled out for condemnation because they allegedly fanned the flames against the witches in order to strengthen the weakening hold of an outmoded orthodoxy. This view seriously underestimates the complexity of witchcraft in the seventeenth-century Puritan community.

Witchcraft may be universal in primitive cultures, but in Western Civilization it was the product of Christianity and modernity. Theologians in the late thirteenth century worked out a theory of human relations with Satan which brought witchcraft within the scope of Christian doctrine. In the following century, the Inquisition identified it with heresy, and secular courts later recognized it as a civil crime. After the Reformation, Protestants vied with Catholics in witch hunts. In England, a stern law of 1604 against witchcraft did not prevent an outbreak of the mania in eastern counties in 1645–47 in which scores of witches were executed. The last execution in England occurred in 1682, although trials of witches continued until 1736. On the continent of Europe, occasional trials and executions took place even in the eighteenth and nineteenth centuries. The first witchcraft trial in Anglo-America occurred in Windsor, Connecticut, in 1647, and the first execution of a witch in Boston took place in the following year. Altogether, 38 individuals were executed as witches in Anglo-America, while many others convicted of the crime escaped execution. As these facts suggest, belief in the reality of witchcraft was endemic in the Puritan world.

The events at Salem Village make it perfectly clear that the learned and powerful were as thoroughly persuaded of the reality of witchcraft as were those immediately involved. The three ancient learned professions, law, medicine, and divinity, were each deeply implicated in the tragedy. If the seventeenth century was, as the philosopher Alfred North Whitehead has called it, the century of genius, it was also the century of witchcraft, and several of the men of genius were as interested in diabolical phenomena as they were in the laws of celestial mechanics. It was the striking intersection of ancient and modern concerns and ways of thinking that endowed the witchcraft episode with much of its historical interest.

Salem Village (not to be confused with the seaport town of Salem) was an inland frontier parish with a history of local quarrels over land titles and ministerial salaries. In January 1692, two adolescent girls in the minister's family showed symptoms of hysteria which were diagnosed by the local physician as bewitchment. It was generally acknowledged that accurate distinctions between bewitchment, diabolical possession, insanity or other forms of physical illness were often difficult to make, and that diagnosis by a qualified physician was essential. Much depended in practice upon the predisposition and medical skill of the attending physician as to whether suspicious symptoms were to be identified as bewitchment or some natural form of illness. Dr. Griggs had previously diagnosed cases of witchcraft, and he did so again in this instance, with dire consequences.

The girls identified as their tormentors a domestic slave named Tituba and two local women, one identified as an "old hag," and the other a woman suspected of immorality. Tituba confessed to being a witch, which doubtless lent credibility to the girls' testimony. They reported that specters in the shape of the accused women demanded that the girls enter into a compact with the devil to promote his diabolic work, and tormented them on refusal. Finding themselves the objects of much solicitous interest the girls identified other witches, and soon the jail was full. It quickly became apparent that the two local magistrates who held preliminary hearings were fully persuaded of the authenticity of the testimony by the bewitched, and were relentless in their vigorous interrogations of the accused parties. When the newly appointed royal governor, Sir William Phips, arrived in the spring, he established a special seven-member Court of distinguished public figures presided over by Lt. Gov. William Stoughton to try the witches before a jury.

The court immediately confronted the thorny problem of specter evidence. Was a victim's testimony of torment by a specter in the guise of the alleged witch acceptable evidence in court? Its acceptance would greatly strengthen the cases against some of the witches, although it would be contrary to the common law requirement of two witnesses to the overt act in capital cases. Judge Stoughton and a majority of the court desired a vigorous prosecution of the witches, and they ruled specter evidence to be admissible. A substantial number of clergymen, on the other hand, led by the Mathers, urged the exclusion of specter evidence, although they had no doubts as to the reality of witchcraft as such.

The issue was of the highest importance because it turned upon conceptions of the extent of Satan's powers and of strategies for dealing with him. It was widely believed that when a witch compacted with Satan a specter or devil was assigned to the witch, taking on his likeness and tormenting his victims. The question before the court was whether the specter could also assume the guise of an innocent person. Stoughton believed firmly that the specter did not have this power, but could only appear to the victim in the form of the witch, and that testimony to this effect was properly acceptable. (Subsequent to the trials he was to insist that no individual had been found guilty on the basis of specter evidence alone.) Cotton Mather on at least three occasions solemnly warned the court against hearing specter evidence. He was persuaded that the devil was fully capable of assuming the guise of innocent and virtuous people, and would not hesitate to do so wherever it would sow doubt and confusion among the faithful. It was both paradoxical and ironic that those who like Stoughton believed Satan's powers to be limited would enlarge the ranks of his victims by admitting the fatal evidence, while those like Mather who conceded the wider scope to Satan's powers would nevertheless deny him the unrestricted use of the judicial process.

Five witches were hanged on August 19, among them the Rev. George Burroughs, a Harvard graduate and former pastor to the Salem Village congregation. Burroughs was a man of dubious reputation who had quarreled with the parish over his salary, and was rumored to have murdered his first wife. From the scaffold, however, he made a dignified and effective protestation of his innocence, and some of the crowd expressed uncertainty as to the wisdom of proceeding with the execution. Cotton Mather, persuaded of Burroughs' guilt, came forward to assure the crowd that the verdict was just, and that they should not be misled by sentiment or sympathy.

Prior to the accusations against Burroughs those identified as witches had come from the lowest ranks of the community, the poor, elderly, illiterate, and unfree; in short, the expendables. It has been suggested that identification of such individuals as witches was a primitive form of social control in which the Puritan conscience expressed its disapproval of stubborn social deviance. Accusations now spread to respectable members of the gentry class: to Judge Saltonstall, a member of the Court who had resigned presumably on the issue of specter evidence; to the mother-in-law of another judge; and even, it was rumored, to the wife of Governor Phips. The fact that none of the latter were arrested did not prevent the rapid growth of uneasiness among the ranks of the privileged. It was noted that no one who confessed to being a witch was executed, apparently on the assumption that such a person's usefulness to Satan was ended; and it was rumored that the sheriff had extorted confessions from accused friends in order to save them from the scaffold.

Governor Phips was now persuaded by Increase Mather to intervene, staying further executions and cautioning the Court on specter evidence. When Stoughton stubbornly insisted upon continuing to hear such evidence Phips dismissed the Court. Subsequently, the Court was reconstituted and tried 52 additional cases, condemning three on whom the Governor stayed execution. Altogether, 19 men and women and two dogs were hanged as witches, and one was pressed to death for refusing to plead. Fifty-five confessed to being witches, while 150 were accused and jailed for varying lengths of time.

Christianity at its best had always been oriented towards God as goodness. It had conceived of sin as alienation from God, the absence of the good. But at times, it had been liable to deteriorate into a morbid preoccupation with sin personified as Satan. A Manichaean dualism of God and Satan, light and darkness then developed. Witchcraft as a Christian phenemenon represented a socio-pathological retreat into an underworld of magic, fear and hatred. For learned and reasonable men like the Mathers to become ensnared in this pathetic delusion a distinctive combination of intellectual and social influences had to come to focus on them.

The historian James Truslow Adams suggested that seventeenth-century dualistic supernaturalism was being challenged by the rising monistic rationalism which was to dominate the eighteenth century. The religious establishment had a vested interest in sustaining the popular belief in witchcraft because it exemplified Satan's intimate involvement in daily affairs. It was true that eleven years earlier Increase Mather had published a book on illustrious providences, natural events such as floods, earthquakes, witchcraft, and demonic possession which testified to divine and diabolic interventions into the regular course of events. Such writings presumably prepared the public mind for the witchcraft episode at Salem Village and promoted the snowballing of hysteria. The Mathers were also concerned over the spread of Sadducism, a belief attributed to the ancient Judaic sect of Sadducees that there were no spiritual agencies at work, either angelic or demonic. In England, the Cambridge Platonists were arguing that it was the current tactic of atheists not to deny God's existence outright, but merely to deny the existence of spirits or witches, thus effectively shutting out either divine or diabolical intervention in human affairs.

Eight years after the Salem episode, Robert Calef, a Boston merchant, published in London *More Wonders of the Invisible World*, a scathing attack on the witchcraft trials and on the Mathers' involvement in them. Cotton Mather promptly denounced Calef as a Sadducee. Calef had not denied the existence of the devil; he merely suggested that Satan could easily discredit God's truth by tempting foolish girls to accuse innocent parties of witchcraft, with the incidental assistance of credulous people like the Mathers. Dispensing with the cumbersome machinery of diabolical providences the devil was perfectly capable of achieving his purposes by natural means. In short, belief in witchcraft was itself a devilish conspiracy to destroy the innocent and subvert God's work in the world. The question at issue between the Mathers and Calef simply concerned the most effective means by which the devil was presumed to operate. Robert Calef was not yet a monistic rationalist, but he was moving in that direction when he separated the operations of mind from the cause-effect sequences of the physical world.

Socially as well as intellectually the witchcraft episode signalled significant impending changes. At the beginning of settlement there had been two social classes: regenerate and unregenerate. The former had ruled through the leadership of clergy and magistrates. During the course of the seventeenth century, as mercantile and landed wealth accumulated, economic stratifications came to parallel the religious distinctions. The religious rulers had been largely successful in absorbing their potential competitors, so that in spite of occasional friction the elect continued to be the economic and political leaders of the community. The witchcraft episode furnished one of the first signs that a new social order was beginning to take shape.

It seems to have been a generally recognized convention that the practice of witchcraft should be confined to the lower ranks of the population. Alleged witches were often quarrelsome persons of unsavory reputation, notorious for their anti-social attitudes and conduct. One of the most disturbing aspects of the Salem episode was its deviation from the usual social pattern. Many of those accused were of exemplary conduct without any previous taint of witchcraft, and some of them belonged to the most privileged ranks of society. It is likely that the conversation in the minister's family provided the girls with a wider range of information about personalities than was available in lower class families. The bewitched girls would have been unrestrained by the sense of deference that must have inhibited those usually accustomed to the demimonde of witchcraft. In any event, the letter of adivce to the Court drafted by Cotton Mather on behalf of thirteen clergymen not only warned against the pitfalls of specter evidence but also expressed concern over the insensitivity of the girls to the niceties of social status! Witchcraft may have been tolerable so long as Satan confined his diabolical stratagems to the common people, but when he extended his snare to judges and governors' wives the matter became much more serious. Increase Mather had great influence with Governor Phips, and as anxiety mounted over the widening circle of accusations he was finally able to induce the Governor to terminate judicial prosecution of witches.

For a brief moment, the common people armed with the weapon of witchcraft had been able to paralyze the entire community. By threatening the rulers with this weapon they effectively compelled the gentry class to give up its previous willingness to accept or countenance witchcraft. Judge Samuel Sewell's celebrated public confession of his error in condemning the witches symbolized the price the gentry must pay for turning aside this first challenge to their hegemony. Puritans abandoned the judicial prosecution of witches not because they ceased to believe in witchcraft, but because prosecution threatened to destroy the social structure of the community.

PART II

The Mind of the American Enlightenment: 1740-1812

CHAPTER 4

||||||||||||||||||||||||||||||||||||||||||||||||||||||||||||||||||||||||||||

The Enlightened Outlook

The present age is an enlightened one. Theories capable of being corrected and improved by experiment, have been greatly elucidated. Principles venerable for their antiquity, have been freely examined, and absurdities exposed. . . . The principles of civil liberty were never better understood. Conviction has generally obtained, that all mankind, of whatever color or descent, are by nature, equally entitled to freedom:— That voluntary associations are the only equitable origin of civil government; and that rulers as well as subjects are limited by the constitution. The rights of conscience, have been set in a clear and convincing light. The idea of attempting an uniformity of faith and worship by *coercion,* is generally acknowledged, to have a much more direct tendency, to make martyrs or hypocrites, than to convince the world that Christianity is from God.

These remarks were made by the Reverend Charles Backus of Somers, Connecticut, in a Fast Sermon preached on April 17, 1788. The Fast Sermon was a traditional way of solemnizing memorial occasions, and a means by which Puritan preachers reminded their flocks of their shortcomings and spurred them on to renewed Christian endeavor. How far the descendants of the Puritan founders had come was apparent enough in the complacent phrases with which the Reverend Mr. Backus assuaged the pangs of his fasting congregation. The clergyman had skillfully touched both the temper and interests of the Enlightenment in America; and in the circumstances one could hardly expect him to have added that it was not an age for fasting.

The chronological limits of the Age of Enlightenment in America can be symbolized by episodes in the lives of two of its greatest representatives. When young Benjamin Franklin returned from Philadelphia in 1724 for a visit to his native Boston, he paid his respects to the elderly Cotton Mather, one of the last representatives of the Puritan mind. A full century later, Franklin's younger contemporary Thomas Jefferson was still alive to witness the phenomenon of an Andrew Jackson representing the new democracy as candidate for the presidency of the United States. Between these ideological frontiers stretched the classic age of enlightened thought.

To assume that enlightened modes of thought were shared from the outset by all Americans of the mid-eighteenth century would be a mistake. Enlightened ideas were originally the peculiar possession of the intellectual and social elite. While there were no barriers deliberately designed to prevent the spread of the new ideas among the mass of the community, the nature of these ideas, as well as the circumstances of their crystallization in America, conspired to prevent their effective dissemination throughout the community. Unlike the configuration of Puritan thought, which was imposed upon the community by powerful sanctions designed to place an impress on each individual, the spread of enlightened ideas was a spontaneous and informal process of diffusion.

The Discovery of America

Although Columbus discovered America as a fact of geography, it remained for the men of the Enlightenment to discover it intellectually as a fact of life and thought. They were the first to crystallize a truly indigenous American mind. The formal elements that composed it were, of course, common to the whole area of European culture, but the experiences of Americans were unique, and so the mood and emphases that they imparted to the common stock of ideas were distinctively their own.

The Puritans had inevitably framed their conceptions of America in terms of the great religious enterprise in which they were engaged. In one respect, America was the "New England" to which they fled in reluctant exile from old England. In another, it was the new Canaan, the land of promise, where the last great battle for the truth and for men's souls was to be waged. It was almost impossible for the Puritans to take America in its own terms. Only as the religious struggle gradually subsided, during the course of a century, were the combatants able to draw breath and look about them at the new terrain in which they found themselves. As they did so, there gradually grew up in their minds a sense that they were living in a new world, both physically and ideally. The exploration of this world was a major preoccupation of the Age of Enlightenment. With fresh eyes and with growing delight, Americans sought out and recorded its wonders and beauties.

Basic to enlightened thought, then, was the awareness of man's relationship to nature, in the form of the peculiar American environment. The activist individualism inherited from the religious mentality of the seventeenth century received a practical and secular expression in several new disciplines designed to master nature, to adjust men more effectively to nature, and to smooth and regularize the relationships of man with man. The political, economic, and social thought of the American Enlightenment assumed man to be an active animal, possessed of reason and spirit, whose peculiar capacity it was to exploit his natural environment for his greater comfort and happiness.

One of the representative documents of the epoch was Thomas Jefferson's *Notes on the State of Virginia,* written in 1781. In accordance with the spirit of the age, Jefferson commenced his book with a vivid description of the geographical features and physical resources of his state. He then described the climate and the flora and fauna of the region, in the course of which he marshaled the evidence to correct the preposterous misconceptions of the New World that had lately circulated among the curious but ill-informed intelligentsia of Europe. Then followed an account of the human inhabitants of Virginia, a subject of special philosophic interest because the region contained representatives of the three great branches of the human species: Indian, Negro, and Caucasian. Finally, Jefferson concluded with a description of the manners and customs of the Virginians, their history, institutions, and ideals. The sequence in which the topics were treated revealed in a general way the logical order in which the enlightened mind arranged its universe in order to understand it. Man could fully understand himself only so far as he could comprehend the larger universe of which he was a part. This universe was a great machine or work of art, which it was man's function to master and use for his own purposes. It was according to God's plan that men should achieve happiness through the exploitation of their environment.

In general, it was neither art nor philosophy for which the age was memorable but, rather, its economic and political science, the beginnings of industry, discovery, invention, and improved methods of agriculture. The symbolic institution of the age was neither church nor college but "The American Philosophical Society, held at Philadelphia for Promoting Useful Knowledge," founded by Benjamin Franklin in 1769, the parent and prototype of a host of local scientific and promotional societies dedicated to research, collection, improved methods, mutual benefits, and advancement of the arts and sciences.

The discovery of America was not, however, something made by Americans alone. It was one of the great intellectual adventures of eighteenth-century European civilization. Enlightened thought in America was in part a product of the reflection of Americans upon their own experiences; but it was also in part the product of Europe's projection upon America of its own hopes and aspirations. America had at least two kinds of influence upon European thought. European intellectuals looked to America for the realization of the good society; they glimpsed there the promised land. They celebrated the virtuous simplicity of the rural way of life, and the self-respecting integrity of the freehold farmer, who might on occasion assume something of the appearance of the noble savage. Much of Franklin's European success was attributable to his skill in subtly capitalizing upon these stereotypes. Even the reputation of the religious sects underwent a transformation. The Quakers, who, at the end of the seventeenth century, had been generally regarded as dangerous fanatics, gradually came to be celebrated for the exalted purity of their morals, while, from the opposite side of the Atlantic, their province of Pennsylvania looked almost like a utopian commonwealth. And the currents of European life that gave rise to these opinions helped to give substance and shape to the hopes and expectations of Americans themselves.

At the same time that Europeans were framing their first conceptions of America, European thought was reacting to the stimulus furnished by information about the New World. The flora and fauna were partly new, and became the objects of extensive research. The native tribes were a source of great curiosity, and their origin the subject of endless speculation. Tales of physiographic marvels circulated with every returning traveler. An aura of exaggerated wonderment hung over much that Europeans wrote about America. Had the New World been created at the same time as the old, or were its remarkable physical features to be explained as evidences of a more recent creation? Were its harsh and forbidding climate and landscapes owed to the previous absence of a civilized hand to subdue and soften its barbarous contours? European speculations on these matters helped to fix the intellectual limits within which Americans were struggling to identify themselves as a people.

Natural Law and Human Right

The thought of the Enlightenment commenced formally with the facts of nature. The ultimate problem for the human species was to define its proper place and function in nature's economy. The older ideas of a chain of being and of design in nature were inherited by enlightened thinkers and incorporated into their more empirical natural science. The Linnaean system of biological classification, in its earlier form, appeared to confirm the idea of a chain of being in nature. The old religious doctrine of design was readily transformed into the principle of intelligibility and purposefulness of nature. This was the confident faith of Jefferson and others that all the facts of life might be rationalized by discovering their proper functions in the cosmic process. Even disease and death were to be justified in the realization that, although the individual derived no benefit from them, the species did.

Charles Chauncy of Boston, one of the most influential clergymen of the age, was so firmly persuaded of the infinite benevolence and wisdom of the Creator that he could find sufficient evidence of them in nature itself, without having recourse to revelation. Should one be so impressed with the imperfections of the human condition as to question the validity of the principle of divine benevolence, let him take a more detached view and he could not but be convinced of it. The world had been furnished with an infinite series of created types of beings, each with its special place and assigned characteristics. Within each species the individuals also differed from one another, so that space was quite filled up "without any void or chasm." The very finite character of each creature testified to divine goodness, since by this means the greatest sum total of happiness was made possible. It was, of course, to be borne in mind that goodness to the whole, and not to any particular part of it, was always the Creator's intention. "The truth is," Chauncy concluded, "the *perfection* of benevolence consists, not simply in the *largeness* of the capacities it bestows upon any beings, but in *fitting* them to the *state* and *circumstances* of beings in *such a situation,* and bearing *such a place,* in the *general plan* for good." In short, whatever is, is not only right but good.

Nature thus came to be regarded as ultimately beneficent, and its processes were idealized as fulfilling the ultimate purposes of life. The evangelical Protestants of the community, to be sure, would not have assented happily to so bald a formulation; but they were, in effect, driven underground and deprived of an opportunity to address themselves fruitfully to the issues of the age. The enlightened mind merged values with facts. As Tom Paine expressed it: "It is only in the Creation that all our ideas and conceptions of a *word of God* can unite." There was a vast respect for the laws of nature and of nature's God. Men armed with a rapidly developing technology saw in the bountifulness of nature in America evidence that those laws were good. The environmentalism that emerged from this context, and that long characterized liberal thought, readily attributed to nature what under other intellectual auspices might have been variously attributed to men themselves or to the gods. In any event, as the enlightened thinker saw it, his function was to exploit nature and thus achieve happiness, which could be secured through a scrupulous regard for nature's laws.

To the eighteenth-century mind, the concept of natural law involved certain connotations not necessarily apparent in the phrase itself. Natural laws implied opportunities, since laws were the keys which opened the secrets of nature for use. Law was a guide to action; it was permissive—not determinative in the religious sense of the law of God; nor compulsive as in the later naturalistic sense. Law regulated the flow of traffic. This conception of natural law explained why it was that men felt no contradiction when they spoke in the same breath of the laws of nature and the freedom of men.

The complacent sense of living in better times which characterized enlightened thought underlay a religious outlook that may be designated as a benevolent and humanistic theism. Jefferson and Paine conceived of God as a master workman or builder who was known to men through His works. There was no sense of spiritual conversion and consequent moral reformation in enlightened religion. The typical thinkers of the age were all moralists, but they did not connect morality with piety. Religion, in short, was reduced to natural religion. After all, a religion of nature was universal in scope, as compared with a religion whose authority depended on an alleged revelation of truth at a specific time and place. As Paine remarked, for all but those to whom the revelation was vouchsafed, the authority of Christianity was mere hearsay. In this the best of all possible worlds, nature and experience themselves furnished sufficient evidence of divine purpose. Although belief in an afterlife was everywhere formally affirmed, enlightened thinkers were completely absorbed in the affairs of this life.

But the fact remains that the age was not irreligious. Its religious convictions arose out of the peculiar circumstances of the time and were an authentic expression of them. Three facets of enlightened religion reflected in the order of their immediate importance the priorities that the issues of the age suggested. First was the moral element. God had woven the moral law into the very texture of things, and perhaps the chief practical function of religion was constantly to remind men of their moral obligations. Because the spokesmen for enlightened ideas in America were also members of a governing class, the social disciplinary function of religion as the custodian of morality was regarded as of the highest importance. While for the most part enlightened thinkers were not devout in the usual sense, they retained their formal religious affiliations and looked with benevolent approval upon the role of the churches as a stabilizing element in society. Tom Paine must, of course, be a partial exception to these generalizations. In its second facet, religion emerged as a rational necessity. No thoughtful man could evade its claims upon him. In various ways, enlightened thinkers from Edwards to Channing stressed the rational element. Finally, religion might appropriately recommend itself as concrete experience. Here one entered the treacherous subterranean regions of the enlightened mind, regions it were well to probe with the greatest caution. The evangelical insistence upon the reality of religious experience was acutely embarrassing to more worldly contemporaries. This was a kind of experience one would prefer not to acknowledge. And so the evangelicals were driven underground and denied a place among the official spokesmen of the age.

The Pursuit of Happiness

Never before or since in American history has a more uncompromising individualism been woven into the fabric of thought. Negatively, this individualism expressed itself in fear of corporate bodies of all kinds and fear of corporate action. In politics, political parties or "factions" were commonly deplored. So also were standing armies, national debts, and powerful governmental agencies. Even the cosmopolitanism of the era reflected a dissatisfaction with the exclusiveness of provincial patriotisms. If there was to be an American nationality, let it stand for values to which all mankind could subscribe with equal enthusiasm. Jefferson, who was particularly effective in giving voice to fears of corporate responsibilities, propounded the quaint notion that each generation should liquidate its own public debts in order not to burden its descendants. In the social sphere, agriculture was glorified as the ideal way of life, while manufacturing and mercantile enterprise were regarded with suspicion. The separation of church and state was one of the great practical institutional accomplishments of the era. In comparison with later times, the age was noteworthy for the relative absence of functional and voluntary associations. Americans were yet to gain their reputation as a nation of joiners and organizers.

Along with its doctrinaire quality, the enlightened mind was notable for its empirical temper. During the period, there occurred a tremendous proliferation of interest in practical subjects. It was as though Americans had suddenly awakened from the long night of religious dogmatism and had turned with fresh eyes and eager curiosity to the physical and social worlds around them. The leading representatives of the age were men with extraordinary variety of interests. Benjamin Franklin, for instance, was not only a scientist and statesman, but an economist, demographer, metaphysician, moralist and journalist. His scientific interests embraced electricity, mechanics, optics, meteorology, and oceanography in addition to his remarkable practical inventive genius. Thomas Jefferson's range of interests was even more impressive. He was virtually a walking encyclopedia. His remarkable zest for the accumulation of data extended to a great number of different fields, and the doctrinaire quality of his mind was fully compensated for in his insatiable appetite for the facts.

It was a happy inspiration which caused the author of the Declaration of Independence to alter Locke's trinity of natural rights —life, liberty, and property—to read life, liberty, and the pursuit of happiness. The Declaration thus accorded official recognition to the ultimate objective of enlightened thought. For the first time in history a society dared to assert for all men the right to seek happiness. This was the supreme radicalism of the age, and because of it men everywhere looked to America with hope or fear according to their own circumstances and aspirations. But it was a radicalism deeply tempered by an abiding skepticism as to human nature.

The provincial gentry among whom enlightened ideas took root were a ruling class—perhaps the most assured and firmly seated ruling class America has ever had—consisting of a closely knit group of planters, merchants, lawyers, and clergymen. But no ruling group in America has ever survived for long, and the enlightened leaders of the eighteenth century knew their world too well to deceive themselves into thinking that their power would last forever. They developed an interpretation of history as consisting of the successive rise and fall of states and classes, which provided an appropriate embodiment of their own expectations. They knew that American society was moving toward social democracy and that eventually democracy would unseat them. In practical terms, their policy was to preserve their privileges and their values as best they could while not foolishly obstructing the inevitable trend of events. The realism of their political thinking reflected these considerations.

It may seem paradoxical that a society which dedicated itself to the pursuit of happiness nevertheless vigorously repudiated the current sentimental and romantic notions about the goodness of the natural man. Human nature was defined in various ways, all of them more realistic than complimentary. The Puritans had worked within a tradition of thought in which they were content to repeat the official Christian affirmations about the nature of the unregenerate man. Enlightened thinkers, on the other hand, attempted deliberately to put that tradition aside and to describe human nature directly as they found it displayed in history and experience. The result was a variety of observations as diverse as the temperaments of the men who made them. Perhaps the most noteworthy testimonial to the continuing influence of the religious tradition was the bare fact that men still found it appropriate to begin with postulates about human nature as something not to be taken for granted.

Man was said to be a rational animal or a tool-using animal. Jefferson liked to explain that the human species had been endowed with an exceptional capacity for adjustment to different kinds of environment; no other known species was found inhabiting such varied regions. To Charles Chauncy, self-love and benevolence were the two "grand principles" of human nature. John Adams insisted that man was dominated by such innate drives as hunger, sex, vanity, and envy. He also remarked on the unusual differences among individuals that was characteristic of the human species. In fact, he said, "the equality of nature is moral and political only, and means that all men are independent." It was only in society with its guarantee of moral and political rights to all that men could be said to be equal in any practical sense.

In the last analysis, the age was agreed that man was fundamentally selfish. This was both a moral and a factual affirmation. It was a way of saying that, because of his nature, the individual man was the basic social unit, and not any class, corporation or nation. Given these conceptions of human nature, the problem for the social philosopher was to shape a social system that would protect men from their own worst impulses. He would be greatly aided in this task by an appreciation of nature's beneficence. The life of virtue could best be cultivated in a rural environment. Nevertheless, man's nature remained the ineradicable source of evil. What then was to prevent the pursuit of happiness from becoming the happiness of the pigsty? How was one to bring out the best qualities in men and repress the others?

The typical moral theory of the Enlightenment was a form of utilitarianism. In the simple maxims of Poor Richard, Franklin gave the utilitarian morality a particularly happy and effective expression. The maxims were especially notable for the distinctive blend of practical and humane values with which he spelled out his definition of happiness. Health, wealth, and wisdom were the ends to be sought by means of a rigorous program of self-discipline. In a familiar passage in his *Autobiography,* Franklin recounted how he had drawn up a list of such virtues as industry, frugality, honesty, temperance, cleanliness, chastity, etc., with a view to their systematic cultivation, first singly and then in combination. Thus isolated, these were the virtues of the Puritan ethic stripped of their theological trappings. For the descendants of Quakers and Puritans, Franklin's maxims simply confirmed the truths that they had absorbed with their mothers' milk. Now, however, these virtues were intended to discipline and socialize the pursuit of happiness by prompting men to defer the immediate pleasure of the moment in favor of the greater good of the morrow. The display of enormous creative energies that marked the careers of so many of the leaders of the age may be attributed to the pervasive influence of the utilitarian virtues.

Franklin's approach to economic and political problems illustrated in a practical way the blending of natural and moral phenomena that was typical of the era. The social scientist began with the fundamental characteristics of the human species as an animal population. The prime feature of life in all its forms, said Franklin in his *Observations on the Increase of Mankind* (1751), was its natural fecundity. The ultimate limit to abundant reproduction was sheer physical crowding and interference with the means of subsistence. Among human populations, the principal limitation upon increase was the food supply, although disease, war, urbanization, and luxurious tastes also played a part. Franklin believed that in no country in his day did the population actually approach its true potential numbers. Everywhere the population could be substantially increased by means of such devices as laws to promote trade and to provide more effective guarantees for the security of property, by mechanical inventions, by curbing luxury and inculcating habits of frugality. In England, for instance, a country widely regarded by contemporaries as overpopulated, the population might, in Franklin's opinion, easily be increased some tenfold.

A spectacular contrast to the long-settled nations of Europe, America was virtually an empty country with an abundance of cheap and fertile land. Franklin had the genius to see that here was a kind of demographic laboratory in which the behavior of a human population momentarily unchecked by the usual limitations could be observed and measured. Here was an opportunity to discover the natural rate of human increase. From such local and fragmentary information as was then available, he concluded that the population of the English colonies in America was doubling in number every twenty years, or approximately in each generation. This was a geometric ratio of increase. He also noted that an average of eight children was born to every marriage. Fifty years later, Franklin's findings were examined by the English demographer Thomas Robert Malthus and generalized in the famous Malthusian law of population, according to which population will always tend to press against the limits of subsistence because it increases more rapidly than does the food supply. For more than a century after Franklin made his estimates, the American population continued to double in numbers every twenty years, as he had predicted that it would.

When he turned to face the great political and economic problems of the British Empire, these natural characteristics of the human population as an animal species conditioned Franklin's thinking.

His insistence in 1763 that Britain should take Canada from France rather than the immediately profitable sugar island of Guadeloupe sprang from his realization of the enormous potential growth in population that Canada promised. Franklin's approach to the controversial aspects of mercantilist economic policy was similarly influenced by demographic considerations. Britain feared the competition of colonial manufactures and prohibited them by various parliamentary acts. Franklin held such legislation to be unnecessary and absurd. Manufacturing, he said, was founded in poverty because it required cheap labor. Americans earned such comfortable livings on their farms that they could not be induced to labor at wages low enough to permit competition with British manufactures. Even the Indians enjoyed comforts of life that by British standards placed them in the gentry class! This was the economic foundation of that glorification of the rural way of life that was rapidly becoming a conventional American attitude.

As a field of formal learning, economics was a branch of moral philosophy. Although the economist undertook to describe a natural economic situation, that situation was not without its moral dimension. Man was always free; and he was always faced with moral choices. The most famous economist of the age was Adam Smith, a Scottish professor of moral philosophy. His *An Inquiry into the Nature and Causes of the Wealth of Nations* (1776) rested on the assumption that if all things in nature, including man, were to act as God wished, the maximum good would result. But, unfortunately, man, being free and less than perfect, was constantly interfering with naturally beneficent processes—to his own pain. Thus, although there was an economic order both natural and good, men must first understand it intellectually and then discipline themselves to behave according to its precepts. The principles of *laissez faire* were the precepts of economic morality, and woe be unto him who failed to regulate his economic activity accordingly.

The basic fact of which economic theory must take account was the abundant reproductive capacity of the human species, with the consequent need for specialized production and exchange of goods and services. The economist undertook to show how these circumstances could be manipulated for good. The disciplining of the individual to act in accordance with economic laws was to be accomplished through Franklin's utilitarian morality. The economic virtues might, of course, be practiced anywhere, but there were especially favored conditions in which it seemed as though the good life was an almost automatic response to a beneficent environment. These conditions were to be found in agriculture. Allegiance to the utilitarian virtues was another source of the sentimental agrarianism of the period. Jefferson's views on this subject are well known: "Cultivators of the earth are the most valuable citizens. They are the most vigorous, the most independent, and most virtuous, and they are tied to their country, and wedded to its liberty and interests, by the most lasting bonds." Franklin, although personally an incorrigible urbanite whose brief venture into farming ended in ennui, expressed the same convictions less sententiously. There were, he said, three ways by which a nation could acquire wealth—war, commerce, and agriculture. War was nothing but robbery; commerce was usually cheating; while agriculture was the only honest way. Here a man received a "real increase of the seed thrown into the ground, in a kind of continual miracle, wrought by the hand of God in his favor, as a reward for his innocent life and his virtuous industry."

In matters of public policy, enlightened thinkers did not display the nineteenth-century tendency to confuse *laissez faire* with economic individualism. They made no fetish of *laissez faire* as such and were fully prepared to intervene in the economic process when necessary in order to preserve economic individualism. Their political economy did not forbid the use of political measures to preserve or extend private enterprise. The state was an instrument to be used like other agencies whenever the welfare and happiness of citizens were at stake. From 1750 onward, Americans freely resorted to state agencies to promote the general welfare by means of subsidy, penalty, or administrative planning. In such cases it was necessary only to show that the individual well-being of citizens would be enhanced.

CHAPTER 5

||||||||||||||||||||||||||||||||||||||||||||||||||||||||||||||||||||||||

From Revelation to Reason

URITAN SETTLEMENT IN THE NEW WORLD had been confined
to New England, with offshoots in Long Island and northern
New Jersey. Elsewhere in British North America, Virginia, the Carolinas, and Georgia were peopled largely by Anglicans. Maryland,
founded as a Roman Catholic refuge, soon came to include many
Puritans, while Quaker-settled Pennsylvania, Delaware, and the
Jerseys had extended hospitality to other faiths, notably to German
sectarians. New York, originally New Netherland, contained an influential nucleus of Dutch Reformed congregations. Early in the
eighteenth century, Scotch-Irish Presbyterians had settled in appreciable numbers in all the colonies from New York to the Carolinas. Thus, by 1740, except in Massachusetts and Connecticut and
in certain solidly Anglican regions of the South, the religious diversity that has since characterized American society was already apparent.

During the second half of the seventeenth century, the religious
fervor that earlier had been typical of most forms of Protestantism
cooled perceptibly. This fact, together with the British policy of
toleration, resulted in the emergence in the early eighteenth century
of a relatively stable accommodation. In most of the colonies, one
faith or another was established by law and enjoyed churchly privi-

leges, but almost everywhere the practical necessity, if not the principle, of toleration of dissenters was grudgingly admitted. During the early years of the eighteenth century, the theory that church and state were necessary to each other as mutual guarantors of a civilized society still generally prevailed. But even in the Puritan colonies a subtle change was occurring. Religion was no longer the dominant interest; although the church remained powerful, it was becoming a vested interest whose privileges were to be balanced in the public mind against its services.

The Great Awakening

The revival of the 1730's and 1740's—the Great Awakening—was an event of major importance for American religion. The clergy of the Reformed churches in America—that is, those of Calvinistic derivation (Puritan Congregational, Presbyterian, Dutch Reformed, and German Reformed)—had been especially conscious of the decay of vital piety within their flocks. The original practice of requiring from each church member a testimonial of his religious experience had been generally allowed to lapse in favor of a simple declaration of faith. Many of the clergy, recalling the holiness and zeal of their ancestors, were in the habit of exhorting their complacent congregations to seek redeeming grace more earnestly. Occasionally these pleas resulted in local revivals in scattered New England parishes—anticipations of what was shortly to break forth on a continental scale.

It was no accident that revivalism originated in the Reformed churches. Regeneration as the Puritans had traditionally conceived and experienced it was the fundamental ingredient of revivalism. As the term signified, the revival was an attempt to renew or revivify the traditional piety. To descendants of Puritans, this meant the ascertainable experience of regenerating grace demonstrated in a sanctified life. Without this doctrinal and practical basis, revivalism would not have occurred in the form in which it did. It is unnecessary to look for sources of revivalism in German pietism or in Wesleyan Methodism. It welled up spontaneously from the latent resources of the local religious tradition. Nor was it until after the revival had been under way in the Reformed churches for some time that non-Calvinistic bodies were able to detach the practice of revivalism from its Calvinistic doctrinal rationale and so to participate in the revival themselves. That revivalism did spread to the non-Calvinistic bodies is, of course, important. But it is not strictly an aspect of the Great Awakening as here defined.

As a connected series of events the revival began in the 1720's and 1730's among the Dutch Reformed congregations of the Raritan Valley in New Jersey in response to the evangelical preaching of Theodore Jacob Frelinghuysen (1691-c. 1748). A native German, but trained in the Dutch Reformed church in Holland, Frelinghuysen came to America about 1719, bringing to the complacent Dutch parishes of New Jersey the intense zeal and high standards of piety and morality that were to fuel the revival in countless Reformed parishes along the seaboard. From the Dutch Reformed, the movement spread to the Presbyterians of the Middle Colonies. William Tennent (1673-1746), founder of the Log College (progenitor of the College of New Jersey at Princeton), had been born in Ireland and had come to Philadelphia about 1716 after studying at the University of Edinburgh. He found the Episcopalians of the Middle Colonies deeply mired in Arminianism and launched a vigorous campaign to rescue the Presbyterians from a similar fate. His son Gilbert Tennent (1703-1764), pastor of the Presbyterian church in New Brunswick, New Jersey, was deeply influenced by Frelinghuysen and became the leader of the revivalist or "New Side" party among the Presbyterians. At the same time, in the 1730's, Jonathan Edwards, a Congregationalist, stimulated a revival in his parish at Northampton, Massachusetts, which spread to neighboring towns in the Connecticut River Valley. All these local revivals were bound together into a common movement by George Whitefield, an Anglican missionary, who toured the English colonies in 1739 and 1740, attracting great crowds and earning much publicity and notoriety because of the emotional fervor of his methods. Whitefield introduced the practice of itinerant preaching, and in his footsteps came a host of imitators, both lay and clerical, whose frequently coarse and injudicious harangues aroused dismay and revulsion among the more genteel and influential elements in the community.

The peak of revival activity in the Reformed churches was reached by 1742. Many congregations were torn apart by bitter quarrels between revivalist and anti revivalist factions. Wherever they were in the minority the revivalists often seceded to form their own congregations, weakening the existing parishes and leaving a lasting heritage of local animosities. After 1742, the situation became stabilized, and an uneasy truce prevailed between the revivalist and antirevivalist parties within the Reformed churches. Sects such as the

Quakers and the General or non-Calvinistic Baptists, which had at first been indifferent to the revival, now began to sense its relevance to their social and cultural circumstances and to embrace it heartily. Although it had originated in the Calvinistic interpretation of the conversion experience revivalism could be detached from that rationale. By itself it proved to be an invaluable technique in religious refreshment and recruitment. For fully two centuries to come, as the population spread westward, the technique of revivalism was to remain one of the major means by which organized religion kept pace in the struggle to Christianize a mobile people.

In the beginning, however, the revival raised certain crucial issues comparable to those presented by seventeenth-century sectarianism. It released forces hostile to the welfare of the Reformed bodies as churches, and, because it arose within these churches themselves, the issues could not be confronted without conflict and bitterness. Each of the Reformed churches was deeply divided into revivalist and anti-revivalist camps. So far as the Congregationalists were concerned, in its effects the revival represented the final disintegration of the Puritan synthesis.

The first issue arose from the practical effort of the revivalists to secure as many conversions as possible. They tended to isolate the concrete religious experience from the conduct of life and to insist upon its necessity for salvation. Mere good conduct was not enough. They set their faces against the trend of practice in the Reformed churches since the later seventeenth century. Opponents of the revival denounced the movement as "enthusiasm," which meant belief in the immediate possession of the individual soul by the Holy Spirit, with some kind of alleged supernatural revelation frequently involved as well. In short, the revivalists believed in a concrete, ascertainable conversion experience, one which sometimes came with shattering impact to the believer. Antirevivalists denounced this as self-delusion. Clearly, the religious community no longer agreed upon an essential element of the religious life on which a century earlier it was solidly united.

A second issue closely related to the first concerned the connection between piety and conduct. The revivalists held that conduct acceptable to God was that which necessarily and inevitably flowed from regeneration. Their opponents, on the other hand, believed that a state of regeneracy could be demonstrated with assurance only in good conduct. Thus the traditional phenomena of the Puritan religious life were divided into two opposed categories, faith and works, in a way in which the Puritans would never have divided them. The revivalists emphasized faith, the subjective part; the antirevivalists emphasized objective good works. Out of the older religious mind, which had never sensed any incompatibility between the spiritual and the material, two worlds were being precipitated.

The sectarian implications of revivalism constituted the third issue. When opposition to the revival was expressed by many of the clergy and laity of the Reformed churches, the revivalists accused these opponents of being unconverted. Most of them did not worship or exhort with the degree of evangelical fervor that the revivalists in practice regarded as one of the signs of a gracious spiritual condition. Gilbert Tennent referred to antirevivalist preachers as "swarms of locusts" who were eating the substance of their innocent parishioners while lulling them into a fatally false sense of spiritual security. The revivalists urged these parishioners to abandon the ministrations of the false preachers and to set up new congregations led by appropriately zealous revivalist preachers. Such separatism was the essence of sectarianism. To divide the churches on the basis of a distinction between allegedly regenerate and unregenerate would, of course, destroy the churchly union of both groups in a congregation identified with the whole local community. Unity was the traditional aspiration of the Reformed churches, an ambition realized most effectively by the Congregationalists of New England. They could not have survived as a church were they to admit that certain of their congregations might require more rigorous standards of piety than others.

As a matter of fact, the revivalists in the Reformed churches were soon forced to back down. In 1742, Tennent reconsidered his advice to separate and shortly afterward retracted it. The antirevivalists, for their part, tacitly agreed to tolerate the revivalists, provided they should cease their attacks on their colleagues and confine their evangelical labors to their own congregations. An uneasy truce was declared in the Congregational and Presbyterian churches.

But if most of the parishes of the colonial churches retained their traditional affiliations through the troubled times of the revival, many individual members did not. A few antirevivalists deserted the vulnerable Reformed churches for the placid security of Anglicanism. Many laymen caught up in the wave of revivalism and discontented with the lukewarm ministrations of their clergymen broke away from the churches of their fathers and went over to the sects. In the long run, the sects, especially the Baptists and Methodists, were the major beneficiaries of the Great Awakening. The institution of revivalism itself passed to the sects, and during the later eighteenth and early nineteenth centuries it became formalized in a standard pattern of ritualistic behavior.

Finally, the Great Awakening was significant in American religious history because it furnished the earliest evidence of the tendency of organized religion to conform to social class divisions. In general, the revival split churches and congregations along class lines. On the whole, the wealthier classes disapproved of revivalism while the poorer people supported it. Jonathan Edwards and Charles Chauncy, leaders of the two factions within the Congregational Church, both acknowledged the class character of the revival. The bitterness of the controversies cannot be understood exclusively in religious terms. In Connecticut, where the conflict was more acrid than elsewhere, the social alignment was particularly clear: the wealthier urban parishes stood firm against the revival; the poorer rural parishes were generally sympathetic. Many Connecticut revivalists left their churches to form so-called "Separate" Congregational bodies. Not one of the Separate clergymen was a college graduate. As the institution of revivalism passed to the sects, the social-class alignment became clearer. So far as they had religious interests at all, the lower classes accepted revivalism without reservations. But among the gentry and middle classes it became suspect for social as well as religious reasons.

In the Age of Enlightenment, the churches no longer furnished the bond of social unity that they had supplied in the earlier period. But their status was a transitional one. Such clerical leaders as Charles Chauncy still spoke in tones of authority on behalf of the entire community in the traditional manner of churchmen. Only in the overtones could one detect a dawning realization that the church was coming to represent only a part of the community and not the whole of it. This meant that the ideology of the Enlightenment was not sponsored by institutions having total social affiliations. The state came to replace the church in this respect, and, as a consequence, the enlightened ideology had a more obviously political than religious orientation. But the state had not yet come to have the moral and practical authority that was to distinguish it in later times. In default of other bases, therefore, the enlightened ideology struck its deepest roots in the gentry, who were most interested in politics.

The revival was also decisive in reshaping the terms in which Americans appraised the current situation and their future prospects.

The early Puritan settlers had identified human history with the operation of God's spirit in the world. They had buoyantly expected that the fulfillment of history in Christ's Second Coming was at hand and that the establishment of the Holy Commonwealth was preparatory to the great event. This millennialist expectation had, however, generally been expressed in a characteristically sober and guarded fashion. Thomas Hooker, the founder of Connecticut, had proposed to reckon the lapse of time leading to the Second Coming in terms of the spreading knowledge of the Truth. Captain Edward Johnson, an early Puritan historian, had further cautioned more zealously impatient Christians that Christ could not be expected to return to reign personally until His spirit and teachings had triumphed in all the churches and kingdoms of the earth. But alas! Far from leading the way toward the millennial day, the Holy Commonwealth could not even hold its own. The sons and grandsons of the Founding Fathers were too realistic to deceive themselves on this matter, and so with a mixture of resignation and despair they relinquished the dream of the millennial Kingdom in their times. In its place appeared a view of history as an endless ebb and flow: God alternately bestowed and withdrew his spirit from the world and thus effected the prevailing state of piety or impiety.

With the coming of the Great Awakening and the spread of revival enthusiasm, the millennial expectation was born again with intense vividness in the minds of many revivalists. The revival itself, with the mass conversions of the godless which attended it, was regarded as a harbinger of the glorious day about to dawn. Millennialism was by no means confined to illiterate enthusiasts. Even the great and passionate Edwards shared in the expectation. He explained the appearance of the revival in America by writing that "this new world is probably now discovered that the new and most glorious state of God's church on earth might commence here; that God might in it begin a new world in a spiritual respect, when he creates the new heavens and new earth." The millennial hope was destined to play a long and prominent role in the history of American thought.

The reaction of opponents to the Great Awakening revealed certain ideas that were destined to become prominent features of the enlightened mind. The Awakening was a social as well as religious crisis, and the reaction to it was both social and intellectual. Opposition to revivalism enabled the antirevivalists to identify the common attitudes and interests that united them. The revival helped form an American ruling class by uniting the local provincial gentry of the seaboard colonies in a common cause of continental proportions. The ideas that the antirevivalists elaborated in the course of their resistance to the revival remained the common property of this ruling class until the coming of the American Revolution split its ranks and a younger generation of leaders broadened the relevance of enlightened ideas to comprehend the interests of other classes as well.

Although the issues at stake in the revival did not ostensibly involve class conflict and many of the participants, no doubt, were oblivious to the social aspects of the movement, certain contemporaries were conscious of the fact that the two parties were divided on class lines and that the revival constituted a threat to social stability. The *Boston Evening-Post,* a paper bitterly hostile to revivalism, warned (Feb. 22, 1742) of its unsettling consequences: "Mechanicks of all Sorts have presum'd to teach what themselves never learn't, and those that serv'd long Apprentiships to other Crafts, have become Divines in a Moment, and with the same emulous Industry wherewith they used to invent *new Fashions,* have made new *Religions.* And as *Idleness* has thus made some *Preachers,* so it has made more *Hearers.*" The same paper again warned its readers a few months later (Apr. 5, 1742): "It is one of the main Disorders and Infelicities of the present Age, that many of the *meanest Rank,* and of *inferior Capacities,* are puffed up with a Pride that is become almost past dealing with. Some of the most contemptible Creatures among us yet think themselves sufficient to direct *Statesmen,* dictate to *Legislators,* and teach *Doctors* and *Divines.*"

Since revival enthusiasm tended to be identified in the minds of antirevivalists with social unrest and the aspirations of less privileged classes, it was to be expected that the interpretation of the revival expounded by antirevivalist spokesmen would be compatible with this judgment. Hence it was that the most objectionable religious feature of the Awakening was its "enthusiasm," the belief in direct inspiration. Enthusiasm had several consequences, all pernicious. The sharp distinction between the regenerate and the unregenerate upon which revivalists insisted was deplorable because it divided the community into two sharply distinguished groups, whereas an increasingly important function of the churchly parish was to unite it or, at least, to minimize the inevitable distinctions that existed. Wherever the Reformed churches were established by law, as in New England, the struggle for their control was a major social conflict. Another objection to enthusiasm centered upon its preference for emotional intensity rather than sanctification as the acceptable criterion of regeneration. This emotionalism occasionally ·expressed itself in demonstrations of uncouth violence, the operation of the spirit being allegedly so powerful as to provoke weeping, the "holy laugh," or physical paroxysms.

The reaction of antirevivalists to these offensive manifestations of enthusiasm was to glorify the disciplined restraint associated with the idea of reason. Reason became one of the key words in the enlightened vocabulary. Eventually, it was regarded as a universal value, the proper possession or heritage of all classes of men. It is useful, therefore, to bear in mind its earlier function as an ideological weapon in the social class conflict. The value of reason as an antidote to emotional extravagance is obvious. Closely linked with it were the virtues of the Puritan moral code, now reaffirmed as the essential embodiments of true piety. When Whitefield visited Boston in the fall of 1740, the *Boston Evening-Post* complained bitterly that among the other evils attendant upon his coming was the fact that "shop-men" and others of that class swarmed to hear his sermons at all hours as a pretext for idleness. The glorification of disciplined sobriety and deep distrust of emotionalism remained a prominent characteristic of enlightened thought.

The qualities of the true Christian as defined by Charles Chauncy threw into sharp outline the expectations of antirevivalists as to the social consequences of religious faith. Truly gracious persons, Chauncy insisted, were *"Partakers* of a spiritual *Likeness* to the LORD JESUS CHRIST, in *Faith;* in *Purity;* in *Lowliness,* and *Humility;* in Love to *God,* and our *Neighbors;* in *Patience, Meekness,* and *Gentleness;* in *Contempt* of the *World,* Contentedness with their Condition, Resignation to God; and in a Word, a *Zeal* to *honour him,* and *do all the good they can in the World."* These were virtues especially fitting to a people who knew how to keep their proper stations in life. All this suggests the early association of enlightened ideas with the interests of privileged classes. The enlightened mind, in fact, expressed the ideology of a social and governing elite. It was not a democratic mind. Later, in the face of the Revolutionary crisis, when such radicals as Tom Paine took over enlightened ideas and generalized them for the benefit of all mankind, many enlightened thinkers were disgusted.

Arminianism

Opposition to the revival served as a catalytic agent to precipitate among the antirevivalist clergy a new and distinctive complex of ideas in the American scene. This was known as Arminianism, an opprobrious epithet long used by orthodox Puritans to designate certain heretical tendencies and now revived by Edwards and applied to opponents of the revival. The leading Arminians were Charles Chauncy and Jonathan Mayhew, both Boston Congregationalists; John Thomson, a Philadelphia Presbyterian; and Alexander Garden of Charleston, Anglican Commissary of South Carolina. Although this discussion of Arminianism is confined to the movement within New England Congregationalism, it could be as well illustrated from Presbyterian or Anglican sources.

The temper and quality of Arminian thought was perhaps best displayed in its prime emphasis upon the benevolence and goodness of God. Whereas the Puritans had stressed God's omnipotence, majesty, justice, and awful inscrutability, the Arminians chose to dwell upon His goodness, mercy, and love. As Charles Chauncy believed, it was God's benevolence that enabled men to love and trust Him. In the 1750's, in the aftermath of the revival, Chauncy wrote his *The Benevolence of the Deity, Fairly and Impartially Considered* (published 1784), a work that ranks with Jefferson's *Notes on Virginia* in epitomizing the enlightened mind. God's goodness was most immediately apparent in His creation. Everywhere, men could see the evidences of goodness in the abundance of creatures each with capacity for enjoyment and in the immense amount of good actually enjoyed. It was, of course, essential to realize that God's benevolence was directed toward the universe as a whole and not to particular parts of it in isolation. The proof of benevolence was to be found in the destinies of systems rather than in the fate of individuals. Future as well as present circumstances were also to be borne in mind, since current irregularities might well be corrected in time. All the good suitable for a universe like the present one actually existed, except where it might be perverted by individuals themselves. Even inanimate nature was so constituted as to bring satisfactions to creatures capable of experiencing pleasure. The sun gave light and heat. The seasons rotated with pleasing variety. And if it was true that not all parts of the globe had been favored with climates so salubrious as that of New England, let it at least be acknowledged that the arctic regions were protected from the worst severities of the cold by a thick blanket of snow!

The great variety of forms of life comprising the vegetable and animal kingdoms provided, for Chauncy, the most convincing evidence of divine benevolence. For this variety revealed a complete creation, one fully stocked with all possible forms of created beings. Each species was a link in the "chain of existence," which constituted a full and coherent whole. From a shortsighted point of view, one might indeed observe many instances of apparent evil; but if these occasions were put in proper perspective, they conformed to the general tendency to good. Thus while some creatures preyed upon others, that fact made possible a larger total of happiness than could otherwise have existed. The same consideration justified death. A succession of individuals was capable of a larger measure of happiness than a single individual. All in all, Chauncy concluded, "the more closely [the wisest philosophers] view the constitution of the world, the more reason they continually find for surprize at the riches of *goodness,* as well as *wisdom,* therein so clearly shining forth."

The fact that men had been endowed with minds enabling them to contemplate all this goodness was, for Chauncy, further evidence of God's beneficent intention. The aspect of external reality that more than any other persuaded the Arminian that God was good was the regularity or uniformity of natural processes. For this regularity demonstrated conclusively that the laws of God's general providence embraced and sustained all things. Although the Arminians thought of themselves as perpetuators of the Puritan tradition in the face of the radical innovations of the revivalists, they nevertheless abandoned much of the Puritan system, including the doctrine of special providences. Man's best evidence of God's goodness was found in the fact that God was not arbitrary. In the faculty of reason He gave men an instrument at least potentially capable of coping with the world in which they were placed. Reason would be worthless in a world dominated by caprice.

The goodness of God expressed itself most effectually in the happiness of His creatures. Man had been so contrived, Chauncy affirmed, that it was his nature to seek pleasure, both for himself and for his fellows. Biologically speaking, the balance of sensations must be preponderantly pleasurable or one could not bear to exist. Pleasure, therefore, was a fact to be taken account of, not a weakness to be apologized for. The Puritan had been acutely conscious of the sin and misery of life. His Arminian descendants undertook to demonstrate that sin and misery are merely incidental if necessary foils for happiness.

The immense amount of happiness that actually existed in the world was the maximum that possibly could exist consistently with the infinite wisdom of the creator. He had so made men that happiness was possible only through a wise and virtuous use of the human faculties. Unlike animals, whose pleasures were merely sensual, man's best happiness resided in his unique capacity to manipulate his environment with the aid of reason. He could thus weight the balance of pleasure in his favor by guarding against injury, providing for want, and refining and diversifying his enjoyments. Unfortunately, men valued the animal pleasures too highly. They forgot that the more enduring satisfactions were found in sobriety, chastity, and moderation—in other words, when the appetites were restrained by reason. Although Chauncy affirmed that the highest pleasures were moral and intellectual, his was not a plea for the life of contemplation or renunciation. He spoke for a class of practical men fully committed to the active management of affairs.

In view of the complacence with which the Arminians contemplated the benevolent intentions of deity, their treatment of the problem of evil was somewhat paradoxical. Evil was produced by men whenever they obstructed the operation of forces ordained by God to be conducive to happiness. Thus men of their own free agency caused evil. In some respects this responsibility was more direct and personal than in Puritan theory. Puritans held all men to be naturally sinful simply because men were human. Sin was a condition to be remedied only by grace. Strictly speaking, the Puritan was not responsible for his sin; he was responsible only for overcoming it with the aid of grace. In Arminianism, however, sin or evil resulted from man's free agency and was directly related to the responsible acts of the individual. Yet, in spite of this fact, evil had become merely incidental to the whole system of nature, the ultimate purpose of which was good. It might be said that evil made possible the conception of the good.

Arminians placed great emphasis upon the principle of freedom of the will. Benevolence in both God and man sprang from free choice; it was a moral and not a mechanical principle. The moral quality of experience, namely, the basic fitness or unfitness of conduct to produce good, was said to bind God as well as man. The moral order of the universe was known to man by means of the moral sense or faculty, "the first power of our nature," Chauncy called it. This faculty enabled men to distinguish good from evil directly, without the aid of reason. It could, however, be atrophied by neglect, like any physical faculty.

Closely related to the moral sense was the faculty of self-determination. The Arminians insisted firmly that without self-determination moral responsibility was an illusion. Edwards had argued that there was no free will because the will was bound to respond to the strongest of the motives presented to it. Chauncy rejected this reasoning as mere metaphysical subtlety. It was directly contradictory to universal human experience. The faculty of self-determination was that power which all men possessed to give motion to their preferences. The Arminians would have echoed heartily the summary verdict of the English wit Dr. Samuel Johnson, who said of the free will controversy that, while reason might be opposed to free will, experience was for it. When reason contradicted the lessons of experience, something was obviously wrong with reason.

Man's free agency, then, was the foundation of the moral world. And it was this very free agency that was the basis of the highest pleasure of which man was capable, namely, the capacity for self-approval on having done well. On the other hand, when men faltered in their moral duty they suffered the pangs of self-disapprobation. These were the psychological stimuli that the Creator had provided in order to accomplish His moral purposes. The Arminians were at great pains to repudiate the determinists, whether Edwardean or deistic. God had deliberately endowed men with freedom of action in order to preserve the moral quality of experience. Chauncy's whole psychological theory was designed to accomplish this purpose.

The minimizing of evil, which was a corollary of the quest for human happiness, was further facilitated by the doctrine of the universal salvation of mankind. Chauncy was the first of the Arminians to embrace the universalist doctrine, and for many years he expressed himself on the subject with great discretion, feeling that the prevailing sentiment in Arminian circles was not yet ready to entertain so radical a dogma. His treatise on the subject remained unpublished for a quarter of a century before it finally appeared anonymously in 1784 as *The Mystery Hid from Ages and Generations, Made Manifest by the Gospel-Revelation; or, the Salvation of All Men the Grand Thing Aimed at in the Scheme of God.*

The focus of Arminian thinking was clearly upon the ultimate maximum felicity to be enjoyed by all men. The influx of humanistic values attendant upon the greater personal security of the age, at least for the privileged class, together with preoccupation with mundane pursuits inevitably fostered the new point of view. For the theologian, the affirmation of salvation for all rested upon the doctrine of universal atonement: Christ's sacrifice atoned for the sins of all men, not merely those who were of the elect. Because of the universal atonement, men were said to face no longer the divine wrath and condemnation that had been their lot after the fall of Adam and before the Crucifixion. Universal atonement necessarily entailed universal salvation. Christ died for all; so all will be happy. In the light of this promise, man's duty, according to Chauncy, was to "acquire such habits, and improve such graces" as would fit him for the joys of heaven at the day of resurrection.

But what of those who persisted in living and dying sinners? God would, of course, punish them; not to do so would encourage misery in the moral world. In good utilitarian style, the theologian undertook to make the punishment fit the crime. For their disobedience, sinners must suffer an appropriate punishment that would "reduce them to a proper temper of mind," after which they would be so chastened as to be capable of rational and immortal happiness. In short, sinners would be reformed in purgatory. Orthodox critics were quick to complain that God's sovereignty was impaired by a theory that enabled men freely to sin and thus frustrate God's design for their happiness. But the Arminian remained steadfast in his conviction that, although men were free, God in his infinite wisdom and power could find a way "to bring *all men* into a state of moral subjection, without breaking in upon their liberty." In the future world, whatever of this worthy task that remained unaccomplished would be completed.

It might well be asked which one possessed the more exalted sense of God's sovereign power: the Puritan, who bound his deity by strict logic and covenant; or the Arminian, whose faith in God's will for happiness supervened both the acknowledged lessons of experience and the dictates of reason? The Arminian clearly had the greater faith in God's capacity for doing the impossible. In any event, there can be no doubt that by the middle of the eighteenth century happiness had become a formidable quality when it could be confidently summoned to bear so heavy a freight.

Deism

Arminianism was the form in which the spirit of the Enlightenment expressed itself among the American clergy. Among laymen the counterpart to Arminianism was deism. The essential ideas of both systems were much the same. The most important difference was in attitude toward the Scriptures. The Arminians found scriptural revelation in no way incompatible with the ideas of natural religion; in fact, they frequently appealed to the authority of revelation in support of their views. The redemptive mission of Christ was, after all, known from revelation and not from empirical knowledge. Deists, on the other hand, were not technically Christians in that they saw no need for scriptural authority, generally dispensing with it entirely. They might take up such parts of the Scriptures as served their purposes, as did both Jefferson and Paine, but it was on their own terms and not in the spirit of men who acknowledged in revelation a higher source of truth. To deists, the Bible was simply a human document that recorded the faith and views of its various authors.

Deism was the natural religion distilled from the mash of eighteenth-century Protestantism. Its roots were as varied as those of Arminianism. Washington and Jefferson had been raised as Anglicans and always maintained nominal affiliations with that body, and with its successor the Protestant Episcopal Church. Franklin and Ethan Allen came out of the Congregationalist tradition. The signs of his Quaker background always remained unmistakable in Tom Paine. Truly, deism furnished the earliest example of what might be called "religion of the lowest common denominator," a phenomenon that was thenceforth to remain a significant if intangible factor in the American religious scene.

A letter written by Franklin a few months before his death to President Ezra Stiles of Yale College effectively caught the calm temper and sedate convictions of the deists. To Stiles's inquiry concerning his religious beliefs, Franklin replied in part:

> I believe in one God, creator of the universe. That he governs it by his Providence. That he ought to be worshipped. That the most acceptable service we render to him is doing good to his other children. That the soul of man is immortal, and will be treated with justice in another life respecting its conduct in this. These I take to be the fundamental principles of all sound religion, and I regard them as you do in whatever sect I meet with them.
>
> As to Jesus of Nazareth, my opinion of whom you particularly desire, I think the system of morals, and his religion, as he left them to us, the best the world ever saw or is likely to see; but I apprehend it has received various corrupting changes, and I have, with most of the present dissenters

in England, some doubts as to his divinity; tho' it is a question I do not dogmatize upon, having never studied it, and think it needless to busy myself with it now, when I expect soon an opportunity of knowing the truth with less trouble.

Deists agreed that while God was the author of nature and its laws, it was not His practice to intervene in the orderly course of mundane affairs; there were no miracles that countervened the natural course of things. Man was possessed of an immortal soul and was rationally and morally obligated to worship his creator. Jesus, who well deserved to be called the Son of God because of the unequaled purity of His moral life, was a great teacher of virtue. The Christian Scriptures were said to contain much wisdom—and much also that was best passed over in silence. But of the reality of the moral order of the universe no deist had any doubt. He acknowledged a principle of compensation whereby the follies and injustices of this life would merit suitable retribution in the life to come.

Deism recommended itself to the gentry because of the universality of its claims. Based as religious truth was upon the universal laws of nature, all rational creatures were obliged to acknowledge its authority. It was no longer enough to set up a holy commonwealth, a city upon a hill which was to safeguard a unique heritage. Religious truth must be such as to recommend itself with equal authority to the intelligence and moral sense of all men. There was no mystery in deism; it claimed no exclusive dispensation. With the deists, cosmopolitanism was a virtue, and sectarianism was to be deplored.

The most extended statement of deistic principles appeared in a book entitled *Reason the Only Oracle of Man*, published at Bennington, Vermont, in 1784, and purportedly written by the Vermont patriot leader Ethan Allen, although believed to have been largely the work of Allen's friend, the physician Thomas Young. The book could have had little influence in its day, since all but a few copies were destroyed in a fire. However, it developed at length several points that were typical of deist thinking.

The ostensible purpose of Allen's book was to show that the only religious truths that man was capable of grasping were to be gained through reason. To this end, it was pointed out that God revealed Himself in nature and that experience, in the largest sense, was man's source of knowledge of the good. When reason was brought to bear on human experience, it was the confident affirmation of the author that the reasoner could not but conclude that God was good; that the happiness of creatures was His object; that this was the best of all possible worlds; and that man should love and adore God for His beneficence. From the vantage point of a later generation, the complacent faith of the deists seemed more striking than their blasphemies.

But Allen was more particularly concerned with affirming man's moral freedom and responsibility against the materialists and determinists. The idea that the universe could have resulted from mere chance he proclaimed to be absurd. Edwardean moral determinism was likewise rejected as based on a false analogy to mechanical action. Nevertheless, Allen did not attempt to demonstrate moral freedom; he merely affirmed it. Freedom of the will was something of which all men were intuitively certain. "The greatest philosopher, and the humble and unlearned peasant, are in this respect on a level, being each of them conscious that they are free." The moral sense that all men possessed expressed itself in the judgments that they framed upon the alternatives of conduct confronting them. God indeed had foreknowledge of man's acts, but He did not foreordain them. Edwardean predestination was morally irresponsible. This was not a very impressive tribute to the oracle of reason but at least it revealed the convictions that lay closest to the heart of the age. Unable to reconcile reason and the moral sense, the deist affirmed that God had created the two distinct realms of being and had happily endowed man with these two faculties in order to cope with each of them. Many years earlier, Franklin had also grappled with this problem and, seeing no satisfactory solution, had abandoned philosophy for more useful pursuits.

Deism functioned chiefly as a means of assuring the intellectual security of its proponents. It had no personal function comparable to the piety of orthodox forms of religion. It played no major part in the lives of its chief proponents, who were men devoted to a variety of secular pursuits. But it was well suited to provide appropriate forms for the expression of the public piety in a community of many religions, and it was so used effectively both by Jefferson and by Washington.

One of the distinctive features of deism was its indifference to the importance of the social organization of religion in ecclesiastical institutions. While it was true that churches were sometimes regarded as socially desirable disciplinary agencies for the mass of the population, the deists showed little inclination to provide their faith with a suitable institutionalization. Franklin contributed indiscriminately to various denominations with condescending good will, but he reserved the appointed times of worship for study. Jefferson's comments on the religious life of Virginia provided a particularly revealing insight into the peculiar paradoxes of deism. Virginia, he remarked in his *Notes,* had originally had a national church (Anglican) established by law. Inevitably the church had persecuted and harassed the sects, those private and voluntary religious organizations that individuals were free to join or leave at will. Nevertheless, the sectarians had grown in numbers and influence in spite of persecution until they were strong enough to force a practical toleration. Eventually the church had been disestablished without precipitating chaos, proving that religion was not a necessary prop to the state. To the continuing complaint of Episcopalians that the sectarians were fanatics, Jefferson replied in effect, true enough; but since they could not be overcome by force, why not try reason? These were the detached observations of a man who appeared to be untouched by the religious convictions that animated so many of his contemporaries.

But when Jefferson came to discuss the social values of the Virginians, his own religious convictions became apparent enough. He roundly condemned slavery for undermining morality and industry; and without morality and industry there could be no public piety, no conviction in the minds of the people that their liberties were the gift of God. Eventually, he prophesied, when the shift in the wheel of fortune inevitably occurred, and God's aid was sorely needed, the Virginians would discover to their sorrow that God had no attribute to which they in their corruption could appeal. God Himself, by "supernatural interference" might even soon bring this day of reckoning to pass. Jefferson here revealed his faith in the omnipresence of God's general providence, displayed both in nature and in "history, natural and civil."

The tolerant and noncontroversial attitude toward the orthodox that was shared by the deists of the gentry class doubtless reflected their appreciation of the need for appropriate institutions to nurture the "public piety." But with the coming of the American Revolution and the broadening of the enlightened ideology in the service of patriotism, deistic ideas quickly permeated all social classes. Orthodox champions were inclined to assess the blame on libertine French officers, but this seemed hardly necessary. As a matter of fact, the influence of deism at the popular level has been grossly exaggerated. But where it did appear, popular deism was distinguished chiefly by its forthright attack on orthodox religion. In the 1790's, a militant deist named Elihu Palmer traveled widely along the Atlantic sea-board, attempting without much success to organize deistic societies analogous to orthodox congregations. The most celebrated expression of the polemical phase of deism was found in Tom Paine's *Age of Reason* (1794-96), written while its author languished in a French prison. Starting with the assumptions of natural religion, Paine vigorously exposed the absurdities and pretensions of revealed religion. Orthodox Protestant groups were accustomed to controversy, but they were unprepared for an attack that rejected all their assumptions, and they could only retaliate with personal vilification.

So far as deistic ideas received institutional embodiment, it was not in any church organization but in Freemasonry, the popularity of which increased greatly in America during the later eighteenth century. Masonry was a fraternal, benevolent, and religious organization whose ritual and principles were distinctly deistic in character. Membership was open alike to Jew and Gentile. By the end of the century, there were said to be eleven American Grand Lodges, 347 local Lodges, and a membership of some 16,000. A list of prominent American Masons reads like a directory of the most eminent men of the period. Although the secret ritualism of the order undoubtedly contributed to the suspicion in which it was widely held, a sense of the competition that it offered to more orthodox religious bodies was also an important factor.

Freemasonry was peculiarly adapted to the spirit of the age. As a profession of faith in the universal ideals of love, brotherhood, justice, and rectitude, it took a position beyond the exclusive sectarianism of particular creeds and proposed to embrace all of them. The symbols of the mason's craft which it adopted represented well the dedication of the age to constructive accomplishment. The humanitarian morality of the order was grounded in history and experience. Fraternity was taking its place beside religious duty. Probably because of the practical fact of organization and fellowship, the moral code of Masonry bulked larger in its scheme of things than did the interest of deists in moral questions, which was, in fact, quite incidental. How far the European stereotype of the good Quaker was actually influenced in its formation by the humanitarian morality of Freemasonry would be a question worth investigation. It is known at least that Tom Paine's deistic morality came from Quaker sources, and that Paine, although not himself a Mason, was deeply interested in the movement.

Revivalism and Enlightenment

Lest one assume that by the end of the eighteenth century the enlightened ideology had come to be generally accepted by Americans a brief assessment of the significance of the pattern of evangelical religious revivalism between 1740 and 1800 will show otherwise. The revival that was known as the Great Awakening among the Reformed churches spread quickly to non-Calvinistic sects and denominations. The sequence of events in Virginia illustrates the process. Samuel Davies, a disciple of Gilbert Tennent, initiated a revival among Presbyterians of the Tidewater region in the 1750's. During the following two decades, the movement spread westward to the Baptists of the Piedmont. It crossed the Blue Ridge during the Revolution and infected the Scotch-Irish Presbyterians in the valleys beyond. Finally, at the end of the century, it reached the rapidly growing Methodists.

By that time, a new generation of New Englanders had forgotten the bitter quarrels that had attended the revivals of the 1740's, and a new wave of revivalism swept the Congregationalist churches there, spreading with migrating Yankees to New York and the Upper Ohio Valley. This was called the Second Great Awakening, but for the religious community as a whole there was no real hiatus between the two revivals; at almost any moment during the sixty years between 1740 and 1800, local revivals were in progress somewhere in Anglo-America, either on the frontier or in longer settled regions.

These phenomena are difficult to deal with in terms of the categories of enlightened thought. So far as the revivals indicated the persisting strength of the traditional Christian supernaturalism, they defined the intellectual, and perhaps even the social, limits beyond which the secular, rationalist spirit of the Enlightenment could not penetrate. But although the religious mind survived the onslaught of enlightened ideas, even in its most uncompromising supernaturalist forms it made certain concessions to the dominant spirit of the age. While the revivalists still regarded man as depraved and in need of regenerating grace, they allowed the Puritan theology of human inability to wither away, to be replaced by a practical and implicit assumption of moral free agency. The institution of revivalism itself, the overt features of which were being rapidly standardized into ritual, symbolized a practical promise to all that salvation was to be had for the seeking. But if the revivalists gave ground on this side, they vastly extended the operations of the Spirit on another. With respect to the substance of sanctification, they replaced the sober virtues of the Puritan ethic with more radical forms of Christian perfection, such as love and self-abnegation. Expectation of the immediate return of Christ to establish His millennial Kingdom was common among revivalists; and it was this expectation that served in part to sustain and justify radical perfectionism by giving assurance that the believer did not have long to wait. A colorful if minor sequence of events in American religious history illustrates these tendencies.

The frontier of settlement in New England during the last quarter of the eighteenth century ran from southwestern Maine across southern New Hampshire and Vermont to the hills of western Massachusetts and Connecticut. In the course of the revivals that periodically swept this region there emerged a new sect called Freewill Baptists. The leader was Benjamin Randall, a former Congregationalist and a convert of Whitefield's. In reacting against the traditional doctrines of the Calvinistic-Puritan tradition, both the Congregationalist and Baptist varieties, the Freewill Baptists proclaimed radical sectarian doctrines. They affirmed direct inspiration and the personal union of the believer with Christ at the moment of regeneration. Sanctification entailed the complete abandonment of sin, an exacting concept of moral perfection that was sustained by the conviction that the Second Coming was about to occur. In typical sectarian fashion, no clerical leaders were recognized. The meetings for worship proceeded as the spirit might move, without formal ritual. They frequently developed an intensity of feeling that resulted in spontaneous movements and gestures and earned for the worshipers the nickname "merry dancers."

At the same time, hundreds of miles away on the southern end of the frontier line in eastern Kentucky and southern Ohio, a similar sectarian movement was under way. It too was an offshoot of an old Reformed church, the Presbyterian. John Dunlavy and Richard McNemar, former Presbyterian clergymen, led a small group who called themselves "Schismatics"—again in deliberate rebellion against the dogmas of Puritanism. Their doctrines were not unlike those of the Freewill Baptists. They believed in direct inspiration and in the same uncompromising obligations of the blessed state of regeneracy, likewise sustained by faith in the immediate Second Coming. Revelations that had been vouchsafed to the leaders led them to the conviction that the Second Coming would occur in the year 1805. In expectation of the great event, the Schismatics spurred one another on with spontaneous exhortations, dancing, singing, and "speaking with tongues," and were subject occasionally to uncontrollable seizures known as "falling" and the "jerks."

Quite independently of these indigenous movements, a quarter of a century earlier, in 1774, there had settled in New York at Watervliet, near Albany, a little band of nine English immigrants who constituted a sect calling itself the United Society of Believers in Christ's Second Appearing. Their leader, Ann Lee, a woman of working-class Quaker antecedents, believed that the Christ spirit had become incarnate in her some four years previously. This second incarnation completed the work of revelation by providing the Christ spirit with embodiment in both the male and female forms. The second incarnation had, of course, been a spiritual and invisible event, and Mother Ann's mission was not merely to proclaim it but also to gather the faithful into a visible community of the righteous that would constitute the promised millennial Kingdom. Entry into the Kingdom was to be obtained by renunciation of sin, and for Mother Ann the symbol and essence of sin was sexual intercourse. Celibacy then was the most obvious mark of distinction between the Kingdom and the social world. Meetings for worship were more-or-less spontaneous affairs at which the worshipers symbolized the renunciation of sin with a kind of dance in which sin was purged from the body by shaking the arms and legs—a ritual that promptly earned for its practitioners the nickname "Shakers."

During the American Revolution, the local suspicion that centered on these recent British subjects effectively isolated them, but in the 1780's they were free to make contact with the American religious community. Emissaries crossed over into New England and proselytized actively among the Freewill Baptists, to whom they were drawn by a sure sense of doctrinal affinity. An appreciable number was converted to the Shaker faith. Little colonies of Believers were scattered through Maine, New Hampshire, Massachusetts, Connecticut, and eastern New York. During the first decade of the nineteenth century, reports reached the Shakers of the revivals in Kentucky and Ohio, and again missionaries set off on foot, carrying the word of truth to the revivalists. McNemar and many of his followers among the Schismatics were converted, and Shaker communities were established in that region also.

The modest accomplishment of the Shakers in making converts

among the revivalists in spite of the difficult obstacle of celibacy was undoubtedly owed to their success in demonstrating the cogency of their beliefs in the light of the faith and hopes of the revivalists. To those who acknowledged the exacting requirement of sinless perfection, the Shakers came with their rigorous but concrete gospel of celibacy. To those who impatiently awaited the Second Coming, the Shakers announced that the great event had already occurred and that with sufficient determination any who wished to do so could enter the Kingdom. The Kingdom itself received tangible expression through the spontaneous development of communitarian settlements composed of groups of "families" specializing in agriculture and handicrafts. These communities were organized by Ann Lee's successors Joseph Meacham and Lucy Wright. At the height of the movement, in 1826, some eighteen communities were scattered from Maine to Indiana. To many backwoods farmers struggling to survive without capital on stony subsistence freeholds, the peaceful stability and order of the prosperous Shaker communities were a welcome testimonial to the fruits of the Kingdom. But since the principle of celibacy precluded the possibility of perpetuation in the usual manner, the survival of Shakerism was wholly dependent upon the continuance in the larger community of the kind of revivalism to which the Shaker doctrine could offer itself as the appropriate fulfillment. These conditions ceased to exist after the middle of the nineteenth century.

Exotic though Shaker doctrines were, they were not entirely immune to secular influences. Mother Ann was not an intellectual and left no writings, but several disciples had received ministerial training and were capable of producing theological treatises in the formal style. These treatises displayed a strong moral repugnance to the traditional Reformed doctrines of predestination, particular election, and limited atonement. Clearly, the Shakers shared with their enlightened contemporaries a more humanitarian and complacent approach to the human situation. In practical terms, the repudiation of the Puritan tradition was even more pronounced. The millennial Kingdom that it was their function to inaugurate was to be characterized not only by celibacy but also by peace, brotherly love, and cooperation. Women were to enjoy full equality with men, and all were to participate fully according to their gifts in the work and worship of the community. The Shaker settlements were an excellent embodiment of the benevolent humanitarianism of the Enlightenment.

The continuing vitality of the religious tradition throughout the later eighteenth century furnishes a clue to the interpretation of the career of Jonathan Edwards, a task that would otherwise be difficult from the point of view of the social history of thought. Edwards is universally conceded to have been the foremost American theologian and one of the most powerful thinkers. He was born in 1703, three years before Franklin and one year before Chauncy, and but for a fatal smallpox inoculation which cut him off in the prime of life, in 1758, he could well have lived to witness the full flowering of enlightened thought. The literary historian Vernon L. Parrington described Edwards as an "anachronism" because of his stubborn preoccupation with traditional religious themes in an age that, presumably, had turned to secular interests and had learned to think in terms of humanistic presuppositions. But Edwards was not an anachronism. He was simply the most profound and eloquent representative of that segment of the community that remained impervious to the complex of enlightened ideas. And following in his footsteps was a succession of able theological disciples who carried the Edwardean piety into the nineteenth century, where the times seemed more receptive to it.

At the same time, Edwards revealed himself in many respects a child of the Enlightenment. It has already been remarked that, to be acceptable to the enlightened mind, religion must be either reasonable or a fact of experience. Most thinkers favored a form of religion that was reasonable. To Edwards, however, religion was both reasonable *and* a fact of experience. The Christian revelation had been designed to assist men in understanding both these aspects. As experience, he was able to revive regeneration as a concrete phenomenon. As reason, he elaborated a closely knit theology based on philosophical idealism. The empirical, analytical, and critical facets of the enlightened mind received no finer expression than in Edwards's two books descriptive of the Great Awakening, *Narrative of Surprising Conversions in Northampton* (1736) and *Thoughts on the Revival in New England* (1740). But for his untimely death, he might have completed his *History of the Work of Redemption,* a history of Christianity designed to show how history was comprehended within God's general providence, a point of view thoroughly congenial to the enlightened mind.

Edwards was a religious mystic who from earliest youth had systematically cultivated the experience of communion with the divine spirit. The environment that proved most congenial to these experiences was found in nature. As he described it: "God's excellency, his wisdom, his purity and love, seemed to appear in everything; in the sun, moon, and stars; in the clouds, and the blue sky; in the grass, flowers, trees; in the water, and all nature; which used greatly to fix my mind. . . . The soul of a true Christian, as I then wrote my meditations, appeared like such a little white flower as we see in the spring of the year; low, and humble on the ground, opening its bosom, to receive the pleasant beams of the sun's glory; rejoicing, as it were, in a calm rapture. . . . My heart panted after this,—to lie low before God, as in the dust; that I might be nothing, and that God might be ALL." For Edwards, the mind prepared itself for communion with the divine spirit by contemplating nature as the image or reflection of the divine.

Edwards's mysticism was the polar opposite of the attitude of the late-nineteenth-century humanists who sought the divine spirit in humanity. Felix Adler, the founder of Ethical Culture, agreed with Edwards that the religious spirit was to be found in experience— but in experience of quite a different sort. Adler sought it in the brotherhood that arises from the doing of good to others; he preached a religion of humanity. Edwards, however, regarded the doing of good as merely a by-product, although an inevitable one, of an ineffable experience achieved through a contemplation of nature as symbol.

It was Edwards's fate to find himself in a society still tinctured by the Puritan religious tradition. He attempted to adapt his mysticism to the religious aspirations of that society. Unlike most mystics, he assumed as a matter of course that the mystical experience should be shared by all men. In this he was true to the Puritan tradition—the whole world ought to be redeemed. So he became a clergyman and proposed to cultivate among men as exalted a standard of spiritual purity as America has seen. Edwards's practical program consisted in reviving the old Puritan piety with its central emphasis on regeneration as a supernatural event. His ministry became an intensive campaign of spiritual education, extended over the years. Beginning in 1735, his parish experienced the first of a series of powerful revivals. The accounts that he published of these revivals did much to spread the Great Awakening.

The revival that Edwards did so much to foster ultimately crushed him. The party of Congregationalist revivalists of which he was the leader was caught between the fanatical enthusiasm of sectarians on the one hand and the contemptuous hostility of the rationalistic Arminians on the other. Edwards was compelled to battle on both fronts in order to save evangelical Christianity from these equally dangerous foes. He clearly appreciated the anarchy that was implicit in the conviction of the sectarians that divine inspiration entailed the imparting of concrete ideas to the believer. At the same time, he deplored what he believed to be the actual or potential materialism of the rationalists who so completely identified the law of God with the material world that no place was left for the independent action of the Spirit. These circumstances forced Edwards to specify in most precise terms the practical consequences that should flow from the work of the Spirit in conversion. In reply to the sectarians, he insisted that the effect of conversion did not consist of the imparting of spiritual truth as such. It was, rather, an emanation like the light of the sun that enabled men to see specific things in true perspective. The most important consequences of the work of the spirit upon the individual —what the Puritan would have called "sanctification"—consisted of a cluster of attributes that reflected the violence of Edwards's reaction from the naturalism of Arminianism. These included a greater veneration of Jesus, a stronger resistance to sin and worldliness, a higher regard for the Scriptures, a deeper understanding of religious truth, and a spirit of love for God and man.

In this heroic attempt to defend the middle ground between Arminianism and fanaticism, Edwards defined a position that proposed, in effect, to purge the Congregationalist tradition of its alliance with the practical and worldly virtues of the Puritan ethic, an alliance that had become so prominent a feature of the Arminianism of Chauncy and his colleagues. But his vision was too exalted and refined to win much support in the practical atmosphere of eighteenth-century America. The great losses in numbers and influence that the Congregationalists suffered as a consequence of the revivals—losses on either wing that culminated in the Unitarian schism at the beginning of the nineteenth century—were symbolized by Edwards's personal tragedy at Northampton. His own congregation rebelled against the rigorousness of the standards of piety that he expected of it and, in an action rare in those times, dismissed him from its service.

CHAPTER 6

〽〽

Natural and Civil History

T HE AGE OF MODERN SCIENCE coincides with the span of American history. The "scientific revolution" of the seventeenth century was primarily an intellectual revolution, introducing a new point of view toward natural phenomena and establishing a new kind of relationship between man and the physical universe. From the modern scientific point of view, physical objects have their own inherent properties and characteristics, which determine their nature and relationships. The scientific observer respects these properties and does not attempt to impose a theory of the nature of things upon his data, save insofar as the theory is demonstrably confirmed by the properties of the things themselves. This is especially so with respect to qualitative and purposive considerations. Human experience, as it is evaluated subjectively, is, on the other hand, peculiarly qualitative and purposive. It would be hard to imagine life without values or will. It is not surprising, therefore, that the earliest scientific theories projected values and purposes in nature. The Aristotelian science that dominated the Western World until modern times found both qualitative distinctions and purposes in nature. These assumptions were deeply rooted and not easily abandoned. Long after Galileo and Newton had reconstituted astronomy, physics, and mechanics without them, they lingered on in the minds of many students to influence scientific thinking.

Natural History

The term *science* in the modern generic sense was not generally used before the middle of the nineteenth century. During the Age of Enlightenment, two terms designated the major branches of science: natural philosophy and natural history.

Natural philosophy embraced physics and mechanics, astronomy and chemistry. These were the fields (chemistry excepted) in which the impact of the scientific revolution was first felt. Perhaps for that reason an analytical approach was more characteristic of natural philosophy than of natural history, while the prestige of the "philosopher," like Dr. Franklin, was correspondingly high.

Natural history was a far more comprehensive field, involving a descriptive approach to all the phenomena of living nature and of physical nature as the environment of life. The first American to hold a professorship of natural history, Benjamin Smith Barton of Philadelphia, left a convenient catalogue of the more specialized fields which it embraced: zoology, botany, geology, mineralogy, paleontology, meteorology, and hydrography (oceanography). But the field of zoology was itself a vast one, for it embraced not only the biology of animals, including man, but also the physical history of man. The latter would now be called anthropology, which Barton subdivided into anthropometrics, linguistics, and ethnology—and was careful to include the study of Indian mounds!

Although the outstanding contributions of Americans to the science of the age were doubtless those of Franklin in electricity and of Benjamin Thompson (Count Rumford) in physics, the principal area of scientific interest was natural history. Through botany and physiology, natural history was closely related to medicine, and many students who worked in the field were physicians. Barton insisted that natural history was in no way inferior to natural philosophy in the questions of general philosophic import that it raised. But in the development of modern science, fruitful advance hinged upon the interplay of theory and factual research, and the field of natural history was too extensive to permit individuals to cope with the rapid accumulation of data. By the middle of the nineteenth century, it was breaking down into its specialized subdivisions. Barton's vision of the regal domain of natural history was gradually displaced by the commonly accepted and less exalted meaning of the term as "nature lore."

Three phases of the natural-history movement in America can be distinguished. The first phase focused upon discovery, description, and classification. This work began with the earliest explorations of the New World and continued into the nineteenth century. Geographical exploration was actually an important aspect of this phase of natural history. The reporting of new species was a regular part of the work of exploring expeditions. Much of the work of discovery and description was carried on by men without specialized training, who identified by European names the species with which they were familiar and assigned Indian names to those that were new. Typical of such reporting was that of John Lawson, a surveyor for the proprietors of North Carolina. Lawson traveled some thousand miles through the interior in 1709 and in his report described sixty-eight species of land birds, sixty-five of water birds, twenty-seven species of mammals, and seventy of fish, besides many trees and plants.

A notable contribution to description was made by Mark Catesby, an Englishman who lived for some years in Virginia at the beginning of the eighteenth century and who traveled extensively to the southward. On his travels, Catesby painted from life specimens of the many species he encountered. Returning to England, he learned copperplate engraving and made engravings from his paintings. The results appeared in three large volumes published between 1731 and 1748, entitled *Natural History of the Carolinas, Florida, and the Bahama Islands,* with two hundred colored engravings. The simple directness and sturdy vigor of Catesby's art are pleasing testimonials to the labors of all those who were engaged in making known the flora and fauna of the New World.

The work of discovery properly culminated in the development of a more adequate system of classifying the forms of plant and animal life than that which had been handed down from the days of Aristotle. This was accomplished by the Swedish naturalist and taxonomist Karl Linnaeus. The binomial nomenclature by which organisms were distinguished according to genus and species was introduced by Linnaeus in 1737. The tenth edition of his *Systema naturae* (1758) was later adopted by international convention as the standard for zoological nomenclature. The basis of the Linnaean classification was structural. It distinguished between plant and animal kingdoms and subdivided each into phylum, class, order, family, genus, and species.

One of the most famous travel reports on America in the eighteenth century was written by a student of Linnaeus, Peter Kalm, who came to America to botanize. Kalm's *Travels in North America* was published in an English translation in 1770. The first American to use the Linnaean system of classification in his work was John Reinhold Foster, who published *A Catalogue of Animals of North America* in 1771.

The most famous American naturalists of the age were the Bartrams of Philadelphia. John Bartram (1699–1777) was a Quaker farmer and physician who became interested in botany. His extensive field trips took him as far west as the Ohio and the Great Lakes, north to the Catskills, and south to Florida. He established in Philadelphia the first botanical garden in America. By personal correspondence, then the common method of communication among scientists, he established extensive contacts with the naturalists of Europe. Linnaeus honored him as "the greatest natural botanist of the age." Bartram was instrumental in introducing into England many native American plants and trees, including the bush honeysuckle, mountain laurel, and wild aster, the magnolia, tulip, and locust trees, red and white cedars, and the sugar maple.

William Bartram (1739–1823), the son, carried on his father's interests. In 1791, he published his *Travels Through North and South Carolina, Georgia, East and West Florida,* a combination of minute scientific description of flora and fauna, adventure, and rhapsodic reflection on the excellencies of nature. The union of natural history with natural religion was perfectly consummated in the younger Bartram. The study of nature revealed to him the infinite subtlety and perfection of the divine craftsman. Every creature of the swamp and forest was an exhibit of this craftsmanship. The beauties of nature were to be described with the same passionate devotion with which the dedicated worshiper sang the praises of his creator. Qualities of character were the common elements that bound man and nature in an intimate union. Bartram habitually personified nature by finding in particular specimens of plant and animal life various traits of human character. The noble savage also appeared in Bartram's comments on the Seminoles, those simple children of nature whose lives were generally animated by the divine principles of honor and reputation. In fact, the complex of sentiments and ideas found in Bartram carry the reader to the threshold of another era. The British and French romantics, Wordsworth, Coleridge, and Chateaubriand, drew inspiration for their romanticism from the *Travels;* and eventually Bartram's attitudes became thoroughly domesticated in the generation of Emerson and Thoreau.

The second phase of natural history might be designated cultural geography, the study of the earth as the habitat for man. The focus of interest here was upon the effects of physiographic conditions on human culture. The result of such an approach to the natural history of man was a variety of theories of environmental determinism.

Cultural geography embraced not only physical geography but also geology, mineralogy, paleontology, and meteorology. Mineralogy and physical geography, being the more practical parts, were the more advanced. But appreciable advances in all these fields were made during the later eighteenth century. In meteorology, Franklin explained the nature of cyclonic storms, while Jefferson appreciated the necessity for a network of weather-observation stations and kept his own careful records for years while urging his correspondents to do likewise. In paleontology, great interest was aroused by discoveries of fossil remains of previously unknown mammals. Physicians trained in comparative anatomy, such as Caspar Wistar of Philadelphia and Samuel Latham Mitchill of New York, did much to introduce system into the classification of fossil species. Exploring expeditions, like that of Lewis and Clark, began to assume something of a modern scientific character by including specialists who brought back voluminous reports of scientific interest.

But while solid advances were being made through the accumulation of information, many insistent questions had to be answered with insufficient knowledge. Some rather fanciful theories were consequently propounded, frequently by Europeans without firsthand knowledge of America. The more encyclopedic writers who attempted to cover the whole field of natural history were especially prone to dubious generalizations. The French scientist and philosophe Georges Louis Leclerc, Count de Buffon was the most influential of these theorists. The first fifteen volumes of Buffon's encyclopedic *Histoire Naturelle* were published between 1749 and 1767 and dealt particularly with aspects of what is here called cultural geography. A comprehensive English edition of his *Natural History* was published in 1812 in twenty volumes.

Buffon's cultural geography commenced with an outline of the geographical and geological features of the terrestrial globe. Historical geology was at that time still in its infancy. There were two schools of thought on the manner in which the earth's crust had been formed, Neptunism and Vulcanism (or Plutonism). The Neptunists were followers of A. G. Werner, a German mineralogist. Werner laid the foundations of geological science with his insistence that the differing rock strata were the fundamental materials of geology. He distinguished five basic strata, some of them formed by mechanical and some by chemical action. Fossil remains of varying complexity correlated with these strata to establish the order of their successive creation. Werner quietly abandoned the Biblical theory of creation. "Our earth," he declared, "is a child of time, and has been built up gradually." In the uneven features of the earth's crust he detected the action both of water and of fire.

Werner hypothesized that originally the earth had been a solid irregular sphere covered with water. All the materials that now composed the earth's crust had been held in suspension or solution in this universal ocean. Over an immense period of time these materials were gradually deposited on the ocean floor, building up the earliest of the geological strata, namely, the granite, crystalline, and transitional. The original core having been of irregular surface, elevated land masses eventually emerged from the waters. Subsequent deposits of material were consequently local in character.

The opposing school of Vulcanists were the followers of the British geologist James Hutton. They rejected the Neptunist theory of precipitation from a universal ocean and emphasized instead the formative influence of volcanic action. The chaotic and overturned geological features to be observed in many localities could not be accounted for, in their opinion, except on the hypothesis of intense heat at the earth's center, bursting forth in sporadic volcanic action.

Buffon was a Neptunist. He assumed that the great continental land masses had emerged from the ocean at different times—a fact of vital consequence for all forms of life. For when he proceeded to zoology and took up the natural history of man, he emphasized the more recent formation of the American continent as the reason for the physical and cultural degeneration of man—and indeed of all forms of life—in the New World. The environment was hostile to life.

Buffon's views were popularized in America by the Scottish historian William Robertson, the first volume of whose *History of America* was published in 1777. Robertson magnified his physiographic determinism by exaggerating the harsh and forbidding features of the American environment. Nature was said to conduct her operations on a bolder scale in America than elsewhere. The mountains were higher, the rivers longer, and the lakes larger. America had a unique climate in which cold predominated and violent changes of temperature were characteristic. All parts of the continent were most unhealthy, being covered with forests, marshes, and swamps, from the stagnant waters of which noxious vapors and putrid exhalations arose to menace the health of man and beast. The miasmatic theory of disease was commonly entertained at that time. Robertson conceded that civilized man could do much to improve these unfavorable conditions, but the American Indians were so primitive that they had been unable to effect any improvements.

The unfavorable environment was then the chief reason why life in America was less robust and vigorous than in Europe. Animal species were fewer in number here and more puny than those of Europe. There was no species in the New World so large as the lion or rhinoceros and none so ferocious as the lion or tiger. Animals common to both continents, such as bear, deer, or wolves, were stunted in America, while domestic animals imported from Europe quickly degenerated here. The native population of America similarly showed the adverse effects of the inhospitable environment. Although quick and agile enough, the North American Indians were not durable. Their hairless skin was evidence of lack of vigor. They were deficient also in the appetite for food and for sexual intercourse; hence the sparse population of the New World. While the distribution of skin color in the Old World varied according to climate, this was not true in the New, where a uniform complexion prevailed from the tropics to the Arctic. The cold climate was doubtless responsible for this remarkable circumstance. Robertson was little concerned with speculation as to the origins of the Indians, although the distribution of animal species suggested to him the probability that men had entered the American continent from northeastern Asia. His major interest was not in derivation but in relationship to environment.

The reactions of Americans to these statements reflected both their access to the facts and their uncertainty as to theory. Jefferson's wide scientific interests equipped him with the facts with which to correct many of the Europeans' errors. Portions of the *Notes on Virginia* were devoted to such corrections. He had for many years kept precise records of temperature and precipitation. He could cite accurate data on the comparative size and variety of animal species in both hemispheres. He could subject Buffon's attempted correlation of body size with temperature and moisture to devastating criticism. And to the charge that the American environment could not produce animals of great size, he was able to exhibit the fossil remains of the mammoth. But historical geology, in either of its contemporary schools of thought, was too advanced for Jefferson and, indeed, for most Americans of that day.

The enormous influence of religion in the American intellectual heritage, and the relatively superficial deviation from it which enlightened ideas represented, became readily apparent when eighteenth-century Americans attempted to reconstitute their ideas about the creation in order to accommodate the needs of historical geology. In this context, Jefferson seemed like a Biblical literalist. It taxed his credulity too heavily to conceive of an omnipotent creator waiting the inconceivable length of time necessary to form the earth's surface either by internal heat and pressure or by precipitation from an aqueous solution. After all, God had created the world as a place for plant and animal life. By attributing efficiency to the creator, Jefferson found it easier to imagine a single comprehensive act of creation than the long-drawn-out processes of the geologists. And so he held stubbornly to his traditional creationism, affirming that God made the earth all at once, "nearly in the state in which we see it, fit for the preservation of the beings he placed on it."

The common assumption of the age that God's processes were "reasonable," employed as Jefferson employed it, seriously obstructed the development of a scientific attitude. In Jefferson's case, it prevented him from appreciating the value of the first steps toward geological science. As late as 1826, the last year of his life, he continued to insist that "dreams about the modes of creation, inquiries whether our globe has been formed by the agency of fire or water, how many millions of years it has cost Vulcan or Neptune to produce what the fiat of the Creator would effect by a single act of will, is too idle to be worth a single hour of any man's life."

The facts of paleontology similarly challenged Jefferson's static creationism. He himself had a deep personal interest in the study of fossils. From fossil remains found in West Virginia he reconstructed the large clawed animal that he named *megalonyx*. In 1807, he dispatched the explorer General William Clark to Big Bone Lick, Kentucky, to dig up the spectacular deposits of mammoth remains that had been found there. No one had ever seen living specimens of these creatures, yet Jefferson persisted in his conviction that the species still existed. Somewhere in the unexplored West it would be found. In God's plan of the creation a place had been provided for every species. None could become extinct without jeopardizing the symmetry of the plan; the chain of being would be broken. "Such is the economy of nature," Jefferson dogmatically declared, "that no instance can be produced, of her having permitted any one race of her animals to become extinct; of her having formed any link in her great work so weak as to be broken." The theory of design in nature later became a particular favorite of orthodox Protestant apologists, but it never received a more categorical affirmation than from the pen of Jefferson.

Such views were not shared, however, by all of Jefferson's contemporaries. George Turner, a member of the American Philosophical Society, disputed the assertion that species do not become extinct. Turner demonstrated that there were two species of mammoth, one carnivorous and the other herbivorous, both utterly unlike any living species; they must both be presumed to be long since extinct. Benjamin Smith Barton also rejected the "purile opinion" that nature does not permit species to become extinct. He saw that the theory was a necessary corollary of the idea of the fullness of the creation, which he also rejected. "There is no such thing as a chain of nature: an absolutely necessary dependence (on this earth) of one species upon another."

The third area of interest was anthropology, or the natural history of man. Speculation was dominated by the assumption of a static creation at a definite moment in the past. It was generally assumed that within certain limits of variability the world with its stock of plant and animal life had been created much as the eighteenth century found it. In the opening number of the *Memoirs* of the American Academy of Arts and Sciences (1780), Governor James Bowdoin of Massachusetts observed that the "beneficent Creator, the first and supremely great naturalist," had endowed man at the creation with the requisite faculties and had instructed him in the skills sufficient to assure his survival. There he had left him to develop further such arts and sciences as he might wish.

Here was the anthropological assumption of the age: man had been created essentially as he found himself to be. What he might do with his faculties and capacities in the way of improvement was, so to speak, his own business. This was the point where civil history grew out of natural history. But even in civil history no radical change or development was presumed to be possible. Jefferson minimized the cultural differences between the barbarian natives of the New World and the civilized Europeans. Without sentimentalizing over the Indians, he emphasized the universal human traits that their way of life accentuated. For after all, "the movements of nature are in a never ending circle," and this applied to civil as well as natural history.

Perhaps the most striking feature of the anthropology of the period was the almost universal assumption that the accumulating facts of human prehistory could be fitted into the Biblical narrative. Fortunately, Biblical history was sufficiently limited in scope so that much other material could be woven around it without raising direct contradictions. Allegiance to the factual veracity of Genesis was not therefore the inhibiting influence that at first glance one might suppose it to have been.

The philosophes of Europe, being more emancipated from the authority of Scripture, had greater freedom to speculate. Voltaire and Lord Kames hypothesized the plural creation of men and animals in the regions they were found to inhabit. Buffon speculated that the North American Indians might have been colonized from the lost continent of Atlantis. Cornelius de Pauw suggested that there had been a separate creation of inferior quality in America.

Most Americans, however, accepted the authority of Genesis as indicating a unitary creation with descent from a single pair. From the Garden of Eden, presumably somewhere in the Middle East, the human species had become dispersed throughout the globe. Since the seventeenth century, a popular theory had held that the Indians were descended from the ten lost tribes of Israel. James Adair, Indian trader and amateur anthropologist, found many linguistic similarities between Hebrew and Indian languages and other ethnographic data to support this hypothesis. President Ezra Stiles of Yale traced two probable routes for the peopling of America. The Canaanites expelled by Joshua had sailed westward through the Mediterranean to Mexico and Peru. Another group had wandered to the East, becoming the Tatars, and eventually reaching America by way of northeastern Asia to become the Indians of North America. Benjamin Barton believed that America had been peopled from numerous sources.

In the meanwhile, western explorers had discovered the prehistoric mounds of the Upper Ohio and Mississippi valleys. For nearly a century, the origins of the mounds remained a topic of widespread interest and speculation. The first accurate and detailed descriptions of the mounds of Ohio, together with analysis of the artifacts that they contained, were furnished by General Samuel H. Parsons in 1786. The quality of craftsmanship of the artifacts was so far superior to the work of modern Indians that the identity of their makers remained an enigma. Peter Kalm was perhaps the first to suggest that the mound builders were a vanished race, possibly of Tataric origin.

The various problems that it confronted thus led the enlightened mind to a preoccupation with the question of origins. This was an issue with which it was peculiarly unequipped to deal. The enlightened mind in America could not cope with the problem of origins because it was unable to take a radical view of history as development. It could not do this as long as it clung to the conviction that God created the universe much as modern men found it. This was the reason for preoccupation with the Biblical narrative of creation: it provided a conventional account of origins which permitted enlightened thinkers to evade all the serious questions that accumulating data were beginning to form in their minds.

After considering and dismissing the various theories that had been advanced to account for the presence of sea shells high above sea level, like those found in the Appalachian Highlands, Jefferson declared that the matter must remain a mystery. Certainly it was incredible to him to suppose, as it had already been suggested, that the floor of the ocean could have been heaved up to heights thousands of feet above present sea levels. Nothing like it was known to history or experience, nor was there any evidence that the alleged forces at work were great enough to accomplish this feat. Yet within a few years, and with no new types of evidence available, Sir Charles Lyell was to maintain that currently existing forces were capable of accomplishing precisely this. Clearly, Jefferson's static creationism was so strong that he could not make the imaginative effort necessary to visualize extensive changes in time.

Civil History

The static view of nature implicit in the enlightened assumption that purpose and value had been built into the creation itself resulted in similarly static theories of human history. The overarching purpose of the creator, whatever it might be, determined the framework within which humanity would work out its destiny.

The several theories of history commonly encountered in the eighteenth century all confined the possibilities of human experience within specified limits, except perhaps for the theory of progress which by the end of the eighteenth century displaced the others and became the dominant American view of history.

The most widely held theory was in all probability that derived from the Christian scriptures. Man had originally been created perfect and had fallen from grace by his own sin. Throughout the long subsequent night of chaos and struggle he had been sustained by the promise of ultimate redemption when the powers of evil would be overcome and the original relationship to the Creator restored. Each of the other theories of history was in some sense a variation on this basic theme.

When on June 8, 1783, General Washington addressed a circular letter to the governors of the newly independent American states, he observed that "the foundation of our empire was not laid in the gloomy age of ignorance and superstition; but at an epocha when the rights of mankind were better understood and more clearly defined, than at any other period." The men of the Enlightenment were acutely conscious of living in a distinctive epoch of human history. They coined the term *enlightenment* to distinguish their age from those that had preceded it. Perhaps the condescension indicated by the term suggests an explanation of the fact that among their multifarious interests enlightened Americans paid little attention to the writing of history. They had more important things to do than to dissipate their energies in the study of the benighted past. Being enlightened, they hardly expected to profit from describing their unenlightened predecessors. It would, of course, be quite incorrect to say that they were ignorant of the past or that they found it entirely useless. Political theorists, for instance, knew much about political history. But their approach was a relatively sterile and narrow one. They used the facts of the past for their own purposes, in order to shed light on their specific problems, and in a didactic spirit.

The basic assumption of enlightened thought that united natural and civil history was the idea of theodicy. The term had been coined by the German philosopher Gottfried Wilhelm von Leibniz to designate those theories that attempted to reconcile the existence of natural and moral evil in the world with God's providence. Natural law was readily identified with the law of God. According to the Reverend Joseph Lathrop of West Springfield, Massachusetts, God governed by general and steady laws. One of these was the fixed connection that He had ordained between virtue and happiness and, contrariwise, between vice and misery. Where piety and virtue existed, a people would rise to importance; without them, misery and slavery would ensue. These convictions were not restricted to clergymen. Jefferson subscribed to the same views and repeated them frequently. The happy contrivance was gratefully acknowledged in his phrase: "virtue and interest are inseparable."

The theodicean assumption was expressed in a sermon preached on the eve of the American Revolution by Ebenezer Baldwin, an orthodox Congregationalist of Danbury, Connecticut. No matter how dark the prospects might be for Americans, Baldwin intoned, let them rest assured that, because of God's infinite wisdom and goodness, whatever He does is done for a wise and good purpose. "Infinite wisdom cannot but do that which is best upon the whole. Calamities are therefore a Part of an infinitely wise Plan, are calculated to answer the best Good of the whole universal System. Every instance of Calamity or Affliction answers some good and valuable purpose; so that what is 'partial Evil is universal Good'." Thus in a universe that is essentially self-equilibrating, evil is rationalized or put in its place.

It was the particular value of history that it taught morality by example. Through history one might transcend the limitations of the immediate situation and, by gaining a larger perspective, see what was "best upon the whole." Within this framework, the utilitarian ethic provided the clue to historical dynamics. The Puritan virtues of diligence, sobriety, frugality, and industriousness, when practiced by a people, were confidently expected to result in a happy, vigorous, and healthy society. But if the cultivation of these virtues was allowed to lapse, a decay of vigor attended by catastrophes of various kinds was sure to follow.

Out of these considerations emerged a theory of history that aptly reflected the peculiar temper of the American Enlightenment. It concerned itself with the rise and fall of states and peoples. The course of history traced a ceaseless ebb and flow, a cyclical movement. Steeped as they were in classical literature, enlightened thinkers were familiar with the use of the cyclical theme in Aristotle's political theory and elsewhere. The idea was also widely current in contemporary British writing, and in a form closer to that in which Americans expressed it. Both John Adams and Jefferson were familiar with Bolingbroke's *Patriot King* (1738), where the life-cycle analogy was applied to the history of nations. Political societies, like animal bodies, said Bolingbroke, have a natural life cycle of infancy, youth, maturity, old age, and death through which they must inevitably pass. No state can contravene nature's universal law by surviving forever. It can, however, prolong its lifespan, if its citizens remain loyal to the healthy principles of social order on which the state was originally founded. So long as they are able to do this, their society will remain prosperous and durable. But if they become corrupted or weakened by their prosperity, the end will soon come.

When Governor Bowdoin inaugurated the proceedings of the American Academy of Arts and Sciences in 1780, he propounded a law of historical development purportedly based on the experience of four great empires: Assyrian, Persian, Macedonian, and Roman.

It is very pleasing and instructive [said the Governor], to recurr back to the early ages of mankind, and trace the progressive state of nations and empires, from infancy to maturity, to old age, and dissolution:— to observe their origin, their growth and improvements, their different government and laws, their variant customs and religion:—to observe the progress of the arts among them, which at first were few and rude, suggested by their wants and necessities, but gradually increasing in number and perfection, in proportion to the enlargement of the community, and as the culture of them was encouraged:—to observe the rise and gradual advancement of civilization, of science, of wealth, elegance, and politeness, until they had obtained the summit of their greatness:—to observe at this period the principle of mortality, produced by affluence and luxury, beginning to operate in them: manifesting itself with greater or less vigour in a variety of ways; and finally terminating in their dissolution, brought upon them by the vices attendant on luxury. Debilitated by these, and incapable of defending themselves against a vigorous invasion, their more hardy neighbors, invited by that circumstance, and perhaps irritated by the insolence, which the national affluence and luxury inspire, invaded and subjugated them. In fine—to observe, after this catastrophe, a new face of things; new kingdoms and empires rising upon the ruins of the old; all of them to undergo like changes, and to suffer a similar dissolution.

The moral cycle of virtue and corruption was closely correlated with a political cycle of freedom and despotism. Eighteenth-century writers charted in detail the cyclical fluctuations of history in which virtuous independence alternated with corruption and tyranny. Rome rose by temperance and fell by luxury according to Oliver Goldsmith, whose friend Edward Gibbon chronicled in detail the sad story of Rome's decline and fall. English history in turn revealed similar fluctuations, commencing with the sturdy virtues of the Saxons, among whom the venerated principles of individual liberty and human rights were presumed to have originated. Paul de Rapin, the French historian whose *History of England* (trans. 1726–31) was admired by John Adams and John Dickinson, portrayed the Saxons as electing their kings democratically, and acknowledging only such laws as they themselves consented to. The succeeding Norman period introduced feudalism and absolutism, and subsequent British history to modern times exhibited a cyclical fluctuation between relatively successful attempts to recover ancient liberties and the imposition of new forms of tyranny. As the conflict between England and her American colonies reached a crisis in the 1770's the Americans readily accommodated their view of the conflict to the cyclical theory. Using the historical analysis furnished by the "True Whigs" of England Americans depicted the course of English history since the Glorious Revolution of 1688 as a long period of decline in which the crown gradually perfected its absolute control of the government through bribery and intimidation. The American struggle for freedom was hopefully to reverse the course of the cycle and inaugurate a new era of liberty and enlightenment.

A distinctive feature of the eighteenth-century form of the cyclical theory of history was the commonly introduced analogy between the life cycle of the nation or people and that of a biological organism. States and societies were believed to pass through the successive phases of youth, maturity, old age, and death. The process might be lengthened by prudence or shortened by folly, as Bolingbroke had suggested, but ultimately it was irrevocable. Those who used the organic analogy invariably placed eighteenth-century America in the stage of youth. Its future was before it, beckoning brightly to a vigorous, young society glorying in the healthy tone of its unfolding powers. The celebrated Pennsylvania revivalist Robert Smith, in a sermon preached in 1781 at the conclusion of the Revolution, spoke of the Americans as a young people not yet having reached maturity, whereas the European nations had passed their zenith. Yet, with characteristic sobriety, he reminded his hearers of the invariable practice of divine providence to lay low those who had been raised high and to exalt the humble. From the lessons of history, men should learn humility and a sense of their own impotence.

The youthful stage of American development was specified more precisely by the Reverend Thomas Barnard of Salem, Massachusetts, in a sermon of 1794. Unlike nations which have arrived at full maturity, and hence have nothing to look forward to except "decline and mortification, according to the course of human affairs," the new United States, he affirmed, can look forward to growth, expansion, and progress in every direction. Exciting though the prospect was, the present also had its peculiar attractions for Barnard. "I should prefer youth and early manhood, ever employed, lively, and full of hope, to complete manhood and old age, when we every day become less active, and less pleased. I should prefer the present period of our nation, for my life, to the more perfect state to which it will gradually advance." So far as those who used the cyclical theory dwelt upon the promise of the near future, they were preparing the way for the idea of progress that would soon obliterate the gloomy eventuality implicit in the organic analogy.

The ultimate cause or motivating force of historical change resided in the restless energy of human beings themselves. As John Adams put it, history shows that all things change. But it was characteristic of enlightened thinkers that they would not allow a stoic fatalism to paralyze the will and energies. All things might change; but they changed for good or ill, and it behooved men to see to it that they changed for good. Just as all activity had its moral dimension, so human history had to be interpreted in moral terms. As Americans used the cyclical idea, the overt indexes of change might be the stages of organic process, but at its heart social change was a moral process. The Reverend Joseph Lathrop of West Springfield, Massachusetts, in 1795, laid it down as a dictum that "all governments tend to despotism." And then he added, "Without virtue and vigilance among ourselves, this will be the fate of our own."

The identification of moral transformation with the organic cycle was made explicit by David Tappan, Hollis Professor of Divinity at Harvard College, in 1798:

Experience proves that political bodies, like the animal economy, have their periods of infancy, youth, maturity, decay, and dissolution. In the early stages of their existence their members are usually industrious and frugal, simple in their manners, just and kind in their intercourse, active and hardy, united and brave. Their feeble, exposed, and necessitous condition in some sort forces upon them this conduct and these habits. The practice of these virtues gradually nourishes them to a state of manly vigor. They become mature and flourishing in wealth and population, in arts and arms, in almost every kind of national prosperity. But when they have reached a certain point of greatness, their taste and manners begin to be infected. Their prosperity inflates and debauches their minds. It betrays them into pride and avarice, luxury and dissipation, idleness and sensuality, and too often into practical or scornful impiety. These, with other kindred vices, hasten their downfall and ruin.

In correlating virtue with youth and corruption with old age, Tappan doubtless thought of social youth as a kind of shorthand symbol to indicate simplicity of institutions and, hence, purity of personal habits. The presumed superiority of America to Europe, an assertion so frequently found in Franklin, Jefferson, and Adams, was essentially a moral superiority rooted in a simple institutional structure. Tom Paine reflected a similar primitivism when, in his *Common Sense* (1776), he correlated the complexities of the British constitutional system with a decadent society and the simplicities of radical republicanism with the virtuous citizenry of the New World. And by the same token, Jefferson trembled for slaveholding America whenever he reflected that God was just, and would eventually call for a fearful reckoning.

The enlightened outlook on the future was one of confident optimism tempered with a realization that all things change and that success was attended by its own peculiar dangers. Jefferson conceded that the American pioneers of civil and political liberty had been lucky both as to time and place. Being the first to establish a free society, they had before them no bad examples to follow. But how quickly and easily the new wine could be soured! "What a tremendous obstacle to the future attempts at liberty will be the atrocities of Robespierre!" John Adams similarly warned of the decline that inevitably followed upon achievement. When nations reached the summit of their glory, "some minute and unsuspected cause" commonly caused their ruin. The destruction of Carthage that removed the threat to Rome also permitted the spread of that debauchery among the Roman citizenry which eventually caused decay and collapse. Americans had no reason to assume that they were exempt from the operation of universal historical laws.

The moralism that permeated the cyclical theory of history was also evident in the theory of degeneration, a distinctively eighteenth century idea that reflected current biological, anthropological, and geographic as well as cultural interests. The empirical, matter-of-fact temper of the enlightened mind had succeeded in separating myth from historical fact, so that the Biblical myth of creation had become literalized. The Scriptures were beginning to be read as historical documents, and the events they described were presumed to have occurred in a literal sense. The creation as described in Genesis had occurred in 4004 B.C., according to the calculations of the Irish Archbishop James Ussher (1581-1656), and within the relatively brief span of time since that year all subsequent changes would have to be compressed. Such an hypothesis was credible only if these changes were presumed to be relatively limited.

The theory of degeneration rested on the assumption voiced by Jefferson that the universe had been created in substantially its present condition. The changes that had occurred represented degeneration within the immutable categories of the creation. In the sense that the original creation was perfect the word "degeneration" carried invidious connotations. But as used by a scientist struggling to accommodate to the assumption of fixity of species the rapidly accumulating data of variations the idea of degeneration came as a godsend, and could be used in a neutral sense.

For anthropologists as well as for historians Adam's sin and fall had resulted in degeneration. Beneficiaries of the Christian revelation may have been at least partially redeemed, but the remainder of mankind still exhibited all the pitiful consequences of degeneracy. Seventeenth-century Puritans had commonly regarded the Indians as spiritually degenerate; in the following century the idea received an anthropological application as well. Samuel Stanhope Smith of the College of New Jersey held that the human species had been created in a civilized condition, since no instance was known of the attainment of a state of civilization by savages unaided by those already civilized. From the original civilized society splinter groups had wandered off, and under the influence of varied environmental conditions had suffered the effects of degeneration as exhibited in their present physical and cultural characteristics. The Scottish historian William Robertson employed a similar assumption in accounting for the albino Indians of Panama. This "degenerate breed" had inherited its albinism and was not to be considered a separate type since true variations were caused by climate and other environmental conditions—a judgment precisely the reverse of that which was to prevail a century later. Degeneration, Robertson affirmed, occurred within an existing type but did not result in significant modification of it.

The theory of degeneration was still current as late as 1866, when the distinguished geographer Arnold Guyot of Princeton declared that the human species had originally inhabited the mountains of Iran, and had been created with Caucasian characteristics. The native inhabitants of other parts of the world displayed degeneration from the original stock to a degree that correlated precisely with the distance of their modern habitat from Iran. By the middle of the nineteenth century such views were invariably employed as an intellectual defense of Protestant orthodoxy and had lost most of their scientific credibility.

The evidences of change that the theory of degeneration was intended to accommodate were eventually to find a more persuasive and congenial rationale in the nineteenth century idea of progress. Although both were theories of change, a radical transformation of mood was necessary before the idea of steady improvement in the condition of humanity could take hold. The principal causes of this transformation were undoubtedly social, but a more strictly intellectual source was to be found in the Christian doctrine of millennialism.

The millennial expectation of Christ's return to earth to establish His kingdom gained a wide currency among revivalists during the Great Awakening. Millennialism then divided into two currents, both of which persisted into the nineteenth century. Sectarians kept alive the more radical version known as premillennialism. Taking certain Biblical prophesies literally, these sectarians looked to the fairly immediate return of Christ to gather the saints and establish His Kingdom on the ruins of earthly principalities and powers. Premillennialism was frequently catastrophic in its expectations; it reflected the determination of Protestant sectarians to resist the encroachment of a more secular outlook.

The more moderate doctrine known as postmillennialism was widely held by representatives of the new type of religious body, known as the denomination, that was emerging at the end of the eighteenth century. Postmillennialists looked for the return of Christ at the end of the thousand-year period; and that period itself was regarded as preparatory to the great event. During it there would occur the gradual spiritual and moral refinement appropriate to the character of the Second Coming in which the millennium would culminate. Postmillennialists were less fervent in their supernaturalism than were the premillennialists. They shrank from the forthright assertion that at some moment in the near future the natural order of things would be disrupted by an invasion of the heavenly hosts. Without denying that the event would eventually occur, they focused their interest on the mundane world in which, they hoped, spiritual and social forces would be at work preparing the way for the "far off divine event."

The ease with which postmillennialism could accommodate itself to a more secular outlook was illustrated in the 1775 sermon of Ebenezer Baldwin to which earlier reference has been made (p. 128). In spite of the impending conflict with the mother country, Baldwin was hopeful for the future. He was confident that the struggling colonies were to become the "Foundation of a great and mighty Empire; the largest the World ever saw, to be founded on such Principles of Liberty and Freedom, both civil and religious, as never before took place in the World; which shall be the principal Seat of the glorious Kingdom, which Christ shall erect upon Earth in the latter days." When he sent his sermon to the printer, Baldwin amplified his prediction in a long footnote. The American population then numbered some three million and was doubling in size every twenty-five years. He expected that this rate of increase would continue for about a century, and at a lower rate for a second century, resulting by 1975 in a population of some 192 million Americans. Because the increase would be the product of natural growth rather than of conquest, the original American principles of civil and religious liberty could be expected to remain intact. Baldwin recalled that divines had calculated the date of the Second Coming from the Biblical prophecies in Daniel and Revelation at about A.D. 2000. At that time, America would be at the height of its glory, while Europe would be sunk in tyranny, corruption, and luxury. Clearly, therefore, the seat of the millennial kingdom would be established in America.

So far as attitudes toward history are concerned, what was significant in Baldwin's postmillennialism was his assertion that "present scenes are remotely preparing the Way" for the Second Coming. The kingdom was to be inaugurated by natural causes, such as the improvements introduced by good government, and by moral refinement. Men could not expect to enter the kingdom without making appropriate preparation for it. For a definite period of time, earthly and heavenly events were to flow together in a common channel, a channel to be characterized by a regular and salutary transformation.

Baldwin's brand of moderate postmillennialism had certain features anticipatory of the nineteenth-century theory of progress. If progress is defined as the assumption that "civilization has moved, is moving, and will move in a desirable direction," then postmillennialism had much in common with it. But millennialism was, after all, the product of the religious mentality, and it foretold, however remotely, the displacement of the natural order by the supernatural. For that reason alone it was not readily available to enlightened minds accustomed to thinking in more mundane terms.

If the idea of progress drew from millennialism a pattern of historical change in the form of a secular trend, it drew also from the cyclical theory the assumption that human experience displayed a universal moralism rooted in a common human nature. Jefferson had held that human nature was the same everywhere, which explained why history revealed the universal alternations between virtue and corruption, power and impotence. "Mankind soon learn to make [self-]interested uses of every right and power they possess." The idea of progress similarly assumed a universal psychology in terms of which society would pursue a steady course of moral and material improvement.

In American thought, the theory of progress was largely a phenomenon of the nineteenth century. Some of its earliest expressions are found in the writings of Franklin during the 1780's. Here he referred to the progressive melioration of the condition of mankind as the result of such basic innovations as printing. The wider dissemination of information that was thus made possible enabled men to substitute responsible government for despotism and thus achieve a larger measure of happiness.

After the War of 1812, a distinctly new note began to creep into the letters of the elder statesmen Jefferson and John Adams. The former wrote that "science had liberated the ideas of those who read and reflect, and the American example has kindled feelings of right in the people. An insurrection had consequently begun, of science, talents, and courage, against rank and birth, which have fallen into contempt. . . . Science is progressive, and talents and enterprise on the alert." Jefferson now redefined the political philosophy of eighteenth-century republicanism as the conviction of those who believe in the "improvability of the condition of man, and who have acted on that behalf."

In his reply, Adams was able at last to set the conflicting theories of history in some kind of perspective. Christians, Jews, Mohammedans, and Hindus, he remarked, all shared the hope of a future state similar to the millennial kingdom. "But you and I hope for splendid improvements in human society, and vast amelioration in the condition of mankind. Our faith may be supposed by more rational arguments than any of the former. I own I am very sanguine in the belief of them, as I hope and believe you are."

The authentic elements of the idea of progress were present in such statements as these. Those elements included the assumption of the cumulative character of technology, belief in the liberating power of science, the enhancement of human dignity as reflected in the idea of social rights, and the steady improvement of the material condition of mankind. But the presence of these ideas in a distinct constellation was an indication that at the beginning of the nineteenth century Americans were ready to enter a new intellectual era.

CHAPTER 7

Republicanism

T HE GENIUS OF THE AMERICAN ENLIGHTENMENT best expressed itself in political thought and practice. While there was little that was original in republican political theory, it displayed a happy facility to adapt itself to circumstances, to comprehend and exploit the distinctive elements in American experience, and to modify practice with lessons drawn from classical and modern history and theory. Never before or after was American public life distinguished by a political leadership at once so experienced in public affairs, so cosmopolitan in its learning and social affiliations, and so firm in its intention to secure the full realization of a distinctively American society and character.

The difficulty in recapturing the political mind of the Enlightenment is due in part to the character of the Enlightenment itself, in part to the relationship of the age to more recent periods of American history. Enlightened ideas did not permeate all ranks of society in the late eighteenth century. They were chiefly the property of the gentry class, an élite group in some respects comparable to the regenerate Puritans. In spite of its cosmopolitan attitudes, its optimism, and its self-confidence, enlightened thinking at the same time displayed a defensive strain that appeared especially in its political thought. The upward thrust of democratic forces released by the revolutionary struggle compelled the more wealthy and conservative elements to examine the problems of freedom and organization with particular care. The threatened tyranny of a monarchical empire on the one hand, and of a democratic mob on the other, fixed the limits within which human and property rights had to be reconciled and protected. Within this context emerged a body of political thought the crowning expression of which in practice was the federal Constitution. The Constitution was an instrument of marvelous economy, and it long survived the enlightened mind that produced it. During the nineteenth century, it became the object of patriotic emotions even as something of its original spirit was being subtly perverted. Nineteenth-century democrats could hardly be expected to read the Constitution with the eyes of the eighteenth-century republicans who had written it. Only in the twentieth century did conscious historical research begin to recover an understanding of its basis in class and economic conflict.

Republican political theory is customarily traced back to the English political writers of the seventeenth century. John Locke was certainly widely read and quoted by American writers, and the Americans who venerated him were products of a similar intellectual background; both were two generations removed from Puritanism, and both were profoundly influenced by that great movement. In both cases, the Arminian modifications of Puritanism had pointed toward a social philosophy of freedom and responsibility, toward a softening of the Puritan social ethic with sentiments of brotherhood and humanitarianism. To emphasize American indebtedness to Locke or to other specific theorists is to minimize the common intellectual tradition on both sides of the Atlantic, a tradition that began with Locke and Harrington and ended with Jefferson and Calhoun. This discussion will take republicanism in America on its own terms and make no effort to establish its relationships to the enlightened political theory of Europe.

Basic Assumptions

One of the fundamental assumptions of republican theory was its distinctive notion of law. The Puritans had taught that God's law is known in part in nature. Locke's friend Sir Isaac Newton, himself a devoutly religious man, had demonstrated with mathematical precision the lawful character of the mutual relationship of all physical bodies. These religious and scientific ideas were blended in the eighteenth century into what was known as natural law, those aspects of experience that demonstrated God's rationality and benevolence.

In the northern colonies the derivation of natural law from Puritan teaching was direct. The Puritans had divided human history into a series of dispensations or epochs: the age of the garden of Eden; the present age of fallen men, when government is necessary; and the eventual age of Christ's kingdom. In enlightened thinking the garden of Eden became the state of nature, separated from the present age by the adoption of the social contract. Even the most secular thinkers of the Enlightenment never quite lost the idea that government is necessary because man is evil; as Tom Paine put it, government, like dress, is the badge of lost innocence.

Outside the areas of Puritan settlement the road by which Americans arrived at a sense of the primacy of law followed a somewhat different course. In the South the earliest articulate group were not clergymen but lawyers, and here the mediating idea was that of the common law. The elder Daniel Dulaney of Maryland, in a pamphlet published in 1728, maintained that the distinguishing mark of a free government is the settled character of its legal structure. In the British Empire this referred both to common law and statute law. Common law, as Dulaney used the term, embraced the law of nature, the law of reason, and the revealed law of God as well as those local customs consistent with good order.

These conceptions of natural law, whether derived from God, from nature, from reason, or from experience, were blended in the eighteenth century to become the bedrock of enlightened political theory and, indeed, to carry over into the democratic thought of the nineteenth century. It is essential here to recall again the distinctive connotation of the eighteenth-century idea of law, its permissive and benevolent implications, and its close identification with right. The Reverend Elisha Williams, former Rector of Yale College, wrote in 1744 that man is free from subjection to earthly rulers because he is subject to the law of nature. In other words, man is free because he is rational.

Another distinctive feature of republicanism, one closely related to the idea of law, was the theory of the social contract. Its indigenous sources were the covenant theology and the colonial charters. The distinction between the state of nature and civil society appeared in American political thinking as early as 1717 in the ecclesiastical writing of John Wise of Ipswich, Massachusetts. By the time of the Revolution, it had become a commonplace. Its chief function was to emphasize the fact that men possessed rights and liberties anterior to government, and which could not be abridged by government. Various reasons were adduced to explain why men had been willing to give up the freedom of the state of nature for the restraints of civil society. Clergymen, such as Chauncy, said that it was because of sin, which necessitated governmental controls. Others cited the uncertainty of affairs that would prevail were men without social regulations. Samuel Cooke of Arlington, Massachusetts, in 1770 gave voice to a characteristic point of view when he observed that government had been unnecessary in the state of nature because property had not existed; but when distinctions of mine and thine began to be made and property had appeared, then government had become necessary.

A third basic assumption was the commitment to constitutionalism. As early as the 1730's references were being made to something called "the constitution." At times, these references denoted something broader than the social contract, since they embraced both natural rights and the powers and forms of government. They referred to the standards against which acts of government were measured. At other times, they referred specifically to the British political system. Here it was assumed that there was an imperial constitution distinguished by a jealous concern for the liberties of the citizen, colonial as well as British. According to the Reverend John Barnard of Marblehead, in a Massachusetts election sermon of 1734, this protection was secured by the "branched" or separated powers of the British government, no one branch of which was permitted to invade the functions of the others.

This conception of a government with balanced or mixed powers became a characteristic feature of republican theory, while it was rejected by radical democrats, such as Paine, who deplored the underlying assumption of a permanent conflict of class and economic interest. The theory of balanced powers as protective of the constitution developed at a time when, after the English revolution of 1688, the several branches of the British government, namely, king, lords, and commons, appeared to offset or equalize each other. Its appearance in America by 1734 antedated Montesquieu's famous exposition by more than a decade. For Americans, the existence of the colonial charters and the perennial struggle to preserve charter privileges against the steady encroachments of imperial administration helped to give the constitutional idea the literal form it has always assumed in American thought.

Human Nature and Politics

Although the men who brought republican theory to its full development in the Revolutionary generation were statesmen and men of affairs rather than cloistered philosophers, they were nevertheless sufficiently aware of the philosophic questions that lie at the basis of political thought that their ideas will always be of interest. Their theory rested upon several assumptions about the nature of man the political animal.

One of the prime characteristics of human nature was its selfishness. This view of man gave republicanism its perennially modern flavor. Man's first need, observed John Adams with typical acerbity, is his dinner; his second is his girl. According to Jefferson, *Homo sapiens* was the only animal species eternally and systematically engaged in the destruction of its own kind. "Lions and tigers are mere lambs compared with man as a destroyer." Selfishness led man inevitably to encroach upon his fellows if he had the power to do so. Both history and divine revelation, Adams affirmed, taught that man is wicked, and the political application of this conviction was made by Jefferson in the Kentucky Resolution of 1798, when he wrote, "free government is founded in jealousy, and not in confidence." These observations, however, were not to be understood as spiritual judgments upon man; this was not strictly a Christian view of human nature. These were simply statements of fact of which political science must take account if it was to complete its task effectively. These facts of human nature did not indicate a fundamental pessimism as to human prospects. Republicans believed that by arranging proper safeguards much could be done to assure human happiness and well-being.

A corollary to this disenchanted view of human nature was the candid acceptance of human inequality as the normal state of affairs. To be sure, the Declaration of Independence said that self-evidently all men are created equal and endowed with the inalienable right to life, liberty, and the pursuit of happiness. Jefferson wrote the Declaration and Adams signed it. In the nineteenth century, these phrases became the cornerstone of the democratic ideology. But it seems likely that the Declaration would have expressed the sentiments of its framers more accurately if it had read that all men were created equal *in the sense that* they were endowed with the inalienable rights of life, liberty, etc., and in this sense only. Neither Jefferson nor Adams believed that men were actually created equal in any concrete sense. Adams provided an illuminating gloss on the phrases of the Declaration when he wrote that "the equality of nature is moral and political only, and means that all men are independent."

Adams was the chief republican political psychologist. He insisted that his speculations were founded not upon natural law or natural rights but upon a realistic apprehension of human nature. Man was a creature of passions, and the passion most germane to political science was the passion for distinction. In its constructive form this passion expressed itself as ambition and emulation. Its destructive forms were envy, jealousy, and vanity. Whatever its guise, this passion gave man his dynamic qualities, whether creative or destructive. However learned or ingenious the lawgiver might be, if his constitutions or edicts were not framed with reference to such an individual, they would quickly reveal their irrelevance. Adams recognized also the innate quality of benevolence, but he insisted that benevolence alone could not balance the selfish impulses. It must be reinforced by emulation and ambition. There seemed to be some mysterious connection between the passion for distinction and the possession of abilities sufficient for its attainment. Whether ambition produced talent or vice versa, Adams could not determine; but, in either event, they always occurred together, and "what God and nature have united, let no audacious legislator presume to put asunder." The inevitable aristocracy that appeared in every society, the constructive utilization of which occupied so important a place in Adams's political speculations, consisted simply of those persons of superior endowment who thrust themselves to the fore in any circumstances.

The political consequence of human inequality was then the universal phenomenon of ruling aristocracies. The choice of the word *aristocracy* was unfortunate, since republican theorists did not intend that it should convey the invidious connotations that it was already coming to suggest in the American vocabulary. They found in history no confirmation of the idea that people are self-governing. Adams distinguished five sources or pillars, as he called them, of aristocracy: beauty, wealth, birth, genius, and virtue. The first three were the older and played much the greater role in history, any one of these always overbearing the latter two. While Jefferson was generally in agreement with this analysis, he was more hopeful that in a "healthy" society genius and virtue would be widely appreciated and utilized in positions of power. Both men concurred in the belief that moral and physical inequalities were transmitted, at least in part, by heredity. The husbandman of Monticello regretted that man did not breed himself to improve the stock as he did his animals. All too frequently greed, ambition, or sentiment caused him to make an unsuitable marriage and breed an inferior offspring. In these circumstances, the best that could be done was to provide some means of detecting the chance appearance of the natural aristocrat of genius and virtue and of bending his talents to the service of society. These were some of the political consequences stemming from the view of man as a selfish animal.

Another aspect of human nature, however, was invariably recognized by republican theory and did much to give that theory its distinctive quality. This might be called the view of man as a moral agent. Freedom and equality, the central ideals of Revolutionary American political thought, were moral ideas, and the purpose of government, both in its forms and in its functions, was to secure these ideals. In their universal concern for freedom of thought and speech as displayed in their Bills of Rights, Americans were grasping the instrumentalities by which right and value were established. It was perhaps no accident that for orthodox Protestants these were the years in which freedom of the will had become the central theological problem.

The sources of republican political moralism were varied. In one sense, value was inherent in the nature of things as properly demonstrated by sound intellectual method. This style of thought led Jefferson in the Declaration to say that good government is consistent with the laws of nature and of God and, furthermore, that it recommends itself to the enlightened judgment of humanity. Jefferson believed that man possessed an innate moral faculty that developed by use. There was also a biological source of the principle of political freedom as a moral value. Jefferson held that, since no two minds were alike, there could be no universal norms for human thought; society could not require uniformity of belief but must be prepared to tolerate wide differences and to teach men to live together with them peaceably. "Difference of opinion," he said, "leads to inquiry, and inquiry to truth." These were the considerations that underlay the celebrated defense of the freedom of thought and speech in his first inaugural address: "If there be any among us who wish to dissolve this union or to change its republican form, let them stand undisturbed as monuments of the safety with which error of opinion may be tolerated where reason is left free to combat it."

The close connection between political and moral theory in the eighteenth-century mind was illustrated in the effective teaching of John Witherspoon at the College of New Jersey, (later Princeton University). Witherspoon made that institution perhaps the leading American college of the Revolutionary period. Although he came to the colonies only in 1768, he was quickly Americanized and threw himself wholeheartedly into the independence movement in New Jersey. He served successively in the Provincial Congress of 1776 that deposed the royal Governor William Franklin and in the Continental Congress, where he signed the Declaration of Independence and sat throughout the war on important administrative committees. After the war he was elected to the state legislature. His final public act was to guide the formation of the American Presbyterian Church.

As president of the college, Witherspoon was accustomed to offer in the junior year his celebrated lectures on moral philosophy; and to make certain that the lessons sank in, he repeated them in the senior year. His students before and after the Revolution included a remarkable number of men subsequently to become prominent in public life: one President of the United States (Madison); four members of the Second Continental Congress; fifteen United States Senators; twenty-four Congressmen; three Justices of the Supreme Court of the United States; twelve state governors; and an appropriate complement of college presidents, clergymen, and professors. Given his forceful personality and interest in public affairs, it seems credible to suppose that Witherspoon had an appreciable influence in shaping the political thinking of his students. Sets of student notes preserved in the college archives provide an intimate glimpse of his style of political thought.

Moral philosophy as taught by Witherspoon consisted of three branches: ethics, jurisprudence, and politics. Each dealt with different aspects of moral obligation in human relationships and was properly studied in conjunction with the others. Underlying moral philosophy was the faculty psychology, including the theory of the moral faculty or conscience. This was the immediate source of the principle of obligation that permeated all branches of moral theory. The obligations that Witherspoon stressed included duties to God, to one's fellows, and to oneself. The latter consisted of the omnipresent utilitarian virtues of self-discipline.

The laws of politics as Witherspoon defined them were a blend of Locke and Hobbes. He commenced in orthodox fashion with the state of nature anterior to the social state, where men possessed the usual complement of natural rights. Man's full potentialities, however, developed only in civil society based on the social compact. In civil society, men relinquished certain of their rights in order to extend and strengthen others. Liberty was a right that should never be abridged. Witherspoon devoted considerable attention to the rights and obligations of property. Prevailing practices with respect to private property were, he believed, a good index of the moral character of any society. Communism might be suitable in small primitive societies or in religious brotherhoods but was certainly not for Americans. For them, private property was necessary as an incentive to labor and as a stimulus to the pursuit of the active virtues. The political importance of property was recognized as readily by Witherspoon as by his lay contemporaries.

Witherspoon reverted to the ethical implications of political theory in his concluding lectures. Civil liberty could not be defended as necessary either to virtue or to personal happiness. Why then was it so priceless a possession? Something of the teacher's eloquent flourish survives even in the undergraduate's notebook: "I suppose it chiefly consists in its tendency to put in motion all the human powers. Therefore it promotes industry, and in this respect happiness, – – produces every latent quality, and improves the human mind. – – Liberty is the nurse of riches, literature and heroism."

A third concept of human nature reflected the scientific revolution. The Puritans had isolated man as a spiritual individual; it remained for the Enlightenment to isolate him as a point of force. The view of man as a force well reflected the dynamic temper of enlightened individualism. One of the functions of the mythological state of nature prior to the adoption of the social contract was to permit theorists to strip man of his social institutions and to see him as he really was, sheer force. Expressions of this conception of man may be taken as evidence of the impact of the Newtonian world view upon political thought. John Adams, for whom the state of nature had little appeal, delighted in recovering the record of man as a force in history.

To the extent that man was a force, the problems of government could be defined as social engineering. The very terminology and approach to political science revealed the extent to which republican thinking was done in mechanical terms. Government was a structure to be organized. A central problem was that of balancing powers. The objective was an orderly relationship of social forces. There were no mystical or transcendental elements in enlightened political thinking, no divine right, no *vox populi vox dei*, no *volksgeist*. When Franklin, never above a timely opportunism, proposed prayer as an aid in surmounting some difficult obstacle in the Constitutional Convention, he was curtly informed that the Convention was not in need of assistance from any foreign power. The framers, said Adams, "had no interviews with the Gods, or were in any degree under the inspiration of Heaven." They employed only "reason and the senses." Americans were basing government for the first time in history upon "the simple principles of nature." The framers always took a sober view of their work, knowing that, like any mechanical contrivance, it would be judged by the success with which it executed its functions. This approach to political questions was obviously related closely to the larger mechanical world view of deism.

Finally, it was typical of enlightened political theory to assume that man was the product of his environment. Locke had rejected the elaborate faculty psychology of Puritanism as so much rubbish, and had replaced it with the simple assumption that the newborn mind was a blank upon which sense impressions were recorded. The mature mind was thus in large measure the product of the specific environment that had impinged upon it. (This did not necessarily imply a denial of hereditary endowments.)

One consequence of this style of thinking was the cult of nature, in which all virtues were ascribed to primitive society while modern civilization was deplored as corrupt and degenerate. The related cult of the noble savage was confined chiefly to Europe where the literary set had had little contact with savages. Its counterpart in America was the almost equally sentimental glorification of the rural way of life which deeply tinctured the political philosophy of republicanism. Jefferson believed that republicanism would survive only as long as small landowners predominated in the community and while acquisition of real property was relatively easy. His reaction to the federal Constitution, a copy of which came to his hand while in Paris, was singularly unenthusiastic. He was confident that, with or without the Constitution, Americans would preserve their liberties "as long as we remain virtuous; and I think we shall be so, as long as agriculture is our principal object, which will be the case while there remain vacant lands in any part of America. When we get piled upon one another in large cities, as in Europe, we shall become corrupt as in Europe, and go to eating one another as they do there." The assumption that liberty and virtue were dependent upon specific social conditions known to be only temporary distinguished eighteenth-century republicanism from nineteenth-century democracy with its consummate faith in man under any conditions.

The Nature of Government

Having formulated these conceptions of the human materials with which political science dealt, the republican theorist was prepared next to consider the nature of government. Perhaps the most striking and revolutionary of all his ideas was the proposition that government was artificial. In one sense this meant that government was man-made. There was no divine right or sanction for it. The social compact came to life in the written constitution; and if the constitution were poorly drawn, it would fail. The republican political philosophers wrote and rewrote constitutions with remarkable fluency, more than a score of them in a generation. Their writings showed a wide and intimate knowledge of the history of governments and of the theoretical classics of political science. In spite of their inevitable conventions of thought, they always approached their task in a practical and pragmatic spirit.

But there was a more important sense in which government was regarded as artificial. This sense involved a distinction between government and society. Society was the term denoting the whole complex of institutions, relationships, and economic activity of men. When society was in a healthy condition it needed little or no government. "That government is best which governs least." Government was superficial. Society, said Paine, is always a blessing, whereas government is at best a necessary evil. While the republicans did not develop systematically the sociology implicit in this distinction, clearly they had in mind some kind of structured image of the good society. This society rested upon an agrarian economy, was distinguished by a large measure of practical economic and social equality, and was dedicated to the cultivation of the utilitarian morality. The function of government was to keep order, to prevent men from tyrannizing over each other. The positive aims of society, whatever they might be, had nothing to do with government. Republicanism consequently never proposed to face the central theoretical problems of twentieth-century democracy, namely, how the general welfare of the community was to be defined, and to what extent it was to be achieved by political action. When, at the end of the eighteenth century, Alexander Hamilton advocated a balanced national economy to be achieved through fiscal manipulation, he spoke as a precursor of the Whig nationalists and not as a Republican.

A fundamental axiom of republicanism was the proposition that sovereignty follows property. President John Augustine Smith of the College of William and Mary, an ardent Jeffersonian, put the matter succinctly in the form of a syllogism: since 99 percent of all legislation relates to property; and since it is the essence of republicanism that the laws should emanate from those on whom they bear; then restriction of the franchise to men of property is good republicanism. While the syllogism was an accurate statement of the republican attitude so far as it went, it ignored an important qualification: it failed to indicate or take account of the fact that enlightened thinkers were also equalitarians. They did not believe that men are by nature equal, as we have seen; they did believe, however, that men have equal rights to property, and that for individual and social reasons of great importance they should have property. In Republican theory property performed a prophylactic function. It made men fit for participation in political society. It sobered men by conferring responsibilities. And its possession was at least a rough index of capacity. While in practice the republicans imposed property qualifications upon the franchise, they were agreed that property should be as widely distributed as possible, that ideally all men should possess property. These were the considerations underlying Jefferson's proposals for the distribution of the public domain. Adams was in agreement when he observed that "the only possible way, then, of preserving the balance of power on the side of equal liberty and public virtue, is to make the acquisition of land easy to every member of society; to make a division of the land into small quantities, so that the multitude may be possessed of landed estates. If the multitude is possessed of the balance of real estate, the multitude will have the balance of power, and in that case, the multitude will take care of the liberty, virtue, and interest of the multitude, in all acts of government." It will be observed that Adams's purpose was to secure equal liberty and public virtue, and that his method was to provide that the interests of each should be identical with those of all.

The principle of majority rule presented the republicans with peculiar difficulties. They were deeply apprehensive of the potential tyranny of the majority, while at the same time they believed that political power should be as widely distributed as possible. How were these convictions to be reconciled? Adams's solution was the ideal one: to make the interests of each coincide with those of all. For practical purposes, however, several other methods were proposed and put into operation. One was the system of checks and balances, the distribution of governmental functions among several independent agencies none of which was empowered to encroach upon the prerogatives of the others. Another was the acknowledgment of the right of judicial review by the courts. Another was provision for the indirect election of important governmental officials, the most cumbersome being the method for electing the President of the United States as incorporated in the federal Constitution. This method was quickly rendered archaic by the formation of national political parties. Another method was the wide dispersal of governmental powers through a series of independent governmental units, from the local to the highest state and national levels. Varying property qualifications for voting and for officeholding should also be considered in this connection, since these restrictions were regarded as proportioning the political participation of the individual to his own capacities.

But the principal method by which republicans proposed to prevent majority rule from degenerating into the tyranny of the mob was to discourage the formation of "factions," the term then commonly used for political parties. The most famous expression of the fear of faction appeared in the tenth number of the Federalist Papers, written by James Madison. The "Father of the Constitution" there argued that the great extent of territory and diversity of conditions found in the United States would serve as the most effective barrier to prevent the formation of national parties. The reason why parties were regarded as injurious was indicated in a sermon preached by the Reverend Joseph Sumner of Shrewsbury, Massachusetts in 1799. Americans, he said, are committed to a government of laws and not of men. They must have confidence in those delegated to make and execute the laws. While it is only prudent to keep an eye on public officials, "all combinations of lesser bodies, to counteract or embarrass public measures, or controul lawful authority, are both dangerous and detestable, as they tend to tumult and faction, and so to anarchy and confusion." Parties were regarded as injurious because they encroached upon the freedom of elected officials who should be chosen because of their ability and integrity and given a free hand within the constitutional limits of their offices. Classical political theory had always affirmed the chief threat to republics to be demagogues backed by their factions. Jefferson's defense of popular government was in the last analysis negative. He believed it to be the most effective bar to the tyranny that breeds on corruption, since the more men that have to be corrupted the more difficult its accomplishment. He favored popular government not so much because it was a good thing in itself but because it prevented evils.

The dependence of the republicans upon classical political theory was especially apparent in their discussion of types of governmental organization. Investigation revealed three types of government: monarchy, aristocracy, and democracy, each the product of a particular kind of society. These types were admittedly abstractions, for rarely if ever did any of them appear in pure form. Historically, governments had displayed various combinations of the basic types, in each instance invariably expressing the character of the people concerned. Most republicans shared the conventional eighteenth-century view that the British government was a mixture of the three types, an opinion to be found as early as the writing of John Wise at the beginning of the century. John Adams, who broke with the Hamiltonian Federalists largely because he was no Anglophile, nevertheless ardently admired the British system because of its perfect mixture of types, each element serving as a curb upon the others. His cousin Sam Adams had declared in 1771 that it would be as unreasonable to assign a preponderant influence to the democratic branch of the government as to the monarchical branch. Shortly after the Revolution, Jefferson warned that to subordinate executive and judiciary to the legislature would be to create "an elective despotism." A balanced division of powers was the ideal solution.

By 1789, however, most republicans were agreed that the character of American society required a government of the democratic type. As the Reverend Samuel Williams of Bradford, Massachusetts remarked: "That government must upon the whole be esteemed best for a people, which is best suited to their temper and genius; to the nature of their soil, and climate; to their situation, extent, connections, dangers, and wants; to ways of subsistence, the occupations, and employments, that nature has assigned to them.—On such, and on all accounts, *a free and equal government* is best suited to our infant and rising state." The debatable issues were matters of detail. The potential tyranny of the majority being the chief weakness of pure democracy, the elaboration of effective devices to forestall this eventuality received considerable attention. John Adams was the most influential man in devising these checks, which were widely experimented with in various state constitutions. The bicameral legislature with differing property qualifications was one method advocated for preventing the poor from tyrannizing over the rich, and vice versa. Such a legislature, balanced with a strong executive and an independent judiciary, was advocated as the mixed type of government best suited to American genius and circumstances. But the most important means of avoiding the evils of direct democracy rested in the principle of representation. Elected officials were expected to act in the best interest of the state as they understood it and not to reflect the whims or passions of their constituencies. The rise of political parties in the first decade of government under the federal Constitution bore witness to the speed with which this principle of republicanism became obsolescent.

PART III

The Mind of Nineteenth-century Democracy: 1800-1860

CHAPTER 8

||||||||||||||||||||||||||||||||||||||||||||||||||||||||||||||||||||

Democratic Social Theory

C HANGE WAS A STRIKING FEATURE of American life throughout the first three centuries, but change was never so extensive or so significant as during the democratic era of the first half of the nineteenth century. In these decades, the territorial limits of continental United States were rounded out through a rapid succession of diplomatic and military triumphs. The peopling of this vast domain behind an ever westward-moving frontier of settlement resulted in the extraordinary spatial and social mobility that was, perhaps, the most important fact of the era.

Prior to the beginning of the nineteenth century, the rate of frontier advance had been relatively slow, perhaps averaging a mile a year and pushing the line of settlement only a little beyond the western foothills of the Appalachians. Now, however, thanks to political control and improved methods of transportation, there was a remarkable acceleration. During the first half of the nineteenth century the line of settlement swept through the middle of the continent to the high plains and, leaping the mountains to the Pacific coast, was pressing eastward into the valleys of the Sierras at a tempo of advance approximately thirty times greater than ever before.

The rate of movement was of great social importance. In itself, the frontier, a mere line of settlement, had little significance. It was the zone of newly settled communities behind it—the subfrontier—that made the frontier an important social phenomenon. The more rapid the rate of frontier movement, the broader the subfrontier zone would be. In this respect, the frontier of the early nineteenth century was by all odds the most important in American history; behind it, an extensive subfrontier unrolled. This was the region of raw settlement, the "backwoods," in which men and families recruited from diverse sources engaged in the heroic task of building new communities. Inevitably, the pioneers reconstituted in large measure the institutions that they had known in their native places, and a traveler acquainted with the region from which the founders of a new community came could usually detect many reminiscences of the place of origin. But pure and simple transplantation never occurred: the sources of the migrants were usually varied, and the new environment always exerted its own peculiar influence. In the last analysis, moreover, the consequence of the westward movement was not so much the modification of institutions as it was the intensification of the spirit of individualism.

In the half-century between 1810 and 1860, the population of the United States increased from slightly more than 7,000,000 to nearly 31,500,000. This great increase in numbers was largely among the rural population. In 1810, more than 92 percent of the population was classified officially as rural; in 1860, some 80 percent still lived on farms.

Until the appearance of the railroad and the telegraph, transportation and communication scarcely kept pace with the rapid expansion of settlement. In 1800, Jefferson required from ten days to two weeks to travel from Monticello to New York. Thirty years later, Calhoun still needed five days to make the journey from Charleston to New York. By 1860, thanks to the railroad, a man could travel from New York to the Mississippi River at Rock Island in two days, although the tier of states beyond the river was then the western limit of rapid transportation. Because of the rapidity of expansion, the available means of communication were taxed to the limit to provide the necessary bonds to hold the country together. Geographical expansion and transportation problems thus retarded the increasing complexity of social structure that normally might have followed upon a fourfold increase in the population.

Agrarian Individualism

A persistent element in nineteenth-century American intellectual history was the theme of agrarian individualism, rendered in warm colors by its close association with romantic sentiments and ideas. One of the first to articulate the agrarian ideal was Michel-Guillaume Jean de Crèvecoeur (1735-1813), a naturalized Frenchman who farmed in Orange County, New York, between 1769 and 1778, and whose *Letters from an American Farmer* (1781) proclaimed the virtues of American agrarianism to an appreciative international audience.

No ordinary farmer, Crèvecoeur was a member of a gentry family who had received a French and English education before going to Canada with Montcalm's army in 1755. As a surveyor he traveled widely throughout eastern North America before settling in New York, where he took the name J. Hector St. John and married into a local gentry family. The publication of his *Letters* in London at the end of the Revolution won recognition for the author in French intellectual circles and focused attention on the revolutionary implications of the new society in America.

It was Crèvecoeur who asked the often-repeated question, what is this new man, the American? He answered that the American was a free man whose independence was assured by the free-hold tenure of land. "What should we American farmers be without the distinct possession of that soil? It feeds, it clothes us, from it we draw even a great exuberancy, our best meat, our richest drink, the very honey of our bees comes from this privileged spot. No wonder we should thus cherish its possession, no wonder that so many Europeans who have never been able to say that such portion of land was theirs, cross the Atlantic to realize that happiness." The farmer was free to think and act as he pleased. Taxes were nominal and government was benign. There was no extremes of wealth and poverty as in Europe, and virtually all American farmers enjoyed a decent standard of living. Ironically enough, the farmer who boasted that he was not obliged to toil and starve for princes or abbots remarked casually that he was a slaveholder.

More distinctive even than his freedom and prosperity was the new complex of psychological traits that characterized the American farmer. Entitled as he was to the full fruits of his labor his acquisitive impulses were given full play. By practicing the virtues of sobriety and industry his comfort was assured. Acquisitiveness thus became a major social virtue. The result was a practical, non-dogmatic anarchism well illustrated on Nantucket Island off the coast of Massachusetts. Five thousand people lived there in peace, Crèvecoeur reported, without police, army, jails, courts or other visible signs of government. These utopian conditions prevailed simply because the inhabitants were fully occupied with pursuits which yielded a modest competence to the industrious. Without idleness there was no misery, and hence no vice or crime.

Crèvecoeur was able to portray the American farmer in an attractive and even glamorous light by making him resemble the natural man, the child of nature, with all of the virtues ascribed by a romantic primitivism. First appearing in enlightened thought as a moral and psychological abstraction, the natural man now became a concrete human being, the farmer. Nature itself, at first a figure of speech, a hypothetical condition or "thought experiment" in which pure human nature could be envisioned, now became actuality—the rich farm land of Pennsylvania or Maryland. One of the marks of transition from the Age of Enlightenment to the Age of Romanticism was the transformation of nature as abstraction into nature as concrete physical place.

The farmer himself recognized the dawn of a new era in America when he chided European savants for failing to perceive the revolutionary significance of American social development. Oriented to the past, learned visitors often showed more interest in Indian mounds and other relics of antiquity than in what was happening before their very eyes. As for Crèvecoeur's farmer, he would "rather admire the ample barn of one of our opulent farmers . . . than study the dimensions of the temple of Ceres." America offered the unique spectacle of social origins, "the very beginnings and outlines of human society." A new intellectual discipline concerned with human betterment was required for its comprehension, one that would come to be known as social science. The new era would be characterized by peace, progress, simplicity, and justice. The hero of this society would be the cultivator of the earth rather than the soldier, saint, wise man, or artist.

Crèvecoeur was one of the first to express the faith in the transforming power of environment which would always typify the outlook of those who believed that America promised a brighter future for mankind. Environmentalism was particularly reassuring in explaining how the ethnically mixed population of English, Scotch,

Irish, French, Germans, Dutch, and Swedes would be transformed into one or more distinctive American types. New laws, modes of living, and social relationships would regenerate the newcomers— a process understood now not in spiritual terms, but as the impact of environment. "Our opinions, vices, and virtues are altogether local: we are machines fashioned by every circumstance around us." Belief in human plasticity was a particularly convenient assumption for Americans faced with the facts of continuing immigration from a variety of sources and in need of a theory that promised an easy and rapid transformation of a foreigner into an American.

The shaping force of environment could be seen in the three major physiographic regions of the new country. The coastal region, inhabited by seamen, merchants, and fishermen, was marked by the bold and enterprising qualities found in all seafaring people. The largest and most important region was that of inland farming. Here was to be found the unique American farmer, purified by his occupation, indulged by the government, gently sustained by religion, and made independent by freehold land tenure. The third "region of the great woods" would later be known as the frontier. Crèvecoeur described it as a cruder version of the farming region. Settled by those who were without financial means, or who had failed in previous ventures, or were by nature lazy and improvident, the backwoods exhibited "the most hideous parts of our society." Poverty, ignorance, shiftlessness, and lawlessness all too often characterized this region of first settlement.

To the individual frontiersman, pioneering in the great woods presented a crucial cultural challenge. Isolated from the civilizing influences of longer-settled regions he was in danger of being transformed into a hunter, "ferocious, gloomy, and unsocial." His wife would be deprived of many domestic conveniences, and worst of all, his children, living like Indians in many ways, might come to prefer the savage to the civilized way of life. The frontier, in short, represented the confrontation of civilization and savagery, illustrating the power of environment to mold society according to the influences exerted in the local situation.

Crèvecoeur's farmer had no doubt that in the end civilization would triumph. The inland farming region was steadily encroaching on the great woods, the pioneering phase usually lasting not more than ten or twelve years. He described the process, not altogether inaptly, in terms of a military metaphor. The pioneers represented a "forlorn hope" or patrol thrust out ahead of the main body of veteran farmers who would arrive in force to take over and secure the first rude improvements of their predecessors. "Such is our progress, such is the march of the Europeans toward the interior parts of this continent."

Fascination with the process of westward settlement was to remain a fixed part of the American mentality as long as unoccupied lands remained. Throughout the nineteenth century, observers were preoccupied with its moral and cultural implications, especially when they shared an Eastern or European outlook. Redemption of the frontier from its potential or actual barbarism was a continuing challenge to be taken up by successive generations of clergymen, educators, and philanthropists. It was not until the end of the nineteenth century, when a frontier of settlement no longer existed, that the sentimentalizing of frontier life began.

Crèvecoeur seems not to have noticed that the inland farmer himself had advanced a large part of the way towards the isolation and cultural deprivation so deplored in the backwoodsman. The structure of American society as Crèvecoeur's farmer portrayed it had shriveled away, leaving nothing but the farm family. Government was virtually nonexistent. Organized religion was withering in indifference. No reference was made to schools or other cultural institutions. By emphasizing the farmer's self-sufficiency Crèvecoeur was able to ignore the actual development of economic institutions that was slowly binding the farmer in a network of trade and credit. Few American farmers would in fact have willingly settled for a mere subsistence agriculture.

It was less Crèvecoeur's intention, however, to provide an accurate account of American farming then to celebrate the agrarian anarchism which he believed to be the distinguishing feature of the new society. Only two institutions appeared to have survived: private property and the family. The three kinds of property were land, its produce, and slaves. The revolutionary psychological consequences of the owner's right to the full product of his labor on the land have already been noted. Since Crèvecoeur undoubtedly disapproved of slavery one may wonder at his perfunctory and parenthetical references to the institution. He seems to have thought of it primarily in terms of forced labor, and since the farmer was himself a laborer, customarily working in the fields with his slaves, the common compulsion to labor was a universal moral obligation that mitigated the evils of bondage. Ironically enough, in his letters the farmer used the familiar form of address practiced by the Quakers.

Aside from property, the only institution to survive the Atlantic migration was the family. Unlike its European counterpart, the American farm family was no longer a unit of a social class. The ownership of land assured its independence and social equality. Standing in the midst of his acres, with his family and dependents about him, the American farmer was indeed lord of all he surveyed.

Crèvecoeur did not recognize the cultural limitations of the rural ideal. Because it did not provide for the adequate maintenance of cultural institutions it entailed a steady deterioration of intellectual life. The country church and the little red school house were not enough to perpetuate European high cultural traditions. The transfer and maintenance of the cultural heritage was to be wholly dependent on towns, where cultural institutions were clustered. Crèvecoeur's farmer acknowledged parenthetically that his wife had warned him not to let it be known locally that he was writing letters to a philosophically-minded English correspondent, since the neighbors would consider it more appropriate that a farmer be wielding a spade rather than a pen.

Crèvecoeur might properly be compared with two other eighteenth-century revolutionaries, Franklin and Paine. Each was at home in three countries, and each was adapt in casting the revolutionary message in an international idiom. Although Crevecoeur was not a political revolutionary—he was in fact a political Tory—he knew and appreciated what was more truly revolutionary in the American situation, namely, the emergence of a new equalitarianism based on widespread property ownership. More effectively even than Paine he voiced the romantic sentimentalism of the first phase of the nineteenth-century democratic movement.

Man and the State

Republican political theory and practice had distinguished between citizenship and suffrage. It had been concerned to secure the natural rights of all men as citizens and to assure their essential civil equality before the law. It had not focused its attention upon suffrage as a central political problem. Seemingly, it was unaware of any inconsistency between the assertion of universal civil rights and the practical restriction of suffrage to property holders. Suffrage had been regarded as a privilege rather than a basic civil right. Given the prevailing Republican assumption as to the relationship between sovereignty and property, it followed that the distribution of suffrage must merely reflect the conditions of property holding at a given moment. Ideally, all men should be property holders and thus qualified for active political participation. In such circumstances, the liberties of all would be most effectively safeguarded. But the realization of such ideal conditions seemed unlikely. In any event, suffrage was presumed to reflect and implement prevailing economic and political realities; it was the by-product of political order, not its precondition.

The central innovation of nineteenth-century democratic political theory was the equation of citizenship with suffrage. Political democracy stood for the right of each individual actively to participate in the elective process, both as voter and as office seeker. The idea of self-government now came to mean government by all. The new point of view received forceful expression in the Virginia constitutional convention of 1829–1830. Petitions of disfranchised citizens of Richmond asserted that suffrage was the right of all men; indeed, that it was perhaps the most important of all rights, since upon its secure possession the enjoyment of other rights largely depended. In support of their claim, the petitioners appealed to the authority of the Virginia Bill of Rights, which they reinterpreted for their own purposes. In that famous document Jefferson had written: "all men, having sufficient evidence of permanent common interest with, and attachment to, the community, have a right of suffrage. . . ." This was the stake-in-society principle; the evidence of permanent interest and attachment being, of course, the possession of a fifty-acre freehold. The petitioners rejected the older assumption that property furnished the best evidence of interest in and attachment to the community. The republican style of political thinking in economic and materialistic terms was now out of fashion. The petitioners couched their appeal in rationalistic and moralistic terms. Patriotism and public spirit must be presumed to be the property of all classes, whereas the economic interest was often a sordid one. And why should agriculture be regarded as a more honorific occupation than the trades or crafts? The numerical majority, said the petitioners, possess the preponderant physical force and therefore have the right to mold the civil institutions of the community according to their will. The principle of majority rule was the inevitable consequence of the new emphasis upon the right of suffrage.

While the struggle to broaden the suffrage base marked the constitutional conventions of the older seaboard states during the early decades of the nineteenth century, universal white manhood suffrage was taken for granted by the constitution-makers of the new states of the Northwest and Southwest. Of the sixteen member states of the Union in 1800, only one, Vermont, practiced universal manhood suffrage, while another, Kentucky, practiced universal white manhood suffrage. Kentucky set the precedent which was to prevail during the first half of the nineteenth century. By 1860, twenty-one of the thirty-three states were practicing white manhood suffrage, while eight retained at least a nominal tax or property qualification. It is significant that the movement to democratize the suffrage was restricted to white men. The new slaveholding states of the Southwest moved as rapidly toward this objective as did the free states. Settlers migrating from slaveholding areas were numerous and influential in the nonslave regions of the old Northwest and the Louisiana Purchase states, where white manhood suffrage was commonly adopted. There the new democracy of white men was erected on the shoulders of black men.

A new theory of representation was implicit in a democracy based on universal suffrage. The citizen could not now be said to be represented adequately unless he himself participated in the electoral process. The older republican theory had assumed that the property holder was an adequate repository for the suffrage because the best interests of the community were represented in him. This was a theory of virtual representation, similar to the British reply to the American charge that the colonies were unrepresented in Parliament. Much of the democratic argument for suffrage extension was directed against the freehold stereotype of rural republicanism, which was now recognized as simply a rationalization of the selfish interests of property holders. It was paradoxical that Jefferson's ideas should be repudiated by those who appealed to his name.

Another paradox of the democratic movement was the tendency in several states to curtail the powers of the representative legislature while enhancing those of the executive. The circumstances in which independent governments had come into being in America were such as to concentrate great powers in the state legislatures. As direct successors to the revolutionary colonial assemblies, the legislatures enjoyed the patriotic approval of the citizenry; the governors inherited something of the onus that had been attached to the royal governors. The revolutionary assemblies frequently had written the independent state constitutions, making no distinction between ordinary statutes and constitutional enactments. These constitutions often curtailed the powers of the governor, while providing for legislative supremacy.

But the gentry found ways to gain control of many of these legislatures, and, as the center of population in the seaboard states moved ever westward, their control was confirmed by disproportionate representation. Movements for suffrage extension and legislative reapportionment in the early decades of the nineteenth century generally found it necessary to circumvent legislative obstruction. This was accomplished frequently by means of a specially constituted constitutional convention, a body having a unique status as the promulgator of a basic constitutional act distinct from and more fundamental than mere statutes. The curtailment of legislative authority was paralleled by a broadening of the powers and independence of the executive.

Perhaps the most important aspect of the democratization of political life was the development of political party practices. Republican theory had deplored party politics in part because it made possible direct majority rule. One of the revolutionary functions of the nineteenth-century political party was to circumvent the constitutional barriers to majority rule erected in the principles of separate and balanced powers. If a single party could control both legislature and executive, its political objectives would be assured, at least temporarily. This tendency culminated in the national administration of Andrew Jackson, where the President as acknowledged leader of his party assumed responsibility both for a legislative program and administrative policies on the theory that his election constituted a mandate from a majority of the people. After Jackson's time, American national political life inevitably found its focus in a succession of more or less effective "administrations," a practical concept that had had no place in the original constitutional assumptions. Within the party itself, management by means of a closed caucus of leaders gave way to the popular convention, which, however, the bosses could usually manipulate.

Other aspects of the democratization of political life included the abandonment of property qualifications for officeholding. Nine of the seaboard states which had originally fixed such qualifications removed them by the middle of the century. Enlightened political society had generally achieved the separation of church and state, but it had not eliminated all religious disqualifications for suffrage and officeholding. These discriminations were quickly abandoned early in the nineteenth century.

Democracy also left its impress upon public policy as distinct from political institutions and practices. The peripheral character of politics as conceived by the enlightened mind was aptly reflected in the judgment of Jefferson expressed in his first inaugural address, when he defined "a wise and frugal Government" as one "which shall restrain men from injuring one another, shall leave them otherwise free to regulate their own pursuits of industry and improvement, and shall not take from the mouth of labor the bread it has earned."

In the age of individualistic democracy, the state was called upon to play a much more important and positive role. Two somewhat related factors accounted for this development. One was the practice of achieving public or socially approved purposes by means of private agencies, to whose aid the resources of the state were summoned. Although federal banking and tariff policies furnished perhaps the earliest examples of this practice, the tactic was more fully developed by individual states during the early nineteenth century. Monopolistic or other privileges were granted by friendly legislatures to banks, toll-road companies, canal companies, or railroads. Public aid was often extended directly in the form of investment of public funds in private enterprises, the so-called "mixed" corporations, of which 144 existed in Pennsylvania alone in the year 1844. The twentieth-century policies of the welfare state, in which the achievement of specified objectives by means of subsidy is so characteristic a feature, are the direct outgrowth of this democratic tactic of achieving public purposes through private enterprises.

The second tendency of democratic legislation that served to extend the sphere and powers of state action developed from the idea of reform. Reform, an idea peculiar to the Age of Democracy, almost invariably sought the accomplishment of its purpose by means of legislation. There was, of course, nothing in the idea of reform itself that necessarily entailed its incorporation in public policy. But the characteristic reform movements—notably public education, civil rights for women, and abolition of chattel slavery—sought to embody themselves in public law. The political philosophy underlying this point of view was expressed by President John Quincy Adams, in his first Annual Message to Congress (1825): "The great object of the institution of civil government is the improvement of the conditions of those who are parties to the social compact. . . . Roads and canals, by multiplying and facilitating the communications and intercourse between distant regions and multitudes of men, are among the most important means of improvement. But moral, political, intellectual improvement are duties assigned by the Author of Our Existence to social no less than to individual man. For the fulfillment of those duties governments are invested with power, and to the attainment of the end—the progressive improvement of the condition of the governed—the exercise of delegated powers is a duty as sacred and indispensable as the usurpation of powers not granted is criminal and odious." Adams may have professed allegiance to the Jeffersonian tradition, but when he charged government with responsibility for the progressive improvement of the condition of the governed he was laying the foundations of the positive state of the twentieth century.

Change and Progress

Enlightened thinkers had understood that changes in manners and morals were induced by changing social conditions. Thus, if a rural people were to become urbanized, many other changes, mostly deemed undesirable, would inevitably follow. But eighteenth-century theorists did not conceive of deliberately manipulated institutional changes accompanied by basic psychological readjustments. Given the assumption of the relative superficiality of politics, it did not occur to them that political instrumentalities might be used for such a purpose.

The nineteenth-century social mind, on the other hand, developed a far more profound and radical sense of the nature and implications of social change. It abandoned the essentially static presuppositions underlying the older notion of cyclical fluctuations and embraced a conception of historical change as a secular trend, which it called progress. The assumption of progress by no means fully defined the new theory of change, but it was one of its most prominent features. Progress constituted a well-nigh universal faith for the men of the early nineteenth century: things tomorrow will be better than they are today. In other words, there is constant change that in its most important respects must be regarded as desirable.

Although most Americans assumed progress to be inevitable, they acknowledged that it could be accelerated or retarded by human effort or folly. In these assumptions they revealed the same mixture of freedom and necessity found in Puritanism or Marxism or, indeed, in any effective social faith. In its American form, the belief in progress was an integral aspect of the democratic idealism: not certain favored individuals or classes but all men were the beneficiaries of progress. The universe itself was progressing. In the florid oratorical style of 1820, the Honorable Josiah Quincy indicated the promise of the cultural and spiritual refinement of humanity that the vision of progress opened to him. " 'Revolutions go not backward!' Neither does the moral and intellectual progress of the multitude. Light is shining where once there was darkness; and is penetrating and purifying the once corrupt and enslaved portions of our species. It may, occasionally, and for a season, be obscured; or seem retrograde. But light, moral and intellectual, shall continue to ascend to the zenith until that which is now dark, shall be in the day; and much of that earthly crust, which still adheres to man, shall fall and crumble away, as his nature becomes elevated." The public discussion of every topic of general interest to the early nineteenth century was framed in some characteristic way by the assumption of progress —whether it be politics and international relations, economics, education, or peace.

The sources of ideas are, strictly speaking, to be found in antecedent ideas rather than in material facts or circumstances. Nevertheless, the material conditions of American life provided the setting within which the belief in progress could flourish. The idea was certainly an appropriate assumption for an active, dynamic society engaged in exploiting the resources of a continent. It undoubtedly helped to focus the energies of the community by reinforcing the utilitarian morality of the cultural tradition.

One element in the idea of progress was drawn from Christian perfectionism. Quakers and other radical sectarians of the seventeenth and eighteenth centuries had made familiar the notion that the interests of Christ's kingdom were to be advanced through spiritual or moral perfection. The more moderate postmillennialists of the early nineteenth century identified the coming of the millennium with a gradual moral improvement. Such a perspective on the affairs of this world could easily be secularized. The blending of religious and secular attitudes at the moment of fusion was apparent in a declaration of faith made in 1843 by the zealous reformer William Henry Channing, nephew of the famous William Ellery Channing and, like his uncle, a Unitarian clergyman. "Therefore, in every sphere, however small, let each declare, that Love is the Law of Liberty, that Faith is forever a Free Inquirer, that Doubt of enlarging Good is virtual Atheism, and Fear of Progress the unpardonable Sin. So let us attest the truth, that the Heavenly Father recreates his universe and regenerates his children, by causing their perennial growth."

The intense individualism of the age at least dictated the major outlines of the idea of progress as a social philosophy. Progress promised the ultimate emancipation of the individual. In the Age of Democracy, man was affirmed to be the prime social reality. Man dominated his social institutions, which he could mold according to his will. The self-realization of individuals thus implied emancipation from institutional restraints—a common romantic theme. Walt Whitman projected his vision of progress in these terms when he wrote in an editorial of 1846: "We are to expect the great FUTURE of this Western world! a scope involving such unparalleled human happiness and national freedom, to such unnumbered myriads, that the heart of a true *man* leaps with a mighty joy only to think of it! God works out his greatest results by such means; and while each popinjay priest of the mummery of the past is babbling his alarm, the youthful Genius of the people passes swiftly over era after era of change and improvement, and races of human beings erewhile down in gloom or bondage rise gradually toward that majestic development which the good God doubtless loves to witness. . . ."

The enlightened ideas of divine benevolence and human happiness were also blended in the new synthesis. The measure of material and intellectual security that had come to exist in the New World, and which was so striking a feature of the age, inevitably left its mark on the intellectual outlook of Americans. In the circumstances, benevolence and happiness were not merely ultimate ideals in terms of which the harsh realities of experience were to be measured; they were goals that men could actually expect to realize, if not in the immediate present, then in the foreseeable future. Progress stood for the attainment of the good life promised by present experience.

Some indication of the firmness with which Americans held to their belief in progress is found in the fact that they were not content with the assumption that progress was to be realized through human effort; they affirmed the existence of a law of progress that guided men's steps in spite of themselves. Senator William H. Seward solemnly informed the Senate in 1854, that "sometimes, when I take an outside position and review the thickly recurring changes through which we have passed, it seems to me that our course has been shaped, not so much by any self-guiding wisdom of our own, as by a law of progress and development impressed upon us by nature herself." In one of its aspects the law expressed itself as an instinctive drive or psychological impulse. The utopian socialist Albert Brisbane believed that an instinct of progress would direct man inevitably to his social destiny, although the reformer insisted that by the use of reason one could greatly accelerate the process. Henry C. Carey, the economist, in a style of reasoning which anticipated the theories of Thorstein Veblen, found in man an instinct of progress that distinguished *Homo sapiens* from other animals. "The first and great desire of man," said Carey, "is that of maintaining and improving his condition." Progress then reflected a basic thrust of human nature.

There was a cosmographic as well as a psychological basis for belief in progress. Geologists were continuing the work begun in the previous era of accumulating the data on the formation of successive geological strata. The fossil remains found in these strata revealed an ever-increasing complexity of organic structures. Professor James Dwight Dana of Yale College, the most distinguished American geologist of the mid-nineteenth century, maintained that this progressive series of organic forms, culminating in man with his immortal soul, furnished convincing evidence of the unfolding of a divine plan. Dana sought to reassure Biblical fundamentalists who were deeply disturbed by his style of thinking. "Science should not be feared. Her progress is upward as well as onward, to clearer and clearer visions of infinite beneficence." The universe itself was undergoing a progressive and purposeful evolution.

The faith in progress proved itself adaptable to a variety of purposes and outlooks. Most Americans doubtless expected the realization of progress in individual well-being. Henry Carey thus understood that faith in progress served as an incentive to economic and industrial activity. As material conditions improved, he anticipated both the harmonizing of conflicting interests and the elaboration of individuality. But social reformers also appealed to the idea of progress, which they expected to achieve through the gradual transformation of institutions. Those reformers who confronted an institutional structure with a concrete proposal for change held a much more radical concept of progress than that which generally prevailed. A widespread faith in progress did not, however, necessarily result in a strengthening of the reform temper. Most Americans looked toward individual fulfillment in personal happiness, material success, or emancipation from current restraints. For them, progress was an opiate that provided escape from their burdens through fantasy.

Progress understood as material comforts and a higher standard of living resulted appropriately enough in the glorification of technology. A writer in the *North American Review* in 1832 indicated how faith in progress was confirmed by technology. "What we claim for machinery is, that it is in modern times by far the most efficient physical cause of human improvement, that it does for civilization what conquest and human labor formerly did, and accomplishes incalculably more than they accomplished." The enthusiasm with which the flood of mechanical inventions was hailed furnished some indication of the breadth of this sentiment. The inventors of the cotton gin, the steamboat, the electrical telegraph, the reaper, the sewing machine, and anesthetics, to mention only a few, caught the public fancy and were quickly enshrined as the popular heroes of a grateful people.

A writer in *De Bow's Review*, commenting in 1846 on the Morse telegraph, ventured to prophesy that "to him who has watched the progress of discovery and invention in the different countries of Europe and America, scarcely anything now will appear to be impossible. . . . We cease to limit the powers of the mind. We cease to draw the demarcation between the possible and the impossible . . . . We limit not what man may achieve, nor determine what is beyond his reach." By institutionalizing and safeguarding the economic rewards for mechanical invention the United States Patent Office did much to rationalize mechanization in terms of progress. The sentimental optimism that resulted from these prognostications was effectively crystallized by the *Democratic Review*, which predicted in 1853 that within half a century machinery would have transformed the world into a utopia. "Men and women will then have no harassing cares, or laborious duties to fulfill. Machinery will perform all the work—automata will direct them. The only task of the human race will be to make love, study, and be happy."

Institutions and Reform

The democratic theory of social change thus presupposed the idea of progress. The analysis of social change became an investigation of the means or method by which progress occurred. During the first half of the nineteenth century there gradually emerged a distinctive point of view that regarded social change not merely as a succession of historical events but as institutional change,—still the prevailing conception of social change.

An institution is a prescribed pattern of social relationships in which the participating individuals are required to conduct themselves according to the rules of behavior determined either by law or, more likely, by the prescriptive force of tradition and public opinion. Institutions serve various socially sanctioned purposes, whether useful, ceremonial, or convivial. They are usually represented by some kind of tangible symbol. They contribute powerfully to the matrix of psychological attitudes that sustains the whole community. Human activity consists for the most part of a sequence of institutionally controlled behavior; men rarely act in a significant way outside any institutional context.

Nineteenth-century democratic thought concerned itself with institutional behavior in a practical way before it had yet succeeded in developing an explicit institutional sociology. In the years immediately preceding the Civil War, the foundations for such a sociology were being laid by certain Southern thinkers, notably George F. Holmes and George Fitzhugh, who were disciples of the pioneer French sociologist Auguste Comte. But the dedication of their theories to the preservation of chattel slavery nullified whatever influence they might have had outside the South. It remained for the naturalists of the post Civil War era to inaugurate a continuing tradition of sociological thought.

Nevertheless, the Age of Democracy was preparing the way for a mature social theory, both by its practical activity in developing voluntary associations and by its growing interest in social reform. The proliferation of voluntary associations coincided with the emergence of a democratic society. In fact, the distinguishing characteristic of democracy from an institutional viewpoint was the flourishing of private voluntary associations. These were large or small, public or secret, incorporated and unincorporated; they were dedicated variously to economic, political, religious, humanitarian, cultural, fraternal, convivial and recreational purposes. Some of them, such as the sectarian religious groups and the older colleges, had deep roots in the past. The later eighteenth century had witnessed the appearance of land companies, Masonic lodges, and revolutionary political organizations. Benjamin Franklin, a pioneer in this as in so many other respects, had organized several forms of civic association, including the library, school, hospital, fire-fighting company, insurance company, and the cultural club or "Junto."

During the early nineteenth century there was an immense growth of these voluntary associations. Alexis de Tocqueville was impressed by the fluency and effectiveness with which Americans formed and used such organizations. There was, he suggested, an inherent connection between democracy and voluntary associations. In a democracy where everyone was relatively weak, such organizations were essential to accomplish anything of significance. The activity of manufacturing and commercial corporations, banks, toll roads, canals, railroads, and agricultural improvement societies certainly confirmed the functional significance attributed to them by the observant and philosophical Frenchman. But voluntary associations served a nonfunctional purpose as well. In the early labor organizations, the fraternal, educational, and benevolent needs of their members shared an importance equal to that of economic objectives. The widespread hostility to Freemasonry during the early years of the century had scarcely dissipated before the rapid growth of Odd Fellows, Druids, Red Men and other secret fraternal orders testified to a need for convivial association that the family and more casual forms of association apparently were unable to satisfy.

A form of voluntary association deserving of special attention was the religious benevolent society. These societies concerned themselves with certain larger aspects of the religious life and were in a sense supplemental to the regular ecclesiastical organizations of Protestantism. The American Board of Commissioners for Foreign Missions, established in 1810, and the American Home Missionary Society, 1826, undertook to coordinate the evangelistic activity of Protestant denominations at home and abroad. The American Bible Society, 1816, and the American Tract Society, 1825, sought through the distribution of Bibles and religious tracts to perpetuate the environment of religious concern within which organized religion could function most effectively.

Apart from their religious influence, these societies were important because of their close connections with another group of voluntary associations formed for the purpose of social reform. These included the American Temperance Society, 1826; the American Peace Society, 1828; the American Lyceum Association, 1831; and the American Anti-Slavery Society, 1833. A deep current of religious sanctity flowed through these organizations, which were a logical expression of the traditional Calvinistic conviction that sanctification should express itself in moral endeavor and improvement. Protestant denominations did not find it expedient officially to follow the admonition of the transcendental preacher Theodore Parker that they should reform the world, but their individual members, both lay and clerical, were free to join voluntary reform associations. These people provided the solid core of the reform societies, and they brought with them the techniques of organization that the earlier benevolent societies had developed. Orestes Brownson, himself a disillusioned reformer, observed sourly that "matters have come to such a pass, that a peaceable man can hardly venture to eat or drink, to go to bed or get up, to correct his children or kiss his wife, without obtaining the permission and direction of some . . . society."

The idea of social reform was a unique element of the nineteenth-century democratic mind. In its most common usage, social reform referred to the reform of specific institutions, such as chattel slavery, war, legal discriminations against women, or the eating of meat. It did not imply, however, that social class barriers must be broken. In the absence of class consciousness, it was inevitable that programs and concepts of reform were aimed at the reform of specific institutional abuses, on the assumption that Americans constituted a single social class and that certain institutional restraints prevented the self-realization to which their ideology taught that they were entitled.

It was true that many of the reform movements of the early nineteenth century did eventuate in legislation, national or local. But the result in most cases was to make the state a moral or cultural agent rather than the instrument of a victorious economic class. The ultimate object of reform was to free the individual from institutional restraints. This objective determined the broad limits within which reforms were effective. Only the monopolistic aspects of the capitalistic economy provoked an appreciable measure of criticism. The small number of communitarian socialist experiments, both secular and religious, have doubtless received more attention than their significance as reform movements would justify.

A quality of paternalism was certainly present in most reform movements, owing to the fact that those who suffered from the institutional restraint in question were usually handicapped in contending against it and needed aid. Thus the Negroes could do nothing by themselves to eradicate slavery. In a different way the drunkard required the help of teetotalers. In reformers' eyes, both women and children were subordinate classes that needed help in escaping from bondage—women from civil discriminations, children from ignorance. Politicians in search of votes doubtless filled a similar paternalistic role for the disfranchised citizens. In each of these cases the beneficiaries of reform might be said to constitute a social class but clearly not in the usual socio-economic sense of that term.

An important by-product of social mobility has been the comparative ease with which individuals could be recruited for the support of movements or "crusades." While the democratic ideology stressed the freedom and self-determining power of the individual, democratic practice revealed how shrewd promoters were able to mobilize these free individuals in support of various enterprises, worthy or unworthy. Social mobilization was an essential feature of the more important reform movements of the early nineteenth century. The formation of a voluntary association was the first major step toward accomplishing the purpose in view, with size of membership and financial resources being considerations of the highest importance. A cynical contemporary described the technique: coin an imposing name; compile a list of eminent citizens as sponsors; finance an efficient secretary with adequate office staff; send out popular lecturers; flood the mails with literature; secure effective press coverage; form local branch societies; and organize women's and young people's auxiliaries. With techniques such as these the American Temperance Society was said to have mobilized 1,200,000 members within ten years. During the years 1836–1840, the American Anti-Slavery Society raised between $26,000 and $50,000 annually from dues, collections, gifts, proceeds from fairs, and the sale of publications. Finally, attention should be called to the ambiguous status of the problem of persuasion *versus* coercion in the reform philosophy. In its initial impulse, the reform movement was educational. It sought to arouse the conscience, to form and focus the power of public opinion upon specific abuses. To these ends the techniques of the voluntary association seemed especially appropriate. In a democratic society in which all individuals were presumed ideally to be self-determining and public-spirited, reform by persuasion was the most effective method of achieving progress. Actually, however, most reform movements culminated in legislation by which the reform was imposed upon an active opposition by the coercive authority of the state, in either its local or national forms.

The enlightened mind had functioned within the context of a society that still retained many of the elements of status and prescriptive rights inherited from the colonial past. In such a context, the state had its recognized place, and state-makers made sure that their creation did not trespass upon its proper limits. These considerations were irrelevant to the democratic theorist. In a classless society of free individuals what could be more natural than that combinations of men should attempt to employ the power of the state for their own purposes? The state thus became the instrument by which reformers might secure their objectives. The voluntary association functioned simultaneously as a means of educating and organizing public opinion and as a pressure group to secure legislation. Many other forces besides those of reform were at work enhancing the power and scope of the state during the nineteenth century, but in any complete account of the history of democracy and nationalism the role of reform must have a prominent place. Reform legislation was frequently far-reaching in its social consequences, so much so as to suggest that democratic legislation could on occasion be so drastic as to deserve the adjective *revolutionary*.

CHAPTER 9

Protestantism and Democracy

T HE RELIGIOUS LIFE of colonial America had organized itself in churches and sects. The church identified itself with the whole society, which it officially represented. While it opposed evil, the church recognized evil as inevitable and attempted to hold it at arm's length. Sects were looked upon as unjustifiable expressions of human rebelliousness and perversity and feared for their divisive consequences. Whenever churchmen could have their way, they provided legal establishment for the church and made things as difficult as possible for sectarians.

The sects, on the other hand, were composed of small groups of dedicated souls whose rigorous standards of piety contrasted sharply with the prevailing indifference of the larger community. So far as practicable, the sectarian sought to isolate himself from contamination by the sinful world. His repudiation of the world was frequently strengthened by his hopeful expectation of the Second Coming of the Lord.

Denominationalism

A significant transformation began to occur during the second half of the eighteenth century. Prominent representatives of both the churchly and sectarian forms of religious body began to converge upon the common ground between their original positions. Eventually, the consequence was a large number of denominational organizations of a type unique in religious history. The same social forces that were receiving expression in the ideology and institutions of political democracy and nationalism were also at work blending the traditions of church and sect in the characteristics of denominationalism. The result was the spontaneity and diversity that came to distinguish American religious life during the Age of Democracy.

Denominational religion grew up in a society that was in the process of dissolving the social class distinctions of earlier times. The lines of discrimination gradually became blurred as many of the overt badges of traditional privilege were abandoned; and this blurring was furthered by the ideological revolution, which prompted men first to speak contemptuously of qualitative social distinctions and later to ignore them. In time, although Americans knew that social distinctions continued to exist, the public creed required them to speak as though they did not.

It remained for the sociologists of the twentieth century to develop a terminology and technique of analysis appropriate to the peculiar American situation. They counseled abandonment of the word *class* and the substitution in its stead of the term *stratification*. After all, when most Americans thought of themselves as *middle class*, the usefulness of that term was seriously jeopardized. The sociologists proposed to examine the overt associations of individuals, as well as their social attitudes toward others, and from such data to construct elaborate diagrams indicating the social strata into which the community divided itself. These strata were said to be "open-ended"; there was considerable opportunity for the individual to change his status. Vertical social mobility was supplemented during the early nineteenth century by the unique geographical mobility of the American population. In parallel columns, Southerners and Yankees moved westward from their ancestral homes into the great valley of the continental interior in a migration that obliterated the social distinctions which had marked the society of the colonial seaboard. Denominationalization was the religious response to these forces.

During the nineteenth century, the denominations occupied the strategic center of American religious life. The surviving churches were inevitably forced into denominational modifications—always excepting Roman Catholicism. The sects, likewise caught in the current of American life, were rapidly transformed into denominations as their members participated in the upward mobility of society. The denominations then replaced the churches as the spawning grounds of sectarian movements. The Methodists and Baptists were most prolific in this respect, although the Congregationalists and Presbyterians were not without their sectarian offshoots. But the attractive power of the forces that shaped denominationalism remained so great that within a generation or two sectarian rebellions were frequently drawn back toward denominational orthodoxy.

Denominationalism became one of the expressions of a national culture, and it was inevitable that denominations should be nationally organized. Those that had been affiliated with the great churches of the British empire, notably the Anglicans and the Presbyterians, reorganized themselves as autonomous American national bodies on the successful conclusion of the Revolution. American Methodists, although they professed themselves to be faithful disciples of Wesley in all matters of faith and doctrine during his lifetime, never wavered in the assumption of their American denominational autonomy. National organization was an appropriate expression of what came to be the distinguishing denominational attitude toward the political realm. Because the denominations shared the democratic ideology of the community, they accepted its political organization; indeed, they went far toward sanctifying the state and accepting moral responsibility for it. Here was one of the prime reasons for denominational suspicion of radical sects and of universal churches, such as the Roman Catholic, which were felt to hold themselves apart from or above the political community.

The peaceful coexistence of a number of denominations was, of course, an essential characteristic of the complex. The state of mind in which Americans could calmly contemplate such a situation represented a revolutionary contrast to the older assumption that social stability required a uniformity of faith and outlook. By 1774, the Reverend Samuel Williams of Bradford, Massachusetts, could express the already commonplace opinion that history had demonstrated the futility of attempting to enforce an official doctrine or discipline. He recognized that the result was a cluster of denominations within a larger social framework. "We have indeed the various names of *Episcopalians, Presbyterians, Congregationalists, Baptists, Friends,* etc. The fierce and bigotted of each party, may be inflamed with a desire of establishing themselves, upon the destruction of the rest. But whatever temporary enthusiasm this may occasion in the minds of a few, it can never succeed. The different parties among us will subsist, and grow up into more large and respectable bodies. And the mutual interests and wisdom of all, cannot fail to perfect that universal toleration and liberty of conscience, which is so generally and well begun."

Behind the point of view of men like Williams was a half-conscious realization of the partial and relative character of the denomination. One of its striking characteristics was its ambivalence with respect to ecclesiastical theory and practice. Denominations had no explicit theory of the church as such. In practice, however, the denominations were among the more important objects upon which the American genius for organization fastened itself. Much of the energy of the religious community was poured into the problems of organization, and a distinctive type of denominational statesman emerged.

The individual tacitly acknowledged that his was one of a number of Protestant bodies and that these bodies had much in common. It was true that in the earlier phase of the denominational era there had been considerable friction between denominations, but with the passage of time they were able to settle down in an attitude of mutual forbearance. Their spokesmen would on occasion refer to "the Church." Sometimes this term referred to the speaker's own denomination; usually it was to something larger, perhaps the whole body of Christendom or, at least, Protestant Christianity. These references usually occurred in the course of an appeal to those general values that the denomination held up as the standard for measuring its own religious condition. In other words, the denominations were beginning to acquire some sense of their fragmentary character.

In their attitude toward the social world of which they were a part, denominations tended to adopt what might be called the principle of limited liability. They acknowledged the fact that their members were citizens, and that the ethical code which all religious groups sponsored might prompt some of these members to adopt a Christian attitude toward public and social questions. But this should be done by individuals in their capacity as Christian citizens and not as church members, in order that their denominations might be spared institutional involvement. Clergymen and laymen might form special organizations, such as reform societies, to promote worthy objects, but they ought not to use the regular ecclesiastical organizations for such purposes. To do so might well divide the denomination, a voluntary organization placed in a competitive relationship to other denominations.

The proliferation of voluntary societies dedicated to various kinds of reform that was characteristic of nineteenth-century America was in part an expression of emerging denominationalism. For reform societies were conveniently adapted to the peculiar relationship to the secular world that the denominationalist assumed. His denomination was, like a sect, a private association that was responsible for nothing but its own religious affairs. But he could easily join with like-minded individuals of his own and other denominations to form a special reform society through which he could undertake to exert upon social life an influence essentially religious. Beginning with societies for Sabbath observance and Bible and tract distribution, the range of interests broadened to include moral reform, temperance, peace, education, and antislavery. The logical culmination of these tendencies was doubtless reached in the proposal dear to the heart of successive generations of Presbyterians that a Christian political party be formed. The independent organization of such activities was the form taken by the denominational compromise between churchly responsibility for the affairs of the world and sectarian indifference.

In the transfer of culture from the coastal region to the watershed of the Mississippi, religion played a prominent role. It did so by modifying both its organizational form and its spiritual outlook in accordance with the tendencies of the time. Denominationalism provided an appropriate religious expression for a stratified but classless society.

The population movement that poured like a torrent across the Ohio and Mississippi valleys and the Gulf Plain in the years between the Revolution and the Civil War presented organized religion with a major challenge. With the exception of a few sects that found places of refuge on the frontier, this movement was composed of unorganized individuals and family groups animated by purely materialistic motives. While in most instances these people took their faith with them, they could not effectively re-establish their religious institutions without aid. The denominational context in which the westward movement occurred was competitive. The groups that gained the advantage in frontier evangelization would reap great rewards. Consequently, the religious bodies that were firmly rooted on the Atlantic seaboard looked upon the westward movement as a challenge both to Godliness and to denominational survival, a challenge that they met with remarkable success. The West was effectively Christianized, and in time it came to be the center of Protestant orthodoxy.

Such colonial churches as the Presbyterian and Congregational adjusted themselves to the denominational outlook and participated actively in the westward movement. But the leading role was shared by three great denominations that had played little or no part in earlier religious history. The oldest of these was the Baptist denomination. Small groups of Baptist sectarians had been present in America from early colonial times. Their great opportunity came with the advance of the frontier. On both Northern and Southern frontiers, the Baptists found their calling as purveyors of a simple, nondogmatic piety expounded by lay preachers who knew how to communicate effectively with uncultivated frontiersmen. The Baptists, who were united by their rite of immersion of adult believers, had learned to live peaceably with the wide divergence of doctrines represented by the Calvinistic and Arminian wings within their own denomination. For them, practical piety was more important than dogma.

The Methodist denomination was the second to come into its own. During the first three decades of the nineteenth century, it experienced a remarkable growth in numbers. The circuit system by which Methodist preachers toured large areas unable to support permanent places of worship was a highly effective adaptation to the fluid circumstances of the frontier. It was reminiscent of the itineracy of the earlier revivalists; and the Methodist circuit riders likewise dispensed a warm evangelical faith in which justification and sanctification as episodic blessings were strongly emphasized.

Finally, the most indigenous product of the interaction of religion and frontier was a new group calling themselves Disciples of Christ. Under the leadership of their founder Alexander Campbell, the Disciples numbered 500,000 by 1865. Part of this growth occurred at the expense of the Baptists, with whom Campbell had for a time been affiliated; part was at the expense of the Presbyterians; the remainder presumably was drawn from the unchurched.

The measure of success enjoyed by these denominations was undoubtedly owed to their greater adaptability to the peculiar conditions of the subfrontier regions. They were content to use many self-trained and lay preachers whose zeal and direct effectiveness more than compensated for the lack of formal schooling in theological doctrines. Although each denomination had its peculiar doctrinal tenets, its major energies were devoted to the enlargement of its fellowship through evangelization. The techniques of revivalism were especially effective for this purpose. Since the days of the Great Awakening, the flame of revivalism had never been completely extinguished, and at the beginning of the nineteenth century, it broke forth in a major conflagration known as the Second Great Awakening. While the older denominations of the Reformed tradition continued to regard revivalism with mixed feelings, the newer groups embraced it without reservations. The revival became an endemic feature of the religion of the West during the first half of the nineteenth century.

The most colorful feature of the revival was the camp meeting. The earliest known camp meeting was a spontaneous affair held under Baptist auspices in Caroline County, Virginia, in 1779. But the usefulness of the institution in thinly settled neighborhoods was speedily recognized, and within a few years camp meetings were a common instrument of evangelization. Perhaps the most famous was the great meeting at Cane Ridge, Kentucky, in 1801, where an estimated ten to twenty thousand worshipers were in attendance. Such meetings were frequently conducted under the joint sponsorship of several denominations or sects, which tended to minimize denominational tenets. A common evangelical Protestantism began to emerge that stressed the need of redemption and God's loving kindness in forgiving those who earnestly sought salvation.

The changing attitude on such matters can be detected in the career of Alexander Campbell, from his early sectarianism prior to the 1830's to his later denominationalism. Campbell had emigrated to the United States from northern Ireland in 1809, settling first in Washington, Pennsylvania, and later in Bethany, Virginia, on the western slope of the Appalachians, one of the great seedbeds of American religious movements. He had been raised a Presbyterian but had early been exposed to independency. Having come to believe in a pure church restricted to regenerate Christians, Campbell approved of the baptism of believers only and naturally gravitated toward the Baptists. He stressed the primitive New Testament ethic of love, brotherhood, and pacifism; and taught a relatively moderate brand of postmillennialism. His sectarian attitude of withdrawal from the world expressed itself in the strong emphasis on separation of church and state and in the advice to his followers to avoid political activity as irrelevant to the proper concerns of a Christian. This opinion has been connected to Campbell's millennial expectations: necessary political reform would be accomplished with the establishment of the Kingdom; in the meanwhile, politics were to be regarded as a "moral pestilence." "Political governments, in their best form," Campbell warned his followers, "are but mere tents for pilgrims to lodge under while on their journey to the great King and Lord of all." He voiced the typical sectarian objection to moral societies that they broke down the distinction between the church and the world, Satan's domain, thus threatening to contaminate the church.

The typical sectarian insisted on the separation of church and state, and in his religious capacity he was suspicious of political activity. But if his sectarian ardor were to cool sufficiently to permit him to enter political life, he would probably espouse a political philosophy of democratic localism. Such a position would be most compatible with the interests of religious sectarianism. It was essentially negative in that it was oriented toward "self-government" in the strict sense. Campbell took such a position when he represented his region in the Virginia constitutional convention of 1829–1830. There he unsuccessfully supported proposals for universal white manhood suffrage and equable representation. It would be a mistake to assume, however, that Campbell's support of democratic practices rested on a positive commitment to the democratic ideology. For many years after the Virginia convention, he continued to argue that as long as men remained degenerate and selfish, democracy was better than monarchy simply because the democratic politician could be gotten rid of more easily. The Jacksonian principle of rotation in office was well suited to "the popular doctrine of our country" that political power corrupted a man; let him be relieved of his temptations in short order.

But as the Disciples of Christ, the religious body of which Campbell was the founder and acknowledged leader, settled into denominational stability, Campbell's opinions on social questions underwent appropriate modifications. Eventually, he came to accept the denominational assumption that one of the most important functions of religion was to Christianize the social order, in the sense that Christian values should permeate society. It was now apparent that the task of religion was more than the saving of souls; for through the work of the church "some are *christianized,* more are *moralized,* and all are in some degree *civilized.*" To this end he advised his followers that it was their Christian duty to vote in order to choose the greater good or the lesser evil. He supported the political campaign for public schools, and he urged Kentuckians to abolish slavery by political action, addressing himself to them as Christians and as citizens. But as the controversy over slavery became more acrimonious, Campbell sought to save his denomination from schism by means of compromise. Although he continued to denounce the evils of slavery and to advocate colonization, he opposed the abolitionists and supported the Fugitive Slave Law. The Disciples were centered in the border regions, and by these means Campbell struggled to preserve their organization from the controversy that split so many of the American denominations.

Denominationalism, then, represented the rapport between religious and secular cultures that was effected in nineteenth-century America. Although each denomination theoretically identified itself with the whole of society, actually it tended to serve the religious needs of a particular stratum. Consequently, the denominations loosely arranged themselves in a rank order that paralleled the social stratifications of the secular community. These distinctions were usually more apparent within individual communities than among whole denominations as such; and there were frequently marked differences in the order of preference or social standing of denominations from one locality or region to another. While each denomination accepted the democratic ideology, each was particularly sensitive to the social aspirations of the class of people who belonged to it. These not-always-commensurable loyalties set up certain tensions that were typical of denominational life. They explained how, on the one hand, the denominations frequently supported the most mercenary forces in American society and, on the other, also produced many courageous critics and reformers who spoke out boldly against injustices and took the lead in promoting those reform movements that were characteristic of the age.

The denominations also gave expression to their relationship to the secular culture in their sponsorship of education. The contrast between denominational dedication to formal education and sectarian indifference or hostility to it was striking. At the primary and secondary levels the denominations supported the public-school movement. But at the collegiate level they did not wait for the state and municipal colleges and universities to appear. They followed the precedent of the great colonial churches that had established and supported the colleges in Cambridge, Williamsburg, and New Haven. During the nineteenth century, some 277 denominational colleges were founded in the United States, a large proportion of them in the newly settled regions of the West. Although denominational bodies frequently contributed directly to their maintenance, these colleges were ordinarily controlled by independent boards of trustees, and, with the passage of time, many of them gravitated out of the orbit of denominational influence.

But this was quite consistent with the essential spirit of denominational religion. Pious though their atmosphere certainly was, the colleges were rarely sectarian in their formal requirements, and the instruction that they offered adhered closely to the liberal arts curriculum that had been worked out in the colonial colleges. Like the denominations themselves, the colleges were more concerned with the inculcation of the spirit of piety than with the propagation of the specific dogmas of their respective sponsors. While they were not, for the most part, institutions for research or scholarship, they took for granted the compatibility of religion and learning. They might well have adopted as their motto an observation attributed to Witherspoon of Princeton: "Piety without literature is but little profitable, and learning without piety is pernicious to others, and ruinous to the possessor."

Democratic Theology

Certain distinctive features characterized the over-all doctrinal profile of denominationalism. This doctrinal complex was democratic, not through any deliberate or conscious effort to develop a theology compatible with democratic ideology but, rather, because the bent of religious thought paralleled that of social ideology. To that degree, they confirmed and reinforced each other and jointly helped to shape that complacency of outlook that was one of the more striking features of the mid-nineteenth-century mind.

Compared with the dogmas of seventeenth-century Puritanism, the democratic theology was primitive. It reflected the needs and outlook of a migratory population that had largely freed itself from the traditions of an educated leadership. For although the denominations loyally supported education, the outcome was of greater secular than religious significance. From the religious point of view, the American population constituted a vast internal proletariat. The evangelical denominations were engaged in dipping down into this mass and "reviving" it in successive waves of religious zeal. This was indeed a civilizing as well as evangelizing mission. Religion contributed immeasurably to the forces of upward social mobility in a democratic society. The schools and colleges that the denominations supported greatly accelerated this mobility of individuals. The character of a man's religious affiliation thus became in part a function of social status, with a change of denominational connection an appropriate expression of changing status. In these circumstances, the effect of formal education was frequently to strengthen the tendencies that led individuals to ascend in the social-denominational hierarchy. Because of the relatively unsophisticated character of the democratic theology, it was difficult for the participating denominations to keep pace with the social mobility of their more ambitious and energetic communicants. Over the course of the century, however, the steady drift toward modernism reflected the force of the social pressure.

There was nothing new in the democratic theology of American Protestantism. Every element of it could be traced far back into Christian history. But in America, the total complex of ideas was new. These ideas stemmed for the most part from the sectarian tradition, while the moderate and practical temper of denominationalism was churchly in quality.

The central element of the democratic theology was its pietism, a simple, undogmatic religion of the heart. Primary emphasis was placed on man's sinfulness, the need for redemption, and God's loving-kindness as revealed in the precious gift of saving grace. This was the vital core of the Protestant tradition, now largely stripped of the surrounding doctrinal garb in which the churches had clothed it and expounded by evangelical preachers with vivid intensity. Formal religion was rapidly becoming a device or a technique for securing regeneration. To the extent that religion thus became an episode, its meaning as process or way of life was undermined.

The practical and activist spirit of American Protestantism expressed itself in the matter-of-fact presumption that man was morally and spiritually a free agent, responsible for his sins. He was obligated to seek saving grace, but he did so with the assurance that, if he sought it earnestly, it would not be denied him. The Baptists particularly stressed free will. The Presbyterians, who clung desperately to the Calvinistic standards of the Westminster Confession, were especially concerned over free-will tendencies in their sister denominations; several schisms in their own ranks involving free will were evidence of the persuasiveness of the doctrine. Among the Congregationalists, in spite of the authority of Edwards, there was a continuous search for a reconstructed psychology that would free the will from the bondage to motives to which Edwards had consigned it. The strength of the drift toward freedom of the will was some indication of the massive impact upon inherited dogmas of the American belief in the free individual.

To the extent that man was believed to be free to seek it, saving grace must be regarded as a promise of which all might avail themselves. Such an implicit universalism came to be widely shared by the evangelical denominations. The Puritan doctrine of particular election restricted to that portion of mankind who had been predestined to salvation virtually disappeared. In New York state and in New England, there emerged a new denomination, the Universalist, challenging the Congregationalists and Presbyterians on this matter and holding that Christ's atonement provided assurance that all men would be saved.

Even more controversial and explicitly sectarian in its derivation was the doctrine of Christian perfection. This was the distinctive tenet of Methodism. The significance of the perfectionist doctrine lay in its attempt to define the substance of that sanctification which every regenerate Christian should show forth in his life and works, for the glory of God. The Puritan had taken a practical and moralistic approach to sanctification; he had tended to think of it as good works, while at the same time cautioning the regenerate believer not to expect immediate or flawless capacity to perform without fault. But to more zealous Christians, such cautious counsels seemed grossly inadequate; nothing less than perfection could be fully satisfying or sufficient. After all, Christ had admonished His followers to be perfect, even as the Father in Heaven was perfect.

What was Christian perfection? The question was not a new one, and during the course of Christian history at least a dozen different definitions have appeared, two of which left a distinctive mark upon nineteenth-century American Protestantism.

The Methodists followed their founder in defining perfection as love. John Wesley had long been dissatisfied with the quality of his own religious faith, and under the tutelage of Moravian friends he underwent a second religious experience of great intensity, out of which came the sense of assurance of God's mercy and love. Thereafter he exhorted his followers to seek such an experience as the fulfillment of the Gospel promise. Francis Asbury and other founders of American Methodism equated perfection with entire sanctification or perfect holiness. This was not essentially an ethical application of the doctrine; perfection was not defined as sinlessness. Rather, it was the realization that salvation from sin is found in perfect love. In Wesley's words: "Pure love reigning alone in the heart and life—this is the whole of scriptural perfection."

With the passage of time, as Methodists developed denominational stability and as many parishes improved their social and economic status, the doctrine of perfection began to lose favor. It had always been susceptible to Antinomian perversions, against which denominational spokesmen had to be constantly on the lookout. But the attractiveness of perfection defined as love was great in the romantic nineteenth century, and, while Methodists in search of respectability found it increasingly embarrassing, others were irresistibly drawn to it. Timothy Merritt and Phoebe Palmer, the leading Methodist perfectionists of the 1830's, recruited a large following from many denominations. The Evangelical Congregationalists and New School Presbyterians who dominated Oberlin College were deeply tinctured by perfectionism. As the main body of Methodists grew cool toward the doctrine, strongly perfectionist wings split off to form the Wesleyan Methodist Church in 1843 and the Free Methodist Church in 1860. The holiness movement of the later nineteenth century came from the same sources. American perfectionism was a rebellion against the older tradition in which sanctification was understood as discipline. The craving for emotional fulfillment could be better satisfied by a doctrine that emphasized the feelings rather than conduct. The Age of Romanticism was a protest against the emotional inhibitions of the Enlightenment, and religion had its own reasons for joining in the protest.

The second brand of perfectionism that affected nineteenth-century Protestantism was sponsored by the Disciples of Christ. Alexander Campbell defined perfection as liberty. Here again, it was through recourse to the sectarian tradition that protest against the dominant influence of the Calvinistic or Reformed churches expressed itself. While the Puritans had incorporated the covenant of works within the covenant of grace in order to give to sanctification its ethical and practical character, Campbell reverted, in effect, to the Antinomians and repudiated the covenant of works. He also made a fundamental distinction between the "law" (covenant of works) and the "gospel" (covenant of grace). Sinful man was said to be utterly incapable of fulfilling the law or of obeying God's commandments. The effect of the redeeming grace of God in Christ, as Campbell expounded it, was to free man from the restraints of the law by releasing him into the liberty of the Gospel.

The ideological significance of these brands of Christian perfectionism should be readily apparent. Man was to be freed from the burden of sin by love; and the essence of freedom was defined as liberation from the bonds of the law. The denominations were thus defining for themselves doctrinal standards that were compatible with the secular ideology of democratic individualism.

The final item in the democratic theological creed was the expectation of the return of Christ and the establishment on earth of the millennial Kingdom. Since the beginnings of Christianity, believers have hopefully anticipated the promised Second Coming. From certain obscure Scriptural passages they have from time to time attempted to calculate the precise moment at which Christ was to return, as well as to establish the relationship of the millennial Kingdom to that event. The literalness and immediacy with which millenarian hopes were expressed furnished a fairly reliable index to the degree of sectarian radicalism of the individual or group in question. The effect of the American revivals of the eighteenth and nineteenth centuries, occurring as they did in the context of the enlightened and romantic climates of opinion, was to wipe away the pessimism implicit in the cyclical historical theory of Puritanism and to plant in many men's minds the hope and expectation that the millennial Kingdom was literally at hand.

There were two schools of millennialist thought during the nineteenth century. The more radical school, characteristic of the sectarian movements that were spawned by the revivals, was that of premillennialism. To the premillennialists, Christ's return was a catastrophic event, a divine irruption into the natural order, in which the existing powers would be overturned and Christ would rule with His saints for a thousand years prior to the final battle with Satan, his destruction, and the day of judgment. The Adventist movement of the 1840's, led by William Miller, was the most spectacular manifestation of a widespread popular interest. It is difficult to reconcile premillennialism with the secular interests of the age. Many Americans in the early nineteenth century must have remained untouched both by the secularism of the Enlightenment and by the practical optimism of the believers in progress.

Postmillennialism was more conservative and practical. Those who held this view regarded the return of Christ in the first instance at least as a spiritual but not as a physical event. They anticipated the millennium as a thousand-year period in which Christ's spirit would invade the world and gradually transform it. Men would be purified, while peace, justice, and brotherly love would eventually reign supreme. Thus the scene would be prepared for the ultimate establishment of Christ's Kingdom. The moderate and hopeful outlook of postmillennialism readily adapted itself to the temper of denominationalism, while premillennialism was generally to be found among sectarians. It is apparent that postmillennialism could be readily accommodated to the secular theory of progress.

Elements drawn from the two schools of millennialism were occasionally blended in a curious hybrid product that may be designated as intramillennialism. The Shakers, who have already been noticed in another connection, believed that the Christ spirit had been incarnate in the founder of their sect, Mother Ann Lee, in whose work the millennium was believed to have commenced. They required only a profession of faith on the part of the believer to enter and avail himself of the blessings of the Kingdom by joining the United Society of Believers in Christ's Second Appearing. The communitarian settlements that the Shakers developed were the practical embodiment of the version of the Kingdom entertained by these wholesome and literal-minded people. A more sophisticated and exotic intramillennialism was entertained by the Oneida perfectionists led by John Humphrey Noyes. Noyes acknowledged his indebtedness to the Shakers for the conviction that the millennium had already begun. Like them, he held the practical task of reformers to be that of establishing social institutions appropriate to the spirit of the Kingdom. From Antinomian perfectionists lurking on the fringes of Methodism, Noyes drew his own doctrine of perfection as love, which, however, he understood in both the spiritual and carnal senses. At Oneida, New York, and elsewhere, he established his own communities in which the institution of complex marriage was the central as well as most notorious feature. Oneida had been a center of radical perfectionism, and it was only from among such people that Noyes appears to have been able to attract followers.

Unitarianism

It would be a mistake to attempt to impose too uniform a pattern upon denominational development and to overlook the distinctive individuality that characterized many denominations. The very designation itself is sometimes difficult to apply. Unitarianism and Mormonism are both cases in point. Each of them deviated in significant respects from the denominational norms, yet each occupied an important place in the religious life of the time, and a commentary, however brief, that omitted any account of them would be seriously deficient.

In the years after the Civil War, Unitarian spokesmen sometimes prided themselves on the fact that their denomination occupied a position on the extreme left wing of Protestantism. More to the point, is a search for the origins of Unitarianism in the Arminian wing of New England Congregationalism as that body attempted to stabilize itself in the years after the Great Awakening. Arminianism laid the intellectual foundations both for Unitarianism and for respectable deism. In some respects, the two were alike, although the Unitarians insisted upon their essential Christianity and continued to worship in a common Protestant fashion.

The Arminians had emphasized freedom of the will rather than Calvinistic determinism. Their principal purpose in doing so was the practical one of stressing the fact that, if the individual were to be held morally responsible for his acts, he must be acknowledged to act with free choice. While this did not necessarily contradict the Puritan doctrine of justification as a divine gift, it did indicate a temper of mind that was likely to lose patience with the traditional Puritan view of human depravity and impotence. Arminian opinions were cautiously expressed by an influential segment of the Congregationalist clergy of New England in the years between the Great Awakening and the Revolution. Because the evangelical Congregationalists were struggling to preserve their solidarity in the face of revivalism, they were not at first inclined to make an irreconcilable issue of Arminianism.

The divergence of views eventually became so great, however, that an open break was inevitable. The Unitarian schism completed the disintegration of churchly Congregationalism that had begun with the defection of revivalistic sectarians in the Great Awakening. The Unitarians took with them many of the wealthiest parishes of the seaboard. The movement was concentrated in eastern Massachusetts, in the very heart of traditional Congregationalism. An essential feature of the Congregational establishment had been the identification of parish with local community. Now, however, it was frequently discovered that, while most of the active church members were loyal to the trinitarian tradition of Congregationalism, a majority of the community were Unitarian in sympathy and in a position to dispossess the minority of the church property. Wherever this occurred, the Congregationalists were forced to organize their own parishes and to accept a denominational status. This transformation had been substantially accomplished by the time of the disestablishment of the Congregational Church in Massachusetts in 1833.

The first openly avowed Unitarian church was King's Chapel in Boston, which took the Unitarian position in 1787. Between that date and 1825, the process of fission was substantially completed. The reorganization of parishes on a Unitarian basis coincided with the rapid accumulation of commercial and manufacturing wealth along the seaboard and at the fall line, which in New England closely coincided. The same social forces that produced liberal religion produced conservative politics and wedded the two together. This class of people had been untouched by the revivals of the early nineteenth century and were predisposed to favor a religious outlook compatible with their urbane and complacent temper of mind.

The Unitarians retained the congregational form of church polity. Unlike the evangelical denominations, they did not throw themselves into home-missionary activity and, except for isolated parishes in New York, Philadelphia, Baltimore, Charleston, and a few other cities, they remained for many decades a regional denomination of relatively small size. But because of the many distinguished clergymen and laymen in its ranks, Unitarianism occupies a prominent place in American intellectual history. It was an integral part of the cultural matrix that produced the "flowering" of New England in the middle decades of the nineteenth century. Unitarianism was notable not so much for itself as for the role that it played as a liberator of minds focused on a variety of cultural pursuits.

The name *Unitarian* referred to the belief in the unity of the deity rather than in the trinity of Father, Son, and Holy Ghost. This doctrine, known as Arianism, was arrived at in New England somewhat later than Arminianism and partially as a consequence of it. Like other Protestants, the early Unitarians insisted upon the Scriptural basis of religious authority, and they professed to be unable to find in the Bible any satisfactory evidence of the divinity of Christ. In the Puritan theology, a relatively stereotyped role had been assigned to Christ. His function was to atone vicariously for the sins of man and thus to make possible the forgiveness that accompanied the sinner's justification. Christ was thus assigned a formal role in the economy of salvation, functioning as an integral part of the promise extended in the covenant of grace. Hence the appropriateness of designating Him the second person of the triune deity.

But as the Arminian wing of Congregationalism moved steadily toward the view that man was to be held morally responsible for his sins, and that he was both obligated and free to strive for salvation, it was not surprising that the Arminians should become increasingly dissatisfied with the traditional doctrines. Salvation came to be regarded as primarily a moral process, in connection with which Christ was the preeminent source of inspiration. And so Christ ceased to be a person of the Godhead and became Jesus the Man, one who represented the most exalted spirituality the world had ever seen, and who died for his ideals.

Humanistic Christianity of this type was not confined to American Unitarianism. It appeared in widely scattered regions throughout the Western World, and wherever it did so, there followed a new kind of literature: biographies of Jesus. In German, the most famous was that by D. F. Strauss, in French, by Ernest Renan, and in English, by J. R. Seeley. In America, such a biography was written by the Philadelphia Unitarian, William H. Furness. These books used the Gospels as sources from which accounts of the life of Jesus were constructed. The lesson or moral that they taught was the power of ideals in history, an appropriately romantic sentiment. For the Unitarians, however, the difficulty of this form of humanistic Christianity was only too apparent. Believing as they did in the truth of the Scriptures, what were they to say about the miracles of Jesus, of which the Gospel writers had been most explicit? Could a mere man be capable of such feats? The solution was an ingenious—and in the long run not very satisfactory—one even to the Unitarians. They created a special and unique place for Jesus part way between God and man, a higher species perhaps, of which but one perfect specimen had yet appeared. Their humanistic orientation was clearly apparent in their assumption that the power to perform miracles was a function of perfection of character.

The most famous of the early Unitarians was William Ellery Channing (1780–1842), a leader whose career epitomized the first phase of the history of his denomination. Channing grew up in Newport, Rhode Island, where he was first identified with the moderate Calvinist party of Samuel Hopkins, one of Edwards's disciples. Fortified with impeccable social connections, Channing attended Harvard College and soon became pastor of the Federal Street Congregational Society in Boston. A man of saintly life and retiring disposition, he disliked controversy, yet he was inevitably drawn into the strife between the conservative and liberal wings of Congregationalism. It was ironic that such a man should have become the most effective critic of the traditional theology that had been reverently handed down from the Puritans. The secret of Channing's success as a controversialist lay in his capacity to appeal to the rising humanitarian spirit of democratic America. He roundly declared the Puritan doctrine of the natural depravity of man to be morally outrageous. It implied a conception of God that was repulsive to all the finer instincts of human nature. Earlier heretics had deviated from orthodoxy on specific points of dogma, and their inconsistencies or errors could be effectively demonstrated. But Channing had gone so far as to substitute humane values for the traditional acknowledgment of God's sovereign will, so that a common ground for effective criticism had disappeared.

The moral perfection of God was Channing's fundamental doctrine. The corollary of this doctrine—or, indeed, the source of it—was his insistence upon the innate dignity of human nature. "The ultimate reliance of a human being is and must be on his own mind." For what can a man know of the attributes of God beyond the capacity of his own mind to discern those attributes? Therefore, "nothing is gained to piety by degrading human nature, for in the competency of this nature to know and judge of God, all piety has its foundation." No better evidence of the hopeful optimism of the age could be found than in the confidence with which such men as Channing found the approach to religious truth through human nature.

The humanistic orientation of Unitarian theism was rendered the more plausible by the urbanity and cosmopolitanism of the people who were the principal lay supporters of Unitarianism. In the years after the Revolution, the merchants of the New England seaboard, freed of British mercantile restrictions, were reaching out for new markets throughout the world. The knowledge and appreciation of cultures different from their own that they thus acquired furnished the background for Channing's assertion that the religious feeling is a natural and inevitable human impulse. Although a great variety of different religions were to be encountered in different regions of the globe, all shared a common basis in their veneration of the highest moral and religious ideals. One's faith in the validity of approaching religion through human nature might quite properly be confirmed by such tangible and universal evidence that man was by nature a religious animal.

In one respect Channing was ahead of his time, even among his fellow Unitarians. He sensed the inevitable drift of humanistic theism toward greater social responsibility, and he did not shrink from asserting the social obligations of Christians, even when his affluent parishioners let it be known that they would prefer to have their pastor preach on other themes.

As a Harvard student, Channing had read the works of the Scottish moral philosopher Adam Ferguson. Here he found the idea that individual regeneration was both a gradual and a social process. Ferguson's moral philosophy had effectively united the social and the providential worlds in a way that was to have a profound influence on American academic thought during the nineteenth century. In the meanwhile, Channing was mulling over the implications of regeneration as a social process. He concluded that regeneration could not be understood simply in terms of the individual, but that it remained incomplete until social regeneration was accomplished. As a young man he had dallied briefly with the ideal of Christian communism, and although he soon gave this up as a practical objective, he never gave up the conviction that the Christian obligation to society is not merely one of charity, but that it is to labor toward a true and lasting social reformation.

These principles were easily translated into a practical program of social reform. Channing was optimistic enough to anticipate an impending "Christian revolution," a new order in which each individual would work for the elevation of his fellows as intelligent and moral beings. One can perhaps detect in this Christian revolution a partially secularized version of Protestant millennialism. And it is certain that the objectives of Channing's revolution were also essential ideals of democracy. The best of all revolutions that Channing proclaimed would culminate in the marriage of Christianity and democracy.

In rejecting the psychological distinctions made by the Puritans between the regenerate and the unregenerate, the Unitarians were emphasizing the common moral nature of all mankind. But if it was only with the mind that man could know God, then the mind was that part of man which approached most closely to divinity. Here was the source both of the intellectualism and of the faith in human nature that characterized Unitarianism. However, the balance between belief in the truth of Christian revelation and faith in the rational powers of the free intellect proved to be difficult for the Unitarians to maintain. Out of their insistence upon the dignity of human nature there emerged the generation of transcendentalists who had little need of historic revelation.

Mormonism

The common nineteenth-century Protestant dream of the millennial Kingdom furnished the dominant motif of Mormon thought. In

1830, there was published at Palmyra, New York, *The Book of Mormon. An Account Written by the Hand of Mormon Upon Plates Taken from the Plates of Nephi,* by Joseph Smith, junior, "Author and Proprietor." Around Smith a religious sect sprang up, first called the Church of Christ and later amplified as the Church of Jesus Christ of Latter-Day Saints. Within fifty years of the publication of the *Book of Mormon,* the Saints had come to number more than 300,000. Their movement shares with Christian Science the distinction of being the most striking indigenous major American religion.

The explanation of the early appeal of Mormonism was to be found in Smith's awareness of the religious needs and interests of his neighbors. Perhaps because of the very fact that he had little formal education his ear was sensitively attuned to the topics of current discussion. He effectively wove these themes into the narrative that flowed in a crude Biblical style from his fertile talent as a story-teller. The "burned-over" region of central New York State, notoriously susceptible to revivalistic appeals, provided rich soil for Smith to cultivate.

Among the local interests that Smith effectively exploited was the speculation which had centered upon the mysterious Indian mounds of New York and the Upper Ohio Valley. For more than half a century prior to 1830 there had been much speculation both in scholarly circles and the press concerning the vanished race that had presumably constructed the mounds before being wiped out by the forebears of the modern Indians.

The *Book of Mormon* purported to be a narrative history of pre-Columbian America. In an age when the Old Testament furnished most Americans with their ancient history, Smith filled a menacing gap in the record by reviving the venerable hypothesis that the New World had been peopled from the Old by a wandering tribe of Israelites. According to his account, at about 600 B.C., the Jewish patriarch Lehi, warned of the impending destruction of Jerusalem, led his family into the wilderness and eventually reached America. Laman, a sinful and rebellious son of Lehi, became the progenitor of the modern American Indians. From another son, the good and faithful Nephi, stemmed the Nephites, a cultured, democratic, and peaceful people whose virtue was rewarded by a visitation from Christ after the Resurrection. The mounds were the surviving relics of their civilization. Constant warfare with the aggressive Lamanites eventuated in the total annihilation of the Nephites, the last of whom, Mormon, buried his records in the hill near Palmyra where the angel Moroni instructed Joseph Smith in a vision to dig them up. It was these records that comprised the *Book of Mormon*. Smith thus furnished his contemporaries with the bonds that linked the history of their physical environment to the Biblical narrative that was the central staple of their religious culture.

The identification of the Indians with the brutal and barbarous Lamanites was in perfect accord with the hatred and fear of the aborigines that prevailed among Smith's contemporaries. In a similar manner, the *Book of Mormon* also appealed to their anti-Catholicism with its thinly veiled references to an iniquitous church with its papal absolutism and inquisitorial instruments of torture. The anti-Masonic movement that had shortly before convulsed up-state New York was also reflected in an account of the machinations of a sinister secret society.

There was much in all this to suggest that Smith wrote his book in good clean fun out of an irrepressible urge to spin a yarn. But around the author and his book there quickly formed a religious sect. Whatever his original aspirations may have been, there can be no doubt that Smith possessed the talent to transform himself effectively from Author and Proprietor to Prophet.

The institutional fragmentation of organized Protestantism that had begun with the Great Awakening had by 1830 produced a welter of competing denominations and sects. Debates over the respective merits of various forms of doctrine and practice were a common form of public entertainment. Among many people of firm practical piety the reaction to such a situation was not one of indifference but of a yearning for an authoritative dispensation of the truth. Smith came to such people with an unqualified claim of authority. His Church of Christ did not rest upon another interpretation of Scripture, as did the Protestant bodies, but upon a special revelation of divine truth vouchsafed to Joseph Smith. This revelation set the Church of Christ apart from all other forms of Christianity, whether Catholic or Protestant. The assurance born of dogmatic authority was thus from the beginning one of the principal assets of Mormonism.

In spite of its assertion that it stood apart from the general body of Protestantism, Mormonism had to address itself to at least some of the prevailing interests of Protestant denominations if it wished to proselytize among them effectively. The principal means by which it did this was to emphasize the common Protestant millennial expectation. Millenarian hopes were not especially prominent in the *Book of Mormon* itself, but as a sect took form and recruits were gathered, the utility of the theme seems to have become increasingly apparent to Smith. His first important convert was Sidney Rigdon, a Disciples preacher and an intense millennialist. Smith received two supplementary revelations, one of which, published as the *Book of Enoch,* was concerned specifically with the millennial promise. It predicted the building of the New Jerusalem to which the heavenly city of Enoch would descend at the last day. In 1831, Smith and his followers moved to Rigdon's communitarian colony at Kirtland, Ohio, which was declared to be at the hither edge of the promised land. The site for the city of Zion was located in Jackson county, Missouri, where the building of a temple and preparations for the great event furnished the dynamic motive in early Mormon history. The phrase "Latter-Day Saints," which was incorporated in the name of the church in 1834, referred to the period of trial and preparation which was believed to precede the coming of the Kingdom. Smith at one time predicted that the great event would occur in fifty-six years. Israel would then be gathered, the ten lost tribes restored, and the faithful would cluster about the throne in Zion. Mormon missionaries cast in vivid and literal terms the expectations that were shared by a large portion of the Protestant world.

Other aspects of Mormon doctrine and practice revealed similar connections with trends in evangelical Protestantism. The Mormons joined with the evangelicals in rejecting such central dogmas of the Calvinistic tradition as particular election, limited atonement, and infant damnation. They held that salvation had been promised to all those who would repent of their sins, and they introduced a unique method whereby those already deceased might be saved through the intercession of living Saints. The practice of adult baptism by immersion provided a common bond with the cluster of Baptist denominations and related bodies.

A more individualistic and sectarian note was sounded by the strong emphasis upon direct inspiration in early Mormonism. Smith's absolute spiritual authority rested upon his prophetic mission to transmit the divine commands that were revealed to him alone. Thus polygamy, which had been condemned in the *Book of Mormon,* was later sanctioned by direct revelation to the Prophet in 1843. The elaborate ritualism and complex hierarchy of officialdom were likewise distinctive features of the movement. It may well have been that in reducing ritual and symbolic rite to a minimum, Protestantism was failing to nourish a common human need. The increasing popularity of fraternal orders with their mystical ritualism bore independent testimony to the prevalence of such a craving.

In common with many other sectarian movements, Mormonism undertook not only to satisfy the religious needs of its communicants but also to provide them with material and social security. The events of Mormon history during the early years immeasurably strengthened this motive. The great migrations of the Mormons to Ohio, to Missouri, back to Illinois, and finally to Utah, together with the immigration of converts from England and elsewhere, were tangible expressions of the quest for the security confidently promised by the leaders. Persecuted and literally driven into the wilderness by the "Gentiles," the Mormons greatly strengthened the cohesiveness commonly encountered in newly formed religious groups. Smith had shared the assumption of many Biblical literalists that the primitive communism of the early Christian church was the form of social organization appropriate to the state of spiritual perfection that was about to dawn. Thus the Mormons were prepared ideologically for the two brief ventures into semi-socialistic organization that the practical exigencies of life in Utah forced upon them. Under the "United Order of Enoch" private property was made over to the church and then returned to the former owner in trust for his use. But direct religious control of the economic life of the community proved to be impractical, and, in the long run, a paternalistic oversight exercised through spiritual and moral authority was found to be sufficient.

CHAPTER 10

The Academic Mind

H IGHER LEARNING IN AMERICA remained on the defensive during the first half of the nineteenth century, in spite of the
large number of colleges established under denominational auspices.
The major problem of the college was to keep alive. Except for a
handful of the older colleges with deep colonial roots, the typical institution was small and handicapped by pitifully meager resources.
Many a Western town that lost its battle for the county courthouse
consoled itself with a college. The mortality among such institutions
was understandably high. Those that managed to survive lacked the
funds to sustain research or to pioneer in the development of new
knowledge or educational techniques. To perpetuate the cultural
traditions that they had received from the past was all that they could
be expected to accomplish. In this respect they were more like advanced academies than colleges. Their history during the first half of
the century suggests little of the excitement aroused by the pioneer
educational theorists of the common school movement during the
same period.

Whatever the shortcomings of the colleges in terms of traditional
standards and objectives of higher education, their major accomplishment was of a different order. They provided moral discipline and an
ordered conceptual pattern of experience for the educated class of a

200

society that was in the process of dissolving many of the traditional supports of social order and intellectual authority. In this respect, religion and higher education stood shoulder to shoulder, making it ordinarily unnecessary for the denominations to interfere with the internal management of the colleges that they supported.

The liberal arts colleges, like the Protestant denominations, were avenues of social mobility. They opened their gates to all who could satisfy the nominal entrance requirements and pay the modest fees. The student who worked his way knew that the tangible benefits from his education would more than compensate for the little discriminations and disadvantages experienced by self-supporting students. While a college education was not then the mandatory prerequisite to training in the learned professions, it opened the way to a variety of careers. The colleges in the nineteenth century thus began to assume the social functions that they have exercised ever since.

But the social role of the colleges in a democratic society was something quite apart from the formal educational function that they undertook to perform. In theory, the object was to provide a traditional liberal arts education. This had been the education deemed suitable for gentlemen, and there had been little change in its substance since colonial times. The intellectual environment of the colleges was not, in most instances, self-consciously democratic. The classical languages and philosophical instruction that dominated the curriculums gave the student little that would provide an immediate practical advantage, while at the same time they set him apart as one possessing honorific skills not shared by a majority of the community. The atmosphere of the colleges was authoritarian, both in the classroom and on the campus. Without deliberately intending to do so, the colleges inevitably assumed a position implicitly critical of the democratic tendency toward cultural leveling, and they were exposed to criticism on the grounds that they produced snobs without practical or useful training. The principal educational issues of the mid-nineteenth century turned upon the demand of academic reformers that college curriculums be revised to serve the technical and practical needs of a democratic society.

In a fluid and expanding community the colleges performed an important conservative function. Somewhat like the medieval Church, they kept alive a great cultural tradition threatened with extinction. The particular use which they made of that tradition was adapted to the peculiar circumstances in which they found themselves. An examination of the substance of the standard college curriculum will show that it assumed the ultimate reality of a fixed and permanent order of natural laws and spiritual values underlying the flux of appearances. A major function of the old liberal arts college was to provide intellectual stability and order in a fluid society.

Protestant Scholasticism

The over-all intent of the liberal arts college was highly ambitious. It was to organize all knowledge, including knowledge of the cosmos, of man, and of society, into a consistent and intelligible whole. The religious organizations that supported virtually all the colleges were sympathetic to this objective because they saw in it only another demonstration of the divine purpose. In a broad sense, a liberal education thus confirmed the beliefs of revealed religion. There was no conflict between chapel and classroom. For this reason, the typical curriculum of a religiously controlled college was in no narrow sense sectarian.

Protestant scholasticism represented a synthesis of seventeenth-century religious ideas with those of the Enlightenment. Its fundamental proposition was the assertion that reality is an orderly and intelligible structure. Facts were apprehended by the physical senses, and their relationships were established by use of the reasoning faculty. When broadly understood by a mature and well-informed intelligence, these facts, whether of nature or of human life, were clear proof of the existence of the deity and His providence. These considerations formed the substance of natural as distinct from revealed religion. One of the most striking indications of the dependence of nineteenth-century thought upon that of the eighteenth century was the importance of the place it assigned to natural religion. Many of the colleges provided a course of instruction called "Evidences of Christianity," consisting of an enumeration of the various aspects of nature and experience that displayed "evidences" of the purposeful character of the creation. Certainty that a broad and informed view of reality would convince any rational creature that the world was comprehended within the laws of God's providence was the reason why colleges under religious control provided broadly humane curriculums.

According to the Protestant scholastic outlook, the organization of knowledge in the various formal fields of study fell into an orderly pattern corresponding to the chain of being in nature. Commencing with inanimate nature, one proceeded to the study of forms of life, to man himself, to society, and ultimately to the deity. Corresponding to this structure of reality were the various sciences or philosophies, the terms still being used interchangeably. There were three major branches of study at the collegiate level: natural, mental, and moral science or philosophy. Natural philosophy embraced the physical and biological sciences; mental philosophy dealt with topics that were to evolve into psychology; while moral philosophy would now be called ethics, with application of general principles to various branches of the social studies.

The three sciences or philosophies were the heart of the liberal arts curriculum. For their proper understanding the student should also be familiar with certain necessary tools, namely, a smattering of elementary mathematics, logic, rhetoric, and foreign languages. These fields of learning were all mutually consistent. Their interdependence in the academic mind was, in fact, one of the striking features of the nineteenth-century educational philosophy. Until after the middle of the century the curriculum was in its essentials a prescribed one. It is true that instruction in the natural sciences was slowly becoming more varied and specialized, at least in the larger and stronger institutions; modern languages were beginning to contest the immemorial monopoly of the classics, and specialized courses in political economy or history frequently were offered. But whatever choice may have been allowed the student in peripheral subjects, the central elements of the college curriculum remained prescribed.

The firmness with which these scholastic assumptions were held imparted to the formal educational experience a predominantly didactic flavor. But Americans have never been impressed by an exclusive intellectualism, and some instinct seems to have prompted college authorities to affirm that knowledge alone was not enough to justify their efforts. The religious tradition with its practical emphasis upon sanctification was doubtless present in the commonly heard assertion that education should develop a balance of character. A report of the Yale College faculty in 1828 announced that a proper education should cultivate the imagination and tastes as well as the reason. It should train the power of invention as well as the memory; it should familiarize the student with literature as well as science. A fully rounded character was thus to be achieved through the cultivation of all the important mental faculties.

Thanks to the fact that the typical college was a small body of students and teachers who lived a semicommunal life on the "campus," the extracurricular literary, forensic, and social activities contributed much toward the realization of the collegiate objective. Perhaps even more in the early nineteenth century than later, the students educated each other outside the classrooms. The literary society libraries that have survived in several college collections are an impressive testimonial to the seriousness with which students supplemented the labors of their instructors. Nevertheless, the formal curriculum by itself fell far short of what would have been required to develop the full range of the faculties and tastes. It remained relatively narrow and predominantly intellectual.

Moral science remained, as it had been in Witherspoon's day, the most important course in the curriculum. Its significance was attested by the fact that it was frequently taught by the president of the college. And since the president was often a clergyman, this vital area of instruction was in safe hands. At the beginning of the century, the moral-science textbook most widely in use was the *Principles of Moral and Political Philosophy,* by the English cleric William Paley. First published in 1785, Paley's book had passed through several American editions by 1830. It represented a continuation of the utilitarianism of the Enlightenment. In spite of his religious affiliations, Paley presented moral theory as the means of achieving happiness, and his enumeration of the virtues conducive to happiness had much the same practical flavor as that of Franklin.

As the reaction against the Enlightenment set in, Paley began to lose favor with college authorities, who objected to his treatment as insufficiently pious. American professors of moral philosophy began to write their own texts, which displayed a more religious tone. The most widely used of the native texts was the *Elements of Moral Science,* by the Reverend President Francis Wayland of Brown University, published in 1835. Wayland's book remained a standard text for nearly half a century. It sold 137,000 copies in thirty years and is said to have been translated into Hawaiian, Greek, Armenian, Nestorian, and Sgaru Kareu. It should be emphasized, however, that Wayland's text and others like it also written by clergymen did not expound a specifically Christian ethics, although they were definitely theistic. They found the basis of ethics, its source, nature, and authority, in the natural order and in the experience of rational creatures rather than in the revealed will of God. Just as natural religion was consistent with Scriptural revelation, so natural ethics was compatible with the Christian law of love.

Moral science was often defined as the science of duty or obligation.

Its scope was wide, embracing the whole range of individual and social life. It was customary to divide the subject into theoretical and practical parts; the former laid down the basic principles of ethics and indicated their connections with mental science or psychology; the latter applied the principles to domestic, political, and economic situations. Witherspoon at Princeton and Francis Alison at the University of Pennsylvania had introduced the subject from the Scottish universities, where it had served to unify religion and learning much as the American situation required. The writings of the Scottish philosophers Adam Ferguson, Thomas Reid, and Dugald Stewart were absorbed by the American writers on mental and moral science and blended with John Locke's psychological theories in their own books.

Moral theorists conceded that their subject was one of the more complex of the sciences because of the great variety of motives and situations involved in human conduct. They refused to be tempted to simplify the subject by adopting doctrinaire economic or sexual theories of human motivation. Yet they entertained the hope that moral science might become exact; not, to be sure, in the positivist sense of the accumulation of the empirical data of all conduct but through the mastery of the peculiar moral data of ethics. For moral law had been wrought into the nature of things by the Creator just as had the physical laws of matter. Neither man nor God Himself could alter this fact. Rightness and wrongness were inherent attributes of all actions.

The moral qualities of experience were apprehended by individuals by means of the moral faculty, or conscience. All men possessed such a faculty, but, like the other faculties, it had to be developed and sensitized by constant use. The cultivation of the conscience was also connected intimately with the functioning of certain other faculties, especially the will and the emotions. Because the data of the moral life did not impinge solely upon the moral faculty, a realistic treatment of moral problems had to commence with a recognition of the complexity of the personality. There was thus a close connection between moral science and mental science, or psychology. Many of the moral philosophers, including Wayland, also taught mental science and wrote texts in that field as well.

The moral faculty was often referred to as an "instinctive" function of the mind by which to probe the moral aspect of situations. The moral-faculty theory was thus distinguished from other types of moral theory. The hedonists, for instance, with their objective of pleasure or happiness, laid the foundations of conduct upon the senses that yield pleasure. The utilitarians likewise emphasized the role of reason when they stressed considerations of expediency. The moral-faculty theory also contrasted sharply with such systems as that of Thomas Hobbes, who traced morality to the dictates of earthly authority, or of Biblical literalists, who found it in the dictates of Scripture.

Wayland insisted upon the close association of the moral and rational faculties. Morality pertained only to rational beings who were free to choose between alternatives of conduct. Both moral and rational acts were made with reference to a given end to be realized. In the case of moral acts, however, the moral quality inhered not in the nature of the act itself but in the intention of the actor. In this respect, the moral-faculty theory stood at the opposite pole from the naturalistic ethics of the late nineteenth century, which took the objective consequences of an act as the sole criterion of its moral quality.

Although the theorists of the moral-faculty school rejected the contemporary British utilitarian and hedonistic ethics of Bentham and Mill, they nevertheless found an important place for happiness. Both the religious tradition and the relative breadth of their own experience as educators and administrators forbade them to overlook the characteristics of the natural man. The physical senses were obviously designed to yield personal pleasure, and they should be used judiciously for this purpose. These faculties were the basis of self-love, as expressed in the love of food, wealth, power, or superiority. The gratification of these desires was possible only in the social context, and one of the principal functions of the moral faculty was to regulate these forms of self-love so that their gratification by one individual would not interfere with the happiness of others.

The ultimate ground or criterion of morality was declared by Wayland to be the fullest use of all the human faculties and powers. Such a realization could not fail to develop and perfect the sense of obligation of each individual to his fellows and to the deity. In the circumstances, this was a remarkably humane and practical code of ethics. It was essentially independent of revealed religion as professed by the Protestant tradition, although the teachers who expounded it would have been most reluctant to make such an admission. Christianity, they said, was the remedial system of truth given to man for his instruction in his fallen state. In other words, what he would know instinctively if possessed of unclouded moral insight must in fact, given his sins, be inculcated authoritatively by revelation. But the spiritual truths of revelation were beyond the proper sphere of moral science, which served only as an introduction to the higher realm.

The second, or practical, division of moral science was concerned with the application of its theoretical principles to the concrete problems of individual and social life. After a brief discussion of man's duty to love God, Wayland developed his treatment of practical ethics by analyzing the laws of reciprocity and benevolence. The law of reciprocity rested on the fact that all men were asserted to stand in a relationship of equality to each other. This was not, of course, an equality of condition, since men were not equally endowed; it was an equality of right to use such faculties as men had been blessed with. The philosopher then sketched the application of the law of reciprocity to problems of personal liberty, property, domestic relations, and political society. The law of benevolence concerned man's charitable obligations to his fellows.

The spirit that pervaded the usual discussions of practical ethics was individualistic and activist if somewhat didactic. In a study of some forty-eight professors of moral philosophy who taught in American colleges between 1830 and 1860, Wilson Smith has shown that most of them were men of affairs who participated actively in the public life of the times. Practical ethics frequently led them to discuss controversial questions of current interest on which they were often made to feel the weight of public opinion. The course in moral philosophy was also important from the point of view of academic knowledge because out of it there emerged, during the course of the century, several of the specialized disciplines known as the social sciences. Economics was the first of such specialized courses, followed by political science and jurisprudence, history, sociology, and anthropology. Whenever one of these specialized courses was inaugurated, the unified spirit of the curriculum was preserved by the simple expedient of assigning the new course to the professor of moral philosophy.

Clerical Economics

One of the basic aspects of early-nineteenth-century American society was the intimate association that existed between democracy and capitalism. The fact that the American population was predominantly rural did not obscure this relationship. Freehold tenure, the extraordinary growth and mobility of the population, rapidly developing means of transportation, the well-established practices of investment and speculation in land—all combined to produce the agrarian capitalist. The political battles of nineteenth-century democratic society were, in their economic dimension, struggles between different types of planter, freehold farmer, commercial and industrial capitalists. Because the institutions and attitudes of capitalism were so pervasive, one would expect to find powerful agencies devoted to their support. It should come as no surprise to find that the principles of moral science as expounded in the college classrooms and textbooks provided a convenient rationalization of the prevailing modes of economic activity.

The academic moral science as it was commonly taught was well suited to furnish intellectual background and support for laissez-faire economic theory and practice. It presumed to be able to deduce a set of valid economic laws from the general principles of ethics universally acknowledged by the cultivated moral conscience of mankind. There was thus a natural economic science, comparable to the physical science the laws of which were found in nature. The complexity of factors motivating behavior should also be borne in mind. Men were animated by selfish as well as by altruistic motives. Indeed, there was little disposition to deny that the faculties of sensation and sentiment were more powerful determinants of action than were reason or benevolence. The desire for pleasure and for the avoidance of pain was the basis of that self-love that all sound moralists had to take into account. Adam Smith, himself a professor of moral philosophy, had demonstrated the relevance of laissez-faire capitalism to these moral principles by equating wealth with pleasure and labor with discomfort; hence the psychological impulse to accumulate capital. From the scholastic point of view, economics might appropriately be designated a "gloomy" science because its processes involved some of the less admirable traits of human nature. Nevertheless, a wise man would reconcile himself to the situation as he found it, firm in the assurance that an economic theory, or any other branch of social theory, that overlooked the selfish aspects of human nature would not fit the facts.

Moral science taught that God had so made men that they had a natural need and desire to gratify their wants. Otherwise life would be deprived of its dynamic element. The problem of practical ethics was to define the social bounds within which men might legitimately gratify their desires. The categories of rights and duties that were the principal subject matter of ethics fixed the terms in which economic problems were to be discussed. Economics dealt with the rights of property and the duties of all concerned in the property relationship.

The earliest courses in political economy in American colleges probably were those offered in 1818 at Harvard and Columbia Colleges. During the following decade, the practice spread rapidly to the older colleges of the seaboard. In many cases the professor of moral science added the new course to his other duties. The texts widely used at first were condensations of Adam Smith's *Wealth of Nations* or a treatise by the Frenchman A. L. C. Destutt de Tracy, which had been warmly recommended by Jefferson. Eventually, American texts replaced the importations, the most successful of which was written by the indefatigable Wayland. By 1906, his *Elements of Political Economy* (1837) had passed through thirty-three editions. Both in Britain and the United States, the introduction of instruction in political economy coincided with the rise of political democracy and with the first appearance of belligerently proletarian writers. Economists of both countries hoped that by teaching the true principles of economic science radical perversions of the truth might be avoided.

The clerical economists started with the assumption that the burgeoning American capitalist economy was a natural economic system, just as the stars in the heavens comprised a natural system, although the economy could admittedly be disrupted by human ignorance or folly. By a happy contrivance of the Creator, it was at once natural and moral. Man's sinful nature alone prevented the two aspects of reality from achieving complete identification. In this respect, the economist and the moralist shared a common responsibility. As Wayland expressed it, "the principles of Political Economy are so closely analogous to those of moral philosophy, that almost every question in the one may be argued on grounds belonging to the other." What better reason need the philosopher cite to confirm his authority as economist? The Reverend John McVicker of Columbia College, the first to hold an American professorship of political economy, insisted that only when economics was studied as a moral science was the range of relevant considerations broad enough to justify the effort as a public benefit.

Clerical economics might well have been defined as the morality of property relations. The sanctity of property rights was a regularly reiterated theme. Professor Francis Bowen of Harvard College agreed with Wayland that the emergence of civilization from barbarism and the subsequent progress of culture had resulted from the stabilization of property rights. Primitive communism undoubtedly had its virtues else the early Christians would not have practiced it. But the academic spokesmen for Protestant orthodoxy in the nineteenth century were addressing themselves to a very different kind of situation. Without becoming apologists for the *status quo* in any vulgar sense, they nevertheless shaped their thinking in terms of the realities of American life in their own day.

The prevailing commercialism required rationalization, and moral philosophers who doubled as economic theorists were excellently qualified to furnish it. They found ready at hand the mixture of Christian realism and hedonism that had first appeared in the Puritan ethic and that the eighteenth-century philosophers had thoroughly domesticated. Man is so constituted, ran the argument, that he seeks pleasure, which can be gratified most effectively through the possession of power. The quest for power results in emulation in order to achieve superiority over others. In a peaceful and civilized society this process takes an economic form, and its by-product is an improved standard of living made possible by the accumulation of goods and services.

At first glance, it might seem as though the complex of motives and sentiments that furnished the psychological underpinning of economic behavior constituted a distinctly lower order of virtues, a kind of moral underworld where the clerical economist might be expected to experience a fastidious repugnance for his task. But providence had unexpected ways of turning unlikely situations to useful purposes. A major need of the nineteenth-century economy was for capital for investment, and, consequently, great emphasis was placed on the assertion that capital was the sum of personal savings accumulated through the exercise of the personal virtues of industry and frugality. The Puritan work ethic was made to serve both an economic and a moral function.

The regulator and governor of the economy was the free marketplace where goods and services were exchanged. In an expanding community the emphasis of economic theorists was upon production and exchange. Only under later and more stable conditions would equal attention be given to problems of distribution and consumption. It was the peculiar beauty of the free market that when allowed to function without interference it automatically established an appropriate level of wages and prices. Interference with the self-regulating activity of the market was denounced by clerical economists in the strongest terms as both economically disastrous and immoral. This condemna-

tion referred both to attempts to influence wages through the union-
ization of labor and to any form of governmental intervention in economic activity.

An exception must be made here for the special problem of the
protective tariff. Clerical economists were divided on this issue. There
was some correlation between the tariff views of teachers and the
principal sources of financial support of their respective colleges.
Where the college relied chiefly on commercial wealth, the clerical
economist tended to be a free trader; where the financial support was
from manufacturing, he leaned toward protectionism.

Clerical economists were agreed that, wherever the market was free
to function without artificial or noneconomic interference, the prices
of commodities that it established might appropriately be regarded as
just prices. What then of the merchant who succeeded in monopoliz-
ing a commodity in order to fix an extortionate price? In principle,
such a practice was uniformly condemned. In fact, however, this was
regarded as an artificial question hardly worth serious consideration.
America was still a nation of small producers and of decentralized
markets. Except for the banking question monopoly had yet to become the burning issue that it would become a half-century later.

The close affinity between economics and morality in the minds of
clerical economists was reflected in the opinion that speculation, as
opposed to the legitimate economic activities of production and exchange, was immoral. In the hierarchy of useful functions, the place
of the banker was appreciably lower than that of the producer or
merchant. This discrimination remained a persistent strain in the
popular mind, especially in hard times when it was a common practice to castigate the moneychangers. Part of this feeling
was doubtless owed to a failure to appreciate all the functions of credit
in the economy. In this connection, Wayland defined money as simply
an ingenious mechanical device to facilitate the exchange of goods
and services. To manipulate the value of this exchange medium,
whether by government or private agencies, was roundly denounced
as iniquitous.

Moralists intent upon demonstrating the congruity of God's providence with the laws of moral and economic science faced a formidable
obstacle in the Malthusian law of population. Malthus had held that,
the procreative capacity of the human species being what it was, there
would in normal circumstances be more people than the environment
could support, resulting inevitably in an indigent class barely able to

survive. The three famous checks by which nature held the size of this class within manageable proportions were famine, pestilence, and war. The more tough-minded of the laissez-faire economists, especially among the British, saw the utility of the Malthusian Law as a naturalistic foundation for their economic theory, and they readily incorporated it into their system. But the American clerical economists, whose religious affiliations were close and whose sense of the congruity of natural and moral law was strong, were repelled by the harshness and nonethical character of the Malthusian analysis. The existence of human misery on any large scale had to be accounted for in human terms, as a consequence of sin and ignorance.

The clerical economists therefore substituted for the Malthusian man–land ratio a man–capital ratio. If population was capable of increasing rapidly in relation to the resources of the physical environment, it was also true, they maintained, that capital could be quickly accumulated. It was capital that, strictly speaking, made possible the employment of labor. The larger the capital fund available, the larger the number of laborers that could be employed. According to Wayland, if the earth were properly tilled and capital wisely invested, more goods would be annually produced than the population would consume. This surplus could be turned into fixed capital, which, in turn, would give employment to larger numbers of workers. "Hence we see that the prosperity of a nation does not depend simply upon the *absolute* amount of its capital, but upon the ratio which its capital bears to its population, and the ratio which is maintained between the increase of both." There would be no indigent class if the increase of capital were sufficient to provide employment for all at decent wages. On the other hand, were the population to increase faster than the capital fund, distress in the ranks of unskilled labor would result. Happily, the former condition prevailed in the United States.

The virtue of this answer to Malthus lay in the fact that capital was presumed to represent the sum of personal savings. It reflected the virtuous life of industry, frugality, and avoidance of luxury. Poverty, on the other hand, was the inevitable consequence of indolence, intemperance, or vice. Wayland did not point out, as perhaps he should have, that the poverty of a specific unemployed worker was not necessarily, according to this argument, the consequence of his own shortcomings; rather his poverty was due to the failure of some potential capitalist. The writer was content to acknowledge the interdependence of men in the economic process with the generalization that, when the capital supply dwindled in relation to the growth of population, the society as a whole would pay for its extravagances in the form of increasing poverty among the lowest class.

Wayland concluded from this analysis that too great importance could not be attached to individual and national frugality. The surplus resulting from frugal habits should be invested in profitable enterprises, whereas its diversion to personal luxuries would defeat this purpose. The same consideration was true of nations as of individuals. Money paid out in taxes was lost to productive enterprise. Although some governmental services were worthy, this was clearly an argument in the tradition of the minimal state. War offered the supreme example of the negative role of the state as a destroyer of capital.

There remained the duty of Christian charity incumbent upon all men. The relief of poverty by means of poor laws or a public dole would both interfere with the natural law of retribution and work economic mischief by diverting funds from constructive uses. The great virtue and advantage of private charity, on the other hand, lay in the fact that the wise benefactor was able to distinguish between laziness and misfortune. The hazards of life being what they were, there would always be ample opportunity to exercise the duty of charity without defying the imperatives of natural economic law. Here, as in other aspects of their thinking, the peculiar blend of economic fatalism and moral exhortation emerged as the distinctive hallmark of the clerical economists.

CHAPTER 11

▐▏║▌▌▌║▐

Romanticism

R OMANTICISM WAS BOTH a temper of mind and a complex of sentiments and attitudes toward life. It assigned a position of central importance to the emotions and intuitions. Because of its emphasis upon the esthetic aspects of experience, the romantic temperament expressed itself most effectively through the arts and literature, although its influence was also felt in many other activities. The current of philosophic idealism that flowed from Germany and England to America in the early years of the nineteenth century furnished the romantics with certain formal doctrines, which were useful both as creative and critical principles. From the idealists, the romantics learned that the human mind was so formed as to be capable of the direct apprehension of the essence of things, as distinct from the concrete particulars with which sensory experience dealt. The result was an emphasis upon subjective experience that sharply distinguished the romantic temper from the rationalism and empiricism of the Enlightenment.

Facets of Romanticism

The romantic spirit was inherently individualistic, and the conditions of American life further accentuated its individualism. In

214

Europe, where tradition and privilege were strong, the romantic was frequently a rebel and a revolutionist. In early-nineteenth-century America, on the other hand, it was tradition that was on the defensive, and the romantic spirit was free to burgeon forth in many forms. The mood of American romanticism was optimistic and constructive. Wasting little of its energies in attack on the inhibitions of the Enlightenment, it turned to the future, to new interests and forms of expression. Thus it represented a widening and enriching of American culture.

The liberation of the expression of the sentiments was an important accomplishment of the romantic movement. The enlightened mind had feared and repressed emotionalism in all its forms. Its emphasis on reason was intended in part to serve this purpose. Chauncy had insisted that God always tempered His benevolence with reason. Hence the preference of the age for verse written in carefully measured couplets after the manner of Pope or for the ordered restraint of the Georgian architectural style. The romantics, however, undertook deliberately to cultivate the sentiments. This involved both the use of new cultural forms and the instilling of the new spirit into old forms.

In literature, prose fiction proved to be an especially effective vehicle. Beginning with the earliest sentimental novels of the 1790's, such as Susanna Rowson's *Charlotte, A Tale of Truth* (1791), and with the first so-called "Gothic novels," such as Charles Brockden Brown's *Wieland* (1798), which was replete with mystery and assorted horrors, a steady and impressive development toward maturity occurred. One line culminated in the precisely constructed mystery stories of Edgar Allan Poe. Another reached full fruition with Hawthorne's *The Scarlet Letter* (1850) and Melville's *Moby-Dick* (1851). Unlike Scott, who chose remote and exotic settings for his tales, the American romantic novelists for the most part favored contemporary and local situations. In poetry, the free forms of verse that replaced the heroic couplet culminated in Walt Whitman's *Leaves of Grass* (1855).

The visual arts were well adapted to express the moods of romanticism. Landscape painting provided an effective form in which to convey the romantic attitude toward nature. The Hudson River School of landscape painters included Thomas Cole, Asher B. Durand, and John F. Kensett. Their representations of nature ranged from photographic likenesses to mystical attempts to communicate exalted sentiments. The sculptor Hiram Powers achieved fame and notoriety with his *Greek Slave* (1843), which celebrated the sensuous beauty of the nude figure. In architecture, the romantic temper was expressed in the Gothic Revival, which began in the 1830's. Although the Gothic style never equalled the earlier classic revival in popularity, the Gothic church designs of Richard Upjohn, commencing with his Trinity Church, New York, in 1839, and the adaptations of Gothic features to the plans for dwelling houses made by Alexander J. Davis were widely imitated.

In all these forms of romantic expression the appeal to a variety of sentiments or emotions was a principal objective. The evocation of a particular mood—be it exaltation, despair, fear, or devotion—was a prime purpose of the romantic, and his success was measured in his ability to command these moods. A great refinement of sensibilities was the result. In a community in which the ethical tradition so heavily outweighed the esthetic, the development of sensibility must be accounted an important accomplishment.

Physical nature played a role of great importance in romantic thought. It functioned as a source both of inspiration and of substantive truth. The poet William Cullen Bryant turned to nature in the spirit of devotion and found there the truest revelation of God. His friend Thomas Cole, the painter, found perfection in nature and sought to convey religious sentiments in his landscapes. Anthony Heinrich, musician and composer, professed to have derived direct inspiration from nature for the themes employed in his "Wild Wood Spirit Chant."

The enlightened mind had conceived of nature as the environment for life and had confronted it with an attitude essentially scientific. But nature was now prepared to play a much more vital role in human affairs. Under her immediate tutelage man was capable of achieving a more heroic stature than in less-favored circumstances. This was the assumption that underlay Cooper's tales of the pioneers, as well as Francis Parkman's histories of the struggle between the British and French for control of the West, which he called a "history of the American forest." The enlightened notion that the husbandman possessed peculiar virtues because of the intimacy of his association with nature was readily taken up by the romantics and pursued to its logical conclusion—the noble savage. Thomas Cole declared that, if human beings were to be introduced into a landscape painting in which the artist was attempting to portray the sublimity of nature, they should be "appropriate savage figures." The hostility to Indians was, however, too pervasive in nineteenth-century America for the "savage" to be a fully satisfying figure. But in the frontiersman who could be represented as half Indian and half white, sharing the nobler virtues of both, a happy compromise was found.

The romanticization of nature resulted occasionally in the complementary conviction that culture was artificial or unnatural. In a suite of five large canvases depicting the *Course of Empire*, Thomas Cole sought to illustrate the tension between nature and culture. The first was entitled "The Savage State, or Commencement of Empire," and portrayed a landscape with a few savages armed with bows and arrows. It was succeeded by "The Arcadian or Pastoral State," a vision of rural serenity with dancing shepherds. The central canvas depicted "The Consummation of Empire." Here a city square framed by immense monumental buildings in the classical style was the scene of a triumphal procession. Façade and pavement had completely displaced the natural landscape. The fourth canvas, "Destruction," depicted the city being sacked and burned by barbarian conquerors. The imminence of tempest and flood accentuated the suggestion that the catastrophe involved the reassertion of nature's supremacy over the works of man. The final picture, "Desolation," revealed a placid landscape in which a few crumbled ruins of the city were all but obliterated in the embrace of the foliage. The cycle of culture was complete. Civilization had been portrayed as a futile revolt against nature. Another group of paintings by Cole, *The Voyage of Life*, depicting the successive states of Childhood, Youth, Manhood, and Old Age, sounded a similarly somber note.

The pessimism of the cyclical theme was never fully satisfying to Cole or to his contemporaries, many of whom criticized the moral of these paintings. The artist himself was happily rescued from his dilemma by a religious conversion. He projected but did not execute still a third group of paintings that would depict Life, Death, and Immortality. He intended that the pessimism of the life cycle should be transcended in the expectation of glory hereafter. Cole's problems suggest the wider difficulty that confronted the romantic temperament in America. The notion that nature not only supported life and culture but would eventually contain and master them ran head on into the optimistic and progressive conviction that civilized man had emancipated himself from the primitive and would continue with the further refinement of culture. The romantic mind never succeeded in reconciling these alternatives, although the pessimistic strain remained a subordinate one in romantic thought.

The romantic temperament emerged from a sense of security, both intellectual and material. The feeling of frustration, also a necessary ingredient, was the inevitable consequence of the deliberate nurture of individuality rather than of any overt obstacles in the real world of experience. If the American romantic was a rebel, he was in rebellion against American inadequacies, not American accomplishments. The sentiments cultivated by the romantic had therefore a certain vicarious and imaginative quality. His well-known predilection for the remote in time and place was the expression of his preoccupation with experiences of an emotional intensity not to be found in the events of everyday life. These experiences were not sought in their actuality, but only in an imaginative creation that yielded for the artist and his public a quality of gratification essentially different from that found in concrete reality.

The material security that made possible the indulgence of the romantic temperament rested upon the rapid growth of the country, the rising standard of living, and the prevailing sense of military security. The intellectual security of mid-nineteenth-century America was perhaps an even more important ingredient. Men were confident that they understood the nature of their world. Its coherence and order were determined by the law and purposes of God. Human history and destiny were comprehended by God's providence. Through the faculty of conscience, each individual was subject to the prompting of the moral law. The assurance that resulted from these circumstances and beliefs provided a sturdy platform upon which to erect the flamboyant structure of romanticism.

While romanticism performed a valuable cultural service in nourishing the arts and sensibility, it did not produce a discriminating social criticism. Its individualism and nonconformity, as well as its preoccupation with man's relationship to nature, resulted in a revolutionary but not a class-conscious point of view. The concern with nature as a tutor tinctured romantic individualism with a bucolic flavor. The romantics perpetuated the notion that the farmer was a more valuable citizen than the urban worker simply because he was closer to the source of virtue. In this respect romanticism was a backward-looking influence. It failed to appreciate its foundations in the first phase of the Industrial Revolution in which improved living standards and lengthened life expectancy gave men the opportunity to indulge their romantic inclinations.

Romantic Democracy

Romanticism found its own distinctive social philosophy in the democratic ideology. Emerson and Whitman have been hailed as the literary spokesmen of a movement that embraced all ranks of society. In the perspective of a century of time, the romantic spirit appears to have united the intellectual and the common man in a homogeneous community. Actually, however, the individualistic element in romanticism was so strong as to border on anarchy, a current that ran as powerfully in politics as in literature. The great political issue of the early nineteenth century was the problem of union precisely because the bonds that united Americans were so loose. Only in Abraham Lincoln did the political system produce a leader capable of the effective fusion of democracy and nationalism.

A cult of personality was one of the forms in which romantic democracy expressed itself. The romantic put his faith in individuality, not in numbers. As Emerson said, when nature had work to do she created a genius to do it. Hence the otherwise paradoxical fact that the democratic movement fashioned for itself the first American popular heroes and welcomed a display of forcefulness in its political leadership. The image of Andrew Jackson created by the opinion-makers of his time revealed the sentimental characteristics that a democratic society preferred to find in its heroes. Jackson was declared by countless editors and stump orators to be an unspoiled child of nature, a self-made man, devoid of the artificial graces of the sophisticated but possessed of great native ability and driven by an imperious will. Here was the masterful leader equally adept at coping with redcoats, Indians, bankers, and slick Eastern politicians. The strict personal integrity and sense of honor, invariably prominent ingredients in these stereotypes of leadership, were extravagantly elaborated by Mason Weems in his biographies of George Washington (1800) and other early leaders.

The great popularity and prestige of oratory was characteristic of romantic democracy. John Witherspoon had shrewdly predicted the growing power of the spoken word when he observed that "democracy is the nurse of eloquence, because when the people have the power persuasion is the only way to govern them." The effectiveness of oratory resided in the intimacy of association between the personality of the orator and the substance of his oration. Its popularity testified to the democratic impulse to identify issues with personalities and to stress qualities of character in the determination of leadership. In earlier periods, the clergy had had a virtual monopoly of the spoken word. Now the platform replaced the pulpit as the principal place for eloquence. It was appropriate that politics should provide the subject matter for the most famous orators of the day, but the range of topics suitable to oratorical treatment was nevertheless broad. The "lecture" became an established institution in every community, appropriately commercialized by the lyceum and similar organizations.

An illustration of the pervasive attitudes of romantic democracy is found in the unlikely field of domestic architecture. Andrew Jackson Downing, architect and landscape gardener, published his *Architecture of Country Houses* in 1850. Downing was a member of the Hudson River School, sharing with the landscape painters of that group the keen awareness of the association between romanticism, nationalism, and democracy. Downing justified a treatise devoted exclusively to domestic architecture with the observation that in a democratic society the architect had an obligation to provide suitable designs of dwellings for all classes of the population; it was no longer justifiable for him to confine himself to monumental designs for public buildings or to stately residences for the wealthy few. An ardent nationalist, Downing strove for a "free and manly school of republican tastes and manners." Buildings should be useful, beautiful, and true—in that order. Truth included suitability of the dwelling to its occupants, adaptation to its site, and honest use of materials. In these respects Downing anticipated the functional theories of Louis Sullivan and Frank Lloyd Wright. The romantic feeling for nature was reflected in Downing's theory of landscape gardening. Nature should be refined and softened by art. The gardener should accentuate the natural features of the site with judiciously planted trees, clumps of bushes, or rock gardens.

For architectural purposes, Downing distinguished three classes in American society: working people, who lived in cottages; farmers, who occupied farmhouses; and "persons of competence," who dwelt in villas or country houses. The object in designing a cottage was to obtain essential living space at minimum cost, with appropriately modest appearance. Downing professed to have achieved these in several two-bedroom designs the cheapest of which could be built for four hundred dollars.

In a republic where there were neither castles of feudal barons nor palaces of princes, the most stately dwellings were the villas or country houses of the well-to-do. Such houses required the care of three or more servants and should be appropriately ornate in style. They should combine truthfulness and beauty with individuality and suitability to the site.

Because 80 percent of the American population lived in farmhouses, Downing felt it appropriate to give special attention to this form of architecture. In countries where serfs did not own the soil they cultivated, no attention need be paid to the style in which they lived. But in a land where virtually every farmer was a proprietor, most of them intelligent and many of them among the wisest and most honored citizens, the architectural needs of farmers were worthy of careful consideration. Downing designed farmhouses in both the English and American styles. The former was characterized by a high, steep roof with overhanging eaves, giving the house a low, squat appearance. The American style, which Downing believed would be generally preferred here, achieved the appearance of "a little more independence and a little less lowliness" by a shallower roof and greater height from ground to eaves. Not only did the American style have the higher rooms required by the warmer summers of the United States, but, in general, it conveyed the impression of the substantial accomplishment to which all American farmers aspired. On esthetic grounds alone Downing himself preferred the English style, but he surmised that the American farmer who was motivated chiefly by a desire to improve his status was less likely to value "that beauty which lies hidden in modesty and simplicity."

Transcendentalism

Prior to the nineteenth century, Americans had acknowledged three different ways of apprehending the most important truths in life. One was the revelation of divine truth in Scripture as professed by all branches of Christianity. Another was the belief in direct personal inspiration entertained by various radical sectarians. The third was the empiricism of the Enlightenment, where sense data were organized with the aid of the faculty of reason. Combinations of these approaches to truth were also possible, as in Arminianism, where revelation and reason were equally stressed. It was noteworthy that in American intellectual history each of these ways to the truth was closely associated with a religious tradition. Even the secular-minded thinkers of the Enlightenment subscribed at least formally to the principles of deism.

Among these alternatives the method of transcendentalism was closest to that of direct inspiration. The transcendentalist believed that spiritual truth was apprehended by each individual instinctively.

American transcendentalism has traditionally been traced to its philosophical source in the writings of the German philosopher Immanuel Kant, whose idealism was the product in part of the attempt to cope with epistemological problems arising from British empirical philosophy. But this was largely a technical derivation for the American transcendentalists. The real animus of their activities was found in the local scene, where a rebellion took shape against the Unitarian synthesis of rationalism and Scriptural authoritarianism. In its reaction against all forms of evangelical piety, Unitarianism had hardened into a cold and formal creed. Even the delicate warmth and refined zeal of Channing's faith had resulted in a marked estrangement from his own congregation when the clergyman responded to the compulsion to support good causes. The transcendentalists were Unitarians, mostly clergymen, who rebelled against their own denomination. It was at this point that the romantic movement in America came closest to making an open break with the past.

American transcendentalism took two principal forms of expression: literary and religious—the essay and the sermon. It was Emerson who perfected the essay form. Many of these essays had actually been written for oral delivery as lectures. They were, in fact, lay sermons. The erstwhile Unitarian clergyman confessed that he had abandoned the pulpit for the lecture platform because he found in the latter a more congenial and sympathetic environment in which to testify to his own unique form of spiritual ecstasy. Certainly the didactic and hortatory qualities of the traditional sermon survived entire in Emerson's lecture-essays.

His disciple Theodore Parker refused to follow the leader's example in abandoning the Unitarian ministry. By steadfastly insisting on retaining his status as a clergyman in the face of virtually the entire body of the Unitarian clergy, Parker eventually won for transcendental doctrines an acknowledged place within the Unitarian denominational fold. Although Parker preached what he called "absolute religion," something broader than mere Christianity, it fell short of the cosmic religion that Emerson celebrated. Without minimizing its importance as a literary movement, in the context of the American scene with its pervasive religious preoccupations, transcendentalism must first be interpreted as a form of religious expression.

Transcendental religion was a mystical conviction of the union of God, nature, and man. In a familiar passage from his most famous essay, *Nature* (1836), Emerson testified succinctly to this mystical union: "In the woods, we return to reason and faith. There I feel that nothing can befal me in life,—no disgrace, no calamity, (leaving me my eyes,) which nature cannot repair. Standing on the bare ground, —my head bathed by the blithe air, and uplifted into infinite space,— all mean egotism vanishes. I become a transparent eyeball. I am nothing. I see all. The currents of the Universal Being circulate through me; I am part or particle of God."

The sense of intimate possession by the Universal Being that is celebrated in this passage established Emerson's position in the radical sectarian tradition. For the customary theological functions and attributes of divinity, he substituted the symbolism and mediatorial agency of nature, and thus freed himself from the theological conventions that traditional Protestant orthodoxy had erected to guard against the anarchy of direct inspiration. The charge of fomenting anarchy left Emerson wholly undisturbed. "Self reliance is God reliance."

The Concord transcendentalist was fully conscious of the fact that his affirmations associated him with certain radical Christian heresies. He insisted that the transcendentalist believed in miracle, in direct inspiration, and in religious ecstasy. He readily admitted himself to be open to the charge of Antinomianism—that is, of subordinating the dictates of the moral law to the promptings of direct inspiration. He believed that each man, having the lawgiver within himself, might properly violate every written commandment. The confusion that would doubtless attend such a situation did not disturb the sage. "Whoso would be a man must be a nonconformist."

The orthodox believer looked back to the one perfect Christian, Jesus Christ, as the source of truth. The transcendentalist, on the contrary, insisted that there had not yet lived a "pure transcendentalist." There had not yet appeared a man who had "leaned entirely on his character," who had lived a purely spiritual life, and who, trusting his impulses and working exclusively for the highest good, had found all his problems solved for him. Emerson believed that such a life was possible because he found the promise of it in nature. "Only in the instinct of the lower animals we find the suggestion of the methods of it, and something higher than our understanding. The squirrel hoards nuts and the bee gathers honey, without knowing what they do, and they are thus provided for without selfishness or disgrace." Here was primitivism with a vengeance. The transcendentalists were adding a spiritual dimension to the benevolent naturalism of the Enlightenment.

It was by immediate intuitive insight that man was said to apprehend the most important truths of life. This was familiar ground to all who were accustomed to the moral-faculty theory. Emerson reaffirmed a widely held opinion when he declared that "in the soul of man there is a justice whose retributions are instant and entire. He who does a noble deed is instantly ennobled. He who does a mean deed is by the action itself contracted." But when the transcendentalist went on to assert that "if a man is at heart just, then in so far is he God," sober-minded co temporaries suspected that Emerson was confusing attribute with essence. They could not down the feeling that transcendentalism was a doctrine in which only moderate and well-bred men could safely indulge themselves.

Nevertheless, the influence of Emerson's doctrine of the intuitive sense of religious and moral truth spread widely and took root among several of the younger Unitarian clergymen. Thus it happened that Emerson, who had been excluded from the Harvard Yard on the grave charge of contaminating Divinity School students, soon saw his ideas effectively expounded by Theodore Parker, who became the most popular Unitarian preacher in Boston. In spite of their commitment to rational theism, however, the Unitarians were a relatively tolerant and adaptable body, and before many years had passed, a transcendental Unitarian, Convers Francis, was appointed to a post in the Harvard Divinity faculty.

The transcendental Christianity preached by Parker and others during the decade prior to the Civil War was an attempt to reconcile Christian revelation with the intuitive sense of divine truth as taught by Emerson. This was not an easy task insofar as the intuitions were to be the ultimate arbiter of what was to be accepted as true. Orthodox Christians, for instance, claimed the entire contents of the Bible to be religious truth, but no one could pretend to discover all this in the intuitions. Parker therefore reduced the truths of Scripture to a few great fundamentals, namely, the existence of God, the obligations of the moral law, the inspiration of Christ's sacrifice, and the promise of salvation. Each of these truths was confirmed by apprehensions of the intuition, and Parker ruthlessly cut away the rest of Scripture as so much useless padding. The principles affirmed both by Scripture and intuition he called "absolute religion."

It is a noteworthy coincidence that at about the same time that Parker was expounding his absolute religion the educational reformer Horace Mann was advocating a very similar "pure religion" as the basis upon which various religious groups could unite in support of public schools. No one faced with equanimity the prospect that public schools might be godless. Mann proposed therefore that the denominations agree that the schools should inculcate the doctrines of pure religion which they shared in common, leaving to each group responsibility for teaching its own peculiar tenets. But Mann, it happened, was also a Unitarian, and his proposal was widely denounced as a plot to infiltrate the public-school curriculum with Unitarian principles.

The transcendentalists felt the full impact of the romantic movement. Their selection from among the moods that romanticism made available was generally creditable. They were incorrigibly optimistic. They displayed none of the exaggerated pessimism that the romantic spirit occasionally generated. Unlike other romantics, the transcendentalists were preoccupied with the present and the future rather than with the past. Emerson reproved his contemporaries for being retrospective; like old men, they were building monuments to the fathers and writing histories. Irving and Prescott were working on their colorful narratives of Old and New Spain, and Bancroft was beginning his lengthy history of the American people. These were romantic histories in the heroic style. But Emerson asked: "Why should we grope among the dry bones of the past, or put the living generation into masquerade out of its faded wardrobe? The sun shines to-day also."

Transcendentalism shared the romantic revulsion against the intellect as the sole means of arriving at the truth. "Pure intellect is pure devil." Such an attitude could easily lead to obscurantism. Yet the transcendental protest against intellectual formalism had much to do with the liberation of creative artistic impulses in a utilitarian and puritanic society that had little use for the esthetic life.

Transcendentalism participated also in the romantic rediscovery of nature. Hitherto Americans had, of necessity, confronted nature as a physical world to be mastered. Nature represented treacherous seas and mountain barriers to cross or the raw materials with which to build a community. But the time had now come when Indians no longer lurked in the woods on the way to Walden Pond; when hayfield, pasture, and woodlot, separated by neat stone walls, had acquired the air of permanence that certified their right to a place in the landscape. Now nature seemed thoroughly domesticated, and in the hands of a consummate artist it was ready to come alive with a cosmic vitality. Out of these circumstances came not only Emerson's *Nature* and Thoreau's *Walden* but also *Moby-Dick* and, somewhat later, the seascapes of Albert Ryder.

For Emerson and for Thoreau, nature performed in addition a special and technical function: it provided the specific symbols that were the key to an apprehension of the Over-Soul or God. Nature was regarded as the conduit through which the spirit of God flowed into man. Like Jonathan Edwards before them, the transcendentalists turned to nature for the most cherished symbols of the spiritual life. Separated from her benign embrace man's soul would wither, just as a plant whose roots were torn from the soil.

Mystical and monistic philosophies have frequently produced fatalistic or deterministic consequences. But this was not true of transcendentalism. The idealism of that philosophy, which held that thought is real and matter of secondary importance, taught that so far as man is a thinker he is a creator. The idealistic current thus flowed through the great American tradition of activist individualism. For this reason, it became possible a century later to regard the transcendentalists as the intellectual spokesmen for their age. It is easy, however, for a later generation to deceive itself as to the extent of the transcendental spokesmanship. Among men preoccupied with material and commercial values the transcendentalists bespoke ideal and spiritual ends exclusively. Thoreau and Bronson Alcott expressed in their lives as well as in their literary labors the contempt they felt for the vast body of their countrymen who were wholly committed to pursuit of the bitch-goddess Success. The divergence between kinds and qualities of individualism was to become ever more crucial in the later history of American civilization.

Harriet Beecher Stowe and Romantic Christianity

Although not a work of great literary merit, *Uncle Tom's Cabin* (1852) is nevertheless a major document of the American mind. In order to appreciate it, one must know something of the religious experience of its author, for although it is generally known as an anti-slavery novel it is more specifically a religious novel. It could only have been written by a profoundly religious person who was prepared to confront the evil of slavery in terms of her own religious experience.

The course of history has obscured the significance of the book because of its peculiar relationship to the development of the sectional conflict. *Uncle Tom's Cabin* is usually thought of as the principal propaganda piece which led to the abolition of slavery, and the author herself promoted this view when she recalled how President Lincoln had greeted her as "the little lady who caused the great big war." By depicting vividly the horrors of slavery she had indeed assisted in mobilizing against it the sentiments and convictions of Americans. Subsequent emancipation served to locate the book in a successful anti-slavery crusade.

Nevertheless, the inferences drawn from these historical circumstances interfere with an appreciation of the profundity of the problem of slavery as Harriet Beecher Stowe confronted it. In 1850–51, when the book was conceived and written, slavery was deeply intrenched and in power. The Democratic party was dominated by its pro-slavery wing, while the Whigs were disintegrating and the Liberty and Free Soil parties had already failed lamentably. The Republican party had yet to appear. The recent annexation of Texas and former Mexican territories had opened up the whole Southwest to slave settlement. The so-called "Compromise" legislation of 1850 was no compromise at all in the eyes of anti-slavery people because it included a fugitive slave act which brought the police power of the Federal government into the local community in a manner unprecedented at that time. Mrs. Stowe was profoundly depressed by these circumstances. When she wrote *Uncle Tom's Cabin* she took it for granted that slavery was an evil with which one had to live. Her book was not a direct plea for abolition in the sense that *Common Sense* had been a plea for independence. One cannot fully understand the book without realizing that in the author's mind slavery was a fact with which one had to come to terms. This realization in turn enables the reader to appreciate more fully the character of the novel as a religious work. While the Christian denounces and resists evil she does not expect to be able to destroy it today or tomorrow.

Harriet Beecher (1811–1896) had been born into one of America's most prominent religious families. Her father, Lyman Beecher, was an outstanding Congregationalist clergyman who was playing a central role in resisting the inroads of Unitarianism while establishing the status of his denomination on the moderate wing of the new evangelical Protestant synthesis. The Puritan distinction between saints and sinners and the need for regeneration as a concrete experience still survived among the Congregationalists, and were expounded with eloquent zeal by Lyman Beecher. Her mother died during Harriet's childhood, and other family tragedies left indelible marks on her. Romantic sensibilities cultivated by the reading of Scott and Byron helped to give form to her feelings of grief. After reading Madame de Stael's *Corinne*, Harriet remarked that "in America feelings vehement and absorbing like hers become still more deep, morbid and impassioned by the constant habits of self-government which the rigid forms of our society demand. They are repressed and they burn inward till they burn the very soul, leaving only dust and ashes." When she was eleven, her sister Catharine's fiance was drowned at sea, and later, her brother George, a gifted young clergyman, accidentally killed himself while hunting. In her anguish Harriet was tempted to doubt the meaning of a world in which talented young men with every advantage could be suddenly obliterated. But at length she found consolation in her religious faith. "The deepest and most powerful argument for the religion of Christ is its power in times like this," she wrote. "Take from us Christ and what he taught and what have we here? What confusion, what agony, what dismay, what wreck and waste! . . . " The Christian promise made intelligible and bearable an otherwise meaningless and chaotic world. This was to be the ultimate message of *Uncle Tom's Cabin*.

Harriet arrived at her own consoling religious faith only after years of anguish and uncertainty. She had experienced conversion at the age of fourteen on hearing a sermon of her father's in which he had turned away momentarily from theological disquisition and had spoken with simple feeling of Christ's love and care for the human soul, "patient with our errors, compassionate with our weakness, and sympathetic for our sorrows." But was she simply indulging a weak womanly craving for support? The stern Puritan doctrines of election, assurance, and perseverance must be satisfied. Harriet's older sister Catharine, with what to a later generation must seem to have been perverse cruelty, threw doubt on the genuineness of the conversion. For twenty years Harriet suffered the agonies of uncertainty before finally arriving at a sense of the sufficiency of Christ's love. "God, the mighty God, is mine, of that I am sure, and I know he knows that though flesh and heart fail, I am all the while desiring and trying for his will alone." She had finally achieved a triumphant consolation snatched from the conventional Congregational theology of innate sinfulness and conversion with its deceptive evidences of assurance. When she lost her youngest child in the cholera epidemic of 1849 she could reflect with resignation that "Christianity enters through the rents and fishers of a broken heart."

Harriet's own religious experience epitomized the general trend of Western culture in the nineteenth century toward humanitarian and humanistic theism. Everywhere, Christian liberals were humanizing the traditional supernaturalism and infusing it with a humanitarian concern for the poor and downtrodden, with a revulsion against violence, and with the exaltation of love and benevolence as the supreme human and religious values. This was a historical and humanistic faith quite different from the theologically centered beliefs of the traditional churches. One aspect of this theism was a new appreciation of the human qualities of Jesus of Nazareth, who taught a simple doctrine of love and forgiveness, and who addressed himself to the poor and lowly. Jesus had lived the life of a mortal man, experiencing all of the pain and sorrow that are the common lot. He died the miserable death of a common felon, leaving only a handful of simple followers. But this was only the beginning of the story of his religion. The Christians steadily increased in numbers until, 1900 years later, they encircled the globe. Their success in Christianizing the world led many of them to believe that the promised return of Christ and the establishment of his millennial kingdom was about to occur. This conception of the religion of Jesus and its future expectations provided the framework in which Harriet located her novel of Uncle Tom.

Between 1832 and 1850 she lived in Cincinnati where she met and married Professor Calvin Stowe of Lane Theological Seminary. Living in genteel poverty on a salary of $600 a year and raising seven children she began to write stories for magazines in order to supplement the family income. Her hostility to slavery was formed at an early age. Lyman Beecher was an ardent opponent of the institution, having preached anti-slavery sermons as early as 1820. An aunt of Harriet's, who had married a West Indies planter, returned with horrifying stories of slave mistreatment. Slave-holding territory was just across the Ohio river from Cincinnati, and Harriet had ample opportunity to collect first-hand accounts of the adventures and abuses of slaves. After the publication of *Uncle Tom's Cabin*, when critics complained that the novel gave a biased account of slavery, she was able to show by the publication of these accounts that many of the episodes of the book were based on actual events.

A traditional argument for the condemnation of slavery, as old as Western civilization itself, was that it denied to a human being the right to his own personality and will, the right, in short, to be a man. One of the striking aspects of the author's delineation of Uncle Tom is the gradual and imperceptible way in which she reveals his character to the reader. A simple Christian slave, hardly literate, who had been taught by a kindly master to read his Bible, which he always carried with him, Tom at first appears to be little more than a pious simpleton. Gradually, the firm character begins to emerge from the simple piety and good-natured kindliness as he meets successive trials with true Christian fortitude. Sold down the river to the cruel and inhuman plantation owner, Simon Legree, Tom finally emerges by virtue of the purity of his character as a force to be reckoned with.

The modern epithet "Uncle Tom" connotes a cringing, fawning sycophant, a Black who accepts the subordinate role assigned by whites. Such a usuage does not provide a reliable clue to Harriet's fictional hero. It is true that Tom did not assert his rights as a man, nor was he a passive resistant in the Gandhian sense. He was what might be called a Christian resistant. Although he counseled submission by his fellow slaves, nevertheless, by virtue of his Christian convictions there emanated from him a strange power felt by all who were in contact with him, a power that infused in the slaves a sense of hope and a new strength with which to bear their afflictions. Simon Legree also sensed this power and knew that he would have to bend Tom to his will or destroy him. He offered Tom the position of straw boss, which would have brought relative security and comfort. When the offer was refused he ordered his minions to beat Tom to death.

In the flush of success following the publication of her book Harriet revealed that this climactic scene had been the first to be written. It had come to her as a vision while attending church service, and she roundly declared that "God wrote that book." The close parallel between the death of Jesus and the death of Tom was clearly intended. Both were tempted by the evil one with the offer of worldly power, and both died secure in the faith that justice would ultimately triumph. Tom's spirit, like that of Jesus, lived on in the little group of survivors who dedicated themselves to the advancement of the Negro race.

Jesus had prophesied that the last would be first, and Harriet was bold enough to apply this prophecy to the Negro race. In one of the remarkable passages of the book in which she paid tribute to the peculiarly Christian qualities of the Blacks, she predicted that the millennial kingdom would be established in Africa.

If ever Africa shall show an elevated and cultivated race,—and come it must, some time, her turn to figure in the great drama of human improvement,—life will awake there with a gorgeousness and splendor of which our cold western tribes faintly have conceived. In that far-off mystic land of gold, and gems, and spices, and waving palms, and wondrous flowers, and miraculous fertility, will awake new forms of art, new styles of splendor; and the Negro race, no longer despised and trodden down, will perhaps, show forth some of the latest and most magnificent revelations of human life. Certainly they will, in their gentleness, their lowly docility of heart, their aptitude to repose on a superior mind and rest on a higher power, their childlike simplicity of affection, and facility of forgiveness. In all these they will exhibit the highest form of the peculiarly *Christian life*, and, perhaps, as God chasteneth whom he loveth, he hath chosen poor Africa in the furnace of affliction, to make her the highest and noblest in that kingdom which he will set up, when every other kingdom has been tried, and failed; for the first shall be last, and the last first.

Christianity addresses itself to two dimensions of human experience: the personal life of the individual and the collective history of the human race. To the individual it offers the cross, while to mankind in general it extends the promise of the kingdom to come. Uncle Tom represents the first of these dimensions, and George Harris, the other principal character of the book, the second. Slavery is the symbol of the ultimate evil in life. Tom's martyrdom exemplifies the way in which the good man is crushed by it. But the Christian is not content simply to accept the way of the cross as a personal solution. He affirms that in the end the good will triumph, the Kingdom of God will be established and evil destroyed. During the nineteenth century, many Protestant Christians in America were eagerly awaiting the coming of the millennial kingdom which they anticipated in the near future. Harriet was of course familiar with adventism, and in the character of George Harris, the St. Paul of her gospel analogy, she sought to personify the millennial expectation.

Harris was a light-skinned mulatto slave whose exceptional abilities aroused the jealousy and hatred of his vindictive owner. Faced with the prospect of separation from his family he decided to run away to Canada in the hope of eventually redeeming his wife and child. In Canada, where he found employment, and later in Europe, Harris completed his formal education in order to serve the interests of his race most effectively. In the final passages of the novel Harriet assigned to him the expression of her views as to the glorious future of the African race when it would finally take its place among the great races of the world.

Two anti-slavery strategies are considered, the Christian strategy embodied in Uncle Tom, and the natural rights strategy represented by George Harris in his earlier or unregenerate period. It was the responsibility of the white Christian to bear witness against the evil of slavery, to attempt to change the public mind by making people more conscious of its iniquity. Thus a frail little woman burdened with poverty, an ineffectual husband, and a large family of children could yet find spare moments in which to write a powerful fictional indictment of slavery.

The slaves themselves should of course be Christianized. Then how was a Christian slave to react to the fact of his own enslavement? Christianity had always professed to be a religion of the poor and oppressed, but it did not counsel rebellion. The believer was to find salvation by taking Christ's yoke upon him. Evil would be transcended, but not destroyed, by the gift of grace. Tom's steadfast faith enabled him to preserve the integrity of his character while submitting to enslavement. His personal triumph in martyrdom prefigured the ultimate victory of Christianity in the millennial kingdom.

Harriet felt strongly that an essential characteristic of the true Christian was the ability to distinguish evil as such from the doer of evil. Slavery was evil, to be denounced with all the fervor at one's command; but the slaveholder was to be pitied, even forgiven. The supreme virtue of Christian love required this distinction. Harriet was careful to introduce in the person of Augustine St. Clare (whose names symbolized two poles of the Christian tradition) a decent and humane slaveholder who agonized over a situation he was powerless to remedy. Simon Legree, on the other hand, was a transplanted Yankee who had gone South to exploit the slave plantation for his own profit. Because she avoided a partisan or regional attack on slavery Lord Palmerston congratulated Harriet on her "statesmanship." Like Garrison, she indicted a whole nation.

In the end, love proved to be the impenetrable armor of the Christian. Legree could destroy the body of his slave, but not the soul, nor indeed his personality. Harriet lived too early to be able to anticipate Stanley Elkins's analogy of slavery and the twentieth-century concentration camp. But Legree's plantation was in a real sense a concentration camp, and what happened there permitted Harriet to declare emphatically that even under the conditions of slavery at its worst the ultimate in evil—the destruction of a personality—need not happen if the slave was resolute in clinging to his faith.

George Harris, Harriet's spokesman for the natural rights anti-slavery strategy, had every reason to be bitter about his abusive treatment by an owner who was in every way his inferior. To his wife Eliza, who counseled Christian submission, George protested that Christianity was a rationalization for people in power. If there were a God, why did he permit such injustice? George had heard too many Fourth of July orations about human rights and self-government to believe that it was his duty to submit to oppression. As a runaway he exulted in the freedom obtained by his own effort. But during the course of his flight he was assisted by Quakers who operated a station on the underground railroad. These gentle people succeeded in converting him to the Christian viewpoint with the argument that regardless of what one might suffer in this life God would make all right hereafter. Stronger than any argument, however, was the personal influence exerted by these pious and kindly people. "This indeed was a home,—*home*,—a word that George had never yet known a meaning for; and a belief in God, and trust in his providence, began to encircle his heart, as, with a golden cloud of protection and confidence, dark, misanthropic, pining, atheistic doubts, and fierce despair, melted away before the light of a living Gospel, breathed in living faces, preached by a thousand unconscious acts of love and good will, which, like the cup of cold water given in the name of a disciple, shall never lose their reward." George's conversion was not so much a spiritual transformation in the traditional manner as it was a change of personality in which a positive and cheerful optimism over the future prospects of his race replaced hatred and despair.

Thanks to the liberation of his will and energies George now determined to devote his life to the cause of African nationalism. Through the hopes attributed to him Harriet expressed her own expectations for the future of the Negro race. Ironically enough, her vision focused on Africa rather than America. A new Negro nation would arise in Africa to "roll the tide of civilization and Christianity along its shores." It would of course display the distinctive qualities of the Negro people. "If not a dominant and commanding race, they are, at least, an affectionate, magnanimous, and forgiving one. Having been called in the furnace of injustice and oppression, they have need to bind closer to their hearts that sublime doctrine of love and forgiveness, through which alone they are to conquer, which it is to be their mission to spread over the continent of Africa." George refused to be deterred by the fact that American colonizationists were using Liberia as a means of evading the issue of slavery. He insisted that he was not deserting the American slaves, since in some unexplained manner a strong African nation would induce free and enlightened America to free its slaves.

In spite of the depth of her human sympathies and her strong sense of justice it is apparent that Mrs. Stowe was incapable of conceiving in concrete terms a multi-racial society in America. Very few white Americans of the nineteenth century were able to do so. She believed that races had their own distinctive characteristics, the Anglo-Americans being "stern, inflexible, energetic," while the Africans were better suited to the anticipated age of universal peace and brotherhood. Until that age came, she took it for granted that the races were to pursue their respective destinies through nation states of their own.

PART IV

The Naturalistic Mind:
1865-1929

CHAPTER 12

||||||||||||||||||||||||||||||||||||||||||||||||||||||||||||||||||||||||||||||||||

The Naturalistic
Pattern of Thought

T HE NATURALISTIC MIND comprised a fairly well-defined bundle
of ideas held by many Americans between the Civil War and
the Great Depression of the 1930's. At no time during that period,
however, did naturalism completely dominate American thinking.
In terms of numbers of adherents, it was probably always in a minority; and since the Depression and the rise of totalitarianism in
Europe, its influence has suffered a sharp decline. But the naturalistic
mind exerted an influence out of proportion to the number of people
who shared its tenets, because it was identified chiefly with articulate
groups of the intelligentsia, such as journalists, literary men, business
spokesmen, and professors. Certain aspects of naturalism were formulated most clearly in the new universities, especially in the natural
sciences and in the newly emancipated disciplines that proudly
called themselves "social sciences."

But at no time did the tenets of naturalism hold uncontested sway
over American thinking. Throughout its lifespan, naturalism was
opposed by the continuing traditions of earlier nineteenth-century
democratic thought. The resulting intellectual controversies helped
to clarify the issues at the turn of the century. Because of its traditional affiliations and commitments, the democratic mind inevitably
resisted certain propositions of naturalism, especially those that bore

upon the conditions of human freedom. With the rise of totalitarian-ism on the international scene during the second quarter of the twentieth century, Americans confronted in practical form issues that they had been debating in the intellectual realm for over half a century. It was inevitable, therefore, that a majority of them should react strongly to totalitarianism on ideological grounds, and that, consequently, certain of the naturalistic ideas should acquire a pa-triotic as well as a moral stigma.

The Social Setting

The naturalistic mind was the first pattern of thought in America to reflect industrial conditions. It was not the product of industrialism alone, but its conceptions of man and society were inevitably colored by the impact of industrialism upon the human consciousness. The rate of increase of the population, so consistently a factor underly-ing previous patterns of thought, fell off sharply during this era. The geometric ratio of growth according to which the population doubled every twenty-five years faltered at about 1890, and thereafter the population, although it continued to increase steadily, did so at pro-gressively lower rates. Numbering over 38,000,000 in 1870, the popula-tion had not quite reached 123,000,000 by 1930.

In itself, however, the declining rate of growth was a less significant aspect of population trends than was the shift from preponderantly rural to urban conditions. Between the Civil War and the Great Depression, American civilization became essentially urban, a trans-formation that can be indicated only very imperfectly by citing the statistics. The U.S. Bureau of the Census, which generously classified populated places of 2500 or more as "urban," found 21 percent of the American people living in urban centers in 1870, while 79 percent were still rural. By 1930 the balance had shifted: 56 percent lived in towns and cities, while only 44 percent remained in the countryside. Earlier nineteenth-century democratic ideals had emerged in a rural environment, and it remained to be seen how extensively urban con-ditions would transform the prevailing intellectual temper and interests. Whatever the results, during this period the city well nigh sucked the life out of the rural regions. Compelling as were the fi-nancial and industrial attractions of the city, they scarcely compared with its intellectual attractions. And by the time of the Depression, the commercialized products of urban culture blanketed the countryside, from which practically every locally autonomous cultural institution had disappeared.

The social effects of urbanization were given a unique twist in the United States by immigration from foreign lands. There were 5,500,000 foreign-born residents in the country in 1870, most of them natives of northwestern Europe. They constituted about one seventh of the total population. The number of foreign born increased regularly to more than 14,000,000 in 1930. Before 1883, immigration derived largely from northwestern Europe, while after that year the principal source was southeastern Europe. Thus, during the decade 1871–1880, some 75 percent of the total immigration originated in the British Isles and Germany, while only 9 percent came from southeastern Europe. But by 1911–1920, only 14 percent came from the former countries, and 77 percent from the latter region. Six million of the 9,000,000 immigrants who entered the country during the first decade of the twentieth century came from southeastern Europe. World War I largely stopped interhemispheric migration. The 4,000,000 immigrants who entered the country in the decade after the war came in large part from other American countries. Recent investigation has dispelled the older assumption made by students of immigration that the so-called "new" immigrants from southeastern Europe after 1883 encountered more severe obstacles in adjusting to the conditions of American life than had their predecessors. Whatever the facts may have been, however, when we confine our attention to the realm of attitudes it remains true that opponents of immigration seized upon the changing character of immigration as the chief justification of their demand that it be terminated.

Although the percentage of foreign born in the total population regularly declined from 14.5 percent in 1870 to 11.5 percent in 1930 —if to those of foreign birth were added their children born in the United States, the so-called "second generation Americans," it appeared that in 1930 some 31.5 percent of the American people were first or second generation Americans, numbering over 39,500,000. The significance of these figures was revealed most strikingly in connection with the fact, well known to students of immigration, that the burden of adjustment to American life fell more heavily on the second generation than on the first. In clinging to their Old World habits and standards in a strange environment, the first-generation Americans succeeded in maintaining their sense of identity and morale. Their children, however, were pulled in opposite directions and frequently displayed characteristics of social maladjustment. The term *marginal man* was coined by sociologists to designate the ambiguous status of second-generation Americans. There were over 25,000,000 marginal men in the United States in 1930.

The geographical frontier that had been so significant a factor in earlier American history was replaced during this period by an industrial frontier. The criteria by which the industrial frontier was located were certainly no more arbitrary than the distribution of two persons to the square mile as chosen by the Census Bureau to designate the frontier of settlement. One such criterion was the value of manufactured product, which rose from 3⅓ billion dollars in 1870 to more than 70⅓ billion dollars in 1930. Nevertheless, the number of manufacturing establishments was still approximately the same at the end of the period as it had been at the beginning, or about 250,000 units. This was the result in part of larger and more efficient units of production, in part of monopolistic concentration. A preoccupation with monopoly control in industry and transportation became in fact one of the great popular political interests of the period. The characteristics and ideology of the traditional economic individualism that survived in the late nineteenth century, especially in rural regions, made the antimonopoly movement inevitable. And although twentieth-century advocates of economic planning and social control frequently were to be found in the antimonopoly ranks, the debate over monopoly was primarily a struggle between different types of capitalistic individualists.

Another aspect of concentration and monopoly under industrial capitalism, although not always recognized as such, became apparent in the labor statistics. There were slightly more than 2,000,000 industrial wage earners in the United States in 1870. This number had increased to only 8,800,000 by 1930. Thus, while the value of industrial product was increasing by about twenty-fivefold the number of industrial wage earners increased only fourfold. Two important consequences stemmed from this situation. Contrary to the expectations of Marxists and others, industrial wage earners were not destined to become a majority of the population. Politically therefore they could become at most an organized bloc of voters with bargaining power. Labor could not expect to "vote in" extensive social changes by weight of numbers. On the other hand, because of the limited expansion of industrial employment opportunities it became potentially possible for a labor monopoly to emerge. This did not occur during the period, but whatever advance toward the effective organization of labor was made, especially among skilled workers on craft lines, pointed toward the emergence of a labor monopoly within the capitalistic framework, rather than toward control of the means of production by and in the interest of labor.

A bare summary of the statistics that indicate the growth of population and development of industry scarcely conveys a sense of the bewilderment, confusion, and disillusionment—at least among more sensitive minds—that accompanied these changes. In the place of the older agrarian civilization there appeared within the space of a generation a rootless and chaotic society, largely devoid of traditions of place, class, or stable institutions. The naturalists felt the full impact of these circumstances, and their thinking cannot be appreciated except in the context of phenomenally rapid social changes.

In one respect, naturalism was the first reflexive reaction of American thinkers to the impact of mass cultural phenomena. But it was a reaction inevitably conditioned by their commitment to the democratic traditions of the older America which had nurtured them. This commitment compelled the naturalists to discharge their social responsibilities by attempting to understand and systematize the confusion that confronted them. They could not turn their backs upon it and retreat into the world of private interests, much as some of them (like Henry Adams) might have wished. Modern sociology is a democratic phenomenon in the sense that it probes with equal sympathy every social stratum and every aspect of the social process. The first major American sociologists were to be found in the ranks of the naturalists. The paradoxical mixture of scientific objectivity and passionate moralistic preachment which their thought characteristically displayed merely revealed ambiguous commitments that they were unable to resolve. The contempt and scorn for the democratic ideology in its more flamboyant forms that they frequently expressed were both a confession of its inevitability and a cry of pain at its failures. Ultimately, it was by means of the resolution of the naturalistic paradoxes that the pathway to the modern neodemocratic revival was to be found.

The Primacy of Natural Law

The naturalistic mind had a peculiar veneration for scientific fact as the most accurate, dependable, and valuable form of knowledge available to man. Scientific knowledge was objective and dispassionate and therefore true. In stressing the truth of scientific fact, the naturalists characteristically contrasted it with the myths, fables, fictions, dreams, or vague impressions of ignorant and selfish men. It was by every right, therefore, that science came to enjoy increasing prestige in the community during the later nineteenth century. Many of the most ardent proponents of this kind of scientism could not themselves be described as scientists in any strict sense of the term; they were merely devotees of a method and a point of view that they believed held the key to a better life.

The earlier naturalists in the years after the Civil War were complacently optimistic because they were confident that scientific truth would gradually replace the accumulated errors and superstitions of the past. Because knowledge was power and power was good and good meant progress, they were under strong compulsion to take an optimistic view of human prospects, even if other aspects of the naturalistic outlook suggested a rather different conclusion. Although science was essentially technique, men had faith in the capacity of these techniques for practical accomplishment. All Americans were conditioned to the activist virtue of practical achievement. Consequently, it was almost inevitable that a scientific outlook should be identified with—or confused with—positive values.

Because they professed to prize verified fact most highly and to distrust speculation, the naturalists tended to be unaware of their underlying assumptions as well as of their debts to the past. Consistency of outlook on the broader questions of life was not one of their virtues. Among their ranks were to be found optimists and pessimists, determinists and believers in free agency, democrats and authoritarians, humanists and theists.

In postulating the primacy of natural law, the naturalists placed themselves in a major American intellectual tradition. But their understanding of this concept and its implications were distinctively modern. Their cosmology was compounded out of the nebular hypothesis of Kant and Laplace, the uniformitarian geology of Lyell, and the organic evolution of Darwin. It assumed universal change under natural law. A century earlier enlightened thinkers had also started with natural law, but at least two important differences distinguished these usages. First, the universe of the Enlightenment was a static one, while that of the newer naturalism was dynamic. For the latter, the basic natural law was the law of evolution. Second, when the enlightened thinker shifted his attention from the physical realm to the social, he transformed his natural laws into natural rights. The modern naturalists, on the other hand, more rigorously carried natural law into the social realm and insisted upon its coercive power over man and society.

The aspect of natural law particularly intriguing to the naturalistic mind was the law of organic evolution, according to which all forms of life were held to be undergoing a gradual transformation or development. The controversies over evolution that for so long occupied the center of attention were in fact only a phase of a much larger conflict of ideas, and they were not always an adequate guide to the nature of that conflict, especially when controversy was precipitated by such an issue as religious fundamentalism.

Naturalists also stressed the universality of natural law as it pertained alike to problems in the physical, biological, and social realms. Since the same law operated in each of these areas, the connections between them were intimate, and transitions were made directly and without difficulty. It was as though the distinction between the social and the biological had been made for some mere practical convenience and was without any basis in fact. Consequently, the naturalist believed it possible to reduce relatively complex social phenomena to relatively simple biological terms, and these, in turn, to even simpler physical and mechanical terms, and by so reducing to understand them. This assumption may be understood by bearing in mind the close affinity between the natural order, the moral order, and the social order in earlier democratic thought. Naturalists perpetuated this assumption, but they subordinated the moral and social orders to the natural.

Whether or not such reductionism contributed to the understanding of human and social problems, it is certain that the coherence of reality assumed by naturalism reinforced the primacy of natural law in its coercive power over the individual. There were no loopholes or interstices in life—or very few. William James, one of the most vigorous critics of naturalism, described the world of the naturalists as a "block universe." Perhaps their major practical problem was to determine the role of the individual in a world governed by natural law. In general, they found very little scope for human freedom. Man was obliged to act out his role in society within the narrow limits of restraints (variously designated as folkways, mores, institutions) over which he had no control. One of their most characteristic contributions was the insistence of naturalists that the individual is the creature of his society. Much of their sociology rested upon this insight. The sociologist William Graham Sumner is sometimes assumed to have espoused moral relativism with his dictum: "the mores make anything right." But this was the scholar's observation; for the practical man it meant that what is, is right because what is, is what has to be.

The very limited freedom man possessed was to be realized in direct proportion to his understanding of the limitations of his situation. Only by knowledge of the social and natural forces impinging upon him did man learn how to maneuver among them and achieve limited objectives, namely, the immediate securities and satisfactions that any solvent society has to offer. In short, there was assumed to be a close correlation between freedom and intelligence. But, unfortunately, the naturalists invented the intelligence test, and they became acutely aware of the abysmal ignorance of the vast mass of humanity. Consequently, their thinking displayed little of that faith in the natural man that had come to characterize American thought, and they were obliged to stand upon a thoroughgoing repudiation of the traditional doctrine of the free individual.

A characteristic emphasis upon the primacy of natural law was sounded in a book by John W. Draper, *Thoughts on the Future Civil Policy of America,* published in 1865 at the conclusion of the Civil War and the beginning of the naturalistic era. Draper was born and educated in England, migrating to the United States in the 1830's. A man of encyclopedic interests, Draper worked in the fields of medicine, chemistry, and physics, rising to the presidency of the medical school of New York University in 1850. His lecture before the British Association for the Advancement of Science in 1860, in which he set forth his evolutionary views, elicited the celebrated exchange between Bishop Wilberforce and Thomas Henry Huxley concerning the latter's alleged descent from the apes. Events such as this drew Draper's attention to philosophical and historical problems, and he subsequently published his histories of the intellectual development of Europe and of the conflict between religion and science.

Draper insisted that natural law controlled the social process just as effectively as it governed the bodily growth of the individual organism. The historian, by relying upon the immutable laws of nature, should be able to predict the inevitable course of human affairs as surely as the astronomer predicted the path of a comet. It was especially important at that moment for Americans to grasp this principle, since they were moving rapidly into an era of extensive social changes. Among the natural laws that determined the life courses of nations Draper specified the influence of climate, the effects of immigration, the political force of ideas, and the "natural course" of national development. Then he blandly added that there were also many other laws, which he did not bother to specify.

The Social Organism

The analogy between human society and a biological organism was one of the more prominent elements of naturalistic thought. By conceiving of the structure of society as analogous to the parts of an organism, naturalists assumed that a clarification of problems and perspective would be achieved. In fact, however, the organic analogy served a useful purpose only in a form so attenuated as to be practically meaningless. But it did accentuate the strong functional flavor of naturalistic social theory. In historiography, the organic analogy suggested a teleological interpretation of history, a point of view emphasizing the realization of an implicit historical destiny that was already well established in American historical thought by the middle of the nineteenth century. It also suggested the study of the history of institutions as a genetic development rather than as the result of the impingement of causal factors mechanically conceived.

The theory of the social organism bulked large in early naturalistic social thought, and it is possible that Herbert Spencer was chiefly responsible for it. Spencer's influence and prestige in America during the late nineteenth century was so great that it is difficult to sketch the history of American thought during that time without noticing his leading ideas. Many of the American naturalists attributed their intellectual awakening to his books. William James observed with a mixture of contempt and envy that Spencer was the philosopher of all those who read no other philosopher. Nevertheless, when he organized at Harvard his pioneer course in physiological psychology, James used Spencer's *Psychology* as a text. John R. Commons, the labor economist, recalled that he had been brought up in Indiana on "Hoosierism, Republicanism, Presbyterianism, and Spencerism." William Graham Sumner used Spencer's *Study of Sociology* as a text at Yale in spite of presidential opposition due, apparently, to Spencer's materialism. A whole generation of literary men, including Hamlin Garland, Jack London, Edgar Lee Masters, and Theodore Dreiser, were indoctrinated with Spencer.

Evolution was the central theme that unified Spencer's encyclopedic survey of human knowledge. He was an evolutionist before Darwin, having sketched the outlines of his system in essays published during the 1850's. Although Darwin borrowed from him the phrase "survival of the fittest," Spencer was not a Darwinian natural selectionist. His conception of evolution owed more to the physical principle of the conservation of energy than to the Darwinian principle of random variations. In what has aptly been described as a famous piece of English lexicography, Spencer defined the process as follows: "Evolution is an integration of matter and concomitant dissipation of motion; during which the matter passes from an indefinite incoherent homogeneity to a definite coherent heterogeneity; and during which the retained motion undergoes a parallel transformation." The definition presupposed a materialistic universe composed of matter and energy.

The evolutionary process as Spencer conceived it had a definite goal: the utmost differentiation of matter into coherent heterogeneous aggregates. At the biological level, including mankind, this differentiation was occurring by means of the struggle for existence and survival of the fittest. Entailing as it did personal hardship and suffering for many, this struggle must nevertheless be accepted as part of an ultimately beneficent process. In his *Social Statics* (1850), Spencer observed sententiously that "the poverty of the incapable, the distresses that come upon the imprudent, the starvation of the idle, and those shoulderings aside of the weak by the strong, which leave so many 'in shallows and in miseries,' are the decrees of a large, farseeing benevolence. . . . It seems hard that widows and orphans should be left to struggle for life or death. Nevertheless, when regarded not separately, but in connection with the interests of universal humanity, these harsh fatalities are seen to be full of the highest beneficence. . . ." Although progress, or social evolution, occurred by means of struggle for survival Spencer did not appear to regard it as any the less certain in its outcome. "Progress is not an accident but a necessity. What we call evil and immorality must disappear. It is certain that man must become perfect."

The naturalistic idea of evolutionary social development accomplished through suffering and death suggests an interesting similarity in the basic patterns of Spencerism and Marxism: an inevitable progression to the good achieved through struggle. Marxism in Europe came eventually to supersede Spencerism as the prevailing naturalistic social philosophy. In America, on the other hand, Marxism never achieved comparable influence.

Since Spencer thought of himself as a scientist rather than as a prophet he did not furnish in any detail the blueprint of the good society of the future that would be appropriate to a perfected humanity. But there were hints of it in his discussion of the social organism. In the twentieth century, his vision would be called totalitarianism. Spencer used the analogy of the biological organism to illuminate his analysis of social problems by indicating appropriate parallels. Human society was like an organism. Its individual members were analogous to the cells of the body. Like the organism, society had specialized functions. Arteries of commerce corresponded to the circulatory system; communications networks were analogous to the nervous system; the processing and consumption of foodstuffs corresponded to the functions of the alimentary tract; the formulation of public policy, to the functions of the brain. While these analogies might not strike a later generation as especially useful or ingenious, it is well to note their implications for social theory. They indicated a new sense of the differentiation of functions in modern society, their interdependence, and a felt need for the subordination of various social processes to the whole. Politically, the organic analogy suggested a repudiation of the traditional compact theory and of natural rights.

Society itself, of course, was evolving along with the rest of the universe. Society in its nineteenth-century condition was most closely analogous to a relatively primitive, undifferentiated type of organism. Spencer himself suggested one of the colonial organisms, such as *volvox,* where specialized cells and functions were beginning to appear but where each cell was still capable of participating in most if not all the life functions. The first requisite of a sound social science was to establish accurately the position of the social organism in the social evolutionary scale at the moment of investigation. Having professed to have done this for his own society, Spencer indicated that the relatively undifferentiated character of the social organism in his own day entailed free competition among individuals as the proper form of social action.

It was of the highest importance that these identifications be made accurately because society was a natural growth, changing according to the universal law of evolution. If ignorant men interfered with its growth, they did so at their peril. Social reformers, do-gooders, and other well-intentioned but ignorant people could do great harm by irresponsibly interfering with social evolutionary processes. Spencer's polemical writings were directed toward this danger. He was particularly exercised over welfare and public-service legislation. But Spencer did not provide precise criteria for the measurement of social evolutionary change, and in their absence his enthusiasm for rugged individualism got the better of him. His only visit to the United States occurred in 1882, when he found competitive enterprise rapidly evolving into monopoly with what might well have seemed appropriate Spencerian spontaneity. Yet he distressed his American disciples profoundly by calling in the reporters and announcing that no such thing would be allowed in England; the state would preserve competitive enterprise by breaking up the monopolies!

In the final analysis, however, in the Spencerian system competitive individualism was clearly but a passing phase of a social evolutionary process. The biological analogy of the struggle for existence was pertinent to the social evolutionary stage in which the naturalists found themselves, and as such it provided a currently authoritative guide for action. But it would be a mistake to assign too inclusive a scope to the principle in reconstructing naturalistic social theory. Students who have recently popularized the term *Social Darwinism* and identified it with the Spencerian school have committed this error by stressing the struggle for existence without indicating clearly the social evolutionary limits within which the concept was restricted. The ultimate anticipations of the naturalists looked toward an integrated society in which there would be no place for competitive individualism as currently understood.

Some of the implications of the organismic theory were developed by John W. Draper. He pointed out that the analogy between the life of the individual organism and that of the nation rested upon a structural similarity. In each, the constituent parts underwent unceasing change. As a physiologist, Draper knew that the death and elimination of cells of the body was the condition of the very life of the organism. A human being weighing 140 pounds took in and discharged some one and a half tons of material annually. Similarly, national survival presupposed the life and death of individuals. The analogy extended to a similarity in the life cycles of individuals and of nations. Each alike must pass through the successive stages of infancy, youth, maturity, and old age. This progression was due, not to the operation of moral laws as an eighteenth-century thinker might have said, but to the physical laws of nature. Life itself was a ceaseless ebb and flow between the organic and the inorganic. One might like to think that the higher organisms were emancipated from the direct control of nature's laws, but this was not to be.

Social evolution, like biological evolution, entailed the increasing differentiation of parts. A growing society was becoming ever more specialized in its various functions and diversified in its requirements of skill and aptitude. Draper insisted, therefore, that equality as a permanent social ideal or objective was absurd. Some must do the menial work, and others, the skilled, responsible, and remunerative work. Given such diversified requirements, true equality was impossible and undesirable. In China, for instance, where the densest population and the most stable government in the world was to be found, intellectual superiority had long conferred the right to rule. Americans, said Draper, in whom the instinct of self-government was strong, were inclined to forget that self-government implied self-restraints voluntarily or spontaneously imposed. Social discipline in Europe was imposed both by moral standards and by force. In America, the force of voluntary self-discipline was exerted chiefly through the appeal to self-interest. In this manner, Americans had, at least momentarily, solved the dilemma of liberty and authority. But however achieved, discipline was mandatory. By thus paying his respects to the economy and efficiency of the current American mode of adjustment, Draper was able to avoid the less palatable compulsive implications of his organic approach to political theory. But these implications were readily apparent in his discussion. They portended a future in which, as population increased and resources dwindled, Americans must inevitably accept increasing measures of regimentation and sharper social distinctions.

The Cultural Anthropological Scale

Because of its evolutionary orientation, naturalistic social theory attached great importance to a proper understanding of the course of social evolution through which mankind had passed in arriving at its current civilized condition. The idea of progress still permeated the intellectual atmosphere in the years after the Civil War, and the earlier naturalists generally incorporated it into their conceptions of social evolution. Only gradually did the tide of events and changing moods in the twentieth century lead later naturalists to abandon progress as a fond delusion.

Thanks largely to the strength of the evolutionary interest, the professional study of anthropology developed rapidly. The most influential of the evolutionary anthropologists among Americans was Lewis Henry Morgan. A native of New York State and educated as a lawyer, Morgan discovered his anthropological interests through personal contacts with the remnants of the Iroquois, to whom he furnished legal aid. In 1878, he published his *Ancient Society,* in which he generalized upon his detailed researches to set forth a comprehensive theory of social evolution.

Surveying the whole history of the human species as far back as knowledge of it was to be gleaned from surviving artifacts, Morgan distinguished seven successive epochs or cultural stages. These stages marked in invariant order the path to the present that humanity had traversed from remote antiquity. The earliest of the stages was designated the Lower Status of Savagery. It terminated with the use of fire and the introduction of fish as food. The Middle Status of Savagery prevailed until the discovery of the bow and arrow. The Upper Status of Savagery ended with the use of pottery. The fourth stage was designated the Lower Status of Barbarism. In the eastern hemisphere, it terminated with the domestication of animals; in the western, with maize culture and irrigation. The Middle Status of Barbarism ended with the smelting of iron ore; and Upper Barbarism with the invention of the phonetic alphabet. The practice of writing had introduced the latest stage, civilization.

It is noteworthy that the distinguishing criteria by which Morgan marked the transitions to higher cultural stages were broadly technological in character. The assignment of a primary role to technological innovation was a fundamental characteristic of naturalistic social thought. Morgan also assumed that cultural stages were cumulative in character; each must succeed its predecessor in the order indicated. A survey of the world's cultures showed that, at each stage of social evolutionary advance, certain societies were apparently incapable of making further progress up the cultural scale. Many such societies had disintegrated, to be known only through archaeological research;

others survived for considerable periods of time in a static condition, ripe for destruction at the hands of a more vigorous invader. Only a few societies had achieved the status of civilization. Of these, the European peoples alone had displayed the degree of technological ingenuity that promised future social evolutionary advance. Thus Morgan provided a cultural anthropological scale against which the social accomplishments of a given society might be measured. That the criteria employed were calculated to work to the decisive advantage of his own society was perhaps not surprising in view of the optimistic self-assurance prevailing in Morgan's day, and in which he fully participated.

The anthropological account of historical cultural development was a late version of the positivistic interpretation of history, of which the classic statement had been made earlier in the century by the French philosopher Auguste Comte. While Comte and the later anthropologists did not always use the same terminology, in both cases history was viewed as a progressive development of institutions and ideas, owed, in the last analysis, to the emergent activity of the reason. The primary role played by technology in initiating epochal innovations as analyzed by Morgan was to be understood as the practical application of the rational faculty to the solution of tangible difficulties, resulting in more efficient tools and methods. The emergence of civilization was a triumph of the practical reason.

Not unrelated to the emphasis upon reason was the important function assigned by many naturalists to the instincts. Instinct psychologies were a peculiar feature of naturalism. In general, the "reason" of the earlier naturalists, a deliberate and self-conscious mental activity, tended to give way to instinctual behavior. Conduct patterned by instinctual impulses was certainly more appropriate to the realistic and detached view of the human situation that became increasingly characteristic of later naturalistic thought. In the writings of Thorstein Veblen, the greatest of the naturalistic anthropologists, the same constructive functions are assigned to the instincts, especially the instincts of workmanship and idle curiosity, that more positivistic thinkers had assigned to the reason.

The theory of instinctual behavior was readily adapted to the positivistic conception of social change with its strong purposive and teleological animus. The developmental character of the historical process could then be explained in terms of the working out of instinctual proclivities. This was the essence of Veblen's theory of history. At the same time, the force of instinct gave a ready explanation of the nonrational character of routine behavior. Instinct was a conservative force, accounting for the persistence of the habits and inertia that moderated the rate of social change. The theory of instinct played an important part in the naturalistic attack upon the older prevailing hedonistic psychology according to which men were presumed to seek their satisfactions with means both cunningly contrived and essentially enlightened.

Differential Social Change

The organic theory of society implied a fixed functional relationship between the various institutions and activities of the social community. The most important of these relationships became explicit in the naturalistic theory of social change. For clarity of statement, it is convenient to shift momentarily from the analogy of organism to the analogy of structure.

Naturalistic social theory pictured social reality as consisting of a structure of several levels. The bottom or basic level was composed of the technological or industrial means by which the society converted nature's resources to social uses. Naturalists were exceedingly conscious of the great importance of the relationship between society and its material environment. Every other social arrangement depended ultimately upon it. Social evolutionary advance was presumed to depend upon the increasing effectiveness of technology. Only insofar as any society could exploit its material resources more effectively through technological improvements could it expect to experience social progress.

The community utilized its material resources through economic institutions. These constituted the second structural level, related most intimately to the technology. Together, the technological and economic levels comprised the material culture of the community. Upon them rose the nonmaterial superstructure, a series of levels composed of political and legal institutions and practices, artistic and intellectual activities, convivial and recreational interests, and religion. The presumed dependence of these nonmaterial aspects of life upon the industrial and economic bases testified to the pervasive materialism of the naturalistic mind.

The theory of differential social change assumed the intimate interdependence of cultural elements in accordance with the foregoing order of priorities. The organic analogy and the reductionist method of social analysis were both appropriate to this point of view. All constructive social changes were presumed to originate in technological innovations. These innovations induced economic transformations, which, in turn, elicited political adjustments. Slowest to change were attitudes and convictions. To reverse this natural relationship of dependence on material changes and attempt to initiate social changes at, say, the political level was regarded by naturalists as at once useless and dangerous. A major object of their scorn was the well-intended but giddy reformer whose ignorance of the law of differential social change led him to injurious tinkering with the social organism.

As the term itself implies, the theory of differential change held that the different parts or levels of society changed at different rates, depending upon their proximity to or remoteness from the prime source of change in the technology. Economic practices were most immediately responsive to industrial innovations, while peripheral aspects of culture, such as the fine arts or religion, were most tardy in their response. No naturalist undertook to formulate precise criteria for the measurement of differential changes or to produce a law of social change applicable to concrete situations. Many of them, in fact, were not apparently conscious of holding a theory of social change that could be as arbitrarily formulated as reconstructed here. But it was nevertheless the pervasive assumption respecting the nature of change in the naturalistic era, and a good many people adopted it who could not in other respects be identified as naturalists.

The closest approximation to a formal statement of the theory of differential social change finally appeared in 1922, when the sociologist William Fielding Ogburn published his *Social Change.* Here the analysis of cultural levels was made explicit. Ogburn distinguished between the material culture, consisting of the technological and economic levels, and the nonmaterial culture, the upper levels dependent on the material. Within the nonmaterial culture, he further distinguished between adaptive and nonadaptive elements. The adaptive culture was composed of the institutions, customs, and beliefs most immediately related to and dependent upon the material culture. Ogburn cited political and legal institutions as illustrative of this category. And within it there were, in turn, degrees of responsiveness to material circumstances. On the line between the adaptive and nonadaptive culture were the domestic institutions, or familial practices. Finally, as illustrative of nonadaptive culture, most remote from the material base of society, Ogburn specified religion. Deliberately or unconsciously, all naturalists similarly analyzed social problems in terms of the relative dependence and responsiveness of specific institutions to the ultimate sources of change.

To designate the lapse of time that occurred between the invention of a new material artifact or technique and the adaptive response of the nonmaterial culture to it, Ogburn coined the term *cultural lag*. In general, the duration of lag was a function of the relative position in the social structure of the institutional practice or custom under consideration. Economic practices presumably responded rather promptly to technological innovation. But in the nonadaptive social superstructure, the lag of response to basic changes might be very great; Veblen, for example, cited a specific instance of a lag of five hundred years as though it was in no way unusual.

Although it remained for Ogburn to coin the term, the phenomenon of cultural lag as he defined it was recognized by all the naturalists. And for all of them it was important because it was a symptom of maladjustment. The implicit major assumption of naturalistic social theory was that progress was realized by closing the gaps between changing material culture and lagging adaptive institutions. In times of rapid technological innovation, such as the late nineteenth and early twentieth centuries, such an approach to social analysis seemed so appropriate that explicit theoretical formulation was unnecessary. Evidences of cultural lag lay about one on every hand. Naturalists specialized in their analysis, and in a sense became experts in sociopathology. The skepticism and pessimism of the movement, especially in its later phases, may be attributed in large part to its preoccupation with these maladjustments.

When, with the lapse of years, it became possible to view the naturalistic era with a measure of detachment, it became apparent that its assumptions were quite arbitrary. Why should one assume the dependence of culture upon technology? Why should the phenomenon of differential change be regarded as evidence of maladjustment? In quest of the answers we may return again to the organic analogy. The appeal of the analogy was undoubtedly owed to its presupposition of a closely knit and interdependent society, in many respects the antithesis of the burgeoning confusion of the early industrial era. To the naturalist, the ideal society was the opposite in most respects of the world in which he lived. It was a society of order and stability, characterized by ethnic homogeneity and the close interdependence of men and institutions. Evolutionary theory assigned an important function to the adaptations to environment effected by organisms. These adaptations were the touchstone by which favorable variations were appraised. The evolutionary significance of a new variation was found in its capacity to afford the organism a new and more fruitful adaptation to its environment. In short, the analogy of organism with its adaptive capacities suggested a closely integrated society in which useful variations (technological inventions) effected prompt adaptations (industrial innovations) and consequent readjustments throughout the body of society. In the biological organism, these readjustments were an integral part of the new adaptation. But in the social organism, the integrative response to the new adaptation was embarrassingly tardy; hence cultural lag.

The elements of the naturalistic theory of social organization and change became widely disseminated in modern thought. The presumed order of priority of social changes originating in the productive process became the source of the pervasive modern assumption that thought merely reflects material conditions and is substantially helpless to alter the natural social relationships determined by these conditions. This, perhaps, explains the paradoxical attitude of Americans who hail the inventor and industrial innovator, no matter how revolutionary the implications of the innovations, but who are profoundly suspicious of social reformers and politicians who offer plausible blueprints for a better social order. Many years later, in discussing the Depression of the 1930's in which the naturalistic era dissolved, the economist J. K. Galbraith neatly caught a typical naturalistic distinction when he observed that "if a man seeks to design a better mousetrap he is the soul of enterprise; if he seeks to design a better society he is a crackpot."

CHAPTER 13

||||||||||||||||||||||||||||||||||||||||||||||||||||||||||||||||||||||||||||

Evolution

T HEORIES OF EVOLUTION occupied a prominent place in the
naturalistic mind because they purported to explain change,
the sense of which was so pervasive in the late nineteenth century.
A measure of critical detachment from the traditional intellectual
loyalties of their contemporaries was characteristic of the naturalists,
and consequently they welcomed the controversies aroused by evolutionism as a convenient means of separating the sheep from the goats.
Naturalists made evolution their battle cry and identified themselves
as partners of the scientists who were engaged in discovering the laws
of the biological world.

It would be a mistake, however, to assume that the naturalists themselves fully grasped the implications of evolution and incorporated
them in a thoroughgoing philosophy of change. The latter task
awaited their principal critics, the pragmatists. With the passage of
time, it became increasingly apparent that the naturalists were unwilling to accept the full implications of the theory of evolution for
social life. Because they imposed upon the evolutionary process their
own hopes and expectations, they were unable to take more than the
first halting steps toward a durable science of social change.

Biological Evolution

American thought in the years after the Civil War felt the full impact of evolutionary ideas largely as the result of the controversies surrounding the work of the celebrated English scientist Charles Darwin, who published his *Origin of Species* in 1859. Darwin's chief contribution was to amass a tremendous volume of data in several related scientific fields purporting to show a gradual evolutionary transformation of life forms. This was by no means a novel idea. For a century prior to Darwin's work, the evolutionary hypothesis had been widely discussed in scientific and educated circles. Americans themselves had played a significant part in this discussion. But the weight of Darwin's evidence was so great that it was no longer necessary to regard evolution as an unconfirmed hypothesis; to many scientists and laymen the fact was at once established, and although several distinguished scientists of Darwin's own generation stubbornly refused to acknowledge the validity of the new principle, after their passing the scientific and intellectual worlds were for all practical purposes united in agreement. The data was of a technical character, but it entitled Darwin to a secure position of eminence in the history of ideas.

At the same time that he presented his evidence to show that evolution did occur, Darwin also offered his own theory as to the cause of the process. He called it natural selection. In the heated controversies following the publication of his book, the facts themselves and Darwin's own hypothesis as to their cause were hopelessly confused. The confusion has been perpetuated by the practice of scientists who have attached the name of its formulator to the theory of natural selection, calling it Darwinism.

Yet one must carefully distinguish the facts of evolution from Darwin's effort to account for them by one of the many causal theories of evolution. With admirable candor, Darwin himself acknowledged that the theory came to him one evening while thumbing over a copy of Malthus's *Essay on Population*. Malthus had held that because of its natural fecundity the human population always presses upon the limits of the supporting power of the environment. Three great forces effectively eliminate the excess of population, namely, famine, pestilence, and war. It occurred to Darwin that here was a theory of selection operating among human beings, which, if broadened to apply to all forms of life, would unify and organize the data of evolutionary changes that he had long been collecting.

Darwin's theory of natural selection may be stated in terms of three principles. (1) From Malthus had come the realization of the significance of the prodigality of life. Organisms reproduce in far greater volume than can be sustained by the environment. Consequently, they will inevitably engage in a struggle for survival. (2) There is universal variation among organisms, no two individuals being precisely alike. At the same time, the peculiar characteristics of each individual are susceptible of hereditary transmission to its offspring. These were purely empirical observations. Darwin readily admitted that he knew nothing of the real nature of variation or of the mechanisms of heredity, although he later propounded some fanciful theories on the subject. (3) In the consequent struggle for survival among dissimilar organisms, those variations proving most advantageous enabled their possessors to survive and transmit their advantages to their offspring, while the less fortunately endowed perished. Such natural selection operating through countless generations was powerful enough, in Darwin's opinion, to produce all the myriad forms of life that have existed.

The theory of evolution by natural selection exercised much the same kind of fascination over the minds of naturalistic thinkers as the image of the Newtonian world machine had exerted upon the men of the Enlightenment. But Darwinism appeared to be much richer in its capacity to suggest analogies and images intriguing to the imaginations of speculative people. This was especially true in the earlier phases of the naturalistic epoch when the romantic mood of mid-nineteenth-century democratic society lingered on to invest the evolutionary formulas with a sentimental coloring derived, perhaps, from the older ideas of mission well established in American society at that time. The idea of a struggle for survival was congenial enough to those who were complacently persuaded that they were destined to emerge triumphant. Even the scientists themselves were not immune to the temptation to sentimentalize over the very laws they were attempting to define. Darwin concluded the *Origin of Species* with the following eloquent peroration:

It is interesting to contemplate a tangled bank, clothed with many plants of many kinds, with birds singing on the bushes, with various insects flitting about, and with worms crawling through the damp earth, and to reflect that these elaborately constructed forms, so different from each other, and dependent upon each other in so complex a manner, have all been produced by laws acting around us. These laws, taken in the largest sense, being Growth with Reproduction; Inheritance which is almost implied by Reproduction; Variability from the indirect and direct action of the conditions of life, and from use and disuse: a Ratio of Increase so high as to lead to a Struggle for Life, and as a consequence to Natural Selection, entailing Divergence of Character and the Extinction of less-improved forms. Thus, from the war of nature, from famine and death, the most exalted object which we are capable of conceiving, namely, the production of the higher animals, directly follows. There is grandeur in this view of life, with its several powers, having been originally breathed by the Creator into a few forms or into one; and that, whilst this planet has gone cycling on according to the fixed law of gravity, from so simple a beginning endless forms most beautiful and most wonderful have been, and are being evolved.

The semimystical overtones frequently found in the writings of the early naturalists are readily apparent in this passage. A central Christian insight had been contained in the Scriptural injunction, "whoso would gain his life must lose it," a dictum confirmed by the miracle of the Resurrection. The naturalist was similarly persuaded that "from the war of nature, from famine and death, the most exalted object which we are capable of conceiving, namely, the production of the higher animals, directly follows. There is grandeur in this view of life. . . ." It seemed as though the unique Christian miracle had been universalized as the very law of nature.

In America, the furor over Darwinism served to call the attention of many people to issues that had been under discussion among scholars for over half a century. In the absence of the scientific specialization that later came to prevail, the field where the problems of evolution were of the most immediate concern was natural history. The domain of natural history was a generous one, including biology and everything from physical anthropology and archaeology to geology as well. In all these areas, problems impinging upon the possibility of evolutionary transformation had received some study, but the most concentrated attention had focused upon anthropology and especially upon the nature of racial differences among men. Evolutionists have always recognized race formation to be an incipient stage of speciation. From that point of view, therefore, discussions of race differences led inevitably to a consideration of the causal factors in evolutionary change. Specimens of the three great human stocks—Caucasian, Negroid, and Mongolian—were comparatively accessible to Americans for study. Without always realizing the significance of their work, the early students of race in America were laying a firm foundation for a consideration of evolutionary theories as such.

Among them may be noted here Samuel Stanhope Smith, son-in-law of John Witherspoon and successor to him as president of the College of New Jersey. Smith published in 1787, the year of the Constitutional Convention, an *Essay on the Causes of the Variety of Complexion and Figure in the Human Species*. Here he argued that racial differences were the product of the adaptation of various groups of men to differing climates, foods, and modes of life. He carefully restricted the operation of these factors to race formation within the human species. Species themselves were held to be the creations of God and immutable. In spite of this qualification, however, Smith employed one of the most famous of the causal explanations of the evolutionary process, that of adaptation to peculiar environmental conditions. Another early student of race was a Charleston, South Carolina, physician, William C. Wells, who anticipated Darwin by calling attention to the parallel between the selective breeding practiced by the stockraiser and the natural selection by which nature fashioned races suited to their native habitats.

A controversy among geologists during the 1840's and 1850's also played a part in preparing for the reception of Darwinism. Sir Charles Lyell, a distinguished British geologist, the first American edition of whose *Principles of Geology* had been published in 1837, propounded what was called the uniformitarian view that the formation of the earth's physical features had resulted from the operation of physical forces uniformly at work from the beginning to the present time. Because of the difficulty of reconciling uniformitarianism with the account of the creation in Genesis, American geologists, many of whom happened to be clergymen, generally subscribed to the opposing school of catastrophists. Led by President Edward Hitchcock of Amherst College, the catastrophists emphasized the distinctive character of successive geological epochs, which they identified with creative acts of God. Darwin himself looked to Lyell as one of his chief mentors, and it would, indeed, have been difficult to reconcile an organic evolutionary theory based solely on natural selection with a catastrophic geology.

The acrimonious controversy in the United States aroused by Darwin's book cannot be understood entirely in terms of the religious and scientific issues it raised, or yet in terms of the natural resistance of people of conservative temperament to the radical reorientation of outlook that it entailed. It was, in part at least, the overt expression of a struggle for institutional power between a vested interest, religion, and an aspiring and vigorous new enterprise, professionally organized science. The course of the struggle can be traced in its impact upon the form and character of collegiate educational institutions in America.

The liberal arts college of the early nineteenth century had never excluded the sciences from its curriculum, but it held them firmly within the embrace of the over-all scholastic outlook. The student received a smattering of physics, chemistry, geology, and natural history—but only a smattering. One "major" only was available: the liberal arts, heavily weighted with the classical languages and moral philosophy. After the spread of scientific interests during the early nineteenth century, accompanied as it was by the rapid growth of scientific societies and professional associations, the time inevitably came when scientists in the colleges insisted upon intellectual independence from an academic outlook intimately associated with traditional religious views and specifically affiliated with the static conception of the universe that had resulted from the fusion of Newtonian mechanics with the natural religion of design. The theory of evolution, and especially Darwinism, came conveniently to the hands of scientists as a weapon in their struggle for institutional influence and prestige. They had merely to insist upon their right to pursue the truth wherever it might lead to place the clerical academic authorities in an embarrassing dilemma.

The first result of the scientific declaration of academic independence was the formation of separate scientific and technical schools: Rensselaer Polytechnic Institute (1824), the Lawrence Scientific School (1847), the Sheffield Scientific School (1858). During the decade of the 1860's alone, some twenty-five scientific schools were founded. The eventual settlement, however, took the form of a compromise. Universities were organized, and scientific schools or divisions were incorporated within them, enjoying a large measure of institutional autonomy and complete intellectual independence. Within the liberal arts college itself, an ideal solution was found in the free elective system of studies. In these circumstances, the scholastic rationale of the old liberal arts college quietly expired, to be replaced by the intellectual anarchy of modern educational institutions.

Perhaps the most important immediate effect of evolutionism upon prevailing American thought patterns was the challenge that it presented to the theory of design in nature. Many scientists as well as religious people believed in the doctrine of design. The Harvard geologist and paleontologist Louis Agassiz, perhaps the best-known American scientist of his day, clung firmly to the doctrine of design until his death in 1873. His Harvard colleague, the botanist Asa Gray, attempted to reconcile natural selection with design, but a theory of design sufficiently tolerant to comprehend the mechanisms of natural selection offered cold comfort to those for whom design represented a universe of order and purpose. In the end, the theory of design was a major casualty of the conflict, rarely surviving except in religious circles.

As the smoke from the controversy over evolution as a process of nature began to dissipate, it became increasingly apparent to scientists that there were serious theoretical difficulties in the way of the theory of natural selection. Objections centered upon Darwin's conception of random variation among individuals of a species. Darwin had assumed that it was upon these variations as transmitted by heredity that natural selection operated. It was relatively easy, however, to test this assumption by controlled breeding experiments with rapidly reproducing organisms, in which the investigator selected a specified character for amplification in successive generations. The results of such experiments showed, not a continuous modification of character as Darwin had supposed, but rather, after a few generations, an embarrassing reversion to approximately the original form. Clearly, Darwin's theory of observable variation as the basis of evolutionary modification was inadequate. Again, as the record of fossil forms was rapidly filled out in the later years of the century, several impressive instances of straight-line developmental or ortho-evolutionary fossil series were discovered that seemed difficult to reconcile with the theory of natural selection acting upon random variations. As a result of difficulties of this sort with natural-selection theory, an influential group of American scientists at the end of the century reverted to an older and discredited evolutionary theory, that of the French naturalist Jean Baptiste Lamarck.

The American leaders of Neo-Lamarckism were the Philadelphia paleontologist Edward Drinker Cope and the biologists Alpheus Hyatt and A. S. Packard. Their theory was more complicated than natural selection, partly because it attempted to explain the origin of individual variations, a matter that Darwinism merely took for granted. Environmental changes in temperature, climate, food, or habitat were believed to be capable of producing changes, directly or indirectly, in organisms experiencing them. The use or disuse of organs or limbs by the creature itself were also believed to be causes of transformation; some seventy known vestigial structures in the human body were explained on this basis. Efforts on the part of organisms to gratify needs or desires were also held to result in modifications of form. Changes of bodily character acquired in any of these ways were susceptible of hereditary transmission to the offspring. Thus the origins of variations were explained in terms of the manifold relationships between the organism and its environment. Neo-Lamarckians had no objection to the Darwinian principle of the struggle for existence, which they incorporated into their theory. They were also concerned with the complications resulting from the mating of dissimilar parents in which a variation possessed by only one parent might not survive in the offspring. To circumvent this difficulty, they insisted upon the evolutionary importance of geographical isolation of variant forms in species formation. Needless to say, the Neo-Lamarckians were no more familiar than the early Darwinians with the principles of Mendelian genetics. The fatal weakness in their theory was their inability to demonstrate the hereditary transmission of characteristics acquired by organisms in the course of their life experiences. Neo-Lamarckism barely survived the turn of the century.

The theory of evolution was widely accepted by Americans for more than a generation before there emerged a competent consensus as to the means by which evolution occurred. In the meanwhile, the explanations offered by the contending evolutionary schools appeared to entail quite different implications for the intellectual and social life of men. Darwinian natural selection assumed that individuals were all different, and that in the inevitable competition for the limited means of subsistence these differences determined which were to be the fortunate survivors and which the unlucky victims. Struggle was man's lot, and should he be inclined to protest the harshness of such a fate let him recall that the result of the struggle was the evolution of ever more beautiful and wonderful forms. Neo-Lamarckism, on the other hand, while it did not deny the reality of the struggle for existence, insisted that in itself such a struggle did not assure evolutionary progress. Progress could occur only when individual creatures through conscious or unconscious effort exerted themselves to establish a more fruitful adaptation to the physical or social environment, and when they had succeeded in transmitting the benefits of the new adaptation to the species, either by inheritance or, it was implied, by training. Clearly, Neo-Lamarckism interpreted the evolutionary process in a more humane and purposeful light. But, unfortunately, it failed to establish its scientific validity.

In spite of the diverging interpretations of the schools, the larger implications of evolution remained the same for naturalistic thinkers. Man's place was clearly fixed in nature, in the order of primates. Nature's methods, whatever they might be, were his methods. The naturalists founded their thinking on the reality of evolution as a natural and social process. And as long as the scientists themselves were at a loss for an authoritative explanation of the precise nature of the process it was not surprising that their disciples should make diverse, and at times fanciful, applications of the theory to the problems in hand.

Evolutionary theory prior to the turn of the twentieth century had furnished the scientific background for naturalistic thought. The subsequent clarification of evolutionary problems that commenced with the rapid development of genetics on Mendelian principles after 1900 largely escaped the attention of naturalistic social theorists, with the notable exception of Veblen, who made a heroic effort to keep up to date in his use of biological concepts. Most naturalists, however, failed to appreciate the significance of genetics in overcoming the theoretical objections to natural selection while at the same time casting the Darwinian principle in quite a different light. Racist theory, for example, which developed out of naturalistic postulates in the early decades of the twentieth century, appealed for authority to scientific principles already outmoded. The more general repudiation of naturalism in recent decades was certainly facilitated by the disintegration of its presumed scientific foundations. In retrospect, the naturalistic movement appears in some respects to be a chapter in the history of the popular misuse of scientific ideas.

William Graham Sumner

The most characteristic of the naturalistic social thinkers was Professor William Graham Sumner of Yale University. Born in Patterson, New Jersey, the son of an English immigrant laborer, Sumner inherited the stern self-regarding Puritan moral virtues in their secularized form. The father painfully put the son through Yale College, while friends financed theological training and provided the Civil War draft substitute. After two years in the ministry, Sumner was called to Yale in 1872 as professor of political and social science.

The remainder of his life was devoted to the study and teaching of political economy and anthropology.

The reading of Spencer and the visual impact of the spectacular fossil series illustrating vertebrate evolution assembled by his colleague, the paleontologist O. C. Marsh, made Sumner a convinced evolutionist. Abandoning the religious doctrine of special creation, Sumner insisted that man had the same status on the planet as any other species, and that his problems must be viewed with the same objectivity with which one studied the animal world.

Sumner heavily underscored the importance of a proper understanding of man's place in nature. Thanks to Malthus, it was now realized that man was engaged in a perpetual struggle with his environment. Whatever liberties or amenities men enjoyed had been wrested from nature by hard work, either their own or that of their ancestors. As an anthropologist, Sumner knew enough of primitive societies to be able to expose the gross fallacy that the savage was a free man; in fact, he was constantly engaged in a grim struggle for survival. Men should not confuse the inevitable struggle with nature with contention among themselves. When men fought one another, they lost ground in their common cause against the environment. Social evolution had occurred primarily because men had painfully learned to cooperate. They had thus been able partially to emancipate themselves from nature's dominion.

The naturalistic attitude toward nature contrasted sharply with that of earlier modes of thought. The struggle for existence was caused primarily by the fact that the environment did not provide enough to go around. Sumner liked to use Malthus's metaphor of nature bidding men to a banquet she had prepared. When the company assembled to find that there were not enough places at the table for all, the guests were obliged to fight for the places in order to survive. It was clear to Sumner that the traditional doctrine of natural rights was a delusion. Man had "no more right to life than a rattlesnake; he has no more right to liberty than any wild beast; his right to the pursuit of happiness is nothing but a license to maintain the struggle for existence if he can find within himself the power with which to do it." In one of his rare genial moods, Sumner conceded that man did have one natural right—the right to make his way out of the world if he could not make his way in it.

As evolutionists, the naturalists were committed to social change. The late nineteenth-century phase of competitive individualism would eventually give place to some more highly integrated system

—an eventuality that they contemplated with equanimity or aversion, depending on their individual temperaments and predilections. Sumner, for one, professed to be happy that he would not have to live to see the new order. If the naturalists were to be pertinently criticized, it would not be for their stubborn and inhumane Social Darwinism but for their failure to indicate the precise steps by which the individualistic struggle of contemporary society was to be transformed into the more closely cooperative society of the future. All the naturalists contemplated some kind of dialectical development of future cooperation out of presently appropriate *laissez faire*. But there was no agreement as to the manner in which this would occur. Sumner's student Veblen came to doubt with increasing pessimism that it would occur. The Marxist theory of increasing misery, class struggle, and proletarian revolution was the most detailed attempt at prognosis in naturalistic terms, although it was unacceptable to the vast majority of early American naturalists. Sumner's theory of "antagonistic cooperation," never fully developed, was another. But, in any event, the early naturalists revealed their commitment to the *status quo* in their apparent distaste for this aspect of their theory, and, while joining battle with humanitarian-minded reformers on questions of public policy, they left the study of current social changes to the radicals.

Many of Sumner's fellow naturalists, and, indeed, later students as well, failed to grasp his distinction between the struggle with nature and social cooperation. It was a fundamental distinction in his system, although generally overlooked because of his stress upon competition and *laissez faire*. Like Spencer, he distinguished between current conditions and future requirements. Individualistic democracy was well suited to the low man–land ratio of nineteenth-century America, which was one of the least cooperative forms of society known. But as population became denser, closer cooperation would become necessary, and democracy as Sumner's contemporaries knew it would be transformed.

Sumner was not using the term *cooperation* in the usual sense of unity of purpose among the cooperating parties. He meant by it the interdependence of men resulting from specialization of function. Labor and management, for instance, were engaged in cooperative effort, even though they might be constantly at each other's throats. This would have been a good illustration, because Sumner believed that, for the most part, people are not cooperative by nature; they do not willingly cooperate. He coined the term *antagonistic cooperation* to indicate the blend of cross-purposes and mutual benefits that characterized the relationship. Such cooperation implied a mutual respect that each owed to the rights of others in their different functions. But men would consent to cooperate only when they were assured of adequate rewards. Sumner believed that laissez-faire capitalism embodied the most efficient forms of cooperation that had yet appeared.

The social struggle imposed by nature took the nineteenth-century form of economic competition. The accumulated capital of the successful competitor provided the means for ever more efficient social organization, which was the essence of social evolutionary progress. Economic liberty, of course, was necessary for the social selective process; and men must be willing to participate in the ever more complex and intimate forms of cooperation that were its outcome. The rapid progress of the previous three or four centuries Sumner attributed primarily to the fact that men were willing to accept both conditions. But economic liberty presupposed economic inequality, and if reformers should succeed in curtailing economic liberty in the interest of equality, the social evolutionary process would come to a standstill. With the growth of social-reform sentiment in the early twentieth century, Sumner's pessimism steadily increased.

Although he did not use the organic analogies in the literal form employed by his predecessors of the naturalistic tradition, Sumner's over-all view of society was nevertheless profoundly organismic in character. The social organism was rooted in the soil, in the sense that it drew its sustenance from nature and developed its character in terms of the richness or poverty of the resources available to it. Society could flourish only as long as it was able to extract nourishment from nature and convert it into social tissue. In other words, as capital was accumulated by labor, the supply of material goods would increase.

The weapon by which the struggle with nature was conducted was technology. Technology was the basis of society; its characteristics determined the form of social organization. A primitive technology could support only a primitive society. Most immediately dependent upon the technology was the economy. Significant economic changes stemmed from technological innovations. Upon the economy, in turn, arose the superstructure of political, legal, and cultural institutions. Constructive social change must necessarily originate at the level of technology. To attempt to introduce changes at any other level would merely disrupt necessary social relationships. Hence the futility of political reform. The function of politics was merely the police function of maintaining order.

The cause of original technological changes was to be found in the pressure of population upon the means of subsistence, which provided the necessary stimulus to inventive effort. To avert the threat of starvation, new technological innovations were made, and these resulted in more complex social institutions, a more intricate division of labor, and, ultimately, a flourishing art and culture. In the last analysis, then, Sumner found the cause of social evolution to reside in the reasoning faculty.

Sumner's analysis of social classes revealed the mixture of descriptive observation and moralistic prescription characteristic of naturalistic social theory. The value of its contribution to society was the criterion used in distinguishing a class. Because social evolution was ultimately caused by the exercise of the inventive intelligence, Sumner appropriately used ability or mental power as the index of societal value, while admitting that luck, health, and common sense also played a part. The socially most valuable, and therefore highest, class was composed of those possessed of a harmonious blend of the best intellectual, moral, economic, and physical qualities. The small number of geniuses and somewhat larger number of talented people composed the top classes on Sumner's scale.

Grouping the entire population of a society according to this qualitative criterion, he expressed the result graphically by a curve of probable error. The bulk of the population, being of mediocre ability, was represented by the bulge in the middle of the curve. At either extreme the line fell away to represent the few gifted individuals at the top and the somewhat smaller number of dependents, defectives, and delinquents at the bottom. Above the dependents was the proletarian class, which consisted of those without a regular trade or means of employment although not dependent. Above the proletariat was a class designated as the self-supporting but unskilled and illiterate. Between these lower classes and the talented at the top was the vast bulk of society, designated the masses.

The masses as Sumner viewed them did not constitute a class but a social core. Much of his social theory depended upon his appraisal of mass characteristics. The masses were by tradition and habit conservative, living "a purely instinctive life just like animals." Mass inertia, to which was to be traced the glacial quality of social change, was not to be confused with the conservatism of privileged classes, which reflected a keen concern for vested interests. The masses were conservative by instinct, resenting the disturbance of habitual routines. The mores, or conventional attitudes and moral standards of society, were rooted in the masses. Social change consisted in the acceptance by the masses of innovations emanating from the privileged classes and assimilated to the mores. These processes, of course, were unconscious so far as the masses were concerned; only the gifted classes were capable of self-conscious discriminations.

The political implications of Sumner's social science were profoundly at odds with the ideological tradition of democratic individualism, no matter how closely the system was intended to reflect actual behavior. In Sumner's opinion, a society composed of equal and unorganized men was incapable of civilization or of order. The masses were always subject to exploitation, whether as laborers, taxpayers, or military conscripts. If they were to participate fruitfully in the political process, they must be organized and disciplined by an effective leadership. To flatter the mass man and cater to his whims as a glorified "common man" was merely to expose him to the political demagogue. The ideal of mass education was a delusion. At best, the leading classes developed institutions of civil liberty out of the mores of the community that assured order, justice, and the accommodation of conflicting interests. "The point which is now important for us," Sumner observed, "is that the masses have never carried on the struggles and processes by which civilized society has been made into an arena, within which exploitation of man by man is to some extent repressed, and where individual self-realization has a larger scope, under the institutions of civil liberty." Nevertheless, Sumner held that neither the masses nor the classes had any exclusive right to rule society. They should cooperate to their mutual advantage.

In the last analysis, society as Sumner conceived it was a vast co-operative enterprise in which men stood grouped about the means of production. Their relationships to each other were determined inevitably by the part that each played in the productive process. The similarity of Sumner's sociology in this respect to that of Marx is apparent enough. The chief difference stemmed from the fact that, whereas Sumner traced the cause of social change back to the in-inventive ingenuity of man, Marx was reluctant to trace it behind the prevailing "mode of production," a complex of factors in which the influence of the social-class relationships involved in the productive process was given prominent emphasis. The emotional commitments of the two naturalists were so different that the points of agreement between them have usually been overlooked. Marx yearned for the classless society of the future and would use violent means to facilitate social development to that end. Sumner, on the other hand, would do all in his power to arrest the process of social change in order to preserve as long as possible the individualistic democracy of his own day. If men should surrender their liberties and responsibilities, it would be to a plutocracy almost as distasteful to Sumner as the empty dreams of reformers and socialists.

In asserting the independence of the social sciences, Sumner perhaps found some satisfaction in repudiating the traditional humanistic authority under which social theory was ultimately resolved into a branch of morality. Sumner had been raised on the theory that found the moral element to reside in the intention of the actor. But the naturalist rejected any such subjective consideration. He stressed the lack of connection between the subjective intentions of the actor and the objective consequences of his act. The latter flowed in a cause–effect sequence from the act itself and might well result in the very situation that it was the ill-informed intention of the actor to avoid. There being no necessary connection between purposes and consequences, it was the function of social science to ignore ethical ideals or social goals and confine itself strictly to the study of cause–effect relationships in the realm of fact.

CHAPTER 14

||||||||||||||||||||||||||||||||||||||||||||||||||||||||||||||||||||||||||

Naturalistic Psychology

W ITHIN THE BROAD FRAMEWORK of the influences that shape human activity, the naturalistic mind distinguished two forces: heredity and environment, the one internal and the other external to the individual. The analysis of evolutionary problems, both organic and social, brought the nature–nurture question to the fore. In various forms, it pervaded naturalistic thought at the turn of the century. Preoccupation with the problem, not the form of its solution, was the distinguishing mark. In the field of psychology, newly reconstituted as a scientific discipline, the nature–nurture emphasis was represented, respectively, by the schools of instinctivism and behaviorism.

Assumptions about the nature of man played as important a role in naturalistic as in earlier patterns of thought. These assumptions fixed the peculiar qualities of the naturalistic mind and influenced the position it took on many of the perennial problems of life. What was new in the naturalistic era was the reorientation of the psychological outlook in terms of a new set of intellectual affiliations. The psychologists were now determined to keep different company. They chose as their closest associates the physiologists and neurologists, and beyond these scientists they gazed with veneration upon the physicists and mathematicians as the exemplars of the scientific method that they were determined to introduce into the exploration of the murky depths of the mind.

In the democratic era, the formal discussion of psychological problems had been designated by such terms as *mental science* or *intellectual philosophy*. The scholastic rationale of organized intellectual life had assigned a fixed place to these discussions and had provided the ultimate concepts with which the psychologist worked. A purposeful God and an immortal soul were realities not to be questioned, and, as if to make sure that they would not be, the function of psychologist was almost universally pre-empted by clergymen. These clerical psychologists were usually expert as well in theology and in the comprehensive field of moral philosophy. In the scholastic scheme of the liberal arts college, mental science occupied the central position between natural science and moral science (the terms *science* and *philosophy* still being used interchangeably). But while by the middle of the nineteenth century, instruction in natural science was passing into the hands of scientific specialists without responsibilities for other fields, instruction in psychology was carefully guarded by the clerical collegiate authorities. Historians have called attention to the remarkable number of general treatises on psychology written by college presidents. McCosh of Princeton, Porter of Yale, Bascom of Wisconsin, Mahan of Oberlin, Wayland of Brown, and Hopkins of Williams—all tried their hands at this genre. Their productions were generally marked by a conception of psychology stressing the purposeful attributes of human nature consistent with the executive energies displayed by their authors. The field of psychology received at such hands a set of official definitions consistent with the character of a society of which clergymen were both spokesmen and apologists.

The term *intellectual philosophy* revealed much of the content and spirit of the older psychology. It conceived of itself as the science of consciousness, and it undertook to show how the mind functioned as it dealt with the subject matter comprising the various categories of knowledge and experience. Particular emphasis was placed upon the cognitive faculties and the intuitions. In order to avoid the antihumanistic implications of Jonathan Edwards's determinism, psychologists throughout the century labored to arrange the faculties of the mind in such a way that their functioning would free the will from the bondage to the motives to which Edwards had consigned it. Thus psychology during the nineteenth century had tended to be both rationalistic and moralistic, providing a convenient basis in human nature for traditional philosophical and social dogmas.

The evolutionary movement accomplished in American psychology a transformation already well under way in Europe. At the end of the century several forces focused upon American psychology and in two decades completely transformed it. The theory of organic evolution postulated the psychic unity of men and animals. Darwin, whose *Expression of the Emotions in Man and Animals* (1872) entitled him to a secure place in the history of psychology, himself suggested that essentially the same psychological mechanisms were found in both realms. Man might possess a greater degree of intelligence than other animals, but intelligence itself, if defined as purposive reaction to an environmental situation, could be traced right down to paramecium. And on the other hand, the new psychology was quick to show the extent to which man was still dominated by primitive and irrational forces of many sorts. Tropisms, reflexes, instincts, habits, subconscious motives, and neuroses were all laid bare for inspection.

Freedom to investigate the new problems was assured by the emancipation of psychology from its traditional metaphysical and theological associations. Oriented now toward the biological and physical sciences, the psychologists quickly organized laboratories of physiological psychology in many of the universities. The new physiological psychology was a somewhat unstable compromise that at least gave the new generation breathing space in which to regroup for an attack on their problems. These problems pointed in various directions. The evolutionary interest posed the problems of development and of variation, which, in turn, led to questions of heredity and environment, child and animal psychology, and the study of racial and individual differences. But at the same time, the physiological orientation required that these problems be dealt with in mechanical rather than vitalistic terms. Psychological facts were reduced to physical reactions, the basic phenomenon becoming a neural reaction. The ultimate development in this direction was the school of behaviorism, in which all the phenomena of mind were described in terms of action. Although the physiological orientation of the new psychology had the virtue of refining methods and sharpening the focus of attention, it tended to restrict the range of legitimate problems to those susceptible of investigation by experimental methods. The attributes and functions of consciousness were explored by carefully controlled forms of the method of introspection. But around the fringes of consciousness lay much unexplored territory, the region of the unconscious. In spite of William James's persistent interest in this area, his followers were inclined to regard it as a slightly disreputable idiosyncrasy of his and to concentrate upon problems more amenable to investigation by scientific methods.

Instinct Psychology

Although physiological psychology continued through the first half of the twentieth century to provide the base upon which psychologists organized and appraised themselves as a profession, its apparent inadequacy for the full range of psychological problems resulted in the formation of several distinct schools of theory. One of the first to emerge was the purposivist or instinct school.

The founder of the movement, William McDougall, was interested in the social applications of psychology. He felt that the prevailing tendency among psychologists to study the nature of consciousness resulted in neglect of those aspects of the subject most relevant to other social disciplines. Therefore, in 1908, he called for a new definition of psychology as the science of mind in all its functional aspects —in other words, a science of behavior. At that time, McDougall was a British subject. His ideas found a ready response in the United States, however, and after World War I he settled in this country, teaching successively at Harvard and at Duke.

McDougall's criticism of the prevailing physiological psychology arose from its failure to account adequately for the active or purposive character of human nature. It could dissect mental processes, but it could not explain their dynamic quality. Furthermore, by preoccupying itself with the study of the normal adult mind by the methods of introspection while neglecting the study of animal, child, and abnormal psychology, it made human nature seem much too rational. McDougall proposed, consequently, to start with the assumption that man was a purposeful or goal-seeking animal and to construct a psychology that would concern itself with the motives of conduct. The psychological elements to which man's purposeful behavior was attributed were called instincts. McDougall proposed to isolate and define the nature of the instincts, and to show how everyday behavior was compounded out of instinctive impulses.

The instinct psychology was first set forth in McDougall's *An In-*

troduction to Social Psychology (1908). Americans were not entirely unprepared for it. The clerical mental philosophies of the later nineteenth century had usually had something to say in passing about the instincts. In a practical way, their authors were inclined to regard man as a purposeful animal. They could appreciate the dynamic approach. Having freed the will from a strict logical dependence upon the motives, they were nonetheless possessed of a healthy respect for the profound influence that the motives could exert upon conduct. T. C. Upham, in the most widely used text of the period, *Elements of Mental Philosophy* (published as early as 1831), devoted a portion to a discussion of "propensities" of the mind, a term McDougall sometimes used as a synonym for instinct. Upham had listed such propensities as self-preservation, curiosity, imitativeness, emulation, approbativeness, acquisitiveness, desire for power, for happiness, selfishness, and so on, a list which offered some instructive comparisons with that later furnished by McDougall.

The goal-seeking quality of human behavior presupposed motivation, and motives were, in turn, explained by McDougall as the expressions of instinctive propulsions. The instinct as he conceived it was an innate, inherited tendency of mind functioning as a primary motive of thought and action. The core of the instinct was an emotional feeling sensitive to certain types of stimulus from the environment. Sensitized by such a stimulus, the instinctive response involved both the emotional feeling and an associated effort to gratify or discharge the emotion. McDougall distinguished the following instincts, each with its associated emotion: the instinct of flight and the emotion of fear; the instinct of repulsion and the emotion of disgust; curiosity and wonder; pugnacity and anger; self-abasement and subjection; self-assertion and elation; the paternal instinct and the tender emotion. Other instincts with less well-defined emotional associations were the reproductive, gregarious, acquisitive, and constructive instincts. All these instincts were believed to be susceptible of modification by being conditioned to new stimuli, and the instinctive response was likewise capable of modification. But the emotional core of the instincts remained unchanged. It was the emotional element in instinctive behavior that was, in fact, the peculiar property of instincts as found in the higher animals and in men. McDougall did not contend that normal adult behavior was the direct expression of instinctive impulses. He held, rather, that the complex sentiments and attitudes of daily life were built with combinations of conditioned instinctive responses, and that the behavior which accompanied them revealed its characteristic blend of love and hate, enthusiasms, rivalries, and similar emotional qualities because of the involvement of the instincts. In the major institutions of society, and in the most commonly recurring patterns of behavior, such as the family, industry, war, or religion, one would expect to find the emotional clues to deep-rooted instincts.

McDougall was aware of his own roots in the old Scottish "moral sense" philosophy that had been so widely received in America. The instincts, like the traditional moral and common-sense faculties, were inherited or innate predispositions of the mind to cope with experience in certain ways. However, a fundamental difference between the two systems was of great practical importance for the modern student who would accept McDougall's invitation to employ the instinct psychology as a means of dealing with social problems. In nineteenth-century democratic thought, the appeal to innate or instinctive tendencies of mind was intended chiefly to supply a basis in human nature for philosophical or theological systems. Hence the instincts that were discovered were inevitably of a moralistic or intellectual character: man was found to possess an instinctive sense of the existence of God or an instinctive moral sense. Naturalistic psychology, on the other hand, was the handmaid of biology, not of philosophy or theology. Its orientation was physiological, not moralistic, and its category of instincts revealed the character of man the animal: the urge to survive, to reproduce, to fight, to flee, to imitate, and to congregate with his fellows. In short, while the older theory of innate ideas had been intended to serve the needs of a traditional culture, the newer reduced culture to nature.

Instincts and Economic Thought

In presenting his instinct theory in the form of a social psychology, McDougall said that his chief purpose was to demonstrate to students of the social sciences the fact that human activity sprang not from moral or rational considerations, or even from considerations of pleasure and pain, but from instinctive propulsions rooted in human nature and derived from the remote past of the species. This was a revolutionary challenge to Americans whose intellectual orthodoxy for the past century could only be described as timid. Students who accepted the challenge would have to engage in extensive theoretical reconstruction in order merely to describe society in the new terms before they could undertake to apply the new principles to the solution of practical problems. Social scientists, however, were not slow to accept the challenge.

McDougall himself attacked classical economic theory as "a tissue of false conclusions drawn from false psychological assumptions." The laissez-faire theory had conceived man to be a rational creature seeking economic ends with enlightened self-interest, motivated by hedonistic values in which the good was identified with pleasure and the avoidance of pain. Pleasure was to be achieved by means of wealth, while pain transformed itself into the aversion to labor. But according to the new psychology, intelligence was always subordinate to the ends determined by instinct, while pleasure was resolved into the satisfaction accompanying the attainment of these ends. Economic theory would have to be reconstructed in terms of the relationship between economic institutions and man's instinctive needs; economic policy should concern itself with the ways in which institutional changes could be made to maximize the satisfaction of these needs.

In the second decade of the twentieth century, many foremost American economists turned to a consideration of these problems. The direction of their thinking was indicated by Thorstein Veblen, one of the most original and stimulating thinkers of the day, in *The Instinct of Workmanship and the State of the Industrial Arts* (1914). As an evolutionist, Veblen had for many years been sharply critical of the static assumptions of economic normality underlying classical economic theory. He now attacked the classical theory on the ground that its psychology was inadequate as well. Veblen held that the instinctive equipment of Western peoples had been fixed in their heredity by the time of emergence from savagery. The subsequent development of barbarian and civilized types of society, a process characterized by ever-increasing acceleration, was to be understood as an institutional development. No significant transformation of the instincts accompanied this institutional development. To the extent, therefore, that modern industrial institutions placed a premium on instinctive qualities other than those actually fixed in the heredity of Western peoples by their selective experiences in the formative ages of their racial life, they were poorly equipped to cope with modern problems; in fact, Veblen described their position as "desperately precarious." It was the relationship between man with his instinctive propensities or needs and the contemporary industrial institutions that Veblen placed at the center of attention and to which his fellow economists addressed themselves.

Professor F. W. Taussig, a prominent Harvard economist, pressed the attack upon traditional economic theory in his *Inventors and Money-Makers* (1915). By building upon a hedonistic ethics and the associationist psychology, the classical theorists had eliminated all but the narrowest of self-regarding motives from their analysis of economic behavior. Taussig concluded that it would no longer do to assume with Adam Smith that the characteristics of man's economic behavior could be deduced from the ultimate faculties of reason and speech. The instincts regarded by Taussig as of greatest significance for economic theory were the instincts of contrivance, collection (rather than acquisition), domination, emulation, and sympathy. With respect to the instinct of contrivance (or workmanship), if man was by nature an "inventor," then one need not adopt the utilitarian explanation that men make things because they find it advantageous to do so. Man works simply because he is happier working than loafing. But this led Taussig to question the proposition that progress in the industrial arts depends upon actual or prospective gain, although he conceded that the direction in which the inventor bent his contriving instinct might indeed be influenced by the hope of gain. Taussig also eliminated acquisition from his list of instincts in favor of collection, largely on the strength of observed behavior of animals. In other words, there was no reason to assume that economic activity depended on the desire to acquire possessions so long as the instinct for accumulation for any of a variety of purposes was satisfied. Taussig agreed with Veblen that modern industrial institutions did not provide sufficient opportunities for the satisfaction of instinctive needs. In particular, the instinct of contrivance was being smothered in many men, which was, perhaps, the reason why classical theorists had assumed as a matter of course that work was irksome.

Professor Carleton H. Parker of the University of Washington introduced a Freudian note into the discussion when he analyzed economic motives before the American Economic Association in 1918. In a broad sense, psychoanalysis might be classified as an instinct psychology, and it was not difficult to fuse elements from the two theories. Parker enumerated the various instincts and indicated how extensively their expression was being frustrated by modern social and industrial conditions. The repression of instinctive needs resulted in characteristic responses of anger or fear and, eventually, in deterioration of character. This was the chief explanation of the pathological violence that so frequently punctuated industrial relations. On the other hand, society was doing little or nothing to find ways to sublimate the expression of the instinct of pugnacity. Parker was a labor-relations expert who had specialized in the study of migratory labor in California. The notorious problems of the casual laborer he attributed to the pathological expressions of the repressed instinctual needs resulting from the unnatural conditions in which such laborers lived. With Veblen, Parker believed that industrial society must move toward a new "normality" in which instinctive potentialities would be realized in greater measure.

In commenting upon Parker's views, Wesley C. Mitchell, the distinguished theorist of the business cycle, echoed the naturalistic conviction that human nature had not changed since the Stone Age, in the sense that the instinctive elements remained unaltered. Institutions, on the other hand, those socially prevalent habits which in any group standardize the behavior of its members, displayed cumulative change. But Mitchell transcended the limits of naturalistic thought when he added that it was the aim of the social sciences to contribute to progress by establishing purposive and intelligent control over institutions. It was therefore the duty of social scientists to press for institutional changes appropriate to the needs of human nature and consistent with current conceptions of industrial efficiency.

The related field of industrial relations was explored by Parker's disciple Ordway Tead. A young settlement-house worker and labor-relations counselor, Tead published his *Instincts in Industry. A Study of Working-Class Psychology* in 1918. Again, the central theme was the unnatural inhibitions imposed upon laboring men by the industrial process. Partly because of the general failure to understand the instinctive bases of conduct, and partly because the frustrations arising from laboring conditions resulted in patterns of behavior among working people that seemed to unsympathetic observers to be capricious or malicious, a deep gulf had opened between the laboring and owning classes. Tead's problem was to make the psychology and behavior of working men intelligible in terms of the universal needs expressed by the instincts. Once a sympathetic understanding of labor's problems had been achieved by means of the common bond of the instincts, it would be possible to shed the fears born of a sense of the alien and come to grips intelligently with the real problems of industrial relations.

These criticisms of the inadequate psychological assumptions of classical economic theory, together with the critics' emphasis upon the necessity of a proper understanding of the relationships between human nature and economic institutions set the stage for the emergence of a new school of economic thought. This was the rather amorphous movement known as institutional economics. In a manifesto on behalf of the new point of view delivered to the American Economic Association in 1918, Walton Hamilton acknowledged that a sound economics must be based on an acceptable theory of human behavior. He agreed that the classical theory had proved deficient in this respect, as it had also failed to appreciate the role played by institutions in guiding human conduct. The reconstruction of economic theory must rest upon an empirical approach to the study of economic institutions. In the long run, the institutional emphasis displaced the original affiliations of the movement with the instinct psychology. Economists made detailed studies of various types of economic institutions. These studies proceeded on the assumption that institutions form and disintegrate in the course of social development, and that the individuals who participate in the process adapt themselves to changing circumstances.

Thus, although the instinct theory was effective in demolishing the psychological foundations of classical economics, it did not make any appreciable positive contribution to economic theory or to other branches of social theory. Instinctivists had always held that the tangible expression of the instincts was susceptible of extensive modification in practice. To the degree that this was true, instincts seemed less significant as factors in social analysis. A more serious difficulty was raised by critics of the instinct theory. An instinct was presumed by McDougall and his followers to be a unit character with a direct genetic correlate. But upon close scrutiny the instinct tended to break down into several components. Consequently, the formation of an "instinct" could be supposed to result from social conditioning, and the alleged hereditary character of the instinct thus disintegrated. Veblen had anticipated this criticism as early as 1914, but he had maintained that, even though the instinct might prove to be a synthesis of psychological elements with life experiences, it still possessed sufficient stability at the institutional level to be of service as an analytical tool for the social sciences. But, in general, social scientists came to share a feeling that the nature–nurture dichotomy was an artificial one. They turned their attention to other matters and, in practice, proceeded on the assumption of the plasticity of human nature.

Behaviorism

The instinctivists represented the hereditarian side of nature–nurture controversy among naturalists. The emergence of their school of thought in the second decade of the twentieth century scarcely anticipated the appearance of another group of psychologists who represented the environmentalist alternative. This was the movement known as behaviorism.

The tendency of the naturalistic mind to explain complex phenomena by reducing them to simpler elements in a conventionally conceived structure of reality has already been noted. This process involved not simply the breaking-down of complex machines into simple mechanisms or of compounds into chemical elements; it implied a whole hierarchy of levels of reality, each of which could be resolved into that beneath it. Thus history was understood in material terms, notably in Marxism and in technological determinism. Or society was reduced to biological elements by means of the organic analogy. Biology was reduced to mechanical or chemical terms. And, finally, mechanics and chemistry were reduced to numbers. The intellectual prestige of science stemmed largely from the fact that it dealt with the lower levels of this hierarchy. The sector of the hierarchy of particular interest at the moment was that where the biological was reduced to the physical or mechanical. The attempt to explain biological phenomena exclusively in mechanical terms was the peculiar feature of the behavioristic school of psychological thought.

The physiological psychology born of the evolutionary movement culminated at the turn of the century in the so-called "functional psychology" of James and Dewey. The functionalists held that consciousness was the instrument or faculty by which the human organism adjusted itself to its environment. Much of this psychology, however, remained speculative in character. Many of the phenomena of mind or consciousness eluded objective scientific tests. They were known only through introspection, or consciousness of subjective mental states. For introspective investigations, a highly trained "subject" was necessary in order to make discriminations of sufficient precision to be of service to the investigator. By strict scientific canons, the method of introspection was an untidy procedure, and the lack of experimental verification of some of their findings was embarrassing to the functionalists.

At the same time, in quite a distinct field of investigation, animal psychologists were working out methods for studying the behavior of animals—needless to say, without reliance upon the method of introspection. The Americans E. L. Thorndike and John B. Watson devised ingenious mazes and puzzle boxes that yielded much information on the learning process in animals. In the most famous of these experiments, the Russian Pavlov discovered the conditioned reflex. Pavlov apparently thought of himself as a physiologist and rejected psychology as worthless. The orthodox psychologists for their part held that, since animal consciousness could not be proved, the study of animal behavior was no proper branch of psychology. It has been suggested that this repudiation accounted for the belligerence of the early behaviorists. In any event, given the objective, measurable data of animal psychology and the elusive aspects of the prevailing functional psychology, it was almost inevitable that an effort should be made to apply the methods of animal psychology to the study of human beings in order to develop a psychology that would deal exclusively with observable, invariant data and yield definite laws of behavior. The resulting behavioristic psychology proposed to develop a science of human behavior in the strictest sense.

The founder of the behaviorist school was John B. Watson, whose paper of 1913 inaugurated the movement. Watson had studied at Chicago under Dewey and J. R. Angell and had then gone to Johns Hopkins, where he worked in the fields of animal and child psychology. Watson's first task as a behaviorist was to prune psychology of its subjective elements. The operation, however, is less appropriately described as pruning than as evisceration. Consciousness was the traditional subject matter of psychology; but what was consciousness? It could not even be defined, let alone measured; it was merely the modern derivative of the old idea of soul. Contemporary psychology was still content to follow the immemorial dualism of body and soul.

The behaviorist therefore abandoned consciousness and all its associated subjective notions. He would have nothing to do with such tainted concepts as sensation, perception, image, desire, purpose, thought, or emotion. The proper data of psychology, Watson insisted, was nothing but observable behavior. This meant acting and talking. Talking consisted either of talking aloud or to oneself—that is, thinking. (Should the reader be tempted to regard this as a rather shabby way of sneaking in the traditional content of psychology by the back door, let it be said that the behaviorists attempted to investigate the observable physiological phenomena presumed to accompany thought, such as movements of the larynx. Where the results were not conclusive, they legitimately pleaded inadequate techniques for measuring so delicate a process.) Another way of defining observable behavior was to identify it as the response to a stimulus.

The stimulus–response relationship was the basic concept of behaviorism. Watson's discussions were little more than a set of variations on this theme. The response to stimulus was always movement in any of several forms. The usual result was said to be an adjustment, which meant that because of the movement the stimulus no longer impinged upon the organism. Fundamentally, the human organism was conceived to be a machine consisting of a set of basic unlearned responses to such stimuli as loud noises, fracturing or blows on the skin, and the insertion of the nipple between the lips. In practice, both stimulus and response were susceptible of being "conditioned." The conditioned stimulus was one that produced a given response by the establishment of an association with the original stimulus of the response in question. Conditioned stimuli were presumed to be practically infinite in number. Likewise, the conditioned response was a response substituted for the original unlearned response. Watson considered Freudian sublimation to be a form of conditioned response.

The social life of man was thus a vast tissue of conditioned behavior. The stimulus–response relationship was a strict cause–effect relationship. Watson held that, if the identity of one was known, it should be possible to determine the character of the other since the relationship was invariant. In Watson's hands behaviorism was, in effect, an extreme development of environmental determinism. Both the stimulus and the conditioned response were external influences that could shape the individual at will.

Watson professed to look forward to the time when there would be a behavioristic ethics. It would be an experimental ethics that would tell men what behavior would be advisable in order to achieve desirable adjustments. He did not provide the criteria for determining what a "desirable adjustment" would be. The adjustment itself was apparently some kind of fully satisfying activity. The criteria of evaluation would probably prove to be hedonistic and intensely individualistic.

Actually, Watson seems to have been less interested in a behavioristic ethics than in developing a predictive science of behavior that would make possible effective social control. The ethical ends to which control would be applied did not greatly concern him. "The interest of the behaviorist in man's doings," he wrote, "is more than the interest of the spectator—he wants to control man's reactions as physical scientists want to control and manipulate other natural phenomena. It is the business of behavioristic psychology to be able to predict and to control human activity. To do this it must gather scientific data by experimental methods. Only then can the trained behaviorist predict, given the stimulus, what reaction will take place; or given the reaction, state what the situation or stimulus is that has caused the reaction." Since most behavior was said to consist of conditioned responses, these responses could be reconditioned. Control of behavior would then be feasible by means of a conditioning program that would prepare individuals to respond appropriately to a series of controlled stimuli.

Twentieth-century theories of social control were developed chiefly by economic theorists and students of public administration. But the potential foundations in psychological conditioning were only too readily apparent. It would be difficult to say how much the development of propaganda techniques and of public-relations counseling owed to behavioristic psychology. But by the middle of the twentieth century, it had become difficult to enthuse over Watson's vision of a reconditioned humanity reacting obediently to the stimuli issuing from some Office of Behavior Control. The idea had been imaginatively explored in its various ramifications by Aldous Huxley, by Arthur Koestler, and by George Orwell. It seemed appropriate that, in due course, Watson himself should become an advertising agency executive, where one fancied him engaged in the conditioning of housewives to demand a certain brand of coffee and accept no substitutes.

CHAPTER 15

||||||||||||||||||||||||||||||||||||||||||||||||||||||||||||||||||||||

Oliver Wendell Holmes, Legal Naturalist

BY THE TIME OF HIS RETIREMENT from the Supreme Court in 1932, Justice Oliver Wendell Holmes had acquired a wide reputation as a liberal jurist and thinker. This reputation rested partly upon his celebrated judicial opinions in which he sturdily defended the civil liberties of dissident individuals, especially the guarantee of freedom of speech and press to social radicals. Even more important, it rested upon his expressed willingness to countenance experimentation with novel ideas and policies, and upon his insistence that the courts should exercise judicial restraint in refusing to read Spencerian *laissez faire* into the due process clause of the Fourteenth Amendment to the Constitution as a means of nullifying legislative attempts to cope with current problems.

Yet those who studied Holmes's career more closely—and among them many of his warmest admirers—were uncomfortably aware of certain aspects of his thought that were conservative or even reactionary. There was, for instance, a harshness in his judgments upon men of good will, a contempt for humanitarianism as an ingredient of public policy, and an expressed preference for the predatory type of individual that his friends usually managed to overlook with embarrassed silence. In fact, it seems most appropriate to designate Holmes as neither liberal nor conservative but as a naturalist.

Holmes's adult career spanned the naturalistic era. Born in Boston in 1841, son of the elder Oliver Wendell Holmes, a distinguished physician and literary man, he enjoyed the social and cultural advantages of a boyhood in the metropolis during its golden age. On graduating from Harvard in 1861, he entered the Union army to follow a distinguished military career during which he was wounded three times. This military experience was decisive in shaping the quality of Holmes's thought. Even less for him than for his contemporary Henry Adams could the Boston background continue to mean what it had meant before 1861. After the war, he took a law degree at Harvard and briefly practiced and taught law before being appointed to the bench. His half-century career as successively justice and chief justice of the Supreme Court of Massachusetts and justice of the Supreme Court of the United States was one of the longest and most distinguished tenures in American judicial history.

Preliminary clues to the naturalistic quality of Holmes's thought were his respectful references to the seminal minds of the naturalistic traditon. He confessed to Harold Laski, "I look at men through Malthus' glasses—as like flies—here swept away by a pestilence—there multiplying unduly and paying for it." "All society rests on the death of men. If you don't kill 'em one way you kill 'em another—or prevent their being born. Is not the present time an illustration of Malthus?" Of Darwin and Spencer he wrote to an English friend, Lady Pollock: "H. Spencer you English never quite do justice to, or at least those whom I have talked with do not. He is dull. He writes an ugly, uncharming style, his ideals are those of a lower middle class British Philistine. And yet after all abatements I doubt if any writer of English except Darwin has done so much to affect our whole way of thinking about the universe." The noble Spencer had suffered a fate that Holmes was disposed to regard as a kind of sacred martyrdom. His original ideas had become hackneyed and commonplace because they were embedded in the texture of modern thought.

The Universe and Man

In typical naturalistic style, Holmes repudiated the naïve humanistic assumptions of earlier American thought. He found in the universe no evidence of purpose or of moral order. As a lawyer, he rejected the belief of Marshall, of Story, and of Kent that human law derived its authority ultimately from the law of nature and of God. He stubbornly refused to agree even with fellow naturalists who believed that nature at least operated according to her own laws in causal terms. His Cambridge philosophy teacher Chauncey Wright had taught him that nothing about the universe could be said to be necessary, and late in life he found this teaching confirmed by the new physics of indeterminacy. He called himself a "bettabilitarian," one who was willing to bet on the behavior of the universe as men experienced it. To remind himself and his friends that they had shed their anthropomorphic delusions, he liked to say that "the Cosmos does not wear a beard."

Repeatedly, Holmes deplored the fatuousness of philosophers and publicists who insisted on the cosmic importance of man. Man, he said, was a "cosmic ganglion," a momentary intersection of streams of energy. Experience, not principle, was his guide; intelligence, if he had any, was his salvation. The only true measure of a man was the total of human energy he embodied. "The final test of this energy is battle in some form—actual war—the crush of arctic ice—the fight for mastery in the market or the court." Man was by nature a predatory animal, and when interests conflicted, force was the last resort. Hence, although he loathed war, Holmes saw little chance of abolishing it. He returned constantly to the theme: life is struggle; "life is action and passion."

Perhaps because he was reared in the older humanistic pre-Civil War world, Holmes felt instinctively obliged to have a faith, even though he professed not to know the truth or the meaning of the universe. His military experience provided the perfect analogy for a man required to act with decision and courage in a world he neither made nor understood. "The faith is true and adorable which leads a soldier to throw away his life in obedience to a blindly accepted duty, in a cause which he little understands, in a plan of campaign of which he has no notion, under tactics of which he does not see the use." The patriotic sentiment from which this faith derived its motive force was to be acquired by exposure to the contagion of those who already possessed it. It could not be instilled by mere argument or persuasion. It was the primitive sense of the identification of the individual with his group. Contemporary psychologists identified it as one of the most pervasive forms of the herd instinct. Holmes set a high value upon patriotic observances, and was himself an effective participant in them, because they were an important means whereby the patriotic sentiment was inculcated. In the last analysis, he judged instinctive loyalty to the group to be the highest feeling of which man was capable.

Holmes was deeply interested in the history of the law, and the problems with which he dealt were of such general philosophic import that it is possible to extract from his discussions an underlying theory of history. This was the typical naturalistic concept of history as the emergence of the human species from savagery into civilization. Within the broad naturalistic framework Holmes's special emphasis was his positivism. Not only was the course of history from the primitive to the civilized; it was also from the irrational and animalistic to the rational and human. The history of law, for instance, recorded "every painful step and every world shaking contest by which mankind has worked and fought its way from savage isolation to organic social life." Thus Holmes asserted his "faith in the prevalence of reason in the long run."

But declarations of faith were not to be lightly made; and in characteristically Holmesian fashion, the declaration once made was immediately retracted in favor of a profession of mere "moderate bias" toward the prevalence of reason. After all, it would indeed be a long run, and in the meanwhile man remained homicidal, cowardly, and irrational. To overestimate his capabilities was a great mistake. Man had amply demonstrated a powerful propensity to believe what he wanted to believe rather than to be guided by reason. This judgment on man's perverse behavior underlay Holmes's contempt for William James's "will to believe." Nevertheless, at the same time, Holmes permitted himself to express the conviction that the papacy and the kind of thinking it represented were doomed to eventual extinction with the spread of rationality. Likewise he noted that already in his own day men found it revolting to be told that no better reason for a rule of law existed than that it had been laid down by Henry IV in the fifteenth century. Thus Holmes, like his fellow naturalists, grasped emergent reason in one hand and surviving irrationality in the other, and was fully prepared to use either as a weapon according to the prevailing mood of the moment.

The typical naturalistic mixture of relativism and absolutism appeared in Holmes's thought. He was a relativist in insisting that the prevailing standards of the moment were created by society and did not derive from universal principles. "The mores make anything right," as William Graham Sumner had put it. Omnivorous reader though he was, Holmes did not discover Sumner until 1929, when he read *Folkways* and saw in Sumner's concept of the mores a formulation of his own conviction that these traditional but changing attitudes and practices determined the principles solemnly declared by the philosophers of the moment to be valid for all time.

But in a more important sense, Holmes's positivistic view of history provided an absolute in terms of which he justified his convictions. The convictions were not to be grounded in the will of society, even though society was acknowledged to have the power summarily to dispose of the dissenter. It was, after all, frequently man's duty to assert his convictions against the will of society, and Holmes as a jurist had served notice that he would defend such an individual to the utmost. No; man's convictions were ultimately to be framed in terms of his own understanding of the social evolutionary emergence of the species from savagery to civilization. The more civilized and scientific values ought always to be espoused. This was the absolute standard to which Holmes resolutely clung.

Society and the Individual

The organic analogy was not employed by Holmes, and his occasional references to the social organism did not apparently have special significance. But he did insist that man was the creature of society, which might dispose of him as it saw fit. The survival of society was the paramount consideration, and to that end society was prepared to sacrifice the welfare of individuals as it might be necessary, whether by the conscription of their lives or the condemnation of their property. In an unpublished opinion of 1917, a war year, Holmes held that if the power either of capital or of labor was exerted in such a way as to threaten the survival of the community then those seeking their private interests at such a cost were public enemies to be dealt with as such. Even when allowance is made for the unusual circumstances, this attitude contrasted sharply with the traditional American doctrine of individual rights anterior to government and to be guaranteed against government. But Holmes was not content to take refuge in exceptional circumstances. "All my life," he decalred, "I have sneered at the natural rights of man."

Holmes's English friend and correspondent Harold Laski was an authority on the political theory of sovereignty. While he undoubtedly admired the erudition displayed in Laski's books, Holmes was impatient with the intricate ramifications of theological and political doctrine that the discussions entailed. Sovereignty, he bluntly informed the scholar, was simply a matter of strength, which varied by degrees. The force a society could bring to bear at a given moment was the measure of sovereignty. One of the most important functions of sovereignty was to create individual rights, which would not otherwise exist. The rights of man meant nothing more than what the crowd would fight for.

Why then did Holmes bother to write his celebrated opinions in defense of such rights as free speech? Because society benefited from free competition in ideas. The social struggle for existence took the form of attempts by individuals to mold the community in accordance with their respective desires. In a civilized society—that is, a rational one—the weapon used in the struggle was free discussion. Under conditions of free competition, men would be persuaded of the utility of a new idea just as they knew how to accept a new or cheaper product. But society was, of course, under no obligation thus to conduct its affairs; and it must have been a source of wry satisfaction to Holmes to note that the recently heightened American sensitivity to civil rights was perhaps less significant as the reaffirmation of a traditional dogma than as a testimonial to the persuasive force of an eloquent judge.

For one who repeatedly affirmed that life was action and passion and that man was a gullible sentimentalist, Holmes had a curiously profound respect for the determinative influence of ideas in history. He supposed that the idealistic philosopher Immanuel Kant had had more effect upon history than had Napoleon; and he assumed that if communism were to triumph, it would be because men would be persuaded of its superior merits. Not only did the progress of society depend on the creative activity of individuals, but this activity was taken in its most important respects to be of a distinctly intellectual character.

While Holmes thus sought to persuade men that social progress depended upon their efforts, he also noted the purely private and personal satisfaction to be derived from creative activity. It was a heroic plunge into the unknown. "Only when you have worked alone —when you have felt around you a black gulf of solitude more isolating than that which surrounds the dying man, and in hope and in despair have trusted to your own unshaken will—then only will you have achieved." There was however a reward, if only a vicarious one, namely, the secret joy of the thinker who knew that a century hence his thought would become the common sense of things, moving men who had never heard of him. His sufficient reward would be "the subtle rapture of postponed power." No passage reveals more eloquently how completely Holmes accepted a social standard of the good.

The path of the law as Holmes traced it had followed the general course of historical development from primitive simplicity to modern organic complexity. The law as it had been formed had always reflected the demands of competing interests. Therefore, if one wanted to know precisely what a rule of law meant, it was necessary to do more than merely analyze the words in which it was stated; it was necessary to study the historical circumstances from which the rule emerged. In earlier and simpler times, the rules of law dealt largely with the rights and wrongs of individuals in private, personal situations. As social circumstances gradually changed with time, these rules remained unchanged, thus inevitably acquiring a somewhat archaic flavor and rendering their reinterpretation necessary. Here Holmes introduced the concept of cultural lag into legal theory. In *The Common Law* (1881), he pointed out that this was a common phenomenon in legal history. The customs, needs, or beliefs of a primitive time led to the formulation of a legal rule. With the passage of time these social usages disappeared, but the rule remained. The reasons for its original formulation having been forgotten, the men of a later age found some relevant ground of policy to reconcile the rule to current conditions. Thus brought into line with current needs, the rule entered upon a new career. Gradually, however, the rule itself, in the course of adaptation to new circumstances, altered. And so the changing forms or rules of the law lagged behind the changing social circumstances that shaped the law.

The law as Holmes conceived it was inevitably remote from the ultimate sources of social and historical change. At any time in the past, it reflected the prevailing customs, opinions, and institutions, arrangements that were dependent upon technology and economy, the basic social determinants. This peripheral position was occupied alike by statutory or administrative law and by the common law. Legal lag was thus inevitable; and when judges reinterpreted the law, they were merely closing the gap between changed social conditions and lagging legal principles. In this light, the function of the law, one might say, was to legitimize history, to put the seal of legality on what had happened. The popular attitude toward the courts as conservative defenders of traditional practices and privileges was accordingly a sound one. To the extent that Americans accepted Holmes's view of the law, they were persuading themselves that they could do little politically or legally to shape the course of human affairs. Holmes himself, however, was more intent upon making a related point, namely, that judges should not attempt to arrogate to themselves functions which should flow naturally and spontaneously from the creative activities of inventors and entrepreneurs.

By the end of the nineteenth century, the current stage of social evolution required that the law should reflect considerations of public interest or utility. Judges, Holmes felt, ought to be guided in their rulings and decisions by considerations of social advantage rather than by the outmoded rationalizations of *laissez faire*. In a democratic society, then in its modern representative form nearly a century old, the legislature was the means by which the public expressed its preference. A judge should not attempt to check such an expression, even though it might contradict his own convictions.

The ambivalence in Holmes's thinking, reflected in his faith in the emergence of rationality and his abiding distrust of irrational men, was nowhere more clearly apparent than in his discussion of the changing character and social role of the law. With the emergence of rationality, the law also should become more rational. "A body of law is more rational and more civilized when every rule it contains is referred articulately and definitely to an end which it subserves, and when the grounds for desiring that end are stated or are ready to be stated in words." Traditionally, the law had been the will of the sovereign, cloaked in its own majesty and applied by the courts. Now, however, it became merely an adapting mechanism, subservient to the deliberately stated end as determined by the popular legislature. This end was, of course, the public utility or general welfare. By his strong and repeated emphasis upon a "scientific" approach to problems of the law, Holmes meant merely that the law was scientific when it served social ends with maximum efficiency. Then it would be functioning perfectly as an adapting mechanism, and it would no longer display the embarrassing symptoms of cultural lag. The judges then would no longer be accused of being the reactionary tools of vested interests.

In modern society, the medium by which the general welfare was to be achieved was largely economic. Holmes urged his judicial colleagues to pay more attention to such issues in the cases before them. The advice to study economics rather than, say, politics revealed Holmes's naturalistic assumption that political life reflected economic conditions, and that the courts could keep abreast of the legislatures if they sensitized themselves to the influences that moved legislatures.

Holmes was always insistent that the law and morality should not be confused. The law ought to be merely a prediction as to what a court would actually do. He admitted, however, that in the past the law had been hopelessly confused with morality, so that the history of the law was "an external deposit of the moral life." One of his chief objects was to sever the remaining fetters attaching law to morality in order that law might be purely scientific,—that is, merely a means to public ends. Revealing his concern to free the present from the weight of the past, he observed that if the legal vocabulary could be purged of its moral terminology it would be rid of "the fossil records of a good deal of history."

The Rugged Individualist

Justice Holmes generally was scrupulous in observing the tradition that members of the Court should abstain from public discussion of controversial current questions. In his private correspondence, however, there was no need for judicial restraint, and his letters reveal him a stubborn individualist contemptuous of the rising reform spirit of the twentieth century. In economic affairs he admired successful men of action, like the railroad builder James J. Hill. Such men were the creators of opportunity who raised the standard of living and added to the comforts of life.

Holmes did not share the concern of so many of his contemporaries for the concentration of wealth in the hands of the few. He was unable to suppress his irritation with such critics of monopoly as Ida Tarbell. They were directing their attention to the irrelevant issue of monopolistic ownership while overlooking the far more important inquiry into who consumed the annual product. The answer was, of course, that the crowd consumed substantially all that there was to be consumed. The luxuries of the rich were trivial, constituting less than 1 percent in value of the total consumption. What difference did it make, asked Holmes, whether Rockefeller or the United States owned all the wheat so long as the people consumed it? To be sure, Rockefeller in pursuit of profit or power would probably manage the wheat more efficiently than would the United States. If, under competitive capitalism, the abilities of the ablest men were devoted to getting the largest markets and the largest profits the end would be economically desirable; the public would be better served than by any other means.

The ideal economic situation, Holmes believed, would be one in which all desirable products were in the hands of a monopolist intent on getting all he could for them. The value of the products would then be determined by the intensity of desires for them, and they would be consumed by those able to buy them. Holmes apparently confused perfect monopoly with perfect competition. At any rate, he made no attempt to define the necessary conditions limiting the freedom of action of the seller so as to compel respect for the competitive positions of the prospective purchasers. Nor did he appear to be aware of the verdict of classical economic theorists that monopolists tended to restrict output in order to increase profits.

Contemporary criticisms of monopoly were believed by Holmes to be essentially sentimental or political in character. He acknowledged, however, that the larger the private fortune the greater the public interest in its administration, and properly so. He himself would have forbidden men of wealth to give to charities not justified by considerations of public policy. At a time when the income tax was a controversial issue, Holmes expressed the opinion that as a subtraction of a part of the annual product a tax was ultimately a burden on the consumer, no matter what form it might take.

In the last analysis, it was the power to command that made a great fortune significant, not the power to consume, where its effect was trivial. Because in any society someone must command, to Holmes it seemed that the test of economic competition in the marketplace was as good a criterion of the capacity to command as any other. It remains only to add that Holmes once good-naturedly noted that his friend and colleague Justice Brandeis thought these economic opinions naïve.

The political opinions of the judge were equally at odds with the contemporary movement for liberal reform. Holmes was skeptical of many of the aspects of progressivism. He referred contemptuously in private to the Progressive era as "the recent soft period of culture," when Americans had become sentimental about human nature, were teaching pacifism, seeking material comforts, and indulging themselves in too much finespun psychologizing. He deplored the tendency of public policy toward collectivism. The chief danger of collectivism would be posed in its threat to individual liberties. In justice to Holmes, it should be borne in mind that his defenses of civil liberties were conducted in the face of popular pressures. He sensed the massive power of public opinion in a democracy, and he was doubly fearful of its effects once collectivist policies had strengthened the potential hold of bureaucratic governmental agencies upon the individual.

Holmes's low opinion of the legislative measures designed to curb or regulate monopoly was consistent with his theoretical indifference to or even approval of monopolistic concentration in industry and transportation. He declared the Sherman Anti-Trust act to be humbug, based on economic ignorance and incompetence. He told a friend, also privately, that the Interstate Commerce Commission was not fit to have rate-making powers. At the same time, however, he confessed that his own knowledge of the inadequacy of such laws was so imperfect that he was fully prepared to enforce whatever laws the public wanted. As he wrote on another occasion, if the crowd wanted to go to hell, it was his job as a judge to help them do it.

It should be apparent enough from all this that Justice Holmes was profoundly skeptical of the popular drift of democratic culture in the United States. Like many of the naturalists who lived into the twentieth century, he viewed with foreboding the demise of the nineteenth-century rugged individualist and the rise of the mass man whose characteristics were projected by naturalistic social theory. At a time when progressive politicians were hopefully talking about curing the ills of democracy with more democracy, Holmes reported with perverse glee the discovery in a book by the archaeologist Flinders Petrie of a formula for plotting the course of civilizations. They "culminate first in art, then in riches, then democratize, and then goodnight."

CHAPTER 16

||||||||||||||||||||||||||||||||||||||||||||||||||||||||||||||||||||||||

Racism

T HE NATURALISTIC MIND with its biological presuppositions devoted much attention to racial problems and assigned an important place in its general social theory to presumed racial characteristics.

In spite of the universalist and humanitarian implications of the democratic ideology, Americans of the late nineteenth century were not innocent of racial and cultural conflict. From the beginnings of European settlement, there had been virtually continuous warfare between Indians and white men. The Indians were abhorred as degenerate savages, and Indian society was systematically destroyed to make way for the white man's culture. It was only after this destruction was complete that the sentimentalization of the Indian and his culture appeared.

The decade of the 1880's was a decisive one in the history of American racism. During this decade the federal courts refused to protect the civil rights of Negroes under the Fourteenth Amendment, thus denying them relief from the restrictions of caste subordination that were being elaborated as a substitute for chattel slavery. In the same decade, the major source of immigration to the United States shifted from northwestern to southeastern Europe. Many Americans of the older derivation were quick to give expression to their fears and resentment, which they put in racist terms. On the West Coast, organized working men of the Kearney movement had already rioted against Oriental immigrants whose competition in the labor markets they feared. A sense of pressure upon the older Americans from diverse ethnic groups stirred deep feelings of insecurity among them and provided the social background for racist theories.

Intellectual Background of Racism

The great popular theory of race in the Western World was the cultural theory of race, or racism. It came to full fruition only in the twentieth century, both in Europe and in America. Racists were prepared to use the physical classifications of the anthropologists when suited to their purposes, but the primary and distinctive feature of racism was its identification of biological race with culture. It identified a race as a group of people having unique cultural characteristics and playing a unique role in history. A race was to be isolated and analyzed by means of its history and evaluated by its cultural accomplishments. Most racists held that the results of their historical investigations were compatible with the findings of physical anthropology. Cultural capacity like physical heredity was congenital. Thus the racist said that the Negro was distinguished alike by his black skin and his cultural poverty.

Outside the South, racist views never had anything like the authority in America that they came to enjoy in parts of Europe. Furthermore, with the emergence of national socialism in Germany and the practical implementation of the racist philosophy in mass racial persecution, a sharp reaction against racist views arose in the United States. After 1941, it was no longer intellectually respectable to express such views. By the middle of the twentieth century, it was necessary to reconstruct the pattern of intellectual associations which had earlier endowed racist ideas with such cogency that many American intellectuals assented to racist propositions and left either forthright or discreet records of their convictions in their writings.

Perhaps the most prominent element in the intellectual background of racism was the scientific study of racial differences according to the principles of physical anthropology. In one respect, racism was a perversion of this legitimate inquiry. The systematic study and classification of races of men on the basis of physical differences had been underway in Europe since the eighteenth century. After the

Napoleonic wars, when European nations maintained both conscript armies and public schools, these institutions became convenient laboratories for the anthropologist with his calipers and tape measure. From the thousands of measurements made there gradually emerged a widely acknowledged pattern of racial distribution.

The results of this research conducted in several European countries were summarized and synthesized in 1899 by a young Columbia University anthropologist, William Z. Ripley, in *The Races of Europe*. The principal physical traits the distribution of which was investigated were head shape (cephalic index), hair texture, eye color, and stature. These varying traits in combination were believed to characterize distinctive racial types. On the basis of these criteria, it appeared that there were three European races. One, the Teutonic, with its center of dispersion in Scandinavia, was characterized by a long head and face, light hair, blue eyes, narrow nose, and tall stature. A second race was the Alpine, centered in the Alpine highlands of Central Europe, and typified by a round head, broad face, medium dark hair, gray eyes, and stocky medium stature. The third race was the Mediterranean, concentrated along the European shores of that sea from Spain to Greece. This race was characterized by a long head and face, dark or black hair, dark eyes, and medium slender stature.

The physical anthropologists were, of course, evolutionists in their theory of racial origin and dynamics. Related races were regarded necessarily as offshoots from the same trunk or stock. Within a given race, a two-fold process was usually underway—upbuilding and demolition. That is to say, so far as the race was isolated from interbreeding with other races, its distinctive physical features became more uniformly distributed among its members. But when intermixture with other races occurred, then interchange of traits followed. William Graham Sumner, who was deeply influenced by certain of the anthropologists whose findings Ripley summarized, furnished a concise anthropological definition of race: "The concept of a race, as the term is now used, is that of a group clustered around a mean with respect to some characteristic, and great confusion in the use of the word 'race' arises from the attempt to define races by their boundaries, when we really think of them by the mean or mode, e.g., as to skin color." A race as thus conceived was a biological subdivision of a species moving either in the direction of uniform approximation of its mean or modal characteristics or toward greater variability due to intermixture with other races.

Because of the unusual mobility and consequent intermixture of the European peoples, one did not expect to find among them perfect racial types. Rather, it was the proportionate distribution of associated physical traits as established by extensive sampling that enabled the anthropologists to trace the racial distributions indicated. The center of diffusion of each race was that region in which the racial traits appeared with greatest frequency, while the boundaries between races were broad zones of physical variability. Ripley reported that the upper classes of Europe had already intermarried so widely that they could throw little light on racial distribution. It was the peasant class that furnished the best raw materials because of its relative immobility. Photographs of conscripted peasants in uniform long furnished the bulk of the illustrations that graced the anthropological studies of racial distribution.

While tracing racial distribution according to varying physical traits, the anthropologists specifically repudiated the older racial theories based on language or skin pigmentation. Linnaeus had distinguished a single European white race, *Homo Europaeus albus*. But the anthropologists appreciated the great variability of skin color, and they knew that as an esthetic factor complexion was subject to "artificial selection." As clues to racial history, the virtue of the features that they chose was relative imperviousness to the selective process. They also insisted strongly on the absence of correlation between racial and cultural boundaries. Language and nationality might well coincide, since a common language was an effective vehicle for cultural traditions. But actually there was little correspondence between political and ethnic boundaries in Europe. Most modern nations were composed of representatives of two or more racial groups. The sentiment of nationality if focused on a specific racial ideal might indeed become a significant ethnic factor through selection. But at the end of the nineteenth century, there seemed little likelihood that such a factor either had had or would have much effect upon European racial history. Ripley believed that a stronger case could be made for the historical influence of religion as a selective factor than for nationality.

The physical anthropologists believed that existing racial types had emerged through adaptation to peculiar local environments. Beneath the variability that had resulted from modern upper class mobility, the firm persistence of local geographical types was revealed by anthropometric research. Language, culture, or customs had little to do with these differences. Occasionally, cultural changes had coincided with the appearance of new physical types, but these were believed to be mere coincidences. Thus the domestication of animals in prehistoric Europe had coincided with the appearance of a new long-headed population from the east; but it could not be proven that the newcomers had introduced domestication.

The evolutionary approach to racial study was taken over by the racists, who incorporated into their thinking such parts of it as suited their purposes. But, unlike the anthropologists for whom the relatively short span of the historical period was insignificant in comparison with the long prehistoric age, the racists focused their attention on the relatively recent past.

A second strand in the racist complex was drawn from the school of evolutionary thought known as Neo-Darwinism. Neo-Darwinists sought to strengthen and perpetuate the theory of natural selection by furnishing new information on the mechanism of heredity, which had been a weak spot in Darwin's original theory. The most prominent Neo-Darwinist was the German biologist August Weismann. Neo-Darwinists distinguished between somatic or body cells and reproductive or germ cells. The latter were said to control the development of body cells, determining the character of the adult individual. In opposition to Neo-Lamarckians, Weismann and his followers insisted that the germ cells were completely isolated from the body cells, and that no characteristic acquired by body cells in the course of the life experiences of the organism could effect the hereditary determiners transmitted to the following generation by the germ cells. The general effect of Neo-Darwinian discussions was to create the impression that there was sound biological ground for believing that individual and therefore racial characteristics were fatally fixed in the germ plasm of members of the race in question, emerging inevitably in successive generations regardless of environmental influence or the activities of individuals.

The Neo-Darwinian emphasis upon heredity emerged also in the new eugenics. Variously defined as the science of human breeding or the art of being well born, eugenics was popularized by Francis Galton, a cousin of Darwin. Galton's most famous book was *Hereditary Genius,* published in 1869, a decade after the *Origin of Species.* Galton made extensive statistical studies purporting to show that exceptional talent was the property of a relatively small number of families and presumably was transmitted by heredity through successive generations. He claimed to find, for instance, that the son of a distinguished father had himself one chance in four of becoming a distinguished man, whereas the son of an undistinguished person had only one chance in 4000 of attaining eminence. A twentieth-century American disciple of Galton, the biologist Frederick A. Woods, came to similar conclusions. He selected the forty-six Americans judged to be the most eminent and found them to be related to each other in the ratio of 1 to 2. The ratio of relationship for Americans in general, however, was merely 1 to 500. Various ingenious checks were employed to eliminate the effect of environmental influences. In the first three decades of the twentieth century, the *Journal of Heredity*, edited briefly by Woods, became the unofficial organ of American eugenists. Data gathered by eugenists were available to racists and were calculated to lend a pseudoscientific aura of detachment to racist writings.

The establishment of the science of psychology on an independent professional basis also resulted in lines of investigation pertinent to racism. As physiological psychology developed in Europe during the latter part of the nineteenth century, chiefly under the guidance of the German Wilhelm Wundt, there was a tendency to use the accumulated data for purposes of generalizing about the standard or typical mind. Americans, on the other hand, found themselves interested in individual psychological differences, and they developed methods for measuring these differences by means of various kinds of tests. The first opportunity to conduct testing on a mass scale was offered by World War I.

The findings of the army psychological tests received wide publicity. Many Americans were startled to learn that the average mental age of army recruits was less than fourteen years. The tests also seemed to indicate, at least at first glance, that there was a close correlation between social and economic status and intelligence. Eugenists seized upon these findings as proof of their contention that good blood would tell. Ethnic differentials were also clearly indicated. "Old Americans" with northwestern European antecedents were found to possess higher IQ's than the "New Americans" stemming from southeastern Europe. The latter, in turn, scored higher than Blacks. These findings were widely accepted as valid by psychologists during the 1920's. In the following decades, however, they were extensively qualified in the light of a new appreciation of the intimacy with which hereditary and environmental influences were blended in the maturation of the individual. But in their raw form, the army test results provided racists with convenient data to support their contention that physical racial differences coincided with differing cultural aptitudes.

The cultural-anthropological perspective on historical development was also an integral part of the racist mentality. It was rooted in the idea of progress, which had conceived of human history as ascending from primitive and simple beginnings to the complex and sophisticated culture of modern times. As previously indicated, Lewis H. Morgan divided the record of the past into a series of epochs within the great divisions of savagery, barbarism, and civilization. It was assumed that these stages represented an ascending order of complexity, and that races must pass through them in the same successive order if they were to advance at all. Research revealed instances of races that had in fact ceased to advance beyond each of the designated stages. Here then was a kind of yardstick for the measurement of the capacity of a race for culture, just as the intelligence test measured the IQ of the individual. At the same time, however, against the background of the thousands of years revealed by the anthropologist's shovel, civilization was seen to be a late and fragile flower emerging from the slow and painful course of social evolution. These were considerations calculated to elicit an exhilarating sense of the magnitude of civilized man's achievement and, at the same time, a sense of the precariousness of the dizzy eminence he had achieved.

On a much smaller scale, a racial interpretation of American history was emerging in the same years. The major tradition of historical thought in the United States had been and was to remain consistent with the spirit of the democratic social philosophy. It was environmentalist in character, finding formative social influences in the frontier, in the freehold farm, the plantation, and in the economic struggles of mercantile and industrial capitalism.

Typical of the increasing dissatisfaction with environmentalist historiography during the late nineteenth century was the historical writing of John Fiske. Fiske was one of the foremost American supporters and popularizers of Darwin. In lectures delivered in England and published in 1885 as *American Political Ideas Viewed in the Light of Universal History*, he attributed American political institutions and accomplishments to the genius of the Anglo-Saxon people. No other race had succeeded in achieving so delicate a balance of liberty and union. The historical roots of this development were to be traced back through the New England town to the English shire and, ultimately, to the primeval Germanic folkmoot whence the political wisdom of the Anglo-Saxon peoples originally stemmed.

Academic political theory, closely related to historical thought and responsive to the same influences, moved toward the abandonment of the natural-rights political philosophy and the adoption in its stead of an organic conception of political society. This tendency was illustrated in the manifesto of a new professional journal, the *Political Science Quarterly*, the first number of which appeared in 1886. The editor, Professor John W. Burgess of Columbia, proposed that students of American constitutional history abandon the static analysis of constitutional problems in terms of legal and political principles. It was high time, he said, that scholars acknowledge that the true foundation of the American union was not the Constitution but geographical and ethnic unity.

Three years later, on the occasion of the centennial celebration of federal government under the Constitution, Woodrow Wilson, a young professor at Wesleyan University, gently undertook to instruct *Atlantic Monthly* readers in the realities of political order. The framers of the Constitution, he wrote, had not been engaged in any experiment. Rather, they had attempted as best they could to provide for the continuance of the principles of English constitutional government in America. Seen in the perspective of a century, it was clear enough to Wilson that the constitutional republicanism of the Founding Fathers and the democracy of the nineteenth century, which had replaced it, were two very different things. Democracy, which traced much of its prestige in Europe to the French Revolution, could never have brought constitutional government into being because democracy was revolutionary, whereas constructive political achievement must always be the fruit of organic growth. "Such government as ours is a form of conduct, and its only stable foundation is character." Wilson declared the so-called "democracy" of America to be a unique expression of Teutonism, nurtured by a long period of self-government in the English colonial system. It had nothing in common with French democracy. "It is a deeply significant fact, therefore," concluded Wilson, "again and again to be called to mind, that only in the United States, in a few other governments begotten of the English race, and in Switzerland, where old Teutonic habit has had the same persistency as in England, have examples yet been furnished of successful democracy of the modern type." Quite consistently, Professor Wilson expressed considerable concern over the threat to this kind of ethnic democracy implicit in the constantly increasing horde of non-Teutonic immigrants flooding into the United States at the end of the nineteenth century.

Cultural Theory of Race

The fundamental assumption of racism was the belief that culture is the product of race, and that therefore a race is identified and characterized by its culture. The racist was impressed by the fact that so few races had succeeded in producing a civilized culture. A detailed discussion of this problem was undertaken by Lothrop Stoddard, a New Englander of "Old American" stock trained in economics and sociology at Harvard. In the decade after World War I, Stoddard published *The Rising Tide of Color Against White World Supremacy* (1920) and *The Revolt Against Civilization* (1922).

Few civilizations had appeared in the long history of the species, Stoddard explained, because few races had been capable of producing civilization. At each stage of social evolutionary advance were to be found races incapable of further progress: among savages, the Bushmen of Africa and the aborigines of Australia; among barbarians, most Asiatics, Negroes, and the American Indians. In modern times, only the Nordic races had proven capable of producing civilization.

The appearance of a civilization was a rare phenomenon in itself, and when one did appear it was highly vulnerable to several disorders that constantly threatened it. Civilization was perhaps only skin deep, as the historian James Harvey Robinson, himself no racist, pointed out in the widely read *The Mind in the Making* (1921). A species members of which had only so recently attained to the civilized state need not be surprised if it did not always behave in a civilized fashion. But racists found cause for alarm in the instability presumed to be inherent in the nature of civilization itself. Stoddard observed that civilization was a cumulative process in which each generation inherited from its predecessor a heavier cultural burden. Yet its hereditary mental capacity was no greater, if in fact it had not deteriorated. Certain thinkers had hopefully adapted the Lamarckian theory of use-inheritance to social processes, and had put forward the view that lessons painfully learned by experience in the earlier stages of civilization might somehow become embedded in the tissue and be ultimately transmitted as instinct; but as Neo-Darwinists the racists sternly rejected such folly. The increasing burden shouldered by successive generations must lead inevitably to what Stoddard called "structural overloading."

Biological regression was another weakness peculiar to civilization. In savage and barbarous societies the process of natural selection regularly weeded out the unfit. But under civilized conditions the natural environment was supplemented and modified by a man-made social environment. Natural selection gave way to social selection, and thus far, modern society with misguided humanitarian zeal had chosen not merely to preserve the weak, the stupid, and the degenerate but to permit them to reproduce their kind. The strong, of course, also survived, but it was well known that they preferred to raise fewer children. The result of the process was a steady deterioration of the racial stock.

The ultimate consequence of biological regression, according to Stoddard, would be a social revolt of those incapable of survival by their own efforts in a civilized society. These "under-Men" were designated as the source of the revolutionary convulsions of modern society. They hated civilization with its complex demands and would gladly destroy it.

Perhaps the most important but little noticed aspect of racist thinking concerned the role of nationality. The means or agency by which race was transformed from a biological to a cultural concept was nationality or the nation-state. It was with respect to this focal function of nationalism that the most widespread participation in racist attitudes was elicited. Among Americans prominent in public life at the turn of the century, both Theodore Roosevelt and the elder Henry Cabot Lodge regularly used the terms *race* and *nation* interchangeably. Both men were historians, and both believed that for the previous thousand years at least the races of the Western world had tended to form nations. They had entered the state-building phase of social evolution; hence the validity of seeking the characteristics of a race in its national history.

In his Romanes lecture at Oxford in 1910, Roosevelt used the evolutionary theme to account for the origin of nations. Just as a new biological species emerged out of a racial variation, so a barbaric race suddenly discovered a cultural specialization that led to the civilizing process. Roosevelt acknowledged that most high civilizations were "artificial" in that they embraced several racial types, bound together by cultural ties. But he emphasized the fact that these were closely related races; and he warned that some racial differences were too great to permit the formation of a common culture if blended together. The man selected by Roosevelt to conduct the foreign affairs of the United States, Elihu Root, stressed the psychological and intellectual capacity that a race must possess in order to achieve the formation of a national union. This capacity consisted of the will and ability to project common political ideals that would serve as the basis for union.

Senator Lodge's thinking on race questions illustrated the way in which racists bent the findings of the physical anthropologists to their purposes. He also acknowledged that there was no such thing as a pure race, ethnically speaking. There were, however, "artificial" races, which thereupon became for him the ultimate reality of modern life. These artificial races were those groups that in the past thousand years had formed the great nation-states: the English-speaking people, the French, the Germans. Race formation and nation formation had been inseparable facets of a single historical experience, reflecting the effects of climate, wars, migrations, conquests, and industrial development. The English-speaking race that had come to dominate so much of the earth's surface had been formed out of an amalgamation of Celts, Saxons, Danes, and Normans. Ethnically, these were closely related groups—an important consideration in racist theory. By the close of the sixteenth century, the ethnic elements were assembled and the era of achievement was about to begin. A similar process had more recently occurred in Anglo-America. To the original English had been added Dutch, Scandinavian, Scotch-Irish, German, Huguenot, and Celtic-Irish elements. Again, these were kindred races, and the greatness of the American republic testified to the happy combination of qualities that emerged from their union.

In an address delivered in 1896, Lodge eloquently set forth the racist theory of the racial basis of culture.

What, then, is the matter of race which separates the Englishman from the Hindoo and the American from the Indian? It is something deeper and more fundamental than anything which concerns the intellect. We all know it instinctively, although it is so impalpable that we can scarcely define it, and yet is so deeply marked that even the physiological differences between the Negro, the Mongol, and the Caucasian are not more persistent or more obvious. When we speak of a race, then, we do not mean its expressions in art or in language, or its achievements in knowledge. We mean the moral and intellectual characters, which in their association make the soul of a race, and which represent the product of all its past, the inheritance of all its ancestors, and the motives of all its conduct. The men of each race possess an indestructible stock of ideas, traditions, sentiments, modes of thought, an unconscious inheritance from their ancestors, upon which argument has no effect.

Since 1875 a momentous change had been taking place. The United States was being inundated by peoples of widely differing racial backgrounds. Lodge skillfully avoided an outright condemnation of these newcomers (he was after all a practical and eminently successful politician from a polyglot industrial state), while at the same time he left with his auditors the certain sense of his conviction that continued immigration of the recent type constituted a grave threat to the survival of the qualities that had made America great. It was a fundamental racist principle that when superior and inferior races were blended the inferior qualities would prevail. Lodge left no doubt of his conviction that this was the crisis which America faced.

American historians writing between 1880 and 1920 reflected a similar point of view, although they rarely dealt with the issue explicitly. Their blending of race and nationality took the form of stressing the essentially Anglo-Saxon or Teutonic character of American life and institutions. They interpreted American history in terms of certain racial-national traits that they believed to be characteristic. These traits consisted of a unique capacity for the reconciliation of freedom and order, a conservative preference for gradual change, and a veneration of tradition—traits that were reinforced in the typically closeknit township pattern of the northern colonies. These were the views of Edward Channing, of Charles M. Andrews, and of Herbert Baxter Adams. Similarly, John Fiske extolled the peculiar contributions of the Anglo-American race as revealed in industrialism, individualism, and the idea of the federal state.

The expression of opinions of this sort among American intellectuals at the end of the nineteenth century was of peculiar interest in view of the increasing ethnic diversity of the American population. It is impossible to avoid the conclusion that, to a considerable extent at least, these racist theories were a rationalization of the fears and distaste of Americans of older extraction who felt that their security was threatened by newcomers.

The practical connection between racist theories and immigration problems was apparent in the attention focused by racists on the questions of assimilation and amalgamation. The term *assimilation* as used by racists usually meant the *Americanization* of immigrants. Newcomers were to be absorbed into the prevailing patterns of American life, relinquishing their former cultural identity. These patterns were, of course, the heritage of the older America derived chiefly from England. Consequently, Americans of English origin tended to favor assimilation. They appraised immigrant groups in terms of the speed and effectiveness of assimilation, and they disapproved of those who resisted assimilation. While assimilation was a cultural concept, Americans implicitly assumed that races of close biological relationship were alone capable of assimilating one another's culture.

John Fiske told an English audience in 1880 that the non-English elements in America were being quickly assimilated to the Anglo-American norm. He acknowledged, however, that these were strains racially close to the English. But by 1894, when he was elected president of the Immigration Restriction League, Fiske was no longer sanguine as to the prospects of assimilation now that immigrant types were deviating more markedly from the older pattern. The difference was no longer simply one of physical features; now there was a qualitative difference, since recent immigrants were, according to Fiske, worthless individuals who had lost out in the struggle for existence. It is noteworthy that discussions of assimilation usually referred to cultural assimilation to the attitudinal and behavioral patterns of older American society. They did not refer to intermarriage. This was symptomatic of how the biological blended into the cultural in racist thinking.

Amalgamation, on the other hand, meant the merging of racial-national characteristics into a new composite type. As commonly used, the term might refer either to biological or to cultural amalgamation. Spokesmen for newer immigrant groups sometimes advocated amalgamation under the term *melting pot*. Each participating group would make some contribution to the new American race. In older and more complacent times, Emerson had bestowed his benediction upon amalgamation.

Racists, however, regarded the crossing of races as highly undesirable, especially where the races in question occupied different places on the cultural scale. Madison Grant, who wrote extensively on racist themes, held that in such crosses the inferior race always swamped out the superior. Similarly, Hugo Münsterberg, German-born psychologist and philosopher of Harvard, attributed the independence and vigor of American society to its Germanic origins, and he warned that the more recent immigrants from southeastern Europe would "drag down the high and independent spirit of the nation to their low and unworthy ideals." Samuel Gompers, founder of the American Federation of Labor and himself an immigrant of Dutch-Jewish origin, declared Oriental immigrants to be biologically unfit for the melting pot because they were congenitally immoral, incapable of self-government, and content with a lower standard of living. Later, by the end of the century, Gompers opposed further immigration from Central and Southeast Europe as well. He was convinced that national survival depended on racial purity. To preserve it, he proposed to restrict further immigration to those capable of passing a literacy test because such persons were more readily assimilated.

A third alternative was more ominous even than the prospects of assimilation or amalgamation—outright displacement. General Francis A. Walker, a distinguished statistician and director of the federal Census, pointed out at the beginning of the twentieth century that the consequences of unrestricted immigration were to be understood in terms of the struggle for existence. It was simply a fact that the descendants of the "new" nineteenth-century immigrants were replacing the offspring of older Americans through the process of more abundant reproduction. In the course of a few generations the country would be theirs.

One of the most comprehensive efforts to deal with racial-national questions in biological evolutionary terms was made by Nathaniel Southgate Shaler, professor of geology and paleontology at Harvard. Born in Newport, Kentucky, of mixed Yankee and Virginia parentage, Shaler had been a student of Agassiz at the Lawrence Scientific School of Harvard, where he graduated in 1862. Although he supported the Union cause, he was always proud of his Southern ancestry and sympathetic with the Southern point of view on race questions. Shaler's views were expounded in *The Neighbor. The Natural History of Human Contacts* (1904).

Like other distinguished pupils of Agassiz, Shaler had gone beyond his teacher to an unqualified evolutionary standpoint. He regarded the *genus homo* as having evolved out of earlier mammalian forms of life and as subject to the same universal natural laws that governed all living things. As a subdivision of a species, a race played a potentially important role in the evolutionary process. Distinctive racial characteristics, if preserved from crossing with those of other races and if adapted to the environmental habitat, might result eventually in the formation of a new species. Shaler stressed the fact that mental as well as physical features were subject to the laws of evolution; each played its part in the raciation and speciation processes. Proof that mental differences were involved in evolutionary differentiation was to be found in the comparison of domesticated with wild races of animals, and in studies of insect life, as well as in human history, where to Shaler's mind the evidence was irrefutable. It was these distinctive mental qualities that gave to the members of each race of the human genus that consensus of understanding or distinctive perceptions so difficult for outsiders to share. In fact, mental differences emerged to distinguish a potential race before its distinctive physical features had yet become fixed. The mental features of the emerging race were to function as a factor in guiding the natural selection of physical characteristics. This, incidentally, was Shaler's contribution to the attempt to bridge the gap between the Darwinian and Lamarckian evolutionary schools.

The Harvard scientist disagreed with most anthropologists by dividing the *genus homo* into several distinct living species. Without indicating precisely how many were to be found, his discussion revealed at least three: white, Negro, and American Indian species. Among the racial subdivisions of the white species he commented at length on the Aryans of northwestern Europe and the Jews. Elsewhere, however, he referred to the Jews as a distinct species. The fact that he was not always consistent in the use of these terms would appear to indicate that Shaler regarded them as loose designations of relative degrees of group difference rather than as mutually exclusive categories.

Within the *genus homo* the racial groups from which species emerged were called tribes. Shaler took for granted the naturalistic assumption that the cultural evolution of the human genus had its place within the broader biological evolutionary framework. It would have been fruitless to ask at what point the one process became the other. But in terms of Shaler's analysis, the shift in emphasis from the biological to the cultural occurred at the tribal stage. In cultural evolutionary terms, the tribal stage corresponded to Morgan's status of barbarism. The previous state of savagery, Shaler held, was one in which "the primitive man is a Philistine with his hand by birthright set against his neighbor of all degrees, animate and inanimate. He must slay when he can and propitiate when he cannot slay, and all with hatred in his heart." Tribalism, on the other hand, represented an advance of great biological and cultural significance. Biologically, the tribe was a race. Its members shared common blood through intermarriage; racial identity was preserved by the prohibition on marriage with outsiders. Thus the tribal race was a potential or incipient species. Culturally, the tribe represented an important social evolutionary advance. The primitive force of hatred, second only to hunger as a basic human drive, which had dominated savagery, was now forced to share man's psyche with the sense of sympathy, born of the peculiar conditions of child rearing with its prolonged infancy. Within the tribe, sympathy was extended to all members, who were bound together by ties of blood, religion, and language. Hatred was now focused upon the outsider.

All species of men were found by Shaler to have reached the tribal stage of social development, although certain of its features were not yet well marked among the American Indians. But even in those groups of men that had progressed beyond the tribal stage, its stamp was still to be seen in certain influential psychological residues. Tribalism had, in fact, developed an organic intensity and moral control that no subsequent social form had displayed. It was, therefore, a great mistake for civilized men to minimize the importance of the survival in themselves of tribal motives.

Only the white species had progressed beyond the tribal stage to the state-making stage that men called civilization. Shaler placed great emphasis on the fact that the modern state was a very recent phenomenon, still in the experimental phase, so to speak. Its principle was the guarantee of equal rights to all its citizens regardless of ethnic differences. An outgrowth of tribal solidarity, it was an expression of Christ's religion of universal brotherhood, itself paradoxically a tribal product. There was already ample experience to demonstrate that the state could be successful only where the ethnic diversities among its people were not great; otherwise it was doomed to failure.

In the meanwhile, the concept of a tribal state, one in which those of common blood were acknowledged to be alone fit for its control, could not be lightly dismissed. Shaler undoubtedly had in mind the antebellum South. Modern men might dream of a more cosmopolitan society, but there was little as yet in experience to justify it. The Southern sympathizer who had witnessed the enfranchisement of former Black slaves issued his warning. Americans were in great danger of underestimating the importance of racial differences. They assumed that in the modern state they could effect the same close relationships among people of diverse races and even species that had been achieved in the tribe. They were attempting to build a state that was, in effect, an enlarged tribe, while at the same time ignoring or suppressing their consciousness of the racial differences within it. American experience had indeed shown that differences of religion and social custom could be reconciled in the modern state; but when it came to the "larger differences" of color, shape, and innate intellectual capacity, Shaler pointed out that the objectives of the democratic commonwealth, namely, equal sharing of the duties and benefits of citizenship, remained everywhere unrealized.

The democratic dilemma should not surprise anyone who troubled to consider the results of European overseas conquests since the time of Columbus. The conquered peoples of other species could sometimes be subjugated, but nowhere had they been successfully assimilated into the cultural patterns of their conquerors. These subject peoples were clearly incapable of absorbing the arts of civilization. An alternative was racial amalgamation, as practiced in Latin America. This was certainly successful in dissolving broad ethnic differences, but the results in other respects, according to Shaler, were "very evil." The hybrid mestizo class was generally weaker, shorter-lived, and without the mental or moral qualities of either parent group. Shaler knew of some individual exceptions among offspring of Indian and European marriages in the United States, but these occasional instances merely proved the rule.

The modern nation-state, like the tribe, was regarded by Shaler as an incipient species. But because of its greater size and ethnic diversity the speciation process presumably advanced at a much slower rate than in the tribe. Shaler knew that the populations of most European nations were ethnically mixed, and, like other racists, he was prepared to acknowledge that the crossing of closely related stocks was biologically advantageous. Hence he approved of the blending of peoples from northwestern Europe in the American population. Nevertheless, the state retained many of the characteristics of the tribe, largely because its people retained the tribal state of mind; as Robinson would have said, they were but newly civilized barbarians. The sympathy that united the group and the hatred that isolated it from other groups had deep psychological roots. Here was the cause of the universal phenomenon of race hatred. But in the modern state, race hatred was not necessarily directed against the foreigner; it might be focused upon the neighbor. It was this ambiguity of human relationships in the modern commonwealth that intrigued Shaler.

The United States provided the student with the ideal laboratory for the exploration of these questions. By a mixture of accident and intention, the Americans had formed a state based on a large number of ethnic groups representing every degree of difference. A singularly varied and intense set of racial feelings was the result. Shaler selected for analysis two examples of race prejudice in America, "the Hebrew problem" and "the problem of the African." His inquiry was conducted with great personal sympathy and sensitivity combined with what he thought to be scientific objectivity. It was apparent to a later generation, however, that his fixed assumption of the objective character of race prejudice founded on awareness of differences closed the very question with which a more careful scientific investigation would have started.

The Jews had survived as a race in spite of dispersion and two thousand years of persecution because of the intensity of their ethnic motivation, in Shaler's opinion. They had refused to forget that they were Jews. Although they had attained legal and civil rights in European states since the eighteenth century, they were everywhere more disliked than ever. Even in the United States, Shaler had noted the rise of anti-Semitism that followed in the wake of the Dreyfus affair of the late 1890's. The heart of anti-Semitism was to be found not in religious differences but in a spontaneous reaction to ethnic differences. The Gentile sensed the innate superiority of the Jew and feared it. He saw that the Jew was at once grasping by nature and fawning by disposition. These objective differences, which Shaler checked by questioning his friends and examining his own reactions, were the basis of race hatred. From a strictly scientific point of view, Shaler concluded that the Jews were the highest species of the *genus homo*. They were the ablest known people, highly moral and humane. Unfortunately for them, however, they had not proved adaptable to the customs of the people among whom they lived. Paradoxically, they were also declared to be somewhat archaic, being deficient in the state-making capacity, in scientific ability, and in the mechanic arts. In all these respects the Aryan race was said to be supreme.

The Blacks, in Shaler's opinion, presented America with its greatest problem. Their history had proven them incapable of progress beyond the barbarian tribal stage. In Africa, they had succeeded in developing a primitive agriculture but no historical sense, no traditions, literature, religion, or social polity. They had thus come to a state of arrested development, incapable of further progress save by imitating a master race. When thrust into positions of power and responsibility in the South during the Reconstruction era, Blacks had proven themselves devoid of any sense of political or social order. On the other hand, candor compelled a student to admit that, in contrast to the Jew, the Black possessed unique physical and psychical adaptability. He also displayed a strong sense of sympathy and a capacity for great faithfulness and affection. His linguistic aptitude and musical talent had often been remarked.

In groping for a solution to its racial problems, Shaler believed that America was fortunate that social evolutionary progress had brought the dominant Aryan race to the point where it could grasp the principles of the Christian religion and the scientific method of investigation. Faith and reason were to furnish the clues to the solution of the problem. Christianity held forth the promise of the extension of the primitive sense of sympathy for the blood relative to all mankind. Fortified with this principle, Aryan Americans would find that on sustained personal contact with members of alien races they could overcome their instinctive aversion to the alien. It was necessary only to make the contact with the stranger, repugnant though the gesture might be, in order to discover the common humanity beneath the surface of racial differences. Shaler set great store by face-to-face associations as a solvent for racial hostilities. He solemnly assured his readers that because of the abundance of such contacts in the South, Southerners had no anti-Black prejudice.

Science, on the other hand, required of Americans that they evaluate their problems objectively. The existing ethnic composition of the population clearly indicated the necessity of ridding themselves of their tribal prejudices if they were to survive as a nation. At the same time, sound biological principles required the prevention of further immigration to the United States of those "who are proven by their history to be unfit for the service of our state." This included all but Aryans and Jews of the "less degraded" sort. Also to be excluded were immigrants from southern Italy, the lower Danube Basin, and the Balkans. Natives of all other parts of the world were to be excluded as a matter of course. Care should also be taken to avoid annexation of territories with alien populations. Aryans and Jews already in the United States should be amalgamated in order to avoid the evil of segregated communities.

Shaler was emphatic that amalgamation of whites and Blacks must not occur in any circumstances. It was common biological knowledge that the hybridization of different species resulted in sterile and devitalized offspring. Moreover, there was said to be abundant evidence that the distinctive qualities that had given the Aryan race supremacy failed to survive in mulattoes. The Black should be content to make a useful contribution to American society as a laborer. He should be trained for agriculture and the crafts but not for the professions. Shaler believed that it would be helpful in the first place to take the Black out of politics by disfranchising him, thus preventing his political exploitation. This could best be done by imposing property and literacy qualifications for the suffrage, on the old republican theory that those with a stake in society should govern. Shaler was not concerned that such tests would disfranchise many whites as well. And tests were certainly preferable to the shameful and humiliating subterfuge of the "grandfather clause." Shaler's ultimate vision was one of a benevolent paternalism, in which the races were bound by deepening ties of sympathy and mutual dependence but carefully segregated in cultural and biological respects.

The pessimism engendered in racist minds by contemplation of the ethnic diversity of the American population expressed itself appropriately enough in a cyclical theory of history explained in racial terms. In 1921, William McDougall, then professor of psychology at Harvard, published his Lowell Institute lectures, *Is America Safe for Democracy?*. The versatile psychologist described the course of history as consisting of the rise and decay of successive national civilizations, each produced by a different race, although the blending of two closely related peoples might also achieve the same happy result. The course of each civilization could be represented by the curve of a parabola. McDougall believed the American civilization to be still in the ascending arc of its parabola, but he was deeply concerned lest certain forces at work within it might turn it on its downward course. He did not believe the decline to be inevitable, in the manner of Spengler's theory. It might be averted indefinitely, although the prospects did not seem bright. The moral and intellectual qualities that were the innate and probably hereditary endowment of each race largely determined the character of its civilization. Results of mass testing of intelligence showed clearly enough upon what ethnic groups American civilization rested. As soon as the potentialities of these people were to become fully realized in civilized institutions decay would inevitably set in.

The usual causes of the decline of civilizations constituted what McDougall felt to be a formidable list. The increasing complexity of civilized life made ever-more-difficult demands on human aptitudes. At the same time, the binding force of custom, so apparent in simpler communities, became loosened, allowing a greater variety of choices, weakening social harmony, and throwing a greater burden on the intelligence of individuals. More leisure and a variety of diversions offered themselves as distractions at a time when the problems of life required more sustained concentration of attention. Dysgenic effects stemmed from military and city life, and from the effectiveness with which social advancement segregated the abler people in a ruling class that then failed to reproduce itself. McDougall was persuaded that race mixing would probably result in reversion to lower biological types, although the findings of intelligence tests that he cited elsewhere had indicated that the scores made by mixed bloods were generally an average of those of the parent groups. Finally, in civilized societies natural selection ceased to operate in its usual fashion to eliminate the unfit. The latter were not only preserved but were even permitted to reproduce their kind and debase the stock, while the abler classes of society tended to become infertile.

The survival of American civilization depended in large part upon the capacity of the better classes to perpetuate their talents in an abundant progeny, while finding some means of preventing or discouraging the incompetent and dependent from reproducing their kind. McDougall did not deceive himself that this could be easily accomplished. But clearly, however, a first practicable step would consist of prohibiting the immigration of the latter types into the country.

A study of racial aptitudes in the American population made by Henry Cabot Lodge in 1891 was intelligible only in terms of the racist conviction that races possessed distinctive cultural characteristics which would be displayed by their respective descendants even when removed from the racial homeland. Lodge classified the 14,243 eminent Americans listed in Appleton's *Encyclopedia of American Biography* according to their racial-national origins. The paternal line of descent was sufficient to determine the derivation of each individual, for Lodge's purposes. He found that of the total number, 10,375 were of English origin, 1439 Scotch-Irish, 659 German, 589 Huguenot, 436 Scottish, with the remaining few hundred widely scattered. In order to offset the long colonial period of English domination, Lodge selected from the same source only those Americans descended from immigrants who had come to the United States subsequent to 1789. There were 1271 eminent Americans in this category, and their distribution by land of racial origin told much the same story: 345 English, 245 German, 200 Irish, 151 Scottish, 88 Scotch-Irish, with the remaining 200 widely scattered.

In the same investigation, Lodge also undertook to analyze the forms in which racial ability expressed itself in America. He found that Irish and Black talent appeared chiefly in religion. This was true also of the Scotch-Irish and the French. The Swiss were strong in the educational field, while Scottish talent appeared chiefly in literature and business. English talent, on the other hand, was so widely dispersed through the various fields of endeavor that none could be selected as peculiarly characteristic. Exceptional versatility as well as talent was obviously a distinctive English trait. In reflecting on his findings, Lodge noted that the capacity of a race to give expression to its aptitudes in America was conditioned by the speed with which it was able to assimilate itself to the patterns of American life.

The practical consequence of racist discussion was the immigration legislation of 1924. While it cannot be said that racism was the sole cause of the policy of restricted immigration, it seems certain that the differential immigration quotas assigned to various nations were the result of racial-national convictions. The annual preferential quota assigned to each country was determined by the proportion of the American population derived from that country. In its effect, the quota system was calculated to protect the cultural and social supremacy of the ethnic groups found by Senator Lodge to have dominated American life down to the end of the nineteenth century. In the five years before World War I, 67 percent of American immigration had come from southeastern Europe; under the quota system the proportion was cut back to 20 percent. In other words, Americans of northwestern European origin were determined not to share their blessings with others.

CHAPTER 17

||||||||||||||||||||||||||||||||||||||||||||||||||||||||||||||||||||||

Thorstein Veblen,
Social Evolutionist

NATURALISTIC SOCIAL THEORY received its most extended and impressive statement from the pen of Thorstein Veblen. The son of Norwegian immigrant parents, Veblen was born on a Wisconsin farm in 1857. The gifted and sensitive boy was not happy in a home environment dominated by a stern and uncomprehending father. A sense of isolation early sharpened the critical faculties. As an undergraduate at Carleton College, Veblen read Herbert Spencer and studied economics with John Bates Clark, experiences that pointed toward major emphases of his life's work. After graduation in 1880, he went to Johns Hopkins for a year of graduate study of historical economics under R. T. Ely. From Hopkins he went to Yale, where he studied philosophy with Noah Porter and socio-anthropology with Sumner. The decisive influence of Sumner could later be detected at many points in Veblen's system of thought. Two years at Cornell concluded his peripatetic graduate studies in 1892. He had not definitely identified himself as either economist, sociologist, or philosopher, a circumstance that militated against the success of a rather uncouth young man in an academic world where disciplinary lines were already becoming tightly drawn.

Veblen's subsequent academic career was a failure when measured by the usual criteria. He was unable, and perhaps unwilling, to retain any of the teaching positions that he held successively at Chicago, Stanford, and Missouri. Although he aroused the interest of a few gifted students, who became enthusiastic disciples, he neglected his responsibilities to the common run of students and was regarded by university administrators as a liability. Friends finally secured for him a position at the New School for Social Research, which he held until his death in 1929. Throughout his life he remained a sensitive, aloof, and satiric spirit, a "marginal man" whose personal alienation from the intellectual institutions of his day undoubtedly underlay the critical detachment with which in his books he dissected contemporary pecuniary culture.

A passage from his first book, *The Theory of the Leisure Class* (1899), announced Veblen's evolutionism. "The life of man in society, just like the life of other species, is a struggle for existence, and therefore it is a process of selective adaptation. The evolution of social structure has been a process of natural selection of institutions. The progress which has been and is being made in human institutions and in human character may be set down, broadly, to a natural selection of the fittest habits of thought and to a process of enforced adaptation of individuals to an environment which has progressively changed with the growth of the community and with the changing institutions under which men have lived."

Veblen was not merely an evolutionist; he proposed more explicitly to make a conscientious application to social theory of the Darwinian concepts of struggle, natural selection, and adaptation to environment. It would be confusing to designate Veblen a "Social Darwinist" because that term has become attached to those apologists for the economic *status quo* who talked more or less superficially about the survival of the fittest in the economic struggle, people with whom Veblen had little in common. Yet Veblen's was the most impressive American attempt to interpret the social process in Darwinian terms. He conceived of social institutions as the result of a selective and adaptive process. So also were the personality types and attitudes prevailing at any given moment. These institutions, personality types, and attitudes constituted total ways of life, which were, in their turn, effective factors of selection. Changing institutions acted to select the individuals with the fittest temperaments, and they, in turn, formed new institutions.

Veblen thus conceived of the social process as an environment, partly human and partly nonhuman, acting upon human beings— the pervasive naturalistic point of view. Selection tended to preserve favorable ethnic types among the varying individuals who composed the population. In communities like those of Europe and America, where the population was composed of several relatively stable ethnic groups, one group would be found to dominate at any given moment, due to selection. Within these dominant ethnic types, the habits of thought of individuals would similarly be subject to selection.

Social institutions must inevitably change with "changing circumstances," Veblen held, because institutions were in the nature of habitual responses to the stimuli emanating from the circumstances. Institutions were defined as prevalent habits of thought about particular relations and functions of the individual with the community. Social evolution was essentially a process of mental adaptation on the part of individuals under pressure of environmental circumstances that would no longer tolerate behavior patterned on previously existing circumstances. Implicit here was the naturalistic assumption of the epiphenomenal character of thought. Thought was regarded as an adapting mechanism, responding to the circumstances presented by the environment. Thus the circumstances of the moment shaped the institutions of the morrow by selection. By the same token, existing institutions, being adapted to past circumstances, were not in accord with existing requirements. They could never fully catch up, because any institutional change was itself a change in the total situation. And so the process went on, *ad infinitum*.

Institutional response to change was always more or less tardy because of the native inertia that characterized men's habits of thought. Men resisted change until prodded from without. Social change depended upon the pressure exerted by the environment upon individuals. If a class of men were sheltered from such pressure, it resisted change. The leisure class, in Veblen's opinion, was such a class. In modern society, the pressure to initiate change usually presented itself in an economic form.

So much for the first general statement of his ideas. The language was vague, Veblen apparently preferring to mask his key concepts in general terms like *circumstances* and *situation*. Fifteen years later, however, in *The Instinct of Workmanship and the State of the Industrial Arts* (1914), he amplified and altered the argument significantly by resolving the changing environmental situation into its component elements. He now asserted the primary role of technology in social change, thus escaping from the circular causation of his earlier book.

Being a thoughtful social evolutionist, Veblen realized that he was obliged to deal with racial groups as well as with individuals. The mutation theory held the center of attention in the biological world at the end of the century. In accordance with this theory, Veblen maintained that the races of mankind had arisen relatively suddenly, by mutation, rather than through the gradual accumulation of imperceptible variations according to the older Darwinian doctrine. Each race was possessed of distinctive physical and mental features. Although in at least one place he asserted the identity of race and nationality, Veblen in general adopted the newly established threefold racial classification of European peoples into long-headed blond Nordics (Teutonics), round-headed brunet Alpines, and long-headed dark-eyed Mediterraneans. (*The Theory of the Leisure Class* appeared in the same year that Ripley published his *Races of Europe.*) These European races were of relatively recent origin, biologically speaking. The youngest of them, the Nordic, was fixed in its characteristics by selection and adaptation to conditions that had prevailed more recently than the conditions to which the other races were adapted. In other words, the Nordic race was less out of date than the others. This accounted, in Veblen's opinion, for the relative dominance of Nordics in modern culture. On a broader scale, it accounted for the dominance of the three European races over all others.

Each of the three European races was a hybrid which bred true. The geographical distribution of each had remained approximately stable since the late Stone Age. And each varied in native endowment for technological and other activities. The hybrid character of these races meant that there was considerable variability of individual characteristics within each of them. Veblen assumed that hybrid variability was the ultimate basis of European cultural development. Because of the unique biological constitution of a race, its history would also be unique. Racial histories could not therefore properly be compared, and there was no universal cultural evolution after the fashion of Morgan and the other naturalists. As a matter of fact, in spite of this denial, Veblen's thinking did involve this assumption whenever he had occasion to comment upon a racial culture in terms of his criteria of savagery or barbarism. It was impossible for him to avoid the universal relevance of his theory of the evolution of culture through successive stages. His actual purpose was merely to deny any invidious racial comparisons. All three European races were well endowed with the instinctual equipment necessary for cultural elaboration. They were, in other words, psychologically qualified for social evolutionary progress.

As environmental conditions changed, the selective forces bearing upon individuals also changed, producing new human types. European cultural evolution since the Stone Age had produced two variants of each of the three European races: peaceable and predatory. These were the products, respectively, of the earlier era of peaceable savagery and the more recent era of predatory barbarism. The law of heredity dictated that the more recent predatory variant would dominate in modern times, with occasional reversions to the older peaceable type. The youngest of the European races, the Nordic, should breed more consistently predatory than the others. Generally speaking, modern man was ethnically a barbarian, although the duration of that age had not been great enough to fix the predatory type without variations.

In spite of his professed interest in economic institutions, Veblen in his role of anthropologist was chiefly concerned with the psychological aspects of social evolution. *The Theory of the Leisure Class* and *The Instinct of Workmanship* both dealt largely with the role of psychic factors interacting among themselves and with institutions. The characteristics of each successive cultural epoch were expressions of various combinations of instinctive impulses crystallized in institutional practices. Veblen affirmed that it was the instincts which had the largest influence in shaping institutions.

Veblen belonged to the instinct school of social psychology. While at the University of Chicago between 1893 and 1906, he had been deeply interested in the work of the physiologist Jacques Loeb, who was investigating the involuntary responses to sensory stimuli that he called tropisms. From Loeb and others Veblen learned that instincts could be broken down into simpler psychological or physiological elements. But he maintained that the concept of instinct was still a valid one for the social sciences, and in 1914 he published *The Instinct of Workmanship,* a detailed investigation of the role of instinct in the social process.

Instincts were defined by Veblen as teleological categories that determined the ends of action. By defining purpose, efficiency, pleasure, and pain they determined conduct. The operation of instincts involved consciousness and capacity for adaptation to an end; they were, in other words, peculiar to the higher animals. In a developed culture, the variety of ways and means by which an instinctive impulse might realize its end was considerable. These ways and means tended to institutionalize themselves as traditions and habits. Instincts did not act separately and independently but in combinations. Veblen's concept of instinct was thus far from that of a simple response to stimulus.

No inclusive list of instincts was furnished by Veblen. Those with the greatest pertinence to his inquiry, and to which he referred most frequently, were the instincts of workmanship, the parental bent, and idle curiosity. Other instincts were fear, arrogance, abasement, race solidarity or conscience, and the self-regarding instincts. There were also tantalizingly vague references to the "propensity" of emulation, to the "proclivities" to construction and acquisition, and to such "traits" as truthfulness, sense of equity, ferocity, self-seeking, clannishness, disingenuousness, pugnacity, and humanitarianism. But it was with the constructive function of the economic instincts in the elaboration of culture that Veblen was chiefly concerned. These were workmanship and parental bent and idle curiosity.

The instincts that made for material well-being and hence for biological survival were workmanship and the parental bent. The latter also expressed itself in concern for the welfare of the community and in interest in efficient effort to that end. These two instincts in conjunction exerted the major influence in working out the customs and standards that gave rise to institutions. They exerted a common-sense control over all institutions, preventing life from becoming "insufferably grotesque." However, fundamental though its effects might be, the instinct of workmanship was apt to give way whenever the pressure from other instincts was great. It was also said to be subject to contamination, to being warped or biased by the activities of other instincts as they functioned within the framework of existing habits and customs. A prevalent emphasis on magic, for instance, would affect the logic and methods of technology and hinder innovation in this field. Similarly, rule by elders, a characteristic of upper savagery and lower barbarism, tended to lessen initiative, to increase the force of constituted authorities, and hence to deflect workmanship from the naïve pursuit of efficiency. Veblen was firmly convinced of the obstructive influence of the instinct of fear expressed through religious forms and institutions upon the functioning of the instinct of workmanship. He asserted that the religious impulse when fully institutionalized might put a stop to all advance in the mechanic arts, thus illustrating how a distorted sense of workmanship when channeled into ritualism could, in turn, contaminate idle curiosity.

Human races were found by Veblen to vary in the distribution of emphases given to the various instincts. This was the reason why racial histories differed. In some of them the paramount influence of pugnacity, fear, and subserviency was only too apparent. The European races, however, were judged to be favorably endowed with the constructive instincts; hence their unique record of accomplishments, a record that Veblen tacitly acknowledged without pausing to gloat over it.

The relative permanence of instincts as part of the biological endowment of races received strong emphasis. While changes in technology and institutions were occurring constantly, changes in hereditary instinctual endowment occurred scarcely at all. Veblen did concede, however, that the European peoples displayed instinctive adaptations to more recent cultural conditions not to be found in the originally pure races from which the modern hybrids were derived. Substantial modifications, then, if not innovations were possible.

The force of instinct could rarely overcome institutional restraints, even though instincts were themselves prime factors in shaping institutions. The historical record was replete with instances where disserviceable institutions had frustrated the expression of the constructive instincts. It therefore appeared to be accidental whenever the development of the institutional structure took such a course as to give effective expression to the positive economic instincts. It was this indeterminate relationship between instincts and institutions that, in the last analysis, gave history its spontaneity and, for Veblen, its poignancy.

Historical–Cultural Stages

Like other social evolutionists, Veblen emphasized the historical analysis of the development of culture. He distinguished three major stages, each subdivided into two substages: earlier and later savagery; predatory and quasi-peaceable barbarism; and modern pecuniary culture consisting of the earlier handicraft era and the present, variously called the commercial era, the business era, or the era of machine industry. Veblen commonly referred to these divisions as industrial or economic stages.

The stage of savagery corresponded to the Stone Age in archaeology, embracing the earliest evidences of human culture. It was an era of great importance and accomplishment, because in it were laid the foundations for all subsequent cultural development. In spite of Veblen's detached and analytical reconstruction of savagery, based largely on inferences drawn from linguistics and archaeology, it contained remnants of the romantic cult of primitivism. Basic technological innovations were made during savagery: first, the domestication of plants and animals, followed by the invention of implements and tools. Peaceable and sedentary conditions must have prevailed to make these accomplishments possible. The parental bent was expressed in the central place assigned to women as cultivators of the soil. Industrial activity was essentially cooperative; there was no ownership, hiring, bartering, property, or prices. It was during the savage era that the European races were formed, and it was their instincts that accounted for these fruitful developments. The instincts of fear and pugnacity were less marked in them than in many other races, and there was consequently less emphasis among them on religious ritual. As for pugnacity, Veblen observed dryly that the capacity to fight was always less important in the racial struggle than the capacity to produce food and children.

In the later phase of savagery, rule by elders became characteristic. This development frustrated the free expression of workmanship and slowed down the rate of technological advance. In the earlier phase, when all had been workmen, it had been the natural tendency to assign a comparable purposive intent to all external objects. But as technological knowledge accumulated, this diffused animism was pressed back into more remote anthropomorphic agencies. The prevalence of such anthropomorphism in the later phase of savagery became an obstruction to workmanship.

When productive methods had improved to the point where a surplus of commodities beyond those necessary for mere subsistence was available and worth expropriating, the transition to barbarism occurred. The central features of barbarism formed a striking contrast to those of the previous age. In the earlier or predatory phase of barbarism, as the term suggests, the state of peace gave way to predation. The character of the struggle for existence now changed from one in which the human group opposed the physical environment to one in which man contended against man. Self-interest replaced the common good as the prevailing ideal. Early forms of private property appeared in war booty, priestly exactions, and the ownership of women. Emulation was the motive behind ownership. The prevailing state of warfare that resulted produced in turn autocratic leadership; patriarchy and monotheistic religion became characteristic expres-

sions of a stratified society. All these developments presumably originated with pastoral peoples who gave expression to their predatory
animus by subjecting their sedentary agricultural neighbors.

The later or quasi-peaceable phase of barbarism represented the
institutional stabilization of the previous tendencies. While warfare
and physical aggression were minimized, the psychology underlying
these practices continued to permeate and color all institutions and
attitudes. A regime of status with a clearly marked social hierarchy
was now accepted by all as normal and inevitable. This hierarchy
ranged from a leisure class at the top to slaves at the bottom. Labor
was now accounted dishonorable as an evidence of poverty. Institutions of conspicuous leisure and consumption were developed, among
the first being an elaborate domestic service. Yet in spite of these stultifying tendencies, a rapid technological development continued,
thanks largely to borrowing from cultures beyond the bounds of the
area occupied by the European races. It was this continued technological development that presumably accounted for the fact that the
barbarian stage in Europe did not, as elsewhere, end in complete
cultural stagnation. Nevertheless, the institutions and attitudes of
barbarism obstructed the expression of the constructive instincts and,
for Veblen, clearly constituted one of the major cultural crises that
man had encountered.

The latest stage of pecuniary culture did not stand in any such relationship of dialectical opposition to its predecessor as barbarism had
stood in relation to savagery. Many features of barbarian culture
continued into modern times. In his own characterization of the pecuniary culture, Veblen spoke of "its institutions drawn in terms
of differential advantage and moved by sentiments that converge on
emulative gain and the invidiously conspicuous waste of goods." The
decisive new element was the modern machine technology. The
foundations of pecuniary culture rested upon what Veblen felt to
be the more-than-fortuitous concomitance of race, machine technology, material science, religious skepticism, and free institutions.

When the predatory culture failed to reach full maturity in Europe, it gave way to the earlier phase of the pecuniary culture, which
Veblen named the handicraft era, lasting from the twelfth to the
eighteenth century. The basis of institutions now shifted from prowess
to security of ownership, resulting in increased application to work,
although accompanied by continuing contention, distrust, chicanery,
and wasteful competition. There was nevertheless a strong revival of
the instinct of workmanship, expressing itself in the growth of handi-

craft, trade, and responsibility in politics. The typical combination of workmanship with ownership brought about an intimate blending of the technological and the pecuniary. The trained workman was the central figure of the era. The life of the community centered on the marketplace where the price system and quantitative habits of thinking were developed. All this reacted back upon the habits of thought engendered by handicraft.

Veblen attributed many of the distinctive features of modern culture to the instinct of workmanship expressing itself through handicraft. Modern science with its central concept of causation was a direct outgrowth of handicraft technology. Democratically organized Protestantism and the national-state system were also somehow related to it. But in a characteristic causal reaction, it was the dynastic wars among these same states that ate up the resources of handicraft and brought the era to a close.

With the development of machines, the craftsman could no longer own his own tools; he became a mere wage worker without prospect of rising to the status of employer, merchant, or businessman. The fruitful emphasis on workmanship that had characterized the beginning of the period thus gave way to pecuniary competition and political anxiety. And yet workmanship remained the pervasive assumption underlying science, philosophy, and theology. It also supplied the major premise in institutional reconstruction looking toward the rights and obligations of the common people. Veblen attributed the persistent survival into his own day of the natural-rights political theory (in the face of conditions presumably no longer pertinent to it) to the continuing relevance of workmanship.

That Veblen should refer to the period since the eighteenth century variously as the "business era" or the "era of machine technology" was perhaps a clue to the uncertainty concerning it in his own mind. Which was its dominant feature? The instinct of workmanship was now less inhibited by pecuniary considerations than it had been in the handicraft era, although they continued to exert a powerful influence. Paradoxically, it had been the growth of commerce that had saved the West from stagnation. The middle class which it nourished favored industrial efficiency, productivity, and technological improvements.

Veblen found the situation of his own day partly favorable to technological advance, partly adverse to it. These trends were reflected in the diverging of class interests. The logic of science and technology was impersonal and mechanical. Workmen and engineers accordingly addressed themselves to labor in a matter-of-fact spirit. The ever-increasing training necessary to operate machines required an educational system that accentuated the matter-of-fact attitude. Owners and businessmen, on the other hand, were motivated by quite different considerations—bargain, price, and profit. They were engaged chiefly in the perpetration of fraud upon the nonbusiness community. The pecuniary principles that animated business-class behavior stemmed from the handicraft era and were partially outmoded. Industry under business control consequently functioned at less than 50 percent of maximum efficiency.

But a more fundamental difficulty was also inherent in the modern situation. Human nature as presently constituted was largely barbarian in its psychological make-up and was consequently not adapted to the mechanistic routine of life imposed by machine industry. Revulsion against industrial discipline expressed itself in religious cults, nature worship, and nervous breakdowns. It seemed to Veblen that modern man was best suited to the conditions of a moderately advanced barbarism; he could not cope with the "unmitigated materialism and unremitting mechanical routine" of the machine technology. This technology had not yet had the necessary time in which to effect institutional changes. It would be even longer before it could affect human nature.

Veblen would certainly have repudiated as naïve the complacent faith in automatic progress still entertained by the first generation of naturalists. His was a detached and critical spirit quick to dissociate itself from the reigning popular stereotypes. Nevertheless, in spite of the uncertain note on which his analysis of cultural development ended, Veblen's conception of history was still one of progress toward the realization of certain values that were emergent in the historical process itself. In spite of his sophistication, the word *progress* occasionally crept into his pages.

The fundamental elements of a culture were said to develop from the instinctual endowment of the race or races participating in it. Because no two races were similarly endowed, Veblen held it improper to compare their cultural products—although, as has been indicated, occasional references involving larger applications of his cultural stage theory appear to contradict this precept. In any event, in his analysis of the culture of the West European races, Veblen distinguished between the constructive economic instincts and the others. His object was to show how the constructive instincts became incorporated in institutions that facilitated their expression—or failed to do so. With this object in view, certain criteria inevitably emerged in terms of which trends and events might be evaluated.

Increasing rationality, taking the term in the broadest sense, was Veblen's ultimate criterion of progress. By this was meant the progressive modification of institutions toward a more satisfying and uninhibited expression of the constructive instincts. These instincts, especially workmanship and the parental bent, exercised a "commonsense" control over institutional elaboration. Whereas the influence of other instincts, if uncontrolled, could result in grotesque life, disserviceable institutions, and imbecile usages.

Native capacity for technological innovation was declared by Veblen to be a fundamental precondition of cultural advance. Production of material goods was thus a rough criterion of progress. This capacity stemmed from the instinct of idle curiosity in conjunction with workmanship. Essential to the free functioning of the instinct of idle curiosity was the matter-of-fact attitude toward the environment—chiefly the physical environment, although such an attitude would presumably carry over to the social environment as well. Finally, Veblen spoke of the "facility of life," by which he meant the state of mind that approved those attainments by which life was made richer, happier, and more secure.

Social Dynamics

The discussion of historical-cultural stages presupposed a hierarchy of priorities with respect to social changes that may now be made explicit. The first and basic proposition was the familiar naturalistic assertion that technological innovation was the prime causal factor in social change. In the opening pages of *The Instinct of Workmanship*, Veblen declared that technological conditions were "fundamental and definitive, in the sense that they underlie and condition the scope and method of civilization in other than the technological respect." The great cultural transformations that established the successive epochs of barbarism and pecuniary culture were attributed to technological innovations. The earliest significant technological achievements, the domestication of plants and animals, made possible the peaceable sedentary culture of primitive savagery upon which subsequent cultural developments were based. At the end of the stage, the transition from savage free workmanship to barbarian industry under pecuniary control resulted from "increasing technological mastery." Again, the development of machinery during the handicraft era brought the period to a close by creating conditions of production in which the craftsman could no longer own his tools and remain self-employed. The era of machine industry followed. But the causal relationship between technological innovation and social change was not conceived by Veblen to be a simple one-way affair. The various aspects of society influenced by technology were capable of reacting back upon and influencing the state of the industrial arts.

The second level of the social structure consisted of the economic institutions, where the impact of technological changes first made themselves felt. Economic institutions might thus be pictured as resting upon and reflecting the character of the technological foundation. The handicraft technology, for instance, produced its own economic institutions and theory, namely, laissez-faire capitalism. Under this economy, at least in its earlier form, the workman and owner were closely identified; market conditions were of great importance; and credit relations were secondary.

All social institutions other than economic were presumed by Veblen to reflect technological and economic conditions. This was a comprehensive category that included not only social customs of all sorts but also the distribution of instinctual emphases and traits of character as well as formal thought. Veblen was reluctant to separate these elements even for purposes of formal analysis because they formed an organic whole. A change at any given point initiated changes elsewhere. This invariably jeopardized vested interests and explained the universal resistance to change, which Veblen appeared to regard as virtually a social law. Because of his interest in the psychic core of institutions, the difference between ideas and social customs was not so great for Veblen as it would have been for many others. The technology and economic institutions prevailing at a given moment would formulate appropriate psychological demands, which, in turn, would operate to select and conserve corresponding personality types. These types would, in turn, achieve a mutual adaptation with existing social institutions. Thus, for instance, during the predatory regime of status social institutions were well suited to the prevailing traits of character: "ferocity, self-seeking, clannishness, and disingenuousness—a free resort to force and fraud." Races well endowed with these qualities would, so long as the conditions remained, be at an advantage.

It was a curious feature of the current situation as Veblen saw it that, while pecuniary economic institutions still tended to conserve the character traits just indicated, the demands of modern machine technology were for traits of honesty, diligence, peacefulness, good will, an absence of self-seeking, and a capacity to recognize causal sequences. But such qualities were clearly a disadvantage to their possessors engaged in the economic struggle. Hence the success of businessmen, for the time being at least, in dominating and extorting tribute from the community.

Formal thought or systems of ideas received little attention from Veblen. He regarded thought as a reflection of social conditions. Its subservience to prevailing economic forces was well illustrated in modern institutions of higher learning. Veblen derived obvious satisfaction from his demonstration of how leisure-class attitudes and interests dominated the colleges and universities of his day. In a more general sense, if ideas were to have any appreciable influence, they must seem pertinent to prevailing conditions. Thus the theory of laissez-faire capitalism rationalized the interests of businessmen of the eighteenth and nineteenth centuries. It was indicative of the inertia of ideas that the theory should still dominate men's minds when the economic conditions that had produced it had so largely disappeared.

Differential Change

Once the scheme of causal priorities had been determined it became apparent that a time lag, often of considerable dimensions, separated the responses of different areas of society from basic innovations. Society was in process of constant change, but different parts of it changed at rates different in relation to each other. If the causal relationships between social phenomena were mechanical in nature, social lag would have been difficult to explain. But Veblen had stressed the fact that social causation was psychological and that resistance to change was a universal trait of human nature.

Veblen expounded the theory of cultural lag in greater detail than any other naturalist. His most famous book, *The Theory of the Leisure Class*, in effect dealt with the behavior and psychology of that class as a special case study of cultural lag. Basic technological changes were presumably a direct reflection of the operation of the instincts of workmanship and idle curiosity. The consequent institutional and cultural changes lagged behind ultimately because they were not immediately responsive to psychological impulses. Institutions represented the inertia of habit and routine. As an example, Veblen cited current business practice and principles, which dated from the era of handicraft and, beyond that, from the unabashed self-aggrandizement of the predatory culture. These practices had persisted down to his own day although they were partially outmoded by the machine technology. The latter, in fact, had not yet had time to register its full effects upon social institutions.

Noneconomic institutions, customs, traditions, and social values were even more tardy in responding to technological change. It had been five hundred years after the introduction of the handicraft technology before the system of civil rights emerged as its institutional expression. In the mental realm, resistance to changes was especially strong, because of the nature of instinct. Veblen reminded his readers of the purposive and adaptive elements present in instinctual behavior. Whenever a race was well adapted to its circumstances, it resisted change. This was appropriate, since its instinctive equipment could not change with changing institutions. Thus it was frequently necessary for Veblen to remark that contemporary Western man was instinctually still a barbarian. He singled out anthropomorphic religion as an example of particularly stubborn persistence of the barbaric frame of mind. Its concept of deity reflected the regime of status, while it perpetuated an attitude of subserviency unsuited to modern industrial conditions. In societies wherever religion had become fully developed in systems of magic and ritual, barbaric stagnation had resulted.

Although Veblen professed to be solely concerned with setting forth an analytical and descriptive science of social change, his professions of impartiality rang hollow when he dealt with the problems of his own day. And indeed, why should he not have identified himself with reason and the life of consistency when the issues were as clear cut as he had presented them? If anything, his detachment seemed a mere pose, best understood as a personal idiosyncrasy. In any event, those institutions and attitudes of the modern world of which Veblen tacitly approved because of their rational or matter-of-fact spirit were the outgrowth of handicraft technology. Among them the scientific method, industrial efficiency, and democratically organized Protestant sects of the more rational variety were to be noted. Although the pecuniary point of view was also closely associated with handicraft, it had, as has been noted, a different origin, and Veblen's attitude toward it was one of distinct disapproval.

The function of the leisure class in retarding change, and in lengthening the lag between technological change and institutions and attitudes, especially attracted Veblen's attention. Since many aspects of leisure-class behavior had no functional value, Veblen elaborated the celebrated concepts of conspicuous consumption, conspicuous leisure, and waste in order to explain the behavior. He also called attention to the extent to which the leisure class dedicated itself to the conservation of archaic traits, chiefly from the barbarian era. It was with ill-concealed satisfaction that he drew parallels between leisure-class mentality and "delinquent class" mentality, emphasizing especially their mutual penchant for sport, gambling, and religion. A curious feature of the modern situation with its fluid class lines was the tendency of the middle class to ape the manners and cultivate the mentality of the leisure class. If the middle class man did not have the leisure to live like the leisure-class man, his wife could at least perform for him vicariously some of the leisure-class functions.

Although constructive or progressive change was held by Veblen to originate at the level of technology, it was also true that decisive changes might originate in the superstructure and react back upon the technological institutions. But such changes were stultifying if not positively destructive. This was because nontechnological institutions and attitudes were expressive of instincts other than that of workmanship. Their influence was likely to contaminate or deflect workmanship and obstruct its development. Effects of this sort have already been cited in other connections. Thus, rule by elders impeded technological progress in the later phase of savagery. Similarly, the well-developed religion of certain barbarian societies had succeeded in halting technological advance entirely. In his own society, Veblen felt that the prevalent sentiments of arrogance and abasement nurtured by pecuniary institutions were a standing threat to workmanship and hence to technological progress.

The institutional and psychological inertia that was the essence of cultural lag sometimes appeared in "derivations" or "transmuted forms" of earlier practices. The conventions of modern business ownership, for instance, were said to be derivatives of ancient predatory culture. Again, the modern invidious distinction between industrial and nonindustrial occupations—the latter alone being honorific—was said by Veblen to be a transmuted form of the barbarian distinction between drudgery and exploit; exploit referred to the special and closely guarded skills, such as those of the medicine man, necessary to cope with the animate as opposed to the inanimate world.

In sum, the psychological response to changed technological and economic conditions was sluggish, and changes in systems of values could be expected to come tardily at best. Moreover, there was a strong psychological tendency to revert to earlier conditions. Great psychological force was exerted upon modern man by the status relations of barbarism, an era that had lasted long enough to leave a firm impress upon the psychological traits of the European races. (Veblen declared it to be a law of heredity that wherever the racial type varied—and the European races had varied when a predatory strain was imposed during barbarism on the peaceable strain of original savagery—the later predatory element would dominate, with the earlier peaceable element in effect recessive.) Consequently, because of these psychological forces, any class or community not subject to the action of forces making for recently developed habits of thought, such as the modern technology, would speedily revert to an older temperament. The modern leisure class was precisely such a class, according to Veblen, since it was sheltered from the stress of the economic struggle. Now it was also true that the blond Nordic race, a relatively young race, was more completely adapted to predatory culture than many races. As a large-scale and spectacular illustration of reversion to barbarism by a Nordic people resulting from withdrawal from the economic struggle Veblen cited the Anglo-American colonies!

Here was a hint of the ultimate practical reason for differential social change. The different parts of society were not equally exposed to the stress of technological and economic forces. The struggle for existence was less exacting of those, like the leisure class, not under economic pressure, and who were consequently less responsive to the demands for institutional change made by the state of the industrial arts. The function of a leisure class was thus the conservative one of retarding social change. This was, of course, owed more to the nature of the situation than to calculation. Aversion to change was in Veblen's opinion common to all men; it had to be overcome by the pressure of circumstances. The very poor, whose energies were absorbed in making a bare living, had no surplus energies for the mental effort necessary to make innovations. Hence they, like the rich, were also conservative—but for obviously different reasons. Thus it appeared that progress was hindered both by want and by luxury. By withholding sustenance from the lower class and reducing its energies, the upper class was perpetuating the conservatism of the community. The example of the conspicuous consumption practiced by the leisure class had a similar effect by enticing the other classes into investing their surplus energies in emulation.

Veblen concluded that cultural lag could not be overcome entirely. It was the nature of things. The institutions of the moment were more-or-less adequate adjustments of methods of living to conditions that had prevailed at some time in the past. The effect of leisure-class behavior was simply to accentuate the inevitable gap between the existing industrial situation and social institutions.

With the passage of time, Veblen became increasingly pessimistic as to the prospects for further fruitful development in West European culture. Part at least of the explanation of his pessimism may be found in personal considerations, as suggested by David Riesman in his psychological study of Veblen. But there were also compelling reasons for concern that thrust themselves up insistently out of the naturalistic reconstruction of social reality. It would have been obtuse of Veblen to have ignored them, given his premises.

As he analyzed the nature of social change, cultural lag was inevitable. It was merely a question whether the nature and direction of institutional change would be toward closing the gap or toward a further contamination and stultification of the instinct of workmanship and of industrial processes. One cause of pessimism was Veblen's sense of the great strength of those institutions in modern society that embodied the predatory animus of pecuniary culture. He was persuaded that "imbecile institutions" usually triumph over life and culture. Hence he could not rid himself of the conviction that the peoples of Christendom were faced with a "desperately precarious institutional situation."

Another cause for pessimism was the racial factor. By the very fact of its exceptionally effective adaptation to the barbarian culture, the blond Nordic race was regarded by Veblen as peculiarly unqualified instinctually for the social demands of machine culture. It showed great difficulty, for instance, in adjusting to the industrial routine of life. The city life required by industry was proving to be lethal to the blond race, as its low birth rate and high death rate in cities demonstrated. To survive at all in an urban environment, Nordics had to maintain conditions similar to those of a "comprehensive clinic"! They were clinging to life in the cities like Englishmen in tropical West Africa—with or without dinner jackets. Veblen did not attempt to forecast the future, and, like his old teacher Sumner, he seems to have become increasingly content not to have to live to see it.

CHAPTER 18

||||||||||||||||||||||||||||||||||||||||||||||||||||||||||||||||||||||||||||

The Science of History

U NTIL FAIRLY RECENT TIMES, historical study was a branch of humane letters. Histories had concerned themselves primarily with public events; and the historian generally conceived of his object as that of edification. Before the latter part of the nineteenth century, the function of historian was largely reserved for gentlemen of means and leisure. Few professorships of history in colleges or universities had been established, while the increasingly exacting standards of the professions left their practitioners little time for the pursuit of scholarly avocations.

A significant change occurred with the growth of universities, which in America coincided roughly with the beginnings of the naturalistic era. Autonomous departments of instruction were organized, including departments of history. Professional training of historians thus began; while at the same time, courses of instruction in history in colleges and universities greatly increased in number, providing employment for professionally trained historians, many of whom were actively engaged in research and the writing of monographs and surveys. Although the publication of histories for the general reading public still continued, much of the new historical output was "professional" in character, which is to say, it was written with strict methodological care for the critical scrutiny of other historians. The institutional setting is relevant to an investigation of naturalistic historiography, for in some degree historians were led to confuse professional with scientific principles.

The study of history in the new universities was closely associated with the study of political science, the two subjects frequently sharing a common departmental organization. The impact of naturalism revitalized academic political theory, and under the influence of naturalism the rather mechanical and formal description of political institutions gave way to a more critical and realistic analysis of the functioning of the political process.

An organic conception of the state was introduced at Johns Hopkins by Woodrow Wilson in the 1880's. Wilson expressed his dissatisfaction with the prevailing legalistic approach of political scientists and urged his students to go beyond the constitution and the laws to the actual life of the state. Those who insisted upon the old legalistic approach "must risk knowing only the anatomy of institutions and never learn anything of their biology." By this he meant that political institutions were embedded in a living social matrix, and that from whatever angle one approached society he would see some phase of government at work. Public law was merely the bare framework or skeleton of the state. A realistic political science as Wilson described it involved not only constitutional analysis but also the study of conflicting economic interests, race relations, imperialism, monopolistic concentration, and political party practices.

Wilson's thinking was profoundly influenced by the English constitutional historian Walter Bagehot, whose analysis of the evolution of the British constitution convinced Wilson that constructive political change is always evolutionary and never revolutionary in character. The application of this dictum suggested a revised estimate of the American Revolution and gave historians a keener sense of the importance of the American heritage from British colonialism. Enlightened political thinkers, who were themselves state-makers, had tended to regard government as artificial. Now, however, naturalistic political theorists accepted the state as given; it was an integral part of society. Men of Wilson's generation had grown up in the somber shadows of the bloodiest war of the nineteenth century, the outcome of which had confirmed the fact that the national state is an ultimate reality.

Another characteristic of academic political science that evidenced the naturalistic influence was its use of the comparative method in studying governments. The theory of organic evolution postulated diverging lines of descent, the comparative study of which would tell much about the evolutionary process itself and about the relationship between existing or extinct species. College catalogues described courses in "the comparative anatomy of vertebrates." Similarly, if states were involved in a social evolutionary process the comparative study of political institutions seemed equally appropriate. Most of the political science textbooks of the late nineteenth century contained at least large sections devoted to comparative analysis. At their best, these comparisons were not made at random but were governed by some principle of genetic relationship of descent.

The Impact of Science

The prestige accorded to science and to scientific thinking was a fundamental characteristic of naturalism. This prestige was sufficient to produce a generation of historians who insisted that history should be written in a scientific spirit. By this they meant that the historical facts should be precisely ascertained from sources subjected to a careful critical scrutiny. Seminars in historical method, usually conducted by medievalists, developed an impressive body of critical principles for the evaluation of historical data. The historian was, of course, to eliminate all personal biases and preconceptions of his own; he was to discipline himself to tell what actually happened. The so-called "scientific point of view" in historiography was stimulated by the rapid accumulation of documentary and other source materials in the great university libraries that sprang up during the later nineteenth century. This wealth of data invited the historian to focus his attention on the technical problems of source evaluation and to neglect broader issues of philosophic import.

Not officially a part of the canons of scientific historiography perhaps, but actually an important feature of the school, was its emphasis upon causal relationships. In an account of the methods taught in his seminar at Columbia in the 1880's, Professor John W. Burgess observed: "We undertake . . . to teach the student to set the facts which he has thus ascertained in their chronological order, to the further end of setting them in their order as cause and effect. And we seek to make him clearly comprehend and continually feel that the latter procedure is the one most delicate and critical which the historical student is called upon to undertake." The ideal of the scientific school of historiography was thus to allow the facts to speak for themselves, especially in their cause–effect relationships.

Well might one wonder why working principles that seemed to be little more than common sense and common honesty should be graced with the majestic garb of science. But at least these principles represented the beginning of a greater critical awareness on the part of historians of the nature of their operations, and they were to lead eventually to a more sophisticated style of historical thought and writing. If scientific method in the most general sense of the term may be taken to refer to those manipulations that produce fruitful results with whatever the material in hand may be, then, perhaps, the doctrines of the early historical seminars may properly be designated as scientific.

Unfortunately, the ideal of the historian without bias, who allowed the facts to speak for themselves, never came to fruition. Since no historian presented his readers with all the facts he could find, some selective principle or "bias" was present. The canons of the scientific school were of no help at this point, and, consequently, the scientific historian's biases were all too frequently unconscious and uncontrolled. Subsequent critics of the school came down upon this weakness with devastating effect. Nevertheless, some of the unconscious biases of the scientific historians were doubly instructive because they appeared in scholars trying to be dispassionate and objective. These biases were frequently aspects of the naturalistic point of view.

One of them was the germ theory of institutional continuity, a biological presupposition that was typical of naturalistic thinking. The theory originated in Germany, passing to England and thence to the United States, where in the 1880's it dominated instruction at Johns Hopkins, then perhaps the most influential university in the country. Members of the germ-theory school of historiography concerned themselves chiefly with tracing the historical evolution of social institutions from their origins to their modern forms. The evolutionary history of institutions, like that of a biological germ plasm, displayed continuity with change. Professor Herbert Baxter Adams, who conducted a celebrated seminar at Hopkins, published in 1883 his *Germanic Origins of New England Towns*. In it he demonstrated how certain features of the town organization could be traced back through the English shire to primitive Germanic sources.

A passage from the Preface to Adams's monograph posed a problem that it did not solve. "The science of Biology no longer favors the theory of spontaneous generation. Wherever organic life occurs, there must have been some seed for that life. History should not be content with describing effects when it can explain causes." It was apparent that in Adams's mind the causal nexus of the scientific historians became confused with the genetic sequence characteristic of naturalism. If he appreciated the theoretical difficulties of applying either one of these concepts to historical studies, he gave no indication of it. In simplest terms, the genetic idea applied to social analysis represented the force of inertia, the tendency of institutions to perpetuate themselves through some inherent property of their own, while at the same time experiencing the changes that are inevitable in both biological and social organisms. In Darwin's terms, the genetic relationship was that of "descent with modification." But how did the causal nexus fit into the genetic? It would appear that Adams was not much interested in causes. His preoccupation with the genetic continuity of the township had the effect of diverting his attention from the more mechanical causal idea, which would have highlighted discontinuities or changes.

Interest in the historical evolution of cultural institutions from their germinal sources was easily identified with a genteel form of racism. In his lectures on American political ideas, John Fiske revealed this tendency to merge the germ theory with the cultural theory of race.

In the deepest and widest sense, our American history does not begin with the Declaration of Independence, or even with the settlement of Jamestown and Plymouth; but it descends in unbroken continuity from the days when stout Arminius in the forests of northern Germany successfully defied the might of imperial Rome. . . . When we duly realize this, and further come to see how the two great branches of the English race have the common mission of establishing throughout the larger part of the earth a higher civilization and more permanent political order than any that has gone before, we shall the better understand the true significance of the history which English-speaking men have so magnificently wrought out upon American soil.

Among Adams's students at Hopkins was a Midwesterner named Frederick Jackson Turner. Turner reacted sharply against the germ-theory interpretation, both for personal and theoretical reasons. The Hopkins seminar tended to center its attention on the institutions of the colonial American seaboard, since they provided the more obvious examples of institutional continuity with the Old World. But Turner was interested in the history of his own West, and he had a strong sense of the emergence there of distinctively new social patterns. The germ theory of institutional continuity was but ill suited to his needs. He turned, therefore, to another facet of naturalistic thought and developed an extreme environmentalist interpretation of regional peculiarities.

The decade of the 1890's witnessed a revival of interest in environmental influences playing upon men individually and upon whole societies. This environmentalism came immediately from the new geography of Guyot, Geikie, and Ratzel, a geography defined by Huxley as the science of man in relation to the earth. Some years earlier, the Englishman Henry Thomas Buckle had popularized a thoroughgoing physiographic determinism. Now, historians on both sides of the Atlantic were ready to apply the idea to specific historical problems. Lord Bryce added a chapter on the influence of environment to the third edition (1893) of his widely read *American Commonwealth*. In the United States, the most ambitious, if unconvincing, interpretation of American history in environmental terms was offered by Ellen C. Semple in her *American History and Its Geographic Conditions* (1903). But much the most famous contribution was that of Turner.

The immediate and lasting appeal of Turner's frontier regionalism was owed to the fact that it emphasized the relationship between culture and environment in a way that was both characteristic of naturalistic modes of thought and reminiscent of the environmentalism of traditional liberalism. It drew upon the earlier nineteenth-century zeal for the free individual, as well as upon the insights of naturalism. Turner emphasized the impress of successive frontier environments on the social organism, resulting in new kinds of social product. As one frontier succeeded another, each more remote from Europe than its predecessor, a social evolutionary process was working to perfect the American democratic individualist. A fundamental postulate of the frontier theory was the absolute power of the environment to limit the directions or forms of social development. The environment of the Old Northwest, on which Turner first centered his attention, was a singularly hospitable one, a circumstance that had the practical consequence of diverting attention from the determinism which was implicit in the theory.

Turner's social evolutionism might be described as Buffonian rather than Darwinian. It emphasized the direct response of the individual to the impact of the physical environment, while it paid little if any attention to the adaptive capacities of the individual as they might be evoked by the environmental stimulus. Hence the persistent question in the minds of later students: What inherent resources in the way of free initiative, of inventive capacity to make new adaptations to the environment, did the *Homo americanus* possess? Because he did not face the question squarely, Turner did not furnish a clearcut answer. He appears to have assumed as a matter of course that the environment evoked the appropriate adaptive response from society. Specifically, it was the free land of the frontier that produced the attitudes and practices called democracy. Whatever may have been the biological or cultural heritage of the frontiersman, the historian did not pause to investigate it. William Graham Sumner would, presumably, have agreed completely with Turner's analysis; and he would have agreed further with the prediction at which Turner hinted in his first paper, that when free land eventually disappeared the democracy that it had produced would disappear with it. However, Turner's deep and genuine enthusiasm for agrarian democracy is not impugned by calling attention to the naturalistic pattern of thinking by which he accounted for its appearance.

A third form of naturalistic historiography might be described as reductionist. The most explicit attempt to write history in this fashion was made by Henry Adams in essays written during the latter part of his life and published posthumously in a volume entitled *The Degradation of the Democratic Dogma* (1919). Naturalists explained complex phenomena by reducing them to simple elements according to the structure of reality as they understood it. Spiritual or psychological facts were reduced to economic or material elements; the social was reduced to the biological; and the biological was explained in physical or mechanical terms.

While it is difficult to measure the seriousness with which Adams set forth the particular principles of historical interpretation contained in these essays, there can be no doubt of his conviction that social and historical phenomena must be understood in naturalistic terms. As he wrote to the American Historical Association in 1894, every conscientious historian since the days of Darwin and Buckle had been busily searching for the laws that would reduce history to an exact science. "That the effort to make history a science may fail is possible, and perhaps probable; but that it should cease, unless for reasons that would cause all science to cease, is not within the range of experience." That he should go on with characteristic perversity to suggest some of the practical complications that would ensue if a science of history were discovered should not be taken to indicate any lack of serious interest in the problem.

Adams proposed to reduce the social process to the terms of a dynamic physical system. The physical concepts that seemed most useful were mass, energy, and velocity. In the science of history, social change was to be designated as velocity. Mental or psychological phenomena represented the release of energy. Energy correlated directly with mass, meaning both the concentration of population and the elaboration of social institutions. The increase of mass and acceleration of velocity effected ever-greater release of energy. Adams predicted that by 1921 the concentration of energy and increase of social velocity would have become so great that whatever might happen would be beyond the comprehension of men like himself and his contemporaries who had not been educated to understand such complex and terrifying conditions.

The rather desperate groping of Henry Adams for scientific laws of history underscored one of the more striking characteristics of the naturalistic mind, namely, its monistic presupposition. The naturalists were engaged in a common quest for certainty in the form of a unitary or all-embracing explanation of experience. Indeed, they may have thought of themselves as the progenitors of a new point of view peculiarly appropriate to the novel circumstances of an industrial age. But in one important respect their point of view was thoroughly traditional: in the face of the chaotic dissolution of the older conventional ideas they sought a traditional refuge by attempting to salvage intellectual unity, order, and an intelligible pattern of experience from the wreckage. These patterns of explanation were as comprehensive as the evolution of species from the first appearance of living cells. The use of evolutionary theories by naturalists was in fact designed to stabilize change by imposing an intelligible sequence upon it.

Henry Adams differed from the other naturalists only in that he early abandoned organic evolution as a developmental sequence. A passage in his *Education* tells how he discovered that the expanding fossil record did not support the assumption of universal development. The existence of species that had not changed over long periods of time dramatized the random character of evolution and destroyed its usefulness for one who sought in it a unifying thread.

And so Adams turned from biological to physical science in his quest for a law to unify history. His ultimate statement was reminiscent of Herbert Spencer's law of development from undifferentiated homogeneity to differentiated heterogeneity. Adams envisaged the course of history as proceeding from the unity of the Middle Ages to the multiplicity of the Nunc Age. He sought in various ways to explain this pattern by means of the laws governing the behavior of physical systems. It remained for the critics of naturalism to give up this kind of monism.

Naturalism and Marxism

In European naturalist thought, Marxism came to replace Spencerism as the prevailing form of naturalistic social theory. Only in England, among European countries, had the Industrial Revolution been attended by the measure of political liberalism and middle-class social development in terms of which Spencer's brand of Social Darwinism seemed to offer a cogent interpretation of social development and public policy.

No such confident generalization can be made about American naturalistic social theory. Clearly defined dogmatic parties have not characterized American social thought in recent times any more than they have typified political organization. During the later nineteenth century, Sumnerian individualism clearly dominated the intellectual scene on this side of the Atlantic. Yet, by virtue of this very fact, the way was being prepared for the sympathetic reception of the Marxian interpretation of history and social process, since Marxism was an authentic expression of naturalism, sharing many of its fundamental postulates. Consequently, in the early decades of the twentieth century, although acknowledged American Marxist intellectuals remained few in number, a pervasive Marxist influence began to permeate the community, leaving its mark upon the work of many students who were not themselves aware of the affiliations and sometimes even the derivation of their ideas.

Anthropologists have demonstrated how readily artifacts and cultural traits are diffused from one primitive culture to another when the circumstances of the receiving community are ripe for the reception. The same must surely be true of the diffusion of ideas in advanced cultures as well. How else can one explain the fact that, although avowed Marxists in America remained divided among small doctrinaire sects, Marxist ideas were readily received and incorporated into their thinking by intellectuals who were not themselves Marxists? The materialist interpretation of history, a preoccupation with the economic basis of the class struggle, and the sense that society formed an interacting organic whole were naturalistic ideas independent of the particular formulation that Marx gave to them. Marxism was little known in America before the twentieth century, and when it came, it sharpened and systematized for political purposes ideas that had been current here for nearly half a century. In these circumstances, it becomes exceedingly difficult to trace the precise limits of Marxist influence.

In the naturalistic view of social reality, a fundamental place and determinative role were assigned to the economic aspects of life, second only to the technological. The evolutionary anthropologists, who were historians in the broadest sense, were among the first to indicate the possibilities of a comprehensive economic interpretation of history. Marx and Engels, working independently, recorded in their correspondence the enthusiasm with which they discovered Morgan's anthropology, which furnished a convenient setting for their analysis of contemporary problems. Historians of the later nineteenth century generally took up other aspects of the naturalistic complex first, before finally coming to the economic interpretation of history. When eventually they did so, it was in circumstances and with results that might suggest a profound influence of Marxism on them. But it would be difficult to demonstrate such an assertion. It seems rather to have been a case of parallel and independent development within the broad confines of naturalistic thought. A single instance will serve to illustrate the process.

The golden age of American socialism was the decade 1905–1915. Socialist political activity reached its peak in the presidential campaign of Debs in 1912, and in local contests in 1916. It was also a time of considerable socialist intellectual activity. The years between 1909 and 1913 witnessed the publication of several of the most impressive landmarks in American socialist literature, including Morris Hillquit's *Socialism in Theory and Practice,* John Spargo's *Socialism,* Louis Boudin's *Theoretical System of Karl Marx,* and William E. Walling's *Larger Aspects of Socialism.* These writers were members of the Socialist Party of the United States, an affiliate of the Second International. In general, they conceived it to be their mission to fuse Marxian socialist analysis with traditional

American democratic values in order to produce a program of economic and social reform appropriate to the needs of industrial America.

Among the books written by socialists during that decade was a brief survey of American history by Algie M. Simons entitled *Social Forces in American History* (1911). This striking book incorporated a series of interpretations that were to become commonplace in the succeeding generation. Simons announced the usual naturalistic themes and point of view. His book was to concern itself with the causal dynamics of American history, not with the surface events, laws, or leaders. Technological innovation was asserted to be the basic cause of social change. The social classes that arose out of the productive process struggled for economic power and, consequently, for the political power to confirm their economic advantages. These struggles resulted in a pattern of social evolutionary development that formed a succession of well-marked historical stages, reminiscent of the anthropological stages from savagery and barbarism to civilization. The social structure as Simons conceived it consisted of the technological base and a series of social classes whose mutual relationship was determined by their respective roles in the productive process. The struggle for power among these classes was the raw material of politics; the outcome of the struggle consisted of those institutional realignments that we customarily characterize as turning points in history.

The application of these principles to the elucidation of the major episodes in American history produced some distinctively new interpretations. Simons discussed colonization and colonial development in terms of the Commercial Revolution in Europe, with its attendant need for colonial markets and extractive enterprises. The American Revolution was an economic phenomenon, to be understood as a conflict over mercantilist policy, land policy, and tax policy, complicated by such issues as debts, smuggling, and paper money. The rising Whig capitalist class in America emerged as the victors, thanks to tacit support from like-minded people in England and to the active aid of colonial debtors with whom an alliance had been formed.

In view of the conflicting economic interests of the two groups, however, it was inevitable that the revolutionary coalition should break down after independence had been won. The capitalists desired a strong national government with the necessary fiscal and regulatory powers to serve their interests. Wage earners, farmers, and debtors, on the other hand, wanted decentralized government. Because they had a political program similar to that of the Populists a century later, Simons referred to them as "populistic." Their objectives were substantially secured by the weak Articles of Confederation. In 1787, the capitalists staged their conspiratorial "counter-revolution" in the form of a constitutional convention ostensibly summoned for the purpose of revising the Articles of Confederation but actually designed to replace them with a strong central government. The convention was, in fact, a committee composed largely of merchants, manufacturers, bankers, and big planters. It drafted a Constitution designed to promote the economic interests of those classes while incorporating ingenious devices intended to frustrate the power of unsympathetic majorities. By the astute maneuvering of ratifying conventions in several states, the Constitution was adopted in spite of the opposition of what was undoubtedly a majority of the American people. Simons, like J. Allen Smith before him, was perplexed by the popular tendency among modern Americans to extol the Constitution as a charter of democratic liberties. Nevertheless, in spite of the fact that it was put over on the American people, the ratification of the Constitution was necessary to the further growth of the nation; it represented progress.

Two themes dominated Simons's account of the years between 1815 and 1860, the development of capitalism and the emergence of a labor movement in response to the challenge of industrial exploitation. The socialist managed to persuade himself on rather meager evidence that labor had played an extremely important role in American history. It had laid the foundation of the great democratic institutions of universal suffrage and public education, and it had secured the abolition of imprisonment for debt and other humanitarian reforms. Simons conceded that this was not yet the organized and class-conscious body that socialists expected "labor" to become. A large majority of Americans were in some sense workingmen, but he did not use the term *labor* in this comprehensive sense either. On the whole, Simons was neither clear nor convincing in his analysis of the role of labor in shaping the direction of American social development. He characterized Jacksonianism both as a movement of expectant capitalists and as a vehicle for many democratic reforms.

Simons described the Civil War as a conflict between two radically different economic systems: the slave plantation economy of the South and the burgeoning industrial capitalism of the North. The slave economy was an "historical atavism" that required Southern control of the federal government in order to assure its survival. The petty capitalist bourgeoisie of the North and West formulated their demands in the platform of the new Republican Party: improved internal communications, tariff protection for local industries, unrestricted immigration to assure a labor supply, a homestead law to hold the allegiance of Western freehold farmers, and no further extension of slavery. The inability of government to reconcile these conflicting economic interests precipitated the conflict. Simons looked upon the Republican program as essentially revolutionary in that it demanded the transfer of governmental control to a new social class, which was to him the essence of revolution.

A final chapter was devoted to an account of the "triumph and decadence of capitalism." Simons had a strong sense that capitalism was moving rapidly toward the fulfillment of its own inherent possibilities. The large-scale industry of the period 1865–1890 had passed into the era of monopoly subsequent to 1890. According to Marxist analysis, industrial monopoly entailed constricted opportunities and the increasing misery that foretold a revolutionary overturn. The panic of 1873 had been the final general panic of capitalism; thenceforth the largest producers would be immune to the fluctuations of the business cycle, and the capitalist economy would no longer possess the power to expand after depressions as it had in the days of its growth. Simons was confident that the socialist commonwealth would emerge in the near future.

That Simons had charted a course into the mainstream of American historiography became apparent after the publication in 1927 of *The Rise of American Civilization* by Charles and Mary Beard, a work which better than any other characterized the distinctive spirit of American historical thought in the first half of the twentieth century. The Beards were not socialists, and Charles Beard is said to have been unacquainted with Simons's book before writing his own. Nevertheless, there was a remarkable similarity between them on several major matters of interpretation. The Beards cut away the Marxian vocabulary and stereotypes. Their skill and knowledge were infinitely richer. But their interpretation of American history was likewise a demonstration of the primacy of economic forces. To be sure, they avowed the operation of a multiplicity of different kinds of causal forces in history, but their own pages left no doubt as to the primacy of economic factors.

The Beards refined Simons's analysis of colonialism as an economic phenomenon. They found the causes of the Revolution to lie in the conflict between London, the economic metropolis, and its colonial economic dependency. On the Confederation years and the Constitution the similarity of their treatment to that of Simons was striking. All saw the essential issue as a conflict between agrarian debtors and merchant creditors. Where Simons had written of the constitutional counterrevolution, the Beards spoke of "Populism and Reaction." There was the same curiously ambivalent judgment implicit in the obvious satisfaction with which the tricks and maneuvers of the constitutional reactionaries were exposed, coupled with solemn assertions that the Constitution was essential to the future greatness of the United States. In their treatment of the Civil War, the Beards again followed Simons's analysis closely. To them, it was also a struggle between two economic societies culminating in a revolutionary transfer of power. In both cases, the revolution was accomplished by the election of 1860. Secession was merely the South's alternative to counterrevolution. Finally, although the Beards did not share Simons's utopian dream of the classless society, they did look toward "social democracy," which meant for them the imposition of such social controls as might be necessary to assure an equitable distribution of goods and services to all classes of society.

One might readily conclude from these parallels that when the socialist intellectuals of the pre-World War I period set out to adapt Marxist analysis to American conditions they builded better than they knew. The enterprise quickly passed from their hands into abler ones, like those of the Beards, where the technical terminology of the Marxist interpretation of history was abandoned but much of the substance retained. Nevertheless, such a conclusion would fail to do justice to the full complexity of the circumstances.

As early as 1916, Charles Beard had listed the names of those whom he regarded as his mentors in the tradition of the economic interpretation of politics: Aristotle, Machiavelli, Harrington, Locke, Madison, Webster, and Calhoun. Marx's name was conspicuous by its absence, and many years later, when someone questioned him on this point, Beard readily conceded that Marx was, like himself, a collateral descendant of these same teachers. The omission of Marx had not been an oversight. The bond that united Simons and the Beards was not a common dependence on Marxism; it was a common participation in the basic presuppositions of naturalism.

All three assumed the same relationship between the physical, organic, and social worlds, each realm resting on the other and understood in terms of it. Simons had stressed the technological basis of culture more than did the Beards, who in this respect were better Marxists than he in subordinating technology to the social environment in which it functioned. All three started with the naturalistic assumption that man's impressive mastery of the physical world held forth the promise that by similar methods man could produce an ideal social science to master the social world. Although they did not propound the organic analogy in so bald a fashion as did Simons, the Beards embraced that point of view in a far more significant way when they deplored the artificial analytical dissections of social reality as practiced by the various incommensurable disciplinary methods of the academic scholars. The result of modern intellectual specialization, they declared, was that "the living organism of human society as a subject of inquiry has been torn apart and parcelled out among specialists." The student must first understand the workings of the whole in order to analyze accurately the functions of any part. To the Beards, the workings of the whole involved the dependent relationships of the naturalistic social structure; and the aspect in which they were particularly interested was the dependence of the political upon the economic. They were convinced that a single principle would yield the deepest insight into the workings of society, and that this was the materialistic principle.

Whether their objectives were ostensibly scientific, reformist, or revolutionary, none of the naturalistic historians escaped the confines of the American national patriotism. In spite of his allegiance to a movement professing to be international in character, dedicated to workingmen without a country, Simons was tracing the origins and character of American democracy with a singleness of purpose that would have satisfied the conventional patriot. His national loyalty was shared by most of the socialists of his generation. It was inevitable for this reason that World War I, by confronting the international commitment with the imperatives of national loyalty, should wreck American socialism. The Beards' nationalism was even more pronounced. In the decade of the 1930's, it veered toward continental isolationism and, in turn, was wrecked by World War II.

CHAPTER 19

|||||||||||||||||||||||||||||||||||||||||||||||||||||||||||||||||||||||||

Moral and Literary Naturalism

PROFOUND CHANGE in the moral climate of American society and thought occurred during the later nineteenth century. The complex of naturalistic ideas was itself perhaps the most important force at work in bringing about this change. In earlier times, the moral qualities of American life had had a distinctly religious cast. The practical character of the prevailing Protestantism was due largely to the custodial function of the denominations as guardians of the Puritan ethic and the other moral virtues clustered about it. But in the years after the Civil War, the Christian view of life steadily gave ground to a more secular frame of mind. This was one of the more important transformations in American history. Religion itself was placed on the defensive by evolutionism and historical criticism, but perhaps even more by the prevailing optimism, prosperity, sense of security, and preoccupation with worldly concerns.

In these circumstances, the traditional belief in the moral order of the universe was weakened in its religious foundations. It was no longer convincing to assert that the voice of conscience was the voice of God. In the naturalistic critique of conscience, it was easy to show that conscience was merely the product of teaching and experience. At the same time, it became possible without fear of reprisal to attack the traditional moral code by attaching to it the stigma "puritanical." It was no longer sufficient merely to separate the Puritan ethic from the Puritan religion, as Franklin had done. The ethic itself was now denounced as mercenary, prudish, hypocritical, and repressive. The moral ideas that naturalism proposed to substitute for the traditional code were implicit in the literary as well as other phases of the movement. But only in a few instances were they systematically developed.

Naturalistic Fiction

The democratic mind of the mid-nineteenth century had expressed itself in literary form in the novels of Cooper, the essays of Emerson, and the verse of Whitman. The naturalism of the postbellum period similarly had its literary movement. Among its early representatives were the novelists Stephen Crane, Frank Norris, Jack London, and Theodore Dreiser and the poets Edgar Lee Masters and Edwin Arlington Robinson. In the earlier novels of the movement written before World War I, several aspects of the naturalistic pattern of thought were readily apparent.

It has already been noted in other connections how the writers of that generation had been stimulated by their discovery of Darwin and Spencer. The obligation was sometimes specifically acknowledged, as when one of London's heroes, the Sea Wolf, after brutally beating a refractory member of his ship's crew, retired to his cabin to soothe his ruffled feelings by reading a few paragraphs of Spencer's *Social Statics*. Even when less obtrusively present, the influence of the great English naturalists gave focus to the native revolt against the reigning genteel tradition in literature. This literary rebellion against the captivity of American letters by Victorian prudery was undoubtedly welcome in that its immediate result was more vigorous writing, while ultimately the way was paved for the more mature and powerful social novels of the twentieth century. In France, Émile Zola had already adapted naturalistic formulas to fiction in such novels as *Germinal* (1885), in which he portrayed individuals caught up inexorably in the impersonal social process, destroyed or tossed to the side by forces they could scarcely identify, let alone control. Here was a variety of themes that seemed to promise fresh and convincing opportunities to a rebellious generation of writers.

Literary naturalism was sometimes defined as pessimistic determinism. It depicted men swept along by omnipotent natural and social forces. In *The Octopus* (1901), Norris wrote that "men were nought, life was nought; Force only existed—Force that brought men into the world, Force that made the wheat grow." On the other hand, however, a kind of fatalistic optimism was equally typical. The individual might be destroyed, but the race went on. Norris consoled himself with the reflection that "the larger view always and through all shams, all wickedness, discovers the truth that will, in the end, prevail, and all things, surely, inevitably resistlessly work together for good." But, in the final analysis, naturalistic fiction was neither optimistic nor pessimistic. Although these qualities were commonly present, either singly or in combination, they served no organic function in the portrayal of the fictional situation. Rather, they merely disinfected the reader, preserving him from the exaltation or contamination of identification with the fictional situation portrayed. This was the common predicament of naturalistic morality in all fields of thought. Unless he was willing to admit the contingent character of the social evolutionary process, the naturalist could not cope with human purpose or conceive of the dignity of freedom. He had lost the Calvinistic art of reconciling freedom with determinism.

A striking characteristic of the early naturalistic novel was its loss of the sense of the dignity or goodness or intelligence of man. In *Maggie, A Girl of the Streets* (1893) Stephen Crane chose to portray people without any of the conventional redeeming qualities. A New York slum family was found living a coarse, degraded, brutal life organized around a few simple stereotyped emotions and gratifications. The daughter Maggie having been seduced, the humiliated family drove her from the house with an outburst of righteous indignation. Without other resources, Maggie was driven to prostitution and eventual suicide. The book shocked many of its readers, one of them protesting to Crane that he had done less than justice to people caught helplessly in an urban slum that had blighted their lives and deprived them of the means of self-improvement. Crane's reply furnished a significant insight into the ambivalent attitude of the naturalistic writer toward his characters. "A person who thinks himself superior to the rest of us because he has no job and no pride and no clean clothes is as badly conceited as Lillian Russell. In a story of mine called 'An Experiment in Misery' I tried to make plain that the root of Bowery life is a sort of cowardice. Perhaps I mean a lack of ambition or to willingly be knocked flat and accept the licking." Conceit was certainly contemptible in any circumstances, but so, it also seemed, was lack of ambition, a judgment that linked

Crane in a curious way with contemporary purveyors of uplift and success literature. The Bowery bums he described had made their adjustment to the environment, but the adjustment was at a level so far beneath that dictated by conventional humanitarian assumptions that it seemed pertinent to Crane to stress the fact.

Naturalistic fiction as well as sociology attached central importance to the delineation of man's place in nature. Technically, nature was indifferent to man. In one of Crane's best short stories, "The Open Boat" (1898), shipwrecked seamen were tossing on tempestuous seas in a lifeboat, unable to run the mountainous breakers to the safety of the beach. As they looked toward the shore they saw on the horizon a windmill, like "a giant standing with its back to the plight of the ants. It represented in a degree . . . the serenity of nature amid the struggles of the individual. . . . She did not seem cruel . . . nor beneficent, nor treacherous, nor wise. But she was indifferent, flatly indifferent." The cosmic and inexorable processes of nature provided the true measure of man's insignificance. As Norris wrote, in *The Octopus:* "Nature was, then, a gigantic engine, a vast, cyclopean power, huge, terrible, a leviathan with a heart of steel, knowing no compunction, no forgiveness, no tolerance; crushing out the human atom standing in its way, with nirvanic calm."

But in spite of these acknowledgments of nature's indifference, the sinister role assigned to her in the Malthusian economy inevitably endowed her with an active malignancy. Man's struggle with nature was a frequent theme in the fiction written during the years in which Sumner was developing the idea in his sociological theory. The locales often chosen by novelists as the setting for their stories underscored their preoccupation with the struggle. Jack London preferred the bleak wastes of the Arctic. The sea and the desert were favorite locales of Frank Norris. Perhaps man's basic virtue was his capacity to survive in the struggle with nature in her most forbidding mien. One of London's arctic heroines, in *A Daughter of the Snows* (1902), chose as her mate the suitor who survived the test of a dangerous canoe trip through the running ice of the Yukon. (This was a novel, incidentally, through which the racist theme also ran.) In Norris's *Moran of the Lady Letty* (1898), the seagoing heroine, a female Tarzan, was determined to select as her mate the man who could throw her in a wrestling match. In the preposterous sequel, when eventually she had met her master, her love, an effete sentiment, proved to have deprived her of her physical strength. When faced with a challenge she could readily have surmounted in her virgin state, she perished miserably.

One of the biological issues that permeated naturalism was the question of heredity *versus* environment, the nature–nurture controversy. Representatives of the movement in literary or social thought were not required to commit themselves to either alternative as evidence of naturalistic orthodoxy. It was enough that they discuss their problems in these terms, emphasizing the determinative influence of heredity or of environment as the circumstances seemed to warrant.

All evolutionists were agreed that the hereditary transmission of variations was essential in the evolutionary process. Evolution was simply the survival of the fittest of these variations and, consequently, their distribution through the population. But curiously enough, no American writer of fiction dealt deliberately with the role of heredity in natural selection, as Zola did. London and Dreiser both started novels in which they seemed to intimate that they were about to do so, but both were diverted. The force of heredity was, in fact, assigned a diametrically opposed function. Through some perversity, the source of which is difficult to discover, these novelists were obsessed, not with the heredity of evolutionary variations, but with the atavistic recurrence of long-submerged primitive traits. This was a fascination similar to the preoccupation of eugenists with the hereditary transmission of dysgenic qualities. As Norris wrote of one of his heroes, McTeague, in the novel of that name (1899): "Below the fine fabric of all that was good in him ran the foul stream of hereditary evil, like a sewer. The vices and sins of his father and of his father's father, to the third and fourth and five hundredth generation, tainted him. The evil of an entire race flowed in his veins. Why should it be? He did not desire it. Was he to blame?"

The force of heredity was the factor that justified the naturalistic concern with atavistic reversion to archetypal forms, a phenomenon so paradoxical in the evolutionists of Spencer's generation who equated evolution with progressive change. They felt free, instead, to follow either of two contradictory lines of thought—or to blend them together, as the spirit moved. They might, and generally did, share Spencer's and Norris's complacent teleological conviction that all things irresistibly worked together for good. But in dealing with a specific situation or problem, they frequently deemed it more illuminating to dwell upon the original or primitive elements out of which the situation had evolved, and in terms of which it was best understood. The search for the primitive took several forms in naturalistic thought. To understand evolution, it was presumed to be necessary to trace back its course; to understand the present, it was necessary to study its roots in the past; to understand man, it was necessary to go with Freud to the child; to understand the race, one must dig with Jung in the roots of the racial unconscious.

The true type, then, for the naturalistic writer, was the archetype. Under the stress of conflict or of a hostile environment, the burden of civilization might drop from a man's shoulders and the brute in him reappear. Whenever this happened, the novelist managed to convey the impression that liberation had occurred. Norris was especially intrigued by this theme. It also explained the preoccupation of the whole group of writers with such primitive activities as fighting, loving, and struggling with the elements.

On the environmental side, the naturalists rendered an important service to American thought by calling attention to the weakness of the traditional democratic ideology in placing reliance upon an uncritical environmentalism. At a time when historians had begun to sing the praises of a vanished frontier, the novelists, in effect, asked them to consider the results had the frontier environment been a hostile rather than essentially beneficent one. Although the more important part of man's environment was social rather than physical, the naturalists believed that social processes were as impersonal and inexorable as those of nature. In his wheat novels, *The Octopus* and *The Pit,* Norris depicted the impersonal forces of supply and demand in the wheat market as they made or broke the characters involved, after the pattern established by Zola in his novel of French coal mining.

Environmentalism was no haven of refuge for one who would escape the cruel laws of heredity. It was merely the other horn of the dilemma. The more impressive works of the group were not concerned with nature or biological problems but with man in society. Dreiser's *The Financier* (1912) was one of the best of these. Dreiser chose to portray not the downtrodden misfit but the American demigod, the financier. As Dreiser depicted him, the financier was not the strong champion who emerged triumphant from the struggle for existence, according to the popular stereotype, but a parasitic growth on the body social. As the book opened, the future financier in his boyhood was witnessing the lethal struggle for survival between a lobster and a squid. But his own subsequent financial success resulted from the realization that he should at all costs avoid a comparable economic struggle for existence. He built his fortune upon circumvention of the open competition of the marketplace by means of contacts that yielded political favors, inside information, exclusive privileges, and "tips" which could be exploited for profit. The moral of his success was to avoid competition wherever possible and to operate in finance rather than in any such usefully productive activity as manufacturing. Dreiser published his critique of the financier as a by-product of the American economic environment in the year that marked the crest of progressivism. It undoubtedly reflected something of the progressive criticism of finance capitalism. It also bore a close resemblance to Veblen's contemptuous analysis of the financier as a "captain of industry." Both critics saw the financier as an atavistic buccaneer or "robber baron" who seized control of the industrial machinery in order to extort tribute from it; both intimated that he was readily dispensable.

Moral Evolution

The moral theory of naturalism always remained confused and difficult. Some naturalists attempted bravely to maintain a pose of amoral fatalism; no moral theory was necessary. Others, the majority, blended their social evolutionism with the self-regarding utilitarian morality that could be easily read into the view of life suggested by the analogy of natural selection. Sumner provided one of the best examples of the latter tendency. He was constantly exhorting his contemporaries to cultivate self-discipline in the face of a total situation about which he insisted nothing could be done. Racist advocates of white supremacy similarly argued that deficiencies of morality, character, and intellect among Negroes were evidence of inferior racial quality. Because the white race monopolized wealth, power, and refinements, it was easy for racists to convince themselves that the conventional moral virtues which were associated with these advantages were necessary and inherent features of the highest levels of social evolutionary advance. Thomas Nelson Page stated categorically that "races rise or fall according to their character," by which he meant the self-disciplinary virtues of the Malthusian and utilitarian tradition.

The exploration of the moral implications of naturalism was extended more systematically by clergymen and philosophers, although the confusion remained. One of the earliest to do so was Minot J. Savage, a popular Unitarian preacher of Boston and New York. Savage, who was an ardent disciple of Spencer, set himself the task of working out the implications of evolution for religion and ethics. Although he remained a member of what professed to be a Christian body, albeit a "liberal" one, he discarded all the elements of traditional Christian supernaturalism. In a volume of sermons entitled *The Religion of Evolution* (1876), Savage taught that man could discover the will of God only through an understanding of the nature and meaning of the evolutionary process, which was the revelation of God's will. Men could no longer accept ethical precepts because they were revealed on a specific occasion in the past. Man had come to realize that this was not the way in which the most important truths in life were apprehended. The principle of evolution indicated a progressive unfolding of truth, in which each age improved upon the wisdom and knowledge of its predecessors.

Lest such an approach seem to preclude the possibility of arriving at an absolute ethical standard, Savage hastened to affirm that that which tended to promote life was the ultimate criterion by which values were to be measured. Virtue was that which made for life or which was advantageous to men. Vice or evil was that which made for disintegration or death. Virtue also made for happiness, since it was happiness alone that made life worth living. Savage strenuously rejected as childish the criticism that such a doctrine would lead to self-indulgence. All mature people knew that self-indulgence was self-defeating. The specific life-giving virtues were known to man neither by revelation nor by intuition, according to the moral systems previously entertained by Americans, but through the accumulated experience of the race. Much of this ancestral experience Savage believed to have become embedded in the living tissue, expressing itself in characteristic instincts, intuitions, and judgments. It was this adaptation of Lamarckian use-inheritance that justified Savage in his complacent assumption that men generally knew without being told what they ought or ought not to do.

The nature of the good, then, was adjustment to the "real facts" of life. The real facts were, presumably, the material conditions and institutional circumstances in which the individual might find himself. Such an adjustment would bring health, happiness, and peace of mind. It was what the biologist might have called successful adaptation. Moral good was defined by Savage as consisting of equitable adjustment between man and man. How the principle of equity was related to the adjustment declared to be the essence of natural good, Savage did not explain.

Evil, on the other hand, was declared to be nonexistent in the traditional sense of being an expression of malignant forces. Evil was simply maladjustment, which brought with it pain, calamity, sickness, and death. It was to be avoided by the use of intelligence. The study of primitive religions showed how uncivilized men, ignorant of the laws of nature, had derived a concept of evil from the conviction that nature was in part diabolical. Increasing knowledge of nature had permitted modern men to make great progress in coping with natural evil. Moral evil was said to consist in the breaking of the universal law of righteousness, namely, the principle of equity or just relationship between men. Savage was persuaded that the ultimate conquest of moral evil would come through a keener understanding of moral laws, reflected in sharper consciences, and in the realization that self-interest truly understood was identical with the interests of all.

Without perhaps being fully aware of it, Savage shared the naturalistic presupposition that ideals or principles were epiphenomenal or peripheral, responding or adjusting themselves to material or social realities. Like others who worked under Spencer's influence, he equated evolution with progress. One aspect of the social-evolutionary process had been the steady refinement of moral conceptions and practices. The good was the more evolved, evil the less evolved conception. It has been noted that Savage defined the good as adjustment to the "real facts" of life. But for the evolutionist, the real facts were constantly changing. Savage shared the naturalistic theory of differential rates of change. As the real facts of technology and economy changed, corresponding changes in institutions and ideas subsequently occurred. Hence it was that ideas of the good at any moment tended to reflect not the real facts of the moment but those that had existed at some time in the past. This was a somewhat unfortunate condition that may be designated as moral lag. Savage pointed out that it was a phenomenon especially significant in times of rapid material and social changes like his own. One of the most important functions of clergymen and teachers was to narrow the gap so far as possible by popularizing theories of the good more in accord with current conditions of life.

As a Spencerian, Savage paid little attention to the bearing of natural selection upon moral theory. Perhaps because of his teleological faith in progress, the means by which the process occurred was of little interest to him. Certain thinkers, however, undertook to explore this relationship. One of them was George F. Wright, an Oberlin geologist and theologian. In an article published in 1880 in the *Bibliotheca Sacra,* Wright found in natural selection certain implications for the moral life not easily reconciled with the bland evolutionary optimism of Savage. Natural selection supposed the inclusion of man within the domain of natural law, and, consequently, it would not support theories of moral free will. Nor would it justify belief in progress, for the evidence showed that degradation and extinction frequently occurred to species under natural selection. As a theologian as well as a scientist, Wright clung to the conviction that natural selection was not incompatible with the traditional religious doctrine of design in nature, but he conceded that the reconciliation could be accomplished only by a "large view" that comprehended the "whole of the relevant phenomena"; a view that one would have to be farsighted indeed to appreciate.

The deterministic implications of the evolutionary point of view for the moral life were fully explored by the lexicographer Antonio Llano, writing in the *Philosophical Review* in 1896. Llano summarily described the historical course of moral evolution as originating in duty, proceeding to right, and culminating in necessity. Morality had originated in conditions of superstition and slavery, which were reflected in its preoccupation with duty, conscience, and compulsion. But the chief feature of social evolution had been the emancipation of the intellect, and reason thus liberated had gradually dissolved the primitive morality of duty, replacing it with the sense of right. In modern times, men were stressing individual rights, many of them espousing a utilitarian morality of enlightened self-interest that assumed a positive individualism. This was, in effect, the position of Savage, for whom freedom seemed to be the end of the evolutionary process.

But Llano was not content to stop here. Since change was inevitable, he insisted upon asking what was likely to be the future course of evolutionary change with respect to morality? He professed to conduct his search for the answer in accordance with the strictest canons of scientific investigation. The naturalist should be concerned with what was most likely to happen, not with what he would like to have happen. Moreover, Llano concluded, "once we have objectized man and included him in the great universal whole, as but one of the infinite cosmical phenomena, we shall cease to be 'morally' shocked or disgusted."

It was already acknowledged in Llano's day that reality was composed of material stuff and that this included human nature. This material reality was governed by natural laws that men were beginning to comprehend. Given these facts, a few men already had sufficient courage to admit that free will was ultimately an illusion. As it became more widely appreciated that men's conduct was determined by their physical organization, which, in turn, was determined by inheritance, environment, and the eternal properties of matter and force, moral feelings based on a sense of personal independence would disappear. It would then be realized that "no man's conduct is *his* conduct; it is simply a manifestation of the way in which the universe exists and moves. There is, then, no vice, no virtue, no duty, and morality . . . must be confessed to derive its authority from superstitious feelings corresponding to inadequate conceptions as to the nature of man and the universe of which he forms a part."

The naturalistic outlook, then, was one that found the traditional ideas of duty or virtue already largely dissolved in self-interest; and self-interest, in turn, was expected to give way to a kind of amoral fatality in which men would realize that what was, was what had to be. So they would come eventually to accept the world as they found it, without protest and, presumably, without hope. Among the novelists at the turn of the century, the same point of view was apparent although rarely free of inconsistencies. Writers celebrated the virtues of the natural man as evidences of sheer animal vitality. The mixture of candor, resignation to fate, and zest for living that their writing usually revealed stemmed from their professed contentment with the universe as they found it, which was the way it had to be. But they had not succeeded in achieving a consistent naturalism free of all romantic involvement or devoid of a lingering conviction that men should be true to their ideals and triumph over obstacles.

Even more important, the course of moral evolution as charted by naturalistic navigators pointed toward a singularly drab and empty future in which men would be obliged to foreswear as irrelevant the whole range of subjective experience involving choice, values, responsibility—exactly those functions found by experience to be the most poignant or exhilarating. If such occasions were to be declared off bounds to the novelist, he would be singularly impoverished in the materials he might legitimately use. He might as well write about animals as men—which of course was what Jack London did with such success in *The Call of the Wild*. But some years were to pass before the full effects of the naturalistic moral cycle made themselves felt.

The End of Naturalism

Although it was doubtless too early to tell with certainty by the middle of the twentieth century, the naturalistic pattern of thought appeared not to have survived the Depression of the 1930's and the world conflict that followed. The causes of its demise were both external and internal. The challenge of events dealt ruthlessly with a philosophy of complacent fatalism. Men were required to act; and, to do so effectively, they needed a positive faith. From the beginning, naturalism had been under constant attack by those who denied its validity, and the trend of events seemed to confirm the critics. Again, many of the issues that had seemed so significant to early naturalists gradually yielded to newer interests, thus robbing naturalism of its apparent cogency and relevance. Evolutionism was a conspicuous example. Finally, the development of naturalistic ideas themselves led to a state of mind that was essentially self-defeating. The latter tendency was succinctly documented in a volume of essays by Joseph Wood Krutch, *The Modern Temper*, published in 1929. Krutch was a literary critic and historian, born in Tennessee, but long identified with New York, both as professor at Columbia and as editor of the *Nation*.

The modern temper was described by Krutch as one of disillusionment, cynicism, pessimism, and resigned despair. In Thoreau's phrase, it was one of "quiet desperation." Although Krutch did not specify the elements of naturalism precisely as they have been isolated in these pages, he clearly attributed the modern temper to disillusionment with the naturalistic pattern of thought. He thought of himself as a product of that tradition, and he sensed that the implications of its doctrines had somehow developed in quite different ways from those anticipated by the first generation of naturalists in the years following the Civil War. In order to understand what had happened to blight its prospects, Krutch undertook his own analysis of the movement.

He noted, in the first place, how an original optimism had given way to pessimism. The first generation of naturalists had been profoundly optimistic. They had witnessed the preservation of the union and the destruction of slavery. The idea of progress, well nigh universally accepted in the early nineteenth century, carried over into the postbellum period to tincture the emerging ideas of the age with its warm overtones. The romanticism of the earlier period had glorified the dignity and freedom of the individual, and the vigorous mood that it created was not to be quickly extinguished, even by new ideas fundamentally alien to it. To be sure, these conditioning factors had nothing strictly to do with the development or implications of naturalistic ideas in themselves, but they did help to fashion a setting or perspective on the new ideas and thus to influence the way in which men tended at first to interpret them. In the light of these factors, for instance, it was inevitable to most men of the generation of Thomas Henry Huxley and Lewis Henry Morgan that evolution should mean progress and that science should seem to be a liberator rather than a destroyer. But after the beginning of the twentieth century, naturalists had become increasingly pessimistic. Since their pessimism was not generally shared by nonnaturalists, it seemed appropriate to assume that it arose from a growing appreciation of the implications of the ideas themselves.

A new and quite unexpected attitude toward science had also manifested itself in Krutch's generation. A fundamental aspect of naturalism had been its scientism, which meant both a veneration for the scientific method as the means of solving all problems and a general outlook based on a philosophy of materialism. Naturalism itself was a kind of philosophy of popular science, and many of its proponents assumed that its doctrines possessed the validity of scientific truths. The optimism of the earlier naturalists had rested in part on the confidence felt in science as the solvent for all problems. By Krutch's time, this early optimism had vanished. Science had, to be sure, dissolved the older ideas of soul, will, and morality. But no sooner had men declared these to be fictions than they began to see that the older ideas had been necessary fictions, and there was nothing at hand with which to replace them. Krutch attributed the widespread disillusionment with science in the 1920's to the fact that, while science had destroyed necessary human values, it had done nothing to repair the damage.

It was with undisguised nostalgia that Krutch looked back to the democratic era before the Civil War. That had been a humane world —man-centered, moralistic, a world of feeling and of qualities. It had been destroyed by the "systematized and cumulative experience called science." The world when looked at scientifically did not display the emotional correspondences that permitted man to interpret it in his own image. His emotional needs remained unfilled because there was no place for esthetics in a scientific world. While scientific knowledge had revolutionized the material world, it had left man's emotions and instincts adjusted to a purposeful and humanized world that no longer existed. It was to this circumstance that Krutch traced the widespread indifferentism and futility of his age, which contrasted so poignantly with the vigorous and self-assured creativity of the previous epoch.

In reconsidering the implications of man's place in nature, Krutch undertook a fundamental critique of the naturalistic outlook. This relationship had been the pivot upon which early naturalistic thought had turned. Although Krutch now saw several aspects of the relationship that had not been apparent to his predecessors, or which at least had not registered upon them with depressing effect, his pessimism was due primarily to his inability to emancipate himself from a point of view that he saw clearly led to futility. Thus Krutch remained a naturalist, and his critique was the more incisive for his inability to emancipate himself from its limitations.

Where the earlier naturalists had stressed the firmness of the bonds that had fixed man to his place in nature, Krutch stressed the radical cleavage which seemed to have opened between man and nature. The pattern of nature as explored by scientific methods bore no relation to the pattern of human emotions. Science had, in fact, divorced man from nature. By greatly enhancing human comfort and security, science had brought into being humanistic philosophies. These philosophies had inevitably emphasized individual well-being, as opposed to the well-being of the species with which nature was solely concerned. By way of contrast, an inspection of the behavior of animals or even of primitive peoples revealed how "in the light of nature" individual well-being was inevitably subordinated to the survival of the group. Humanistic attitudes consequently meant a weakening of the group. From this point of view, it was apparent that the religious belief in immortality was to be regarded as a surviving relic of animal virtue, since it compensated for self-sacrifice with the promise of the hereafter. But as religious skepticism was spread by the scientific frame of mind, life was expected to justify itself, and its values consequently had meaning only for individual consciousness and not for nature.

It appeared to Krutch therefore that humanistic values were the ultimate enemy of those natural impulses that made the life of the species successful: to reproduce abundantly even at the pain of discomfort or privation; to sacrifice for the young, or for the group. Consequently, as societies civilized themselves they inevitably became decadent. The quiet desperation of Krutch's generation arose, in part at least, from a dawning realization that it must choose between "a stable, essentially animal existence and the dangerous—ultimately fatal—life of the society which starts out in pursuit of purely human values." But Krutch knew well enough how men confronted with these alternatives would be likely to choose. It furnished but another reason for reverting to a cyclical interpretation of the historical process.

The social-evolutionary emergence of mankind from savagery through barbarism to civilization, which constituted the most pertinent interpretation of history for the earlier naturalists, emphasized a basic or secular trend upon which much of their optimism rested. Now, however, Krutch found history to consist of a series of cyclical fluctuations as civilizations rose and fell. The organic analogy resided not in the structure and related functions of society but in its life history. Society, like the individual organism, was to grow old and die. In its childhood, it was dominated by imaginative fantasies in which the universe seemed to be made for man. But with the growth of society, these childish fantasies were replaced by objective scientific knowledge. Nature was now seen to be indifferent or hostile to man; skepticism became widespread; finally pessimism set in.

Implicit in Krutch's discussion was the assumption that the truly creative impulses had expressed themselves in the construction of myths, value systems, and religious dogmas, while reason, on the other hand, merely revealed the cold world of fact. This invidious distinction contrasted sharply with the conviction of earlier naturalists that intelligence was the creative force upon which the social process hinged. It now seemed apparent that the decline of civilization coincided with the flowering of intellect. A decay of national vigor inevitably followed because of the contradiction between human and natural virtues.

Krutch designated the beginning of the twentieth century as the approximate point at which the earlier optimism and complacence of naturalists began to give way to pessimism. Prior to the turn of the century, they had been wholly absorbed in working out a mechanistic and materialistic concept of the universe in which man's place was fixed. Thereafter, as they explored more fully the moral and practical implications of their creation, they began to realize that they had sprung a trap upon themselves.

PART V

The Contemporary Neodemocratic Mind

CHAPTER 20

The Critique of Naturalism

AT NO TIME DURING THE YEARS between Appomattox and the Great Depression of the 1930's did naturalistic ideas hold undisputed sway over the American mind. A reaction against them set in as soon as they had appeared. In the spirit of this reaction the social philosopher Lester Frank Ward in 1906 characterized naturalism as "the philosophy of despair that has come to dominate even the most enlightened scientific thought." Ward prescribed an active individualism as the effective "remedy for the general paralysis that is creeping over the world, and which a too narrow conception of the law of cosmic evolution serves rather to increase than to diminish." The reaction to naturalism was controlled by the continuing appeal of the traditional American democratic ideals. It took the form of a reaffirmation of these ideals, modified somewhat in the light of modern conditions. The early twentieth century thus witnessed the coexistence in America of two antithetical bodies of values. To this fact may be attributed at least something of the peculiar intellectual confusion that characterized the era.

Neodemocracy

The American democratic ideology had emerged in the early nineteenth century as a spontaneous product of the interaction of social and economic conditions with the cultural and intellectual traditions of the American people. Although the Americans of the Middle Period had been acutely conscious of belonging to a new and distinct civilization, they were nevertheless unable to objectify their society and call it democratic with the degree of self-consciousness that would be possible for their descendants of a century later. A perceptive foreigner, Alexis de Tocqueville, who studied the United States in 1830, was perhaps the first to characterize the society of the New World as democratic. But it was not until the early twentieth century that an American President—Woodrow Wilson—is said to have used the term *democracy* as synonymous with *the good society*. By mid-twentieth century, the normative usage of the word *democracy* had become a universal cliché. The Swedish economist Gunnar Myrdal, who knew the United States intimately, remarked in 1944 that no other people was so thoroughly committed to a bundle of articulated verbal symbols as were the Americans.

These circumstances explain the essential conservatism of the neodemocratic ideology. Twentieth-century Americans were attempting to preserve a traditional set of values and attitudes in the face of newer antithetical ideals. A society has little occasion to formulate its ideals explicitly until it is challenged by external or internal adversaries. The reaction to naturalism took the form of a more self-conscious preoccupation with the democratic values that were challenged by naturalism. The rise of totalitarianism in the middle third of the twentieth century presented Americans with the spectacle of naturalism in action. The nature of their response to it, in spite of the force of the traditional isolationism, was inevitably conditioned by the previous ideological struggle.

The emancipation of the individual from the theoretical restraints imposed by naturalism was, perhaps, the most important ideological feature of neodemocratic thought, although this fact tended to be obscured by the concern of Americans with the practical issues of public policy. The nineteenth-century individualistic ideal, together with many of the practices that gave it meaning, continued to show surprising vigor in the following century in view of the extensive changes that had occurred. The Progressive political reform movement of the first two decades of the twentieth century conceived of the ideal of social progress in individualistic terms. And after the heat of partisanship had dissipated, it was also apparent that the New Deal was likewise concerned primarily to preserve traditional values and institutions by making expedient compromises where necessary.

Nevertheless, a significant realignment was occurring. The older individualism had had firm roots in the agricultural–commercial capitalism of the preindustrial era. With the coming of industrialism the social and economic conditions that had nourished individualism were largely transformed. In these circumstances there occurred a shift in the basis of individualism from economic conditions to legal and civil rights. The significance of this transfer will be discussed at greater length in another place. It is enough to say here that much thought has been devoted to the best means for securing and extending the civil liberties of individuals as the essential precondition of all other forms of liberty. Considerable gains have been made in the effort to guarantee civil liberty to individuals and to groups and classes to whom it has traditionally been denied. But it would be foolish to overlook the fact that in a society dominated by a crass and tasteless machine culture powerful forces are brought to bear on all to compel uniformity and to stamp out individuality, both of thought and action.

Another change concerned the conditions of security. In earlier times, an adequate measure of security had been offered to the individual by the sparsity of population and the unfolding economic opportunities of the New World. In theory, security was a by-product of a life governed by the practice of the Puritan virtues. In practice, however, the matter seems to have been largely taken for granted. The growing disrepute of the Puritan ethic at the end of the nineteenth century was a significant indication of a dawning realization that its presumed practical efficacy was a snare and a delusion. In the twentieth century, security was not infallibly to be had through any relatively simple prescription of hard work and self-discipline. Americans turned to deliberate measures to achieve it. They sought security from external danger by means of military power, and they sought security from internal danger, chiefly impoverishment, through government financial assistance of various kinds.

The quest for security had much to do with the circumstances in which the democratic ideology sought to perpetuate itself. Because the state emerged as the most effective instrument for the guarantee of security, the state experienced a rapid expansion of its functions and powers. But the resort to public agencies meant that a powerful equalizing force had come into play. To guarantee security is to equalize in an important sense, especially when the cost is assessed in accordance with capacity to pay. The consequence of these tendencies was to proceed toward the transformation of the traditional ideal of equality of opportunity into some measure of actual equality in the form of social security. In short, security, which was formerly a by-product of individualism, was now to be guaranteed by society even at the expense of some measure of individual freedom. What the ultimate effects of these tendencies upon individualism would be, could scarcely be predicted at Mid-century.

The intimate union of the democratic ideology with the sentiment of nationalism was another distinctive feature of neodemocracy. Two world wars in the twentieth century served to provide a world-wide context for American democracy, at the same time that these wars released revolutionary forces that revealed the democratic aspirations of suppressed peoples everywhere. Again, it remained to be seen whether Americans would be capable of assuming the world leadership for which their prior experiment in democracy had potentially qualified them.

Genetics and Evolution

The repudiation of naturalism has not involved a repudiation of science or of the scientific method. Americans have not lost any of their practical enthusiasm for the material benefits and constructive achievements of applied science. Rather, since the critique of naturalism involved a repudiation of some of the deterministic consequences of the application of presumed scientific method to human affairs, modern thought has more effectively adapted scientific thought to human purposes and is prepared to make effective use of science in many areas where the naturalistic mind did not find it necessary.

Biology had occupied the central position in the scientific canon of naturalism, and the Darwinian principle of natural selection was the "law" that afforded the principal insight into the operations of nature and society. On it depended for their validity the principles of the struggle for existence and the survival of the fittest.

But the theory of evolution that prevails among scientists in the twentieth century is appreciably different from classical Darwinism or Neo-Lamarckism, and it does not perform in modern thought a function comparable to that of Darwinism in the naturalistic pattern.

An event of major importance in the history of science and of thought was the rediscovery in 1900 of the earlier work of an obscure Austrian geneticist, Gregor Mendel. The laws of heredity that Mendel laid down provided a theoretical basis for the experimental science of genetics, which at once assumed a central position so far as problems of evolution were concerned. The new science was concerned with the genetic determiners or genes, discrete particles from which the bodily characters of organisms are developed through interplay between genetic potential, environmental forces, and the activities of the organism during growth. The influence of genetics in reformulating the general theory of biological evolution has been so great that it is only proper to distinguish the modern theory from Darwinism and all other earlier theories by designating it as genetical evolution. The development of the genetical theory has been predominantly an Anglo-American enterprise. A list of its more distinguished proponents would include Thomas Hunt Morgan, Julian Huxley, Theodosius Dobzhansky, and Sewell Wright, geneticists, and George Gaylord Simpson, a paleontologist.

Although the genetic influence is essentially conservative, determining the overt similarity of offspring to parent, nevertheless it is in mutations and other alterations in the genetic materials that the most important sources of evolutionary transformations are found. Each individual organism possesses a unique complement of genes. In reproduction, the genes of the parent germ cells are reassorted, so that the offspring is both like and unlike either parent. Apart from the regular changes resulting from the continuous reassortment of genetic material through successive generations, there are occasional variations due to mutations of the genes themselves. Individual genes combine to govern complex bodily characteristics, but without blending or merging with each other. Here was the reason for the universal variation among individual organisms that Darwin had observed but could not explain.

While the voluminousness of the data that Darwin cited to confirm the fact of evolution was impressive, it was nothing in comparison with what was available in the twentieth century, especially in the field of paleontology. The earlier controversies among evolutionists over the random or directional character of evolutionary modifications have been resolved in the realization that both tendencies have appeared under specific circumstances which can be explained. Since Darwin knew nothing of the nature of genetic mechanisms he had to deal with the overt characteristics of organisms rather than with their genetic constitutions. He could describe the results of evolutionary processes so far as the evidence was available; but the true nature of the causes eluded him. This meant that the universal variations among organisms upon which his theory of natural selection rested proved to be largely irrelevant.

The theory of natural selection in its modern form is significantly different from the formulation given to it by Darwin. Darwin had defined natural selection as the survival of the fittest in the struggle for existence. The modern evolutionist, however, regards the struggle for existence as largely irrelevant to a sound explanation of the evolutionary process. He defines natural selection much more simply as differential reproduction: organisms participate effectively in the changing stream of genetic transmission in proportion to the number of their offspring. Those organisms having a larger number of offspring tend to be better integrated with the environment and, hence, better able to exploit it. Natural selection thus tends to direct the evolutionary process toward such integrations; and adaptation, or adjustment of the organism to its environment, is accomplished in large measure through the operation of natural selection.

Natural selection thus conceived is ordinarily a peaceful process. Veblen understood this perfectly when he observed that from the evolutionary standpoint it was more important to produce food and children than to emerge victorious from combat. How often had a conquered people swallowed up their conquerors? The advantage in differential reproduction is ordinarily the consequence of superior integration with the environment, more efficient utilization of the food supply, better care of the young, the avoidance of intragroup discords that might hamper reproduction, and the capacity to monopolize and exploit new environments where competition with other species can be avoided. Simpson has also pointed out that intra- and extragroup relationships should always be distinguished when analyzing the total environment of an organism. Where intragroup relations involve struggle—as, for instance, war in the human species—the consequence might be deleterious to successful adaptation to the total environment. In general, however, if the term *struggle for existence* is to be retained at all it should be borne in mind that as it pertains to natural selection the struggle does not typically involve overt struggle. The individual organism, including *Homo sapiens,* is usually unconscious of the process.

The first consequence of the genetical theory of evolution for intellectual history was withdrawal of scientific support from the naturalistic sociological, political, and moral theories that justified themselves in part by appealing to the presumed validity of the

struggle for existence and survival of the fittest in the literal competitive sense as essential to evolutionary progress. Although this
was a negative consideration, it was a matter of great moment
for the intelligentsia at least that the prestige and authority of science
no longer appeared to support certain features of the naturalistic
outlook. On the positive side, genetical evolutionary theory led to a
new approach to the race question, an approach that entailed a
drastic revision of the naturalistic theories of race.

Naturalists had employed both physical and cultural characteristics as the criteria for racial distinctions. The physical anthropologists, from whom the racists took their racial biology, were accustomed to designate the physical features characteristic of each race
and to classify individuals racially as they might approximate one
or another racial norm. The practice presupposed blending inheritance, what Dobzhansky has described as a vestige of the immemorial
blood theory of heredity. It assumed that the individual blended the
dissimilar features of his parents, so that an inbred racial group
would eventually come to share universal common racial features.
Racist theories of racial purity, and convictions as to the consequences of racial crossing, rested implicitly on the validity of these
assumptions. These theories fortified the conception of racial groups
as ranging all the way from the ideally pure race, composed of individuals sharing uniformly the distinctive racial characteristics, to
the polyglot mixtures of two or more races with wide individual
variability.

In recent years, the application of genetic principles to the study
of racial problems has resulted in a drastic modification of the older
anthropological approach. Geneticists define a race as an intrabreeding population that consequently shares a common pool of genes.
These genes are discrete units distributed in distinctive ratios
through the population and are regularly reassorted through successive generations by means of the process of chromosome division
and combination in reproduction. In the human species, no two
individuals (except identical twins) possess precisely the same genetic
constitution. When one race is distinguished from another, the real
difference resides in the fact that each race contains within its population a different proportion of the genes or gene complexes chosen
as the basis for racial distinction. Such a choice would, of course,
be quite arbitrary, save insofar as the chosen genetic factors might
have adaptive significance in the local environmental context. But

it is of vital importance to note that the genetic differences among races are proportionate differences, referring to races as whole groups. They do not refer to individual members of the races in question, who may or may not possess the distinguishing genetic characteristic of the race, even though the parents and offspring of the individuals in question might possess it. So far as the individual is concerned, racial designation has nothing to do necessarily with his own physical or genetic characteristics; it has to do solely with his participation in an intrabreeding group.

Certain anthropologists, notably Ashley Montagu and Ruth Benedict, have grasped the significance of genetic principles for racial study and have attempted a fresh statement of the social implications of a sound racial theory. In a study aimed at Nazi racial theories, *Man's Most Dangerous Myth: The Fallacy of Race*, published in 1942, Montagu suggests that, although one may properly speak of human races as a biological phenomenon, in practical terms it is undesirable to do so, since a scientific conception of race is so far removed from the misconceptions that have long been associated with the term in its popular usage. He employs such neutral terms as human *variety* or *ethnic group*. These anthropologists repudiate their predecessors who attempted to distinguish races on the basis of differing physical features that were presumed to be transmitted from one generation to another as whole complexes. In fact, gene units may vary independently. Although there is a legitimate basis for distinguishing races within many plant and animal species, it is probably impossible to make similar distinctions among men. Human varieties are much more mixed than are those of plants and animals, with much intergrading between ethnic groups. Biologically speaking, human differences are relatively insignificant.

The racist correlation of physical and cultural traits—the essential element in racist theory—rested upon convictions that transcended the limitations of racial genetics. It depended in the last analysis upon an interpretation of history. The geneticist knows of no evidence that mental selection comparable to the natural selection of physical traits has ever been operative. He declares mental characteristics to be cultural; at least without known physiological basis. In biological terms, human racial groups form and dissolve rapidly, and in this process social factors are important; they shape and enforce the caste restrictions that perpetuate ethnic groups. But here the student moves from the biological into the social realm.

No scientific evidence is known to support the racist assumption of the inferiority of racial hybrids. Where objective evidence to this effect has been cited, it is usually to be accounted for as the consequence of the handicaps that result from social discrimination. From a biological point of view, interbreeding between ethnic stocks is regarded as probably advantageous. The phenomenon of hybrid vigor that frequently results is owed to the dominance of previously recessive genes. In any ethnic group, a certain variability of physical characters resulting from some outbreeding is regarded as desirable from the standpoint of survival, since the group is then better equipped to perpetuate itself under a maximum variety of selective possibilities.

Because the early intelligence-test programs furnished the racists with presumably objective evidence of differences of racial intelligence, the subsequent re-evaluation of those test results was an important episode in the discrediting of racism. The army tests of World War I showed significant differences of IQ for various ethnic groups, and the results were widely cited as evidence of superior and inferior racial intelligence. During the 1930's, however, the findings were re-examined, and the earlier interpretations largely qualified. Two well-known authorities, C. C. Brigham and T. R. Garth, who had earlier accepted the validity of the army tests, later repudiated them on diverse grounds. Otto Klineberg summarized the prevailing opinion of 1941 when he held that a test score does not adequately indicate or measure inherited mental ability, since a host of social and environmental factors peculiar to the circumstances of the individual play a part in his performance on the test. Among such factors, Klineberg specified motivation, schooling, socio-economic status, language, and cultural interests. Here was but a single instance of the growing realization that nature and nurture cannot be separated but are interacting aspects of a single process. As Dobzhansky put it, heredity is never actuality, only potentiality; the actual always mixes the hereditary potential with environmental influences.

The refinement in theories of heredity made possible by genetic science was accompanied by a more critical analysis of the social effects of the physical environment. The opulence of the New World environment had reinforced the tendency of historic American liberalism to think of nature as beneficent. Perhaps in reaction to the culmination of this tendency in romanticism, the naturalists veered toward the Malthusian interpretation of nature as harsh and deterministic. The most extreme form of environmental determinism could doubtless be found in Watson's behavioristic psychology, where all action—and all of life is action—is conceived in terms of response to external stimulus. The dependence of reaction upon stimulus is so direct and complete that, according to Watson, it should ultimately be possible to predict the response wherever the nature of the stimulus is known. This assigns a purely passive role to the individual. Whatever the technical utility of the behaviorist doctrine may be for problems of research, an increasing number of social scientists outside psychology are coming to regard it as a totally inadequate explanation of the functioning of the human individual in practical situations.

A more moderate and widely accepted form of environmental determinism appeared in the historiography of Frederick Jackson Turner and the frontier school. Turner's theory that frontier experience had been the source of American democracy was almost universally accepted by historians during the first quarter of the twentieth century. Since 1925, however, many students have questioned both the validity of the generalization and the deterministic assumptions underlying it. In that year, a Stanford University historian, J.C. Almack, branded the frontier thesis as both materialistic and deterministic. He pointed out that these features, which if recognized would have jeopardized its popularity, were masked by the generally accepted puritanical notion that the self-reliance of the pioneer and the hardships of his rugged existence promoted individual and social well-being. During the next two decades, Turner's work was repeatedly subjected to searching and critical examination. By the middle of the century, it was probably generally agreed that American democracy was as much the product of cultural traditions and interests as of material conditions, and of the older settled regions as well as of the frontier.

Neodemocratic thought emphasizes not man's subordination to the environment but his capacity to exploit it. The term *adaptation* no longer means what it meant in Darwin's or in Turner's day: adjustment of the organism to its environment. Here was one of the most important deterministic elements in naturalistic thought. In Darwin's concept of natural selection, the physical environment was conceived to confront each organism with rigid standards of selection in terms of which the organism survived or was eliminated. Nature made her choices as definitely if inscrutably as ever Calvinistic deity had saved or damned. Now, however, adaptation means interaction of organism and environment. Each kind of organism has its peculiar environment. The most significant genetic variations are those that enable the organism to enter and exploit a new environment. The advantages that *Homo sapiens* enjoys over other species may be measured in part in terms of the number and variety of environments to which he has access, immeasurably the most important being the cultural environment.

Out of the thinking of scientists on these related problems there emerged in the years after the Great Depression certain principles that were believed to provide a biological basis for democracy. The first principle came with the realization that the diversity of mankind rests upon genetic uniqueness and variability. Dobzhansky has pointed out that, even if it were true that human personality were wholly or partially determined by the mechanisms of Mendelian heredity, the theory of individualistic democracy would still be the social theory most compatible with human biology. According to democratic theory, the individual finds his place in the social structure as determined by his own personal qualities and activity. Genetically, the same individual possesses a unique biological endowment, so that theoretically he is equipped for a unique social role without reference to hereditary social status.

A second principle concerned the inviolability of personality. Genes are substantially immune from external controls. Mutation rates can indeed be effected by radiation and other agencies, but the nature of the mutations is unpredictable. A revival of Lamarckism occurred in the Soviet Union during the later years of the Stalin era, led by Trofim Lysenko. It was asserted that by controlling the environment specified changes in the organism could be effected. Anglo-American geneticists working on Mendelian principles knew of no valid evidence to support such claims, and for a few years the world of genetical science was divided along ideological lines. After a short time, however, the Lysenkoist movement appeared to have collapsed.

Finally, it is necessary to note the passing of the dogma of the social organism. Biological processes occur in particular organisms whose differences constitute their individuality. Biology does not recognize a social organism. Genetics cannot admit functional specialization within a species beyond a very crude limit. Each individual organism must be a sufficient unit. At the beginning of the century, Lester Ward exposed the basic fallacy of the organic analogy. In a biological organism, the whole is sentient and the parts, insentient. In the so-called "social organism," on the contrary, the whole is insentient, and the parts—that is, the individuals who compose the society—are alone sentient. The social organism can thus exist only for the parts and not for the whole. The objective of social evolution must be the enhancement of the interests of individuals, not their subordination to some hypothetical social personality.

The Diversity of Cultures

The anthropologists had provided the most explicit formulation of the theory of cultural evolution, although the concept permeated the thought of the Western World during the naturalistic era. It was appropriate, therefore, that anthropologists should undertake the critique of the idea. An early instance of such a critical re-evaluation was Franz Boas's *The Mind of Primitive Man* (1911).

Boas was able to view the theory of cultural evolution through the successive stages of savagery, barbarism, and civilization with sufficient detachment to see that it was happily calculated to flatter the accomplishments of Western man, but did not do justice to the experience of many other peoples. It was a technological and materialistic interpretation of culture, and Boas was not inclined to accept the naturalistic assumption that technology was basic to other cultural accomplishments or that it correlated with them in some universal way. It was also apparent that the materialism of the theory rested upon an assumption of the psychic unity of mankind; otherwise the cultural evolutionist could not have taken it for granted that similar technical innovations would everywhere produce similar cultural consequences.

The accumulated anthropological data available to Boas made it apparent that the sequence of technological innovations had not been substantially uniform among all peoples, as Morgan had assumed it to be. Pottery, for instance, did not always appear in societies otherwise well advanced. And the same was true with respect to the use of metals, stabilized agriculture, or the domestication of animals. Thus it appeared that an advanced culture need not have passed through each of the successive stages that the evolutionists regarded as invariant.

The analogy of biological evolution had seemed to confirm the naturalistic assumption that men had started from a general lack of culture and had developed everywhere along approximately similar lines; that social development had proceeded from simplicity to complexity. But the available evidence did not support these assumptions. Rather, it appeared to Boas that opposing tendencies toward complexity and simplicity were commonly found to intercross. If the student were to concentrate, as Morgan did, on the history of technological or industrial development, a development that depended on rational activity, the facts would indeed show a progression toward greater complexity. But types of activity that did not depend on rationality would not show such a progression. The languages of primitive societies are usually highly complex, while the civilized languages are crude by comparison. The rhythmic structure of primitive music is similarly complex.

In short, naturalistic anthropology selected types of data in order to build a case for social evolution in terms favorable to the outlook and self-esteem of Western men. When attention was focused on the material culture, there did appear to have occurred a steady accumulation of artifacts and tools. By further assuming that the nonmaterial culture depended on the material, naturalistic anthropologists could postulate a universal cultural evolution.

To twentieth-century students, however, it became increasingly apparent that the evolutionary anthropologists had drawn the world's cultures into a unitary pattern of development by emphasizing certain of their similarities while ignoring their differences. A more tolerant acknowledgment of cultural diversity thus came to replace the earlier insistence on a universal pattern of cultural evolution. Veblen possibly had sensed some of these weaknesses in the older theory, for although the standard sequence of savagery, barbarism, and civilization had an important place in his system, he restricted its application to the history of the European races and was careful not to generalize about cultures beyond the area of European settlement. More recently, the sociologist W. I. Thomas, having rejected the evolutionary approach, summarized the modern consensus on the matter. Thomas declared differing cultures to be the result of differing interpretations of experience. Such an approach to culture as a phenomenon of thought upended the naturalistic structure of social reality with its technological and economic bases. The new emphasis on the approach to a culture through a study of its mentality was popularized by Ruth Benedict in her widely read comparative study of primitive societies, *Patterns of Culture* (1934). Here the material was chosen to illustrate the great variety of psychological attitudes upon which a given society may draw in composing the specific constellation of traits that characterize it. A new tolerance began to emerge from a deeper appreciation of the essentially unique qualities of each culture.

The theory of cultural lag was an integral part of the materialistic interpretation of history. It presupposed the naturalistic structure of social reality, in which the nonmaterial aspects of culture were presumed to respond more-or-less tardily to changes in the technological and economic foundations. Inevitably, therefore, the idea of cultural lag would sink or swim with the naturalistic outlook. Its declining popularity in the years since the Depression was less the result of specific criticism directed against it than of the gradual fading of the whole naturalistic point of view in terms of which it seemed to furnish a significant insight into the nature of the social process. The involvement of the Marxist version of naturalism in the international tensions of the times introduced a controversial note and helped to sharpen the reaction against dogmas that thus became ideologically tainted.

Although cultural lag still survives in contemporary thinking about social change, especially among students interested in practical problems of social disorganization and control, it has been subjected to critical scrutiny and is used more judiciously than in Ogburn's day. Cultural lag eventually came to be recognized as essentially a normative concept rather than as the purely descriptive formula that naturalists apparently held it to be. It dealt with the maladjustments or disintegrations that allegedly resulted from differential rates of change in related social phenomena. But "maladjustment" and "disintegration" are highly subjective and elusive categories. Close inspection showed that judgments of value were usually implicitly involved in situations where the concept of cultural lag was employed. With the growing demand among sociologists for more objective methods, the theory has passed from the center of attention. Like the larger theory of cultural evolution of which it became an integral part, cultural lag seemed by the middle of the twentieth century to be relevant chiefly where technological or economic phenomena were obviously involved in the situation under scrutiny. In other types of situation, wherever a sense of the dominance of material forces was weakened, the theory of cultural lag had become far less persuasive than it was to an earlier generation.

||||||||||||||||||||||||||||||||||||||||||||||||||||||||||||||||||||||||||

CHAPTER 21

Democracy and Public Opinion

T HE POLITICAL THEORIES appropriate to a democratic society
have much to say about the nature and functions of public
opinion. No better evidence of the continuing vitality of the democratic tradition in the twentieth century was to be found at the
intellectual level than the increasing attention that centered upon
this topic. In fact, the isolation of public opinion as an aspect of the
social process, and the analysis of its character and significance, was
a distinctive feature of neodemocratic thought.

The modern preoccupation with problems of public opinion has
been the product chiefly of practical tendencies in recent industrial
and political life. Industrial capitalism requires mobile and febrile
types of individuals whose interests and energies are easily aroused
and focused upon ever-shifting needs and social goals. Stimulated
by consumer needs as channeled through the mass media of communication, the modern citizen has been conditioned to be peculiarly responsive to the varied facets of his social environment. It
is with such individuals that the modern theory of public opinion
is concerned.

Nineteenth-century democrats devoted little attention to the problems of public opinion. A plausible explanation was furnished
many years later by Walter Lippmann. In every political ideology,

said Lippmann, there is a central unexamined assumption, a basic axiom on which the system rests. In the democratic ideology, this axiom is the sovereignty of public opinion. Powerful if largely unconscious forces inhibit the examination of the central assumption lest its validity be questioned or repudiated. Thus it was that in democratic America the central article of political faith remained for long veiled in the innermost sanctuary of the public piety.

Progressivism and Direct Democracy

The debate on the nature and functions of public opinion that continued through the Progressive era down to World War I was conducted within the framework of assumptions that had grown up around the structure of constitutional institutions in the United States. During this phase of the debate, the attention of participants was firmly fixed upon the political role of public opinion. It remained for later scholars to probe the broader sociological and psychological aspects of the subject. In a sense, the discussion during the Progressive era completed the corpus of commentary on classical constitutional theory. It summed up a century of thinking and experience on that aspect of political theory which the constitutional fathers had carefully circumvented, namely, popular sovereignty.

When eighteenth-century republicanism had asserted that political society rested upon the consent of the governed, it was, in effect, proclaiming the sovereignty of public opinion. As Jefferson put it, governments were republican to the extent that they expressed the will of the people. But having agreed upon this fundamental axiom, men were still confronted with the complex and politically crucial problem of translating public opinion into public policy. This was no simple equation. Republican theorists were acutely conscious of the pitfalls in translating the will of the people into the law of the land. Public opinion provided the raw materials of political life, and the science of politics, in Madison's phrase, consisted of the "refinement and enlargement" of these raw materials into the pure elements of public order. Human nature, as we have seen, was acknowledged to be a complex of good and bad, wisdom and folly, selfishness and altruism. Government must nourish the good and discourage the bad, not by means of policy but through the instrumentalities by which government was effected. The political institutions themselves then had a vital connection with the articulation of public opinion.

The republicans proposed to refine and enlarge public opinion into law through representation. The evil consequences of converting public opinion in its raw form into legislation was only too apparent in the direct democracy of the city states of antiquity or in the somewhat less direct form of the agrarian-dominated legislatures of certain of the contemporary American states—Jefferson's "elective despotisms." In all these cases, the result was "confusion and intemperance." Much thought was bestowed by republican constitution-makers upon the problems of representation, and ingenious analyses of it were advanced by them in defense of their labors. Together with the principle of mixed and balanced governmental powers, they expected representation to serve as an effective bulwark between the "sudden and violent passions" of the mass of citizens and the orderly processes of government.

In later times, it became so common in popular parlance to equate democratic government with the will of the majority that it is necessary to remind ourselves that this idea was not one of the conventional assumptions of republican theory. The framers of the Constitution conceived of society as composed of various interest groups, each of which was inevitably concerned with its own selfish welfare. One of the functions of government was to mediate between these interests, which it could do only if it was so constituted as to be immune from effective control by any one of them. In such a predominantly rural community as eighteenth-century America, much the largest of these interests numerically was the small farmer group. Given the prevailing freehold suffrage qualification of the American states, this group constituted the most serious threat to a public policy of harmonized interests. Although republican theory required of the statesman a national outlook transcending his interest affiliation —and many of the best of them achieved it—it would be asking too much to expect that republican theorists as a body, most of whom represented interests other than that of the small farmer, would stress a theory of majority rule that would, in practice, play into the hands of a single interest. And so they emphasized the distance between public opinion in the raw form and its ultimate embodiment in public policy. The former, which might be called the immediate will of the majority, was apt to be transient, passionate, ill advised, and delusive; the latter constituted the mature will of the community and was presumed to be sound, informed, dispassionate, and durable.

During the nineteenth century, the representative legislative institutions into which the Fathers had instilled their political philosophy solidified into the modern bicameral stereotype, about which swirled all the political changes of a bustling commercial civilization. Suffrage was extended, and political parties assumed their modern, loosely federated form. Industrialization generated political pressures of an intensity unknown in the eighteenth century, while the complexities of urban life confronted governing bodies with problems of administration with which they were utterly unprepared to cope. By the last third of the century, these pressures had resulted in the effective subjection of representative political institutions by business interests working through boss-controlled political machines. The result was a mounting wave of criticism of the representative principle, culminating in the Progressive sponsorship of various forms of direct democracy.

Many advocates of direct democracy regarded the introduction of the initiative and referendum as an effective reassertion of popular sovereignty. This was the view of Frank Parsons, propagandist for direct legislation. Successively civil engineer, lawyer, law professor, and reformer, Parsons was one of the most active workers for Progressive reform at the urban and state levels. Because sovereignty necessarily implied effective control, Parsons reasoned, the people could be said to be sovereign only when their elected representatives acted as their agents. But actually, he pointed out, the representatives had usurped control and had taken government into their own hands. By controlling law, business, and property, they had succeeded in transforming government into an "elective aristocracy," selling the fruits of sovereignty to monopolists. The historical background of this situation was filled in by Charles A. Beard in 1911. The United States had begun with practically omnipotent legislatures, powerful bodies that created and filled offices, granted charters to public and private corporations, levied taxes, and incurred debts at pleasure. But they shortly began to abuse their trust, and a succession of popularly elected constitutional conventions had sought to impose restrictions upon legislative power. The theoretical distinction between a basic popularly elected constitutional convention and the regularly constituted legislature thus gradually emerged during the nineteenth century. At the same time that these conventions curtailed the powers of the legislature, they increased the powers of the executive, who seemed to reflect more directly and effectively the popular will. Beard called attention to the way in which the best of the modern governors, notably Theodore Roosevelt, Wilson, La Follette, Hughes, and Folk, dominated their legislatures. The methods of direct democracy by which the Progressives proposed to restore sovereignty to the people were felt to be consistent with this trend of constitutional development. The initiative permitted a relatively small number of voters to initiate legislation and secure its adoption if successful in obtaining popular ratification. Similarly, the referendum would permit a small number of voters to require reference of a legislative act to popular vote. Both these procedures with their various modifications were designed as checks upon the mistrusted legislatures. Thus it was proposed to "cure the ills of democracy with more democracy."

The virtues of direct democracy, as Parsons enumerated them, revealed the utopian quality of his political ideology. Direct democracy would purify political life by attracting better men to active participation and by minimizing partisanship and the role of parties. It would elevate the press and act as an educational influence on the electorate. The equalitarianism implicit in the movement appeared in Parsons's conviction that it would promote the diffusion of wealth by depriving the rich of their disproportionate influence. Labor would then receive its just deserts. At the same time, however, the unfit would be effectively disfranchised, since only the more intelligent and public-spirited citizens would take the trouble to understand issues and vote. Thus it appeared that Parsons, in effect, divided political society into two classes on the basis of intelligence and public spirit, the techniques of direct democracy being the political weapons of the intelligent and public-spirited class. But he assumed that among a people "fit for free institutions" the latter class would comprise the majority. Majority opinion, therefore, could safely be accepted as superior to minority opinion. Because he assumed that virtue was in the majority, while he identified the minority with ignorance and "special interests," Parsons was prepared to commit public policy directly to the majority, and he gave little thought to the rights of the minority.

Parsons recognized the vital role of public opinion in direct democracy. In practice, he abandoned a professional and academic career in order to form and guide public opinion more effectively by means of written and spoken propaganda. Although he proposed to commit the political process directly to the wisdom of majorities, he was at the same time determined that they should share his point of view. He knew as a matter of fact that the proponents of direct democracy were concerned for good government in the interests of the whole people; and the moral indignation with which he chronicled the corruption of representative bodies rested upon the assumption that his disgust was widely shared. Nevertheless, these circumstances deluded Parsons into the false impression that, beyond a common indignation at corruption, public opinion would remain united upon a positive political program providing for public ownership of utilities and other reforms that he for one felt to be clearly in the public interest.

It fell to the twentieth-century conservatives to formulate the critique of the principles of direct democracy, in the form of a reaffirmation of the traditional theory of representation. One of the most eloquent of the conservatives was the elder Senator Henry Cabot Lodge of Massachusetts. An occasion for the expression of his views was provided in 1907 by the introduction of a public-opinion bill in the Massachusetts legislature authorizing that body to submit issues to the public by ballot in order that the legislators might inform themselves of the state of current opinion on pending matters of legislation. Senator Lodge was strenuously opposed to such a referendum, even for informational purposes. It would destroy the traditional relationship between legislator and constituency upon which he conceived the success of the American political system to depend.

The central conviction in Lodge's thinking on this subject was the dependence of political liberty upon a sound theory and practice of representation. The Anglo-American political tradition had perfected liberty because it had developed representative institutions to a degree hitherto unapproached in political history. Greece and Rome, by way of contrast, had lost their liberty—although they practiced purer forms of democracy than were to be found in modern states—because their representative institutions were deficient. Liberty, then, as history showed, was the product of a durable representative system. Lodge readily acknowledged the responsiveness of the representative principle to public opinion. He insisted upon the importance of making adequate provision for the public discussion of public issues. This was one of the major virtues of the representative assembly: it provided a forum for responsible debate. The devices of direct democracy, on the other hand, made no provision for discussion. The voter was to be presented with a ballot upon which he was expected to express a preference with or without the benefit of discussion of the issues, as the circumstances of the individual case might determine. Lodge thus attempted to turn the weapon of public opinion upon opponents who must have thought themselves in firm possession of it.

The traditional classical cycle of political deterioration reappeared in Lodge's conviction that the devices of direct democracy would undermine the responsibility of representative bodies and foster the all-powerful executive. This would follow because the confusion that would inevitably result from the direct rule of public opinion would induce a growing desire for the stability and order that a despot would promise to provide. In a more realistic vein, Lodge scrutinized the prospects of the initiative and referendum in the light of his extensive political experience and of the evidence accumulating in states where these devices were already in use. What was to prevent the politician from taking control of the initiative and referendum just as he had succeeded in capturing the political parties? The politician was even then demonstrating his capacity to manipulate primary elections, which had been heralded as a means of circumventing boss-dominated nominating conventions. Experience with the initiative and referendum indicated that only a small proportion of the eligible voters were participating, much smaller than the number casting ballots for candidates for office whenever the two occasions coincided. Lodge interpreted these facts to indicate that the people did not actually favor direct democracy. The facts also indicated to his mind that the initiative and referendum were not in reality to be regarded as a means of assuring the sovereignty of public opinion; rather, they were a device for the control of government in the interests of a small, active minority.

In the last analysis, direct democracy assumed the existence of a reservoir of public wisdom, expressed directly by the majority. Lodge refused to acknowledge the validity of this assumption. The people, he observed, were prone to act unwisely, especially in the heat of passion. He recalled the Know-Nothing movement in Massachusetts at the middle of the nineteenth century when the coercive measures proposed by the popular majority were averted by the wisdom and restraint of the legislature. Lodge concluded that the traditional practice of representation rested on a valid concept of the will of the people; while modern theories of direct democracy, although professedly animated by a zeal for the general welfare, actually handed over government to a small portion of the people, namely, those who voted.

A more sophisticated exposition of the suitability of direct democracy for the purposes of social reform than that of Frank Parsons was provided by Charles A. Beard, who, with B. E. Shultz, published *Documents on the State-Wide Initiative, Referendum and Recall,* in 1912. To the realistic historian, the initiative and referendum were the means for serving special interests, just as the representative legislature had so frequently proven to be. Beard did not equate these techniques of direct democracy with the expression of public opinion. He readily acknowledged that experience with referenda in various states showed that a minority could capitalize on the indifference and inertia of the majority, although he was inclined to believe that questions of major importance generally received an appropriate amount of attention. He was also at pains to distinguish between the size of a vote and generalizations about the intelligence or apathy of the electorate. A small popular vote on a technical question simply indicated the good sense of many citizens in abstaining.

But who were the special interests for the achievement of whose purposes Beard believed the techniques of direct democracy to be peculiarly suited? They were the social reformers, the small number of "interested and enlightened persons" with whom proposals for reforms originated. To secure the enactment of a reform in a representative legislature, it was necessary to win the support of a majority consisting largely of "those who know little or nothing about it," compromises and deals being an inevitable accompaniment. The use of the initiative permitted the reformers to circumvent the requirement of a legislative majority and, incidentally, permitted them to preserve their integrity also. They could appeal directly to the public; if the public were interested a large vote would result; if not, then a small one. "If, in real practice," Beard concluded, "we should demand the deliberate and carefully formed will of a majority of all of the voters of a commonwealth or their representatives on every important measure, progressive and enlightened legislation would be difficult indeed to secure. All that we can ask of a law, in a democracy, . . . is that it shall be reasonably acceptable to that vague thing which we call public opinion." Beard thus appeared to conceive of public opinion as a fluctuating mass of informed, or at least interested, opinion on public questions, the degree of interest being likely to reflect the nature of the question at issue.

The qualitative criterion that appeared in Beard's analysis was fully developed by A. Lawrence Lowell in his *Public Opinion and Popular Government* (1913). Lowell was a Harvard political scientist, later president of that institution, best known for his studies of

English and European governments. His analysis of public opinion in a democracy was the most comprehensive to appear during the Progressive Era, and it remained the most penetrating critique of the problem within the terms of traditional political concepts.

Public opinion as Lowell understood it was an aspect of the prevailing climate of opinion, or basic framework of beliefs generally accepted by the community. An opinion might be defined as a public opinion when its implementation was accepted by the minority in spite of its opposition. Such voluntary acquiescence was the mark of popular government, which could exist only where men were agreed on the ends and methods of government, while disagreeing on concrete issues. Only in these circumstances could the minority freely accept majority rule, knowing that the agreement on fundamentals was the bulwark assuring its survival. Otherwise, popular rule would degenerate into the tyranny of the majority. This was, of course, a profoundly conservative point of view, since public opinion was acknowledged to sanction only those acts that did not disturb the basic framework of society upon which all were agreed. Lowell conceded that in societies where sharp divergences of opinion on vital political questions existed there could be no public opinion and hence no popular government. Democracy therefore must work within clear-cut limitations as to legislative innovations. Thus although he equated democracy and public opinion, Lowell sharply distinguished the latter from the will of the majority. Public opinion could exist only where there was a general acceptance and approval of existing arrangements in all fundamental respects.

Lowell was disturbed by the recent tendency in political thought to replace the older democratic concept of harmony of interests with theories of class conflict and conflict of interest. The newer realism merely accentuated cleavages over racial, economic, and other irreconcilable issues and thus destroyed the conditions under which public opinion could exist. A successful democracy, he felt, was one where the limitations of public opinion were understood and where divisive issues were not needlessly raised.

The limits of a true public opinion were further restricted by the insights of naturalistic psychology. It was no longer permissible for the political theorist to accept the older assumption that man was a rational creature who intelligently sought selfish objects. Man was now known to be a "creature of assumptions," whose strongest impulses were often generous. These assumptions were not ordinarily reasoned but were acquired unconsciously and from unknown sources. Politically, these ephemeral opinions would, of course, have to be reckoned with, even though they might be blind prejudices of the sort that popular government was supposed to discourage. Nevertheless, Lowell carefully distinguished between such prejudices and true public opinion as it emerged from the general structure of community convictions and attitudes. True public opinion was an expression of tempered conviction and usually concerned itself with matters of principle. Although it was conceded to be possible to form public opinion on matters of fact, here the opinion must be informed in order to qualify. People must know the relevant facts on an issue if they were to form a public opinion about it. This they would be rarely able or willing to do—quite apart from the fact that public affairs were daily becoming more complex. It was necessary, therefore, to have experts to whom complicated and technical matters could be delegated. This was Lowell's ultimate justification of representative institutions.

Public opinion as Lowell conceived it was an expression of the crystallized moral sentiment of the community, a "brooding omnipresence in the sky," as Justice Holmes might have described it. It would be unrealistic to expect that every public issue would evoke a response that could properly be called an expression of public opinion. Nothing could be farther from Lowell's point of view than the mechanical concept of public opinion as something to be found and measured by polling on arbitrarily selected topics or by the mere counting of votes.

Given the elusive and impalpable character of public opinion, the function of the political system in a democracy was to simplify the issues of public life to the point where public opinions might be crystallized. It was the function in other words of mediating between the complexities of administration and the limitations of public comprehension and conviction. The role of the political party, as Lowell understood it, was to focus the attention of the public upon issues that had to be solved and to simplify them to the point where the electorate could say yes or no. In practice, the parties usually resolved issues into personalities, the candidates for office, among whom the voters seemed to find it easier to make their choice. Lowell was convinced that the American two-party system gave the most effective expression to the sovereign public opinion. It offered simplified alternatives for choice, whereas the multiple-party system of European parliamentary states must necessarily form governments composed of unpredictable coalitions with compromise policies more remote from control by public opinion. Nevertheless, it remained a fact that much of the technical work of government must be done without the sanction of public opinion.

In the light of his discussion of the theory of public opinion, it was apparent that Lowell would reject the assumption of Progressives that direct democracy provided more effective implementation than did the representative system. He appreciated the reasons that underlay the criticisms of legislatures (although he thought them perhaps somewhat exaggerated), but he pointed out that the proper remedy was to elect officials responsive to the public will, not to abandon the system. The initiative and referendum were certainly inadequate as a means of giving expression to public opinion. They made no provision for adequate discussion, and they provided no safeguards against misuse. Even if public opinion were to be defined in the most vulgar sense as the mere will of the majority, a plebiscite was still not necessarily a clear indication of public opinion; motives in voting were often mixed, and issues were rarely so presented as to offer the adequate alternatives. Lowell noted shrewdly that although proponents of direct democracy accused elected representatives of not reflecting the opinions of the people who had elected them, nevertheless whenever elections to office and issues of initiative or referendum were placed before voters simultaneously the men invariably received more votes than the measures. This to Lowell's mind indicated a persistent preference which should not be ignored. It was a sound instinct that led men, being what they were, to delegate their political business to responsible representatives.

"Being what they were" was the clue to Lowell's persistent effort to think of political problems in terms of a realistic view of human nature. The community, he concluded, was composed of some good people, some bad ones, and a large number of well-meaning but indolent people indifferent to all but their own narrowly conceived personal interests. The test of any institution was its fruits in these circumstances, not those of some ideal utopia where all men were presumed to be animated by a zeal for the public welfare.

In the final analysis, Lowell was prepared to defend the theory of representative democracy because it stood for certain values, namely, responsible action in the public interest. So far as the will of the people reflected a considered judgment of current issues, representative government should be responsive to that will. Public opinion was thus the link by which government and people were united in a democracy. But the practical limitations of public opinion as a bemused sovereign must be clearly recognized and respected.

Making and Measuring Opinion

The American experience in World War I caused a significant shift in approach to the problems of public opinion. Prior to the war, it was assumed that these problems were to be dealt with as aspects of political theory; attention focused upon the role of public opinion in the social process. The issues debated were matters of value—the uses and abuses of public opinion. On the question of opinion formation, the interest of students centered upon the relationship to desirable social goals.

After the war, however, there was a sense in which interest in public opinion as traditionally conceived ceased to exist. Students were now concerned primarily with the way in which the opinions of individuals were formed, with the techniques for recording these opinions, and with the making of statistical computations of them. The great philosophic questions that had preoccupied the previous generation now seemed to be settled; the sovereignty of public opinion was taken for granted, and it remained only to learn how to manipulate it. The central questions were now: What do individuals think about specified subjects, and how did they come to think that way? How can they be made to think the way we want them to think?

With American entrance into the war in the spring of 1917, President Wilson created a Committee on Public Information that was to serve both as a censorship and propaganda agency. The chairman was George Creel, a journalist and political pamphleteer. It was the function of the committee as Creel conceived it to convert a peaceful and individualistic democracy into a monolithic war machine. To achieve this object, Creel took the positive approach. He would give his fellow citizens war aims that would arouse their enthusiasm and thus greatly intensify their contributions to the war effort. The voluntary censorship that the press accepted permitted the Creel committee to interpret the flow of events in a manner consistent with the point of view it sought to propagate. Thus the war of 1917 became the first ideological war in American history. Creel shrewdly harnessed to his purposes that traditional democratic idealism which had recently been revivified in the Progressive movement. This was to be a war for the preservation and extension of democracy and for the destruction of autocratic militarism. President Wilson was of great assistance to the propagandists. The evangelical and humanitarian zeal with which he phrased his war and peace aims furnished the positive goals of the war effort. He interpreted the struggle as "the war to end war." America had entered it in order to "make the world safe for democracy." Those aspects of the Fourteen Points that had the greatest popular appeal had to do with the national self-determination of peoples and with the promise of a new era in international relations. The enemy, on the other hand, was made to stand for everything that was the opposite of the democratic ideology: tyranny, militarism, cynical disregard of treaty obligations, and inhumanity.

There was nothing essentially false or artificial about this justification of the war by appeal to the deepest convictions of the American people. But the nature of the situation made it almost inevitable that convictions were intensified into obsession and uneasiness into fear, while regimentation reinforced voluntary effort. Symbols were thus substituted for ideas, while people were taught to think in stereotypes. The crudeness of many devices employed by the Creel committee to play upon public feeling suggests that Americans must have been more naïve at that time than they were during World War II. But it is also possible that the committee overplayed its hand. Part at least of the popular cynicism of the 1920's was born of disillusionment with the peace settlement, and many Americans relished the exposure of the deliberate wartime manipulation of opinion. The word *propaganda* became a household term connoting substantial falsehood.

The wartime manipulation of opinion by propaganda techniques drew the attention of Walter Lippmann to the problems of opinion formation. He saw at once that censorship was an inevitable aspect of propaganda, because censorship barred the individual from access to the real environment of facts. A false or pseudoenvironment could then be effectively imposed by propaganda. But even in the best of circumstances, could the average individual be expected to know his world with sufficient accuracy to justify the democratic theory of the sovereignty of public opinion? The result of Lippmann's deliberations was the publication in 1922 of his *Public Opinion,* a book concerned largely with the obstacles to the formation of opinions suited to the functions of public opinion as traditionally conceived. Like other notable studies by Lippmann, this one was a preface to the subject.

What had been done deliberately in wartime appeared in fact to be a special case of the distortion that always entered into the formation of opinions about the external world. Man's normal behavior, Lippmann observed, was governed by certain symbolic pictures or fictions, representations of his environment made by himself, varying in adequacy from the hallucinations of the madman to the precise discriminations of scientific hypotheses. Whatever the source, these images were essential because the environment was too complex to be acted upon directly. They so often misled men because the images were uninformed, ill considered, distorted by ignorance, fear, or prejudice, or because they were deliberately manipulated.

Viewing the world in these circumstances, the individual framed what Lippmann called stereotypes, value-laden judgments reflecting his position, aspirations, and sense of values. These stereotypes were preconceptions that influenced the process of perception; or they were prejudices in terms of which one found meaning in the confusing flux of events. The stereotype was the product of that blending of personal and subjective considerations with perceptions of the external world which constituted the unique experiences of each individual. Such stereotypes were necessary and inevitable. One could question only their quality, which was determined largely by the individual's philosophy of life. If men were more conscious of their own stereotypes, they could at least hold them at arm's length in order not to be strangled by them. But they must realize that the stereotype was simpler and more rigid than the flux of events, and hence that it would always tend to frustrate effective action.

Public opinion as Lippmann understood it was the complex of mental images and stereotypes in terms of which men acted in groups. He rejected as too simple the theory of Lowell that a public opinion was a moral judgment upon the facts. It was rather "primarily a moralized and codified version of the facts." Prevailing stereotypes largely determined the facts men saw and the light in which they saw them. Public opinion was thus intimately involved in the life history of the group and, to a large degree, was the spontaneous reflection of it. In practice, the formation of a public opinion involved the transfer of individually centered emotions by means of conditioned responses to vague common symbols, such as those representing Americanism. These symbols were customarily cultivated by such authoritative individuals as parents, teachers, friends, and one's superiors. These were the real opinion-makers. Symbols thus used were the agents both of solidarity and of exploitation.

Seen in this light, the democratic assumption of a society composed of self-sufficient individuals was substantially false. Mass decisions must necessarily be extremely simple in a world of great complexity. In fact, the mass could do no more than choose between alternative courses of action. Moreover, the qualities of men that were involved in the process of opinion formation were those least suited to the framing of adequate judgments. While men habitually formed their opinions in terms of what was familiar, interesting, or dramatic and personal, they ought, of course, to make a conscious effort to understand the issue at stake, which would require labor, patience, equanimity, and the expenditure of time and money for information. These qualities were essential for an understanding of the external world.

It was all too apparent to Lippmann that the traditional nineteenth-century democratic theory had never faced the problems of opinion formation. It had taken the political competence of all men for granted and had given no thought to the means by which the public was to be informed. It had perhaps assumed that opinions were formed spontaneously. The explanation of so notable a gap in the democratic rationale was found in the historical circumstance that American democracy emerged in small and relatively isolated communities. Here public opinion might quite naturally be presumed to be the spontaneous response to local situations generally understood by all. But political issues would have to be restricted to local matters if the public were to act competently under such a presumption, and it was a sound instinct which prompted the nineteenth-century democrat to isolate himself so far as possible from the larger world outside. Isolation and security were essential to that kind of democracy. "Every good foreign observer," said Mr. Lippmann, "has been amazed at the contrast between the dynamic practical energy of the American people and the static theorism of their public life. That steadfast love of fixed principles was simply the only way known of achieving self-sufficiency. But it meant that the public opinions of any one community about the outer world consisted chiefly of a few stereotyped images arranged in a pattern deduced from their legal and moral codes and animated by the feeling aroused by local experiences."

Adequate methods for establishing the character of the real social world had taken shape only recently, subsequent to the emergence of the complacent democratic theory of public opinion. These methods consisted of "measurement and record, quantitative and comparative analysis, the canons of evidence, and the ability of psychological analysis to correct and discount the prejudices of the witness." It seemed to Lippmann as though now for the first time continuous and accurate reporting of the unseen social world was possible. It was in the light of these modern methods that the inadequacy of the traditional theory had become apparent. The political institutions associated with that theory, especially the representative legislature, had declined in prestige and effectiveness chiefly because of inability to inform themselves adequately. The legislative investigations by which the Congress, for instance, sought to inform itself seemed to Lippmann to be a relic of barbarism, a form of legalized cannibalism.

The older democratic theory had tended to transform the problem of public opinion into an issue of civil liberty. It assumed that the truth would prevail if it were given an opportunity to be heard. But Lippmann did not share the positivistic view of history that seemed to make this assumption tenable. He was acutely aware of the difficulty of discovering the truth about distant and complex questions. The traditional theory had also quite logically attached great importance to a free press as the means of disseminating adequate information. Lippmann questioned the utility of this function also. "News" as printed in newspapers and the truth about the external world were rather different things. The news signalized events, while the truth was concerned with the relationship and analysis of all the relevant facts as a basis for effective action. These functions coincided only to a small degree. Perhaps it was such reflections as these that led Lippmann to develop his own style of commentary on the news which was for many years to lend distinction to American journalism.

Convinced as he was of the inadequacy of the traditional theory, Lippmann formulated a neodemocratic theory of public opinion. Instead of assuming that men instinctively make wise laws, one should insist on creating the conditions in which human political capacities might operate at maximum efficiency. In practical terms, this would mean the provision for minimum standards of income, health, education, housing, and leisure. These were the essential preconditions to effective utilization of adequate information about the external social world. Without them, men always would remain unequipped with the resources necessary to cope with their world. But beyond these preconditions there must be agencies of fact-finding experts to compile and disseminate information about subjects of vital political interest. Only by access to the facts thus made available could the public come to grips with the social environment by dispelling the censorship, stereotypes, and distortions to which it is normally subject. An intelligence bureau of the kind Lippmann proposed would be of even greater aid to the legislator and administrator than to the public. Personal representation would then be supplemented by representation of the facts. The leadership of informed experts was a central element in Lippmann's vision of the future. An active political science he felt to be essential as an instrument of effective political democracy.

The propaganda efforts of wartime had made many men conscious of the great tangible stakes to be won through the manipulation of opinion. One of these was the astute public relations counselor Edward L. Bernays, whose *Crystallizing Public Opinion* was published in 1923. A nephew of Sigmund Freud, born in Vienna, Bernays was brought to the United States at an early age and grew up in New York City. As a member of the Creel committee, he had had first-hand contact with opinion manipulation on a mass scale. The function of publicity agent had long existed, but Bernays sought to transform a mere occupation into a "profession," and to enhance its dignity by providing its activities with a quasi-philosophic rationale. His greatest publicity stunt was to transform the publicity agent into the "Public Relations Counselor."

Although the chief activity of the public relations counselor remained that of promoting the business of his client through advertising, Bernays developed a general theory of public opinion to support and dignify this activity. It rested on Lippmann's concept of the stereotype and on the insights of naturalistic psychology. Public opinion, Bernays believed, consisted largely of dogmatically held convictions or prejudices. Because of their deep psychological roots, these stereotypes were relatively impervious to manipulation. The wise public relations counselor would not attempt therefore to change public opinion but merely to amplify or articulate it for his own purposes. He should learn to play skillfully upon the prejudices of the public in order to promote the interest of his client. By attaching the interests of the client to a public stereotype, it was possible to effect a rearrangement of public loyalties that would be to the advantage of the client. Thus, for instance, if the product or service of the client could somehow be associated in the public mind with the patriotic sentiment, the good will of the client would be greatly enhanced. There were many ingenious ways by which this might be accomplished. From his experience with the Creel committee, Bernays had come to realize the importance of press manipulation. The fact that most of the early public relations counselors were former newspaper men testified to the practical importance of familiarity with the means of access to communications media.

Bernays did not attempt to conceal the cynicism of the new profession. The sovereign public opinion provided a court of last resort and relieved the individual of responsibility for moral discriminations. The only difference between education and propaganda, said Bernays, was the point of view. Education is what we believe in; propaganda is what we do not. Public opinion was not to be confused with considerations of value. It was after all the product of crowd psychology. The only test of truth was the power of the idea to get itself accepted in the marketplace.

Perhaps the chief significance of public relations counseling was the testimony it bore to the increasing politicization of American life. The area of private relationships was steadily receding before those in which the public was conceded to have an interest and to be a participant. The formal regulation of economic enterprise by political agencies was only part of this politicization, and perhaps the less significant part. Interests of all kinds were now finding it desirable to cultivate a favorable public reception. By learning to court public favor, the public relations counselor was necessarily flattering the public. By representing his client to it in a favorable light, he was, in effect, declaring it to be the arbiter of the fortunes of his client. By creating public demand for the goods and services of his client, he was to that degree extending the scope of public opinion. These tendencies were usually viewed from the opposite point of view from that taken here, namely, as examples of the attempt to manipulate opinion for the advantage of special interests. But while this certainly occurred, it seems more significant to emphasize the extent to which public opinion was being extended, if not actually created, into areas where it had formerly been of little importance. To create new force when one thought that he was merely engaged in manipulating power that already existed was surely the essence of irresponsibility.

Empirical investigations of the opinions of individuals by means of a questionnaire or "poll" became commonplace during the second third of the twentieth century. By generalizing from the findings of such polls, the strength of public opinion on many specific issues was allegedly measured. Many commercial and academic organizations became engaged in this activity. The framing of questionnaires free from distortion or ambiguity, and the complex statistical problems of sampling, gave opinion-polling an intellectual respectability that it scarcely warranted on other grounds.

In perfecting techniques for sampling the opinions of individuals on public questions, the pollsters lost sight of public opinion and its problems as traditionally conceived by political theory. By eliciting casual responses to questions, the pollster was actually creating a partially fictitious opinion that he called "public opinion," and he was largely oblivious of the profound consequences of this irresponsible act of creation. The pressures for conformity that drew increasing attention from uneasy observers resulted, at least in part, from the deliberately cultivated sensitivity to whatever was alleged to be public opinion. Lindsey Rogers, an unfriendly critic, observed that the pollsters thought they were taking the pulse of democracy when in fact they were merely listening to its baby talk.

Among the more well-known pollsters was George Gallup, educated at the University of Iowa and a teacher of journalism before organizing in 1935 the American Institute of Public Opinion. In a lecture delivered at Princeton in 1939 on "Public Opinion in a Democracy," Gallup set forth his conception of the political role of public opinion. He reverted to the presuppositions of direct democracy. The traditional processes of representative democracy were inefficient because the will of the people was not known with any certainty. Elections and the representative system expressed the popular will only imperfectly. Now, however, the new technique of the sample survey enabled the research worker to discover public opinion accurately and, hence, to voice the sentiments of the people on vital issues promptly. As to the accuracy of his findings, pre-election surveys when checked against election results showed a maximum error of only 3 or 4 percent. Thanks to these techniques, the function of political leadership, according to Gallup, was that of discovering and executing the general will. But lest this seem less than completely reassuring, he then shifted his ground and remarked that the survey poll merely improved the traditional methods by which the elected representative had always sounded the opinions of his constituency.

CHAPTER 22

||||||||||||||||||||||||||||||||||||||||||||||||||||||||||||||||||||||

Walter Lippmann's Politicoanalysis

T HE FIRST INTELLECTUAL LANDMARK in Walter Lippmann's long and distinguished career as an observer and commentator on public affairs was the publication in 1912 of his *Preface to Politics,* when the precocious author was only twenty-three years old. The book has been described as a contribution to Theodore Roosevelt's Bull Moose campaign of that year. It was much more than that. It was a major contribution to the literature of American political theory as well as a testimonial to the richness and variety of political thought in the Progressive Era.

The Making of a Journalist

The son of a New York City manufacturer, Lippmann entered Harvard in 1906. While a student there he discovered "how the other half lived," and with youthful zeal plunged into the radical movement. He joined with John Reed to organize the Harvard Socialist Club and identified himself with the rapidly growing Socialist Party. Even more influential for Lippmann's intellectual development was his association with Graham Wallas, an English social scientist then teaching at Harvard, who was working on the book published in 1908 as *Human Nature in Politics*. From Wallas, Lipp-mann acquired a conviction of the importance of founding political theory upon a sound understanding of human nature as revealed by modern scientific psychology.

Although democracy was seemingly triumphant in the Western World at the beginning of the twentieth century, Wallas was persuaded that democratic political theory was nevertheless in a low state because theorists were neglecting its proper foundations in human nature. There were, of course, implicit psychological assumptions in their theories, but because the assumptions remained unexamined they were all too often naïve and untenable. Thanks to the naturalis-tic psychological revolution, it was no longer permissible for the political theorist to ignore the importance of the unconscious or the force of instinctive impulses. The easy alliance of hedonism and ra-tionalism that had supported nineteenth-century democratic individ-ualism had dissolved, and the political philosopher was faced with the task of installing a substitute foundation that would stand up under the probing of modern scientific inspection.

Political convictions, then, as Wallas conceived them, were not intellectual inferences from nice calculations of means and ends. They were tendencies prior to thought and experience, express-ing such basic impulses as fear, affection, ridicule, and the desire for property. The mental processes by which political opinions were formed were nonrational and only partly conscious. Furthermore, politically significant objects must be susceptible of symbolic repre-sentation before they could effect a mass appeal. "The empirical art of politics," Wallas concluded, "consists largely in the creation of opinion by the deliberate exploitation of subconscious non-rational inference." To men of Wallas's generation, the moral implications of an analysis of politics which reduced that art to the manipulation of men through an appeal to their prejudices were profoundly dis-turbing. How much worse would political life become when politi-cians learned from the philosophers to do deliberately what they were already doing more or less haphazardly? Wallas was keenly apprecia-tive of the danger that lurked in the implementation of his own theory of politics. To forestall it, he urged a more realistic public education in politics, emphasizing at the same time the moral respon-sibilities of citizens.

From Graham Wallas the young Lippmann passed to the post-graduate tutelage of the celebrated muckraking journalist Lincoln Steffens, whom he served as assistant in 1910. Steffens had achieved fame a decade earlier with a series of spectacular exposés of political corruption in several of the largest American cities. Certain of his articles, originally printed in *McClure's Magazine,* were gathered in a volume published in 1904 entitled *The Shame of the Cities.*

Steffens was not one of those superficial progressives who thought that all that was necessary to overcome political corruption was to get government back into the hands of the people. His investigations revealed how corruption ramified from the officeholder and the boss to embrace the businessman and indeed the most respectable classes of the community. Steffens found that the businessman, the typical American citizen, was everywhere a bad citizen, whose pursuit of wealth led inevitably to the corruption of political life. Yet business leaders invariably maintained an attitude of hypocritical self-righteousness.

Although Steffens traced the sources of corruption to the very core of American life, the diagnosis did not disillusion him of his conviction of the fundamental soundness of Americans. He reminded himself that they had achieved much that was memorable in science, art, and business in spite of the corrupt condition of their politics. In exposing the hypocrisy of American life, it was Steffens's aim and expectation to appeal effectively to the civic pride of an apparently shameless citizenry, promoting a reformation in political morality. Such a faith in the capacity of the democratic ideal to appeal to men's better nature, strengthening them in the struggle against their own selfish and antisocial impulses, was to become a permanent element in Lippmann's thought. He may well have acquired it in part from Steffens, in whom it had survived the fires of disillusionment.

Lippmann was now ready for a brief venture into practical politics. He joined the newly elected Socialist city administration in Schenectady, New York, as secretary to Mayor George R. Lunn. But he quickly became disillusioned of the possibility of accomplishing socialization at the local level in a capitalistic environment, no matter how sincere and determined the reformers might be. Bidding farewell to the Socialists Lippmann retired to the Maine woods in the summer of 1912 for quiet study and writing in the company of Alfred Booth Kuttner, an early American Freudian. The theories of Freud exercised a dominant influence on the book Lippmann was about to write.

Although Freud's ideas everywhere remained controversial for many years, they had a warmer reception in the United States than elsewhere. While he was still largely unknown outside professional psychiatric and psychological circles, and generally ridiculed or ignored within them, Freud was supported and encouraged—although not necessarily accepted—by a small but influential group of American psychologists and psychiatrists, including William James, President G. Stanley Hall of Clark University, and Dr. Morton Prince of Harvard. In 1909 he was invited to lecture at Clark, the first academic recognition he had received anywhere. Lippmann was acquainted with Freud's leading American disciple and translator, Dr. A. A. Brill, and he participated in many of the early discussions of psychoanalysis among New York's intellectuals.

Sigmund Freud was a Viennese neurologist and psychiatrist who developed his own system of psychotherapy called psychoanalysis. It was based upon a theory of the development of personality worked out in the course of the search for an effective treatment of the class of disorders called neuroses. For nonmedical purposes, Freud's general theory of personality was of greater significance than his analysis of mental illness or his system of therapy, although these were integral parts of a single system. In assessing Freud's influence, it should be noted that the principles of psychoanalysis were found in the structure of the normal healthy mind and exhibited in the routine of daily conduct. They could thus be used to elucidate everyday situations not necessarily of a pathological character.

Freud's theory of personality was a thoroughly naturalistic system of psychology. It was an evolutionary theory, conceiving of the development of personality as a process analogous to the growth of a physical organism. One of the classic forms of evidence in support of the theory of evolution had been drawn from embryology. Studies of the developing embryo revealed a succession of forms similar to its evolutionary sequence of development. According to the famous "law" of von Baer, "ontogeny recapitulates phylogeny" —that is, the phases of the development of the individual organism recapitulate the evolutionary stages through which its own forebears have passed. Similarly, Freud held that the personality was the product in part of the life experiences of the individual, the product of growth, so to speak; but it was also in part the product of a racial heritage, the substance of which appeared in the common or universal symbolism of dreams. But the analogy should not be pressed too far. Whereas in von Baer's law a rapid recapitulation was noted in the earliest stages of the course of development of the organism, in Freud's psychology the primitive racial heritage continued to lurk in the unconscious of the mature individual, exercising a profound influence upon his character.

A prominent place was assigned to the instincts. Freud emphasized especially the sex instinct, the death-wish instinct, and the ego instinct. He held that conflicts between the demands of the instincts gave rise to neuroses. Life was conceived ultimately in terms of energy. Its processes involved the expenditure of energy. Mental disease was injurious to life because its symptoms entailed an expenditure of mental energy, both in themselves and in the effort to combat them. The dynamic emphasis in Freud's theory was very strong. He repeatedly insisted that mental phenomena should not be merely described and classified, which had been the sterile endeavor of the older psychiatry. They should be studied as developments of the conflicting forces in the mind. They were to be understood as expressions of striving toward goals—that is, the achievement of satisfactions required by the primitive elements of the self. Thus man might be said to be a goal-seeking animal. Lippmann may well have noted the relevance of this concept of man for modern American political theory attempting as it must to cope with problems in which issues of public policy were invariably central.

Great importance was attached by Freud to the unconscious. He held that mental processes were essentially unconscious, only a small portion of them emerging into consciousness. Psychoanalysis thus concerned itself chiefly with the unconscious, with "the refuse of the phenomenal world." Every mental process began in the unconscious, and it might or might not emerge into consciousness. When it failed to emerge, it was said to be repressed. An impulse subject to repression was unknown to the ego, and consequently it retained its psychic energy. Whereas if the impulse entered the consciousness its energy was discharged either in realization or rejection, and it became merely a memory without dynamic properties. Neurotic symptoms were said to be the product of the dammed-up energies of unconscious mental processes. If these mental processes could be brought into the consciousness, the symptoms would then disappear because the accumulated energy would be discharged. Thoughts were said to pass from the unconscious to consciousness when permitted to do so by the censorship barrier. To pass the barrier, they must be "respectable," conforming to the acknowledged public standards or mores of the day, since the criteria of the censorship mechanism were conventional values, especially those implanted in the individual by the parents during infancy. Thoughts that remained in the unconscious, however, displayed all of the primitive selfish character of the sexual, death- and pleasure-seeking instincts. These unconscious thoughts reflected both infantile impulses and the remote past of the species. They formed themselves in visual images rather than in verbal forms, and they assumed symbolic representations for common events or experiences. In a partially disguised form the character of the unconscious was familiar to every individual in his dreams.

Freud was a strict psychological determinist in both the functional and historical senses. He maintained that forces in the unconscious mind determined the whole mental life of the individual, although the nature of these forces were unknown to the individual. The famous analytic technique of free association of ideas depended for its validity upon this assumption. The patient was invited to say whatever came into his mind. The analyst knew, however, that these were not random, disconnected thoughts but were determined by inner impulses of the unconscious, to the character of which they thus furnished clues. Freud was also a historical determinist in his strong emphasis upon certain universally recurrent mental patterns or attitudes originating in concrete events in the primeval past and transmitted in the racial memory, such as the incest taboo.

In the light of the foregoing attributes and assumptions about human nature, it clearly remained Freud's problem to indicate how the civilized and socialized individual was fashioned out of the "veritable hell" of his innermost nature. How could freedom and responsibility properly be attributed to man whose very thoughts were found to be formed by forces of which he had neither knowledge nor control? Freud's answer to the challenge was contained in the concept of *sublimation*. Under the pressure of the struggle for existence, the ego instinct, which was held to be more flexible and adaptable than the other instincts, had discovered that it must frequently sacrifice the gratification of its primitive impulses for the sake of survival or for a common or social advantage. Sacrifice, however, was not the right word. Impulses rather were sublimated; their energies were turned aside from their original selfish goals and invested in other socially more valuable objects. The creative energies from which the highest products of civilized talent sprang were thus found to be sublimated forms of originally egoistic, sexual, and anti-social impulses.

Politicoanalysis

The book that Walter Lippmann wrote in the summer of 1912 was called *A Preface to Politics,* and in it may be seen the evidences of the intellectual forces to which he had been exposed. Although he was a Progressive, Lippmann had no great faith in direct democracy as a solution to prevailing political problems. His Progressivism revealed itself in the closely related questions that he posed at the outset of his study. Why was it that many people who should have been interested in politics were not? Why was it that in a country that prided itself upon its democratic political institutions political indifference was the key to so many of its shortcomings? Lippmann was convinced that the answers to these questions lay in the totally artificial conception of the nature of politics that generally prevailed. It was universally assumed, said the young intellectual, that the ideal objective of politics was to "do good," to pass the right laws in accordance with some clearly defined public policy calculated to secure the general welfare. But this conventional ideal of politics, he concluded, was so palpably inappropriate to current conditions that many people were turning away from politics in boredom.

There was a sense in which Lippmann's judgment upon the triviality of politics as conventionally conceived and practiced might be taken to constitute a wise philosopher's verdict upon more than a century of American political experience. It did indeed seem as though the broad stream of American life through the nineteenth century had found its channels by virtue of its own varied properties and forces. Its politics had been little more than eddies upon its surface. But the year 1912 was one of the last years in which such a generalization would have contemporary relevance. Thereafter, insistent issues of public policy would revivify the conventional and traditional notion of politics that Lippmann had confidently discarded.

The politicoanalysis by means of which Lippmann proposed to reinvigorate political thought was postnaturalistic in the sense that it rested upon the psychology of the unconscious and recognized the force of irrational motivations and instincts. But the object of his analysis, like that of psychoanalysis, was to guide the expression of these impulses to constructive ends, to salvage the rational from the irrational. If the suitability of psychoanalysis to provide a model for such a purpose be questioned, let it at least be remembered that psychoanalysis was individually oriented. It was concerned with the needs of the individual personality, and with the disorders that arose, it claimed, from the suppressed expression of these needs. Its outlook was thus compatible with the long American tradition of individualism. Quite appropriately, on the other hand, the totalitarian regimes of the second quarter of the twentieth century, which required the subordination of individuals to official purposes, quickly suppressed psychoanalysis, the Communists in 1929 and the Nazis in 1933.

Lippmann's point of view was essentially humanistic. Social and political institutions had no merit in themselves save insofar as they served the purposes of men. He divided men into two categories. Routineers were those who thought in terms of existing social machinery and who subordinated men to it. Their social role was largely passive, and Lippmann devoted most of his attention to the second type, the inventors, men who had a sense of the dynamic quality of society and who put the individual at the center of their philosophy. Politicoanalysis proposed to deal with political problems in terms of these personality types. The inventors were active, willful, aggressive men who seemed to be the creators of their environment rather than creatures of it. Because of them, government was a continual process of creation, new forms being invented to meet new needs. Power naturally gravitated to the inventors. They were usually found in control of the institutions through which power was most effectively exercised. Typical power-wielding institutions were industries, labor unions, banks, churches, universities, and the press.

Lippmann regarded the conventional distinction between the political and nonpolitical as artificial. The total life of the community was necessarily relevant to politics. He was groping for a new conception of politics that would embrace all and yet not strangle all in the totalitarian embrace of traditional political forms. Lincoln Steffens had taught him how politics inevitably involved the major activities of the community, whether production or prostitution. It was the narrow and artificial conception of politics, Lippmann concluded, that had given rise to the "invisible government" of boss and businessman, the normal and healthy expression of whose power was repressed by the conventional view of politics.

The twentieth-century American society that Lippmann undertook to analyze was in many respects sick. He found its economic life "morbid" and "perverted." Its politics were "feckless" and "literally eccentric." Following the analogy of psychoanalysis, the method of treatment required a historical analysis of the American people.

According to the Freudian explanation of mental illness, the needs or wishes of the personality were repressed in the unconscious by a censorship composed of the prevailing moral standards of the community. Because they were repressed, these needs retained their psychic energy, which would subsequently break out in the symptoms of illness. The treatment prescribed by Freud was analysis of the life history of the patient in order to bring the repressed material to the light of consciousness, where it would then discharge its energy and lose its capacity to induce illness.

When Lippmann undertook to make a social application of the psychoanalytic technique in the hope of curing the ills of democratic America, he was therefore logically required to turn historian and to inquire exhaustively into the early experiences of his patient. His investigation, however, was perfunctory; no psychoanalyst would have been satisfied with it. His findings were nonetheless revealing. The investigation sought to discover what had happened during the childhood of the American people to result in such an unhealthy political development. The findings would doubtless be painful to the feelings of the patient but, it was to be hoped, salutary. It appeared that the Fathers (Constitutional) had imposed certain restraints upon the activity of the infant republic. They had imposed mechanical limitations upon the exercise of governmental power because, although they had had faith in man in the abstract, they had feared their own fellow citizens (and their sons?). These constitutional restraints were taboos, resulting in the repression of vital needs of the community. The eventual outcome was the pathological symptoms of "invisible government," the corrupt alliance of boss and businessman deplored by all good Progressives.

The Fathers had inculcated in the young republic the abstract principles of liberty, justice, and equality. But the infant proved to be stubborn and contrary and seemed to be more interested in making money and in abusing his fellows. Every taboo was admittedly born of an original need, but it tended to live beyond the time of its relevance. Besides constitutional fetishism, other taboos to which Lippmann felt that Americans had been subjected were the sanctity of private property, the notion of vested rights, competition, and prosperity. The result of these restraints was the morbid political neurotic of 1900. His symptoms were corruption, trusts, class conflict, the amnesia of political indifference, and a cultural life in many respects infantile.

The respectable citizen, the reformer who manned the censorship barricade armed with the Puritanic morality that constituted the American superego, was shocked by the appearance of these pathological symptoms. Ignorant of the nature of the disease or of the remedy, he could only attack the symptoms. Feverishly he went to work setting up Sherman Acts against business combination or obtaining injunctions against labor organizations. The result was worse than futile. In repressing the expression of the vigorous economic id, the reformer was inducing the politicopathology of corruption, the "cracking and bursting of the receptacles in which we have tried to constrain the business of this country."

In connection with Lippmann's discussion of American fixation upon the constitutionalism of 1787, it is of interest to note that in the Freudian theory of dreams the manifest dream as it was apprehended by the dreamer was a disguised or distorted form of the underlying latent dream thought, the meaning of which was thus hidden from the dreamer himself. The disguise of the latent dream thought was accomplished by means of the omission, modification, and regrouping of material in the manifest dream. The interpretation of dreams therefore required in the first place the expert reconstruction of the latent dream before its interpretation could be attempted. Lippmann did not undertake a detailed analysis of the American dream of constitutional origins. He was content merely to suggest the politicopathological function of the dream in perpetuating the taboos of constitutional fetishism, and thus he missed a fine opportunity to analyze the long tradition of pietistic historiography in which, it might not improperly be said, the dream recurred with monotonous regularity. But by a happy coincidence, a contemporary of Lippmann's, the historian Charles A. Beard, was at work on a study that, in effect, furnished such an analysis. Beard published his diagnosis in a controversial book entitled *An Economic Interpretation of the Constitution* (1913). The patient was scandalized to be told by Dr. Beard that behind the manifest dream of the Constitutional Fathers with their sanctimonious government of laws and not of men lurked the latent dream material that revealed a clique of selfish investors bent primarily upon making a killing on their speculation in worthless public securities. Clearly, Freudian realism was not incompatible with the widespread impulse to re-examine the established pieties of public as well as private life.

Lippmann found the solution to the ills of American society in a social and political application of the concept of sublimation. The object to be kept steadily in view was always the use of human power for human purposes. Society by its very nature generated power, and while this power could be repressed only with pathological consequences, men could hope to guide its expression to beneficial ends. The enactment of moralistic laws against tendencies believed to be injurious was the method of the taboo, "as naïve as barbarism." Effective reform must offer attractive virtues as a substitute for attractive vices. In William James's phrase, there must always be a "moral equivalent" for evil. "The same energies," said Lippmann, "produce crime and civilization, art, vice, insanity, love, lust, religion. . . . Only by supplying our passions with civilized interests can we escape their destructive force."

Applied specifically to the problems of politics, the concept of sublimation helped Lippmann to clarify the relationship of politics to the other areas of social life. Politics must adjust itself "to the movement of real life. The only way to control our destiny is to work with it." The skill of the statesman consisted largely in his ability to trace the line between the inevitable and the contingent, yielding where necessary and acting positively where possible. This was a thoroughly naturalistic point of view. But what distinguished Lippmann from the naturalists was his insistence upon exploring and exploiting the limits of freedom. The qualification for true statesmanship, as he conceived it, was an understanding of the nature of the "social movements," "dynamic currents," and "actual needs" of society as expressed in trusts, unions, opportunities for women, racial aspirations, educational needs, radical movements, sects, journalism, clubs, and so on. But the function of statecraft was to develop and guide these forces to constructive social ends. The means that it was to use (and here the therapeutic analogy was especially pronounced) were not statute and administrative bureaucracy but "criticism, organized research, and artistic expression." Because properly conceived, "politics would be like education—an effort to develop, train and nurture men's impulses."

Since the object of politics was to work with the forces that expressed themselves in social movements, it might appear that Lippmann was inclined to minimize the importance of the political aspects of life. And, in fact, he did say that political institutions provided only a fragment of real government. This was fortunate too, for if the nation's destiny were determined solely by its formal politics, there would be little hope of improvement. But in a more important sense, every aspect of life had its political significance. Lippmann incorporated this conviction in his concept of sovereignty.

Sovereignty was found to reside in all the manifold social forms in which personality expressed itself. Sovereignty was power, and power gravitated inevitably to the dominant personality types that, as we have seen, tended to control institutions. How then could Lippmann speak of democracy guiding the expression of power in society when he appeared to deny the effective sovereignty of the majority expressed politically? The answer lay in the representative character of political institutions, the importance of which in Lippmann's mind was never tarnished by corruption or by the popularity of direct democracy shared by many Progressives. The most important function of democracy was to select effective political leaders. When it did so, then the full potentialities of political institutions would be realized and the ultimate educational function of politics effectively exercised.

Lippmann was an ardent admirer of Theodore Roosevelt. Such a President as Roosevelt was a real inventor. He added to the resources of life, especially with his irrigation, conservation, and inland-waterway projects, with the Panama Canal, and with his sponsorship of the "country life" movement. Thus democracy could decisively effect the incidence of sovereignty by placing a dominant personality type in the presidency. The state then became a creative force.

CHAPTER 23

||||||||||||||||||||||||||||||||||||||||||||||||||||||||||||||||||||||||||||

Pragmatism

P RAGMATISM HAS OFTEN BEEN DESIGNATED, either in condescension or approval, the most indigenous and distinctively American of all the schools of formal thought. Pragmatism originated in the United States, and before the waves of influence it excited had subsided, its impact had been felt from England to China. Although the triumvirate of leading pragmatists—Charles Sanders Peirce (1839–1914), William James (1842–1910), and John Dewey (1859–1952)— were all native New Englanders, the movement has never been identified narrowly, like transcendentalism, with that region. Chicago, with which city Dewey was for a time closely identified, would seem to be a more appropriate locus for the pragmatists than Boston. In the early years of the twentieth century, pragmatism assumed a central position with respect to ideological issues in American society. As an expression of the new democracy, its importance was comparable to that of transcendentalism in the older nineteenth-century democracy.

A Philosophy of Change

Philosophical systems had traditionally been concerned with the permanent realities and truths that were said to lie beneath the flux of appearances. The pragmatists reversed this assumption. They insisted on the changing character of reality. Nothing could be said to be fixed for all time. Every act was an experiment, the outcome of which was more or less uncertain. To be aware of this fact was to be in a position where one could deal intelligently with contingencies; not to be aware of it was to be at their mercy. Existence consisted of a succession of qualitatively unique events. The immediate givenness of experience was an integral part of life as an organic process, and the pragmatists deplored its subordination to more abstract considerations, where thought was distinguished from action or feeling from cognition.

An acute consciousness of change is characteristic of the modern mind, and in this respect the pragmatists were certainly products of the age. It was not simply a matter of the surface changes in institutions and habits. Much more important were the authoritative indexes of change furnished by modern science, which showed that process is the only universal. The world of Newton with its supposedly permanent natural laws had given way to a changing universe in which the only universal law was the law of probability. Modern science, according to Dewey, conceived of law as a constant relationship among changes. What the scientist endeavored to establish was "a correlation of changes, an ability to detect one change occurring in correspondence with another. He does not try to define and delimit something remaining constant *in* change." The first task of philosophy was to work out the significance of this scientific discovery. How was the conduct of life to be rationalized in these circumstances? This was the major task of pragmatism; and to accomplish it, the philosopher need not first turn aside in the traditional manner to establish a general theory of reality, or metaphysic, which was declared to be unattainable. It was perfectly possible and permissible to investigate a specific situation without taking the nature of the universe into account.

Although science had destroyed the old absolutes, it had given men a new one—the scientific method. The pragmatists were tremendously impressed with the accomplishments of the scientific method. It had revolutionized both the physical and physiological aspects of life. It was so inclusive, so penetrating and universal in scope, as to demand philosophic formulation. The pragmatists went far beyond the naturalists in their dedication to it. Especially in Dewey's version, pragmatism was little more than an application of the scientific method to human and moral problems.

Scientific method was the method of inquiry: observation, experiment, the framing of hypotheses, and the use of reflective reasoning. It was a method self-corrective in operation, which identified inquiry with discovery. In its light, the usual preoccupation of philosophers with epistemological problems seemed irrelevant. A person firmly committed to the scientific method should not be disturbed by the upsetting of any specific beliefs he might hold because he would retain security of procedure.

Pragmatists asserted the functional character of thought. They rejected the common-sense notion of thought as something going on in the brain, something subjective and immaterial, as distinct from the objective external world. Ideas were said to arise in and through experience, which meant the active interaction between the human organism and its physical and social environment. Mind was the product of experience. The pragmatists rejected the "spectator theory" of knowledge. Mind should not, however, be regarded as a passive product. Each individual is unique, and his creative activity may well result in a unique contribution. "Thought," said Dewey, "represents the suggestion of a way of response that is different from that which would have been followed if intelligent observation had not effected an inference as to the future."

A social emphasis was especially strong in Dewey. Men acquire the materials of intelligence from the community, and their possibilities are limited by what they are. "Science is an affair of civilization, not of individual intellect." Dewey regarded traditional dualistic philosophical systems as products of sharply stratified societies in which passive contemplation was the privilege of ruling classes, while purposeful physical activity or labor was the badge of a menial status. Pragmatism, with its functional monism, its identification of thought with creative activity, might justifiably be declared to be an authentic philosophic expression of democracy.

In their social theory, the pragmatists were staunch individualists. Philosophically, they held universals to be means to specific ends. In practical terms, the welfare of the individual was to be the end, society the means. The aim of education was the enrichment of the life of each individual, and the task of education was to make available to each child his full social inheritance. Unlike the naturalists, who were unable to emancipate themselves from a rather narrow biological view of the human situation, the pragmatists insisted that the most significant part of the environment of modern man is social. It consists of his personal associations, his language, customs, tools, and institutions. In a civilized community, communication is the central social function. Thinking, which may be defined as preliminary discourse, is an integral part of communication. It is not too much to say that man becomes human through interaction with his social environment. All events are subject to revision and adaptation when communication occurs.

The functional moral theory expounded by the pragmatists was probably the most controversial aspect of their whole position. They believed that it was no longer possible for moralists to insist upon immutable or universal norms as the only protection against moral chaos; moral subject matter was just as relative to particular times and places as scientific subject matter was now known to be. Dewey declared moral values to be immanent in the facts of primary experience. Moral judgments were directed to the reorganization of that experience in such a way that conflicts might be eliminated and impulses liberated. All acts are moral in the sense that, wherever a choice of better or worse acts is confronted, there is a moral choice. The experimental point of view made every quality a moral good so far as it contributed to the amelioration of existing evils. The moral significance of science was thus emphasized, because applied science had done so much to elevate the human condition. The functional emphasis was apparent in Dewey's insistence that moral values existed only when something had to be done to remedy the evil or deficiency in a concrete situation.

Because each moral situation was unique, the burden of moral conduct rested squarely on the intelligence of the actor. Moral judgment and choice must precede action. In Dewey's words: "Our moral failures go back to some weakness of disposition, some absence of sympathy, some one sided bias that makes us perform the judgment of the concrete case carelessly or perversely." In a pluralistic universe where values are relative to specific situations, the ends of life must be of a personal or private nature. As seen through pragmatist eyes, man is a creator. Happiness, or what Dewey called "consummatory satisfactions," is the product of successful integrations of experience. By transforming his environment in such ways as to enhance the welfare of himself and his fellows, man realizes the highest satisfactions.

Living as he does in a world that is insecure because it is incomplete and constantly changing, man has a deep psychological craving for security. The pragmatists recognized the inevitability and indeed the legitimacy of this need. But they pointed out that nothing in experience justified belief in ultimate certainty. To seek it too persistently was not only to neglect the novel but to ignore the reality of evil as well. After all, the age of pragmatism was also the age of Christian Science. In Dewey's opinion, "quest for certainty that is universal, applying to everything, is a compensatory perversion." William James had divided mankind between the tough-minded and the tender-minded. He liked to think of himself as a "Rocky Mountain tough"; and, indeed, we may include the pragmatists among the tough-minded breed in the sense that they relished the hurly-burly of life and found their highest satisfactions in its activities. Dewey found such security as he required in the scientific method of inquiry. Armed with security of procedure, he was not disturbed by the prospect of the upsetting of specific substantive beliefs that he might hold.

Pragmatism drew several of its ideas from naturalism. The two systems had enough in common so that their relationship may profitably be explored in some detail. For the pragmatists as for the naturalists, science furnished the central inspiration. Furthermore, both movements focused attention upon organic evolution and sought to base a philosophic outlook upon it. For each, evolution suggested a new way of thinking that eventually was bound to effect politics, morals, and religion as well as natural knowledge.

But the pragmatists, not the naturalists, insisted upon working out the full implications of the evolutionary emergence of novelty in the biological world. An early instance was furnished in Dewey's reaction to Thomas Henry Huxley's widely read essay *Evolution and Ethics* (1893). Starting with naturalistic premises, Huxley had confronted an insoluble dilemma: How was one to reconcile natural selection with the ethical process? At best, moral values were to be maintained in the face of nature by the force of a civilized will, much as a gardener keeps his beautiful flowers free of the weeds. Otherwise, natural selection imposes its own inexorable conditions. Huxley's dilemma was framed by the environmental absolutism that was the common presupposition of naturalistic thought.

Dewey insisted in reply that the ethical process could not be opposed to the natural process, when their relationship was properly understood. In terms of natural selection, each imposed its own conditions of fitness. The function of environment in serving as a selective criterion for variations was a far more complicated one than the naturalists had assumed. The variations most fruitful of new developments were those that circumvented the standards of selection currently in force; they tapped a hitherto unexploited environment. Only such a conception of the situation did justice to the truly creative role of unique variations. What was true of the biological realm was equally true of the human and civilized world. The development of intelligence and social organization meant that the social environment was the most distinctive aspect of man's total environment. Here the kinds of possible variations were infinite. The capacity of civilized man for the reconstruction of his environment was one of his most striking qualities. Dewey pointed out that the unwritten chapter in the history of the idea of natural selection was the chapter on the evolution of environments. This was the chapter that the pragmatists proposed to write.

The pragmatists thus broke down the dualism of organism and environment that the naturalists had established with the rigid conception of environment employed in their version of natural selection. Instead of a simple profile against which variations were to be measured, environment was envisaged by the pragmatists as a boundless potentiality, the possibilities of which could be realized only through the test of fruitful variations. This solution of the naturalistic dilemma led back to the favorite pragmatic doctrine of the unity of organism and environment as participants in an interactive process. Heredity and environment were not to be regarded as mutually exclusive categories. The hereditary potential could become actual only as the end-product of interaction with the environment. The play of intelligence was an integral aspect of this process because of the intimate connection between knowing and doing. The bearing of these ideas upon educational theory should be readily apparent.

Dewey rejected both the major brands of naturalistic psychology. Instinctivism he dismissed curtly as simply a lazy man's way of avoiding the investigation of the roots of certain types of activity. Behaviorism was worth more serious attention, for Dewey also insisted upon the unity of thought and activity. However, he held intelligent behavior to be more than a mere response to a stimulus. Intelligent behavior is purposeful behavior, guided by meanings. The situation that evokes it is one which is so confused that it does not produce a behavioristic response. In these circumstances, the object of reflection is precisely to reorganize the situation so that confusion is resolved into meaning, and purposeful action may occur.

In his social analysis, Dewey frequently employed the naturalistic theories of social structure and social change. His emphasis on the creative role of intelligence expressed itself appropriately enough in a sense of the primacy of technology. He understood his own era as one in which technology had resulted in corporate institutions of production but had not as yet caught up the lag of social institutions and attitudes that still reflected the influences of the vanished age of individualistic democracy. There was much in Dewey's social thought that was reminiscent of Veblen. Nevertheless, the principle that distinguished Dewey and the pragmatists from the naturalists was the firm and characteristic assertion of the creative potentialities of intelligence. Here was a universal tool applicable in every concrete situation. When the history of thought is viewed in its social context, as in the present book, the pragmatic emphasis on intelligence is seen to have held practical implications which were diametrically opposed to the passivity and despair that were the ultimate outcomes of naturalism.

Pragmatism and Progressivism

Pragmatism was an authentic expression of the Progressive social philosophy. Here the principal role was played by Dewey, the only one of the founders of the movement to survive the Progressive Era. Dewey believed that under the impact of science modern philosophy must inevitably shift from the contemplative to the operative. It must concern itself chiefly with "rationalizing the *possibilities* of experience, especially collective human experience." Philosophy was thus brought to bear on human affairs in a highly practical way, and especially on the reform of institutions and habits, in order to realize the full potentialities of life. Dewey was no mere cloistered academic. Scores of articles dealing with matters of current public interest, published in the *New Republic* and other progressive journals, and several popular books testified to his participation as a journalist in the main current of affairs.

Although Dewey frequently emphasized the pertinence of the scientific method of hypothesis and experiment in dealing with social problems, he also acknowledged that there was a branch of science especially concerned with social reality, namely, historical analysis by the genetic method. The study of history was a kind of vicarious experience; it taught men how to achieve both intellectual and practical control in order to secure a desired result. Only the breadth of his wisdom and the catholicity of his interests prevented the philosopher from reducing history to the status of a branch of public administration. The purposes or "desired results" which Dewey was determined that history should serve were the ideals of progressive democracy. Viewed from this perspective, the history of modern times displayed a shift of interest from matters eternal and universal to practical and temporal affairs; in a word, from religion to science. With this shift, the authority of institutions and classes had rapidly decayed, to be replaced by the free individual armed with the scientific method. The moral and psychological consequence of the shift had been the emergence of the idea of progress with its intimation of infinite perfectibility.

The modern age was to Dewey the age of rationalism, an age to be understood in terms of the spread of creative intelligence. Its problems were those incident to the partial and incomplete domestication of intelligence in the community. When the scientific point of view had first emerged in the seventeenth century, it had been opposed by such vested interests as the church, while the mass of the population had remained indifferent. Subsequently, however, the printing press, newspapers, telegraphic communications, and finally public education sensitized the people to questions reserved in earlier times for the intelligentsia. The zeal of the fundamentalists in their crusade to secure laws forbidding the teaching of evolution in the schools seemed to Dewey an instructive example of social lag in the diffusion of intelligence. The public could now participate in the discussion of a scientific question even though it was unable as yet to comprehend the issues intelligently. The schools had not yet succeeded in converting emotional and prejudiced habits of thought into a scientific attitude of mind. "The fundamental defect in the present state of democracy is the assumption that political and economic freedom can be achieved without first freeing the mind."

The pragmatists had a vivid sense that pragmatism was itself a product of these distinctive forces that were shaping the modern community. Lewis Mumford expressed a familiar opinion of pragmatism when he sneered that James's philosophy was merely a warmed-over hash of the outlook of the Gilded Age. Dewey did not bother to deny the allegation. He conceded that there was indeed a similarity between James's thought and the attitudes of pioneer America. He likewise claimed a connection between his own later version of pragmatism and industrialism. He thought of industrialism as inevitably conditioning the corporate spirit of neodemocracy, just as James's individualism had reflected the older democracy.

These associations suggest a more precise historical context that embraces both phases of pragmatism, namely, the Progressive Era. Progressivism was a complex set of attitudes that looked both ways. Its individualism expressed its allegiance to the pre-industrial past. Its enthusiasm for science and technology signified its acceptance of machine civilization. And its faith in progress revealed its confidence in the future. The Progressives were conservative in their determination to maintain the continuity of traditional values in a world of change. Their program of reform was a cautious, ambiguous one, shaped by their determination to mitigate the full revolutionary consequences of industrialism, as those consequences were being forecast by the naturalists. Pragmatism was also a philosophy of change, which it envisaged as a process of "reconstruction," proceeding step by step as governed by the dictates of the critical intelligence. The pragmatists felt themselves fully at home in the current of Progressivism.

Democracy was the central social ideal of pragmatism. Dewey defined it as "faith in individuality, in uniquely distinctive qualities in each normal human being; faith in corresponding unique modes of activity that create new ends, with willing acceptance of the modifications of the established order entailed by the release of individualized capacities." In spite of the emphasis on the individual, Dewey's sense of the importance of the social was also very great. He made constant references to "communal life," "shared culture," communication, and the common. He repeatedly insisted that under industrial conditions the realization of democracy must be a cooperative enterprise.

This concern with the individual and the social furnished the framework for Dewey's definition of government as arising out of the distinction between public and private affairs. He held human acts to have two kinds of consequences: those that affected the people immediately engaged in the transaction in question—these were said to be private acts—and those that extended beyond the parties immediately involved so as to affect the welfare of others—these were public acts. Whenever these indirect consequences were recognized, and an effort was made to regulate them, some of the attributes of the state came into existence. Thus a prime function of government was the regulation of activities ultimately private in their origin or intention. It would be hard to find an approach to political theory more appropriate than this to the spirit of Progressivism.

In the bleak light of normalcy in the early 1920's, after World War I had ended Progressivism, Dewey undertook a postmortem examination of the Progressive Era. The spirit of the times suggested a more critical analysis of American history than he might have made earlier. His central problem was to explain why political liberalism in America was so fragile a flower. He found the answer in the peculiar character of American democracy. The Enlightenment had nurtured a revolutionary point of view in science and philosophy that had found its social expression in nineteenth-century democracy, with its ideal of freedom and equality of opportunity. While this ideal remained the genuinely spiritual element of the American tradition, it had never been fully realized.

Rather, during the nineteenth century, democracy had become closely identified with evangelical Protestantism. In Dewey's opinion, the fusion of democracy and religion had produced results at once admirable and deplorable. The heart of democracy was the American middle class, a fairly prosperous and well-disposed people, moderate in outlook, sympathetic to reform, pacifism, and public education but largely devoid of taste or discrimination. The middle class had emerged in its most heroic proportions in the South and the Middle West. There it held together a diffuse, heterogeneous, mobile population; and there the influence of evangelical Protestantism was strongest. Dewey readily conceded that the churches had performed an important social function in maintaining a basic decency and order in an expanding society. But their concept of cultural life had been narrow; they grasped power in the form of moral authority; and they perpetuated a reign of mediocrity. It was to such degrading influences that Dewey ascribed the failure of democracy to find the kind of leadership to which eighteenth-century republicanism had proudly resorted. Democracy had no place among its leaders for such intellectuals as Jefferson, Franklin, or Adams; its dislike of privilege focused itself with special resentment upon the cultivated and the expert. In the twentieth century, William Jennings Bryan best represented this spirit. Bryan's anti-evolution crusade reflected the popular fear of whatever seemed to threaten the security and order of a precariously held civilization. The fundamentalist insistence upon uniformity of belief revealed the need of the insecure for conformity.

Progressivism, as Dewey now sadly realized, had been a kind of moral crusade. Bryan, Theodore Roosevelt, and Wilson had been revivalists whose activities had expressed "moral emotions rather than the insight and policy of intelligence." It was because of this weakness that World War I had destroyed Progressivism. The emotionalism of political habits of thinking was readily focused by the propagandists and opinion-makers upon war issues. Indeed, it would not have been difficult for Dewey to have shown how the idealism of Progressivism was adapted by the Creel committee to war aims calculated to arouse the patriotic enthusiasm of the public. But he was more concerned with the bitter intolerance and coercive suppression of minority opinions that accompanied the drive for unity in the war effort. A temper of mind began to emerge with the preparedness movement of 1916 which in the end proved fatal to Progressivism. The events of the war years showed many Americans to be "social fundamentalists," enlightened in scientific or religious matters but prejudiced, emotional, and ignorant of political and economic affairs. The effect of the war upon such an immature people was to render them unwilling and unable to recapture the mood of prewar Progressivism.

The years of normalcy were a bitter hangover from the emotional binge of wartime. Dewey's disillusionment was reflected in his appraisal of the contemporary scene as well as in his historical interpretation. The synthesis of elements that had produced nineteenth-century democracy was clearly inadequate to twentieth-century industrial conditions. For here it spawned the pecuniary culture of a crass and sordid Social Darwinism that was oddly at variance with the mawkishly sentimental rhetoric of sweetness and light that resounded through every "service club." There must be a new democracy based on a new form of individualism consistent with industrial conditions.

American socialists had long dreamed of the Cooperative Commonwealth; and at a time when the socialist movement was perceptibly wasting away, Dewey's new democracy seemed to point toward a socialized order. The modern mentality is at odds with itself, he believed, because, while industrialism is collective by its nature and results, men insist that its motives and compensations shall be private. They are consequently bewildered because a unified mind entails a harmonious relationship between human purposes and the consequences actually effected by behavior. Dewey's analysis of the industrial situation was strongly reminiscent of Veblen. But unlike Veblen, he did not despair of the future. He insisted that he was a meliorist, neither an optimist nor a pessimist but one who believed that, by the use of intelligence, current conditions could always be improved. Socially, the possibilities of such improvement turned very largely upon an effective educational program.

Progressive Education

Dewey's intense and abiding interest in formal education was a natural consequence of his philosophical position. Beginning in the 1890's, he exerted an enormous influence on American primary and secondary education, through experimental schools and teacher-training programs, first at the University of Chicago and later at Columbia University Teachers College. His little classic, *The School and Society,* was published in 1899, and his major work, *Democracy and Education,* appeared in 1916. Representative of the school of thought that grew up around Dewey was John L. Childs's *Education and the Philosophy of Experimentalism* (1931). For more than half a century, the theory and implications of progressive education remained a topic of great and sustained interest.

As an educational philosophy, progressivism rested squarely on certain psychological assumptions. Man's primary experience, like that of all other animals, is an active process of doing and under-going. This experience is ultimately tangible, and not primarily cognitive in character. Knowledge is, in fact, only one form of experience, and secondary and derived at that, no matter how important may be its contributions. Also, the qualities of primary experience are esthetic; they are feelings, directly connected with sensory experiences. In these terms, the good life consists in the richness and variety of the satisfactions that primary experience yields. The function of knowledge is thus instrumental; its object is to regulate the events of primary experience. To "know" an object is to understand its possible consequences for experience. Activity directed by anticipated consequences is behavior controlled by meanings. Thinking arises out of problems. It is simply an attempt to resolve ambiguous situations into experiences the consequences of which have been foreseen. Thus in the largest sense, education is life, and vice versa. The key to successful living is the capacity to solve problems, and to this end the scientific method provides the educator with a central inspiration.

Dewey had been among the first to insist upon the modern genetic theory of the relationship between the organism and its environment. This relationship is one of interaction between the primary elements of experience. It is the given condition of life, with which analysis must start. The implications of this view for educational theory are readily apparent. The self develops out of its experiences, and not simply out of the unfolding of inborn capacities. Education may thus be defined as learning from experience. It must proceed in terms of the specific needs and interests of each child—that is, his current experience. If the student is to learn anything of value from his educational activity, it must be connected with his current experience; otherwise his schooling will become artificial because divorced from the stream of life as he experiences it. Motives as an incentive to learning are very important, and motives come from the child's reactions to concrete situations.

Progressive educators were proudly conscious of the fact that their pedagogical theory constituted a revolutionary departure from traditional American educational theory and practice. They insisted that, in divorcing its concept of knowledge from experience and from physical activity, the older educational philosophy was perpetuating an abstract and artificial concept of knowledge. It was, in fact, perpetuating the ancient dualism of mind and body. Dewey acknowledged, however, that in the fervor of their rebellion against the traditional point of view, his disciples sometimes went to the opposite extreme and failed to maintain contact between expressional activities and the intellectual possibilities of these activities. So keen was their awareness of change that they insisted that the object of education was not to transmit fixed beliefs or to build habits which might dominate behavior. Rather, its objective was to facilitate the reconstruction of experience by equipping the child to cope with novel situations by means of self-controlled behavior. In order that the individual might deal successfully with unique occasions, much importance was attached to the training of the intellect not merely as an adapting mechanism but as a creative force capable of fashioning new adjustments.

Since the time of Horace Mann, American philosophies of public education have been firmly rooted in the democratic ideology. But no educators have insisted more strenuously on the relevance of their theories to a democratic society than the progressive pedagogues. The unique needs of each child must receive individual attention. The progressives found this ideal difficult to reconcile with a rigid and prescribed curriculum. Properly conceived, the results of education should be freedom, initiative, and activity. To secure these outcomes, the teacher should think of himself as a partner of the pupil, since authority in another person was clearly undesirable. The facts of the situation were the only authority to be acknowledged. The old-fashioned classroom with its rigid discipline, rote learning, and authoritative dispensation of truth was palpably incompatible with the nurture of mature, self-disciplined, and intelligent adults. The best hope of democracy, said Dewey, is the school. Here must be developed emotionally mature and self-reliant individuals if democracy is to survive.

Like certain religious modernists who diluted their religion to the point where they could identify religion with life itself, progressive educators made the mistake of identifying education with the whole of life. John Childs declared education to be its own end, coextensive with experience itself. Education as preparation for the future was thus supplanted by education focused on "rich and vital living *now.*" From this point of view, formal schooling merely accentuated a perpetual process during important years of individual development. Nevertheless, rich and vital though the *now* of childhood might be, the progressives did insist, if in a roundabout way, on preparation for the future. The school, they said, must be in vital contact with the activities of the community and not be isolated from them. But these activities were for the most part the activities of adults and not of children. The one day of the year in which a school boy sits behind the governor's desk hardly accomplishes the effective fusion of child and adult. The community, in short, continued to insist upon the distinction between childhood and adulthood even if the educators did not. And yet John Childs was prepared to assess the value of a school in terms of the quality of interaction with the wider social life of which the school is part. In learning to cope with living issues, children do not require mechanical drill or compulsory learning. They will be found to acquire naturally the necessary skills as these are needed.

The older America had clearly been an adult's world. Its schools had effectively functioned to mold each generation of youth in the image of its forebears. It had regarded adolescence as a period of training to be passed through as quickly as possible. Progressive educators rejected this paternalism. Not the least revolutionary of their accomplishments was the liberation of the young from the old by dissolving the differences between them. The activities of the young were to be regarded as equally important as those of adults. At the same time, school was to be a place where children "grew up" by learning to cope with problems of the real world under controlled conditions of optimum desirability.

Dewey's educational philosophy suffered an ironic fate. The prime object of his theory was to develop in individuals the capacity to reconstruct reality in order to achieve more enduring satisfactions. His emphasis upon reconstruction was strongly intellectualist in character. He repeatedly stressed reliance on the scientific method of observation, hypothesis, and experiment. Such traditional educational objectives as the memorizing of an established body of knowledge, the inculcation of discipline, of patriotism, or of conformity were all discarded in favor of a mental cultivation calculated to equip the student with the most difficult of attainments, namely, the capacity to cope with novel situations. Yet the progressive ideal was curiously perverted by the obvious prolongation of youth that characterizes twentieth-century America. It became increasingly evident that the schools and even the colleges were places where children, instead of growing up, retained the privilege of remaining children. The progressive education movement came under vigorous attack for abandoning the traditional intellectual content of the curriculum in favor of such things as personality development and "life adjustment." Complaints were heard that the products of progressive schools, although presumably well-adjusted, frequently did not know the multiplication table or the elements of grammar—both of which might be justified as useful aids in the reconstruction of experience.

CHAPTER 24

||||||||||||||||||||||||||||||||||||||||||||||||||||||||||||||||

The Varieties of Religious Experience

T HE PROTESTANT DENOMINATIONAL ADJUSTMENT to the secular culture of American democracy allowed for considerable mutual interplay between religious and secular elements. Through the mediatorial role of the denominations, the democratic idealism acquired much of its religious quality; the denominations, on the other hand, were readily responsive to currents in secular culture. It was the pervasive influence of the ideology of democracy that induced influential segments of the Protestant denominations to choose from among the total cluster of religious values and attitudes those most compatible with the humanistic assumptions of the secular culture. At the same time, the secular culture drew upon the religious temper in order to endow its social ideals with a spiritual quality. Hence, much of twentieth-century religious life can be interpreted either as a response to the democratic ideology or as a reaction against its implicit humanism.

A Social Gospel

The deeply embedded religious tradition of the American people survived the age of naturalism and kept alive the moralistic and

429

humanistic values of the democratic ideology during the naturalistic era. The strength of the religious tradition is indicated in the fact that its expression was not confined to the clerical spokesmen who usually represented the religious point of view. Beginning in the 1880's and continuing into the twentieth century, a prominent and influential group of lay scholars in the social sciences brought religious principles to bear upon the social problems of the age.

During the early nineteenth century, the moral and spiritual orientation of organized Protestantism had become profoundly individualistic. Religion was an affair of the individual with his Maker. Repentance, salvation, sanctification—all were understood in private, personal terms. The catalogue of religious virtues presupposed an individualistic society. The dogmatic and inflexible character of moral and psychological assumptions was, in fact, a bulwark of support to the individual faced with bewildering institutional change and social fluidity.

However, the denominational adaptations to the social and economic conditions of the agricultural-commercial civilization of the early nineteenth century was not calculated to prepare Protestants to confront the problems of the industrial era. The individualistic social ethic combined with the traditional assumption that piety was a personal issue to raise a formidable obstacle to the recognition of the social dimension of religion.

It was the more remarkable therefore that so many individuals displayed a religiously sensitized conscience when confronted with the social consequences of industrialism. Because of the limited-liability principle involved in the denominational adjustment, one would not expect to find denominations as such taking a formal stand on matters of this sort. Eventually, several of them did make pronouncements on the social responsibilities of religion, but for many years the question was agitated by individuals by means of the spoken and printed word. Among the laymen who were active advocates of a social gospel were the prominent economists Richard T. Ely and John Bates Clark and the sociologist Charles Horton Cooley. The significance of the lay, as distinct from the clerical, social gospel stems from the fact that these men addressed themselves as Christian scholars to the educated secular community and not as laymen to the religious community. They were convinced that a sound approach to the social problems of the age was to be found only with the aid of religious values.

The social gospelers shared a deep sense of the need for social unity and human solidarity. Their chief criticisms of contemporary industrial society centered upon the widening gulf between classes with the consequent loss of sympathetic understanding, upon the selfish complacence of the rich and the bitter resentment of the poor, and upon social strife and the threat of revolutionary violence. Their responses to these conditions were essentially religious in character. They took it for granted that the achievement of social harmony was a religious function. One might employ scientific methods of diagnosis, but an effective cure required action governed by religious truths. The sense of the need for social solidarity was sharpened in the minds of social gospelers by the prevalence of the naturalistic theory of cultural organicism. Clark declared in 1880 that the organic nature of society forbade the artificial segregation of the religious life from political and economic affairs. The laissez-faire concept of the economic man seemed to him as artificial as worship in a vacuum. Both rested on a partial and inadequate view of human nature.

Implicitly or explicitly, the social gospelers assumed that organized Protestantism was failing to secure the unity of society, partly because it continued to sponsor the old individualistic gospel and partly because of the limitations of its own institutional character. Although they continued to write in the typically vague Protestant fashion about the social responsibilities of "the Church," Clark at least was partially aware that ecclesiastical fragmentation into a large number of denominations and sects was a fundamental aspect of the problem. The lay social gospelers were members of large middle-class denominations. They were aware that their own denominations were without appreciable representation in the working class. Thus "the Church" itself failed to display an example or working model of that comprehensive solidarity which the larger society so desperately needed. Clark was convinced that a socially stratified hierarchy of denominations was both un-Christian and undemocratic. But he concluded sadly that little could be done. Clark betrayed some sympathy for the old Puritan state church because of its social function of unifying the community upon a platform of Christian ideals. But it would have been scandalous at the end of the nineteenth century to have advocated the reunion of church and state, and Clark did not do so.

The social gospelers were agreed that the ultimate solution of the social problem lay in the great principle of Christian love. The doctrine of the Fatherhood of God, declared R. T. Ely, provided the only universal bond among men. By virtue of this doctrine all men were brothers. Christian love found its supreme expression in service to one's fellow men. Social welfare thus became the criterion for all conduct. The ideal family relationship furnished the image of the Christian society. In the family, all were bound together by love. While the members of the family were not equal either in possessions, in talents, or in authority, these abiding inequalities were submerged in love. In this vein, Clark declared that the church must take the lead in solving the labor problem by showing that this was a moral issue involving arbitration, profit-sharing, and cooperation.

Finally, the social gospelers shared a belief in the immanence of the divine spirit in the social process and in a gradual refinement of spiritual values that pointed toward the coming of the Kingdom. The older belief in progress, the newer theory of social evolution, and the ancient Christian millennial expectation were blended together to provide a historical framework in which the ideals of the social gospelers were to be realized. These were sober-minded and practical men who were nevertheless moved by the conviction that the selfish and competitive society of their own day would be gradually transformed by a cooperative and communal spirit. Clark did not hesitate to designate the ultimate social ideal as "Christian socialism."

Laymen, such as Clark and Ely whose denominational affiliations were orthodox, accommodated their social evolutionism to the eschatological promises contained in the Christian revelation. Less orthodox thinkers placed greater emphasis on the emergence of ever more refined and exalted ideals during the course of the historical process itself. Charles Horton Cooley maintained that as society evolved toward organic wholeness its social ideals, which had emerged through the successive concepts of community, nation, and mankind, would open upon vistas of a greater life, continuous with the earlier concepts in some ways, immeasurably transcending them in others. In his book *The Social Process* (1918), Cooley attempted to generalize the social obligation of religion by observing that "the human mind must ever conceive some kind of a life of God or 'kingdom of heaven' answering to its need of a satisfying universe." While his fellow countrymen were convulsed in the struggle of World War I, Cooley remarked that the essence of modern religion was a kind of higher patriotism hardly separable from the nobler ideals of the nation. Patriotism, at the same time, took on a distinctly religious flavor. Cooley anticipated that religious and social worship would continue to converge upon each other without, however, becoming fully merged. No more than Clark was he enticed by the vision of a state church or a church state. But at least the church must embrace and promote the highest social ideals and functions in the realization that the salvation of individuals was possible only through the salvation of society.

The clergymen who sponsored a social gospel during the closing decades of the nineteenth century had at least one thing in common with the laymen: they spoke for themselves as individuals and not necessarily for their respective denominations. In no denomination did the group of social-gospel advocates constitute more than a small minority, albeit a vocal one. Eventually, in 1908, the Methodist General Conference adopted a resolution endorsing social-gospel principles, to be followed shortly by a similar pronouncement of the Federal Council of Churches. These resolutions, however, had little practical effect, and in the Middle West at least the impact of the social gospel upon the larger Protestant bodies was relatively superficial.

The preachers of a social gospel first appeared in the pulpits of urban parishes where their congregations represented the larger middle-class denominations with ancient churchly traditions. The social situation of these clergymen was much like that of the secular progressive reformers of the following decades. Episcopalians and Congregationalists led the way, followed somewhat later by Methodists and Baptists. In these bodies, the social gospelers were, however, more than balanced by fundamentalist wings that continued to stress the old individualistic evangelical piety. By mid-twentieth century, it was apparent that no denomination had in any substantial way been transformed by the social gospel.

The most representative and influential of the clerical social gospelers was Washington Gladden. A Congregationalist with clerical and editorial experience in several industrial towns and cities, Gladden knew at first hand the urban industrial situation in North Adams and Springfield, Massachusetts, Brooklyn and New York City, and Columbus, Ohio. His moderate and hopeful outlook was marked by his sympathetic understanding of the problems and aspirations of laboring people and by his conviction as to the proper mediatorial role of religion. He preached and lectured constantly on the whole range of social questions, and his writings had a wide influence.

In accounting for the ills of contemporary society, Gladden placed primary responsibility on the inadequacy of the traditional Protestant piety. By conceiving of salvation as a private matter between man and God, Protestants had forgotten the social nature of righteousness and had misconceived the law of love. The social tensions of industrial society were due to the failure of Christians to realize that the law of love governed the whole of life. Secondary responsibility was assigned to naturalistic materialism and determinism. It was the duty of Christians, said Gladden in 1902, to insist that human society is "under the sway of spiritual motives; that it is constantly undergoing renovation through the ideals which men entertain and the choices which they make; that human nature is modifiable, and is constantly being modified, under the influence of the divine Spirit, so that social standards and ruling ideas are gradually changing from generation to generation."

In one respect at least, naturalism had served a useful function. It had familiarized men with the evolutionary theory of "an orderly progress in creation." This was necessary in order that they might grasp Saint Paul's conception of Christianity as a "normative germ or force planted in the very heart of the creation, and working itself out in the slow processes of history." Here was Gladden's version of the doctrine of divine immanence. The normative germ or force working in history was the Christ spirit, namely, sympathy, love, and self-sacrifice. However, Gladden preserved some shreds of orthodoxy. He insisted that God's revelation of Himself in nature was only partial; the deeper truths of incarnation and redemption were not to be found there, but only in Scriptural revelation.

The blending of the Christian doctrine of divine immanence with the secular theory of social evolutionary progress resulted in a moderate brand of postmillennialism in which the Kingdom was envisaged as in process of formation by means of forces already present and at work. Righteousness, peace, joy, and love existed even now and gradually would gain wider dominion and control. These were the essential elements of the Kingdom. Few contemporaries had a closer firsthand knowledge of the social evils of the early industrial era than had Gladden. His mediatorial services in industrial disputes were widely appreciated both by labor and by employers. He offered no easy or impractical solutions. He was well aware of the peculiar social limitations of the Protestant denominations in dealing with problems involving the conflicting interests of social classes. Yet his Christian optimism remained unimpaired, thanks to his abiding faith in the coming of the Kingdom. In the face of the depression and industrial strife of the 1890's, this faith remained unshaken. "The thought of the world is gradually being freed from superstition and prejudice; the social sentiments are being purified; the customs are slowly changing for the better; the laws are gradually shaped by finer conceptions of justice. There are reactions and disasters, but taking the ages together, the progress is sure."

The variety of attitudes toward social and religious questions that the loose bonds of denominationalism made possible was well illustrated in the contrast between Washington Gladden and his fellow Congregationalist George Herron. If Gladden represented the conscience and idealism of the urban middle class, Herron spoke in the rebellious tones of Midwestern agrarianism. A native of Indiana and educated at Ripon Academy, Wisconsin, Herron achieved sudden fame with a sermon preached in 1890 at Minneapolis on "The Message of Jesus to Men of Wealth," a ringing social-gospel exhortation. The following year he was called to the Congregational Church in Burlington, Iowa, a parish typical of those that supported social-gospel preachers. Two years later Herron took a professorship of Applied Christianity established for him at Grinnell College by a wealthy Burlington parishioner. Herron was equally effective as teacher and as preacher. Swept along perhaps by the effectiveness of his own rhetoric, he soon found himself on the radical fringe of the social-gospel movement.

Herron was acutely conscious of the drift of the larger Protestant denominations toward humanistic modernism. He also saw that beyond the complacence and prosperity of middle-class parishes was much bitterness, poverty, and despair. Somehow, these two phenomena were related. The preacher called for a return to doctrines something like those of early-nineteenth-century evangelical Protestantism. In these traditional dogmas he found the key to the solution of the social, economic, and moral evils of the modern age. Chief emphasis was placed on the divine-human mission of Christ. "In Christ is revealed all that God is, and all that man is to be; he is God in man and man in God." Christ was to be realized in history with the Second Coming. Justice, love, and brotherhood would then reign supreme.

Herron managed to combine in a curious way the major types of millennialism. His insistence that through self-sacrificing imitation of Christ the Kingdom would come, and the fervency with which he denounced iniquitous institutions, recalled the catastrophic expectations of the premillennialists. But unlike the premillennialists, he was unwilling to abandon the world as beyond redemption. His perfectionism was of a practical, moral variety. Christ could save men from sin if they would only imitate Him. The "new messianic day" would then dawn. In other words, the Kingdom was to come by transforming the world, not by destroying it. Herron insisted that institutions as well as individuals must be saved from sin. On every side he confronted the paradox of moral man and immoral society. "A corporation, greedy, godless, vicious in many of its operations, consists of men famous for their piety and benevolence. A nation governed by men of eminent Christian character goes mad with the spoils of unrighteousness. . . . A church containing many sincere, teachable, self-sacrificing Christians is as powerless a moral institution in the community as the town pump." Iniquitous institutions must be sacrificed to the same end that Christ was sacrificed before God could bring order out of chaos.

The anticipated transformation, obviously, would be a drastic one. Herron was both a revolutionist and a socialist. In a volume of sermons entitled *The New Redemption* (1893), the prairie prophet stressed the contrast between the selfishness and immoral anarchy of competitive capitalism and the equality, security, peace, unity, and brotherhood that would characterize Christ's kingdom on earth. The establishment of the Kingdom would be accomplished only through suffering and self-sacrifice. "Whoso would gain his life must lose it."

Herron's radicalism was utterly incompatible with the commitments of middle-class Congregationalism. After two years of increasing estrangement from denominational and college authorities, he was compelled in 1895 to relinquish his post at Grinnell. Subsequent divorce and remarriage led to the removal of his name from the official roles of the Congregationalist clergy. Herron's deviation from denominational orthodoxy might conceivably have resulted in the formation of a new sect. His peculiar blend of Christian perfectionism and millenarianism with socialist utopianism was by no means unique in the history of American sectarianism, and Herron possessed the personal magnetism to have drawn a small following with him. Actually, however, he found congenial associations among the democratic socialists of the Socialist Party, which he joined in 1901. The ideals of love, brotherhood, cooperation, and self-sacrifice that he had preached from the pulpit he carried over into the secular socialist movement. These ideals found a sympathetic response among the socialists, who formed what might quite legitimately be regarded as a humanistic sect.

Modernism

The most direct and characteristic religious expression of the neo-democratic ideology was found in the movement known as modernism. In a broad sense, modernism represented tendencies that had been at work in the secular culture at least since the eighteenth century. The movement came into focus in the first three decades of the twentieth century, when most of the modernist books were written and sermons preached. This was the era when, according to the *Catholic Encyclopedia*, there was "an infatuation for modern ideas," namely, humanism and humanitarianism.

As a movement of religious thought and feeling, modernism, like the social gospel, cut across denominational lines. Its strength lay in the larger Protestant denominations, at least outside the South. While it captured no denomination completely, except perhaps the Unitarians, a small body, it deeply influenced the Congregationalists, Methodists, Baptists, and Disciples. Modernism also left its mark on Reformed Judaism and was attractive enough to Roman Catholics to warrant papal condemnation in 1907. Nevertheless, it produced no specific organizations of its own except for an occasional "community church." The present summary of modernist ideas is based on the writings of two Chicago modernists, Edward Scribner Ames, a Disciple, and Shailer Mathews, a Baptist.

Modernism may be described as a religious expression of the democratic ideology and practices because the modernists freely acknowledged the derivation of their faith from the secular culture. This of course, in no way qualified its essential Christianity in their eyes. The democratic movement of the early nineteenth century had produced powerful ideological currents that resulted religiously in the recrudescence of doctrines previously deemed to be heretical but that now appealed to many Americans as peculiarly timely and appropriate. These doctrines of free will, universal salvation, and various kinds of perfectionism were blended in a new form of evangelical Protestantism. Later in the century, the same ideological forces produced the social-gospel movement. Crusading movements for freedoms of various kinds were undertaken and consummated, all in the name of the democratic ideal. By 1918, it seemed to Ames that men all over the world were struggling to realize "an actual and visible society of righteousness, justice, and love." Modernism, according to Ames, was to be the twentieth-century religion of democracy. The only alternatives were premillenarian fundamentalism that despaired of worldly progress and equated human misery with the approaching day of judgment, or scientific materialism with its determinism and ultimate pessimism.

Modernism was also a product of humanism and personal security. Humanism implied a man-centered orientation, a tendency to look at things from man's point of view. Personal security was the result of the great technological, economic, and medical revolutions that, since the beginning of the nineteenth century, had doubled the life expectancy of the average individual and provided for more fortunate classes a measure of leisure and comfort which had previously been dreamed of only by impractical utopians. Humanism and personal security closely reinforced each other. Mathews affirmed that religion always springs from human needs, a thoroughly humanistic point of view. A religion that cannot meet these needs is therefore merely a social encumbrance. It was appropriate that an age which was so impressed with the uniqueness of its own modernity should believe that its religious needs were also unique. Mathews pointed to democracy, social equalitarianism, the rapid accumulation of scientific knowledge, national and racial aspirations, and a keener sense of social obligations as areas in which the needs of the age were focused. These were the issues upon which religion must concentrate.

In fact, the larger the measure of personal security that prevailed, the more varied and demanding human needs proved to be. In the meanwhile, the preoccupation of the modernists with human values and needs in the context of the rapid extension of human control over the material world produced a situation in which many of the concerns of traditional religion—although not all of them—no longer had any meaning. And so there disappeared from modernism all superstition and all concern with those parts of religion that dealt with miracle, supernatural ritual, and dogmatic creed.

Modernists cordially accepted science as in no way injurious to religion. They even assigned to it a central place in their thinking. Mathews defined modernism as "the use of the methods of modern science to find, state and use the permanent and central values of inherited orthodoxy in meeting the needs of a modern world." It was not so much the accomplishments of science that impressed the modernists as it was the implications of the scientific method: patient inquiry into the nature of things, intellectual integrity, and freedom of thought. The specific aspect of scientific method that most concerned Mathews was its application to historical study. The result was the freeing of history from the grip of theological dogmas to speak for itself as an objective social process. The great importance of sound historical method to the modernists is apparent once it is realized that their understanding of the character and needs of the modern era depended upon an "objective" interpretation of history.

Convinced that history demonstrated the emergence of reason, the refinement of humane values, the emancipation of suppressed classes, and the accumulation of material comforts, the modernists, of necessity, regarded religious orthodoxy as a largely outmoded heritage from the past. The dualism and supernaturalism of traditional Christianity were at best implausible. The alleged historic revelation of a Word of Truth, confirmed by miracle, was now seen to be nothing but a primitive religious myth. The modernists insisted upon a complete merging of the spiritual with the secular. As Ames put it, "the Christian life may be regarded as just life itself at its best." Every act was to become an act of worship, every thought a prayer. Religious truth was not revealed on unique occasions in the past but was found in every experience.

It appeared to Ames by 1918 that modernism was so firmly established that it could be described in a book entitled *The New Orthodoxy*. He specified three basic tenets of modernism. First, reverence for life. Men must not evade the religious obligation to study their experience with scientific rigor. Jesus's teachings, for instance, reflected such keen observation and profound insight into the problems of life that they were of universal validity. Ames presumably referred to the moral teachings of Jesus rather than to his messianic claims. In any event, whatever wisdom men possessed was the product of the total experience of mankind. Second, love for one's fellow men. The democratic ideology had generated an idealism that pointed men's aspirations inevitably toward a good society based upon social justice. Justice, in turn, depended ultimately upon love. Finally, faith in the progressive character of human experience. Progress might not be inevitable, but one could not expect to get the most out of life unless he believed in the possibility of improving the world. "The Christian attitude of faith is that the world has immense possibilities and that these may be realized through the industry, intelligence, and good will of men working in harmony with the highest knowledge and deepest convictions they possess."

Ames was one of the radical modernists. Others were more concerned than he to retain what hold they conscientiously could upon Christian dogmatic traditions. Mathews declared that democracy and science were not enough; humanity must be regenerated. For such moderate modernists the central Christian doctrine was incarnation, and modernism might be appropriately regarded as exemplifying the radical culmination of this doctrine. During the nineteenth century there had been a growing tendency among Protestants, both in Europe and in America, to interpret the dogma of the incarnation as a necessary ethical implication of the outpouring of God's love into the creation. The divine spirit incarnate in Christ was diffused by the modernists throughout the universe. God's spirit was believed to be incarnate in the world, working through the social historical process, expressing itself in the highest values of the community, such as love, brotherhood, justice, and good will.

In attenuated forms, the doctrine of incarnation was susceptible of being drawn out into a wide variety of attitudes. Henry Demarest Lloyd, reformer, socialist, and humanist unaffiliated with any religious body, professed his faith in the ever more refined morality emergent in the historical process: "the growth of the God within in the likeness of the God without." Lloyd proclaimed the one true church, the church of the deed.

The roots of modernism in the social gospel were suggested above when attention was called to the common denominational locus of the two movements. In traditional Christianity, good works had always been regarded as the culmination or necessary consequence of religious piety. In modernism, where there was no piety in traditional terms, good works might readily become the central phenomenon of religion—Lloyd's religion of the deed. As Ames put it: "We are rapidly making this devotion to human welfare religious." A logical tendency of the modernist movement, therefore, like the social gospel before it, was to transform the churches into social-welfare agencies. Sometimes an individual participated in both movements, as did Shailer Mathews, who proudly observed in his memoirs that his *Social Teaching of Jesus* (1897, but published earlier as journal articles) had been a pioneer social-gospel document.

The logical thrust of modernist thinking toward a social gospel had become evident much earlier. In 1876, Felix Adler broke with the Free Religious Association, a pioneer modernist organization founded in 1867 of which Adler himself had served as president, because he felt strongly that the Association should not evade as it did the social obligations of the type of humanistic religion to which it was committed. Adler formed his own organization, the Ethical Culture Society, which was intended to concern itself actively with social reform. In fact, however, Ethical Culture became just another modernist church, retaining as the symbol of its original intent an abiding interest in education. It was perhaps wise and certainly consistent with the limited-liability principle of Protestant denominationalism that the modernists did not commit themselves actively to a social-reform program. Had they done so they would have put themselves at the mercy of the unpredictable course of events. Indirectly, however, there can be little doubt but that Protestants of modernist outlook furnished important support for progressive and reformist programs during the first half of the twentieth century, from the days of Theodore to those of Franklin Roosevelt.

Medicine and Religion

The two great philosophical principles that underlay the popular thought of the nineteenth century were idealism and materialism. The pervasive influence of materialism has already been chronicled in the discussion of naturalism. One of the most spectacular triumphs of the materialistic point of view occurred in the rapid development of medical science during the century, as a result of the use of materialistic hypotheses in the related medical sciences of physiology and pathology, biochemistry, bacteriology, and pharmacology. The accomplishments of medicine lent strength to the view that the knowledge of the behavior of matter as governed by physical laws would yield a complete account of reality.

Idealism was driven underground during the latter part of the nineteenth century, to become the peculiar property of clergymen, professors, and women. But it could not be suppressed entirely, and it broke out in bizarre or partially disciplined forms, such as New Thought or Christian Science. These movements reflected the failure of naturalistic materialism to recognize or to deal adequately with certain kinds of human experience and thus to satisfy certain human needs. They also reflected the declining spiritual vitality of the middle-class Protestant denominations, which were rapidly becoming formal social institutions without any moving religious spirit. The social-gospel movement was one form of protest against this situation, and the Emmanuel movement was another.

Before considering the Emmanuel movement, note must first be taken of the influential theories of William James on religious experience. A new and unusual combination of scientific interests appeared in James. He was a doctor of medicine and a psychologist of renown who nevertheless scandalized the profession by maintaining a life-long interest in spiritualism and psychic research; he assisted in the introduction of Sigmund Freud and his ideas to America; he was one of the originators of the pragmatic philosophy; and he wrote a distinguished treatise on *The Varieties of Religious Experience* (1902). James combed the literature of religious "experience," using that term in the strict sense of designating communion with the divine spirit, in order to analyze in psychological terms what had occurred. There were innumerable autobiographical accounts of such experiences, and James took them at their face value as the record of authentic happenings. His analysis suggested that at the moment when the "experience" occurred, a barrier between the conscious mind and the subconscious mind dropped so that the particular identity of the finite self was momentarily merged or in contact with a larger something called God, resulting in an influx of power and sense of well-being.

By thus employing the controversial theory of the subconscious or subliminal self, James set the stage for a renewal of interest in the psychological aspects of religion. To describe its central phenomenon as he did, in an analytical but sympathetic spirit and in the vocabulary of psychology, seemed new and fresh. Denominational Protestants who had largely forgotten their evangelical traditions found the approach stimulating. A few seized the opportunity to put the new ideas to work in a rather original way.

The so-called "Emmanuel movement" was initiated by Elwood Worcester, pastor of the Emmanuel Church (Episcopal) in Boston. Worcester had combined clerical with psychological training in Germany, where he had taken the doctorate under the celebrated psychologists Wundt and Fechner. He was called to the Emmanuel parish in 1904, where be began a fruitful collaboration with his pastoral associate, Samuel McComb.

By the beginning of the twentieth century, Episcopalianism had replaced Unitarianism as the socially élite religious denomination of Boston, and Emmanuel was perhaps its strongest parish. It conducted an extensive program of social services, with a settlement house in the slums, a Y.M.C.A. branch, and a staff of trained social workers. Yet Worcester knew that something vital was missing. His parishioners gave generously of their money, and the poor appreciated the charity, but the church lacked spiritual power. Men no longer turned to it passionately, to be transformed by its spirit and message. The social gospel was one form of response to this situation, but Worcester rejected the social gospel with the shrewd observation that it offered an archaic theology made palatable by a full stomach. He concluded that something much more radical was needed, namely, the recovery for the church of Christ's power as healer of the sick. Worcester sensed more keenly than most of his contemporaries the intimate connection between peace of mind and health of the body.

To appreciate the Emmanuel movement, it is necessary to bear in mind the medical situation at the end of the nineteenth century. The dominant materialism of medical theory and practice offered the practicing physician no rationale with which to cope with functional nervous disorders. Illness was understood to be an organic disorder to be treated by physical means. If no lesion could be detected, the patient's symptoms could only be dismissed as "imaginary." Worcester estimated that nearly half the illnesses from which men were suffering were of a nature with which the medical profession was unprepared to deal. These were functional disorders in which personality, mind, or moral nature appeared to be the controlling factor. An inevitable response in the absence of an effective medical psychiatry was the appearance of healing cults, such as Christian Science, which went to the opposite extreme of denying physical reality entirely.

In these circumstances, Worcester and McComb developed a distinctive religiotherapy that blended Christian faith in Christ's healing power with Jamesian mysticism, pre-Freudian psychiatry, and hypnosis. A parish clinic was established for the treatment of functional disorders, the principal technique used being suggestion. The practice grew rapidly and attracted wide interest. Many articles and books were written, including *Religion and Medicine* (1908), in which Worcester and McComb collaborated with Dr. Isador Coriat, an eminent neurologist and psychiatrist. Within three years, some forty Protestant parishes had established pastoral clinics for the treatment of nervous disorders. Worcester and his associates organized a course of instruction for the training of clinical workers in 1908.

The religiotherapeutic theory of the Emmanuel movement tolerated no conflict with professional medicine. It proposed to deal only with those disorders beyond the scope of physical medicine. Prospective patients were first to be examined by a medical practitioner in order to determine whether their disorders were organic or functional in nature. Only illnesses in the latter category were to be treated. The therapy rested on the assumption of the existence of a subconscious self underlying the conscious mind. The subconscious was believed to exercise in many ways a controlling influence upon the conscious mind. Personality disorders were said to be caused by the existence of fears, phobias, and obsessions in the subconscious; cures were to be effected by replacing these morbid constructs with healthy ones. Worcester and several other clergymen interested in the work discovered that they possessed hypnotic powers, which they occasionally used as a means of making direct contact with the subconscious, especially in cases of drug addiction or alcoholism. But their principal method was suggestion, employed in a series of interview treatments. Patients were assured that there was hope for any sufferer who would place himself in the current of good and high thoughts. He would find a renewed and transformed life in which faith would replace despair.

Since it was apparent that the cure of functional disorders required a change of personality, one might well ask, change to what? The answer was to be furnished by the church. The positive reconstruction of personality was to be shaped by the basic Christian values and outlook. Christianity was peculiarly suited to perform the therapeutic function because it required the throwing off of the burdens of self through trustful dependence upon a sufficient power. Both the surrender of self and the will to be saved were characteristic features of psychiatric treatment. Without faith on the part of the patient, nothing could be done for him. As McComb put it: "Trust in God draws together the scattered forces of the inner life, unifies the dissociations of consciousness created by guilt and remorse, soothes the wild emotions born of sorrow or despair, and touches the whole man to finer issues of peace and power and holiness."

The fate of the Emmanuel movement may well have been determined by its relationship to the medical profession. Because it was in no way disposed to question the validity of physical medicine, which it merely sought to supplement, the movement committed itself to the good will of physicians. From the beginning, Worcester worked closely with doctors and enjoyed their confidence. He was supported by several of the leading American neurologists and psychiatrists, including S. Weir Mitchell and Morton Prince. But as the movement spread, and practice was undertaken in some instances by well-meaning but incompetent people, the medical profession generally withdrew its support. In spite of some opposition to psychiatry in medical circles, there was strong and successful pressure to organize psychiatric training and practice as a recognized branch of professional medicine. The result of this salutary tendency was to discredit those who practiced psychotherapy without medical training. The movement was also weakened by identification in the minds of many people with rapidly growing Christian Science. Perhaps the lasting contribution of the Emmanuel movement was to furnish added inducement to the medical profession to enter the field of functional disorders, to recognize psychiatry as a legitimate branch of medicine, and to support research and practice in that important field.

When Sigmund Freud lectured on psychoanalysis to medical students at the University of Vienna in 1915 he reminded them that the training which they had received was exclusively materialistic in character. They had been taught the anatomy and physiology of the organism and had learned to understand its functioning and pathology in biological and chemical terms. But they had been taught nothing of the psychical aspects of life, and Freud accused them of harboring a general attitude of suspicion toward emotional phenomena as being outside the range of data susceptible of scientific investigation. The result of such ignorance, in Freud's opinion, was abandonment of a large area of potential medical practice "to the quacks, mystics, and faith-healers whom you despise." While the rise of Christian Science cannot be attributed wholly to the failure of nineteenth-century medicine to cope with functional and emotional illness, the new faith served the needs of many who found no aid elsewhere.

Christian Science shared with Mormonism the distinction of being the most striking and successful of indigenous American religious movements. Although its rapid growth was largely a twentieth-century phenomenon, the train of ideas and events that culminated in the organization of the Christian Science church traced back to the eighteenth century. Among the scientists at that time there was widespread interest in the phenomena of magnetism. According to one of the explanatory theories, a subtle magnetic fluid pervaded all things, directed by some indwelling spirit. The currents of this fluid were believed to affect the animal body as they flowed through it; by proper manipulation of the flow, the health of the organism could be assured. A shrewd Austrian named Friedrich Anton Mesmer (1733?–1815) elaborated these ideas into a therapeutic technique and established a lucrative and fashionable medical practice in Paris until he was repudiated by the French Academy of Sciences. Mesmer designated the fluid "animal magnetism," and undertook to control its flow by means of manipulation and passes at the patient. In the course of practice he discovered and used hypnotism, without, however, understanding its nature.

Mesmer's theories circulated widely, and in the following generation were being employed by a practitioner of Portland, Maine, named Phineas P. Quimby (1802–1866). In the earlier phase of his practice, Quimby used an indirect and cumbersome method of diagnosing the illness of his patients. He hypnotized a medium who in trance described to him the feelings and subjective condition of the patient. The physician then analyzed the report and prescribed the cure, usually some innocuous herbal remedy. Subsequently, Quimby discovered that he could dispense with the hypnotized medium and deal directly with the emotional condition of the patient. He regarded illness as the manifestation of false belief. His deep interest in theology, and specifically in the cures effected by Christ, led him to call his system Christian Science.

Among Quimby's patients was a chronically hysterical woman named Mary M. Patterson, better known as Mary Baker Eddy. Mary Baker had grown up in central New Hampshire near the Shaker village at Canterbury, and she may have absorbed some of the mysticism that was strong in the Shaker communities during the middle of the nineteenth century. She had suffered for years from a variety of psychosomatic disorders. As a patient and student of Quimby during the years 1861–1866, she was not only restored to health but became an enthusiastic disciple. She carefully studied the manuscripts he had written, with a view to becoming a practitioner herself. Subsequently, she strenuously rejected the assertion that she was in any way indebted to Quimby, although the eventual publication of Quimby's manuscripts left little doubt on the matter. Be that as it may, Mrs. Eddy's significance in history does not stem from the theories of Christian Science, whether original or borrowed. Her genius lay in converting the crude psychotherapeutic theories of Quimby into a religion and in founding a new church upon it. She purged Quimby's Christian Science of its material fluid substance and acknowledged the reality of spirit alone. Even within the bounds of her own system, Mrs. Eddy was said not to have been a successful practitioner. Her talent was that of the teacher, organizer, and administrator. Possessed of a magnetic personality and imperious will, she gathered and disciplined a body of devoted followers. Her book, *Science and Health, with a Key to the Scriptures,* was first published in 1875, and the Church of Christ, Scientist, was chartered four years later.

Although the immediate antecedents of Christian Science may have been in the mesmeric school of therapy, much more important was the great tradition of idealism as represented in Emersonian transcendentalism and Shaker mysticism. Mrs. Eddy proclaimed God or Infinite Mind or Good—synonymous terms—to be the only reality. This was unadulterated idealism. But it was certainly not a common-sense point of view, and to be persuasive to unreflective minds it must be presented with simple, dogmatic authority.

In its Christian Science form, idealism received several characteristic emphases. Mrs. Eddy taught that Infinite Mind or Intelligence was omnipresent. Christian Science was sometimes said to be nothing but correct thinking—that is, communion with Infinite Intelligence. Each thought should be a fresh act of contact with the Infinite. Such a doctrine might appear to open the door to claims of direct inspiration or mystical experiences, but such tendencies were not to be characteristic of Christian Science. In fact, the dogmatic authority of the church was strictly maintained. Finally, one must impersonalize his sense of person, and dematerialize his sense of things. Thus he would be enabled to shake off the false sense of sin, disease, and death. In spite of its denial of material reality, it would seem, paradoxically enough, that Christian Science was attempting to recover Christ's promise of life everlasting, not in the Heaven of nineteenth-century Protestants but here and now.

In its zeal to triumph over the flesh, Christian Science offered its own brand of perfectionism. Sin, pain, death—all aspects of the false world of matter—were declared to be nonexistent. Orthodox Christians had always regarded evil as a very real thing that even the best of men never escaped entirely. And at the same time there had always been a few who were impatient with the requirement of unending war against something that could never be vanquished. Such rebels developed the conviction that justification through Christ's sacrifice was sufficient to free the flesh from its mortal limitations, and they gave voice to their faith in doctrines of Christian perfection. It should also be borne in mind that during the nineteenth century, romantic Protestantism had placed increasing emphasis upon God as love. As an expression of genteel sentimentalism, romantic optimism made it increasingly difficult to account for the abiding evidences of sin and mortality. For people who enjoyed a degree of personal security never before known, the misfortunes which yet continued to befall them possessed a terror they would scarcely have evoked in sterner times. Christian Science drew its clientele from those who failed to find satisfaction in the middle-class denominations of modernist orientation. It was strikingly successful in persuading comfortably situated urban dwellers in a materialistic and humanistic civilization that everything except God, Goodness, Love, and Intelligence was the false imagining of mortal mind.

Christian Science doctrine and practice placed the perennial problem of liberty and authority in sharp focus. The powerful subjective element in Mrs. Eddy's teaching, its mystical tendency, would doubtless quickly produce anarchy were it not disciplined by a powerful and authoritarian ecclesiastical organization. The rigidity of discipline developed by the Christian Science Church came to exceed even that of Roman Catholicism. The early history of the movement was littered with expulsions for heresy and insubordination.

During her lifetime, Mrs. Eddy ruled her church with an iron hand. After her death in 1910, the question inevitably arose as to the ultimate source of authority for her followers. Would it be Mrs. Eddy's teachings as found in *Science and Health* or would it be the directors of the Mother Church? The former was an open book, which anyone could interpret to his own satisfaction; the latter was a body of men which represented the continuity of institutionalized authority. In 1922 the Supreme Court of Massachusetts answered the question in favor of the Directors and against an opposition group that had contended that ecclesiastical authority should be subordinated to religious truth. Since that time the Directors have exercised unchallenged authority over doctrine and practice.

The aspect of Christian Science that has attracted the greatest interest, both within and outside the movement, has been its healing mission. This was the inevitable consequence of the founder's preoccupation with religiotherapy. Because illness was declared to be an error of mortal mind, the sufferer would find relief by purging his mind of error through contemplation of the Infinite Goodness. Wherever suggestion of this sort was appropriate to alleviate the condition of the patient much good was doubtless accomplished. Mrs. Eddy was practical enough to concede that the supremacy of mind over matter could scarcely be established without considerable conditioning. A convenient recourse to bone setting and surgery was thus provided those who were not yet firm in the faith.

CHAPTER 25

||||||||||||||||||||||||||||||||||||||||||||||||||||||||||||||||||||||

Social Control
and Planning

ONE OF THE MAJOR PROBLEMS confronting the neodemocratic mind was to discover the effects upon nineteenth-century democratic values of the peculiar social conditions of the twentieth century. It was then necessary to decide what positive measures, if any, were necessary to preserve democratic values. The democratic faith of the nineteenth century had arisen spontaneously from a combination of the intellectual heritage with social and economic conditions peculiarly suited to democratic and capitalistic individualism. Social thought had inevitably reflected this spontaneity in the complacence with which it had overlooked many of the perennial tensions of social life. But in the twentieth century, the spontaneity was largely gone, and the preservation of the traditional ideology required deliberate appraisal and the manipulation of institutions. Hence, neodemocratic thought concerned itself largely with the exploration of the meaning of the social community and with the place of the individual in the community.

The range of practical possibilities available to Americans was not great. The stability of their institutions and the continuing vitality of the democratic tradition inculcated a matter-of-fact conservatism that discouraged social radicalism. Marxian socialism, for instance, had been of little importance in American thought and even less in politics. The United States had not reproduced the experience of European countries where socialism had emerged out of capitalistic and democratic tendencies during the nineteenth century. It was not likely, therefore, that the United States would turn to socialism in any of its orthodox forms. But it was likely that conditions would dictate the continuing elaboration in a pragmatic spirit of what had come to be called "social controls."

Controls, Formal and Informal

The term *social control* was first used by Edward Alsworth Ross in his book *Social Control,* published in 1901. As a sociologist, Ross was familiar with the assumptions of naturalism, which, however, he rejected in large part. The direction of his thinking was indicated by the question: Given the individualistic, self-centered characteristics of man, how was it that society, which was after all merely a large group of individuals, got its work done? Ross answered the question by pointing out, in the first place, that man also had more sociable characteristics, such as sympathy, a sense of justice, and the power of resentment. Much more important, however, were informal social controls, forces of which until recently men had been largely unconscious. Informal controls included custom and tradition, educational and religious influences, propaganda, public opinion, class attitudes and loyalties, and the influences emanating from group participation of all kinds. Informal controls were exercised largely through persuasion or by means of the processes of socialization, although in some of its forms coercive pressure of considerable intensity might admittedly be exerted. Finally, there were formal social controls implemented by law, either statutory or judicial, and promulgated by agencies designed for that purpose, with coercive powers in the form of penalties for noncompliance.

Ross was concerned primarily with the informal type of social control. These were the most pervasive forces in the community. Simpler societies were governed almost completely by them. But even in a complex industrial community most of the disciplinary force was exerted through informal controls. In calling to men's attention the pervasive character of these controls, Ross was indicating one of the most striking features of modern Western civilization. Out of awareness of the scope and nature of informal controls came the possibility of exercising management through deliberate manipulation. The distinctive feature of the group of students of social control following Ross was their conviction that, if informal controls satisfied social needs effectively, this would be the best possible state of affairs.

Ross's exploration of the psychological nature of informal control suggested rather more complacent conclusions than might occur to a later generation more experienced in the practical arts of propaganda and indoctrination. He was concerned to show how an original informal restraint gradually achieved voluntary acceptance. Men check or stimulate one another in ways they would be reluctant to apply to themselves. They approve a new form of control because it restrains other people. But by a gradual process that might be called social magic, the control first imposed by force comes to be accepted as just, egoism thus being transformed into altruism. Personal conscience as formed in this process is merely a reflection of crystallized public opinion.

Ross had been concerned with the whole range of social control, but among his followers interest centered chiefly on the regulation of economic activity. John Maurice Clark, an economist of Columbia University, published *Social Control of Business* in 1926, a book which passed through many printings and was widely studied in subsequent decades. Clark built upon the foundations that Ross had laid. He held that formal social controls rested on the vast body of informal controls and could be enforced only with their support. No matter how extensive the formal controls might be, it remained a fact that "most of the controls in business must always be moral in character." Wherever informal controls failed to provide for some public need, formal control would have to be exercised, usually by means of legislation. Whatever may have been their preference for informal ones, students of economic control were inevitably concerned largely with legislative and administrative controls. They retained the characteristic conviction, however, that formal controls should be limited to those essential to achieving the social goals set by the community. The practical significance of their distinction between formal and informal control lay in its fresh approach to problems that had previously been discussed in terms of *laissez faire* and public regulation.

In his review of the history of the Industrial Revolution, Clark was at pains to show that, at each stage of its development since the eighteenth century, society had imposed appropriate formal controls. In the late eighteenth century, the theory of *laissez faire* had been elaborated to justify the attack upon the mercantilist restraints upon economic activity. But this did not mean that when laissez-faire capitalism emerged triumphant it did not develop its own form of controls, chiefly for the purpose of regulating and protecting the practices of economic individualism. Among such devices Clark specified measures for military defense, for protection of person, property, and health, for public revenue, for the control of inheritances and bequests, and for the regulation of the appropriation of goods not yet private property.

More recently, the consolidation of the factory system under the auspices of the corporation meant that large-scale enterprise was no longer private in the traditional sense. Nor did big business any longer behave according to the theories of *laissez faire*. Accordingly, at the opening of the twentieth century, the community began to impose further controls as practice appeared to warrant them. Among them were regulation of railroad and utility rates; irrigation, reclamation, and flood control; regulation of communications; air transport regulation; antitrust legislation; banking and exchange regulation; Social Security insurance; minimum wage and collective bargaining provisions; pure food, drug, and marketing laws; and local zoning and planning regulations. Most of these controls originated in the Progressive movement at the beginning of the century. They reflected the desire to fortify and strengthen the individual in his right of access to the traditional economic opportunities. In a sense, the protection of rights involved the curtailment of liberties. In any event, its solicitude for the economic rights of the individual put the Progressive movement in the neodemocratic tradition. The New Deal, as Clark understood it, belonged in the same tradition. Its policies indicated the unwillingness of Americans to accept the full consequences of the business cycle. Most of its measures were concerned with efforts to influence the level of economic activity and to alleviate the human distress resulting from the Depression.

In accordance with this interpretation of recent American history and with his understanding of the social values that it revealed, Clark propounded a theory of control appropriate to American circumstances. The ultimate end to which control of economic activity should be directed was the refinement and extension of the institutions of social and economic democracy. This was taken to mean political self-government, equality of economic opportunity, the absence of special privileges, and the reward of merit. It also implied leisure, security, a decent minimum standard of living, and opportunities for individual self-development. The criteria by which controls should be appraised reflected the conviction that informal controls were preferable to the formal type. Coercion should be economized, and intelligent use made of incentives and motives. Controls should be flexible and adaptable, awake both to experience and experiment. The agencies for the exercise of business regulation should be those centers of power most intimately involved in business operations. These included employer organizations, labor unions, cooperatives of all kinds, even professional associations. Clark insisted that the state was at best a clumsy instrument for the exercise of control, the use of which should be avoided so far as possible. He could hardly deny, however, the nature of the American economy being what it was, that further extension of political controls was almost inevitable.

Should these controls be implemented in the spirit indicated by Clark, the result would hardly be the dictatorship loudly prophesied in certain quarters. No one could deny, however, that a further extension of political controls would certainly underscore the growing importance of the public administrator. The tremendous development of administrative functions of government in the twentieth century was paralleled by an increasing interest in the formal training of administrative personnel. By the middle of the century, most universities had instituted courses in public administration, and a vast literature on the subject had appeared.

Dwight Waldo made a study of this material in order to discover the social values and political outlook of those who both in practice and by their writings were determining the intellectual atmosphere in which future public administrators were receiving their training. The study revealed that public administrators were fully committed to the democratic ideology and to representative political institutions. They approved of the subordination of administration to legislative direction and control. Their zeal for efficient public administration stemmed in part from scientific management in industry and in part from the good-government spirit of Progressivism. The venerable principle of separation of powers nevertheless presented a dilemma that the administrative mind could solve only at the expense of the legislative power. Administrative efficiency presupposed unified administrative authority, with concentration of adequate powers in an executive officer. Inevitably, therefore, the literature of administration tended to emphasize the extension of executive powers and the subordination of legislative freedom to continuity of policy, budgetary limitations, and executive initiative. A practical embodiment of these ideas had already appeared in the city-manager and commission forms of local government.

Democratic Planning

Discussions of planning in the United States inevitably provoked two fundamental questions. The first was economic in character: Was planning compatible with the nature of the economy? Would it not destroy whatever vitality was left in the system of free enterprise? Theoretically, over-all social planning did appear to be incompatible with classical laissez-faire capitalism. But the American economy of the second third of the twentieth century could scarcely have been regarded as a good specimen of traditional capitalism. Its distinguishing characteristic was corporate enterprise, which had largely supplemented but not entirely replaced individual enterprise. The extent to which economic planning within the corporate structure itself rather than market activity had come to control the policies of large corporations was dramatically revealed in the Depression of the 1930's, when to the surprise of many observers these corporations failed to respond to the decline of business activity in the way in which they were expected to react, according to the prescription of the traditional economic theory. The conditions of quasi-monopoly or oligopoly that had come to prevail in the more highly industrialized branches of productive enterprise manifested themselves in imperfect competition and price rigidity. These circumstances resulted in a depression pattern that departed from expectations based on traditional concepts; but they were of interest in the present context as evidence of the extent to which industrial policies had come to reflect planned considerations stemming largely from fixed commitments rather than from the state of the market. As a result, a major lesson of the Depression was the realization that the character of the economy was changing so rapidly that many of the generalizations founded on traditional concepts were no longer relevant.

There was, of course, in the business community a deep rooted antipathy to the idea of bureaucratic social planning by public servants. Nevertheless, widespread public interest in the problems of planning in the United States was a direct product of the Depression; and here, curiously enough, it was the businessmen who took the lead. Such organizations as the Chamber of Commerce of the United States and the National Association of Manufacturers were prominent among those who came forward with proposals of measures to combat the Depression. Many of these proposals advocated industry-wide planning, especially with reference to the allocation of raw materials and the regulation of marketing practices within the industries in question. The object in most cases was to raise prices by reducing the rigors of competition.

Social radicals at that time generally shared with businessmen the conviction that economic and social planning was incompatible with existing political and economic institutions in the United States. Marxian socialists interpreted fascism in its various forms as the extreme development of capitalism, and they were highly successful in propagating this dubious generalization among many liberals as well as radicals. Professor Sidney Hook, an influential independent Marxist, declared that wherever the capitalist form of economy was retained and planning was imposed upon it (by the state, presumably), fascism would be the result. Thus it appeared that neither industrialists nor socialists believed that there could be comprehensive public planning under the existing American system.

The second fundamental question was political in character. Was social planning possible in a democracy in which the majority will was free to express itself on policy and personnel in frequent elections, and in which the political power of organized pressure groups was admittedly very great? These problems did not embarrass planners in totalitarian countries. In the Soviet Union, for example, the theory and practice of democratic centralism that provided for mass political participation was deliberately arranged not to jeopardize the continuity of policy and control which was essential to the rigid, long-range planning that characterized Soviet development. Clearly, a practicable theory of planning in the United States must take cognizance of the distinctive economic and political features of American society. It must be so framed as to recommend itself to the business community as compatible with its welfare, and it must be sufficiently flexible to adjust to changes of political opinion.

Cognizant of these limitations, a somewhat vague but nonetheless distinctive school of thought concerned with planning in a democracy emerged under the auspices of the New Deal. Partly a product of the Depression, these planners nevertheless believed that the Depression itself was a manifestation of a growing and therefore fundamentally sound economy. Planning as a means of mitigating the fluctuations of the business cycle seemed to be a pertinent function in a dynamic economy. Prevailing political attitudes and institutions dictated, however, a negative rather than positive approach. Planning should be regulatory rather than initiatory in its means; it should offer inducements rather than attempt to coerce. It should be educational and therefore long range rather than immediately political in its methods. But before taking up the thought of the New Deal planners in more detail, it would be appropriate to consider the resources of American historical experience upon which the planners might draw.

To most Americans, the term *planning* conveyed the idea of more or less precise predetermination of the details of future action. It had not occurred to many of them that, by any standard, the most successful planning would be that which achieved the desired result with a minimum of detailed regulation. Perfectly executed planning would consist in planting in men's minds an idea that would prompt them of their own volition to seek the desired goal according to plan. The Puritan deity was the perfect planner, so to speak, when He so made men that they thought they were acting of their own free wills when in fact their conduct had been determined from the beginning. In terms of such an approach, one might search American experience for those decisive events or policies from which had flowed a train of consequences of positive effect in shaping the development of American society.

One of the earliest and most influential of these episodes was the adoption of the land-use policy set forth in the Northwest Ordinances of 1784–1787. Here was one of the most far-reaching acts of social and economic planning in modern history, in that the acts specified a pattern of land-use distribution calculated to create and perpetuate a society of freehold farmers. These principles were reaffirmed in a long series of subsequent legislative acts, and, in spite of many imperfections and concessions to special interests, their effectiveness could be measured by contrasting agricultural development with the unplanned exploitation of American mineral resources during the same period.

Of equal importance was the tradition of a balanced national economy, which necessarily involved the notion of planning. Alexander Hamilton's famous report on manufactures set forth the original conception of a balanced economy of industry, agriculture, and commerce, the balance to be achieved by tariff, banking, and currency legislation. As an aspect of economic nationalism the idea of a balanced economy, maintained if necessary by planned policies, was to be a perennial element in American history. The New Deal re-

458 / THE NEODEMOCRATIC MIND

covery program had also as its goal the maintenance of a balanced economy. Several types of economic manipulation were used, more or less successfully, to bring agriculture and industry into "parity" with each other at suitable levels of economic activity. Agricultural prices were to be restored to the level of 1909, while industrial prices were to reach the level of 1925. Whatever the measure of success achieved, it was undeniable that here for several years large-scale measures of public economic planning were in effect.

Another type of planning of increasing importance was connected with the utilization of natural resources. Beginning at the middle of the nineteenth century, Americans undertook the first scientific surveys of their physical resources in land, minerals, timber, and water. At the federal level, several independently authorized surveys were consolidated into the United States Geological Survey in 1879. The second director was Major John Wesley Powell, who laid the foundation for a scientific approach to the study of resources utilization and conservation. Powell had drawn national attention by his exploration of the canyons of the Colorado in 1869. In the course of his travels in the West, he had ample opportunity to ponder the meaning of the increasing aridity west of the 100th meridian of longitude. He was perhaps the first American to understand the connection between erosion and waterway control on a continental scale. By contrasting the Missouri basin with that of the Colorado, he was able to isolate many of the factors that made each a distinctive physiographic unit. Millions of people lived in the Missouri Basin, their lives subtly linked by its physiographic processes, of which they were largely oblivious except in times of flood. The arid Colorado Basin, on the other hand, was virtually empty, but its sheer potentialities fired Powell's imagination. By devising policies appropriate to its conditions, men could make the Colorado also support a flourishing civilization. Thus Powell developed the idea of multipurpose river-basin control for the planned utilization of the water, agricultural, grazing, timber, and mineral resources of the region.

A chief disciple of Powell was W J McGee, a self-trained geologist and ethnologist from Iowa, who joined the Geological Survey in 1882 and became Acting Chief of its Bureau of Ethnology ten years later. To Powell's interest in the conservation of natural resources, McGee added the conservation of human resources. Under the relatively simple conditions prevailing in primitive societies, he believed, one could study many of the problems that in more complex forms baffle modern civilization. Using the Indian cultures of the Southwest as the source of his data, McGee proposed to make the Bureau of Ethnology a kind of social-science laboratory for the development of techniques to implement social planning and control.

Through his contact with Gifford Pinchot, McGee was instrumental in interesting Theodore Roosevelt in conservation. He drafted a plan in 1907 for the creation of the Inland Waterways Commission, which was the first national agency to be charged with the consideration of resources utilization as a unified problem. McGee also organized the Conference of Governors held at the White House in 1908, out of which came the National Conservation Commission. Pinchot described him as "the scientific brains of the conservation movement." As an editor of the *National Geographic Magazine*, McGee made it an influential factor in mobilizing public opinion in support of conservation.

"The greatest good for the greatest number for the longest time" was McGee's motto. His philosophy of democratic social planning rested on an anthropological theory of social evolution. Governmental functions had emerged out of the primitive family, passing successively through administrative, legislative, and judicative phases before entering the present executive phase. The next succeeding phase now beginning to emerge McGee termed the determinative phase. In it, the people themselves were to exercise power directly rather than through designated representatives. It would witness the full realization of the democratic ideal. McGee displayed the characteristic contempt of the scientist for politics and politicians. Under direct democracy there would be no place for either. These views placed McGee at the ideological center of the Progressive movement with its faith in the procedures of initiative, referendum, and recall. An inevitable consequence of the emphasis on direct democracy was a more intensive cultivation of public opinion. In the interests of river-basin control, McGee was active in promoting the organization of pressure groups, such as the Rivers and Harbors Congress, and the Lakes-to-Gulf Deep Waterway Association. He also wrote popular articles for magazines. Pioneers in resources planning like McGee found nothing inappropriate in developing a program of planning in a democratic society. They were persuaded that disinterested experts could bring the people to share a common understanding of their own best interests.

Problems somewhat similar to those presented by the effort to utilize the resources of a physiographic region arose in metropolitan areas of great population density. By 1934, more than seven hundred city and some eighty-five county or regional planning boards had been established. Most of these boards were of an advisory, non-political nature, concerned with the evaluation of transportation systems, land use, and public-works projects. But they sometimes possessed far-reaching authority through the formulation and over-sight of zoning regulations and other forms of building restrictions. City dwellers knew how decisively regulations of this sort could achieve a planned result in a rapidly expanding industrial environment.

A federal agency originally called the National Planning Board was created in 1933. It was President Franklin D. Roosevelt's desire to establish a central planning board as a regular function of the federal government. Its dominant figure was Frederick A. Delano, an uncle of the President. The political status of the Board always remained precarious, because it had little money to spend and few friends outside the inner New Deal circle. After several reorganizations with changes of title, it was finally killed by the Senate in 1943, ostensibly for reasons of economy. The Board was purely advisory. It was to make studies of the character and utilization of the resources of the community, including the land and its products, the population, industrial potentials, and the need and feasibility of various kinds of public works. It was also to make statistical studies of economic and demographic trends. At that time, the wide divergencies in the best-informed estimates of current unemployment was a dramatic illustration of the inadequacy of statistical information on a most important subject. Finally, the Board was also to serve as a clearinghouse for the coordination of the planning activities of various governmental agencies.

In its first annual report, issued in 1934, the Board set forth a philosophy of democratic planning appropriate to the character of the American government and economy. It placed great emphasis on the flexible, pragmatic character of planning as a day-to-day process of research and adaptation. "Planning does not involve the preparation of a comprehensive blueprint of human activity to be clamped down like a steel frame on the soft flesh of the community by the United States government or by any government." Moreover, planning preferably should be undertaken on a local scale, where it would adapt itself to local conditions with maximum effectiveness. It was not held desirable to centralize planning in Washington. Finally, sound planning should acknowledge as its objective the release of opportunity rather than the regimentation of activity.

Wherever restraint might be deemed necessary, it should be used with caution. Rather than embrace all the activities involved, the control should be placed at a strategic point where its influence would permeate the system and accomplish the desired result, much as a traffic light at a busy intersection regulates the flow of traffic in the region. The essence of successful planning was said to consist in the capacity to detect these strategic points as tensions developed about them, and to devise effective means of regulation. The ultimate values in terms of which planners should frame their recommendations were those to be found in the Preamble to the Constitution, where the ends of government were stated to be justice, defense, liberty, and the general welfare. It was assumed that these were mass values, pertaining to the whole people rather than to any privileged class.

In spite of the planners' assertion that planning should preferably be carried on at the local level, when they came to list the means available for the implementation of planned policies, it was apparent that most of these were devices available only to state and federal governments. Among the instrumentalities by which governments might foster planned objectives, the Board listed the following forms of governmental activity, all well known to American practice: (1) government purchases from firms cooperating with its policies; (2) taxation and tariff manipulation; (3) public-works programs and relief benefits; (4) commodity price supports, or crop reduction payments; (5) judicious use of the yardstick technique of government competition, as in power production; (6) various forms of direct assistance to private enterprise, as in RFC-type loans to business or as in the operation of the United States Employment Service. In these devices the federal government at least possessed ample power and a variety of means with which to induce the community to participate in its programs.

The widespread fear of economic depression following World War II led to the creation in 1946 of the Council of Economic Advisers, to which certain of the functions of the old National Planning Board were assigned. The Council was charged particularly with the study of economic trends, and with the recommendation of fiscal policies appropriate to changing economic circumstances. Perhaps because of its eminently practical and apparently more limited objective, the Council did not arouse the hostility that the National Planning Board had encountered, and it managed to survive several changes of party administration.

In the long run, the war experience itself might well come to have a prime influence on the theory of control and planning. Over-all military and civilian objectives were formulated, in terms of which the material and manpower resources of the nation were allocated by administrative authority. Wage and price controls were imposed. Yet, in spite of the enormous waste and destruction of warfare, an amazingly high level of civilian prosperity was maintained. In the light of this experience, J. M. Clark's dictum that the state was a clumsy instrument of control might well require re-examination. The Depression and the war that followed produced a number of thinkers, many of them with practical administrative experience in war and peace, who were reconciled to the use of the state as an instrument of control and planning. They had found that when emergencies necessitated the imposition of controls by the state upon the free enterprise economy, the result, far from being destructive, was a level of employment approaching the maximum and a marked improvement in the standard of living of the lower income groups. In view of these accomplishments, it seemed likely that the state was destined to play an increasingly active role as an agency of planning and control.

CHAPTER 26

Liberty and Loyalty

T HE IDEAL OF CIVIL LIBERTY has been one of the most cherished American traditions since the eighteenth century. In spite of recurrent tensions of national life that jeopardize their exercise, civil liberties have found powerful support in the courts of law and in the convictions of many thoughtful citizens through successive generations. At the same time, the connotations of the term itself, and the kinds of situation to which it has been thought to be relevant, have passed through a distinct historical evolution. This course of development has been charted by the development of the democratic ideology itself. In no other area can more persuasive evidence be found of the continuing vitality of the democratic ideals in the twentieth century.

The Evolution of Civil Liberty

The revolutionary struggle for independence culminating in the drafting of state and federal constitutions furnished the context in which the American people first faced the problem of providing for the protection of civil liberties. Enlightened leaders of opinion in America were well aware of the strength of the tradition of individual liberty in British society. Their first impulse was to contend for the traditional rights of Englishmen against a regime that appeared to betray those rights. After independence had been won, the heritage of bitterness and suspicion bequeathed by the internal conflicts that accompanied the struggle expressed itself in the widespread fear that the newly established American governments might exercise the same arbitrary powers that the imperial government had employed, and thus destroy the principal advantage of independence. It was this fear that led to the appending of ten amendments to the federal Constitution, the so-called "Bill of Rights." These amendments guaranteed to individual citizens the enjoyment of specified civil liberties, notably freedom of religion, speech, press and assembly, the right to bear arms, and to a jury trial, and freedom from unreasonable search and seizure.

The civil liberties specified in the federal Bill of Rights were intended explicitly to serve as a guarantee against possible infringement of rights by the federal government. Similar civil-rights statutes were enacted by several states. The notable feature of all these enactments lay in the implicit assumption that the prime threat to civil liberty was to be found in the potential exercise of arbitrary power by government. Whatever validity such an assumption may have had did not derive solely from the revolutionary struggle through which the American people had just passed. It was also an inevitable product of the assumptions of republican political theory.

Enlightened political theory and practice made an implicit distinction between the natural rights that all men were held to enjoy and the organization of political society in which active participation was restricted to a specially qualified class of citizens, the property holders. This distinction was a fundamental one in republican social and political philosophy. The law was held to be universal in scope and uniform in its application—"all men are equal before the law." But statute law at least was not the product of a political society in which all men were qualified to participate. Given this discrepancy between the scope of the law and its source, between universal natural rights and the inevitable discriminations of statutes, the defenses of individual liberties were inevitably erected against the possibility of encroachment by governmental authority. Experience and theory thus combined to make plausible the assumption that the principal threat to liberty was to be found in government.

During the era of individualistic democracy prior to the Civil War, the distinction between universal natural rights and restricted political privileges was obliterated for white Americans. The foundation of government was broadened to permit the participation of all free men. Men no longer were conscious of the earlier need for protection from government; after all, they controlled the government. It was a confused period, with tendencies working in opposed directions. The chief threats to civil liberty were private or spontaneous. There was occasional mob action, unrestrained by complacent or sympathetic authorities, against unpopular minorities, whether Catholic, Mormon, or Masonic. In spite of the growth of democracy, there was less concern for civil liberty under pristine democratic conditions than there had been earlier. Prevailing conceptions of the federal nature of the Union were such that the federal government did not concern itself with protecting the liberties of citizens of states. Thus Chief Justice John Marshall observed in 1833 that the Bill of Rights was not applicable to states, but only to the federal government.

At the same time, however, the democratic era was also the age of humanitarian reform movements. Animated by the democratic idealism, the reform sentiment culminated in the abolition of slavery and in the adoption of the Thirteenth, Fourteenth, and Fifteenth Amendments to the federal Constitution, which freed the slaves and guaranteed civil and political rights to freedmen. It was an age in which there was relatively little concern for protecting the rights of citizens from each other; yet an age so committed to the ideal of liberty in the abstract that it created a whole new class of citizens from former slaves. Had the generation of the emancipators been more realistic and less doctrinaire they would have paid more attention to civil liberties. They would have realized that freedom from bondage without the guarantee of other basic civil liberties might indeed represent progress but left much to be desired.

Only in the second quarter of the twentieth century did Americans become concerned in a conscious and deliberate way with the problems of civil liberties. When they did so it was in the spirit of governmental paternalism. The prevailing assumption was that civil liberties are jeopardized not by malevolent government but by mass emotions, and by the selfish interests of individuals or groups expressed directly or through governmental agencies wherever the latter could be manipulated for the purpose. The historical situation was completely reversed when the federal government finally emerged as the prime guardian of the civil liberties of citizens.

The protection of liberties was to become a special function of the federal courts. Prior to the Civil War, although the federal courts refused to protect the liberties of citizens, they were indirectly preparing the way for this function. In the celebrated case of *Marbury* vs. *Madison* (1803), in which the principle of judicial review was asserted, Marshall also declared: "The very essence of civil liberty certainly consists in the right of every individual to claim the protection of the laws, whenever he receives an injury. One of the first duties of government is to afford that protection." Where the Chief Justice referred to government he obviously meant the courts.

The principle of judicial review established the federal courts as the guardian of the Constitution, as opposed to the rival theory of the Jeffersonians, who would reserve constitutional interpretation to the member states of the Union. The victory of judicial review became a fact of great importance when, after the Civil War, the Thirteenth and Fourteenth Constitutional Amendments were added, because these amendments were intended to guarantee the liberties of citizens against infringement by states. According to Section I of the Fourteenth Amendment: "No State shall make or enforce any law which shall abridge the privileges or immunities of citizens of the United States; nor shall any State deprive any person of life, liberty, or property, without due process of law; nor deny to any person within its jurisdiction the equal protection of the laws." For more than half a century following the adoption of this amendment, however, the federal courts generally refused to find in its clauses any sanction for the protection of civil liberties. In vain did attorneys attempt to persuade the judges that the "privileges and immunities" of citizens consisted of the civil liberties specified in the Bill of Rights. It was not until 1931 that the Supreme Court for the first time invalidated a state law on the ground that it deprived a citizen of a liberty guaranteed in the Bill of Rights "without due process of law." Freedom of the press was at issue in this historic case.

Subsequent to 1931, the federal courts moved rapidly to extend their protection to all the basic rights of speech, press, assembly, and religion. Within the span of a generation, the principle at least if not the uniform observance of nationalized civil liberties secure from infringement by state action seemed well established. The legislative branch of the federal government also became increasingly sensitive to the issue of civil liberties. From 1936, when a Senate subcommittee held hearings on violations of civil liberties in labor disputes, to 1957, when Congress enacted the first major civil-rights legislation since Reconstruction, this issue remained a staple ingredient of politics. It was noteworthy, on the other hand, that the states for the most part had not kept pace with the federal government. Only eighteen states had enacted civil-rights statutes by 1948, although many types of individual or informal infringement of civil rights were beyond the scope of effective federal purview.

Loyalty

The principle of civil liberty was an appropriate form in which to express the idealization of individualism. In this respect, individualism was more than a term describing a particular form of social behavior. It denoted a normative way of life to which successive generations of Americans more or less explicitly committed themselves. The individualistic ideal thus entered into the definition of the national creed. It helped to give the United States its national personality in terms of which attitudes toward both domestic and foreign issues were shaped. Because loyalty to the nation was evoked in part by the national personality—that is, the democratic ideology with its individualistic ideal—the relationship between personal liberty and national loyalty became a peculiarly sensitive and interesting one.

In times of international tension and conflict, the scene necessarily widened. Americans then were obligated to distinguish between the legitimate freedom of individuals and disloyal intent to overthrow the government or social system. This distinction presented the greatest difficulties precisely for those Americans who were most deeply committed to the ideals of civil liberty.

Virtually all Americans have agreed that liberty does not shelter the individual from acts of treason, sabotage, or espionage as defined by the Constitution or statutes. But, short of these overt acts, was every form of dissent or avowed revolutionary intent to be protected by the cloak of civil liberty? If not, where was the line to be drawn between legitimate right and subversive intent? At one extreme were those who placed civil liberty at the heart of their conception of the democratic ideal. This was the tradition of Jefferson, of Oliver Wendell Holmes, and of William O. Douglas. It might appropriately be called the tradition of liberalism. At the other extreme were those who subordinated civil liberties to patriotic loyalty. Although the precise principles of these loyalists remained elusive, they frequently appeared to be motivated by an ethnic or economic animus. They often confused loyalty with their own programmatic objectives.

The equation of democracy with civil liberty was a central aspect of neodemocratic thought in the twentieth century. In the face of the mounting pressures that made for conformity, the liberals sought in institutionalized civil liberties a bulwark for the protection of individuality. They proposed, in effect, to detach individualism from its traditional economic nexus and to associate it with social values: with freedom to speak and to disseminate information, freedom of assembly, and freedom to implement religious convictions. Modern liberalism thus defined was precipitated by revulsion against the race and class theories of naturalism and as a consequence of the totalitarian denial of individual rights.

The liberal point of view toward the problem of loyalty found an early expression in President Jefferson's Inaugural Address of 1801. The United States had been struggling to confirm its independence and establish its identity in the community of nations during the previous decade when Europe had been convulsed by the French revolutionary wars. The issues of foreign policy were further complicated for Americans by conflicting sympathies and ideological commitments. The Federalist administration of John Adams, moved by a mixture of patriotic and political motives, had enacted the repressive Alien and Sedition laws and had used them to silence outspoken critics of the administration, ostensibly in defense of national security.

In the heated political atmosphere that Jefferson himself characterized as the "revolution of 1800," the newly elected Anti-Federalist President assured his fellow citizens that there would be no reprisals. Even those who favored the dissolution of the Union or the establishment of a monarchy or a dictatorship would be allowed to "stand undisturbed as monuments of the safety with which error of opinion may be tolerated where reason is left free to combat it." Jefferson carefully restricted the issue to freedom of speech; it was "error of opinion" with which he was concerned rather than overt acts. Nevertheless, he revealed the characteristic confidence of the liberals that through unrestricted freedom of speech a consensus would crystallize which the public-spirited citizen might contemplate with complacence.

Jefferson's modern successor was Justice Holmes. Like Jefferson, Holmes relied upon uninhibited freedom of speech as the best if not the only means of forming a viable public opinion. The point at which the collective right of self-protection should take precedence over free speech was defined by Holmes as the point where an utterance "produces or is intended to produce a clear and imminent danger" of some substantive evil to the community. Here was the point where speech was translated into treasonable act. In his famous dissenting opinion in the Abrams case (1919), Holmes again sketched the philosophic outlook in terms of which free speech performed so central a function. He believed that if men would only take a sufficiently detached and comprehensive view of human history, they could not fail to see that the good was best achieved by free trade in ideas, "that the best test of truth is the power of the thought to get itself accepted in the competition of the market," and that men's purposes were worthy of realization only when they could survive such a truth test.

Holmes believed that the Bill of Rights with its safeguards for free speech committed constitutional government in the United States to the experimental philosophy. So long as they remained dedicated to that philosophy, Americans "should be eternally vigilant against the attempt to check the expression of opinions that we loathe and believe to be fraught with death," up to the point where interference was necessary in order to save the country. The experimentalist would not, of course, experiment with giving up experimentalism. Like Dewey, Holmes would turn to the history of constitutional government to demonstrate that mistakes inevitably followed upon the suppression of freedom of speech. Ultimately, however, Holmes's pragmatism was supported by his positivism. It was his faith in emergent reason that sustained the conviction that the truth would emerge triumphant from the test of competition in the marketplace.

A generation later, Holmes's mantle was inherited by Justice William O. Douglas, who attempted to adapt the test to markedly different circumstances. In 1951, the Supreme Court reviewed and upheld the conviction of eleven Communists for conspiring to teach revolutionary doctrine. In his dissenting opinion, Justice Douglas reaffirmed the liberal conviction that free speech was essential to the very existence of democracy. To the list of its virtues he added a valuable therapeutic function. Through the airing of ideas, free speech released pressures that would otherwise become destructive. "When ideas compete in the market for acceptance," declared Douglas, in language reminiscent of his predecessor, "full and free discussion exposes the false and they gain few adherents. Full and free discussion even of ideas we hate encourages the testing of our own prejudices and preconceptions. Full and free discussion keeps a society from becoming stagnant and unprepared for the stresses and strains that work to tear all civilizations apart."

Douglas would have made a somewhat different application of the "immediate danger" test. Rather than fix the test inflexibly at the point where speech became imminent act, Douglas would be guided by the general state of affairs. Whenever times might be critical and public opinion in a tense condition, speech must be acknowledged to possess an inflammatory potency it did not have in normal circumstances. In their application of the immediate-danger test, the courts should take into account the current state of public opinion. In applying the test to the utterances of Communists, the key consideration would be their organizational strength and tactical position. Should these be found to constitute a clear and present danger, the Justice would presumably approve the suppression of Communism. But because the government had not considered such evidence to be germane to the case, Douglas believed that the court did not have the evidence upon which to frame an opinion.

In a concurring opinion in the same case, Justice Robert H. Jackson took a position that probably was widely shared by thoughtful Americans concerned to disentangle freedom of speech from the imperatives of national security. Justice Jackson pointed out that Holmes had propounded the clear-and-present-danger test as a means of dealing with anarchist propaganda. The anarchists in question had printed and scattered a few leaflets attacking the United States government for allegedly attempting to prevent the consummation of the Bolshevik Revolution. The anarchists had been unorganized and without financial or other support. Their act was quite literally an effort at persuasion; and the issue presented was clearly the issue of free speech.

The issue presented by the case of the eleven Communists was, in Justice Jackson's opinion, quite a different one. Communism was a highly disciplined international organization, the principal object of which was the seizure of political power by the most effective means, legal or illegal. The Communists admittedly had no interest in freedom of speech except as it might be used to confuse or weaken their opponents. Jackson reviewed the methods by which the Communist *coup d'état* in Czechoslovakia had recently been accomplished. Building its strength under the shelter of civil liberties, the Communist Party there ruthlessly suppressed all liberty as soon as it seized power. It was apparent to Jackson that, while the clear-and-present-danger test may have been appropriate to the philosophy of anarchism, which advocated the use of violence as a means of over-throwing existing institutions, it fell far short of furnishing adequate protection against the subtle and varied techniques of subversion of which the Communists had demonstrated their mastery.

The Smith Alien Registration Act of 1940 had made it unlawful to advocate the overthrow of the government by force or violence or to form an organization or circulate material designed to attain this end. The eleven Communist leaders were convicted of conspiring to accomplish the purposes forbidden by the act. Justice Jackson believed it to be fully appropriate to deal with Communism as a conspiracy. Prosecutions for conspiracy were well known in American practice. And on none of the occasions when labor unions, trade associations, or news agencies had been subject to such prosecutions had the courts permitted a plea of freedom of speech to serve as a cloak of immunity from prosecution.

Sidney Hook took much the same position as that of Justice Jackson. The object of both men was to define the practicable limits of free speech in the face of the kind of threat that organized international Communism posed for traditional American values and social practices. Both held that only those who were sincerely dedicated to freedom of inquiry as a permanent ideal and method were entitled to the immunity of free speech. No Communist, they believed, could be so dedicated. For the Communists admittedly put loyalty to the party above all else; for confirmation one need only turn to a study of Communist parties in action to be convinced of their opportunism.

Neodemocratic thought substituted the ideology of democracy for the materialistic assumptions of the earlier naturalistic era. In an age of international tension and ideological conflict it was inevitable that Americans should identify their social ideals with the state, thus blending social values with patriotism. But in spite of the paternalistic form in which the modern quest for effective civil liberties expressed itself, the interest in this issue lay close to the heart of the democratic enterprise. Democracy in its earlier forms had been nourished and strengthened by the economic opportunities and the rough measure of social equality that had prevailed in a decentralized and expanding society. It seemed likely to survive in a much more closely knit and interdependent twentieth-century world only if it could be successfully detached from its original social nexus and find in the ideals of civil liberty an animus sufficient to sustain the spirit of democracy.

CHAPTER 27

The Old Left
and The New

URING THE FIRST THREE AND a half centuries of American history the steady growth of the country in size, wealth, power, and opportunity provided relatively poor soil for the growth of radical criticism. The broad generalities of the democratic ideology offered sufficient support for most individuals pursuing rewarding careers. When specific problems were identified efforts might be made to correct them in a practical manner without the felt necessity for a comprehensive restructuring of the social order. Insofar as there was an indigenous radical tradition it reflected the pervasive spirit of individual autonomy in a type of anarchism that glorified the free individual. Henry Thoreau and Benjamin R. Tucker represented this tradition during the nineteenth century. At the same time, a reaction against excessive individualism took the form of communitarianism, in which those who felt the need of mutual support drew together in a closely-knit communal order.

The Old Left

The period of the Old Left, approximately the first half of the twentieth century, now appears as a kind of political interlude closely related to the last generation of massive European immigrants. For it was immigrants who brought Marxian socialism to America, and whose children and grandchildren failed to perpetuate it.

Karl Marx derived from the philosopher Hegel the idea that the historical process is a basic dimension of reality and that this process should be guided towards the realization of ideals of brotherhood, justice, and equality. Marx stated his ethical ideal in the doctrine: "From each according to his ability, to each according to his needs." The possibilities of change were limited by the existing conditions at any moment because change must develop out of these conditions. Marx was a close student of his contemporary society in Western Europe, especially of what he took to be its dominant feature, the institutions of industrial capitalism.

Rejecting the enlightened ideals of rational accommodation, harmony of interests, and individual fulfillment, Marx emphasized a romantic glorification of conflict. All history, he taught, is the history of class struggle. He would foment conflict by setting employee against employer, and wherever it did not exist he would attempt to stimulate it by awakening a sense of class consciousness and teaching people to perceive the conflict of interests of which they had previously been unaware.

Industrialism in Europe had grown up within traditionally class-structured societies. Industrial capitalists (bourgeoisie) readily accommodated themselves to the existing class structure, assuming a privileged position and often intermarrying with aristocrats. At the same time, the new industrial labor (proletariat) had no difficulty in perceiving their lowly status in traditional class terms. Thus although Marx focused on the industrial relationship his analysis was reinforced and made relevant to workingmen by the larger social structure of Europe. In America, where such a social structure did not exist, it proved to be very difficult to inculcate class consciousness in Marxist terms. Perplexed Marxist theoreticians repeatedly asked why there should be no socialism in the United States, one of the most industrialized nations. They could only speculate that American labor was "backward" in lacking a sophisticated sense of its own proletarian status, as a consequence of which it could not appreciate the logic of socialist doctrine. Such an analysis implied that a primary task of American socialists must be educational. But as has been pointed out in Chapter 18 of this book the socialists were more successful in inculcating

Marxist doctrine in intellectual circles than in the ranks of labor. Immigrants who brought to America their sense of class distinctions often found that attractive career opportunities were open here to them or their children, tempting them to put personal goals ahead of class solidarity. Perceptive radical leaders often sadly noted this fact.

Marxist theory affirmed that the industrial mode of production was the determinative social relationship, and that the national state was one of its products. Government was said to be simply a committee of the bourgeoisie. The theory permitted little latitude in decision making by the state, since unless it acted irrationally it must act in the interests of the bourgeoisie. The fact was, however, that during the century between 1850 and 1950 most industrialized states did not behave as though their governments were committees of the bourgeoisie. They pursued policies suggesting an overriding conception of national interest transcending particular class interests. On the basis of his theory Marx could hardly have predicted one of the great facts of the twentieth century, namely that successful socialist revolutions would without exception occur in economically underdeveloped countries. The economic evolution of capitalism did not bring the crisis of class conflict and revolution in highly industrialized countries that Marx had predicted. It did, however, bring revolutions in underdeveloped countries against economic penetration and control by foreign capital. By mobilizing nationalistic sentiment local patriots were able to expropriate foreign investments. They demonstrated that the unifying force of national sentiment was stronger than the divisive force of class antagonism.

Classical Marxism had been founded on the Hegelian dialectic of thesis, antithesis, and synthesis. It assumed the historical resolution of opposites in a series of confrontations and syntheses. The Marxian expectation of revolution was an appropriate version of the dialectical view of history. On the other hand, the prevailing nineteenth- and early twentieth-century view of history, at least in America, was that of linear progress through technological advance, social reform, education, and social planning. The theory of progress assumed a gradual and relatively smooth course of improvement. The so-called revisionist socialists accepted the linear progressive theory. They believed that socialization could be achieved, at least in democratic and parliamentary countries, by legislative means, peacefully, and with legal continuity. They adapted themselves to the existing political process, forming political parties that appealed to a broad spectrum of middle-class voters as well as to laboring men.

The conciliatory tone and outlook of the revisionists was well expressed in the writings of Morris Hillquit (1869-1933), a leading theoretician of the Socialist Party of the United States. In his *Socialism in Theory and Practice* (1909) he addressed himself to the relationship between socialism and reform, indicating how socialists would carry through by legislative means a series of economic, political, and social reforms to their logical fulfillment in a socialized society. Hillquit searched for areas of agreement with non-socialists, and minimized the rigidities of dogma. He flattened out the conflicts of the dialectic and softened the violence of revolutionary rhetoric. Most importantly, he sought to get out of the restricted ethnic circles in which Marxism had first appeared in America in order to propagandize among native Americans. His efforts were characteristic of the main line of Socialist Party leadership from Eugene Debs and Victor Berger to Norman Thomas.

A basic dilemma for orthodox Marxists had always been the problem of "immediate demands." If revolution was to be the outcome of increasing misery among working people would not improvements in wages and working conditions alleviate their misery and thus defer the revolution? On the other hand, if socialists were to refuse to endorse such remedial measures and sit by passively awaiting the collapse, what chance would they have in bidding for labor support against reformist parties demanding immediate improvements in working conditions? The question was equally pressing in terms both of party policy and union tactics. Orthodox Marxists attempted to cope with the problem by integrating reform proposals into their general revolutionary objectives. They would so manage reform agitation as to strengthen the revolutionary movement, win converts, and confuse bourgeois reformers. Reform thus became a tactic to be used in the revolutionary struggle. On the labor front they would attempt to capture existing unions or organize "dual" unions in order to guide their activity toward revolutionary objectives. The consequent subordination of immediate to ultimate objectives often looked like cynicism.

Revisionists, while reaffirming the socialist view that a total transformation of society was necessary, distinguished between reforms that promoted their objective and those that simply bolstered the existing system. Most important to them was the effort to indoctrinate the unions with the socialist philosophy. Hillquit noted that only in England and the United States did union membership exceed the socialist vote—in the United States by a factor of more than five to one; elsewhere in Europe the reverse was the case. It was essential to teach American union members that their object of enhancing their own share of the profit from their labor through higher wages correspondingly decreased the employer's share. In theory, the end result of increasing wages would be "the entire elimination of the capitalist's profits—the socialization of industries." The object of the socialists was to open the eyes of labor to a clear vision of this end result.

One of the principal obstacles to the socialist indoctrination of labor was the leader of the American Federation of Labor, Samuel Gompers (1850-1924). After emigrating to New York in 1863, Gompers had joined the cigar-makers union, of which he rose rapidly to leadership. As a devout Marxist he learned German in order to read Marx's major work, *Das Capital*, then untranslated into English. He chose union organization rather than party activity as the best means of promoting the socialist cause, his militant leadership resulting in his being blacklisted and locked out for striking.

The secret of Gompers' success as a union organizer was to confine his efforts to skilled crafts where disciplined locals with trained leaders and strike funds could for the first time in American labor history exert effective pressure on employers. As these techniques were gradually developed Gompers found himself increasingly at odds with the socialists, who attempted to capture control of his union. After the organization of the AFL in 1886 he battled continually and successfully to exclude the socialists from control. But for many years to come he continued to use the socialist rhetoric of the class struggle, contrasting the selfish and grasping capitalist with the miserable defenseless worker. His unionism had grown out of the radicalism of his Marxism with its immediate demands. It became increasingly apparent, however, that the survival and success of the unions depended on the successful negotiations of contracts with the employers, and that the socialist critique of capitalism infuriated employers and made negotiation more difficult. It was also important to create the image of the union as a responsible, business-like organization able to stabilize the labor market for the mutual benefit of the contracting parties. Out of these considerations grew what came to be known as "pure and simple" unionism.

Gompers never abandoned the ideal of gaining for labor a progressively larger share of the total wealth of the community, and Hillquit, in a famous Congressional hearing, attempted to draw from him a socialist interpretation of this objective. Did not Gompers foresee the time when labor would receive the full value of the product of its labor, a classic definition of socialism? Gompers replied in pragmatic style that workers preferred to deal with problems of the moment rather than speculate about an ideal future. He now rejected the assertion that his program led logically to socialism. He foresaw rather an indefinite extension of the existing system of industrial employment.

Gompers foresaw more accurately than the socialists what was to come to pass. Labor and management would reach wage agreements at the expense of the consuming public in higher prices. For their part the socialists failed to anticipate the role of a benevolent government in supporting the right of labor to organize and bargain collectively. Nor did the conditions of industrial competition result in the decreasing wages which the socialists anticipated. The higher wages and prices resulting from negotiated settlements simply created inflation which was passed along to consumers and government to manage as best they could.

In the largest sense, the failure of Marxism in the United States was the failure to anticipate the kind of social order that would emerge from a mature industrialism. Instead of a class conscious proletariat there appeared an amorphous mass which lacked precisely those characteristics and attitudes traditionally associated with a working class. The attempt of the socialists to cultivate class consciousness in the mass was notably unsuccessful. Marxism was largely confined to certain ethnic minorities, and as these groups experienced assimilation they generally abandoned their radicalism.

Since in later times it became fashionable in certain New Left circles to speak disparagingly of the Old Left it would be appropriate to note its achievements, which were undoubtedly more considerable than any the New Left would contribute. It has already been noted in an earlier chapter of this book that the lasting impact of the Old Left was upon intellectual life rather than on industrial life. Throughout the twentieth century there has been a succession of writers and scholars who have analyzed American public issues in terms of the conflicting interests of social-economic classes. At the institutional level the Old Left was able to organize itself in a number of political parties. Some of these remained largely ethnic in composition, but others, notably the Socialist Party, succeeded in attracting a broad spectrum of support. Thanks to its willingness to participate in conventional electoral politics the Old Left shared a common bond with the majority. Its newspapers, magazines, clubs, and publishing houses all gave it an institutional durability that permitted it to survive for nearly a century.

The New Left

If the Old Left had been an exotic interlude, a passing phase of the process of assimilation of foreigners into the permanent fabric of American life, the New Left was a spontaneous and indigenous expression of native impulses, "as American as apple pie." The anarchism and communitarianism inherent in American conditions welled up spontaneously in the New Left, some of whose best spokesmen combined these seemingly opposed principles in their criticism and projects. To the extent that the spontaneity of the movement is emphasized it would be superfluous to look for sources or antecedents in earlier events or thinkers, and particularly in the Old Left. One would look rather to contemporaneous circumstances of American life for those features that would explain or illuminate the peculiar characteristics of the New Left as a protest movement.

There was an ironic sense in which the New Left possessed at the outset an advantage that the Old Left never succeeded in achieving—it was a proletarian movement. As early as 1954 the literary critic Richard P. Blackmur pointed out that the only surviving proletariat in America consisted of students, highly educated young people for whom society had no appropriate use. These young people were alienated because they were uprooted. Their education had not, for the most part, prepared them for functions society needed or appreciated, while at the same time its deficiencies left them without adequate internal resources. Blackmur found a comparable situation in many parts of the world, and everywhere it portended explosive consequences.

The term proletariat was of course being used in a very special sense. Far from being impoverished or illiterate the students who were to constitute the New Left came from relatively affluent homes with educated parents. The context of their rebellion was not economic or materialistic in terms that the Old Left would have understood. It was psychological and deeply personal. If the patron saint of the Old Left was Marx with his economic analysis of social ills, the patron saint of the New Left was Freud with his therapeutic treatment of sick personalities. The object of the one was to transform, and the other, to cure both self and society.

It was symptomatic of the spirit of the movement that a distinguished psychiatrist, Kenneth Keniston, should have been closely associated with a working group of young radicals, intimately involved in their activities and eliciting from them revealing insights into their personal motives and behavior. Keniston found that the deep personal commitment of the radicals was a product of their own experience filtered through received moral values rather than the acceptance of a new ideological dogma. Keniston agreed with Peter Blos and Erik Erikson that most American youths of similar backgrounds did not experience the pattern of adolescent crisis characteristic of young Europeans as described by Freud. American youths turned from their families to peer-group cultures and thus minimized the classic Freudian adolescent rebellion against the family. By the same token, they often missed the adolescent phase entirely, with unfortunate consequences for the total maturation process. The young radicals, on the other hand, were found to have had a more traditional kind of family experience, with deep involvement and a consequently sharp struggle for emancipation. In their rebelliousness they found their parents ineffectual and antiquated. The psychiatrist knew of course that in the end these painful experiences would result in stronger adult personalities.

Keniston also found in his young associates an "identity crisis" of an ethical nature, in which prevailing social values were questioned and normal adult roles were rejected. At this point the rebellious adolescent became a radical. But there was still no basic discontinuity with the past. He retained the core values with which he had grown up: honesty, kindness, deference, the need for achievement. There was continuing concern about hostility, aggression, and violence. The very preoccupation with these basic values, however, often led to reconsideration and rejection of prevailing religious beliefs and public policies.

The first impulse of these sensitized young people was to work within the system in order to reform it. Poverty projects in the slums, the Southern civil rights movement, sit-ins, opposition to the Vietnam war, all expressed their sense of concern over the discrepancy between the professed ideals of the community and its actual practice. In his analysis of the psychology of commitment, Silvan

Tomkins has shown how in a society undivided by class barriers those who enjoy a relatively secure status may become involved vicariously in the sufferings of the less fortunate and identify with their grievances. Keniston appropriately noted that many Americans in no way identified with the radicals shared these feelings of guilt and concern while simply lapsing into cynicism and apathy. The widespread feeling of powerlessness with its invitation to indifference was in fact a major feature of twentieth-century American politics.

A central doctrine of the radicals that placed them in the tradition of the Left was their anti-capitalism. Most of the ills of the world, its wars and colonial empires, its exploitation of colored races, its enormous depersonalized institutions, its tendency to bring ever larger areas of life under the control of remote bureaucracies, its sordid commercialism, all were traced to the malign influence of international capitalism. This was not, however, the capitalism of Marx with its immiseration of labor, tottering on the brink of collapse. It was the powerful military-industrial complex of war lords and industrialists whose firm grasp on society was described by the sociologist C. Wright Mills in his book, *The Power Elite* (1956). Far from alienating labor, modern capitalism had succeeded in subverting and capturing organized labor, so that no revolutionary activity could be expected from that quarter. Also from the Old Left came the idea that capitalism culminated in totalitarian suppression of personal and civil liberties. In radical discussions of the evils of the system the word fascism was bandied about lightly.

Although there was general agreement within the New Left that a thorough-going revolution was necessary, the manner of carrying it out was never specified. The Marxist tradition of an organized and disciplined political party providing a vanguard of revolutionary leadership was repugnant to most radicals with their profound aversion to externally imposed discipline. There were, to be sure, within the broad confines of the New Left Leninist, Maoist, Trotskyist, and Castroite factions, but they were neither large nor influential enough to give doctrinal coherence to the movement. Most radicals seem to have accepted the verdict of Mills that parties and legislative bodies were no longer available as agencies for fundamental change. Jerry Rubin remarked that politics is not how you vote, it's how you live your life. While the radicals thus disavowed politics as an instrument of change their aversion to violence foreclosed the other traditional method of implementing change through direct action. There was a sense in which the radicals with their doctrine of total revolution resembled the intramillennial perfectionists of the nineteenth century who inaugurated the Kingdom of Heaven on earth by the simple expedient of taking up a new style of living.

In his "Letter to the New Left" (1960) Mills called upon the intellectuals to furnish revolutionary leadership. Not many of them came forward, perhaps sensing the radicals' widely publicized mistrust of the older generation. Such leadership as scholars like Mills, Marcuse, or William Appleman Williams did provide was strictly literary, and rarely of a public or programmatic character. For their part, the radicals mistrusted all leadership as inconsistent with their ideal of participatory democracy.

It was not surprising that the New Left as a student movement should have focused much of its discontent on the colleges and universities. The intimate relationship between the Vietnam war, compulsory military service, and the ROTC programs seemed to imply complicity in hated public policies. Some of their critics perceived the higher educational institutions to be vital arms of the corporate liberal establishment. The "class structure," the systematic "laying on of culture," and authoritarian dispensation of truth were offensive to students who preferred more permissive learning situations. To many of those who had enrolled without specific technical or professional objectives academic life seemed futile and irrelevant. Most fundamental, however, was the radical rejection of academic objectivity. Modern higher education in America nourished the ideal of the dispassionate search for truth. Such a search, especially in the social sciences, was now declared to be pious hypocrisy masking a compliant acceptance of the status quo. It allegedly fostered a culture of leisured elites. Mills called for a rejection of empirical neutrality in social thought. Let the student candidly proclaim his principles and organize his materials so as to promote their realization. The New Left was in danger of taking flight from actuality into the subjective realm of desire.

One of the most important if elusive aspects of the New Left was its deep preoccupation with immediate shared experience. The impersonality of every-day life, the fragmentation of human relationships under bureaucratic conditions, and the formalities of coat-and-tie etiquette suddenly became profoundly depressing. Direct and open sharing of even the most intimate feelings and experiences were found to be highly rewarding. Shabby, casual clothing, and unkempt hair and beards symbolized the revolt against anonymous business-like conventions. Keniston found that young radicals were deeply concerned about their personal relationships, perhaps because of the conflicts with their parents attendant upon their rebellion. As the gap between generations opened it became more important to establish rewarding relationships with one's peers.

The New Left political principle of participatory democracy reflected in part this preoccupation with the personal encounter. The reconciliation of anarchistic individualism and the communal impulse was to be achieved through participation in the decision making process at all levels, although it was difficult to conceive how it would work beyond the local level. Local autonomy and decentralization were important principles to the New Left. In Carl Oglesby's words, "any decision not made by the people in free association, whatever the content of that decision, cannot be good." The implication was clear, on the other hand, that any decision made by the people in free association could not be bad. All of the chief statements by New Left leaders contained versions of the traditional American democratic ideology, stressing its libertarian, equalitarian, and humanitarian content. Spokesmen were quite conscious of the utopian strain in their thinking, and often referred to it. Their rebellion was against all integrated social structures, against the over-organized and the business-like. They attempted to return to the primitive, simple, earthy modes of earlier times as symbolized in the resurrection of nineteenth-century frontier dress styles.

The sense of being disinherited outsiders was very strong in the young radicals. It was as though the break with their parents had severed their ties with society in general. A new sociology structured in terms of their detached perspective on society was needed since the Marxist proletarian orientation was no longer relevant. An engaging attempt to furnish such a sociology was made by Paul Goodman in his book *Growing Up Absurd* (1956). A novelist and social philosopher, Goodman was also a gestalt therapist whose discussion of social topics showed the preoccupation with personal adjustment typical of the New Left. From the disenchanted perspective of the radical student the enemy was the Organized System, the Establishment, or Rat Race, composed of government, corporations, and labor unions, or in human terms, managers, organization men (hipsters), and wage workers. In scathing terms Goodman denounced the iniquities of the System. It corrupted every aspect of life and denied one's essential humanity. It was no wonder that the young, deprived of the stimulus and challenge of a humane and civilized order, should grow up absurd.

Two options were available to those repelled by the System. They could join the Beats or the Independents. The Beat Generation consisted of those who had dropped out of the System because of its falseness and who had chosen poverty as a style of life in preference to the mindless huckstering of the Organization Men. To the Beat, work was no different from shoplifting, or "ripping off," as it was euphemistically called. The Independents, on the other hand, were a widely heterogeneous group including old-fashioned people, eccentrics, criminals, gifted and serious people, rentiers, freelancers, infants,—and, of course, Goodman himself. The Independents had little in common besides their aversion to the System. Radical students would no doubt have been assigned to the Independent category.

In the absence of an adequate theory of social change the New Left was tempted to attach too much importance to the issues of the moment, risking the chance of being left behind by passing events. One such issue was the problem of abundance. Everyone seems to have assumed that abundance was here to stay. Many radicals shared Goodman's sense of outrage at the crass mercenary values, the mindless pouring out of goods, the waste and gadgetry of industrial mass production. On the other hand, the communitarian anarchist Murray Bookchin welcomed abundance as the agent to free men from the psychology of scarcity. The grinding, self-denying work ethic of the preindustrial era had finally resulted in the technology of abundance. Now that the problem of scarcity had been solved the old ethic was outmoded, to be replaced by a new ethic of joyous, carefree, sensuous living. Bookchin left unclear what effect the new ethic would have on the continuation of abundance. Would goods and services continue to pour forth in automated plenty while humanity lounged on flowery beds of ease? Or would the knowledge that scarcity had once been banished be sufficient to reconcile radicals to more modest expectations? Bookchin's own vision of decentralized and ecologically balanced communes suggested the return to a more austere if doubtless healthier standard of living. But when the long period of prosperity during which the New Left flourished should finally come to an end the preoccupation with abundance would doubtless acquire a dated flavor.

After 1970 the New Left disintegrated as quickly as it had formed.

The coincidental withdrawal of American forces from Vietnam and the ending of compulsory military service seemed to lend credence to the view that the radicals had tied their cause too closely to the flux of public events. But the underlying circumstances of American life had not changed, and Kenneth Keniston analyzed the demise of radicalism in terms consistent with his earlier account of its emergence. He noted especially the shattering realization of many radicals that they had violated one of their most cherished principles in using or flirting with violence. Deaths by bombing, however unintended, brought the sobering realization that fellow-radicals were pursuing a course which could not be condoned. The tranquility that now settled on the campuses suggested to the psychiatrist the analogy of the neurotic patient who refuses to face his problem and prefers to live with his neurosis. The young radicals were tempted to give up the effort to change society and to retreat into a private world of communes or of mystical oriental contemplation. The psychiatrist could only offer the wholesome advice to eschew any feelings of exclusive self-righteousness and to continue to work for a more humane social order with all of the dedication and hard work of the older professionalism.

CHAPTER 28

||||||||||||||||||||||||||||||||||||||||||||||||||||||||||||||||||||||||||||||||||||

Ethnic Pluralism: The Experience of American Jews and Blacks

N O MODERN NATION POSSESSES a population more richly varied in ethnic composition than the United States. If racial or ethnic distinctions within the human species arose originally through tribal isolation and intramarriage, American life now represents the potential and actual mixing of races, the ethnic and cultural consequences of which remain unpredictable. It has often been said that the historic significance of America lies in its experiment with democracy. No less significant is its attempt to fashion a viable multi-ethnic society.

Like other colonial nations, the United States recruited its population from a variety of foreign sources; while unlike many of them, it virtually decimated its indigenous native Indian population. Whether the modern American was descended from "settlers" or "immigrants" was simply a matter of priority in time; while decent from slaves or Indians remained, of course, a serious handicap. In any event, the circumstances of the recruitment of American population made inevitable a kind of ethnic struggle for existence. By virtue of prior settlement and early numerical superiority the Anglo-Americans survived as the fittest, and imposed upon the new society their own intellectual and cultural standards.

For the first three centuries of American history—until about 1920—intellectual life was dominated by Americans of English extraction. Then quite suddenly Jewish-Americans rose to prominence in literary, scholarly, artistic, and professional fields. The critic Walter Kerr observed that "the American sensibility itself has become in part Jewish, perhaps nearly as much Jewish as anything else." More recently still, Negroes have begun to play an active role in intellectual life, and it is not inconceivable that black Americans may in the near future be as conspicuous in high cultural activity as the Jews are today. The changing ethnic bases of intellectual life invite attention to aspects of intellectual history that are often ignored.

Ethnocracy

The early dominance of Anglo-Americans in intellectual as well as political and social life resulted in a traditional form of ethnocracy, defined as a nation dominated by a particular ethnic group. Most of the nations of Western Europe were ethnocracies of this type, in which a dominant race held sway over various ethnic minorities. It was probably inevitable that a theory of racial nationalism should have appeared, in which nations themselves were considered to be the appropriate creative expressions of the abler and more aggressive races. In the earlier chapter on racism we have already seen how spokesmen for Anglo-American culture at the end of the nineteenth century adapted this view to American circumstances.

Theories developed to rationalize and justify the imposition of national policies on ethnic minorities could also be appropriated by the minorities and turned against their masters. An important aspect of nineteenth-century liberal nationalism consisted of nationalistic movements of liberation by such subject peoples as Irish, Czechs, Belgians, Norwegians, and others whose awakening sense of racial-national identity expressed itself in cultural as well as political forms. Along with revolutionary movements for political independence went cultural revivals in which the spontaneous traditions of folk culture were reworked by creative artists in the internationally recognized high cultural forms of fiction, drama, verse, and music. The ethnic-nationalistic implications of these creative activities were widely recognized, and many a creative artist suddenly found himself a national hero. The patterns of ethnic struggle within

European nations are helpful in identifying parallel developments in America.

Given the circumstances under which the American national union was formed, together with the continuing immigration of new-comers of varied ethnic backgrounds and without deep attachments to the country, the bonds of union long remained precarious, and divisive forces were to be deplored. The idea of assimilation which became the dominant American expectation of its ethnic groups was the inevitable response of a restless and uneasy people seeking national identity and solidarity. The idea of assimilation presupposed that ethnic minorities should conform to the social and cultural norms of the dominant Anglo-Americans. The speed and effective-ness with which a given ethnic group could achieve assimilation largely determined the merit of that group in the eyes of the majority. The "races" most closely allied historically to the English, namely, the Scotch, Irish, Germans, French, and Scandinavians, generally achieved assimilation most rapidly, and were regarded therefore as the most desirable additions to the American popula-tion. The word assimilation as used in this sense should be care-fully distinguished from amalgamation or race mixing in which the elements contributed by each group were to be blended in a new composite form. One should also note that these processes might occur in either the social and cultural or biological realms, or both.

The assumptions of intellectuals as well as popular opinions on ethnic relationships were profoundly affected by the progressive evo-lutionary theories that underlay late nineteenth-century ethnic na-tionalism in Europe and America. The economic and military su-premacy of the European nations was explained and justified by theories of historical development which conceived of the powerful nation-state as the fitting fulfillment of a long evolutionary sequence of events. It was a rare scholar who could so far dissociate himself from the obvious trend of modern history as to suggest that the present supremacy of the West European races might be but a brief and passing moment in history. The ideas of the Chicago sociologist Robert Ezra Park (1864–1944) furnish an excellent illustration of the pervasive influence of racial-national thinking in evolutionary terms.

Park was one of the most influential of the early sociological theorists in America. At the University of Chicago in the second and third decades of the twentieth century he helped to organize the so-called Chicago school of sociology, in which a group of students and disciples pursued many of the teacher's insights in a wide range of specialized investigations. Park himself had begun life as a newspaperman and had acquired a reporter's knowledge of several of America's largest cities before turning to academic life. After graduate work in philosophy at Harvard he went to Germany for a doctorate in sociology, writing a dissertation at Heidelberg on mass theory. For seven years Park was associated with Booker T. Washington at Tuskeegee Institute in Alabama, remarking in later years that he had learned more about the realities of human society at Tuskeegee than he had previously found in books. At the University of Chicago he trained a number of distinguished students of both races, including E. Franklin Frazier, Charles S. Johnson, Louis Wirth, and Edward B. Reuter.

His German training at the turn of the century exposed Park to the strong social evolutionary emphasis that William Graham Sumner had encountered there a generation earlier. Social life was understood in terms of a dynamic process of interaction in which change was the only constant. The basic forms of interaction were competition, conflict, accommodation, and assimilation. Civilization itself was believed to be the consequence of the contacts between migrating tribes in which the interaction processes, in spite of the confusion, conflict, and suffering that ensued, resulted in progressive development. This "catastrophic theory of progress" found the origins of modern national peoples in the hybrid races of western Europe. Out of the clash of wandering tribes came stabilized patterns of organization imposed by conquerors within which social structures mutually beneficial to both conquerors and subject peoples emerged. Isolation and a consequent condition of peaceableness, on the other hand, bred cultural stagnation. Harsh though it might seem to modern sensibilities, war came "as a saving angel" to invigorate and launch an era of progress.

Park found that in the modern era, migration was characterized not by the warlike clash of wandering tribes but by the peaceful migration of individuals. The constructive consequences remained the same. The repetitive routines of institutionalized behavior were disrupted, and out of the collective responses to feelings of unrest new and potentially fruitful adjustments emerged. The effect of this process on individuals was intellectual and psychological emancipation. A sense of individuality replaced the older feeling of folk solidarity. Park was wholly persuaded of the progressive implications of this process. He contrasted the earlier pattern of "culture" which bound sedentary rural peoples in a tight web of institutions, with the more recent "civilization," which concentrated people in cities and emancipated them. The urban dweller was the epitome of the modern civilized man—literate, rationalistic, humane and cosmopolitan. Park had high hopes for the future of American civilization, no matter how painful at times the accommodation to novelties might be.

One of Park's concepts especially useful in understanding American race relations was the theory of marginality. Migration from one society to another, especially from a rural culture to a civilized urban community, resulted in a marginal individual, one who had lived in two worlds in both of which the act of migration had left him more or less a stranger. The marginal man was a cultural hybrid, sharing the life of two distinct peoples, unable or unwilling to break completely with his past traditions, and not wholly accepted, because of ethnic prejudice, in the new society. He experienced a characteristic tension, depression, and uncertain self-image. But he also gained a wider horizon, a keener intelligence, and a more rational and detached point of view. As examples of marginality Park cited especially the Jewish immigrant and the American mulatto who migrated from the rural South to the Northern cities.

Another concept especially applicable to black-white relations was the theory of social symbiosis. The race relationship emerging out of the original contact and conquest was a symbiotic interdependence in which the dominant race exploited the conquered race without intermarrying with it (at least in principle). Such had been the result of the forced transportation of African slaves to the New World. Symbiosis was not a social relationship in that each race was expected to maintain its own society. Under rural conditions it might survive for a long time as peonage, serfdom, or chattel slavery. Park believed that the influence of urban civilization tended to break down the symbiotic relationship and replace it with a more flexible and individualistic social-class relationship. He thus viewed race relations in the dynamic context of social evolution from culture to civilization. He was basically optimistic because he shared the nineteenth-century faith in progress conceived as the breakdown of isolated and static cultures under the impact of world-wide civilizing urban influences. It was a point of view appropriate to those who took for granted the world dominance of Western European civilization.

It should not be overlooked that the prospect of assimilation to Anglo-American norms had great appeal for many immigrants because of the manifold forms of liberation contained in the American promise. European ghetto dwellers knew more of the image of America as the land of the free than they did of the actualities of American economic and social life. But for at least a few of the more able and energetic of the newcomers the promise of opportunity did in time become the actuality of achievement. For such, the inevitable process of assimilation was virtually equated with emancipation, even while it involved a new language, new customs, and the abandonment of many religious and cultural traditions. One such creative individual was Mary Antin (1881–1949), a child of the Russian Jewish Pale. Although the Boston ghetto in which her immigrant family found itself was in most respects worse than the environment from which the family had come, it did provide through its public school system the avenue through which the gifted girl could escape to the great world of learning and letters. When eventually she came to write her autobiography Mary Antin could consider her life story the exemplification of fulfillment, in which the loss of her Jewish orthodoxy was more than compensated for by her new cosmopolitan literary culture. "Nothing more pitiful could be written in the annals of the Jews," she concluded; "nothing more inevitable; nothing more hopeful."

The metaphor of the "melting-pot" celebrated in Israel Zangwill's play and frequently heard in discussions of immigration at the turn of the century referred to the mixing or amalgamation of ethnic traits out of which a distinctively new American form would presumably emerge. Zangwill, however, was an English Jew, and no American immigrant spokesman or student of immigration elaborated a detailed exposition of the idea. In the eighteenth-century, it may have seemed credible to an observer like Crevecoeur that the closely allied nationalities of Northwestern Europe would indeed experience amalgamation in America. But in the twentieth century, the likelihood of fusing together European, Asiatic, Oriental, and African in a new amalgam seemed remote indeed. The legal objective of the integration of public institutions and non-discrimination in employment and housing still fell well short of either assimilation or amalgamation, since the primary-group relationships which are the ultimate tests of these processes are not necessarily altered or affected by integration. Furthermore, when attention is given to the tensions generated by the Jewish identity crisis, or to the anguish of persons of Negro ancestry who contemplate passing for white, we realize how painful a process the melting-pot can be.

A major intellectual revolution was inaugurated early in the twentieth century with the work of the anthropologist Franz Boas. Even while Park and his disciples were putting the finishing touches on the theory of the evolutionary development of races and cultures, Boas was beginning the demolition of the theory. In *The Mind of Primitive Man* (1911) and many subsequent publications he discredited the traditional evolutionary view that racial, linguistic, and cultural developments were all part of a single evolutionary sequence, to be evaluated by a single scale of achievement. In rejecting the orthogenetic or unilinear view of social evolution Boas showed that the historical development of technology, religion, art, language, and moral ideas did not follow a single course from simple to complex. Each culture revealed its own unique patterns determined by unique historical circumstances, and each must be understood in its own terms in order to appreciate its peculiar qualities.

Boas did not deny that the history of industrial development did indeed show a progressive sequence of increasing complexity. He merely rejected the naturalistic assumption that technological innovation was a universal foundation on which analogous cultural forms were erected. He also rejected the racist view that cultural achievement was sufficient evidence of innate racial superiority. Careful comparisons of anatomical features indicated that human biological features deemed more advanced were randomly distributed among numerous races.

In an earlier era, when the self-confidence of Europeans was still running at flood tide, Boas's critique would have been found perverse and unpersuasive. But in the second half of the twentieth century, after the collapse of European empires, the rise of Asiatic superpowers, and the emergence of many newly independent colored nations, the intellectual arrogance if not the confidence of Western intellectuals collapsed. It was no longer possible for white scholars to defend the superiority of Anglo-American culture on evolutionary grounds, or to assume that the non-white elements in the American population would inevitably assimilate to the Anglo-American norm. Boas's cultural relativism now seemed timely and helpful. A new mood came to prevail in which one could consider more dispassionately the peculiar merits of each ethnic culture without making pejorative distinctions among them. In the new climate of opinion an appreciation of America's ethnic pluralism would come to flourish.

The decline of theories of evolutionary assimilation and the rise of cultural pluralism coincided with a new consciousness of ethnicity. The ethnic group possessed a distinct combination of racial traits, religious or cultural traditions, and national origins. Although these independent variables play roles of greater or less importance in individual cases, it is the combination that gives the ethnic group its durable character. Few ethnic groups can in fact display all of these attributes, and in their absence, strenuous efforts may be made to supply the deficiency. A fully developed ethnicity thus becomes an ideal in which a group feels that its potentialities will be ultimately realized. Consciousness of ethnicity in America arose out of the multi-ethnic situation, and was undoubtedly accentuated by the defensive feelings of minority groups. Irish-Americans and Negroes both responded to discriminatory treatment by cultivating their respective ethnic identities. By contrast, the Anglo-Americans enjoyed such a secure domination prior to World War II that they had little occasion to develop ethnic consciousness. Throughout the nineteenth century, their generalizations about the nature of American society usually revealed a striking "ethnic blindness" as they extended their own values and expectations to the whole society, oblivious of their possible irrelevance to other ethnic groups.

The strength and subtlety of ethnic bonds vary greatly from one group to another, reflecting cultural resources and historical experience. In a color-conscious society color alone may be sufficient, as in the case of Afro-Americans, to forge the bonds of ethnicity even though a distinctive cultural or religious heritage has been obliterated, and a historical nationalism must be painfully fabricated. Among the Jews, where racial identity is dubious, the remarkable congruence of religion and historical experience combine to produce a deep and powerful sense of ethnic identity. Zionism and the revival of Hebrew both express the thrust toward ethnicity.

The traditional American moral commitment to liberty and equality, together with the legal commitment to integration, might seem to counteract the thrust toward ethnicity. The policy of integration undertakes to assure equality in educational and employment opportunities, as well as equal access to all kinds of public facilities. But the achievement of effective measures of integration does not necessarily imply progress towards assimilation or amalgamation. It may in fact be the symptom of a maturing relationship among several ethnic groups, in which each is assured a fair share of the privileges of citizenship. Nathan Glazer has pointed out that so long as the primary social groups which are the ultimate guarantors of ethnic group identity are not directly involved in integrated activities, integration offers no threat to the survival of ethnic identity.

Ironically enough, it is in the mass society in which primary social bonds are loosened and individuals feel isolated and alienated that the impulse to seek refuge in ethnic identity expresses itself. The reassertion of the primitive blood bond binding the ethnic group coincides with the deterioration of the monogamous nuclear family, as though the failure of the family tempts men to fall back on the race. The absence in the mass society of a firm social class structure also provides a fertile soil for the growth of ethnicity. If there were a clearly marked social class structure the ethnic groups would have to accommodate themselves to it. If, for instance, the American social-economic elite were to approximate the characteristics of a ruling class the prospects for viable ethnic group relationships would be dim at best. But in the absence of such a class, it seems realistic to ethnic leaders to monopolize both the primary and secondary relationships of their followers, and thus create societies within society.

The Jews

Ethnic consciousness, according to the Chicago School, originated in the conquest and subjection of rural peoples by warlike invaders who built the cities that became the political and cultural centers of the nation states of Europe. In each of these states a dominant race imposed its civilization and order upon subject peoples. Thus the English subdued and incorporated the Welsh, the Scotch, and the Irish in the British nation. Similarly, the modern Austrian empire consisted of a varied and complex group of ethnic peoples whose relationships and rights were regulated with constitutional nicety. Stimulated by the economic opportunities of the cities and the cultural vitality of their urban rulers these subject races gradually awoke to a sense of their ethnic identity. Throughout the nineteenth century, dawning ethnic consciousness expressed itself in movements for national independence as Irish, Norwegians, Belgians, Catalans, Czechs, and other subject peoples sought the realization of ethnic aspriations in sovereign states of their own. Ethnic aspirations, as the Chicago scholars understood them, represented the awakening of rural folk cultures to the wider and richer possibilities of urban civilization for the realization of which ethnic independence and solidarity were believed to be essential.

Park and his colleagues believed that the analysis of the development of ethnic consciousness in Europe was also applicable to the experience of ethnic minorities in America. The immigrant peasants who migrated to the United States were subject to the same kind of "civilizing" urban influences they would have felt had they remained in Europe or Asia. As the children and grandchildren of immigrants responded to these influences and began to assimilate the prevailing norms of American culture they could be expected to display the symptoms of marginality, being fully at home neither with the new culture nor the old. The experience of American Jews and Blacks furnished striking illustrations of several aspects of developing ethnic consciousness.

The Diaspora or dispersion of Jews throughout the western world had resulted in extensive intermarriage with Gentiles. Religion rather than biological race furnished the bond of modern Jewish ethnicity. In America, there was little besides religion to unite wealthy old colonial Sephardic Jews of Portuguese origin with impoverished immigrants from the Russian Pale. As late as 1880 there were only some 230,000 Jews, largely of German and Portuguese origin, in a total American population of fifty million. Thereafter, persecution in the Russian empire, together with glowing reports of wider opportunities in America, brought a swelling flood of Jewish immigrants who raised the American Jewish population to three and a half million by 1920, half of them living in New York City.

The Yiddish-speaking Jews from eastern Europe who comprised most of the recent immigration had not had a previous history of high cultural achievement. They had remained largely untouched by the eighteenth-century Enlightenment which had emancipated the Jews of western Europe and inaugurated extensive cultural and racial assimilation. Restricted to the Pale of Settlement and to densely populated ghettoes the East European Jews had of necessity focused most of their cultural energies on their religion. Ambitious boys had little choice but to prepare themselves for careers as rabbis by long and intensive study of the Talmud. The intense preoccupation with religion was reminiscent of that of the Puritan settlers, three centuries earlier.

Many of the features of old-world ghetto life were preserved in the densely populated neighborhoods of the seaboard cities where the immigrants first settled, notably in New York. However harsh the conditions, there were significant advantages which the newcomers and their children were quick to exploit. Educational opportunities were free, the political system was locally responsive to pressure, careers in the police and other patronage positions were available, and there was no longer the threat of official or popular violence. Moreover, many of the Jewish immigrants were not peasants and the transit from one ghetto to another was far less difficult than the adjustments to the urban environment faced by rural folk, whether immigrant or American. Nathan Glazer has pointed out that many of the immigrants arrived with well-developed middle class values of thrift, sobriety, ambition, desire for education, aversion to violence, and the ability to defer immediate gratifications for long-run objectives. These qualities undoubtedly facilitated the Americanization process.

In any event, in a remarkably brief time after the beginnings of mass immigration a cultural explosion occurred, of which Yiddish was the vehicle, and adaptation to American life the principal burden. A flourishing Yiddish press and theater helped to break down distinctions between Polish, Russian, and Rumanian Jews, while common concerns with socialism, Zionism, or trade unionism also tended to mold a single ethnic community. The popular Yiddish culture which flowered in the first two decades of the twentieth century was a striking expression of the emerging ethnic identity, and although of relatively brief duration, was extremely influential in preparing second and third generation Jews for professional, artistic, and literary careers, as well as a wide range of business opportunities.

The popular culture of theater, press, and music hall with its ethnic themes nurtured local talents, many of whom came eventually to be known to a national audience. The Yiddish Art Theater, founded in 1918, with Max Gabel as impresario and Maurice Schwartz as principal actor, came to be celebrated as the best repertoire theater in America. Abraham Cahan, journalist and novelist, edited the Yiddish *Forward* with distinction. The fiction of Sholem Aleichem and Sholem Asch helped to elevate Yiddish to the dignity of a literary language. Popular entertainers, such as Al Jolson,

Eddie Cantor, and the Marx brothers commanded a national audience, while the playwrights S. N. Behrman, George S. Kaufman, and Elmer Rice moved beyond ethnic themes to topics of perennial concern. Music in the European ghetto had had little prestige, being commonly provided by barbers. But in America it quickly came to have great prestige and wide practice, thanks in part to the celebrity achieved by such distinguished musicians as Elman, Heifetz, and Menuhin.

The central emphasis on justice in the Jewish religious tradition, together with ethnic solidarity and compact ghetto living combined to produce a strong and characteristic social conscience among the New York Jews. Trade unions quickly developed among the garment workers. Summer camps in the Catskill and Pocono Mountains, often maintained by the unions, combined educational and service functions with recreational activities. Radical politics was particularly attractive to Jews during the Yiddish cultural period. Socialist, Socialist Labor, and Communist parties all attracted numerous members from Manhattan's lower East Side, where many interparty battles were waged.

The decline of Yiddish culture coincided with the ending of mass immigration in the late 1920's, and with the entrance of Jews in increasing numbers into the mainstream of American life. For such people Yiddish was now irrelevant, and in order to hold its readership the *Forward* began to publish English-language supplements. Franklin D. Roosevelt's New Deal, with its sympathetic labor policy, undermined the appeal of socialism for Jewish garment workers. Their union leaders, Sidney Hillman and David Dubinsky, who had served prison terms in Tzarist Russia for radical activities, now became national political powers as advisers to Roosevelt. At the same time, as their economic status improved, many Jews moved out of the Manhattan ghetto, breaking up the dense concentration of people that had sustained ethnic solidarity.

Because the historic core of Jewish ethnicity was its religion, the response of the religious Jew to life in America would largely determine the fate of their ethnic group. Wherever religion is primarily a matter of faith or belief and only in a minor degree ritualistic, as in most forms of Protestant Christianity, assimilation of the believer to American norms can be accomplished with little risk to the survival of the religion. But where ritual is of primary concern, as it is with Jewish Orthodoxy, conflicting demands of religious and secular life may be very difficult to reconcile. Loyal adherence to the rituals will foreclose many forms of secular activity and dictate a secluded life. This was indeed one of the reasons why the voluntary European ghetto had come into existence in the first place. To the degree that it might prove difficult to maintain a voluntary ghetto in America the survival of a vigorous ritualistic religion would be threatened.

As though in response to this threat, many American Jews practiced two forms of compromise, each in its way representing degrees of assimilation, Reform Judaism and Conservative Judaism. The Reform movement had originated in Germany early in the nineteenth century in response to the opening up of Jewish life to the secular culture of the Enlightenment. Its greatest development occurred in America, where the object of the reformers was to accommodate the Jewish faith and tradition to a liberal democratic society. Many of the traditional rituals that had stood between the Jews and social and cultural assimilation were abandoned: Kosher food, the Saturday Sabbath, religious schools, and traditional garments and hair styles. A new emphasis on the universal spiritual authority of God replaced the older tribal nationalism. Sermons were preached in English, women were accorded equality, and congregational autonomy replaced rabbinical authority. In many respects Reform Judaism resembled Unitarian Christianity, and cordial relations often developed between the two groups.

Had it not been for the massive immigration of East European Jews at the end of the nineteenth century it is conceivable that Reform Judaism might have become the principal form of Judaism in America. Conservative opposition to the Reform movement coincided with the latest wave of Jewish immigration, and over the years was to draw increasing strength from the descendants of Yiddish-speaking immigrants. Conservatives attempted to sustain a historical conception of Judaism as the total way of life of a people rather than as a mere profession of belief, in the Protestant Christian manner. The affirmation of Judaism as a religious civilization would appear to signal a return to Jewish Orthodoxy, but in fact the Conservatives took a position somewhere between the Reformed and the Orthodox. They would preserve the Hebrew liturgy, the dietary laws, and the traditional Sabbath, but in other respects would accept and participate in the social and cultural life of the Western countries.

Being a tribal religion perpetuated in families as distinct from a proselytizing religion the Jewish faith is threatened by intermarriage with Gentiles. Jewish men marry non-Jews more frequently than do

Jewish women, and children tend to follow the religion (or non-religion) of their mothers. Jewish law holds the children of a Jewish mother and non-Jewish father to be Jews by birth-right; but if the mother is non-Jewish they must be converted. The rate of inter-marriage in America clearly reflects the local density of the Jewish population, and perhaps also the length of time since immigration. In New York, between 1908 and 1912, only 1.17% of Jewish marriages were mixed; whereas in Iowa, between 1953 and 1959, 42.2% of marriages involving Jews were mixed. The break-up of the big city ghettoes posed a long-range threat to the survival of the religious component in Jewish ethnicity.

If the period of Yiddish culture in the early twentieth century facilitated the rapid entrance of Jews into American professional and high cultural life, by the same token it speeded up the processes of assimilation. Jewish writers who observed or were themselves involved in the process were able to report at first hand the tensions and conflicts that were the symptoms of marginality. One of these was the journalist Abraham Cahan, whose novel, *The Rise of David Levinsky* (1917) was inspired by William Dean Howells' *The Rise of Silas Lapham* (1885). Howells had chronicled the moral perils encountered in making the transit from rural to urban civilization in America. Cahan now explored the parallel case of the Jewish immigrant.

Levinsky was a Jewish immigrant who had begun life as a Talmud student in the Russian ghetto, but whose aims in America were quickly modified (or corrupted) by the prevailing mercenary standards of New York. In order to make money quickly in the garment industry he resorted to various shabby or illegal devices, including an offer of marriage in order to obtain a girl's dowry, misrepresentation of his financial position, and inducement of employees to kick-back part of their wages in order to undersell competitors. Levinsky rationalized such practices by espousing the currently fashionable Social Darwinian philosophy of dog-eat-dog. The traditional mores of the Jewish community were quickly eroded by such a transformation. Although he contracted with the parents for a conventional Jewish marriage to a girl he did not love, the engagement was broken off when he fell in love with another girl. In fact, the romantic love that Americans sentimentalized rendered the traditional familial control of marriage archaic. Nevertheless, Levinsky's romances never came to satisfactory fruition, his bachelor-hood serving as a symbol of his inability to achieve fully satisfying and rewarding personal relationships. In the end, the seemingly successful millionaire confessed to his loneliness and sense of failure, the marginal man who had abandoned his birth-right without finding a satisfying new life.

In the broadest sense, American society has threatened the ethnic identity of each of its immigrant peoples; at the cultural level through assimilation to the prevailing norms of secular life, and at the biological level through inter-marriage. This threat has given rise to a characteristic crisis of identity. The sociologist Manford Kuhn sensed the pervasiveness of this crisis when he devised his famous "Twenty-statements test," in which the respondent was asked to give twenty answers to the question: Who Am I? Analysis of typical responses revealed an all-too-frequent wavering and uncertain self image. In a mass society, consciousness of ancestry is not as common or useful a form of self identification as it is in class-structured societies. Nevertheless, American Jews, whose original and primary ethnic bond in religion has been threatened by fragmentation into Reform, Conservative, and Orthodox parties, to say nothing of lapsing into irreligion, have been increasingly driven back on Jewish ancestry as their primary bond. As one of their leaders remarked, one can change one's religion as readily as one's clothes or one's politics; but one cannot change one's ancestors. Something of the Jew would always remain in those whose forebears were Jewish. There was a pathetic note perhaps in the appeal to ancestry in a society in which ancestry counted for so little.

Park's disciple Everett Stonequist attributed little significance to ancestry when he remarked that the only remaining distinguishing mark of the Jew was his consciousness of being a Jew. Hence the perennial problem of the modern individual Jew: to be or not to be a Jew. By the simple act of denying his identity the Jew could escape from it, unlike the Black whose color marked him irrevocably. Thus the Jew found himself in an agonizing realm of choice. If he was to remain a Jew, how would he affirm it? By going back to the synagogue; by becoming a Zionist? Or if he chose to relinquish his Jewish identity, what then was he? Were there sufficient compensations in being simply an American? Would the thought of his former Jewish identity return to plague him? Questions such as these cast doubt on the utility of the theory of the melting-pot with its assumption of the easy abandonment of ethnic identity.

The career of Ludwig Lewisohn, literary critic and novelist, furnished a poignant commentary on the problems of marginality and identity. Born in Berlin in 1882 of secularized Jewish parents, Lewisohn had come with them to Charleston, South Carolina, as a child, and had become fully assimilated to the Anglo-Protestant culture of the South. Although his parents were socially isolated, he did not attribute this, nor his own failure to make a college fraternity, to anti-Semitism. But when he went to Columbia University for graduate work in English and American literature he was told candidly that although he had deliberately dissociated himself from his German-Jewish background and was immersed in British-American literary culture his Jewish identity would nevertheless effectively bar him from academic employment. Little wonder that he should have been struck by the ironic contrast between the ideology of freedom and the reality of ethnic discrimination.

As Lewisohn recalled later, in his autobiography *Upstream:* "I didn't know how to go on living a reasonable and reasonably harmonious inner life. I could take no refuge in the spirit and traditions of my own people. I knew little of them. My psychical life was Aryan through and through. . . . I can, in reality, find no difference between my own inner life of thought and impulse and that of my very close friends whether American or German. So that the picture of a young man disappointed because he can't get the kind of job he wants, doesn't exhaust, barely indeed touches the dilemma. I didn't know what to do with my life or with myself."

What he did in fact was to redirect his scholarly interests to Germanic literature and the writing of fiction, while earning his living as a teacher of German. In his bitterness he noted that "the notion of liberty on which the Republic was founded, the spirit of America that animated Emerson and Whitman, is vividly alive today only in the unassimilated foreigner." The expression of pro-German sympathies during the First World War brought Lewisohn's academic career to an end, and during the 1920's and 1930's he joined the American expatriates in Paris, from which vantage point he could lampoon the puritanical philistinism of popular American culture.

The pain of rejection undoubtedly heightened his restlessness and need for a "principle of coherence" which he envied in his Anglo-American friends. He finally found this principle in a reaffirmation of his Jewishness. It now became apparent to him that the process of assimilation to nineteenth-century liberalism begun by his father in Germany had been a tragic mistake. In denying significant differences between Jew and Gentile the emancipated Jew was indulging in a covert form of Anti-Semitism, since in fact he preferred Gentile traits to his own. "The instincts of one's blood were treated as mouldy Ghetto prejudices." As an intellectual Lewisohn would still take possession of the high culture of the West, but he would shape it creatively as a Jew. "The doctrine of assimilation, if driven home by public pressure and official mandate, will create a race of unconscious spiritual helots. We shall become utterly barbarous and desolate. The friend of the Republic, the lover of those values which alone make life endurable, must bid the German and the Jew, the Latin and the Slav preserve his cultural tradition and beware of the encroachments of neo-Puritan barbarism—beware of becoming merely another dweller on an endless Main Street; he must plead with him to remain spiritually himself until he melts naturally and gradually into a richer life, a broader liberty, a more radiant artistic and intellectual culture than his own."

Lewisohn's aversion to assimilation received appropriate expression in his conversion to Zionism. By declaring themselves a national people the Jews would be better able to preserve their ethnic identity. The hopes for the reestablishment of a national Jewish state were now focused on Palestine, but until such time as that state were to come into being Lewisohn urged the Jews, wherever located, to demand minority cultural rights as the best means of preserving their distinctive national character.

The secularization of individuals like Lewisohn made it clear that religion was but one element, even if the major historic one, in the ethnic complex. Many secular Jews now resumed an active religious life as the only way to preserve their Jewish identity. Involvement in the Zionist movement was another such method. Early in the twentieth century the American Zionist leaders had been German Jews identified with the Reform movement, while the Yiddish-speaking Jews had been generally indifferent or opposed to Zionism. But after the rise of Nazism and the European Holocaust there was a growing realization among descendants of the Yiddish-speaking immigrants that assimilation or secularization were no refuge from fanatical racist persecution. The establishment of a sovereign Jewish state capable of defending itself might well be the best guarantor of survival. Many American Jews now became Zionists and active supporters of the state of Israel.

Demands for American financial and diplomatic aid for Israel precipitated a lively debate in Jewish magazines in 1950. If the Jews were a nation whose legitimate aspirations were fulfilled in the independence of Israel how could the American Zionist also be loyal to the country of his birth? This question had always been posed to Zionists, but with particular insistence following the creation of Israel and the highly organized American campaign for its support. The journalist Dorothy Thompson, who, although not herself a Jew had been married to one, felt free to inform American Jews that sovereignty was indivisible, and that in the United States, unlike the USSR or the old Austro-Hungarian Empire, there were no legally recognized national, racial, or religious minorities. Jews had come to the United States individually as nationals from other countries; here, they or their descendants became American citizens owing loyalty to this country. She rejected the idea of a world-wide Jewish nation to be gathered in Zion as incompatible with the obligations of American citizenship.

The historian Oscar Handlin replied that Thompson's fears were groundless, as well as based on false premises about the nature of American society. There were in fact no minorities in America because there was no majority. Groups were free to organize and dissolve on passing issues. Americans of different origin had long expressed lively interest in foreign countries. The Irish-Americans, for instance, had shown a passionate concern for Irish independence, at one time even organizing an Irish government in exile. Multiple loyalties, far from being injurious, could be powerful factors in sustaining the freedom and autonomy of the individual citizen.

Conflicting loyalties had always been a basic dimension of American experience if for no other reason than that all Americans, apart from the Indians, were descended from immigrants. Especially in time of crisis they were prone to suspect one another of disloyalty. During the First World War, German-Americans were often held in suspicion, while during the Second World War, Japanese-Americans were placed in detention camps. In another dimension, the Federal Constitution itself created dual loyalties when it provided for a sovereign nation of sovereign states, a legal conundrum which remained unresolved for nearly a century until settled in the most decisive fashion by military conquest of the seceding Southern States. But within the bonds of political union Americans continued to enjoy a broad area of personal freedom within which to work out their ethnic relationships.

Robert Park's theoretical cycle of ethnic interaction proceeded through phases of competition, conflict, and accommodation to eventual assimilation. Especially during the phases of conflict and accommodation the distressing symptoms of marginality were expected to appear: alienation, deracination, identity crisis, and various forms of anti-social behavior. Marginality, however, expressed itself in strikingly different forms. Among ordinary people it took the commonly undesirable forms of anti-social behavior and social disorganization. But among talented people it released the individual's creative powers. The latter function of marginality was often cited as an explanation of the striking release of Jewish creative energies during the middle decades of the twentieth century.

Another uncertainty resided in the culminating phase of assimilation. Did assimilation mean a complete absorption of the ethnic minority in the dominant patterns of American life, so that no distinguishing marks remained to identify it? Or was there some intermediate stage at which the assimilative process would achieve a measure of accommodation sufficient to satisfy all parties while leaving to the minority a saving area of autonomy in which to preserve and cherish its own distinctive traits? The latter seems to have been the hope of the ethnic pluralists, who conceded the overarching requirements of economic, political, and other public forms of community life, but who hoped nevertheless to preserve the distinctive cultural patterns that gave value and style to the lives of the individuals constituting each ethnic group.

Afro-Americans

According to Park's theory of ethnic relations, a dominant racial nation centered in its cities imposed its rule upon a rural subject race. The impact of urban culture on this subject people inaugurated a series of cultural developments, the ethnic cycle, which resulted in ultimate emancipation through the development of a mature ethnic identity. Park believed that this theory illuminated the experience not only of ethnic minorities in Europe, but also of American immigrants and Afro-Americans, who, in this context, should be considered to have been involuntary immigrants. It was admitted that acceptance by the American majority was accelerated or retarded by the degree of physical difference separating the immigrant group from the native Americans, but it was nevertheless assumed that sooner or later these differences would be overcome. Park's disciple Emory Bogardus studied the native American response to Chinese, Japanese, Philipino, and Chicano immigrants and identified in each case a "race relations cycle" passing from initial hostility to eventual acceptance of the newcomers. Bogardus assumed that the same cycle would govern black-white relations.

The most striking aspect of the early history of African slaves in America was their capacity to survive under the most forbidding circumstances. In spite of the often lethal conditions under which they were forced to labor they continually increased in numbers, thus passing the ultimate test with spectacular success. A comparison of the African with the native Indian response to the impact of Anglo-American culture is instructive. The Africans adapted to it successfully and survived. On the other hand, were it not for the protective custody of reservations, the Indians would probably not have survived into the twentieth century. The reasons for the differing responses are no doubt complex, but it is possible that the adaptability of the Afro-American was due to the completeness with which his native African culture was stripped from him. He was left with no cultural defenses with which to resist westernization. The stubborn resistance of the Indian was made possible by the surviving elements of native culture he was permitted to retain. In any event, within the bonds of slavery the Afro-American learned a new language, and acquired a new religion, and formed monogamous nuclear families, which according to the anthropologists are the basic cultural artifacts.

How much more he would learn from white Americans became readily apparent in the succession of distinguished leaders of the Black race following Emancipation. One of the first of these was Booker T. Washington (1856?–1915) whose autobiography, *Up From Slavery* (1901), ranks with Franklin's autobiography as a classic American success story. Representative of the first generation of emancipated slaves, Washington always thought of himself as a Southerner, speaking to the problems of rural southern Blacks. Ironically enough, however, thanks to the personal influence of a succession of Yankee teachers who had gone South to labor on behalf of the Freedmen Washington acquired principles and traits of character often held to be typically Yankee. He developed a boundless ambition to succeed, happily combined with a selfless devotion to the welfare of his race. Not only did he make a religion of hard work, but he extolled the value and dignity of manual labor. He was confident that "merit, no matter under what skin found, is, in the long run, recognized and rewarded." He possessed extraordinary patience, and was willing to wait for the rewards of industry which he knew to be inevitable. He counseled the Blacks to make progress in the conventional American manner by acquiring useful skills, amassing property, gaining an education, and thus win the confidence and respect of the white majority.

From his white teachers and patrons Washington acquired and mastered the attributes of gentility, recognizing the social value and prestige that still attached to that tradition. All of his public utterances were dignified, moderately phrased, restrained and eminently civilized. He openly professed to admire the dignity and courtesies of the old-school southern gentlemen, seeing in gentility a potential common bond transcending the barriers of racial discrimination. Thanks in part to such rapport it became part of his strategy to appeal to the sympathy and support of "the better class of whites" against the mass of whites among whom he located the principal opposition to Black objectives. The gentry style was eminently suited to the tactics of accommodation and conciliation Washington always followed.

By failing to insist that Blacks be immediately accorded the full measure of political and civil rights Washington has often been accused of settling for a second-class citizenship. He accepted the naturalistic assumption of the primacy of economics over politics, believing it fruitless to hope that Blacks could improve their situation by political means before their economic position was strengthened. During Reconstruction the Freedmen had looked to the Federal Government for all their needs, while the Radical Republicans, intent primarily on punishing the white South by putting Blacks in office, had adopted a reconstruction policy that was false, artificial, and forced. It was obvious to Washington in retrospect that the Blacks would inevitably be recompensed for this folly in hatred, contempt, and discrimination. Political rights, he believed, would come eventually and spontaneously, and in the meanwhile southern Blacks should look for leadership to the best whites in their local communities. Nevertheless, he always deplored the disfranchisement of Blacks, proposing as a kind of compromise a literacy test for the suffrage to which both white and black would be subject.

In his invincibly positive, optimistic, and progressive outlook Washington was an excellent representative of progressive America at the turn of the century. He was fully convinced that race prejudice was a function of provincial ignorance, to be swept away in the advancing tide of popular enlightenment. He refused to yield to bitterness over the treatment of Blacks, and often came close to saying that they would fare better in direct proportion to their merits. In a remarkable passage in his autobiography he observed that "notwithstanding the cruelty and moral wrong of slavery, the ten million Negroes inhabiting this country, who themselves or whose ancestors went through the school of American slavery, are in a stronger and more hopeful condition, materially, intellectually, morally, and religiously, than is true of an equal number of black people in any other portion of the globe." His ability to see the problems and frustrations of the moment in the longer perspective of continuing racial contacts anticipated Robert Park's race relations cycle. Perhaps the best that could be said of Washington was that in the face of grim realities he got the most out of limited possibilities.

In a practical sense, Washington was a pragmatist, centering his attention on immediate needs and refusing to speculate about ultimate objectives. He may have envisioned, as Park did, the ultimate assimilation of American Blacks, but he did not project such a resolution in specific terms. Rather, he seems to have anticipated the development of a prosperous and cultivated Black race sharing all the benefits of high civilization, and living in peaceful and cordial relations with other races. For the moment, he emphasized the economic foundations for such an order, its trades, skills, and professions. Washington was not a nationalist in the sense of anticipating a future in which a Black nation would live in self-sufficient isolation from other nations. As a rural Southerner he assumed that the black and white races would continue to live in close contacts and interdependence. In a famous speech at the Atlanta Exposition of 1895 he spoke of "interlacing our industrial, commercial, civil, and religious life with yours [whites] in a way that shall make the interests of both races one." A clenched fist seemed an appropriate symbol for such intimate interdependence. But at the same time, each race should maintain a separate social life, as autonomous as the fingers of the hand. Washington's metaphor of fist and fingers was doubtless intended to reassure southern whites that he had no designs on social segregation, but the time would come when the metaphor would serve as well to symbolize the theory and practice of integration.

The immediate effect of Washington's accommodationist policies and influence was to fashion a black social structure parallel but subordinate to the white. Those who supported him tended to be

those who profited the most from serving a segregated community—
the black businessmen, professionals and teachers, as well as those
who needed white patronage and approval, since whites generally
admired and supported Washington. But the Tuskeegee leader failed
to halt the general deterioration of race relations at the end of the
century, and there developed among professional men and intellectuals a more militant opposition to his leadership.

The principal spokesman of the militants was W. E. Burghardt
Du Bois (1868–1963), a sociologist and journalist. Du Bois had
grown up in a white community in western Massachusetts, and had
discovered his black identity as well as his mission of service to his
race only on attending Fisk University in Nashville, a black school.
He had a much stronger ethnic consciousness than had Washington,
for whom the background of slavery was more significant than
racial identity. Apart from the clash of powerful personalities the
conflict between the two men concerned the appropriate role of
agitation in achieving Black objectives. Du Bois shared with Washington and all progressives the democratic idealism, the common
heritage of Blacks as well as whites. But he insisted vehemently
upon the equal rights of Blacks, including the suffrage, equal educational and employment opportunties, and the abolition of caste distinctions. Unlike Washington he believed strongly that economic
advance depended on the full exercise of political rights, without
which many economic opportunities would always remain closed to
Blacks. Leadership should be furnished by a highly trained and
dedicated corps to whom Du Bois attached the term "the Talented
Tenth." The production of such a leadership required first-class
universities rather than the vocational-technical schools favored by
Washington.

In an essay of 1897 on "The Conservation of Races" Du Bois set
forth his view of ethnicity as a dynamic process to be realized
historically in a fully developed ethnic culture. It was probably inevitable that the racist thinking prevalent among white intellectuals
at the turn of the century should also have infected the Blacks.
Du Bois defined a race as a vast family of human beings, "generally
of common blood and language, always of common history, traditions and impulses, who are both voluntarily and involuntarily
striving together for the accomplishment of certain more or less
vividly conceived ideals of life." Each of the eight or more races
of the world develops a particular ideal and makes a distinctive contribution to the ultimate perfection of human life. It was inevitable

and appropriate that each race should seek the forms of sovereign nationality in which to cultivate the racial impulse. Great Britain thus exemplifies the English genius for constitutional liberty and commercial freedom; Germany, the German's zeal for science and philosophy; France and Italy, the literary and artistic flair of their respective peoples. The Black race had not yet arrived at a comparable state of maturity, so that one could not be equally specific about its racial bent, although one could note that already it had given America her only indigenous music, fairy tales, pathos and humor. Du Bois was emphatic that one could be both black and an American. So long as there remained substantial agreement among all Americans as to their laws, language, and religion, and when all enjoyed equal economic opportunities, the races could live peaceably together, each pursuing its own racial goals. It was apparent that at the outset of his career Du Bois shared with Washington the vision of a multi-ethnic society based on common access to essential opportunities and services.

In his later years Du Bois became increasingly pessimistic about the prospects for the Black race in America. Loyalties to his race and his country became increasingly difficult to reconcile. He had long been an active promoter of Pan-Africanism, an effort to unite Blacks throughout the world against white injustice and exploitation. Pan-Africanism, like Zionism, represented the interests of an ethnic group that could not be fully realized in America. In the end, he came to a Marxist-Leninist conception of imperialism as the world-wide exploitation of colored races by the white race. He identified himself with the emerging black nations of Africa, and died in Ghana.

Throughout most of his long career, however, Du Bois's program for his race was thoroughly liberal, civilized, and genteel. He believed in the value of educated leadership because the world to which he aspired for the Blacks—the only world worth having—was the larger world of civilized high culture. He had once defined social equality as "simply the right to be treated as a gentleman when one is among gentlemen and acts like a gentleman!" But at the same time, he understood the necessity for the conversion of landless peons into landowners, and for the development of a Black business class. He had faith in the efficacy of the political process, believing that the ballot was a potent weapon with which to counteract the perennial economic exploitation of the weak by the strong. He was also a liberal with respect to the implications of social mobility for race relations. It seemed only reasonable to him as it had to Washington that the "best" people of both races should show the least signs of discrimination, and he could not reconcile himself to the fact that the opposite was often the case: that the elites were completely separated while at the bottom of the social scale, in saloons, gambling halls, and brothels the color line often disappeared. His disillusionment with these processes undoubtedly led to his ultimate renunciation of liberalism.

Robert Park considered color to be only one of numerous ethnic traits, and he refused to admit that color differences might be so important as to remove a relationship involving color from the larger category of ethnic relations. He himself had enjoyed a long and intimate association with Blacks, feeling so much at ease among them that he could on occasion successfully pass for black. Nevertheless, the deep emotions which have created the "color problem" have clearly injected into black-white relationships factors hardly present in many other ethnic situations.

It has often been observed that in contrast to the practice in many other countries white America does not recognize a distinct mulatto class, but forces mixed bloods into the Black population where they have furnished most of the leadership. Over a century or more this leadership had been essentially moderate and accommodating, looking towards social assimilation and full participation in American life. When Park's student Edward Byron Reuter studied American mulattoes in 1918 he took it for granted that a leadership group of mixed blood aspired to an ultimate condition of whiteness. Guided by their mulatto leaders American Blacks could be expected to move towards assimilation. Reuter believed the mulattoes to be more sensitive to and resentful of racial discrimination than were the Blacks. The mulattoes provided him with classic cases of marginality. Their restless intelligence and ambition accounted readily enough for their leadership role, while their moodiness and psychological instability testified to the burdens of living between two worlds, fully accepted in neither.

Several Black writers during the decades prior to 1930 echoed this white interpretation. They were associated with the so-called Harlem Renaissance, a cultural flowering in the Black New York ghetto comparable to the period of Yiddish culture among the Jews. In the fiction of Claude McKay, James Weldon Johnson, Wallace Thurman, and Nella Larsen, Harlem functions both as the ghetto from which the emancipated Black escapes and the refuge without which he never feels at home. These writers were fascinated with the problems of the light-skinned person of mixed ancestry who could pass for white but whose denial of his Black identity created agonizing psychological conflict. Nella Larsen, in particular, probed this problem with a delicate insight into stages of mind reminiscent of Edith Wharton and Henry James.

During the 1920's, while some Blacks were still thinking in terms of the ethnic cycle of assimilation, others were advocating separatist Black nationalism. Marcus M. Garvey (1887-1940), a Jamaican who came to the United States in 1916, organized the Universal Negro Improvement Association to promote the creation of an independent Black nation in Africa. Garvey's organization, which soon claimed a million members, was the first mass movement of American Blacks. Although it soon collapsed without achieving its objective of large-scale repatriation to Africa it did mark the first significant challenge to the moderate leadership of the mulattoes.

One of Garvey's primary concerns was to preserve the identity and integrity of the Black race, and he professed sympathy for those who, like the Ku Klux Klan, shared a similar concern for the purity of the white race. He bitterly denounced as traitors to their race those "colored" leaders who were consciously or unconsciously promoting cultural assimilation and biological amalgamation with the white race. In an apparent effort to undermine the prestige and influence of the mulatto leadership he accused them of snobbishly looking down on Blacks while associating preferably with whites. Du Bois and Walter White of the National Association for the Advancement of Colored People were singled out for particular criticism. Garvey's hatred for whites was so great that he would discourage all forms of economic and social integration. The various types of business enterprise promoted by the U.N.I.A. were intended to make the Blacks as self-sufficient as possible until such time as they could emigrate to Africa.

Although the Back-to-Africa movement shortly collapsed and Garvey himself was convicted of mail fraud and deported to Jamaica several of his ideas remained staple elements of militant black nationalism. The obstacles to the development of black nationalism were formidable. American Blacks had no distinctive national language or literature. Following the massive migration to northern cities they no longer could lay claim to a geographical region of habitat. Apart from Christianity there was no distinctive religion shared by an appreciable number. Their economic life remained wholly dependent on the white community. They perpetuated no distinctive manners, customs, or traditions. And finally, the racial memory did not run behind slavery to a tradition of past greatness. Their one distinctive attribute, color, they had been taught to regard as a stigma rather than a source of pride. Black nationalists nevertheless vigorously attacked each of these deficiencies in order to stimulate ethnic pride and consciousness.

Although Black nationalists have for the most part focused their attention on Africa as the original home of the Black race they have also on occasion called for the creation of a Black nation in some portion of the United States. In more recent times the nationalist movement has also intersected with Marxist-Leninist revolutionary doctrines, resulting in the equation of the economic exploitation of colonial peoples with the subjection of the colored races. None of these nationalist movements have enlisted the permanent allegiance of large numbers of American Blacks. As a component element of ethnicity in America it is noteworthy that for so many ethnic groups the return to a former homeland remains impractical. This fact tends to give to ethnic nationalism in America a nostalgic, dreamlike quality. The national homeland, whether it be the Irish Free State, Israel, or the independent black nations of Africa, functions as a source of pride rather than as a practical haven for the ethnic American.

Although Christianity early gained a powerful hold on the rural Blacks of the South it has been challenged in the black ghettoes of northern cities by new and exotic religions, the largest of which is the Nation of Islam (Black Muslims). This nationalistic religion provides the Blacks a direct link with Arab Africa. It teaches an original black creation and assigns a diabolical role to whites as minions of Satan. Its devotees form a "nation within a nation," passively awaiting the impending destruction of white society, which is the will of Allah. In view of the vital role played by Christianity in the historic assimilation of Blacks no challenge could be more profound than this repudiation of the universal proselytizing mission of Christianity.

Unlike the exclusive claims of religion the demands of cultural nationalism could be compromised. It was quite possible for a Black to share an appreciation of jazz music as the principal form of Black cultural expression with equal enthusiasm for the art, literature, and learning of Western high culture. Militant nationalists, however, were tempted to maintain that jazz was a distinctive expression of the Black genius and in some sense an exclusive possession. The chief virtue of jazz for ethnic nationalism was its popular character. It welled up spontaneously from the soul of the Black people. Black nationalist spokesmen in the nineteenth century had been cultivated men whose nationalist aspirations were modeled on the highest values of Western Civilization. Subsequent to the Garvey movement, however, the cultural elite no longer furnished nationalist leadership. Speaking in the name of the black masses militant nationalists demanded that the black cultural elite subordinate their interests to the welfare of the race as the militants conceived it. Black studies programs in colleges and universities often demanded a curriculum concerned exclusively with topics of interest to Blacks rather than with preparation for successful careers in a multi-racial society.

These militant expressions of ethnic nationalism occurred at a time when the Black middle class was growing rapidly, when employment opportunities were improving, and when the exercise of political rights had resulted in a growing number of Black Judges, Congressmen, legislators, and big-city mayors. These incongruous facts suggest that as the Black community increases in strength and improves its relative position its bonds of unity will weaken and diversity of opinion will become wider. In former times, weakness and oppression unified the Blacks behind a leadership that made the best deal it could get with white America. By the 1970's, they were strong enough to assert a measure of independence, and a diversity of views appeared, consistent with the range of problems that were still very real for Black Americans.

Suggestions for Further Reading

From the very large literature on American intellectual history the titles listed below will enable the reader to pursue further many of the topics discussed in the text. The principal sources used have been mentioned in the body of the text and are listed in the Index alphabetically by author. The bibliography is therefore confined to secondary works.

Part I: THE COLONIAL RELIGIOUS MIND

Perry Miller, *The New England Mind: The Seventeenth Century* (New York: Macmillan, 1939; Cambridge: Harvard University Press, 1954).
Still the most important book on the Puritan mind, although focused narrowly on the Federal Covenant school of theology.
Perry Miller, *Errand into the Wilderness* (Cambridge: Harvard University Press, 1956; Harper Torchbook).
Chapter III of these collected essays on early American religion, "The Marrow of Puritan Divinity," provides a convenient summary of covenant theology.
Alan Simpson, *Puritanism in Old and New England* (Chicago: University of Chicago Press, 1955).
A brief survey, emphasizing the divergence of the two branches of Puritanism.
Edmund S. Morgan, *Visible Saints. The History of a Puritan Idea* (New York: N.Y.U. Press, 1963; Cornell Paperback).
Corrects Miller's interpretation in certain important respects.

Samuel Eliot Morison, *The Puritan Pronaos, Studies in the Intellectual Life of New England in the Seventeenth Century* (New York: N.Y.U. Press, 1936. Reissued, 1956, as *Intellectual Life in Colonial New England*).

A survey of the educational, literary, and scientific interests of early American Puritans.

William G. McLoughlin, *New England Dissent, 1630-1833* (2 vols. Cambridge: Harvard University Press, 1971).

An important supplement to Miller's exclusive emphasis on Federal Puritanism.

Robert Middlekauff, *The Mathers. Three Generations of Puritan Intellectuals, 1596-1728* (New York: Oxford, 1971).

An important pioneering reinterpretation of Cotton Mather.

Alan Heimert, *Religion and the American Mind: From the Great Awakening to the Revolution* (Cambridge: Harvard University Press, 1966).

Traces the democratic and revolutionary movements to evangelical revivalism.

Sydney V. James, *A People Among Peoples. Quaker Benevolence in Eighteenth-Century America* (Cambridge: Harvard University Press, 1963).

Traces the development of Quaker humanitarianism.

Lawrence A. Cremin, *American Education: The Colonial Experience, 1607-1783* (New York: Harper & Row, 1970).

A comprehensive history defining education as the transmission of culture.

Clinton L. Rossiter, *Seedtime of the Republic* (New York: Harcourt, Brace, 1953).

Analyzes the contribution of Puritanism to the development of American political thought in the colonial period.

Part II: THE MIND OF THE AMERICAN ENLIGHTENMENT

Max Savelle, *Seeds of Liberty. The Genesis of the American Mind* (New York: Knopf, 1948).

An encyclopedic study of American culture in the generation prior to the Revolution.

Bernard Bailyn, *The Ideological Origins of the American Revolution* (Cambridge: Harvard University Press, 1967).

An excellent study of the thinking of American revolutionary leaders.

Gordon S. Wood, *The Creation of the American Republic, 1776-1787* (Chapel Hill: University of North Carolina Press, 1969).

A balanced account of the intellectual and institutional history of the Revolutionary period.

Michael Kraus, *The Atlantic Civilization: Eighteenth-Century Origins* (Ithaca: Cornell University Press, 1949).

A survey of cultural relationships between America and Europe.

Ralph Barton Perry, *Puritanism and Democracy* (New York: Vanguard, 1944).

The ideological implications of the relationship between Puritan and Enlightened patterns of thought.

Perry Miller, *Jonathan Edwards* (New York: Sloane, 1949).

An intellectual study emphasizing the power and originality of Edwards's mind.

Isaac Woodbridge Riley, *American Philosophy. The Early Schools* (New York: Dodd, Mead, 1907).

A review of the eighteenth-century schools of idealism, deism, materialism, and realism.

Charles Conrad Wright, *The Beginnings of Unitarianism in America* (Boston: Beacon Press, 1955).
An able analysis of American Arminianism within New England Congregationalism.

Alice M. Baldwin, *The New England Clergy and the American Revolution* (Durham: Duke University Press, 1928).
The revolutionary patriotism of the Congregationalist clergy related to doctrines of divine law and natural rights.

Daniel J. Boorstin, *The Lost World of Thomas Jefferson* (New York: Holt, 1948).
A brilliant analysis of the intellectual outlook of Jefferson and his circle.

Adrienne Koch, *The Philosophy of Thomas Jefferson* (New York: Columbia University Press, 1943).
The relationship of Jefferson's ideas to contemporary French and Scottish schools of thought.

David Brion Davis, *The Problem of Slavery in Western Culture* (Ithaca: Cornell University Press, 1966).
A comprehensive history of the intellectual response to slavery down to 1800.

Herbert M. Morais, *Deism in Eighteenth Century America* (New York: Columbia University Press, 1934).
A useful survey, although the influence of deism is over-estimated.

Part III: THE MIND OF NINETEENTH-CENTURY DEMOCRACY

John William Ward, *Andrew Jackson, Symbol for an Age* (New York: Oxford, 1955).
The characteristics of democratic ideology as reflected in the popular image of Jackson.

Henry Nash Smith, *Virgin Land. The American West as Symbol and Myth* (Cambridge: Harvard University Press, 1950).
An important study of changing attitudes towards the West.

Richard Slotkin, *Regeneration Through Violence: The Mythology of the American Frontier, 1600–1860* (Middletown: Wesleyan University Press, 1973).
Richly detailed analysis of mythic content of frontier literature.

Marvin Meyers, *The Jacksonian Persuasion: Politics and Belief* (Palo Alto: Stanford University Press, 1957).
A distinctive interpretation of the Jacksonians as nostalgic conservatives.

Francis Otto Matthiessen, *The American Renaissance* (New York: Oxford, 1941).
A classic study of the principal romantic writers.

Richard W. Lewis, *The American Adam: Innocence, Tragedy and Tradition in the Nineteenth Century* (Chicago: University of Chicago Press, 1955).
Analyzes the response of romantic writers to various facets of the American situation.

Leo Marx, *The Machine in the Garden. Technology and the Pastoral Ideal In America* (New York: Oxford, 1964).
A central metaphor for the literary imagination during the period of industrialization.

Arthur A. Ekirch, *The Idea of Progress in America, 1815–1860* (New York: Columbia University Press, 1944).
A useful survey of expressions of the idea in a variety of contexts.

Joseph Dorfman, *The Economic Mind in American Civilization*, Vol. II (3 vols. New York: Viking, 1946–49).
Excellent summaries of the ideas of economists in the early nineteenth century.

Albert K. Weinberg, *Manifest Destiny* (Baltimore: Johns Hopkins University Press, 1935).
A study of ideology as reflected in rationalizations justifying territorial expansion.

David Brion Davis, *Homicide in American Fiction, 1789–1860: A Study in Social Values* (Ithaca: Cornell University Press, 1957).
A perceptive study of democratic society as mirrored in fiction. Of wider interest than the title indicates.

Ernest Lee Tuveson, *Redeemer Nation: The Idea of America's Millennial Role* (Chicago: University of Chicago Press, 1968).
A history of the types of millennial doctrine in American Protestantism.

Ray Allen Billington, *The Protestant Crusade, 1800–1860. A Study of the Origins of American Nativism* (New York: Macmillan, 1938).
An analysis of the social sources of anti-Catholicism.

Richard M. Huber, *The American Idea of Success* (New York: McGraw-Hill, 1972).
A history of changing ideas of success.

Richard Hofstadter, *Anti-Intellectualism in American Life* (New York: Knopf, 1963).
A study of the social and cultural sources of anti-intellectualism throughout American history.

Louis Hartz, *The Liberal Tradition in America* (New York: Harcourt, Brace, 1955).
Contends. that America has no other tradition of political thought than liberalism.

Allen Guttmann, *The Conservative Tradition in America* (New York: Oxford, 1967).
Distinguishes the various conservative elements in American history.

Neil Harris, *The Artist in American Society. The Formative Years, 1790–1860* (New York: Braziller, 1966).
A perceptive account of the first attempt of artists to establish their social identity in a democratic society.

William R. Taylor, *Cavalier and Yankee. The Old South and American National Character* (New York: Braziller, 1961).
An account of the formation of distinct regional character types as reflected in literature.

Clement Eaton, *Freedom of Thought in the Old South* (Durham: Duke University Press, 1940).
A study of the intellectual and psychological consequences of the defense of slavery.

William R. Stanton, *The Leopard's Spots. Scientific Attitudes Towards Race in America, 1815–1859* (Chicago: University of Chicago Press, 1960).

An account of the racial ideas of the so-called American School of anthropology.

George M. Fredrickson, *The Inner Civil War. Northern Intellectuals and the Crisis of the Union* (New York: Harper & Row, 1965).
Explores the wide range of responses to secession and war.

Rush Welter, *Popular Education and Democratic Thought in America* (New York: Columbia University Press, 1962).
A history of the educational ideals of spokesmen representing various segments of American society other than professional educators.

Part IV: THE NATURALISTIC MIND

Richard Hofstadter, *Social Darwinism in American Thought, 1860–1915* (Philadelphia: University of Pennsylvania Press, 1944; rev. ed. Boston: Beacon Press paperback, 1955).
The study in which Social Darwinism was defined and identified as a movement of thought.

Stow Persons, ed., *Evolutionary Thought in America* (New Haven: Yale University Press, 1950; Archon Books).
Essays on the impact of the evolution idea on various fields of thought.

Henry F. May, *Protestant Churches and Industrial America* (New York: Harper, 1949).
A study of the response of Protestantism to industrialism at the end of the nineteenth century.

Philip P. Wiener, *Evolution and the Founders of Pragmatism* (Cambridge: Harvard University Press, 1949).
An analysis of the role of the evolution idea in the development of pragmatism, emphasizing Wright and Peirce.

Thomas F. Gossett, *Race: The History of an•Idea in America* (Dallas: Southern Methodist University Press, 1963).
A comprehensive history of racial ideas since colonial times.

John Higham, *Strangers in the Land. Patterns of American Nativism, 1860–1925* (New Brunswick: Rutgers University Press, 1955. Atheneum Press).
A history of ethnic discrimination culminating in the National Origins legislation of the 1920's.

William H. Jordy, *Henry Adams: Scientific Historian* (New Haven: Yale University Press, 1952).
A critical analysis of Adams's successive historical theories.

Charles Albro Barker, *Henry George* (New York: Oxford, 1955).
A biography, including a careful analysis of George's ideas.

Joseph Dorfman, *Thorstein Veblen and His America* (New York: Viking, 1934).
A meticulous examination of the development of Veblen's intellectual life.

Arthur Mann, *Yankee Reformers in the Urban Age* (Cambridge: Belknap Press of Harvard University Press, 1954).
The activities of New England humanitarians and civic reformers at the end of the nineteenth century.

Donald H. Fleming, *John William Draper and the Religion of Science* (Philadelphia: University of Pennsylvania Press, 1950).
A biographical study of a representative naturalist thinker.

Luther L. and J. Bernard, *Origins of American Sociology; the Social Science Movement in the United States* (New York: Crowell, 1943).
A history of social-science theory in the nineteenth century.

Fay B. Karpf, *American Social Psychology: Its Origins, Development, and European Background* (New York: McGraw-Hill, 1932).
A useful review of European and American theories since Hegel.

Sidney Fine, *Laissez Faire and the General Welfare State: A Study of Conflict in American Thought, 1865–1901* (Ann Arbor: University of Michigan Press, 1956).
A review of the range of theories on public policy.

Robert Green McCloskey, *American Conservatism in the Age of Enterprise* (Cambridge: Harvard University Press, 1951).
An analysis of the ideas of Sumner, Stephen J. Field, and Carnegie.

Jurgen Herbst, *The German Historical School in American Scholarship* (Ithaca: Cornell University Press, 1965).
A history of the impact of German historical thinking on the social sciences in America.

Part V: THE CONTEMPORARY NEO-DEMOCRATIC MIND

Henry Steele Commager, *The American Mind. An Interpretation of American Thought and Character since the 1880's* (New Haven: Yale University Press, 1950).
A survey of principal trends in twentieth-century thought.

Morton G. White, *Social Thought in America: The Revolt Against Formalism* (New York: Viking, 1947; Beacon paperback).
An important study of Dewey, Veblen, Beard, Becker and Holmes as "antiformalists."

Paul K. Conkin, *Puritans and Pragmatists. Eight Eminent American Thinkers* (New York: Dodd, Mead, 1968).
Emphasizes moral and intellectual continuities since colonial times in the work of major American thinkers.

Henry F. May, *The End of American Innocence. A Study of the First Years of Our Own Time, 1912-1917* (New York: Knopf, 1959).
A detailed examination of a significant transitional period in American cultural history.

Jean B. Quandt, *From the Small Town to the Great Community. The Social Thought of Progressive Intellectuals* (New Brunswick: Rutgers University Press, 1970).
Focuses on the preoccupation of Progressive intellectuals with preservation of the values of personal association.

Christopher Lasch, *The New Radicalism in America, 1889–1963: The Intellectual as a Social Type* (New York: Knopf, 1965).
Concerned chiefly with the life styles of a variety of rebellious critics.

Cushing Strout, *The Pragmatic Revolt in American History: Carl Becker and Charles A. Beard* (New Haven: Yale University Press, 1958).
A careful analysis of the relativism of these historians.

Robert D. Cross, *The Emergence of Liberal Catholicism in America* (Cambridge: Harvard University Press, 1958).
An account of Catholic modernism or "Americanism" at the end of the nineteenth century.

Lawrence A. Cremin, *The Transformation of the School. Progressivism in American Education, 1876-1957* (New York: Knopf, 1961).
The Progressive movement in education is broadly defined, with Dewey the central figure.

Gerald N. Grob, *Workers and Utopia: A Study of the Ideological Conflict in the American Labor Movement, 1865-1900* (Evanston: Northwestern University Press, 1961).
An analysis of issues during the period when the ideology of American labor was yet to be defined.

August Meier, *Negro Thought in America, 1880-1915. Racial Ideologies in the Age of Booker T. Washington* (Ann Arbor: University of Michigan Press, 1963; Ann Arbor paperback).
A detailed analysis of the controversies over the programs for Black advance.

Nathan I. Huggins, *Harlem Renaissance* (New York: Oxford, 1971).
An account of the first major cultural movement among Black writers and artists.

Allen Guttmann, *The Jewish Writer in America. Assimilation and the Crisis of Identity* (New York: Oxford, 1971).
The response of American Jewish writers to the prospects of assimilation and the loss of Jewish identity.

Ronald Berman, *America in the Sixties: An Intellectual History* (New York: Free Press, 1968).
A comprehensive account of the major intellectual movements of the decade.

John P. Diggins, *The American Left in the Twentieth Century* (New York: Harcourt Brace Jovanovich, 1973).
Traces the radical tradition in its various guises from the Old Left to the New.

Alfred Kazin, *On Native Grounds* (New York: Reynal & Hitchcock, 1942).
A history of twentieth-century American literature.

Herbert Wallace Schneider, *Religion in Twentieth-Century America* (Cambridge: Harvard University Press, 1952).
A comprehensive analysis, emphasizing recent changes.

Elmer Talmage Clark, *The Small Sects in America* (Rev. ed. New York: Abingdon, 1949).
A sociological study of religious sectarian movements.

Index